D0606500

Astrology

Astrology Louis MacNeice

Doubleday & Company Inc.,
Garden City, New York

©1964 Aldus Books Limited London
Library of Congress Catalog Card No. 64-18633

First published in 1964 by Aldus Books Limited,
Aldus House, Conway Street, Fitzroy Square, London W1
Distributed in the United Kingdom
and the Commonwealth by
W. H. Allen & Company,
43 Essex Street, London WC2
Printed in Yugoslavia

Contents

1 The art of the stars

In June 1941 the Nazis locked up all the astrologers in Germany, partly because their activities were considered unsuitable (if not subversive) in the National Socialist state. This remains one of the more famous, if backhanded, tributes to one of the most diehard of the arts. A similar tribute occurred in the British House of Commons in June 1942. A Conservative M.P. asked the Minister of Information, Mr. Brendan Bracken, "whether his attention has been drawn to the fact that astrologers are predicting that Germany is on the brink of collapse; and whether he will stop astrological predictions about the war in order to counteract the risk that addicts of astrology will relax their efforts?" The minister replied: "Astrologers seem to have the misfortune to be perpetually in conflict. And, as no sensible person takes their predictions seriously, I cannot ask our overworked censors to meddle in their mysteries."

Mr. Bracken showed himself more lenient than the Nazis, or than certain ancient Roman emperors who used to deport their astrologers. But perhaps the astrological profession is not as powerful in modern Britain as it was in Nazi Germany or ancient Rome. Nevertheless, Mr. Bracken was wrong. Many sensible people *do* take the subject seriously. Astrological almanacs and newspaper horoscopes are eagerly read by millions all over the world, many of whom believe or would like to believe at least part of it. And astrology has many addicts in Western countries today among the educated and the sophisticated.

The Dumb-Bell Nebula in the Vulpecula galaxy photographed by a 200-inch telescope at an American observatory. Astronomers are constantly revising their ideas about the universe in the light of fresh discoveries; yet modern scientific advances have never affected the world-wide popularity of astrology today.

In France the astrological author André Barbault has expounded the Zodiac with great elegance and relish (he will tell you that Louis Armstrong is a typical *Aries* character—*"ardeur et improvisation forcenée"*). In Germany the heavier guns of scholarship and of psychological and statistical analysis are trained upon such targets as "astro-biology." In the U.S.A., as in Germany, there has been a serious attempt to correlate modern astrology with the findings of modern psychology.

One of the veterans of American astrology, Dane Rudhyar, describes his art as a "system of symbolical life interpretation." He also calls it "the algebra of life" and, unlike some other of his colleagues (astrologers have always disagreed), flatly denies that it has any empirical basis. In England astrology is on the whole treated more frivolously, or at least on a lower intellectual plane, but it is easy to find British intellectuals who believe there is "something in it." In evidence, however, they usually either refer you to German, French, or American publications, or quote what some mysterious Hindu once said to them in India.

In other countries today astrology retains her old position as queen of the "sciences." In India it may not be true that (as some Indians allege) most of the more conservative members of the cabinet regularly consult astrologers; but it is certain that below cabinet level astrology permeates every sphere of life. Indian astrologers tend to work with collections of allegedly ancient *ready-made* horoscopes (known as *nadi granthams*) written on palm leaves. To the Western way of thinking this may smack of common fortune telling, but many Europeans have returned from India much impressed by what these palm leaves have told them about themselves. And Santha Rama Rau, a westernized Indian writer married to an American, has confessed that a return visit to India converted her from her American-style skepticism. She mentions a friend of hers, a Bombay businessman, who never makes an important decision "without first consulting his astrologer." For that matter, this has been said of J. P. Morgan. According to one authority, the most famous modern American astrologer Evangeline Adams was one of Morgan's advisers.

Professor Morris Carstairs, a social psychologist in Edinburgh University, has made a detailed study of an Indian community and has concluded that Hindus consult astrologers in order to discover their own real wishes: "With the initial premise of this self-centered view of the world, the Hindus' unshakeable belief in astrology became more comprehensible." But there are some Indians who find the whole practice a nuisance. One of them writes of the ubiquitous astrologers: "They draw a red herring across every practical problem—choice of profession, marriage, journeys, treatment in illness—and in truth disturb and upset every practical arrangement."

Many countries in the Western world, at various stages of history, have similarly come under the influence of this very peculiar body of beliefs that has been building up through the ages. That influence, and the reasons for it, is the subject of this book. But, first of all, what *is* astrology?

Even in our skeptical age, astrology numbers many well-known intellectuals and artists among its followers. Right, the Irish poet W. B. Yeats (1865-1939), who was fascinated by the irrational; far right, a pencil sketch of his uncle George Pollexfen, who taught Yeats to cast horoscopes. Below left, the British composer Gustav Holst at his piano, and, right, the cover of a recording of his suite *The Planets* (composed in 1919). Holst's interest in astrology inspired this composition—a musical interpretation of each planet's traditional astrological character.

GUSTAV HOLST
THE PLANETS

nxa

PHILHARMONIC PROMENADE ORCHESTRA and members of the LONDON PHILHARMONIC CHOIR
Conducted by SIR ADRIAN BOULT

Left, the American writer Henry Miller (born 1890), whose enthusiasm for astrology has lasted throughout a long literary career. Though he does not claim to "live" by it, Miller admits to finding "disturbing accuracies in everything that concerns astrology."

All persons who give any credence whatsoever to any form of astrology must hold one belief in common: that there is some kind of relationship between the stars and human beings. It may not be a relationship of cause and effect (i.e., the stars may not directly influence human beings). But relationship there must be. To put it colloquially, the stars are part of our set-up.

But for many people today, at least in Europe and America, astrology is mainly a matter of horoscopes and predictions; the ordinary man, being selfish, wants to hear about himself and his prospects. The widest appeal, therefore, is much the same as that of fortune telling with crystal balls, cards, etc. (Astrologers have themselves sometimes gone in for such sidelines, though this is usually much frowned upon by the more serious theorists and practitioners.) Some hardheaded students of the subject believe that a good astrologer *can* make successful predictions, but that he does this without really knowing (consciously, that is) what he is doing. The stars are just as much props to him as the Tarot cards are to a fortune teller, or the lines on the hand to a palmist. The real active agent is his own intuition.

But other believers in astrology regard the prediction of events as its weakest side, and would prefer the art to be restricted to the diagnosis of character, and, at most, the assessment of an individual's *potentialities*. At this they think that it can be of the greatest use socially. The modern English astrological writer Rupert Gleadow maintains that "the comparison of horoscopes is the only certain way of making marriage not a lottery but a partnership." Many astrologers today claim that they can act not only as marriage counselors but as advisers on health, education, and careers.

Above, a scene from the film *Nine Hours to Rama*, recently made in India. The police believe that killers will try to assassinate Gandhi at an astrologically auspicious moment; here two detectives consult an astrologer to find out when that moment might be. Reliance on astrological prediction is widespread in India today, and has been for centuries: Above left, a Nepalese palm leaf horoscope containing prognostications for the years 1362-66. Left, a more recent example of the Indian astrologer's art: a decorative motif of bulls (symbolizing the sign of Taurus) from the horoscope of a 19th-century prince of Lahore.

The subject indeed has many forms and applications, whose order of importance varies according to time and country. Astrological medicine, which in the first century A.D. brought a fortune to a doctor in Marseilles, no longer enjoys a vogue in Western Europe, yet doctors can be found who believe in it. (The American astrological magazine *In Search* has featured articles by Dr. W. M. Davidson and Dr. William Gutman, both practicing medical men.) Similarly, while run-of-the-mill practitioners rest their claims on the hoary antiquity of what skeptics have called this "fossilized science," the intellectuals among modern astrologers are anxious to liberate their subject from the dead hand of tradition. A leading Swiss astrologer, Karl Ernst Krafft (who figures in an extraordinary story to be recounted in Chapter 7), once went so far as to write: "The tradition is like a rotting corpse, and should not be brought to life again." A similar line is taken by several of the leading Americans.

Even within traditional astrology, if we look back through the centuries, we find a great range of beliefs—from the ancient (and medieval) conception of the stars as gods or divine animals (typical question: What food do they eat? typical answer: Purer food than we do) to the 15th-century Italian humanists' comparison of the star-man relationship to a struck harp that sets the strings vibrating in some other harp that no one has touched. And astrology has usually attracted a wide range of adherents. In early 16th-century France, the distinguished court physician Cornelius Agrippa accepted astrology (though he renounced it later) at about the same time that the famous obscurantist prophet Nostradamus was writing his scrambled verse quatrains that have since given much pleasure to lovers of puzzles and prediction.

Many of Nostradamus's prophecies are not overtly astrological, but this is true also of many predictions in astrological almanacs; anyway, it was as an astrologer that people thought of Nostradamus in his own day. And his mystificatory technique in his writing is typical of a certain kind of astrologer through the ages. The French of his verses is not only the (to us) difficult French of its period; Nostradamus often deliberately misspelled words, and used anagrams, portmanteau words, and telegraphese. So his statements about the future are open to widely differing interpretations, though many commentators have agreed as to the meaning of some quatrains (such as several that apparently foretold the French Revolution).

In the same period astrology numbered among its famous supporters men like Paracelsus, the Swiss physician and alchemist; Melanchthon, the German theologian and friend of Luther's; and Cardan, the Italian physician and mathematician. In 16th-century England, Queen Elizabeth's astrologer, John Dee, could assert that "Astrology is an art mathematical . . ." while his greater contemporary Francis Bacon was writing: "As for Astrology, it is so full of superstition, that scarce anything sound can be discovered in it." (Yet even Bacon could later add: "I would rather have it purified than altogether rejected"— a feeling that has been echoed by the present-day attitude of astrologers like Krafft, quoted above.)

Some astrologers consider their craft an "occult" one; others think it is as much a matter of fact as any empirical science. In 1899 an American astrologer using the pseudonym "Gabriel" (such pseudonyms having long been fashionable) wrote in a book called *The Gospel of the Stars*: "Unlike religion, astrology is based not on faith but on facts. The religious man believes; the astrologer knows. Experiment and observation are his guides." But some of his colleagues at the time were combining their "science" with theosophy, which claims to be in direct touch with the "divine essence," transcending both observation and reason. (The Theosophical Society was founded in the U.S.A. in 1875.) Some years ago a very successful English editor of astrological magazines, who used the alias of "Alan Leo," wrote: "I believe every human being belongs to a Father Star in Heaven or Star Angel . . . ."

Left, a scene from the American film *Love is a Many Splendored Thing* (1960). Two lovers consult a Chinese fortune teller to find out whether they will have a long and happy life together. All the world seems to love a fortune teller—which (since most people equate astrology with prediction) explains much of astrology's popularity.

Right, some prophetic verse written by the 16th-century French astrologer and seer Nostradamus. The stanza printed in green has been translated thus:
By night shall come through the forest of Reines,
Two parts Voltorte Herne, the white stone,
The black monk in grey within Varennes,
Elected captain, causeth Tempest, fire,
blood running.
It has been interpreted as a prediction of the capture of France's Louis XVI in 1791, while fleeing to Varennes (disguised as a monk) to escape the revolutionaries.

CENTURIE IX.   143
XX.
De nuiĉt viendra par la foreſt de Reines,
Deux pars vaultorte Hene la pierre blanche,
Le moyne noir en gris dedans Varennes,
Eſleu cap cauſe tempeſte, feu, ſang tranche.
XXI.
Au temple haut de Bloys ſacre Salonne,
Nuiĉt pont de Loyre Prelat Roy pernicant,
Curſeur victoire aux mareſts de la lone,
D'ou prelature de blancs aburmeant.
XXII.
Roy & ſa cour au lieu de langue halbe,
Dedans le temple vis à vis dupalais,
Dans le jardin Duc de Mantor & d'Albe,
Albe & Mantor poignard langue & palais.
XXIII.
Puiſnay joüant au freſch deſſoubs la tonne,
Le haut du toiĉt du milieu ſur la teſte,
Le Pere Roy au temple ſaint Salone,

The more serious modern astrological writers often tend toward caution. Louis de Wohl, for instance, who after a long residence in Germany went to live in England, was not unduly modest: According to himself, he conducted a one-man astrological war with the Nazis. Yet even though de Wohl can write: "A man who plunges blindfold through the London streets is distinctly safer than a man without a horoscope," he can also write of astrology in general: "Let us get this straight from the start: it is not prophecy. It is dealing not with certainties, but with tendencies. It has a fairly wide margin for error—but it works."

But prophecy, of course, is just what the ordinary man wants (hence the popularity of *all* kinds of fortune telling). And in practice de Wohl went in for something very like it. For example: "It was clear to me, as to every student of astrology who knew Hitler's horoscope, that he would launch his great attack against the West when Jupiter was in conjunction with his Sun, in May 1940."

Curiosity about the future is a primary reason for the continuing popularity of astrology. Another reason for many people (though astrologers have often been at pains to deny this) is the almost cosy appeal of fatalism: In times of either stress or failure you can always pass the buck to the stars. But perhaps equally important is the delight most people take in *classification,* especially in the classification of themselves and their friends: "Are you Virgo?" "Oh no, I'm Leo." The bulk of any popular book of astrology is given up to the human characteristics attributed to the influence of the heavenly bodies, whether they are the planets or the signs of the Zodiac. Even animals, plants, precious stones, etc., come under this influence. These will be discussed again, but some samples may be given here from an early 19th-century English astrologer, the first "Raphael" (another celestial pseudonym—real name R. C. Smith):

"Saturn," writes Raphael, "is by universal experience acknowledged to be the most powerful, evil, and malignant of all the planets." Among persons he represents (among others) grandfathers, paupers, monks, and gravediggers; among animals cats and dogs "and all creatures delighting in filth and breeding from putrefaction"; among plants hemlock, hellebore, poppy, mandrake, night-shade, and moss; among trees willow, pine, yew, and cypress; among birds the crow, owl, and cuckoo; among places deserts, churchyards, and all "muddy dirty stinking places, wells, and nuisances of every description." His wind is the east wind and his favorite mineral is lead.

This grouping of interrelated creatures and objects has the same appeal as certain card games with their sequences, flushes, and so on. It all goes back to the basic concept of *sympathy,* which we shall find stressed over and over again when we come to look at astrology's history. There is sympathy between the parts of the universe, between things celestial and things terrestrial. From this stems a whole system of *correspondences,* the most famous perhaps being those between the signs of the Zodiac and the parts of the human body, constituting the so-called "Zodiacal Man."

The city of Jerusalem, usually assigned
to the sign of Virgo. Most kinds of
terrestrial objects—from cities to
blades of grass—have been classified
by astrologers in terms of the influence
of planets or Zodiac signs.

There is something in this concept of natural correspondences that attracts
the mystic in us. And there is an equally strong attraction for the poet in us,
or at any rate for the patternmaker. The same Raphael becomes uncommonly
eloquent on this principle of sympathy: He speaks (the following quotation is
much boiled down) of the "simple and easy but beautiful theory, which pre-
sumes that the same sympathetic power which causes the iron and magnet to
attract each other, . . . the same occult influence which drives the frantic herd
about the pastures; which provokes the gadfly to vex the steed; . . . which
seizes with fits of temporary madness the owl and raven; which affects the
brains of the maniac *or which circulates through all living nature, pervading
all, disquieting all*; . . . this universal sympathy or instinct (for all instinct *is*
sympathy) is neither more nor less than the secret but powerful influences of
the heavenly bodies."

The pigeon-holing technique of astrology is also extended to the hours of the
day, historical periods, and towns and countries. Algiers is assigned to Scorpio,
New York to Cancer, London to Gemini, both Jerusalem and Paris to Virgo,
Hamburg to Aquarius, and Oxford to Capricorn. Scotland, according to the
modern astrologer Maurice Wemyss, "is particularly influenced by Capricorn 26

[each Zodiacal sign consists of 30 degrees], a degree of 'caution,' and its ruling planet Saturn." The U.S.A. is under Gemini and Portugal under Pisces. The seven-day week is apportioned among the planets: Saturday is Saturn's day, Sunday the Sun's day (*Sonntag* in German); in French, *mardi* (Tuesday) is Mars's day, and *mercredi* (Wednesday) is Mercury's day (*mercoledì* in Italian).

These conceptions also survive in the very vocabulary of most modern languages. In English the word "saturnine" is connected, just as much as Saturday, with the planet (which in turn got its name from a god). Similar words are "jovial" and "mercurial," while the English "disaster" and French "désastre" derive from the old Greek word for star. For many people these associations may be as unfamiliar as the ancient doctrine of the four humors, which also survives in modern languages in words like the English "sanguine" and the French "mélancholie." This doctrine, like that of the four elements, was very much involved with astrology; indeed, some modern astrologers still make use of it, as they also make use of the ancient parallel of microcosm and macrocosm. The figure of the so-called Zodiacal or astrological man is just one illustration of this doctrine. And medieval astrologers often combined their craft with that of alchemy, which also presupposes mysterious correspondences in things.

Forms and varieties

Traditionally, astrology was divided into *natural* astrology, foretelling the motions of the heavenly bodies (now absorbed into astronomy), and *judicial* astrology, which interprets these motions in terms of terrestrial life. This latter has many subdivisions, the most important today being undisputedly *genethliacal* astrology, or the art of erecting and interpreting individuals' horoscopes.

Four types of "judicial" astrology, which interprets the heavens in terms of life on earth. Left, some of the people that gathered on Mont Blanc in Switzerland in anticipation of the end of the world (forecast by an Italian astrologer for July 14, 1956). This kind of prediction is "mundane" astrology, which foretells events of national or international importance like earthquakes or revolutions. A more popular form today is "genethliacal" astrology—casting and interpreting the horoscopes or "natal charts" of individuals. Right, an American astrologer with some of his clients' charts.

Casting horoscopes to answer questions is called "horary" astrology ; below right, an Italian fortune teller outside a Naples law court undertakes to answer litigants' questions by this method. "Meteorological" astrology is weather forecasting. Below left, a page from an Austrian calendar for 1962 showing the first nine days of January ; below them at the bottom of the page are Zodiac signs, and above them symbols for different kinds of weather.

But this was a late comer; it was preceded by *mundane* astrology, the chief interest of the Babylonians (the inventors of the science) who were concerned only with the fortunes of the state or of the king as head of the state. They naturally paid particular attention to such conspicuous phenomena as eclipses of the Sun or Moon. In some circles, these (and comets) are still assumed to portend grand-scale happenings. For Raphael, in his *Manual of Astrology* (1828), an eclipse of the Moon on November 3, 1827, boded no good to the British nation (which was at the time brewing up for the first parliamentary Reform Bill). Raphael's illustrator made a great deal of the occasion: Britannia sits downstage on the left covering her eyes, a bull is being strangled by a snake, upstage right is a gesturing skeleton. Not only national but world-wide disasters are foretold in mundane astrology—disasters like the threatened deluges in 1186 and 1524, neither of which came off. One of the most recent examples of such mundane miscalculation was on February 5, 1962; from the Indian point of view (but not the European) there was a conjunction of all the main planets in Capricorn, which many Hindu astrologers said would mean the end of the world. Crowds of Hindu holy men sat up all night for it in Delhi.

There is also *horary* astrology, extremely popular in the 17th century but now disapproved of by some astrologers. It consists of answering questions by making horoscopic calculations for the moment at which they crop up. Ingrid Lind, author of *Astrology and Commonsense*, writes: "To me this savours of the bead

Left, 13 cards from the earliest existing pack of Tarot cards (made in Florence in the 15th century) depicting an astrologer (top) and the 12 signs of the Zodiac. Tarot packs (though not all containing astrological cards) are still used today for fortune telling. Another form of divination sometimes linked with astrology is palmistry—reading the future from a hand. Above, a palm marked with planetary hieroglyphs from a book by the 17th-century English occultist Robert Fludd.

curtain and fortune-telling booth and I will have nothing to do with it." On the other hand, Rupert Gleadow, in his book *Astrology in Everyday Life,* appears to find it both useful and amusing: "If a letter or telegram arrives to announce, for example, an unwelcome visitor whose journey may possibly be postponed, a horoscope set up for the moment when the telegram was read will set all doubts at rest by announcing quite simply whether the visit will take place, and if not why not."

Gleadow, who seems to get great fun out of his astrology (and even the most hardboiled rationalist would find that it affords amusing parlor games), is also prepared to accept *medical* astrology. He says we should watch the 12 "biochemic cell salts," which are essential constituents of the body and which can be related to the 12 signs of the Zodiac. Thus the Libra salt holds the balance (Libra of course *means* balance) between the acids and the alkalis. "It is a good rule," Gleadow writes, "that if any sign contains an afflicted planet [i.e., one that is badly "aspected"; see later], the body will need the salt corresponding to that sign." The 12 cell salts are usually accepted by astrologers in the U.S.A.; but some (in spite of the tempting parallel with the Zodiac) have decided that this was oversimplification, and have added a few more to the tally. On medical astrology generally, a veteran American physician has written: "The doctor needs astro-diagnosis worse than he can ever realize until he has used it for some years."

As for *electional* astrology (the art of horoscopically choosing exactly the right moment for an enterprise), Gleadow warns us to watch the date for laying a foundation stone, or the moment the champagne bottle sends the new craft down the launching slip.

Aside from these general divisions, there are many related sidelines, such as the use of astrological "images" or amulets, or *physiognomical* astrology, concerned with the facial characteristics connected with the stars' influence. As an illustration of the astonishing lengths (or minutiae) to which astrologers can go, consider the "Sabian Symbols" of the American astrologer Marc Edmund Jones, which are presented by Dane Rudhyar in his book *The Astrology of Personality.* Jones devised a separate symbolic image for each of the 360 degrees in the Zodiac. He also halved each sign (containing 30°) to make 24 "spans" (15° each) with different qualities or characteristics assigned to them.

Jones's image for the eighth degree of Aries (under the "Span of Realization") is: "A woman's hat, with streamers blown by the east wind." Jones's explanation: "First real attempt at self-exteriorization and embodiment in consciousness. Individualizing Eastern forces are suggested." For Aries 30° (the Span of Examination) the symbol is: "Young ducklings disport themselves merrily upon a pond." Explanation: "Essential social co-operativeness and appreciation of selfhood." For Cancer 4° (the Span of Expansion): "A hungry cat argues with a mouse before eating her." Explanation: "The urge to self-justification through intellectual sophistry or social-ethical considerations. Sense of self-righteousness."

For Cancer 8°: "Rabbits in faultless human attire parade with dignity."
Explanation: "Reaching out to participation in a higher order through imitative
behavior." For Sagittarius 29° (the Span of Detachment): "Perspiring fat boy,
eager to reduce, is mowing lawn." Explanation: "Desire for fitness inherent
in all human beings."

The whole subject seems as involved as a vast Hindu temple (and just as
capable of decadence). We will try to avoid as many of the more obscure astrological byways as possible, in order to maintain a view of the forest as well as
the trees. And, as a further help, here is a short glossary of some of the basic
horoscopic terms that will crop up in later chapters:

Ecliptic: The apparent path of the Sun through the sky. From the earth it
appears to describe a great circle.

Zodiac: A band of sky extending about 8° on each side of the ecliptic.
This band is the racetrack of the planets; with the exception of Pluto (which
we cannot see) we never see them outside it. In orthodox, traditional European
astrology this band is divided into 12 segments, each of 30°, known as the

Signs: Though these have the same name as the Zodiacal constellations—
Aries, Taurus, and the rest—they are not to be confused with them. The difference will be explained later.

Houses: There are 12 of these too, but they are not the same as the signs
(or as the constellations). Astrologers use several different systems of houses,

Some astrological terms explained in
diagrams: Right, the signs of the Zodiac
and their traditional symbols. Below left,
the ecliptic, the Sun's apparent path
around the earth. Below right, the
distribution around the ecliptic of the
12 signs of the Zodiac—which are also
assumed to move around the earth—in
relation to the 12 houses (separated by
"cusps"), which are fixed.

Aries	♈	Libra	♎
Taurus	♉	Scorpio	♏
Gemini	♊	Sagittarius	♐
Cancer	♋	Capricorn	♑
Leo	♌	Aquarius	♒
Virgo	♍	Pisces	♓

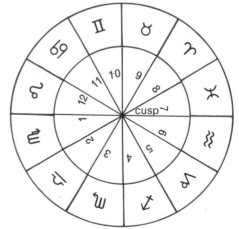

but whatever the system the houses (unlike the signs) stay put. Think of the ecliptic as a clock face: The signs keep moving around it like the hands, while the houses keep their places like the figures.

Cusps: The dividing lines between one house and another. Owing to the disagreement about house division, one man's cusp can be another man's blank.

Medium Coeli (*or M.C.*): Latin for mid-heaven. This is the point above the observer where the Sun "culminates" at noon. Its opposite number is the *Imum Coeli* (*I.C.*). A vertical line drawn between these two points crosses at right angles a horizontal line connecting the ascendant in the east with the descendant in the west.

Ascendant: Technically, this is the degree of the ecliptic that is rising above the eastern horizon at any moment. But more generally the term is used to designate the rising *sign* (which is of the utmost importance in horoscopes).

Angles: The cross formed by the ascendant-descendant horizontal line and the M.C.-I.C. vertical line (or meridian). The angles add importance to any planet found on or near any of the four arms of the cross.

Transit: When a planet passes over a sensitive spot in your natal chart it is said to be "transiting" it. Say your ascendant degree at birth was 23° Taurus. It is known (from astronomically compiled tables) when a certain planet is going to transit that point, so it is easy for the astrologer to tell you to expect certain effects at the time of transit.

Right, the 11 planets with their symbols. Below left, the positions on the ecliptic of the medium coeli (noon), the imum coeli (midnight), ascendant, and descendant. The lines joining these points (which produce the "angles") form the basis of any horoscope chart. Below right, examples of planetary "aspects": Mercury (colored red) is shown in "opposition" to Neptune; in "conjunction" with Venus; in "sextile" with Saturn; in "square" with Uranus; in "trine" with Mars.

Sun	☉	Jupiter	♃
Earth	●	Saturn	♄
Moon	☾	Uranus	♅
Mercury	☿	Neptune	♆
Venus	♀	Pluto	♇
Mars	♂		

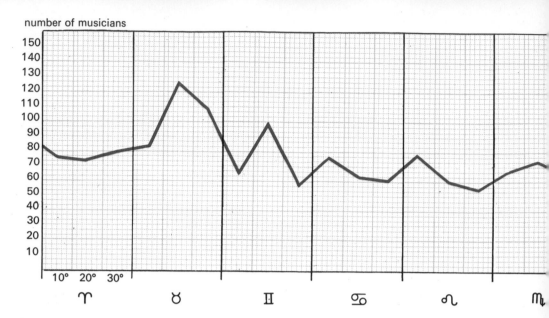

number of musicians

A graph based on the results of
a statistical investigation of traditional
astrology made in 1939 by the great
Swiss astrologer Karl Ernst Krafft.
For this experiment, Krafft took the birth
dates of 2817 musicians, which he allotted
to their correct signs of the Zodiac.
The resulting curve shows that the number
of births varies little from one sign to
another. The highest peak is found under
Taurus—but, traditionally, this sign has
no association with musical talent.

Aspects: These are established geocentrically, like most of astrology. You draw a line from the center of the Earth to one planet and another line to another planet and measure the angle between them. (Don't confuse this with the "angles" just mentioned.) As the whole Zodiacal circle in which the planets travel is 360°, a planet rising is 180° away from a planet setting. Two such planets are said to be in

Opposition: Traditionally a bad aspect, though some modern astrologers dispute this. The opposite of opposition is

Conjunction: Where two planets are very close together (say, within 8° or 10° of each other). This aspect can be either good or bad; it depends on the planets concerned. There are other aspects, but here are the major ones:

Sextile: Two planets 60° apart. Good.

Square: Planets 90° apart. Bad.

Trine: Planets 120° apart. Very good. Unlike a conjunction, it does not matter here if one of the planets concerned is a traditional "malefic." The English poet Dryden, in an epitaph for an admired young lady, writes:

> *For sure the milder planets did combine*
> *On thy auspicious horoscope to shine,*
> *And even the most malicious were in trine.*

The minor aspects have names like *quintile* (72°), *sesquadrate* (135°), and

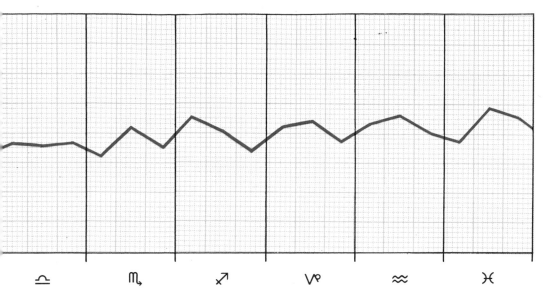

$\underline{\Omega}$ $\mathrm{M}_{\downarrow}$ $\nearrow$ $\mathrm{V^{p}}$ $\approx$ $\mathcal{H}$

quincunx (150°), but we need not bother with them here. There is, however, something called an

Orb : If aspects were limited to the *exact* degrees of the definition, they would not crop up nearly so often as they do. Astrologers allow a margin of about 7° for sextile and about 12° for conjunction or opposition of Sun and Moon. This margin is the orb.

The presence of all this apparently scientific procedure (in a subject so often connected in modern minds with quackery, magic, and occultism) can be ascribed to the fact that, whether astrology now is a "fossilized science" or was never any more than a pseudo-science, it originated in the wish that is at the heart of science—the wish to make sense of the universe. When astrology began, in ancient Babylonia, it was inseparable from *astronomy*. And the two, as we shall see, were not divorced until the time of Sir Isaac Newton.

Attacks and defenses

During its very long history many attacks have been made on astrology, sometimes on rationalist grounds, more often on religious or moral grounds. The astrologers have naturally defended themselves, and the arguments on both sides have been endlessly repeated through the centuries. It should be noted that such opponents of astrology as the Christian Fathers attacked it not because it was a false science but because they thought it was a *science*. Also, some of the attacks on astrology (like Francis Bacon's, quoted above) assume there is something in it, or could be something if only its exponents were more knowledgeable or more scrupulous.

Bacon's demand .for a sane astrology is echoed in our own time by some deeply inquiring minds in Germany. Great efforts have been made in that country to vindicate astrology as a science (i.e., statistically; the French seem to have started this). Various experiments have been made from this angle, the object always being to prove that the diagnoses of astrologers are correct more often than pure chance (as indicated by the laws of probability) would allow. Sometimes the experimenters compare the horoscopes of a large number of people belonging to an easily defined group, such as lunatics or musicians. If a certain pattern in the natal charts recurs too often for the "laws of chance," this is taken as proof of the relationship between human beings and the stars. About 1900 a French artillery officer and amateur astrologer named Paul Choisnard made this sort of investigation into the horoscopes of people of outstanding ability; but he dealt with them only by the hundred. Later, in Switzerland, K. E. Krafft claimed to have made 60,000 observations of the charts of musicians and painters, and to have achieved positive results.

More recently various tests have been made by psychologists, the most famous of these by Carl G. Jung (as will be recounted later). In America in 1960 an Illinois psychologist, Vernon Clark, ran a test using a group of 20 astrologers and a control group (for comparison) of 20 psychologists and social workers. Each of the 40 persons was given 10 horoscopes (of persons unknown) and 10 case histories and was asked to pair them off. According to Mr. Clark, the results of the control group came out "almost exactly at chance"; those of the astrologers were higher. Similar results were obtained from a second and more complicated test on the same lines.

Some modern defenders of astrology, abandoning statistics and empirical criteria in general, have tried to prove that it was in the same category either

Above, a Babylonian boundary stone from about 1200 B.C. showing a king and his daughter at the feet of a goddess; above them are Venus, the Moon, and the Sun. Left, a 16th-century portrait of John Dee, court astrologer to Queen Elizabeth I. Astrology's prestige—gained from long association with royalty—declined in the Renaissance, when printed books gave its mysteries to a wider public. Right, pages from one of the earliest printed books on astrology (1485).

as mathematics (which is assumed to be non-empirical) or as mystical religion or the arts. Some astrologers have insisted that the aesthetic mode must now supersede the ethical; others, especially in America, are trying to make astrology either a substitute for or a culmination of religion.

Some of these controversies on the validity of astrology will appear in the historical chapters of this book. A distinction between "signs" and "causes" was repeatedly and forcibly drawn in past debates; some said the stars were one and some the other. This inevitably involved a discussion of free will, which proved as much of a red herring as it does with philosophers proper. Though the arguments repeat themselves through the centuries, the tone of voice usually varies according to the period and country and also according to the intellectual level or social class of the debaters.

As regards class, astrology for long was considered a *royal* science or art; astrologers (who themselves formed an elite) were accepted attendants upon the kings of Babylon and Assyria, the emperors of Rome, popes in the Middle Ages, and the great ducal families in Renaissance Italy. But by the 16th century, in spite of the fact that John Dee was patronized by Queen Elizabeth and Nostradamus by the queen of France, the social decline of the art was apparently concurrent with the appearance of annual astrological almanacs, which are still popular today. And the almanac makers were rapidly followed by the parodists. For example, in 1544 there appeared in England a satirical pamphlet entitled *A Merry Prognostication* containing the following stanza:

But I say if the ninth day of November
Had fallen upon the tenth day of December
It had been a marvellous hot year for bees
For then had the Moon been like a green cheese.

Some classical examples of almanacs from an intermediate period can be found in the writings of an English astrologer who called himself "Zadkiel the Seer." In his *Herald of Astrology* (later renamed *Zadkiel's Almanac*) published in 1832, he made predictions for 1833. In his 1834 publication he reprinted some of these predictions together with notes on their fulfillments. Sample prediction: "About the 12th [of February 1833] a vexatious event happens in London." Fulfillment: "A baronet's lady sent to the House of Correction on this day." For 1836 Zadkiel predicted: "About the 9th February lamentable events occur in Ireland; accidents by water will there be frequent." Fulfillment: "On Sunday the 14th inst., a sailboat from Limerick was upset in a squall and went down, when of 15 persons on board only three were saved."

These specimens are typical of almanac predictions from the Renaissance down to our own day. Almanac makers also of course make frequent predictions about international events; but here they tend to play safe or hedge and are rarely overspecific. For example: In April the British government brings out its budget. In *Old Moore's Almanac* (a long-established and popular specimen of its kind) for 1963, the first prediction for April states: "This year the political situation demands a soft budget, but the economic circumstances require a tough one."

For the decline of the royal art there were several probable causes, most of which overlapped each other. Chief of these perhaps were the Reformation, which cast doubt upon all forms of traditional authority or superstition; the increasing use of the vernacular where previously Latin had sufficed; the invention of the printing press and the rapid increase of printed books; and of course the Renaissance spirit of scientific inquiry. To take just one of these: The traditional astrology that was derived from Ptolemy (second century A.D.), so long as it was confined to manuscripts, remained the property and mystery of a few. Once it got into print, it gained in popularity but lost in prestige. Besides all this the telescope was now on its way.

By the 17th century the "scientific revolution" was really gathering force. But at the same time England produced her most popular astrologer, William Lilly, whose name is still honored in most modern astrological textbooks. Yet Lilly's milieu was very different from that of his predecessors in, say, 15th-century Italy; he descended or was forced to descend to repeated undignified mud throwing and squabbling, not only with the enemies of his art but with various rival practitioners who would have liked to take over his following. After Lilly's time astrology lost even more respectability, but made a comeback toward the end of the 19th century that has continued in our own time.

Above, Britain's King Edward VIII (later
Duke of Windsor) broadcasting his abdication
speech in December 1936. This event was
foreshadowed by a newspaper horoscope
(right) cast for his niece Princess Margaret at
the time of her birth in 1930, which predicted
events of great importance affecting the
fortunes of the princess in her seventh year.
This kind of general and often vague
prediction has been (since the 16th century)
a feature of most popular almanacs and
astrological periodicals.

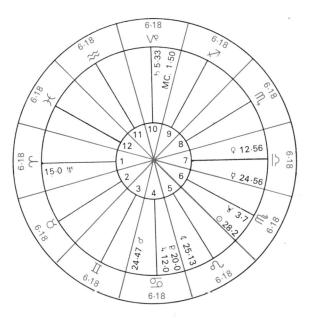

While most of our historical retrospect will naturally be devoted to Europe, it should be remembered that from very early times until today astrology has flourished—and with less fluctuation—in most Eastern countries. The prevalence of the art in 20th-century India has already been mentioned. Indeed, Indian astrologers claim that it was the West (as far back as Ptolemy or earlier) that learned from them. But there are very important differences between Hindu and Western astrology. For one thing, the former presupposes a belief in reincarnation. And the Hindus also have a different conception of the Zodiac.

In China, where astrologers had ranked very high from long before the time of Christ, the great Venetian traveler Marco Polo found them still very powerful in the 13th century. He recounts that in the great city of Kanbalu there were about 5000 astrologers and soothsayers provided for by the emperor. They used astrolabes and made weather forecasts (*meteorological* astrology) but also foretold such things as epidemics, wars, and conspiracies. Moreover, they were great exponents of electional astrology. No one would undertake a long journey without first consulting an astrologer; and no astrologer would give such advice until he knew the year, month, and hour of the would-be traveler's birth.

In a quite different part of the same huge empire, subject at that time to the Mongol Kublai Khan, Marco Polo explains how astrologers there could hold up funerals. No upper-class family would allow any one of its members to be cremated until the astrologers had examined his natal chart and fixed a day for cremation according to the planets or signs. Such a day might be six months off, which meant ordering an extra thick coffin and a large amount of preservatives and deodorants. And sometimes, for good measure, the astrologers would insist on the body being removed from the house along some particular line—which often entailed making a hole in the wall.

Astrology had a long run in China. As long as the old empire lasted, astrologers were as important at court as they had been in ancient Babylon. Thus even the tough old Dowager Empress Tzu Hsi, who ruled China at the time of the Boxer Rising, owed her occasional vacillations in policy to the intervention of astrologers. And when she was buried at 5 A.M. on November 27, 1909, it was the astrologers who had chosen the hour for the funeral. The site of her tomb had been chosen about 35 years earlier when, again thanks to the astrologers, the remains of a former empress had to be shifted to make room.

Mao Tse-tung presumably cares for none of these things. But in most other parts of the Far East astrology appears to be still flourishing. In what used to be Indochina astrological flags feature in the public processions, while there is a 200,000-strong federation in Japan to which professional astrologers belong, as well as palmists, graphologists, etc.

In most countries there are differences in the systems employed by astrologers and in the emphasis given to different aspects of astrology; at the same time there has been a good deal of interplay between most countries in Europe and Asia. In the old civilizations of Mexico and South America, centuries before

The Crown Prince of Sikkim (a province
in northern India) and his American
bride at their wedding in March 1963.
In accordance with Eastern custom,
astrologers were asked to select a
favorable wedding date; their choice
postponed the ceremony for a year.

they had any contact with Europe, some form of astrology was apparently practiced that was almost certainly different from European or Asian forms.

The literature on astrology is vast, and to read much of it at a time leaves one punch-drunk. Most of it is repetitious and much of it is tendentious and ill-written. Also, since the time of the Roman poet Manilius (first century A.D.), and the Greek astronomer-cum-astrologer Ptolemy, whose books are the first two extant that deal with the subject in detail, expositions of astrology have by their nature been cluttered up with technicalities, many of which seem arbitrary to many people (including some astrologers). By now there are so many things to consider in a horoscope that, while it may mean extra work for a scrupulous astrologer, to others it affords a ready let-out. For instance, people who read newspaper astrologers usually assume that your dominant Zodiacal sign is decided by what day of what month you were born on. But Rupert Gleadow writes: "It cannot be often enough repeated that one can be born under any sign of the Zodiac on any day of the year." The confusion will be cleared up in the next chapters.

The literature on astrology is not, of course, confined to sheer textbooks or to those "ephemerides," tables of "houses," etc., which are your necessary tools if you want to cast horoscopes. There is also a mass of casebook material, including *retrospective* horoscopes of famous people or of other things such as the city of Rome or the German Republic. There are the stories of notable predictions, correct or incorrect, and the stories of notable astrologers who made a fortune at court or got themselves burned at the stake. There are great rivers of polemic, for and against, and there are lyrical or mystical effusions by people for whom astrology was primarily neither a science nor an art but a religion. There are allegories and plays and parodies, and, lastly, the descriptions of astrologers or their practices in non-astrological writings such as Chaucer's *Canterbury Tales.* The literature ranges from the cuneiform clay tablets of Ashurbanipal's library in ancient Assyria to the latest almanac, from St. Thomas Aquinas to newspaper columnists like Britain's Gipsy Petulengro, from the adverse philosophical analyses of Cicero in ancient Rome and Pico della Mirandola in Renaissance Italy to a knockabout parody entitled: *Shinkin ap Shone her Prognostication for the ensuing year, 1654 . . . Printed for the Author, and are to be sold at his shop at the Sign of the Cows Bobby behind the Welsh Mountains.*

A sampling of the enormous assortment of astrological literature: top left, a description of the qualities of Libra from a 15th-century English manuscript; top right, two pages from a 19th-century Indian astrological text, depicting the Zodiac signs used in Eastern astrology. Bottom, a selection of modern astrological journals published in Europe.

Authors from different times and countries will be quoted in the course of this book, often on particular aspects of astrology. At this point it may be appetizing, as a sort of hors d'oeuvres, to provide a few typical remarks made by writers on astrology in general:

(a) Astrology is the science and art of describing persons and events of the past, present, and future by correctly interpreting maps of the sky drawn up for the appropriate moments and places.

(b) The heavens don't affect our will . . . but they do affect our bodies.

(c) . . . the foolish little daughter of the respectable reasonable mother astronomy.

(d) Astrology is essentially conservative (in the strict sense of the word), sedative, private, unsocial.

(e) I am convinced that the problem of the inequalities of the human race can only be successfully solved by a knowledge of astrology.

(f) At length I learned that wholly and altogether it was based upon no other foundation but upon mere trifles, and feignings of imaginations.

(g) If we listen within ourselves for a moment, then we can hear the breathing of planetary forms.

(h) There is some physical sympathy that makes earthly things depend upon celestial.

(i) . . . *cette chimère d'Astrologie.*

(j) There's not even a blade of grass, however infinitesimal, that is not ruled by some star.

(k) I believe God rules all by his divine providence and that the stars by his permission are instruments.

(l) Astrology stands first among those superstitions of which she is both mother and foster-child.

(m) From the scientific point of view, there is little hope of proving that astrological correspondence is something that conforms to law.

(n) Some astrologers say or write things *after* the event and pretend they had predicted them beforehand.

(o) If astrology is true, why bother with anything else?

These quotations, in the above order, come from the following array of authors:

(a) Rupert Gleadow, already mentioned, who seems (though he is very readable) to have stopped writing books about astrology.

(b) Marsilio Ficino, the founder of the Platonic Academy in 15th-century Florence.

(c) The pre-eminent 16th-century astronomer Johannes Kepler, who cast horoscopes as part of his job and made many confusing pronouncements on the subject.

(d) Tom Harrisson, founder of Mass Observation (a British sociological research organization), who wrote an article called "Mass Astrology" in the British weekly paper *New Statesman* in 1941.

(e) Alan Leo, already mentioned.

(f) Henry Cornelius Agrippa, already mentioned, 16th-century France.

(g) Louis de Wohl, already mentioned.

(h) The Jewish philosopher Philo, who lived in Alexandria in the time of Christ and made allegorical interpretations of the Old Testament.

(i) Voltaire, 18th-century France.

(j) One Rabbi Eleazar, quoted in the 13th-century *Zohar*, a mystical work compiled by Spanish Jews.

(k) William Lilly, already mentioned, 17th-century England.

(l) Pico della Mirandola, late 15th-century Italian humanist.

(m) The psychologist Carl G. Jung.

(n) The 14th-century French mathematician and ecclesiastic Nicole Oresme.

(o) An ancient Roman, about whom little is known, named Arellius Fuscus.

The variety of the names of these authors is nothing to the names that stud the average astrological textbook, some of which we too shall have to use more than once. Names like Mardukshakinshum and Adadshumusur, Adam, Abraham, Enoch and Solomon, Nechepso, Petosiris and Berosus, Nigidius Figulus and Hermes Trismegistus, Alexander of Tralles and Isidore of Seville, Alkindi and Albumasar, William of Auvergne and Moses Maimonides, Marbod and Gerbert, Adelard and Abelard, Albertus Magnus and Guido Bonatti, Madame Blavatsky and Baron Sobottendorff. Also Raphael, Zadkiel, Sepharial, and Gabriel, whose real names were Smith, Morrison, Old, and Hingston. If this looks as forbidding as the New York telephone directory, it does at least (just like that directory) bear witness to the cosmopolitan character of the subscribers.

Such is the cosmopolitan and venerable background to all the goings-on of astrologers both big and little; to the Archbishop of York whose sudden death in his garden was attributed by his enemies to the book of astrology he had hidden under his pillow; to the egg, hatched in Rome in 1680 with markings suggesting a comet, that touched off dozens of sermons and solemn theses in Germany; to such pronouncements as "All moles are the result of the influence of the planets" or "A doctor without astrology is like an eye that cannot see" or "The Sun, Moon, and stars were created on Wednesday, April 22nd, 6 P.M., about 4002 years before Christ"; to, in our own day, an astrological columnist in a Sunday newspaper who answers personally 100,000 letters per year; and also to certain German astrologers working out horoscopes with the aid of eight hypothetical trans-Neptunian planets that hardly anyone elsewhere has heard of. (In the U.S.A. some astrologers have gone even further by postulating at least 18 unknown planets.)

But through all this great range from the sublime to the ridiculous and underlying all the variations, mystical or whimsical, ingenious or plain silly, two things can always be found: a certain sense of mystery, and a certain hankering for harmony. Later chapters may indicate how traditional astrology originated with the first and attempted to satisfy the second.

2 Planets and personality

In a modern city we tend not to notice the stars. But even today, if we are alone in the country, they almost force themselves upon us, and they still excite wonder and a kind of distant affection. To the ancient civilizations, especially those that enjoyed clear skies, the stars were extremely familiar but also extremely puzzling. They were always there (or at least always returning), but with the exception of the two "luminaries"—the Sun and Moon—they never had any immediate effect that one could feel in the way one feels a change in the weather. You cannot grasp the rays of the stars in the way you can grasp any terrestrial object, animal, vegetable, or mineral.

There was another worrying thing about the stars. Most of them—the "fixed" stars—appeared vastly more stable and predictable than other natural phenomena. But a small minority seemed disturbingly wayward. These were the planets (the word comes from a Greek word meaning "wanderer"), which the Babylonians had called the "stray sheep." Sometimes they appeared to go forward, sometimes to go back, sometimes to stand still. It was probably in Mesopotamia that men first pondered the relations between the fixed stars and the straying ones, and first thought that they affected human life.

So began astrology. Very early it had been noticed (especially by shepherds and navigators) that however the Sun, Moon, and other planets may seem to wander, they do not just wander anywhere in the heavens. They keep within a

An 18th-century British "orrery" (named after the Earl of Orrery)—a clockwork mechanism that demonstrates the positions and motions around the Sun of the six planets known at that time, with their accompanying moons. Men have known since the 18th century (some guessed earlier) that the planets, including the earth, revolve around the Sun. But, in spite of astronomers' findings, astrologers still work from an earth-centered conception of the universe and treat the Sun and Moon as planets.

definite track, which eventually was called the Zodiac and divided into 12 parts bearing the same names as 12 of the constellations. The ancients decided that the position of the planets within the Zodiac at any one time must be what affected human beings. By the time of the Christian era the Roman poet Manilius could take as an established fact this significant interrelationship of planet and Zodiacal constellation (or "sign"):

No sign nor planet serves itself alone,
Each blends the other's virtues with its own,
Mixing their force, and interchanged they reign,
Signs planets bound, and planets signs again.

It was some time before the 12 signs of the Zodiac were identified and named. But the planets—Mercury, Venus, Mars, Jupiter, and Saturn—were known to everyone almost from the start. As, of course, were the Sun and Moon, which for millennia were also to count as planets. So before we consider the signs (which have been of great importance in astrology for at least 2000 years), it seems proper to look at the traditional pictures of the planets.

These pictures are highly anthropomorphic: Though some of the more sophisticated modern astrologers would like to explain this away as a convenient means of summarizing the planets' effects on human beings, even they sometimes find themselves talking as if the planets were human neighbors to be liked or admired or feared. The leading British astrologer Ingrid Lind writes: "I find that I come more and more to regard some of the planets at least as having distinct personalities." She adds (on the assumption that each of us contains *all* the planets, rather in the way that each of us contains the same set of organs) that the relationship between man and the planets resembles that between an actor and the various roles he must play: "If our Jupiter is weak he must be rehearsed until he no longer spoils the part with illtimed buffoonery."

(Incidentally, because astrological books and authors are so numerous, and repeat each other so much, I shall be quoting in this chapter and the next from only a few of them, selected on the sampling principle. One of them will be a 15th-century French work called *The Kalendar and Compost of Shepherds,* which not only is a valuable source of traditional astrological thinking but manages to make the most ancient commonplace fresh. Ptolemy has proved useful, as have the 19th-century authorities, mentioned in Chapter 1, "Raphael" and "Zadkiel." Aside from these, my principal sources have been modern books by such astrological writers as Ingrid Lind, Margaret E. Hone, A. J. Pearce, Furze Morrish, Rupert Gleadow, and W. J. Tucker—many of whom were mentioned in Chapter 1.)

The names we use today for the planets are Latin god-name equivalents of the earlier Greek god-names, which the Greeks themselves had matched to the god-names of those pioneering stargazers the Babylonians. Thus Mercury is a translation of Hermes (the Babylonian Nebo), Venus of Aphrodite (Ishtar), Mars of Ares (the red Nergal), Jupiter of Zeus (Marduk), and Saturn of Kronos

(Ninib). One would naturally assume that Babylonians, Greeks, and Romans (and for that matter Egyptians too) all called their planets *after* their gods. But a few astrologers maintain that it happened the other way around; i.e., that a certain planet was found to affect people's love-lives and that a goddess was then invented to represent this planet and was called Ishtar or Venus.

Nevertheless, before the Greeks gave their planets the names of gods (whom they had *already* invented), they seem to have given them names derived from their visible characteristics: Venus was the Dawn-bringer and Mars, because of his red color, the Fiery One. It seems possible that they changed to the god-names when they met with the astronomy-cum-astrology of Babylon. But perhaps after all we are not up against the old hen-and-egg dilemma (did god or planet come first?), because in early cultures these distinctions were often irrelevant. In Babylon some of the heavenly bodies *were* gods—or should we say some of the gods were heavenly bodies? Or should we say certain gods controlled certain heavenly bodies? Anyway, the great triad in that country was Sin the Moon-god (who was masculine and the most powerful), Shamash the Sun-god (feminine), and Ishtar, the goddess of love. Symbols of all three appear in stone carvings from the 14th century B.C.

This historical background will be considered further in later chapters. The immediate business here is to introduce the cast, the broad lines of whose behavior have hardly altered for over 2000 years. And a very strong cast it is. As an English astrologer put it in the 17th century, "you must know that the seven planets are the seven rulers of the world, by their different natures, and are God's instruments." Among the ancients the normal order of the planets, based

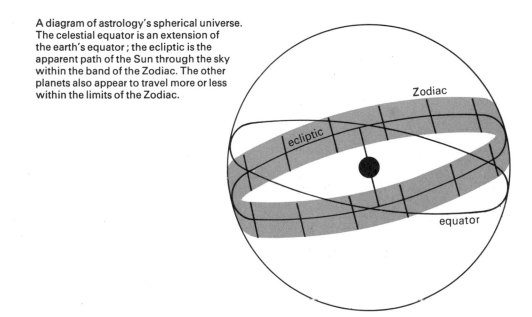

A diagram of astrology's spherical universe. The celestial equator is an extension of the earth's equator; the ecliptic is the apparent path of the Sun through the sky within the band of the Zodiac. The other planets also appear to travel more or less within the limits of the Zodiac.

The seven planets of traditional astrology
as depicted in the 15th-century French
astrological work *The Kalendar and Compost
of Shepherds*. Below the planets are the
12 signs of the Zodiac as they appear in
a 15th-century edition of a ninth-century
Arabian textbook. Each planet is said to
"rule" two Zodiac signs (except the Sun
and Moon, each of which rules one) ; here
the signs are shown in the same colors
as their ruling planets.

on their supposed distance from the earth, was : the Moon, Mercury, Venus, the Sun, Mars, Jupiter, and Saturn. (There are inscriptions at Nineveh, however, with the peculiar order : Moon, Sun, Jupiter, Venus, Saturn, Mercury, Mars.)

When astrologers say that someone is a typical Jupiterian or Martian or other type, they mean that he displays some or all of the qualities associated with the planet, and they assume that this planet was in some way dominant at the moment of his birth. There are various ways in which a planet achieves dominance : For one thing, each planet is the "ruler" of one or two of the Zodiacal signs. Thus Mars is the ruler of both Aries and Scorpio ; if he is found in either of these at the moment of your birth, he will tend to make you not only more of an Aries (or Scorpio) type but more of a Mars type. (This applies whatever the position of the sign.) As will be seen in Chapter 3, the Aries man has much in common with the Mars man, just as the Leo man has with the Sun man, and so on. A planet has a similar (though lesser) effect if it is in a sign that is sympathetic to it. Technically, this is known as "exaltation" ; Mars has his exaltation in Capricorn.

Some other factors that enhance the power of a planet are the following : If a planet is found at any of the four highly sensitive points in the heavens—the ascendant, its opposite the descendant, the mid-heaven (M.C. or medium coeli), and its opposite the imum coeli or I.C.—it will have something extra to say to you. So will a planet that is the ruler of the sign rising at your birth : If you have Taurus rising, Venus (the ruler of Taurus) will have more strength in your horo-scope. The same is true of a planet that is the ruler of your Sun-sign : Venus will again be strengthened in your horoscope if you are "born under Taurus" by being born between April 21 and May 21. (Serious astrologers, by the way, would not admit that this necessarily merits the label "born under Taurus.") Lastly, a planet can become prominent or dominant in your natal chart if it is strongly "aspected" by other planets. But aspects are a complicated subject that will be dealt with later.

All this should be enough to indicate that there is more than one way of becoming a "planet type" or of being "born under" any planet. The same is only too true of being "born under" any Zodiacal sign. And of course all the possible combinations and permutations that these factors supply not only give the astrologer a chance to show his skill but can also provide him with a let-out if his predictions go wrong.

Now let us turn to the characteristics of the individual planets, taking the Sun first, since he is pre-eminent in modern astrology. (Though modern astrology is not anthropomorphic, I prefer to call the Sun "him," the Moon "her," etc., in accordance with mythological tradition and also because, like Ingrid Lind, I am tempted to think of the planets as having "distinct personalities"—which would obviously not be neuter.) For people who read only the newspaper "pre-diction" columns, the Sun-sign (i.e., the Sun's position in the Zodiac on the day of one's birth) is the only thing in astrology that matters. Even through the long geocentric ages (and astrology still carries on as if the Sun went around the earth) the Sun was always unique. Some of the ancient Romans called him "the chorus-master of the planets." The point does not need laboring ; after all, the Sun is something that hits you. The centuries-old Hermetic writings on astrology, alchemy, magic, and so on describe the stars as visible gods of whom the Sun is far the greatest. The Sun's astrological symbol, or hieroglyph, is a dot within a circle: The circle is said to symbolize eternity or primal power; the dot pinpoints the emergence of that power.

Sun ☉

According to the British astrologer Margaret E. Hone, the "keywords" of the Sun (i.e., words that express the aspects of human personality connected with the Sun) are *power, vitality,* and *self-expression.* In contrast with the Moon, who represents the female principle and the unconscious, the Sun stands for the male principle and consciousness. Traditionally, he was neither a good planet like Jupiter and Venus nor a bad planet like Mars and Saturn. He had something of both, like Mercury. On the other hand, Indian astrologers tend to consider him powerful but on the whole malefic. For them the Sun controls the heart and the Moon the mind; but the latter, luckily, is generally considered to be the more powerful.

The Kalendar and Compost of Shepherds describes the Sun as "a planet of great renown and king of all the planets . . . he is hot and dry of nature, and the planet Saturn is to him full contrary." As for his effects on human beings, "all men and women that be born under the Sun be very fair, amiable of face, and their skin shall be white and tender, and well colored in the visage with a little redness. . . . They shall be clean and good of faith and shall be governors of other people. . . . The children that are born under the Sun shall desire honor and science, and shall sing very pleasantly. And they shall be of courage good and diligent, and shall desire lordship above other people. . . . And of all the members in man's body, the Sun keeps the heart as most mighty planet above all others."

Ptolemy states that of the seven ages of man the Sun controls the fourth, from about 20 to 40 (though other authorities apportion the ages differently). The Sun naturally rules Sunday; but, as the *hours* of the day were also shared out among the seven planets, on the Sun's own day his particular hours were the first, eighth, fifteenth, and twenty-second. The child in the womb was thought to be ruled by the Sun during the fourth month when the heart was formed. On the hand he rules the third finger. And Ptolemy (who attributed diseases to the planets as well as to the signs of the Zodiac) makes the Sun responsible for afflictions of the sight, brain, heart, sinews, and right-hand parts.

Toward the end of the ancient world, mystical thinkers made much of the strange behavior of the heliotrope, the plant that, like the sunflower, turns its flowers to the Sun. The fifth-century Neoplatonist Proclus writes: "Thus the heliotrope moves itself in so far as it is easy for it to move, and if one could only hear how it beats the air as it turns on its stalk, one would understand from this sound that it is offering up a sort of hymn to its King, of such kind of singing

Right, an engraving of the Emperor
Napoleon (based on a painting by the
Italian artist Toffanelli). Napoleon's
personal power and energy would be
ascribed by astrologers to the Sun's
prominent position in his horoscope. The
Sun is one "planet" whose traditional
astrological qualities have a factual
basis : It *is* a source of life and power.
Below, its energy is stored in a modern
solar power station in Israel.

as a plant can manage." This is one of the more obvious "correspondences" so much favored in the first Christian centuries and in the Middle Ages. Among the animals, vegetables, and minerals that the Sun rules are such obvious ones as the lion, the marigold, and gold.

But more important than the Sun's patronage of actual lions is his rulership of the Zodiacal sign Leo. The Sun and Leo both pull in the same direction, and the account of the Leo type of man in Chapter 3 will fill out the picture of the Sun type. This means that if in your natal chart you are born between July 23 and August 23 (which makes Leo your Sun-sign) and also born about sunrise (which makes Leo your ascendant, since naturally the Sun's sign rises when the Sun does) your solar and/or Leonine qualities should be doubled or more than doubled. Such a doubling-up is not necessarily an advantage, especially since the Sun is not necessarily a "good" planet. "Too much Sun," writes Ingrid Lind, "tends to make the individual overbearing." She also points out that you can have too much Sun, regardless of your Sun-sign or whether the Sun was rising or not, if there were at your birth too many planets in Leo (which is *always* the Sun's own sign).

It has already been emphasized that no planet can be assessed as if it existed in a vacuum. Its influence varies according to the sign in which it is found. The textbooks say that the Sun in Taurus or Pisces makes you rather short, in Virgo or Sagittarius tall, while in Capricorn he gives a "mean stature." But this material belongs more to the next chapter. Something else that affects the Sun's or any other planet's influence is the whole pattern of the sky—i.e., the aspects— at the moment of birth or any other moment of importance. The American astrologer W. J. Tucker says that the Sun and Venus in conjunction lead to a "finely poised character" (both Chopin and Bernard Shaw were born under this conjunction) while the Sun and Jupiter in opposition or square (both bad aspects) lead to financial entanglements.

From very early times eclipses of the Sun were regarded as portents of great events, usually disasters. The same of course was true of eclipses of the Moon; Ptolemy attaches enormous importance to both. Now that mundane astrology is so much overshadowed by genethlialogy, astrologers tend not to bother so much with eclipses. When they do they prefer to deny, in the words of the late A. J. Pearce, that "the mere eclipse portends anything." What counts again here is the over-all picture, the relative planetary positions. Pearce instances an eclipse of the Sun visible in England on September 7, 1820, at a time when the bad planet Mars was nearly in opposition to the bad planet Saturn in Aries, the ruling sign of England. "Within a few months England was on the verge of revolution." Great stress was traditionally laid on where the eclipse itself takes place; for example, in Libra it might cause ecclesiastical schism, while in Cancer it might make the fruit crops go bad.

Sun-worship—the exaltation of the Sun into the supreme deity (sometimes the only one)—has been common at various periods and in various countries.

Above, sunrise at England's Stonehenge, an ancient circle of stones probably used for Sun worship. In many past societies, the view of the Sun as the most powerful of the planets (a view shared by astrologers) led to worship of the Sun as the supreme god. Elements of this worship still survive today : Right, a participant in the centuries-old Swiss ceremony of goose-cutting (held every year at Lucerne) wears a Sun mask—perhaps a relic of some forgotten Sun ritual.

For that matter, in Baghdad about A.D. 900 there was a sect that prayed to the spirits of the planets. The ancient Persians sacrificed to the Sun; in Egypt as far back as the second millennium B.C. King Akhenaton attempted to overthrow the long-established polytheism and substitute a monotheistic Sun-worship; and in the declining days of the Roman Empire the Sun was proclaimed the supreme god on the Capitol. Of course, astrologers do not necessarily regard the Sun (or any other heavenly body) in a spirit of worship. There have been many astrologers who thought of *all* the heavenly bodies as divine beings; there have also been many who denied that they were anything more than inorganic objects. For all that, of the heavenly bodies that have been deified, the Sun (alias Sol, alias Helios, alias Shamash) takes first place. The only possible runner-up to him is the Moon, alias Luna, alias Selene, alias Sin.

Moon ☽

The fast-traveling and ever-changing Moon traditionally and obviously stands for the female principle (in spite of the Babylonians, who curiously made the Moon male). She brings out the lyrical vein in astrologers no less than in other people. The American astrologer Evangeline Adams writes: "She is the lustral water and the mystic bearer of the Holy Grail." In a different style the *Kalendar of Shepherds* says: "Such men and women as be born under the Moon shall be lowly and serviceable, and very gentle . . . and they shall be well favored both man and woman, and their faces shall be full and round. . . . They hate lecherous talkers and speakers of ribaldry. . . . They shall gladly go arrayed in many colored clothes, and they shall soon sweat in the forehead. Also they will have great desire to be masters and mistresses over great streams, rivers, and floods, and shall devise many proper engines to take fish and to deceive them. . . . And the lights and the brains of man are under the governance of Luna." The word lunacy, of course, comes from Luna; in the 16th century, Paracelsus taught that lunacy grows worse at the full and the new Moon because the brain is the moon of the microcosm.

In the Middle Ages, when some astrologers held that different historical periods fell under the sway of different planets, it was suggested that the Moon was in command when Sodom and Gomorrah were destroyed. This seems to fit with the *Kalendar*'s conception of the Moon as a patroness of chastity. But there are other facets of the lunar image. According to Raphael, the Moon is especially responsible for rather low-grade persons and sailors, for amphibious animals, all shellfish, such birds as geese and swans, such plants as seaweed, melon, cucumber, and mushrooms, and, among places, sewers.

The connection with water is obvious: From early times men had noticed the Moon's effect on the tides. Menstruation was also (understandably) referred to the Moon. In more recent times a lunar periodicity has been observed in the behavior of land crabs, palolo worms, and certain sea-urchins. The Moon, like the Sun, rules only one sign—Cancer the Crab (which is a "watery" sign). At one time astrological physicians advised that purges should be taken while the Moon is in a watery sign, the others being Scorpio and Pisces. The Moon has also been held to be involved in nearly all cases of drowning. And Rupert Gleadow writes that a dominant Moon may give you long, thin, damp hands.

Margaret Hone gives as the Moon's keywords *response* and *fluctuation*. The Moon governs babyhood and is concerned with the passions and emotions and also with changes in health. Unlike the Hindus, Western astrologers do not allow her control of the mind; for them the intellectual planet is Mercury. She is, however, of great importance if you want to marry.

W. J. Tucker assumes that the human character is threefold and gives its three components the somewhat arbitrary names of "individuality," "personality," and "temperament." Individuality, he says, is the product of the solar position and is "superconscious" (Evangeline Adams once defined individuality as the thing we feel behind a handshake); personality is of the lunar position and is subconscious; temperament is of the ascendant and is just plain conscious. The American astrologer Zoltan Mason states that the Sun represents your relationship to the divine spirit, the Moon your soul, and the ascendant your physical body. Australia's Furze Morrish holds that the Moon represents the pull of matter (subconscious) and the Sun the pull of spirit ("superconscious" again). Anyhow, whether the Moon is linked with the soul or with matter, the subconscious character seems to be a constant. So it is no wonder, in these days of psychoanalysis, that the Moon's position in the horoscope is considered by many astrologers to be almost equal in importance with the positions of the Sun-sign and the ascendant sign.

A "lunar" type as depicted in a modern French handbook of astrology. Such a childish "moon" face with its innocent, naïve expression can be (according to "physiognomical" astrologers) the result of the Moon's prominence in a horoscope.

Above, a 17th-century French engraving depicts the Moon's rays affecting the minds of women. Astrologers may not be able to prove the Moon's effect on the mind, but they can show that it (like the Sun) has *some* influence on earthly things—for instance, on the sea. Right, a diagram shows how the Moon's gravitational attraction creates high tides : It draws up the sea at A, leaving low tides at B and B[1]. Astrologers often go a step or two further and say (in effect) : The Sun and Moon affect the nature of the earth, so it is likely that they also affect peoples' natures. And if this can be said of the Sun and Moon, why not of the other planets as well ?

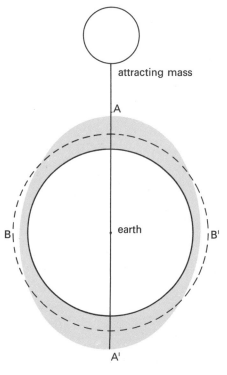

attracting mass

A

B   earth   B'

A'

Once again it is the over-all pattern that has to be considered. Tucker explains that, while the Moon in Gemini gives you the personality of a very successful commercial traveler (which seems to imply that what makes a salesman is the subconscious), the Moon in Capricorn will make you very disagreeable if you don't control yourself. Napoleon, he adds, had the Moon in Capricorn. The Moon in Scorpio is generally considered dangerous or undesirable, while the reason that Shakespeare did not invent his own plots (according to Evangeline Adams) was because he had his Moon in Taurus. As for aspects, the Sun and Moon in sextile or trine (both good aspects) are supposed to help you to get what you want, though perhaps you will get it too early.

The Moon's connection with health has always made her prominent in astrological medicine. The 17th-century English satirist Samuel Butler, in his burlesque poem *Hudibras,* caricatures William Lilly (the most famous astrologer of the day) as one who

>   . . . *with the Moon was more familiar*
> *Than e'er was almanack well willer.*
> *Her secrets understood so clear,*
> *That some believed he had been there,*
> *Knew when she was in fittest mood,*
> *For cutting corns or letting blood.*
> *When for anointing scabs and itches,*
> *Or to the bum applying leeches;*
> *When sows and bitches may be spayed,*
> *And in what sign best cider's made. . . .*

It is quite clear that in Butler's and Lilly's time many people did take the Moon into account when going about their household business. But other people flew higher, into more nebulous realms. A treatise in 1652 explains how "to extract a white milkie substance from the raies of the Moone." All you need is a glass and a sponge; but it is not clear what you do with the substance when you have it. In all such practices the *phase* of the Moon was always of utmost importance. In the Hermetic writings the peony is assigned to the Moon as one of her special plants; we are told that it grows as she waxes and wilts as she wanes. If you are going to use this flower for medical or magical purposes you must pluck it while the Moon is waning. On the other hand, the American astrologer Max Heindel held that surgical operations should be performed when the Moon is waxing. And medieval alchemists had found their experiments were more successful when the Moon was both waxing and ascending.

The use of the Moon in astrological medicine or magic had most respectable precedents. In Constantinople in the sixth century A.D. a physician at the court of the Emperor Justinian recommended that gout could be cured by inscribing a verse of Homer on a copper plate when the Moon is in Libra or Leo. In the Renaissance it was thought that dreams come true when the Moon is in any of the four "fixed" signs—Taurus, Leo, Aquarius, and Scorpio. The idea that the

Moon is concerned with diseases of the stomach, the womb, and "all left-hand parts" goes back to Ptolemy. And in relation to the four temperaments or "humors" or "complexions," she was connected by some with the melancholic (though more usually that humor belonged to Saturn).

So much for this "subconscious" lady. Let us now turn to a planet who, if anything, is almost too conscious. His hieroglyph is equated by some astrologers with the *caduceus*, the wand that was always carried by the god Mercury (or Hermes) in his double role of divine herald and conductor of souls to the underworld.

Mercury ☿

"The fair planet Mercury," says the *Kalendar of Shepherds*, is "very full and dry of nature" and is "lord of speech, as the Sun is lord of light. . . . Who so is born under Mercury shall be subtle of wit . . . [that is, and always has been, Mercury's first characteristic] and shall be very crafty in many sciences. . . . He shall ever follow and resort to them that be of good manners, and shall be fortunate on the sea to use the course of good merchandise." Mercury is the traditional patron not only of intellectuals but of merchants. He is also the patron planet of transport.

But the Mercury man, according to the *Kalendar*, will not have it all his own way. "He shall be very gracious, and he shall have harm by women, and when he is married, men shall not set so much by him as they did before." All the same, "he will have great love to ladies and gentlewomen, but yet they shall not be masters over him. He will be a very good man of the church or a religious man, and he shall not love to go to a warfare. . . . He shall love well to preach and to speak fair rhetoric language, and to talk of philosophy and geometry."

The *Kalendar* details other intellectual, artistic, and commercial activities and ends : "He shall be servant to some great lord or else a receiver of his money." (The original god Mercury himself had been something of a lackey on Olympus, always running errands for the greater gods.) "He shall have a high forehead, a long visage, black eyes, and a thin beard. He shall be a great pleader in the law, and will meddle with other men's deeds if they do not well and say against it."

There has been general agreement that Mercury stands for the intellect and for most types of communication, whether mental or physical. Not surprisingly, however, he is undependable; astrologers have named him "the chameleon among planets" (compare the adjective "mercurial") and have explained that he is neutral because, in the aspects, he takes color from other planets but does not give color in return. This idea goes back to Ptolemy, who says that Mercury is "generally speaking in nature like whatever of the planets may be associated with him." By Ptolemy's time he was also firmly established as the ruler of two signs, Gemini and Virgo. Rupert Gleadow, who calls him a "sexless planet," points out that both these signs are "somewhat lacking in emotion."

The Russian writer Leo Tolstoi (1828-1910), right, typifies the great intellect and powers of expression that are among the qualities associated with the planet Mercury—the ruler of Tolstoi's Sun-sign, Virgo.

Left, the Roman god Mercury, in a French bank's advertisement for travelers' checks. In both mythology and astrology, Mercury is considered to be the patron of commerce and transport : Thus the two roles here symbolized by the god are equally typical of the planet.

Mercury can make you a genius; he can also make you a crook. The original god had been both, as is shown by the early Homeric *Hymn to Hermes,* in which he is described (in Shelley's translation) as

A schemer subtle beyond all belief;

A shepherd of thin dreams, a cow-stealing,

A night-watching and door-waylaying thief

who yet, while still an infant, went on to invent the lyre, killing a tortoise to use its shell for the purpose. An English earl in the reign of Elizabeth I cited this traditional idea of crookedness to bolster up his attack on astrology in general, taking Mercury's influence as an example of unjust determinism: "If by nature no man ought to spoil or rob another, how cometh it to pass that Mercury, disposed thus or thus at the time of our birth, enforceth theft?"

In the field of diseases Mercury has been held responsible for ailments both of speech and of thought and for troubles in the bile and the buttocks (or, as Pearce puts it, "mania, apoplexy, convulsions, impediments of speech, coryza, and dry cough"). His day is Wednesday (French *mercredi,* Italian *mercoledì*) and, according to Ptolemy, in any man's life he rules the period from four to 14 when education is most necessary. Mercury's finger is the little finger, and physiognomical astrologers allot him the bridge of the nose. Three lines on the bridge of the nose denote eloquence and wit; more than three denote loquacity and deceit.

The planet Mercury, like Venus, owing to its *actual* nearness to the Sun, is always seen from the earth as lying in a sign near the Sun. Consequently Mercury and Venus are comparatively often found in conjunction. In spite of the frequency of such conjunctions an 18th-century English astrologer, Ebenezer Sibly, used one of them (retrospectively) to explain the French Revolution: "The active position of Venus and Mercury, conjoined, denotes much restlessness and instability in the councils of France, which seem distracted by the arbitrary will of the Gallic Queen, here represented by Venus, upheld and assisted by light, volatile, time-serving men, pre-noted by Mercury."

Similarly, Raphael says that Mercury is concerned among human beings with philosophers, secretaries, merchants, teachers, ambassadors, "and all ingenious clever persons" (with whom Raphael includes astrologers) but also, when he is in a wrong position, with thieves. Among the beasts of Mercury, Raphael continues, come "all such as are of quick sense, ingenious, inconstant, and swift; also such as are easily taught by man," including the ape, fox, weasel, hare, squirrel, hyena, and spider. Among fishes there are "the mullet and all swift reptiles"; among birds "all those that are naturally witty and inconstant," like the nightingale, blackbird, parrot, swallow, jay, and jackdaw; among places schools, tennis courts, fairs, markets, bowling greens, libraries, and counting-houses. According to modern astrologers, Mercury is also the ruling planet of the telephone system, radio, and other means of communication. Altogether a versatile, volatile planet.

As for aspects, it is generally considered that Saturn, having such a different and therefore complementary nature, is the best influence on Mercury. Saturn also has a steadying effect upon the next planet to be considered.

Venus ♀

Venus, whose hieroglyph is used in zoology to indicate that an animal is female, is a good and beneficent planet but does not always make a character strong. In ancient Babylon, under the name of Ishtar (goddess of love), she was the most powerful heavenly body after the Sun and Moon and her eight-pointed star is often found carved on the Babylonian boundary stones. She was traditionally known as the "lesser fortune" (Jupiter, another beneficent planet, was the "greater fortune"). She governs adolescence and is the giver of harmony, being especially influential in personal relationships and (more surprisingly) in money matters. Evangeline Adams holds Venus liable to produce "the dilettantes of the world"; she can make you graceful or lazy, gentle or indecisive. This is where Saturn is needed. As Pearce puts it: "If Venus be afflicted, there is a tendency to dissipation. A friendly ray of Saturn to Venus is exceedingly useful in steadying the character."

Her signs are Taurus and Libra, and she is very closely connected with the malefic Mars, as she was in mythology with the god of the same name. (Homer

A 15th-century woodcut depicting
the pleasure-loving, sensual Venus type.
On the left, Venus herself.

53

A third-century B.C. statue of the ancient love goddess Ishtar, who was identified by the Babylonians with the planet that we know today as Venus.

The French actress Brigitte Bardot, whose film roles have made her one of the modern world's "love goddesses"—and whose Sun-sign is Libra, a sign ruled by Venus.

tells a story about them being caught together in a net.) Mars stands for sex where Venus stands for love; if they are in a good aspect to each other, it bodes well for any lovers who are concerned. If they are in a bad aspect, then don't do it!

Raphael assigns to Venus "all such animals as are amorous in nature," such as the swan (which he also gives to the Moon), kingfisher, swallow, turtledove, lobster, salmon, and dolphin. Her flowers include the violet, rose, and lily, and she also rules many fruit trees. Among winds hers is the south wind, and her day is Friday (*vendredi, venerdì,* etc.). Pliny, the Roman author of the *Natural History,* thought that this planet had a *direct* influence on terrestrial beings through scattering some kind of genital dew. According to the textbooks she can (as one would expect) make you very beautiful, but when she appears in some of the signs she does nothing of the sort. Pearce writes that Venus in Capricorn "gives but a mean stature, pale sickly complexion, face thin and lean, hair dark or black." (In Pearce's discussion of hair color, Venus provides a good example of the variations caused when the same planet is found in different signs: The score seems to be three to four real blondes, three real brunettes, the rest in between.)

As usual, Venus and "her properties" are most sympathetically described in the *Kalendar of Shepherds.* She herself is "the gentle planet Venus, and it is a planet feminine, and she is lady over all lovers." As for her properties, the man or woman born under Venus "shall be a very gay lover, pleasant and delicious, and most commonly they shall have black eyes and little brows, red lips and chests [cheeks?], with a smiling cheer. They shall love the voice of trumpets, clarions, and other minstrelsy, and they shall be pleasant singers with sweet voice . . . and shall greatly delight in dancing and gambols with leaping and springing, and will use playing at the chess, and at the cards and tables, and desire oft to commune of lust and love, and covet oft sweetmeats and drinks as wine and be oft drunken, and oft desire lechery and the beholding of fair women, and the women of men in likewise, and use fleshly lust oftentimes."

The Venus types, as here described, seem to be more sensual than in modern astrology, where sensuality comes rather from Mars. But the sensuality of the *Kalendar* Venusians is not of the violent "dark god" type. The passage continues: "They will desire fair clothes of gay color and fine with rings of vanity, and all vain pleasure of the world, with fair and rich clothes, and pelts and precious stones. They shall love flowers with sweet smells. *Yet shall they be of good faith* [italics mine], and they shall love others as well as themselves. They shall be liberal to their friends. They shall have few enemies. If they be brown [of face] they shall be well proportioned of body. If they swear it is true, ye may believe them. And Venus governs the thighs of man." Easy on the eye, as they say, but also nice to know. The *Kalendar* writes very differently of Venus's opposite number, Mars, whose very hieroglyph is the opposite of hers, a symbol of male aggression.

Mars ♂

"This planet Mars is the worst of all others, for he is hot and dry, and stirs a man to be very wilful and hasty at once, and to unhappiness. . . . He causes all wars and battles. . . ." After stressing the old war-god character of the planet (in Homer Ares had been a most disagreeable god), the *Kalendar* comes on to the man born under Mars who "in all unhappiness is expert. He shall be a nourisher of great beasts [this would suggest violent stallions, bulls, and maybe bear-baiting dogs of the mastiff variety]. He is full of malice, and ever doing wrongs. Under Mars are born all thieves and robbers that keep highways and hurt true men, and night workers, quarrel pickers, boasters, and scoffers. And these men of Mars cause war, murder, and battle, and will gladly be smiths or workers on iron, light fingered and liars. . . . [The Mars man] is red and angry with black hair and little eyes. He shall be a great walker, and maker of swords and knives, and shedder of man's blood, a lecher and speaker of ribaldry, red bearded, round visaged, and good to be a barber and letter of blood, and to draw teeth, and is perilous of his hands. And he will be rich of other men's goods." In fact, as we should say now, a very fine specimen of an extravert. (In ancient times the planet seems to have been also identified with that notable performer Hercules.)

This is the traditional Western picture of Mars and the Mars man. But it should be pointed out that in ancient Egypt the planet was called Horus—the red Horus. This fact is used by the modern scholar Robert Eisler in *The Royal Art of Astrology*, a book that is violently hostile to that art; Eisler makes the point that Horus, in whatever form, was a favorite figure in the Egyptian pantheon, so there could not have been any question of turning him into a "malefic." Modern astrologers do not try to make Mars good but at worst they regard him as a necessary evil. Without him no one would have martial qualities, and no one would be either feared or loved when he wanted to be.

Margaret Hone gives as his keywords *energy, heat, activation*. The two signs ruled by Mars—Aries and Scorpio—both show the same dangerous energy. In Ptolemy's queer scheme of things, in which different countries were governed by different planets and signs, both Gaul and Britain were closely linked with Mars and Aries. "For the most part," writes Ptolemy, "their inhabitants are fiercer, more headstrong and bestial" than other people. Fairly recently a French astrologer who called himself "Papus" explained the English character by the fact that England's ruling planet is Mars and her national sign "the monstrous sign of Aries": The pure English type, the "John Bull," was according to Papus essentially Martian. But he wrote this while that type was still comparatively common. Nelson, who was not a John Bull but who certainly was successful in battle, was born with Mars rising in the second Martian sign of Scorpio. The great German soldier Wallenstein, one of the heroes of the Thirty Years' War and himself a devout believer in astrology, seems to have regarded this planet

Left, the great British military leader Field Marshal Lord Montgomery signs the terms of surrender with Germany in May 1945. Astrologers would attribute his military success to the favorable influence of Mars, which is the ruling planet of England and of Montgomery's Sun-sign, Scorpio. Right, an artist's impression of some quite contrasting Mars attributes: The features express the fierceness and brutality that are said to result from the planet's *adverse* influence in a horoscope.

as his patron; at any rate, this is suggested by a ceiling fresco in Prague entitled "The Triumph of Wallenstein."

Raphael, as usual, outlines the chief spheres of the planet's influence: Mars is concerned not only with military men but with surgeons and barbers and "all such as use implements of a sharp nature, all trades wherein fire is used." The creatures proper to him include the "mastiff, wolf, tiger, panther, and all such beasts as are ravenous and bad," also sharks and "all stinging water serpents and hurtful fish," and, needless to add, all birds of prey. His plants include thistles, brambles, nettles, ginger, pepper, garlic, "and all trees that are thorny or prickly." Among his minerals are bloodstone, asbestos, iron, and brimstone, and he is the patron of such places as furnaces, distilleries, and butchers' shops. His day is Tuesday (*mardi, martedì,* etc.), which in the Middle Ages was considered the best day for blood-letting.

Ptolemy points out that Mars dries up rivers and causes the loss of crops. A maleficent planet, Ptolemy also explains, causes *injuries* when it is rising as distinct from *diseases* when it is setting. As regards diseases, Pearce (who was strongly opposed to vaccination) states that unless Mars afflicts either the ascendant or the luminaries "there is little if any liability to take smallpox." Traditionally, Mars was known as the "lesser infortune" and Saturn as the "greater infortune." (Saturn was always considered the most powerful of the planets.) Of these malefics, Saturn's effects have been compared to a consumption, Mars's to a fever. Inevitably, the relations between them are to be watched. Mussolini had them in conjunction, Hitler in square, and Goering in opposition. It is a relief to turn from these infortunes and attend to the "greater fortune."

Jupiter ♃

Jupiter is the tycoon planet and it is after him, since he is also known as Jove, that people are described as *jovial.* His keywords are *expansion* and *preservation*; Papus describes him as "un mélange de père, de patriarche, et de roi." Mythologically, of course, Jupiter (the Greek Zeus) had been the king of the gods, as had Marduk at one time in ancient Babylon. The great 13th-century Dominican doctor Albertus Magnus argued that the pagan assignment of the thunderbolt to the *god* Jupiter was a mistake due to the influence of the *planet* Jupiter in bringing about thunderstorms. (Dominicans could not accept the pagan pantheon but some of them could accept astrology. And, astrologically, they regarded Jupiter, together with the Sun and Mercury, as one of the planets who patronized the Christian religion.)

In spite of Albertus Magnus and others, the traditional character of this planet continues to remind us of the old Greco-Roman father figure who would have been so at home on any board of directors or in any senate or country club. Of all "lucky stars" he is the most patently lucky. He can see through illnesses and he can help you to survive disasters. He is rather like those good old rich men in Dickens. This "noble planet," says the *Kalendar of Shepherds,* "is very

Pope John XXIII (1881-1963). Jupiter was
a strong influence in the pope's horoscope,
since it rules his Sun-sign, Sagittarius,
and was at the mid-heaven at his coronation
in November 1958. And the pope's career
reflected Jupiter's astrological association
with patriarchs and ecclesiastics.

pure and clear of nature, and not very hot, but he is all virtues. And there are
fixed in Jupiter two noble signs of love; the one is Pisces and the other is
Sagittary, signs of no evil nor unhappiness. This planet may do no evil; he is
best of all the other seven. He keeps the liver of man and maintains it joyously."

Whether he can do evil or not, Ingrid Lind and other astrologers admit that
he *can* cause boredom or embarrassment. The Jupiter man tends to get things
too easy, to talk too big, to deceive himself. The *Kalendar* is unaware of these
dangers and portrays the Jupiter man as a model of physical cleanliness, virtu-
ous living, and good clean fun. It is not suggested that he has much intellect
but "he shall be a fair speaker and say well behind a person. He shall love green
color and grey. He shall be very happy in merchandise, and shall have plenty
of gold and silver, and he shall love to sing and to be honestly merry. And of
the man he governs the stomach and the arms."

On the other hand, Raphael makes Jupiter responsible for quacks, cheats,
and drunkards—but only when he is weak in the chart. When he is strong, he
produces men like judges and archbishops. His beasts include "generous crea-

tures of most descriptions" and his places include palaces, courts of justice, and wardrobes. Pearce assigns to him not the stomach and the arms but "the lungs, the blood, and viscera." Some astrologers say that the typical Jupiter sins are more of omission than commission. Furze Morrish suggests that the proper "sublimations" for Jupiter people are "religious methods and philanthropy, ranging from conviviality to devotion." As to his aspects, Jupiter in square with Mars will exaggerate the Martian effects. And throughout history special importance has been attached to the "great" conjunctions of Jupiter and Saturn, that cold old planet who is our next subject.

Saturn ♄

Until fairly recent times Saturn was the most distant of the known planets. His distance made him seem both slow and cold and these qualities were enhanced by the traditional character of the god Saturn (the Greek Kronos) who got identified with Chronos—i.e., Old Father Time—scythe and all. (In the Middle Ages, Saturn was said to carry a scythe or a sickle because he does more execution when receding than when advancing.) And just as Kronos, before Zeus, had been king of the gods, so Saturn in many times and places was thought of as the most powerful single planet—perhaps because he was a notorious malefic. The Roman historian Tacitus wrote that "of the seven stars that rule human affairs Saturn has the highest sphere and the chief power." Like many of the ancients and their successors, Tacitus would have assumed that the highest sphere (i.e., the greatest distance from the earth in the center of the system) actually conferred the chief power.

Saturn is the governor of old age and his keyword is *limitation*. He is essentially cautious; even the ancient Babylonians called him the "steady one." (He is the ruling planet of Scotland.) As far back as Tacitus, Saturn was considered the planet of Judaism: Tacitus uses this to explain the Jewish observation of the Sabbath, which was also Saturn's day. In the Middle Ages the famous Scottish astrologer Michael Scot, contrasting him with Jupiter (the patron of true believers), points out that Saturn is the patron of pagans and Jews, who are as slow to believe as the planet is slow in getting about the sky.

Raphael's description of Saturn was quoted in Chapter 1. *The Kalendar of Shepherds* is equally eloquent: "When he reigns there is much theft used and little charity, much lying, and much lawing one against another, and great prison-

A 15th-century German allegorical picture of Saturn and some of the types of people associated with this planet. Saturn, depicted as a horseman, rides in the sky above his two Zodiac signs, Capricorn and Aquarius. To astrologers, Saturn's influence is mostly malignant, causing misfortune, disease, and death—indicated here by the criminals in the stocks and on the gallows and the hobbling cripple. Some less unfortunate Saturn types portrayed are the farmer (plowing), the gardener (digging), and the tanner (skinning a horse).

ment, and much debate, and great swearing. . . . And old folk shall be very sickly, and many diseases shall reign among people, and specially in the chief hours of Saturn. And therefore this planet is likened to age, as hard, hungry, suspicious, and covetous, that seldom is content with anything. For Saturn is enemy to all things that grow and bear life of nature, for the cold and stormy bitterness of his time." Where Venus and Jupiter are warm and moist, Saturn is traditionally cold and dry and so is linked with the humor of melancholy. According to the ancient Hermetic books, his plants include the asphodel and the house-leek.

The qualities assigned by the *Kalendar* to Saturnian types seem an odder mixture than with most of the other planets. "He that is born under Saturn shall be false, envious, and full of debate, and full of law. And he shall be cunning in curing of leather, and a great eater of bread and flesh. And he shall have a stinking breath, and he shall be heavy, thoughtful, and malicious; a robber, a fighter, and full of covetousness; and yet he shall keep counsel well and be wise in counseling, and he shall love to sin wilfully." Not all these traits seem in keeping with the planet of old age and caution. No more does what follows: "He shall be a great speaker of tales, jousts, and chronicles. He shall have little eyes, black hair, great lips, broad shoulders, and shall look downward. He shall not love sermons, nor go to church."

The *Kalendar* goes on to recount how vindictive Saturn people are and how "cold in charity." Their favourite color, of course, is black. Much of all this is derived from Ptolemy, who also noted that Saturn makes you hairy-chested, but only when he is rising. In Hindu astrology the planet is given an equally gloomy character: He is personified as lame, clothed in black, with long nails and teeth, and "skilled in all kinds of wickedness." In spite of this bleak picture, Saturn, like Mars, is needed in the heavenly kaleidoscope. Ingrid Lind (who presumably would not accept the more lurid details in the *Kalendar*) writes: "A person with a good Saturn is like a plant with sound roots."

In the Middle Ages Saturn was much connected with magic. Some even thought that for magical purposes he was more use than the Moon. On astrological images (small amulets inscribed with astrological symbols and designed to do the wearer good or his enemies harm), Saturn was represented as a man riding a dragon, holding a sickle, and dressed in black or a panther skin. What powers were attributed to him are shown by the remarks of a 13th-century bishop of Paris who was extremely interested in astrology but would not go so far as to admit "what is so celebrated among the astrologers . . . viz., that a statue will speak like a man if one casts it of bronze in the rising of Saturn."

In Renaissance Florence the scholar Marsilio Ficino (a protégé of the Medici family) worked out his own doctrine of melancholy—the *saturnine* humor—as the one of the four humors that most influenced intellectuals. In fact he tried to turn Saturn into a good planet and was proud that it featured largely in his own horoscope. Kepler also had Saturn prominent in his horoscope; skeptical though he was about the practices of astrologers, he could write quite seriously: "With me Saturn and the Sun operate together: therefore my body is dry and knotty, not tall. The soul is faint-hearted, it hides itself in literary nooks; it is distrustful, frightened, seeks its way through brambles and is entangled in them. Its moral habits are analogous." One more historical example: In the 17th century William Lilly described the hard-drinking Welsh clergyman who had taught him astrology as "the most Saturnine person my eyes ever beheld . . . seldom without a black eye."

Saturn's Zodiacal signs are Capricorn and Aquarius. Pearce, in supplying his usual catalogue of the effects of the planet in all 12 signs, finds few in which Saturn makes for an agreeable temperament. Of his own signs, Saturn in Capricorn is most unfortunate, but in Aquarius, apart from crooked teeth, he gives you a *mens sana in corpore sano.* Of the others, Saturn in Aries makes you "quarrelsome, fretful, and austere," in Taurus "avaricious, secretive, and envious," in Gemini "perverse, selfish, and austere," and so on. A notable exception is Saturn in Sagittarius, which makes you "affable, obliging, generous, honest, and upright, merciful to an enemy, and constant to a friend, profuse in promises through excess of good nature."

Other astrologers are more ready to recognize the helpful side of Saturn. Evangeline Adams writes: "The Saturn position of any man represents his wisdom; that is to say, his innate and accumulated experience." She instances

The Russian leader Joseph Stalin (1879-1953), whose Sun-sign, Capricorn, is ruled by Saturn. Many astrologers have called Stalin typically "saturnine," pointing out that his personality seemed to reflect the planet's astrological nature—somber, melancholy, and suspicious.

Gladstone and Woodrow Wilson as Saturnian types and also notes that self-made persons often come under Saturn. The 19th-century German astrological writer Countess Wydenbruck gives as Saturn characteristics "selfishness, reticence, diplomacy" and "disappointment, delays, constriction in every respect," and then adds "hard work and perseverance."

In the matter of aspects, where Jupiter tends to exaggerate, Saturn tends to limit or devaluate. Venus is the planet of personal relationships, but Saturn in too close conjunction with her will limit your power to make friends. Tucker maintains that while Saturn in sextile or trine (both good aspects) with the Sun will make you philosophize, Saturn in sextile or trine with Jupiter can contribute to genius—as with Bismarck and Dickens. More important still is Saturn in conjunction with Jupiter, which can lead to outstanding genius as with Shakespeare and Newton; but this same conjunction can also cause frequent attacks of gloom. Morrish points out that Saturn, who is especially concerned with the mineral kingdom, is the planet you want in the second house (the house, among other things, of finance) if you're after a mining contract.

For millennia Saturn was the farthest planet known to astrology or, for that matter, to astronomy. Then in 1781 Uranus was discovered. The impact of this most startling event will be discussed later; here we may confine ourselves to his characteristics, which have gradually accrued to him through the observation (or invention) of astrologers.

Uranus ♅

As has been observed by modern astrologers, the hieroglyph for Uranus looks like a television aerial, and they have now agreed that among other things he stands for mechanical inventiveness. Louis de Wohl (who was mentioned in Chapter 1) goes so far as to attribute the inventions of World War II—including radar, penicillin, V-1s and V-2s—to "Uranus running amuck," adding that his worst but perhaps most typical invention was "that dreadful super-Uranian thing made of uranium 235—the atom bomb." (Some astrologers, however, blame the bomb on Pluto.) He is also held responsible for the Industrial Revolution with which, some say, his discovery more or less coincided.

He is also regarded as the planet of rebellion and eccentricity; but, because it takes him seven years to pass through a single sign of the Zodiac, most astrologers agree that his influence falls on generations rather than on individuals. Pearce, however, holds that he can be very powerful in nativities when in aspect to the Sun or Moon, and attributes the mistakes made by earlier astrologers to their ignorance of his existence. He considers Uranus "very inimical to conjugal happiness" but admitted that there was not really as yet enough evidence about him.

Raphael (writing at a time when Uranus was still called "Herschel" after his discoverer) describes his effects as "truly malefic." The first Zadkiel, though also considering him more potent for evil than for good, adds that he might

Some astrologers regard the planet Uranus as the patron of the heavens (relating it to the Greek sky god Uranus) ; others connect it with mechanical invention. Right, a 16th-century German woodcut shows that these two ideas were linked long before the discovery of the planet Uranus : A curious human peers through the vault of the universe and sees the mechanism that moves the stars. Another "heavenly" mechanism is the steam engine (below right), driven by two wheels called "sun and planet wheels." This machine was patented by the British inventor James Watt in 1781—the year that Uranus was discovered. Below left, Russia's Yuri Gagarin, the first astronaut. The date for his flight into space (April 12, 1961) was favorable in astrologers' terms—partly because Uranus and the Sun were in trine (which is regarded as a good aspect).

lead to a "great love of truth." But Zadkiel makes no mention of machinery—nor of democracy, with which some modern astrologers associate Uranus.

But even now astrologers seem in considerable disagreement about this planet. Some make him (like Neptune, the next planet to be discovered) a patron of things occult. An American astrologer at the end of the last century noted that the planet "lorded it in the ascendant at the birth of Mrs. Annie Besant" (who was the second president, after Madame Blavatsky, of the British Theosophical Society). Furze Morrish (who is himself much influenced by theosophy), in calling for a "World Aristocracy of Integrated Minds," wants as his pioneers men like Franklin D. Roosevelt in whose chart Uranus is positively emphasized. But, he adds, this could hardly happen under the "democratic" electoral system.

On the other hand, Rupert Gleadow insists that Uranus is a supporter of democracy. (His anthropomorphic account of the struggle between Uranus and Saturn for the rulership of Aquarius will be summarized in more detail in Chapter 6.) His point is that Aquarius represents the ordinary man and that Uranus by rights should be his ruler since Uranus represents, among other things, international collaboration and the brotherhood of man. On the same assumption, some astrologers have entitled Uranus "the emancipator." Ingrid Lind rather hedges her bets by associating this planet with "change (revolutionary, disruptive, dictated)." Most astrologers would agree that he is concerned with change; the question is what *kind* of change. Gleadow is banking on a change in the right (i.e., truly democratic) direction and therefore opposes Uranus not only to the repressive Saturn, but to the mysterious and sinister Neptune.

Neptune ♆

According to Gleadow, Neptune stands not only for *sensation* but for "the absorption of the self into something great and wonderful"—such as modern dictatorships. Margaret Hone and Ingrid Lind give as his keywords *nebulousness* and *impressionability*, which might possibly have applied to the Nazi masses but do not seem to fit, say, the Soviet Union or Communist China. On the other hand, Gleadow considered Hitler a typical Uranian, which makes it the more confusing when he lines up Neptune with Saturn against Uranus. We can sympathize with Zadkiel who wrote soon after Neptune's discovery: "Nothing has been satisfactorily proved as to the nature of this planet, astrologically, hitherto." He added (rather surprisingly, since Neptune was also the Roman god of the sea): "So far as we know, he seems to be dry, warm, and genial, or of fortunate 'influence'." But later astrologers, agreeing that nothing has been proved about the planet's nature, have not endorsed this individual view.

Countess Wydenbruck includes among Neptunian characteristics emotional genius and mysticism and, "if badly aspected, drunkenness, drugs, fraud." Ingrid Lind, who suggests that with slow-running planets the *transits* are the things to look for, notes that Neptune's transits lead to muddle, and adds: "It really takes a strong and sane man to control the Neptune in him." It must be remembered that it takes this planet 15 years to pass through one sign, and that neither he nor Pluto can get around the Zodiac in an individual's lifetime. As Evangeline Adams put it, he has more to do with the *Zeitgeist* than with individuals. She suggests that, historically, Neptune in Leo may have been responsible for national revolutions, in Virgo for great lawgivers, and in Sagittarius for artistic revivals or new ideas in religion. Furze Morrish, who assigns the five senses to the five "older" planets, connects both Uranus and Neptune with extrasensory perception (E.S.P.).

Margaret Hone, thinking of Neptune's nebulous character, points out that he was discovered in 1846, the same year in which ether was first used in surgery. She also connects his discovery with the introduction of gas lighting. As with

Gleadow's remarks about Uranus, many people may fail to see why the *discovery* of a planet should be responsible for anything. One possible answer available to modern astrologers lies in the suggestion that the time was ripe for *both* the discovery of Neptune and the first use of ether and gaslight.

Some astrologers (rather obviously connecting the planet with the god) would like to transfer to Neptune the rulership of Pisces, which traditionally belongs to Jupiter. Some, apparently also working by association of ideas, attribute to him occupations to do with the sea (which Raphael had given to the Moon). In the same way Pearce, not having had long acquaintance with Neptune, is cautious about him, suggesting that he might give one a bent for foreign travel. As for the qualities of sensationalism and nebulousness and mysticism and mediumism and so on, these too may well have been suggested to astrologers by the enormous distance from us of this planet and by the mere chance of his name. (On this second point, however, some astrologers are capable of replying that the planet himself—or perhaps the whole starry set-up—imposed the inevitable name upon the people who thought they were inventing it.)

Russian revolutionaries in 1917 firing on their tsarist enemies. Although astrologers disagree as to the spheres of Neptune's influence, some have suggested that this planet in Leo causes revolutions. The slow-moving Neptune was last in this sign at the time of the Russian Revolution.

Whether Neptune himself is as eccentric or not as they say he is, he certainly seems to make some human beings so. Max Heindel, wanting to equate the planets with "the seven spirits before the throne of God" (excluding the Sun and Moon, which the ancients had counted as planets, but including the earth and Uranus), disposed of Neptune by stating flatly that he "does not really belong to our solar system." What *is* Neptune then? Answer: "The embodiment of a Great Spirit from the Creative Hierarchies which normally influence us from the Zodiac." This was written in 1919. Today Furze Morrish, whose bugbear is jazz, assumes that Neptune of all planets is the one to remedy this: With his entrance into Libra (which of course represents balance) we may find, he hopes, "a change from the abominable, destructive, and maniacal type of music." He even adds optimistically: "Ugly music could be banned."

That leaves us with little far-flung Pluto, compared with whom (in terms of being known about) Uranus and Neptune are veterans. He has not as yet even acquired a proper hieroglyph.

Pluto ♇

Pluto was not discovered till 1930 and many astrologers are still naturally reluctant to diagnose his significance. Presumably Max Heindel, if he were alive, would explain that he had just dropped in from the Zodiac. Pluto is as far away again as Uranus and his apparent motion is only one and a half degrees a year, so it would seem safe to say that he is even less concerned with the human individual than Uranus and Neptune. Ingrid Lind, however, ventures the opinion that he may be "associated with divorce and re-marriage"—but then such things these days are practically a mass movement. On the other hand, Gleadow considers Pluto very important just because he is so slow-moving: In contrast with the Moon, who is transiting all the time, Pluto barely makes a dozen transits in a lifetime.

Unlike other astrologers, who connect this planet with Scorpio or Pisces, Gleadow says that Pluto appears to rule Aries (what would Mars say?) and that, when he was in Gemini, he produced the airplane. He adds: "Of course it must not be thought that Pluto had no influence before he was discovered." Furze Morrish says that Pluto's entrance into Cancer led to a wave of sensationalism and World War I and his entrance into the next sign, Leo, to World War II and dictatorship. Margaret Hone gives as his keywords *elimination, renewal, regeneration.* She connects him with the blackout in World War II (association with the kingdom of Hades?) and with the eighth house, which is the house of death.

The discovery of Uranus fluttered the astrologers for some time but they eventually adjusted; however, they are still having trouble adjusting themselves to Neptune and Pluto. Some astrologers now, at least in Germany and the U.S.A., follow the principle that attack is the best form of defense and are casting and interpreting horoscopes with the aid of a whole set of hypothetical planets lying on the *far* side of Pluto. These planets are properly equipped with names as well as with orbits, but, because there is no astronomical evidence of their existence (though some *astronomers* are, in fact, looking for a trans-Plutonian planet), they will be ignored in this chapter.

As far as the "old" planets are concerned, the traditionalists among modern astrologers (which means the vast majority of them) still use them in interpreting horoscopes very much as they were used by Ptolemy. It must be repeated that the planets are regarded as having influence *only* in relation to each other and to the signs of the Zodiac. And with the signs, just as with the planets, it must always be remembered that there are a great many factors and relationships to be considered before it can be established that so-and-so is such-and-such a "type." With that word of warning we can turn now to the signs of the Zodiac themselves, without which the planets would be not just wandering but lost.

St. Paul's Cathedral above the smoke of the
London Blitz in 1940. Many astrologers assign
explosive and destructive qualities to Pluto,
and regard the planet's discovery in 1930 as
the starting point of a period of darkness
and violence that culminated in world war.

3 The signs of the zodiac

For the sake of convenience (but quite incorrectly) the planets were considered in Chapter 2 more or less on their own. In this chapter the signs of the Zodiac will be treated in the same way, though always with the reservation that, in Ingrid Lind's words, each sign, planet, or other element of a horoscope "has its own characteristics, and like the ingredients of a cake before mixing can be seen and described separately. But, as any cook knows, separate ingredients when treated and mixed produce totally different results." In fact, the Zodiac considered apart from the planets is like an empty stage or empty race track.

The more confusing technicalities, such as the vexed question of "houses," need not concern us at this stage, though I should repeat the warning that the 12 houses, to which astrologers have attached such importance for centuries, do not coincide with the 12 signs of the Zodiac. But we will come to these questions later. Now we are going to concentrate on the signs.

The name "Zodiac" comes from the Greek word *zodiakos,* meaning "to do with animals." This in turn is derived from the Greek *zodion* (strictly *zoïdion*), meaning "a little (painted or carved) animal." The plural *zodia* was used by Aristotle for the Zodiacal constellations, presumably because the ancients pictured many (though not all) of them in animal form. The Zodiac itself, which contains these little animals, is a circular band of sky spreading some eight degrees either side of the ecliptic (the path of the Sun), and it is only within

An illustration from a 15th-century
French text depicting the relationships of
the seven planets to the 12 signs of the
Zodiac. Within a conventional portrayal
of the Zodiac band (with the earth at the
center), a personification of each planet
is shown linked to the signs it rules:
For example, Mars (an armored knight)
is joined to Aries and Scorpio.

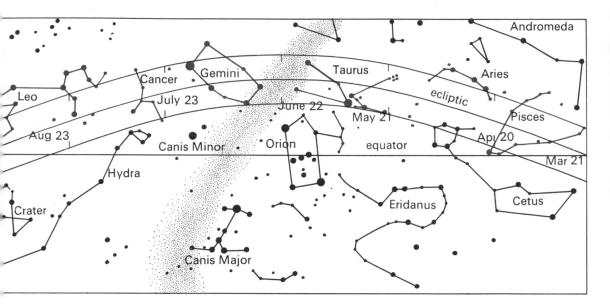

Left, Capricorn the Goat (with the figure of Aquarius visible in the background), as personified in *The Celestial Atlas* of John Bevis, printed in England in 1789. The drawing is superimposed on a map of the constellation; but (as with most Zodiac signs) the shape of the figure has little in common with the pattern of the stars.

Above, a star map relating the actual Zodiac constellations to the imaginary Zodiac band. Due to a "shift" in the stars' positions over many centuries, the dates of the Sun's entry into each constellation no longer correspond to the dates still used by astrologers. For example, the Sun now "enters" Taurus in May, not in April.

this band that the planets are seen from the earth. Astrology always has been, is, and always will be geocentric; but the *astronomical* reason that the planets appear to confine themselves to the Zodiac is that their real orbits around the Sun are all more or less in the same plane. The Zodiac does not lie flush with the "celestial equator" (an imaginary extension of the earth's equator) but is hitched at an angle to it, rather in the manner of a cowboy's belt.

When the Zodiac was divided into the 12 signs is not known for certain, but it was certainly long after men had identified the planets and endowed them with astrological significance. Here another distinction must be made. Within the Zodiac there are 12 constellations (though once, it seems, there were only 10). These bear the same names as the 12 signs used by astrologers; but astrologically they have nothing to do with the case. If you are told that your Sun-sign is Aries—which means that the Sun was in that particular sign when you were born between March 21 and April 20—this does not mean that you were born under the actual group of *stars* known as Aries. Once upon a time the Sun *was* (or appeared to be) among that group at that time of year; but he is not there now, thanks to what is known as the "precession of the equinoxes" (a very slow shift in the sky pattern, as observed from the earth, that takes 25,800 years to come full circle). The signs that most modern astrologers deal with are 12 exactly equal sections of the total circle of the Zodiac. Each section measures 30° and it makes no difference what fixed stars are contained in it.

This disconcerting fact provides ready ammunition for opponents of astrology. Robert Eisler (whose polemic book *The Royal Art of Astrology* was mentioned earlier) pounced with joy on this divorce of the two Zodiacs. "If it is conceivable," he wrote, "that the sector in which Taurus stood two thousand years ago can still impart 'Taurine' qualities to children born or conceived when this sector was just rising above the horizon, why is this 'Taurine' influence of a constellation which is no more there—i.e., of a pure memory-image—not overwhelmed by the quite different influence of the stars of Aries, which *are* actually there now, for everyone to see?" Eisler would certainly have an almost unanswerable point if modern astrologers (like many of their predecessors who were only too ready to talk about "radiation," etc.) really believed that the stars exercised a direct *influence* upon human beings. But most of them do not believe this. They consider, as did some astrologers in the Middle Ages and the Renaissance, that the stars are merely "signs," not "causes."

In a passage much quoted by modern astrologers, Carl G. Jung wrote that all of us, being born at a given moment and a given place, are invested for life with the qualities of the time of our birth. According to himself, Jung was not presupposing a *causal* relationship but rather relying on that presumed "unity of things" which has so often been a cornerstone of astrology. Anyhow, many astrologers find it logical to attach such importance to the moment of birth; some even claim that there is a mass of empirical evidence (like the statistics referred to in Chapter 1) proving that, other things being more or less equal, people born at the same time (i.e., under the same stars and planets) tend to have certain characteristics in common.

But some more sophisticated modern astrologers, who stress the psychological side of their art, are usually embarrassed by the mass of astrological lumber in their attics. They feel vulnerable to charges like the one made in *Chambers's Encyclopaedia* (1959) that "the fundamental flaw in the whole system of astrology is the arbitrary character of the presuppositions made." In an attempt to get rid of these arbitrary elements, there is accordingly a modern movement away from traditional astrology.

For all that, the pictures of Zodiacal human types given by such a cultured and amusing astrological writer as André Barbault still remain pretty traditional and, if only from an aesthetic point of view, it would be a pity to scrap some of the more "arbitrary" detail. In fact, since ours is a period when people have a passion for classifying each other (compare Jung's "psychological types"), Barbault has watched his detail and provides a set of self-consistent pictures. He also is very well aware of the poetic or symbolic appeal of his subject matter. But with most of the moderns, psychology is what they go for. Rupert Gleadow writes: "The chief advantage of studying astrology is that it gives the power to understand the feelings and temperaments of others." Which, as he says, can be very useful when asking people to dinner or contemplating marriage.

How or why the signs got the names that they share with the constellations we do not really know. Of the constellations, Leo is the only one who looks

Many of the Zodiac signs we use today can be traced back 3000 years, though their exact date of origin is uncertain. Three of the earliest known representations are from Babylonian *kuddurus* (boundary stones) of the 10th century B.C.: Sagittarius (with two heads, a man's and a lion's), Capricorn, and (right) Scorpio.

anything like his name. Some people have tried to derive the Zodiac names from seasonal activities—Virgo from young girls harvesting and Pisces from the fishing season—but this often seems conjectural and forced. Gleadow denies "that the signs were named after the constellations with which they once coincided." He thinks it was the other way round: that the signs—the mechanically bacon-sliced 30° strips of Zodiac—"were named symbolically after the effects they were found to have, and that these names later became attached to the constellations." This seems very odd, especially if one thinks of the effects ascribed to some of the signs. Why should the quality of tenderness, for instance, make people think of the name Crab? Or fixity of purpose suggest the name Water-carrier?

Traditionally, the 12 signs fell into groups of three in accordance with the four elements—so that there are fiery, earthy, airy, and watery signs—and into groups of four in accordance with the three "qualities"—so that there are "cardinal" (i.e., predominant), "fixed," and "mutable" signs. The ancients stressed some other groupings: male and female signs, human and brute signs, single and double signs, land and water signs, and also mixed signs such as Capricorn, the goat-fish. Ptolemy gives four categories: "solstitial" (Cancer and Capricorn), "equinoctial" (Aries and Libra), "solid" (Taurus, Leo, Scorpio, and Aquarius), and "bicorporeal" (Gemini, Virgo, Sagittarius, and Pisces). The first and second of these groupings make good sense but some of that arbitrariness already mentioned seems to have crept into the third and fourth.

The groupings by elements and qualities seem to be of primary importance to most astrologers. In 17th-century England, the famous William Lilly pointed out that the great conjunction of Saturn and Jupiter in 1603 was "their entrance into the fiery Triplicity." By "triplicity," which he also called "trygon," Lilly meant the triangle made by the three *fiery* signs—Aries, Leo, and Sagittarius. "This Trygon is called by Ptolemy the first of the Zodiac; and by the Arabians, the fiery Trygon." Lilly also remarked that this "trygon" was always connected with "memorable and notable changes in the Church and Commonwealth: . . . great actions and alterations have happened under it." He added, by way of proof, the fact that James VI of Scotland became king of England in 1603. (Incidentally, this dissertation on the great conjunction was published about 40 years after the event.)

Most astrologers hold that it makes a great difference whether you are fiery, earthy, airy, or watery. In early 19th-century Britain, John Varley, author of *A Treatise on Zodiacal Physiognomy,* wrote: "The fiery trigon . . . contains the spirited, generous, magnanimous, and princely natures. The earthy trigon, Taurus, Virgo, and Capricorn, contains the careful, sordid, and penurious qualities; the aerial trigon, Gemini, Libra, and Aquarius, contains the humane, harmonious, and courteous principles; and the watery trigon, Cancer, Scorpio, and Pisces, the cold, prolific, cautious, and severe qualities." (Not all of this attribution of qualities would be endorsed by modern astrologers.) Varley added, but without giving statistical evidence, that vastly more people are born under "the earthy, melancholic Saturnine, and the watery, phlegmatic signs" than under the other two groups.

In the 20th century America's W. J. Tucker (drawing on another American, Max Heindel) explains the psychological differences between the cardinal, fixed, and mutable signs: A cardinal sign (i.e., Aries, Cancer, Libra, or Capricorn) has a dynamic influence, though lacking directive power, and affects your conscious mind; a fixed sign (Taurus, Leo, Scorpio, or Aquarius) awakens your desire-nature, makes you stubborn but dependable, and affects your subconscious mind; a mutable (Gemini, Virgo, Sagittarius, or Pisces) deals with your super-conscious. Heindel had also asserted, specifically in regard to the treatment of invalids, that with the cardinal signs you can expect co-operation from the patient, whereas the fixed signs (such as bovine Taurus and arrogant Leo) are so fixed in their ways that they are difficult to handle.

Louis de Wohl distinguishes between signs that encourage the man of action (such as Aries, Scorpio, and Sagittarius) and signs like Gemini and Virgo that encourage the man of system. If you are born under the latter you might well make a Chief-of-Staff, but don't go near the front! Of the relationships between signs, all astrologers hold that some signs are mutually congenial and some are not; for example, many astrologers would advise a Pisces type to marry a Cancer but not a Virgo. Gleadow maintains very plausibly that the greatest contrasts are between adjoining signs, as between Taurus and Gemini. And he differentiates between the behavior of the "trigonal" or elemental groups: "The fiery signs, for example, eat a great deal, not from greed, but because their internal combustion proceeds very rapidly."

The traditional order of the signs—Aries, Taurus, Gemini, Cancer, Leo, Virgo, Libra, Scorpio, Sagittarius, Capricorn, Aquarius, Pisces—represents, according to Ingrid Lind, "a progress from primitive unity and simplicity to complexity." This notion of Zodiacal evolution has been elaborated by much less orthodox astrologers, such as Furze Morrish. For Morrish the circle of the Zodiac is a pilgrimage. The first six signs, beginning with Aries ("nescience" or ignorance), represent the achievement of full objective consciousness (culminating in Virgo) and the latter (or homeward?) six represent "evolution into the subjective states, or yoga." The 12th sign, Pisces, corresponds to the ascension into heaven (which should comfort those Pisceans who have been told by popular books of astrology that they are just a lot of woolgatherers).

Aside from these groupings—the relationships of the signs with one another—the signs also form other relationships. As already mentioned, from the time of the Greeks and Romans the signs were distinguished according to their planetary rulers: Many, say, of the Sun's qualities would be found to characterize the sign Leo; many of the qualities of Venus would be associated with her signs Taurus and Libra; and so on. There are also relationships between signs and houses, between signs and "aspected" planets. And, as another kind of relationship, the apportioning of parts of the human body to the signs was considered gospel even in ancient Rome, where the first-century A.D. poet Manilius wrote (in a 17th-century translation):

> The Ram defends the Head, the Neck the Bull,
> The Arms, bright Twins, are subject to your Rule:
> I' th' Shoulders Leo, and the Crab's obeyed
> I' th' Breast, and in the Guts the modest Maid:
> I' th' Buttocks Libra, Scorpio warms Desires
> In Secret Parts, and spreads unruly Fires:
> The Thighs the Centaur, and the Goat commands
> The Knees, and binds them up with double bands.
> The parted Legs in moist Aquarius meet,
> And Pisces gives Protection to the Feet.

These relationships (or correspondences) are just a few of the "ingredients" referred to earlier. One can easily agree with Rupert Gleadow that "with so much material to go on one is never long at a loss to analyse anyone in terms of the Zodiac."

But before we enter this gallery of 12 archetypes, one very popular fallacy must be ruled out. To be, say, an "Aries type" you do not need Aries as your Sun-sign; i.e., you need *not* have been born between March 21 and April 20.

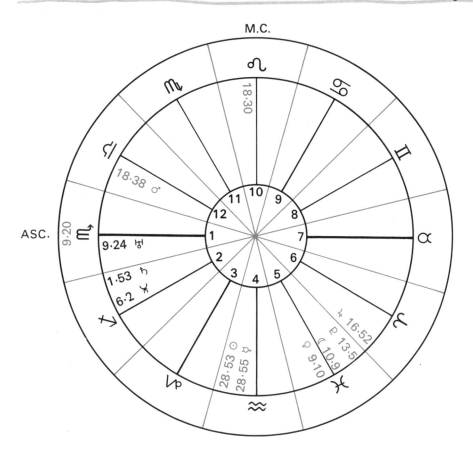

One should know one's Sun-sign—as practically everyone does—but there are two other things, as suggested in the last chapter, of at least as great importance in and to a horoscope. These are, first, the position of the Moon in regard to the planets in the Zodiac, and, secondly, the ascendant, the sign that was rising above the eastern horizon at the moment of birth. If you were born at sunrise—i.e., if your Sun-sign and ascendant coincide—the effect of the sign, as one would expect, is taken to be greatly enhanced. The same is true if the planet that "rules" the sign is present in it at the time of birth. And the story does not end here; there are yet other things in the whole pattern of the heavens (as we saw in Chapter 2) that can make you an Aries type: For instance, Aries may be neither your Sun-sign nor rising when you are born, but if there are enough planets in conjunction in Aries (no matter where Aries is in your horoscope) this may be enough to make you an Aries type.

It should be added that very few people are "pure" Zodiacal types. The great majority are noticeably influenced by more than one sign. This is where the really subtle astrologer (of whom there are not so many) can show his skill in *interpretation*. Even the most naïve astrologer would not claim that there are only 12 types of human being; but we will now look at the 12 *basic* types, giving just a hint here and there of the countless possible variants.

Right, the American poet Edgar Allan Poe (1809-49). Poe's life and writing were haunted by a morbid obsession with violence and death—both associated by astrologers with Scorpio. Poe was "born under" Aquarius; but Scorpio is in the ascendant in his horoscope (left). In many horoscopes, the ascendant sign (or other features) can be more influential than the Sun-sign.

Aries the Ram ♈

March 21 to April 20. The hieroglyph for Aries looks like a ram's horns (though Morrish says it might just as well represent a fountain). A cardinal, fiery sign, ruled by Mars: cardinal in that it serves as the ignition key for the year, fiery in that it symbolizes the explosive suns of spring. This is the sign of the vernal equinox when the ecliptic crosses the equator and day and night are of equal length. To the ancients it seemed natural to begin the astrological year on March 21 with the first degree of Aries (0° Aries), though the people in the southern hemisphere were not consulted about this. That Aries is a "priority" sign in almost every respect is shown by the instructions given in some of the early Hermetic writings as to the use of "Zodiacal plants" for magical purposes: Whatever the plant and whatever other sign is concerned, it should be picked and its juice extracted when the Sun is in Aries.

Aries is in general the adventurous pioneer sign and, like all the other signs, has the vices of its virtues. It had been assigned to Mars and its basic character established by the time of Ptolemy, and the association of Britain with Aries goes back to that time. The traditional qualities of the Aries man were briefly and

Courtesy: Museum of Modern Art, New York

80

clearly outlined by Raphael in the early 19th century: "Aries, the house of Mars and exaltation of the Sun, . . . is a vernal, dry, fiery, masculine, cardinal, equinoctial, diurnal, moveable, commanding, eastern, choleric, violent, and quadrupedian sign." It will be remembered that, apart from the sign that a planet "rules," there is usually another sign in which he feels particularly at home; this is the sign in which he is said to have his "exaltation." So Aries's fiery furnaces are kept doubly stoked, by Mars who rules it and by the Sun who is exalted in it.

On the other hand, a planet who is not at ease in Aries is Venus, as should be obvious from her character given in the last chapter. André Barbault stresses that the fire of Aries, in contrast with that of the other two fiery signs, Leo and Sagittarius, is the *primal* fire that both creates and destroys. So the Aries type of person tends to be an impetuous juvenile type taking no thought for the morrow. And not only juvenile but primitive: Ingrid Lind says there is something of the cave man about him.

There is a general agreement about the character of the Aries man: He is an enthusiast, tough, rather reckless, impetuous always and irritable sometimes, and he falls in love like a thunderbolt. Aries moves much too fast for the Taurus

Left, *Starry Night,* painted by the Dutch-born artist Vincent Ván Gogh (1853-90). The explosive quality of the painting reflects the fire and passion that are usually said to be the dominant qualities of the first sign of the Zodiac, Aries (which was Van Gogh's Sun-sign).

Astrologers in the past considered that Aries may sometimes cause a ram-like appearance. Above, two drawings from a 17th-century Italian book of physiognomy representing Aries and its human counterpart.

type (to be discussed next) and is exasperated by the fussiness and exactitude of Virgo. From early times astrologers have also described his physical characteristics, making him strong, with powerful shoulders, and so on. After a warning about Zodiacal morphology, Barbault suggests that the Aries type does tend to look like a ram (Gleadow writes that "his nose, even when small, has an energetic arch") and notes that he walks rapidly and has a strong, quick hand-grip. He is something of a menace as a driver, and does not like wearing a hat. As for Aries women, in dress they don't wish to follow the fashion but to lead it; on the other hand, they are almost aggressive in their non-use of make-up.

As examples of Aries types, Barbault gives Louis Armstrong (who invented "hot" jazz), Marlon Brando, George Sand ("the first feminist"), Savonarola, and St. Teresa of Avila. To prove the point that two Aries types can be thoroughly Aries and yet, owing to the positions of the planets, in many ways very different, he contrasts two French writers, Baudelaire and Zola. Each of them had a notable conglomeration of planets in Aries but whereas Zola had the Sun, Moon, Mars, and Pluto, and at that in trine (a good relationship) with Saturn, Baudelaire had the Sun, Venus (bad, as just mentioned, in this sign), Jupiter, and Saturn—and at that in the eighth house, the house of death.

Morrish's evolutionary theory has already been mentioned. According to this scheme—in which the whole Zodiac symbolizes the universal "Wheel of Life and Death"—Aries, the first sign, represents ignorance (at whatever level) in contrast

A drawing of the French writer Honoré de Balzac (1799-1850). Balzac's Sun-sign was Taurus; to astrologers, his personality and even his appearance expressed the sign's strong, earthy character.

with the last sign, Pisces, which represents universality (at whatever level). Focusing in, Morrish makes the first three signs stand for "unit germination." Aries here stands for the male creative impulse (to be quickly followed by the traditionally feminine sign, Taurus, which represents *matrix* or matter). Morrish, like many artists, believes in the fertilizing effects of conflict, and stresses the importance of Zodiacal opposites; for example, "in a physical analogy Libra (air) is required to enable Aries (fire) to 'burst into flame.'" As well as making Aries play the male to the female matrix of Taurus, Morrish makes him stand for motion in contrast with the Taurine inertia. This evolutionary scheme of Morrish's, which involves the concept of yoga, is a peculiarly modern outcrop to which we shall return later. But, on the traditional premises, he has not miscast either Aries or Taurus. We can now turn our attention to the latter.

Taurus the Bull ♉

April 21 to May 21. To the layman it may seem comic that Taurus should be feminine, but the horned moonface of its hieroglyph certainly looks less aggressive than Aries' hieroglyph, which is almost all horns and nothing else. Moreover, Taurus is a fixed and earthy sign, and is ruled by the opposite of Mars, the gentle Venus. It is not surprising that Taurus is slow and long-suffering, in fact "bovine"; the hostile Robert Eisler even suggests that he was never a bull, only an ox, and quotes the ancient Roman champion of astrology Firmicus Maternus to the effect that this sign is responsible for the birth of impotent people and perverts. But most astrologers have been less insulting. A slow sign, yes, but a sure sign certainly. Nor is the Taurus type traditionally a sissy: Pearce writes that he is "slow to anger but, when provoked, furious."

Just as Aries was connected with both Mars and the Sun, so Taurus is connected with the Moon as well as with Venus. Barbault describes the Taurus type as essentially a *ruminant*, a creature of a leisurely rhythm who tends to walk slowly looking at the ground, obedient to the law of his sheer weight. The physiognomists, of course, make him *look* like a bull: thickset, thick-necked, and thick-lipped, with a broad forehead, wide nostrils, and a tuft of hair on the forehead. Countess Wydenbruck notes that he is "not very intelligent," but everyone agrees that he can be a tower of strength. Barbault, in discussing Freud (whom he makes a Taurus type) and his Taurine psychological universe, moves from the love of the child for its mother to the conclusion that "we are here at the heart of Taurus, which represents the meat-safe of the Zodiac . . . and, through displacement of the oral tendency, the strong-box of the Zodiac."

Working on the same strong-box lines, Tucker finds in Taurus a symbol of the Golden Calf; but he concedes that the Taurus man worships money not for itself but for the pleasure and ease it will bring him. He adds that, if the Taurus man does have enough money to eat well, he should cut down on the carbohydrates. He is a reliable husband and family man, pays his debts, and enjoys a joke; but too much of the "ruminant" quality can make him slothful.

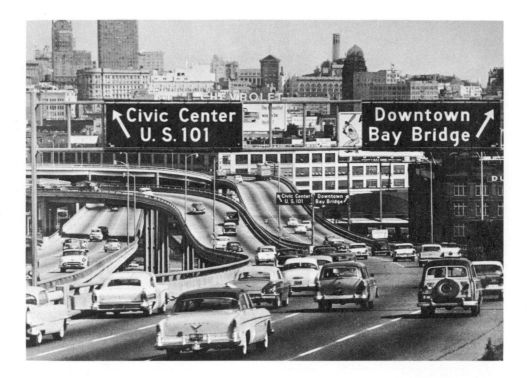

Cars speeding along the San Francisco
freeway against a background of towering
skyscrapers suggest the speed and material
progress that characterize the American way
of life. Mobility and energy are qualities
of Gemini—the sign that is particularly
associated with the United States.

Right, the British actor Basil Rathbone
as Sherlock Holmes in the film version of
The Hound of the Baskervilles (made in
1939). The great intellect of the fictitious
detective is a typical characteristic of
Gemini—the Sun-sign of Holmes's
creator, Arthur Conan Doyle.

The two points to remember are that Taurus is essentially fixed and essentially earthy. Gleadow instances as Taurine types George Washington and Arnold Bennett. Barbault gives Balzac and Karl Marx as well as Freud. Marx had Taurus as his Sun-sign and it contained at his birth both the Taurine females, the Moon and Venus. Dialectical materialism, Barbault says, falls naturally under this sign. The next, the first of the airy signs, is a very different kettle of flying fish.

Gemini the Twins Ⅱ JANE M.

May 22 to June 21. A mutable, airy sign, Gemini is ruled (easy to guess) by Mercury. The word "dialectical" might be applied here too, but more in the original Greek sense where "dialectic" meant conversation—a quick and most argumentative conversation, full of twists and traps and contradictions. All astrologers agree that the Gemini type enjoys argument; after all, this comes naturally to a double man, born under a double sign. Barbault stresses this "bipolarity" and points out that Gemini rules the lungs with their double process of breathing in and breathing out. He adds that if Aries symbolizes the original fire at the source of life, and Taurus the condensation of this life in a material form (as it were, an egg), it is when the process arrives at the stage of Gemini that this egg is polarized and we meet the differentiation into the masculine and feminine principles.

Morrish, in a not altogether dissimilar way, having equated Aries with the male creative impulse and Taurus with the matrix, takes Gemini to stand for that "self-conscious entity which is the result" (being the third and last sign in his phase of unit germination). And in a discussion of "astro-symbolism" in which Aries represents motion and Taurus inertia, he makes Gemini represent "rhythmic balance or oscillation." Also, Morrish finds in the hieroglyph of this sign two pillars, one light and one dark, a "portal through which every human being must pass." Alternatively, he suggests that the two uprights of the hieroglyph, traditionally equated with the "heavenly twins" Castor and Pollux, could as well be equated with two apes—the divine ape of intelligence and the chattering ape of imitation. This last piece of symbolism brings us back to dialectic or, we might as well say, to the good and the bad sides of Mercury.

Being both mutable and airy, Gemini is intellectual but fickle. (Pearce describes the Germini type as having "disposition fickle, understanding good.") Ingrid Lind writes that he goes to "extremes of rationality" and possesses the "ability to live a double life." It has often been claimed by astrologers that many intellectuals are born under this sign. But, as indeed is often the case with intellectuals, the Gemini person is often emotionally cold. His congenial signs are Aquarius and Libra; he would not get on with cosy old Taurus. When we are told by Gleadow that Gemini is "pure intellect" and that no one is more mobile (a word frequently used of this sign), it is surprising to find him quoting Queen Victoria as someone who was born with Gemini rising.

Unfortunately, Gemini is the patron not only of intellectuals but of egocentrics and, in some cases, of lunatics. Thus another British monarch, the notorious George III, is quoted by Raphael as an example of the *bad* influence of Gemini, "the sign remarkable for producing insanity" when the planetary picture goes askew. But in the late 19th century (after Raphael) a study of a number of well-known cases of insanity was made by the British scholar Richard Garnett; while he was struck by the frequent conjunction of Mercury and Saturn, he found Gemini featuring only once in his chosen group of mad monarchs.

As regards the minor characteristics of Gemini people, Tucker notes that, if this is your Sun-sign, you may be inclined to vegetarianism. Barbault observes that Gemini women prefer two-piece suits and checkered materials. The physiognomist John Varley writes: "Gemini, though a beautiful and human sign, yet occasionally gives to persons born when it is rising [note that he is concerned with the ascendant, not the Sun-sign] a strong resemblance in the head and neck to the characteristic forms of goats, kids, and deer."

This sign stands for nervous energy; the United States is said to be very much under its influence. Among people born with Gemini rising many astrologers include Dante, Kepler, Wagner, Bernard Shaw, and Clemenceau. Barbault includes Conan Doyle in his list of Gemini types; he adds that Sherlock Holmes is a "popular Gemini hero." On the debit side, apart from producing madmen, it can (like its ruler Mercury) produce crooks and very selfish people. Once again, in moving from this sign to the next, we find a complete change of atmosphere.

Cancer the Crab ♋ *Jeff.*

June 22 to July 22. In spite of its name, Cancer is a homey, motherly sign, but also perhaps the most vulnerable. It is the sign of the summer solstice, from which it will be nine months before Aries comes around again; it can therefore be regarded as a symbol of fecundation and conception. As with the other signs, Barbault makes much of its position in the year, forgetting that many other countries have their spring and summer at different times from his. But on the symbolism of this sign and the psychology of Cancer people, he is at his most eloquent and suggestive. Because it is a cardinal sign and the first of the watery signs, he treats it as symbolizing the primal water—*les eaux-mères*—in the same way that Aries symbolizes the primal fire. It therefore stands for our ancestral origins, all organic life being assumed to have begun in the waters. It also stands, like the sea, for both intuition and introversion. It is the one and only sign ruled by the Moon, so Cancerian qualities are very much the same as the lunar qualities described in Chapter 2. The Moon, it will be remembered, is Our Lady of the Waters.

In accordance with this watery character, Barbault says that the Cancer type tends to be *un végétatif*. And the Cancer man (it is easier to be a Cancer woman and work it out in motherhood and the home) is often unduly feminine; as Pearce puts it, "effeminate in constitution and disposition." Cancer people can

Above, the French novelist Marcel Proust
(1871-1922), whose introversion and
sensitivity typify Cancer (his Sun-sign).
Above right, the modern artist Salvador
Dali represented as a fetus in an egg.
This "return to the womb" idea also ties up
with Cancer (linked with fertility and
birth), which was Dali's ascendant sign.

easily become "drowned in their own insecurity" : They are over-emotional and
sub-active. But there is another side to the picture. In its earlier pictorial representations, Cancer was drawn as a crayfish, a creature that can give one a terrible
nip. And even crabs, however soft inside, have a very hard shell and are difficult
to dislodge from their chosen crannies. So throughout the centuries this sign
has stood for tenacity. Not only for tenacity of purpose but also for tenacity of
memory—especially memory of childhood. Which brings us round to the home
again. "*Cherchez la mère*," writes Barbault, "*et vous trouverez le Cancer!*"

This sign, however, stands for not only motherly people but mother-fixated
people. Being extremely sensitive, it is in fact a sign of many colors and moods.
Many astrologers consider that it makes excellent teachers (or actresses) and in
it Barbault distinguishes what appear on the surface to be two quite different
types : the stay-at-home, sufficient-unto-the-day type and the explorative, castles-
in-the-air type. (Actually he would not claim that these are more than subtypes.)
The examples that he gives of Cancer people include Byron, Cocteau, Salvador
Dali, Rembrandt, Rousseau, and Schubert. And he refers to the great stress laid
upon *intuition* by the philosopher Bergson, who had his Moon in Cancer.

Earlier astrologers laid less stress on the profundities and sensitivities of this sign and more on its crab nature. According to Varley, Cancer tends to give "a crabbed, short-nosed class of persons, greatly resembling a crab in features, when viewed in front; these persons resemble crabs, also, in the energy and tenacity with which they attack any object." And in spite of his shy and retiring nature a Cancer friend can be a social asset. Gleadow advises anyone about to give a dinner party: "If you want to know about food or wine ask Cancer." (He adds unkindly: "And if you want someone who will not object whatever you do choose Pisces.")

Morrish, in his ladder of Being (or, more strictly speaking, of Becoming), makes Cancer the first of three rungs representing gestation and birth. (He suggests that the hieroglyph could stand not only for crab-claws but for breasts.) The Zodiacal opposite to Cancer is of course Capricorn, an earthy no-nonsense sign that does not suffer from hypersensitivity. The signs that Cancer gets on with are Pisces and Taurus; but in *mundane* astrology Cancer and Capricorn are bracketed together, not only because they are both solstitial signs (one summer, one winter) but because they are the traditional fields for world-wide disasters. A third-century B.C. astrological missionary from ancient Babylon to Greece named Berosus taught that, when all the planets are in conjunction in Cancer, there will be a universal conflagration (a summery type of disaster); when they get together in Capricorn, there will be a universal deluge.

So there is Cancer, the only sign ruled by the Moon. Water, water, every-where—but also tenacity and patience, maternal love, understanding of others, extreme sensitivity, and introversion. And next door to it, with the usual dramatic juxtaposition, what should we find but the only sign ruled by the Sun?

Leo the Lion ♌ Mike woody cleryh

July 23 to August 23. A fixed and fiery sign. With Leo, Ingrid Lind begins by picking on the apparent paradox "or contradiction . . . in the thought of fixed fire." The answer, she says, lies in "molten gold," but she could also perhaps have used her cookery ingredients analogy. She goes on to contrast Leo with the first fiery sign, Aries, who is anything but fixed. Aries is impulsive and restless; Leo, like the Sun, stays put on his throne. People born with Leo rising include Bismarck, Garibaldi, Huey Long, and Picasso. Among those who had Leo as their Sun-sign were Lorenzo de Medici, Louis XIV ("le Roi Soleil"), Napoleon, and Rubens.

This, then, is obviously an extravert sign; it has produced far more than its share of presidents both in the U.S.A. and in France. As to the physical characteristics of Leo men, Pearce attributes to them "a large, fair stature, broad shoulders; prominent and large eyes; hair generally light and often yellowish; oval, ruddy countenance; of a high, resolute, haughty, and ambitious temper." Varley less flatteringly describes the Leo physiognomy as "most resembling a lion, especially in the nose and retreating chin; such as the profile of King

The Italian fascist leader Benito Mussolini (1883-1945) was born with the Sun in Leo. The planet and the sign have a similar astrological character; when combined (as in Mussolini's horoscope) they are said to lead to aggressive ambition and power seeking.

George III." Barbault distinguishes two physical types of Leo—the Herculean and the Apollonian—but they are both athletic and fine figures of men. He instances Dumas *père* as an almost pure specimen of the Herculean type. As for Leo ladies, Barbault notes that they go in for *la grande toilette*.

The Sun in Leo is at his greatest strength, and it is this strength that is the essence of this sign—the strength of a fire that has now been brought under control and is harnessed to useful ends. Morrish (in his psycho-evolutionary scheme) brackets Leo with Cancer as the "fundamental positive and negative polarities underlying everything." Barbault contrasts Leo with Cancer: In Cancer the umbilical cord has not yet been cut; it is Leo who breaks out into independence. But though independent and very full of himself, the Leo man is far from anti-social: "His ego disappears in his vocation" and he is a great worker. However passionate and ambitious he may be (with him "*vouloir c'est déjà pouvoir*"), Barbault says, his ruler the Sun acts as a sort of internal gendarme. Not that he always obeys this gendarme. As with any other sign, the types can go wrong. One should specially beware of Saturn in Leo, a sign in which he is "in exile": This can produce people like Cesare Borgia.

There seems no need to stress the animal symbolism of Leo—the king of beasts, etc. His 30° of the Zodiac are filled with roaring. But when we step over the border between this sign and the next we perhaps hear a typewriter, or a

89

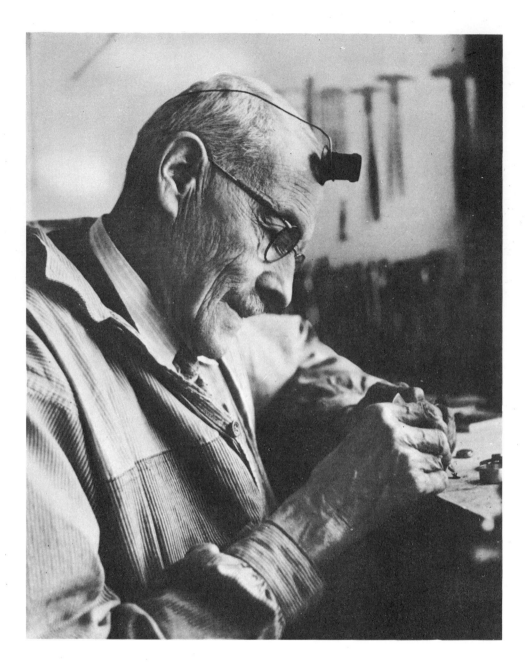

A Swiss craftsman assembling a watch
exhibits the precision and attention to
minute detail that astrology connects with
the sign of Virgo—which, appropriately,
is the patron sign of Switzerland.

vacuum cleaner, a secretarial voice drily reading the minutes, a whispered aside of criticism. We have entered territory where everything must be "just so"— floors must be swept, files must be kept, *i*'s must be dotted and *t*'s crossed, beds (in all senses) must be properly made.

Virgo the Virgin ♍

August 24 to September 23. A mutable, earthy sign, ruled by Mercury. Ingrid Lind once again asks straight away: How can earth be mutable and mercurial? And the answer yet again is in the other ingredients (though, as she says, this internal conflict does tend to make a Virgo type a worrier). Gleadow calls Virgo "perhaps the most earthbound" of the 12 signs, but her earthiness is very unlike the earthiness of Taurus: Mercury could never rule Taurus. In fact the earth gives Virgo common sense and Mercury supplies an unusually keen intelligence. The two together make for disciplined thinking and acting. Cardan (Girolamo Cardano), the famous 16th-century Italian physician, mathematician, and astrologer, was grateful to the Mercury in his horoscope; Mars, he said, was casting an evil influence on both the luminaries, so "I could easily have been a monster, except for the fact that the preceding conjunction had been 29° in Virgo, over which Mercury is the ruler." N.B.: Virgo is a *human* sign.

Virgo is thought of as the patroness of critics and craftsmen, but not of creators or commanders. Louis XIV, though he had his Sun in Virgo, is regarded as a Leo type owing to the position of the planets in his horoscope. But Virgo is a great deal more than a sharp-tongued and keen-eyed housewife. It is the patron sign of Switzerland (which was to be expected), but also of Paris and of cats (no doubt because cats are so neat). Morrish connects it with diet and also with psychology. And Tolstoi is accepted by astrologers as a Virgo man, having had not only the Sun and Mercury in the sign but the Moon as well. Which would suggest that Virgo *can* be creative sometimes, though perhaps what is most obviously Virgonian about Tolstoi is the exact and conscientious way in which he tried to lead a new life in his old age.

Virgo is traditionally represented holding a sheaf of corn and, in western Europe at least, its time of year is the time of harvest, which means both fulfillment and desiccation. The idea of granaries may connect with Virgo's place in the picture of Zodiacal Man; it is assigned (in the phrase of the *Kalendar of Shepherds*) "the belly and the entrails"—i.e., it rules the digestive system. Barbault typically pounces on this to prove that the ancients anticipated modern Freudian psychoanalysis: What we find in the Virgo types is the "anal complex," hence their tendency to hoard things. But he admits that there is a small subspecies of Virgo in which the anus is equally important but plays an opposite role—"*anal relâché*" instead of "*anal contrôlé*." Ivan the Terrible was one of these; such people are really more like Scorpio. There is also, says Barbault, a somewhat larger subspecies of "ambivalents," who are holding back one moment and letting go the next.

A painting by the Italian artist Canaletto
(1697-1768) of the Grand Canal in Venice.
Libra (which was Canaletto's Sun-sign) is
the sign of harmony and balance—qualities
that are suggested by the symmetry of the
painting's composition and the detailed
representation of the architecture.

Anyway, the traditional Virgo type is somewhat dry and cold, a fusser over detail, a discriminator, a rationalist, a perfectionist, yet prepared to sacrifice himself. Barbault suggests that if the Pisces man is like an astronomer brooding on the infinite spaces, the Virgo man is like a biologist with a microscope. For Morrish, Virgo is the third of his second group of three signs, the triad that denotes gestation and birth. So here Virgo, in spite of the name (but compare the harvest symbol), represents "conscious birth into the outer world, and objective powers of observation and selection." The sign is a halfway house:

You can go no further in the way of *objective* consciousness. But at the same time it is the beginning of "the cycle of evolution from the material back to the spiritual."

As already mentioned, the remaining six signs represent for Morrish "evolution into the subjective states, or yoga." The next sign, Libra, the first of the third triad, represents *collective* germination. But whereas Virgo (as halfway house) stands for the *first* stage of discrimination, with Libra there begins a second stage, which means the control of emotion.

Libra the Scales ♎

September 24 to October 23. A cardinal, airy sign, ruled by Venus. One would not expect to find Venus as Libra's ruler (it has little in common with the other Venusian sign, Taurus) but Venus, as we saw in the last chapter, stands for harmony and so can promote a proper balance not only between persons but also within an individual. So the Libra type is easy to get on with, being diplomatic, gentle, and tolerant. Tucker comments that this type has "many of the traits common to the Chinese race." (This was before China went Red.) Being the other equinoctial sign, Libra is the opposite number to Aries, and we could well imagine that it might do Aries some good. But this is contrary to the opinion of most astrologers who think that any two signs 180° apart *must* be opposed to each other in every sense, just as planets are when in "opposition." There are, however, a minority who think that such opposed signs would naturally *complement* each other, and certainly the signs of the spring and autumn equinoxes would seem to be a case in point.

Note that Libra is the only one of the signs that is inorganic; thus it seems quite fitting that Varley summarizes its "elementary notions" as follows: "Libra, independently of its appearing in the world's horoscope, to mediate the Zodiac horizontally, and to balance, as it were, the sign Aries, has been found to signify straight lines and regular buildings, and the sublime uninterrupted horizon line of the sea; it represents also the blue color of the sky and the distances." We might add, thinking of this blue seascape, that the Venus who rules Libra is more the Venus Anadyomene of Botticelli than the sensual goddess who prompted the Wife of Bath.

The picture that emerges of the Libra person is a sociable, cultured, and courteous person, perhaps only too pleased to sparkle in embassies. He seems to be humanist, empiricist, and eclectic, and almost entirely lacking in aggression. He would do most things for peace and finds it very difficult to say no. Perhaps his chief virtue is that he can see both sides of a question; his chief failing that he is too easily influenced. As for the Libra woman, she is extremely *soignée*. Barbault includes among Libra types Erasmus, Katherine Mansfield, Gandhi the apostle of non-violence, and, as its typical painters, Boucher and Watteau. Libra could hardly frighten anyone. We now move on to a sign that has long had a sinister reputation.

93

The Dutch-born spy and *femme fatale* Mata Hari (1876-1917). Astrologers relate Scorpio to both eroticism and death ; and they would detect its sinister influence on Mata Hari (Scorpio was her Sun-sign), whose career of amorous and political intrigue ended with her execution.

Scorpio the Scorpion ♏

October 24 to November 22. A fixed, watery sign, ruled by Mars. Traditionally, people were frightened of Scorpio, since it is the eighth of the signs, and was thus often related to the eighth house, the house of death. Varley gives it rather alarming physical characteristics: "Scorpio has been occasionally found to afford to one class of human form when it is rising, a near approach to serpents, in the expression of the countenance, especially in the eyes and mouth; and when doing or saying cruel and bitter things, they are apt to be assimilated to the nature of snakes, scorpions, etc." This animal symbolism has been made much of by most astrologers, but it is surprising to find a scorpion, usually encountered in hot, dry countries, established as a watery sign. (All the same, we are told that some modern Scorpio types excel at skin diving.)

The watery significance of Scorpio has been explained in different ways. Ingrid Lind says it is "the tidal wave of the thundering weight of Niagara." On the other hand, Barbault contrasts it with the water of Cancer (the source) and the water of Pisces (the ocean) and makes it essentially stagnant, the kind of water that is found in marshes. This does not seem to fit with the energy and passion attributed to Scorpio characters, but Barbault no doubt is basing this diagnosis on the fact that Scorpio is a *fixed* sign; after all, Cancer is cardinal and Pisces is mutable.

Stagnant or tidal, Scorpio is very peculiar. Barbault points out that the scorpion is the only animal that can kill itself (whether deliberately or not) by stinging itself with its tail. And he describes the sign as "the cemetery of the Zodiac." But readers who think themselves Scorpio types need not be alarmed: Scorpio has enormous stamina and can make a comeback like a phoenix. Having Mars as its ruler, it shows two main Martial qualities: aggressiveness and eroticism. Barbault writes that "the most murderous sign is also the most fecund." And to explain the apparent contradictions in Scorpio he once again, as with the preceding sign Virgo, calls in the anal complex. The Scorpio infant gets its first taste of power on the pot—and it will never look back.

Some modern astrologers prefer to think that it is the newcomer Pluto, rather than Mars, who is the ruler of Scorpio. This would only emphasize the dark side of the sign, Pluto being the lord of the underworld. To look on the bright side of the sign, we are told that though the Scorpio man doesn't set out to please and doesn't like taking advice, he can be very good company just because he enjoys things so much. We are also informed that he often excels as a physician or a practical engineer and that Scorpio women make excellent cooks —and tend to have sexy voices like Edith Piaf. Born with Scorpio rising (which, according to some, endows a man with Spartan qualities) were Nelson, Kemal Ataturk, Goering, Mussolini, Franco, Nietzsche, Goethe, Victor Hugo, and Edgar Allan Poe. Goethe's great hero Faust has been taken as a Scorpio type. Dostoevski, Goebbels, and Madame Curie had it as their Sun-sign. Scorpio, being simultaneously fixed and watery, is like the two preceding signs, Libra and Virgo—complex if not self-contradictory. The next sign, Sagittarius, being mutable and fiery (which seems to make more obvious sense), is comparatively straightforward.

Sagittarius the Archer ♐

November 23 to December 21. Ruled by Jupiter, Sagittarius is accordingly an expansive sign. From ancient times it has been represented by a centaur drawing a bow, which is why Ptolemy classed it as a "bicorporeal" sign, and many astrologers nowadays lay stress on this double nature. So after all it is not 100 per cent straightforward. With its animal half and its human half, it provides a good theme for a sermon or, as Barbault puts it, gives the "best image of sublimation." It has its four feet (or hooves) firmly on the ground and yet is shooting at the highest targets. On its centaur make-up Varley comments that, whereas its human half signifies "the deliberation or temperate resolves of humanity," its latter half "often exhibits more of the excessive impulses and nature of a race-horse, an animal most specifically described by Sagittarius." It is this latter half that may affect you if you were born roughly between December 6 and 20; it can lead to nasty accidents.

As one would expect with a ruler like Jupiter (see Chapter 2), it is a *success* sign. Abraham Lincoln and Cecil Rhodes were born with Sagittarius rising, and Winston Churchill had it as his Sun-sign with Venus also present. (Countess Wydenbruck, however, did point out that Churchill's horoscope shows him "likely to be subordinate to others in his profession.")

As to the *fire* of Sagittarius, Barbault describes it as a purifying fire, very different from that of either Aries or Leo, and suitable to later middle age when the desires of the flesh are waning but the spirit can still have a burning desire for social, political, intellectual, or spiritual objects. Morrish writes: "Whereas Aries represents the red, smouldering fires of creation, and Leo the yellow-golden fire of organized mentality, Sagittarius represents the blue fire at the heart of the flame. This is the hottest part of the flame." Sagittarius always wants to go further: He is a born explorer and adventurer and loves the wide open spaces. Everything he does is done in a big way. In music the Sagittarian type is Beethoven.

In the Zodiacal Man, Sagittarius is connected with the thighs, which brings us back to the power of horse and horseman. Many astrologers use this horse motif literally as well as symbolically. We are told that many Sagittarians are very horsey (and for that matter doggy) people: The eccentric and dynamic Queen Christina of Sweden, who dressed like a man, was mad about horses and also had something of a "horse face." (So had Milton, who was born with Sagittarius rising.) We are also told that the typical Sagittarian is "as strong as a horse." He has a very healthy appetite and in middle age has a tendency to *embonpoint*.

America's James Thurber (1894-1961)
often illustrated his humorous essays with
cartoons of which the best-known are
probably "Thurber's dogs." An affinity
with animals is a key characteristic of
Sagittarius (Thurber's Sun-sign)—an
association that perhaps originated from the
idea of the sign as half-man, half-beast.

He is a very strong individual but, like Jupiter his ruler, is a good mixer and, indeed, finds himself only in communal concerns. Barbault does suggest that there is an introverted subspecies (where Saturn dominates) whose member is concerned with the "beyond" within himself, but the typical Sagittarian throws himself into things outside himself, sometimes even achieving a "global vision." He has a hearty handshake, slaps his cards on the table, and tends to be euphoric. It is a little hard to recognize him in Morrish's system, where he stands for the "abstract, higher consciousness." But then Sagittarius has to conclude the second of Morrish's four stages, the stage of "control of emotion": In this sign human emotions have to emerge from animal desires (the centaur again) and these emotions, in turn, must be directed into lofty aspirations—the arrow must leave the bow. Morrish squeezes his next and third stage, the "control of wind," into the confines of one sign only, which is naturally our next sign.

Capricorn the Goat ♑ Grandpa z.

December 22 to January 20. A cardinal, earthy sign; also an equinoctial sign, the equinox of course being the winter one. So Capricorn's ruler, predictably, is frosty old Saturn. "One does not invite to dinner the same evening Leo and Capricorn"; so writes Gleadow and, if you look back in this chapter to the account of Leo and in the previous chapter to the account of Saturn, you will have a notion of what Capricorn is like. With this sign one is (in western Europe) at the midnight of the year, so no wonder Morrish makes this the stage for "control of the mind." Tucker says that if Capricorn is your Sun-sign you should avoid alcohol in any form, if it is rising you will be inclined to be very pessimistic, and if you have the Moon in Capricorn you will be very disagreeable if you don't exercise control—witness Napoleon.

In the mid-19th century, when astrology was getting more mixed up with Biblical symbolism, Frances Rolleston (author of an odd book called *Mazzaroth*, the Hebrew name for the Zodiac) equated Capricorn with the kid of sacrifice. But then she had already equated Aries (of all the signs!) with the lamb of innocence and meekness. From more orthodox angles A. J. Pearce ascribed to this sign a "disposition subtle, collected, calm, witty, and yet melancholy" and Ingrid Lind speaks of "action allied with caution and commonsense." Through the ages Capricorn has been more often than not represented as a goat *with a fish tail*: Varley comments that while some Capricorn people look like goats, others look like fish. Symbolically, however, we can go deeper—or higher—than that: This is a fish with ambition that would like to clamber up the mountains.

Barbault stresses the opposition—and complementary relationship—of Capricorn and Cancer: Cancer is to Capricorn what the mother is to the father, the base to the summit, etc. In Capricorn we are getting away from matter (compare Morrish). Collectivization is coming in and the state or religious conscience may take over. Saturn is casting a chill or a shadow and yet he may be a liberator. If Saturn the ruler is actually in this sign, then everything is cut to the bone:

You get people like Kant and Mallarmé. Among other Capricorn types Barbault instances Queen Elizabeth II (Capricorn rising and in sextile to Saturn, so strongly Saturnian), the stolid Marshal Joffre (both Sun-sign and ascendant), Kepler (of whom more later), Pasteur, Woodrow Wilson, and, above all, Stalin. The last named had his Sun in Capricorn, in aspect with all the slow-moving planets, Mars, Jupiter, Saturn, Uranus, and Neptune. Get the idea?

Capricorn people are thought to be born traditionalists, yet they are not so much disciplinarians as diplomats. They like traditional ceremonies, religious or

The yearly spectacle of the state opening of Britain's parliament is an example of the pomp and ceremony that surround the British monarch. Such a concern with tradition and ritual is usually associated with Capricorn— the ascendant of Queen Elizabeth II.

civil, and are upset if they are dressed wrongly for the occasion. It is also conceded that many of them are religious in a deeper sense; this might provide a bridge from traditional astrology to Morrish's astro-psychology. For Morrish, Capricorn is the gate to the spiritual life just as Cancer was the gate to "form-life." We are now getting into yoga (under Capricorn, like a yogi, one practices control) and are on the brink of spiritual rebirth, which for Morrish is represented by the next sign, the last but one in the Zodiac.

Aquarius the Water-Carrier ≈

January 21 to February 19. A fixed, airy sign. Aquarius's ruler is traditionally Saturn, though some astrologers (such as Varley) prefer to promote Uranus or at least make him co-ruler. This sign provides some of the most graceful illustrations to medieval textbooks and has long been thought of as a particularly *human* sign; Gleadow calls it "the only completely human sign in the Zodiac." But there seems to be a divergence of opinion as to whether he represents the ordinary man or an especially gifted man. On the former premise he is linked with democracy, on the latter with science and the capacity for abstract thought. This was the Sun-sign of Galileo, Francis Bacon, and Darwin.

Some years ago the French amateur astrologer Paul Choisnard investigated the horoscopes of 119 outstanding intellectuals and claimed to have found that under only three signs was the incidence more than average—Gemini, Libra, and Aquarius. These, of course, are the three *airy* signs and the symbolism of air here is obvious. Traditionally Aquarius rules the circulation of the blood, and this has been correlated with the circulation of ideas. If Uranus is brought in, one would expect to find Aquarians showing the characteristics of that planet (like mechanical inventiveness) and also what Ingrid Lind calls the "Uranian urge to disrupt." Miss Lind, on the assumption of co-rulership, would like to distinguish Saturnian Aquarians from Uranian Aquarians. Rupert Gleadow, writing of the so-called "Aquarian Age" (see below), foresees the spread in the immediate future not only of such Uranian effects as machinery and inventions, but of "world-wide organizations, . . . international collaboration, and the Brotherhood of Man."

The Aquarian, unlike his predecessor the Capricornian, is no respecter of tradition or convention (otherwise he would not be so well equipped for scientific research). But he *is*, in the best sense of the phrase, a respecter of persons because, once again, he is human. He pours out the water freely: "Your need is greater than mine." He can be tactless, though, and other faults ascribed to him are obstinacy (after all, this is a fixed sign), fanaticism, and (more surprisingly) inefficiency. Countess Wydenbruck describes him as "popular yet solitary, often abnormal." It has been observed that Aquarius men often have beautiful profiles but tend to look unduly feminine. But this is not mentioned by that old traditionalist Pearce, who merely says that the Aquarian is "of prepossessing appearance and good disposition," and has a "long and fleshy face." Here we have a minor inconsistency, since in another passage describing the influence of Aquarius as a Sun-sign, Pearce speaks of "a round full face," and again goes on to mention "good disposition, though tinctured with pride and ambition; artistic or scientific."

Apart from the scientific thinkers already mentioned, other people who had Aquarius as their Sun-sign were Abraham Lincoln, Franklin D. Roosevelt, and James Dean. Edward VIII (the Duke of Windsor) was born with Aquarius as his ascendant sign.

To return to the "Aquarian Age": Many astrologers block out history in periods of roughly 2000 years, each such period falling under the tutelage of a particular sign. This is dictated by the movement of the vernal equinoctial point (i.e., 0° Aries), which goes very slowly backward through the signs (because of the "precession of the equinoxes," mentioned earlier). So in the last 2000 years B.C., 0° Aries was in Aries the constellation. Then it moved into Pisces— very suitably, since the Piscean Age coincided with the Christian era, and the fish was an early symbol of Christ. As to whether the Aquarian Age has yet begun, astrologers disagree. Ingrid Lind thinks that it has, and ascribes to it much the same characteristics as Gleadow: "All the modern trend of thought and invention." For Morrish also, but in a different way (since what he is

The American film actor James Dean (1931-55). Astrologers would label his sensitive good looks as typically Aquarian —and Aquarius was Dean's Sun-sign. Equally typical of this sign was the youthful spirit of rebellion against convention that James Dean stood for during his career and, especially, after his death.

concerned with is *subjective* development) Aquarius is "the awakener." For him it is the sign not of the scientist but of the yogi—"the development of spiritual consciousness through contemplation." This development will be completed in the next sign, which he takes as representing the "cosmic ocean."

Pisces the Fishes)(

February 20 to March 20. A mutable, watery sign. To be both mutable and watery might be thought to be overdoing the fluid element; traditionally Pisces types are liable to lack both stability and precision. But the ruler of this sign is Jupiter (though some would substitute Neptune), which tends to correct the balance. The water symbolism is made much of by astrologers (Pisceans are said to be wonderfully adaptable and to make good actors) but the actual fish reference has mostly been dropped. Varley provides an example of the latter: "Pisces was found to signify persons who were employed in fishing, and in other watery concerns. . . . It is a sign under which many fishmongers are born . . . and some of the persons born when it is rising approximate to fishes in their eyes, which are somewhat conspicuous and phlegmatic."

Modern astrologers do not mention fishmongers but they stress the fact that Pisceans at their best are idealists and, at their worst, drifters. They are not individualists and in fact seem hardly conscious of their own individuality. And they certainly are not go-getters: They are gentle, shy, sensitive (often hypersensitive), vague, and prone to melancholy. Some retire from ordinary life by drifting (astrological textbooks always warn them against drink); others retire into lives of dedication, in cloisters or hospitals. They are extremely malleable, often hesitant, and keep changing course; Barbault says that the Piscean voluntarily loses himself in a labyrinth. When they lie it is not usually intentional but just part of their general confusion. The Moon in Pisces is dangerous for she encourages fantasies and hallucinations. At one extreme the Piscean can lapse into schizophrenia.

All this being so, it is not surprising that some of the artists born under this sign (it could be said to be a natural sign for artists) should have had tragic careers. It was the Sun-sign of the unfortunate German poet Hölderlin, who went mad. Nijinsky was born with Pisces rising, and also went mad. And the pessimistic German philosopher Schopenhauer was born under Pisces with Saturn very prominent in his horoscope. A tragi-comic example from fiction is Dickens's Mr. Micawber in *David Copperfield*, a person who (according to Gleadow) "is notoriously Piscean."

The Polish-born pianist and composer Frédéric Chopin (1810-49). Chopin's career, devoted to romantic music and romantic love affairs, ended in early death. Elements of love, art, and tragedy are all attributes of Pisces, which was Chopin's Sun-sign.

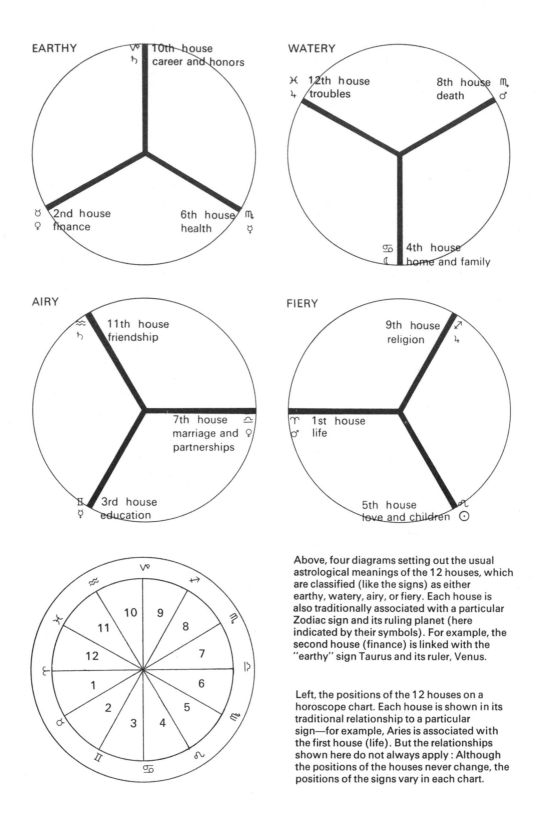

EARTHY

♈ 10th house
♄ career and honors

♉ 2nd house
♀ finance

6th house ♍
health ☿

WATERY

♓ 12th house
♃ troubles

8th house ♏
death ♂

♋ 4th house
☽ home and family

AIRY

♒ 11th house
♄ friendship

7th house ♎
marriage and ♀
partnerships

♊ 3rd house
☿ education

FIERY

9th house ♐
religion ♃

♈ 1st house
♂ life

5th house
love and children ☉

Above, four diagrams setting out the usual astrological meanings of the 12 houses, which are classified (like the signs) as either earthy, watery, airy, or fiery. Each house is also traditionally associated with a particular Zodiac sign and its ruling planet (here indicated by their symbols). For example, the second house (finance) is linked with the "earthy" sign Taurus and its ruler, Venus.

Left, the positions of the 12 houses on a horoscope chart. Each house is shown in its traditional relationship to a particular sign—for example, Aries is associated with the first house (life). But the relationships shown here do not always apply : Although the positions of the houses never change, the positions of the signs vary in each chart.

On the brighter side of the picture, Pisceans are very lovable people because they are very loving. Not only is Pisces ruled by Jupiter (which tends to redress the shyness, neurosis, etc.) but it is in this sign that Venus is exalted. And, true to the oceanic nature of the sign, the Piscean tends to "lose himself" in love. In Morrish's scheme there is a similar merging or fusion but here it is a "liberation" in the symbolic ocean of the cosmos: We have reached the highest point of yoga or spiritual consciousness, the top of the Zodiacal ladder. As usual, this is Morrish's own formulation, but he also accepts the traditional idea of the Piscean Age and, unlike Gleadow and others, deplores the fact that it is passing: Everywhere he sees a "characteristic destruction of Piscean values."

With this sign we have come the full circle of the Zodiac. It is hoped that the rather sketchy summary of the signs in this chapter will at least throw some light on the historical chapters to follow. There has not been space here to say much about "mixed" Zodiacal types; but some very important matters, such as the effect of the aspects, will be discussed again in Chapter 8, which will also give a glance at such things as "transits" and "revolutions." In that chapter we shall also see how astrologers disagree as to "house arrangement."

What the 12 houses mean, however, has been fairly well established since ancient times, so, as the houses will be referred to here and there in the historical chapters, it is worthwhile ending this chapter by giving very approximately their traditional significations. (Remember that, though they may have affinity with the respectively numbered signs, they do *not* coincide with them. The seventh house, say, is always in the same position; the seventh sign is not.)

First house: The life of the individual, the self, his general potentialities.

Second house: His possessions (compare old strong-box Taurus), finance, etc.

Third house: Education; relationships with what Americans call one's "peer-group."

Fourth house: Family origins, parents, home.

Fifth house: Loves, recreations, children.

Sixth house: Hard work, health, domestic chores. (Compare poor Virgo.)

Seventh house: Marriage, partnerships, enmities, etc.

Eighth house: Death. Also inheritances.

Ninth house: Higher life of the intellect and spirit. (Compare Sagittarius.)

Tenth house: Social life, profession, reputation, honors, etc.

Eleventh house: Friendships, objectives.

Twelfth house: Troubles of various kinds, illnesses, betrayals, disgrace.

There is a Latin mnemonic distich that puts these in a nutshell:

Vita, lucrum, fratres, genitor, nati, valetudo,

Uxor, mors, pietas, regnum, benefactaque, carcer

and that can be translated: Life, lucre, brothers, father, children, health, wife, death, duty, career, benefits, prison.

And now, having assembled our cast of both planets and signs, let us go back into history and see how the first directors or stage managers managed them.

4 The ancient world

According to one modern astrologer, echoing historians from the early Christian era, "Adam was instructed in astrology by heavenly inspiration." Without bringing Adam into it, the fact remains that astrology *is* of great antiquity. The brand practiced in Europe today derives originally from ancient Mesopotamia. The Greeks and Romans tended to call all astrologers "Chaldeans" (i.e., Babylonians), while their name for a horoscope was "Babylonian numbers."

In these beginnings astrology was still intertwined with astronomy, which had come into being when people began to ask for an accurate time reckoning. Such a time reckoning was required for agricultural purposes, but most of all by religion. Religious ceremonies had to take place at fixed dates, so the astronomers were the priests. A Babylonian priest in the early days must have been something of a commissar : The land belonged to the gods, and the priests were the gods' stewards. (In other countries farther east, such priestly astrologers retained their powers till fairly recent times—for instance, the Brahmin *purohitas* who published the Hindu almanac, and at a word from whom parents abandoned their babies.)

The dry, cloudless Mesopotamian climate is naturally favorable to astronomy ; in Babylonia the priests were observing the heavens from the third millennium B.C., and many of the fixed stars and constellations (such as the Pleiades and Orion) were known and named by them. The 12 signs of the Zodiac probably

Part of a second-century A.D. Roman relief showing the casting of a child's horoscope. A nurse presents the child to its mother, while two women (probably two of the three Fates) read the child's future in the "celestial globe." By Roman times astrology had become for most people an accepted part of everyday life.

Left, a 20th-century B.C. copy of an older Babylonian clay tablet recording the movements of the planet Venus and omens indicated by her risings. Such records were compiled by Babylon's priests (represented, right, by a statue of 2700 B.C.), who were both astronomers and astrologers, and who predicted (and guided) the future of the state and its rulers. Priests in modern India (like the Hindu holy man, below right) are also partly astrologers: They use astrology to choose the best dates for religious festivals, weddings, and other ceremonies.

came later. But what we think of today as the astrological approach seems to have been there from the start.

The idea that the stars condition human behavior and fortunes rests on the notion that the world is *one*—a whole of interdependent parts. This world is full of correspondences between things above and things below—in the way that the ziggurat (the holy mound) in any Sumerian temple was a meeting place between heaven and earth, where the gods could converse with men. In other words, the ancient world seems to have automatically correlated human experience with natural phenomena.

The determinism (or fatalism) that this correlation implies can have been no more discouraging, before the development of science, than the concept of the world as an unintelligible plurality ruled by blind chance. So, though astrology today may look to many people like sheer superstition, we should not forget that it made very good sense at a time when man was at the mercy of a great many uncontrollable forces—the elements, warlike neighbors, the gods. Perhaps one reason why men of the old civilizations turned to the stars was to find an antidote to the precariousness of life.

The first Babylonian Empire lasted into the first millennium B.C., when the Assyrian came down like a wolf on the stars and made Babylon's lore his own. The Assyrians were modified and humanized by the people they conquered. Their capital was Nineveh, but they preserved and respected the civilized city of

Babylon and the cuneiform texts in its temples. Among such texts were many dealing with those Siamese twins, astronomy and astrology. The Assyrian king Ashurbanipal compiled a library of clay tablets from the earliest days of Babylonia down to his own time. In these latter texts the astronomical records become surprisingly detailed; the stargazers had been working overtime.

This wealth of detail was needed for fortune telling. But in Babylon and Nineveh the fortune to be told was that of the state, not of individuals—except the king, who himself personified the state. It was partly for this reason that astrology never had the wide popularity in Mesopotamia that it was to achieve in Greece or Rome.

In Ashurbanipal's library many letters from priests to their sovereigns illustrate this narrow application of astrology. The tone is appropriately dry, the objects utilitarian. One priest writes to Ashurbanipal: "This eclipse of the Moon that took place has destroyed the lands . . . . It has cast down the land of Amurru and the land of the Hittites and again the land of the Chaldeans. It is favorable for the king my lord . . . ." Eclipses, being such a sensational phenomenon, naturally concerned the priests a good deal, but their predictions were often inaccurate: "As for the eclipse of the Sun, it did not take place. It is over. The planet Venus is approaching the constellation Virgo. The appearance of the planet Mercury is approaching. Great wrath will come."

A ceiling from the Egyptian tomb of Sethos I
(1300 B.C.), decorated with constellations,
including the lion, the bull, and (unique to
Egypt) the crocodile. These figures are not
Zodiac signs : Astrology did not develop
in Egypt until the sixth century B.C., over
2000 years after it started in Babylon.

During the sixth century B.C., astrology caught on in Egypt. (Later, in Roman times, Egypt was to claim that she had been the pioneer in this field; but in fact she did not turn to it until long after the great days of the pharaohs.) At the same time, scientific inquiry was bursting out in the Greek cities of Asia Minor—first of all in Miletus with the famous Thales (the first European who could properly be called a scientist). Not that the Babylonians were finished; their greatest achievements in astronomy proper were to come. So far as time reckoning went, the Greeks could still learn from the Babylonians. And the Greeks were also to become the pupils of the "Chaldeans" in astrology, though not for a few hundred years. It should be noted that, whereas in Mesopotamia astronomy proper was developed later than astrology, in Greece it was the other way around.

Astronomically, then, the Babylonians made great strides—though one would not guess this from, say, the Book of Daniel, where Nebuchadnezzar's wise men ("the magicians, and the astrologers, and the sorcerers, and the Chaldeans") were invariably defeated by Daniel. (But then all the Hebrew prophets were good at propaganda. The "Second Isaiah," pronouncing God's judgment on Babylon, cries out with relish: "Let now the astrologers, the stargazers, the monthly prognosticators, stand up and save thee from these things that shall come upon thee. Behold, they shall be as stubble; the fire shall burn them . . . ." etc.)

Ruins of a Greek amphitheatre at Miletus in southwest Turkey. The city was the birth-place of Thales, founder of the "Ionian" school of philosophy. Thales was concerned with scientific observation rather than metaphysics; because of his influence, astrology suffered a temporary setback.

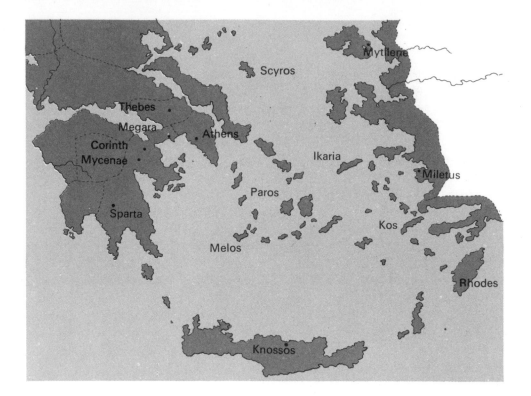

It was astrology, not astronomy, that seems to have declined during the sixth century B.C. Possibly, when Babylon lost her imperial power, the skies were observed more for their own sake or for the old time-reckoning reasons than in order to bolster up the government. Anyhow, it looks as if astrology entered a slump period (except in Egypt). In view of the "Enlightenment" that swept the Greek world during the next centuries, one might have expected it never to emerge from this slump. But history does not work like that.

The inquiring mind of the Greek Enlightenment did not arise in a vacuum; it was conditioned by politics that were conditioned by economics that were conditioned by geography. Mesopotamia had to be politically centralized, largely because the water supply desperately needed strong government control. So the pattern was one water supply, one ruler, one religion—and hence one hierarchy of priests, who also monopolized what science there was. Greece was entirely different: a congeries of city states in remote mountain valleys and islands where centralization, whether political or religious, was not possible. So whereas science in Babylon never got out of the temple, in Greece it never got into it.

Thales and the sixth-century "Ionian Physicists" certainly had no time for astrology—though this does not prevent some modern astrologers from including them in the fold. It is easier to lay claim to Pythagoras later in the century—as, of course, astrologers do—because, unlike Thales, he had a religious bent. It has been said that Pythagoras put the "supernatural" back into astronomy. In particular, his mystique of numbers and his famous "Harmony of the Spheres" would make him irresistible to name-collecting modern astrologers.

dome

heavens

wall

earth

oceans

chamber of water

In the separate city-states of ancient Greece (left), science (including astrology) flourished independently of religion—unlike centralized Babylon, where science was the monopoly of the priests.

Above, the Babylonian idea of the universe: The earth lies enclosed beneath the dome of the heavens, surrounded by oceans and resting on a chamber of water. Below, the universe as conceived by Philolaus of Tarentum, a fifth-century B.C. Pythagorean. Pythagoras had believed that the earth was at the center, but Philolaus substituted a "central fire" around which the earth, a "counter-earth," the seven planets (including the Sun and Moon), and the fixed stars revolve, all attached to spheres.

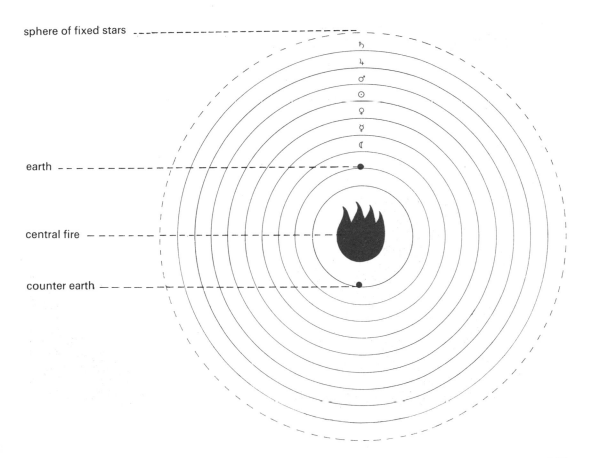

sphere of fixed stars

earth

central fire

counter earth

Like the Babylonians, Pythagoras and his followers saw the universe as a system of correspondences, a unified whole made up of interlocking component parts. This is especially clear in Pythagorean astronomy. The universe, as the Master himself conceived it, was still geocentric (as it had been for the Babylonians). But the Babylonian earth-disk had now become a sphere; Pythagoras was probably the first to maintain that the earth is round. The planets (which still included the Sun and Moon) and the fixed stars were fastened to spheres or wheels that revolved round the earth in concentric circles, each humming on a different pitch, the whole constituting the "Pythagorean Scale."

This sort of geometrical perfectionism (which was extended by Pythagoras's followers, and by others, like Plato) imposed a sort of deep freeze on the universe and encouraged others to give up careful observation. Nevertheless, later centuries did see further original work in Greek astronomy. In the third century B.C., a very careful observer called Aristarchus developed the concept of the heliocentric universe, and so anticipated Copernicus by 17 centuries. But no one believed him, and the universe remained geocentric and rigid. As the astrologer's universe is also geocentric and rigid, this retrogression of astronomy can be considered one of the probable causes of the coming triumph of astrology in Greek life.

But it was not, of course, the only cause. All the ancient Greeks were by no means well-balanced, clear-eyed rationalists. There was in the Greek character and culture what Nietzsche calls a "Dionysiac" or irrational strain. After the fifth century, and largely owing to the internecine wars of the tiny Greek city states, a great gulf seems to have developed between the few—the intellectuals— and the many; the former were no longer at home in society. Among the intellectuals the result was the appeal of new individualist cults like Stoicism and Epicureanism; and among the masses, a falling back into superstition and a renewed interest in magic. Various new and very un-Greek orgiastic cults were being imported from countries like Phrygia and Thrace. And Alexander's conquests had an effect on Greece like that of Renaissance sea voyages upon Western Europe.

Particular results were an increase of interest in the ancient East and better communications between Greeks and "barbarians." Some of the latter started visiting Greece not only to acquire culture, but to spread it. All this prepared the ground for the astrologer.

In 280 B.C. the Babylonian astrologer Berosus set up a school in the Greek island of Cos. And in the second century B.C., a number of popular manuals— especially one supposedly composed by an imaginary pharaoh, the *Revelations*

Left, the Greek fertility god (and god of wine) Dionysus, depicted with two followers on a sixth-century B.C. vase. The orgiastic cults associated with the worship of Dionysus were one expression of the "irrationalism" of ancient Greece, which made way for astrology's comeback around 200 B.C. Such cults were not confined to Greece: Right, a second-century A.D. Roman statue of Cybele, a fertility goddess of Phrygian origin.

of Nechepso and Petosiris—began to circulate widely. Practicing astrologers appeared as far afield as Rome. Chaldean astrology became the vogue.

One more reason might be suggested for the Greeks' embracing astrology. For some centuries these rationalist people had been intellectually free, their own masters. Perhaps the responsibility became too heavy—and so they preferred to give up their self-rule and place themselves in the hands of an astrological Fate.

But astrology among the Greeks (as, later, among the Romans) turned into something different from what it had been in Babylon. These younger and more individualistic peoples asked the stars not only about the nation or its rulers, but about each man's personal destiny. Astrology became primarily *genethliacal*—which, of course, is a Greek word. The long queue for horoscopes had started.

Rome and the stars

The Romans, though in many ways a practical and hard-headed race, were superstitious from the start, always fussing over omens of thunder or intestines or the flight of birds. This tendency, plus the influence of Greek culture and thought, opened the floodgates to astrology. For the more cultured Romans of the Republic, the new form of divination made more sense (and implied a wider view of the universe) than their own traditional forms.

But astrology appealed to the masses as well. One of the first Roman mentions of the subject was an objection (by the third-century B.C. poet Ennius) to various vulgar quacks, including *"de circo astrologos"*—which means not astrologers who perform in the circus but those who hang around the circus grounds. Ennius's remark, of course, shows that astrology didn't appeal to everyone. Many of the great men of the Roman Republic opposed it. In the second century B.C., the Elder Cato warned farmers not to go consulting "Chaldeans." And in the first century B.C. a sustained attack on astrology was launched by that versatile character Marcus Tullius Cicero.

In this last chaotic period of the Republic the Romans were taking to horoscopes as if they were drugs. They seemed only too willing to swap their uneasy (if not illusory) political freedom for a tyranny that offered peace and quiet. Cicero, however, fought to forestall the break-up of his traditional world. His efforts included writing the *De Divinatione*, an attack on all forms of divination including astrology. "Superstition," he wrote, " . . . has usurped nearly everyone's wits and scored over human silliness."

But Cicero's opposition was in vain against the prevailing mood of the early Empire, reflected by the poet Manilius's statement : "The world is ruled by Fate; there are fixed laws for everything." These words are appropriate to the reign of Augustus. Whatever was the case before, the stars were now running on time.

By the second century A.D., the horoscopic "science" was fully developed. Most of the astrological lore of preceding centuries was gathered together in Claudius Ptolemy's *Tetrabiblos,* which has been described as "the world's greatest astrological textbook." Ptolemy was concerned with the "celestial bodies" not

The ancient Greek personification of Gemini
(from an 18th-century star map). The Greeks
took their mythology into the skies by
identifying constellations with gods and
heroes. Gemini was seen as the twin
gods Castor and Pollux.

ETVS.OPINIO.EST.IAM.VSQVEAB.HE
*roica ducta temporibus eaq̃ & p. r. & omnium
gentium firmata confensu uersari quandam in
ter homines diuinationem quam graeci mann
cen appellant. ud est presensionem & scientiam
rerum futurarum. magnifica quaedam res & salu
taris si modo est ulla. quaeq̃ proxima ad deorũ
uim natura mortali possit accedere. Itaq̃ ut alia nos melius multa
q̃ graeci sic huic prestantissime rei nomen nostri a diuis graeca ut
plato interpretatur a furore duxerunt. Gentem quidem nullam ui
deo neq̃ tam humanam atq̃ doctam. neq̃ tam imanem tamq̃ bar
baram quae non significari futura &a quibusdam intelligi prediciq̃
posse censeat. Principio assirit ut ab ultimis auctoritatem repetam
propter planitiem magnitud inemq̃ regionum quas incolebant cũ
caelum ex omni parte patens atq̃ apertum intuerentur traiecho
nes motusq̃ stellarum obseruauerunt. quibus notatis quid cuiq̃
significaretur memoriae prodiderunt. qua in natione chaldei nõ
ex artis sed ex gentis uocabulo nominati diuturna obseruatione si
derum scientiam putantur effecisse. ut predici possit. quid cuiq̃ eue
turum & quo quisq̃ fato natus esset. Eandem artem etiam egyptii lõ
ginquitate temporum innumerabilibus pene seculis consecuti pu*

Left, a page from a 15th-century manuscript of Cicero's *De Divinatione* (which was written about 44 B.C.). Astrology was only one of the forms of divination that the Romans used (and that Cicero attacked). Below, a second-century A.D. bas relief of another popular form—seeking auguries from the entrails of a bull. Other societies before Rome practiced entrail divination : Right, a head imitating intestines, used for fortune telling in seventh-century B.C. Babylon. Far right, a fourth-century B.C. Etruscan mirror case depicting entrail divining. And oracles as well as entrails gave views of the future : Below right, a fifth-century B.C. Greek bowl showing King Aegeus of Athens consulting the oracle at Delphi.

only as astrologer but as astronomer. It was Ptolemy who invented what Arthur Koestler has called "the ferris-wheel universe," a cumbrous affair that, though accepted by everyone down to the time of Copernicus, was laughed at by Milton in *Paradise Lost*:

> *With centric and eccentric scribbled o'er,*
> *Cycle and epicycle, orb in orb.*

Ptolemy's assertion of the value of astrology (or, more precisely, of the value of knowing your future) is double: On the one hand, foreknowledge can reconcile you to your fate; on the other, once you know the dangers to which you are predisposed, the better equipped you are to avoid them. You can take precautions against your own temperament just as against bad weather.

The Greeks seem to have been the first to combine astrology with the doctrine of the four elements (fire, air, earth, and water) or the four basic qualities (hot, cold, dry, and moist). Ptolemy writes: "The ancients accepted two of the planets, Jupiter and Venus, together with the Moon, as beneficent because . . . they abound in the hot and the moist, and Saturn and Mars as producing effects of the opposite nature, one because of his excessive cold and the other for his excessive dryness . . . ." He applies the same treatment to the signs of the Zodiac: Leo and Cancer are warmest; Capricorn and Aquarius, which are opposite to them, are "cold and wintry" signs.

Ptolemy, in his discussion of genethliacal astrology, is not a little shifty on the subject of "starting points." In general astrology, "we have to take many starting points, since we have no single one for the universe"; but with individuals "we have both one and many starting points." Having rashly conceded that the best would be the moment of conception, he hurries on (since hardly anyone knows his father all that well) to claim that the moment of birth is good enough. (This conception-birth dilemma still worries modern astrologers. But we might add that, long before Ptolemy's time, the authors of the *Revelations of Nechepso and Petosiris* had got around it by assuming that the sign the Moon was in at your conception will be in the ascendant at your nativity.)

Left, a horoscope from the earliest printed
edition (produced in Venice in 1482) of the
Tetrabiblos, Ptolemy's vast compilation of
astrological information. Above, an
illustration (from an atlas printed in
Amsterdam in 1661) of the Ptolemaic
universe—the rigid geocentric system that
remained unchallenged for over 1000 years.
Around the earth rotate the seven planets
(*septem orbes planetarum*), each depicted as
a god driving a chariot. Each planet's
hieroglyph is indicated on its orbit.
Beyond the planets is the sphere of the
fixed stars, marked with the signs of the
Zodiac and their symbols.

By Ptolemy's time, astrology had triumphed throughout the Roman Empire, the emperors themselves often leading the way. The early emperors may have kept their tame astrologers for the same reason that many too powerful men have done since—simply because their high position gave them little sense of security. The young Augustus, though a hardheaded and calculating person, was so impressed by the glorious future foretold to him (by an astrologer named Theagenes) that he published his horoscope and struck a silver coin stamped with Capricorn, the sign under which he was born. Tiberius had a favorite astrologer called Thrasyllus (another Greek name; under the Empire the Greeks in Italy made corners in whatever needed wits). The crazy Caligula was said to have been warned of his impending death by a *mathematicus*—i.e., astrologer—called Sulla.

In A.D. 52, under the next emperor, Claudius, the astrologers were expelled from Rome. (The historian Tacitus called the decree "ruthless but ineffectual," adding that nearly everyone at the time believed that each individual's future is predetermined from birth.) But Nero returned to the old ways and consulted astrologers. He was told by some of them that if he had to leave Rome, he would find another throne in the East; one or two even specified the throne of Jerusalem.

Not only the emperors turned to the stars. Even in a thesis on architecture, there is a passage that implies that astrology was common knowledge—and practice. When drawing the ground-plan of a theatre, the thesis says, the best procedure is to inscribe four equilateral triangles in a circle "as the astrologers do, in a figure of the 12 signs of the Zodiac, when they are making computations of the musical harmony of the stars."

Right, the ruins of a Roman theatre (about A.D. 30) near Arles in France. Above, a plan of the theatre, based on the astrological method of drawing four equilateral triangles to form the circular figure of the 12 signs of the Zodiac.

Left, a coin minted about 19 B.C. in Spain (then part of the Roman Empire) during the reign of Augustus. The coin shows the emperor's birth sign, Capricorn, operating a rudder attached to the world globe (symbolizing Rome's rule over the world).

An engraving of Trimalchio's feast, from
an 18th-century Dutch edition of Petronius's
Satyricon. According to Petronius, the food
merely symbolized the Zodiac (beef for the
Bull, etc.). Here the artist has depicted
each dish in the *shape* of a Zodiac sign.

The establishment of astrology in Rome comes in for its share of mockery in the *Satyricon*, a picaresque novel by Petronius, part of which describes a vulgar and fantastic banquet given by a vulgar and fantastic "self-made man" named Trimalchio. This provincial freedman (freedmen, or emancipated slaves, had become very prominent at this time from court circles downward) displays his "culture" by serving a plate of titbits representing the signs of the Zodiac—beef for the Bull, kidneys for the Twins, a barren sow's paunch for Virgo.

Later, Trimalchio expounds the Zodiac as follows: The heaven in which the 12 gods live turns into an equal number of figures—the Ram and the rest. So anyone born under the Ram has plenty of flocks and wool and a hard head into the bargain. And so on. He himself was born under the Crab: "So I have many legs to stand on." Trimalchio also assigns butchers and perfumers to Libra, poisoners to Scorpio, cross-eyed men to Sagittarius, innkeepers and men with water on the brain to Aquarius, and to Pisces chefs and rhetoricians. "And so," he concludes, "the world turns like a mill, always bringing some misfortune, so that men are either born or die."

In A.D. 77 (nine years after Nero's death) there appeared a massive work that was to have a great influence on the Middle Ages: the *Natural History* of Pliny the Elder. This book begins with the stars. Pliny says in his first sentence that it is right to believe that there is something divine in the world and in the sky. There is no one, he says, who does not want to know his own future and who does not think this is shown most clearly by the heavens. This remark clearly indicates the mental climate of the day.

But a generation later this climate apparently didn't suit the gloomy satirical poet Juvenal. In his longest satire, an attack upon the female sex, Juvenal finds one of the gravest faults of women to be their susceptibility to oriental cults— and to astrology.

And Mankind, ignorant of future Fate,
Believes what fond Astrologers relate.

A woman, says Juvenal (as translated by John Dryden), will consult an astrologer for the most abominable reasons:

From him your Wife enquires the Planets' Will,
When the black Jaundice shall her Mother kill:
Her Sister's and her Uncle's end would know;
But, first, consults his Art, when you shall go.

Juvenal's attack on oriental cults stemmed from his general hatred of all things foreign. By his time, of course, Rome was thoroughly cosmopolitan. The Roman Empire, an astonishing conglomeration of countries and races, was geographically more unified and socially more standardized than the British Empire ever was. In literature and the arts, Greece had taken her captor captive long before the Roman Republic came to an end. And by the time of the emperors, the Asian provinces of the Empire were also exerting a powerful influence over their mistress.

From Egypt (which had been annexed in 30 B.C.) came that peculiar bundle of mystery, the cult of "Hermes Trismegistus" (Thrice Greatest Hermes), with which astrology was closely linked. The name "Hermes" is Greek of the brightest water; but the voice is a dark voice, linking primitive and medieval man, the witch doctor's medicine and the old wives' tale. Hermes was not, of course, a real person. Like Nechepso and Petosiris, he was literally a name to conjure with.

The Hermetic literary corpus consists of 17 or 18 fragments (it was once believed that Hermes wrote more than 20,000 books); but this is quite enough to show the appeal of these esoteric doctrines. According to Hermes, there are seven human types, corresponding to the seven planets, and the 12 signs of the Zodiac govern different parts of the human body. This is the notion of the Zodiacal Man, mentioned earlier and still current today. It is based on that ever-recurring concept of *correspondences*. Hermes writes:

"The macrocosm has animals, terrestrial and aquatic; in the same way, man has fleas, lice, and tapeworms. The macrocosm has rivers, springs, and seas; man has intestines. The macrocosm contains breaths (the winds) springing from its bosom; man has flatulence. The macrocosm has Sun and Moon; man has two eyes, the right related to the Sun, the left to the Moon. . . . The macrocosm has the 12 signs of the Zodiac; man contains them too, from his head, namely from the Ram, to his feet, which correspond to the Fish."

This general principle of correspondence, which may well go back to the days of the pharaohs, became greatly elaborated in the Hermetic scriptures. In particular, the authors of these works went in for medical astrology. Different ailments were assigned to the various signs of the Zodiac or their subdivisions, the decanates. (A sign can be divided into three decanates of 10° each.) Stomach troubles belong to the first decanate of Virgo, lung troubles to Cancer's second, while gout falls under both Aquarius and Pisces. As in most forms of astrology, these Zodiacal influences have to be correlated with those of the planets. The ears, for example, are ruled by Saturn, the brain by Jupiter.

The correspondences were extended to include, among other things, stones (certain stones are in "sympathy" with certain decanates, and help to effect a cure if the image of the decan is engraved on the stone and worn as a ring). Plants and herbs play an important role: The peony, for instance, is medically useful for anointing, for plasters, and for fumigation, and is otherwise helpful in business affairs. The directions for the peony's use are detailed: You must look for it when the Moon is waning, you can start operations when the Sun has

An illustration of the "Zodiac man" from a 14th-century German astrological manuscript. The figure shows the correlation of the signs of the Zodiac with parts of the human body. Man is ruled by the stars from his head (by the Ram) to his feet (by the Fish)—one example of the constantly recurring idea of "sympathy."

127

entered Virgo, you must be in an open place, and you must come equipped with a properly consecrated piece of seal skin. On this skin you must draw certain magic signs, then fix it around the root of the peony with genuine raw silk, uttering at the same time a long repetitive prayer, followed by incantatory words in Chaldean, Syriac, and Persian.

A further system of correspondences includes the individual fixed stars. The theme is the quadruple relationship of star, stone, plant, and talisman (or magic image). The talisman is to be engraved on the proper stone, under which the plant is inserted. Some examples of these correspondences are the following (the names in the text being usually the Arabian ones):

Aldebaran—ruby—spurge—a god or man fighting; Alhaioth (Rigel)—sapphire—horehound—a man about to amuse himself with chamber music; Alhabor (Sirius)—beryl—a kind of juniper—a hare, or a pretty young girl; Regulus—garnet—celandine—a cat or a lion, or a seated dignitary; Alchimech Abrameth (Arcturus)—jasper—plantain—a man dancing or playing, or a horse, or a wolf.

Many of the Hermetic prescriptions are primarily medical; but many more are obviously magical. Magic (in the form of incantations, talismans, etc.) had been in use medically and otherwise long before the Hermetic writings got to Rome. What is new here is the adulteration of astrology with such practices. But perhaps this was inevitable once astrologers, instead of confining themselves to foretelling things, set themselves up as healers.

Enter certain Christians

Certain facts about the second century A.D. clearly differentiate it from the preceding century. Where there had been a series of bad emperors, there came a series of good emperors, culminating in the philosopher-ruler Marcus Aurelius (A.D. 161-80). Yet in this same period Rome for the first time had seriously to contend with two of the chief disruptive forces that were to undermine her—the barbarians outside and the Christians inside.

Marcus Aurelius fought the former and persecuted the latter, and managed to stave off both of them temporarily. But neither the Danube in the one case nor traditional Roman culture in the other proved a strong enough bulwark. And where the traditional culture failed, so also did the modern eclectic culture that included the oriental cults and astrology.

At the same time that Ptolemy was summarizing the astrological knowledge that had been accumulating for centuries, counter-attacks on these beliefs were being prepared in various quarters, both pagan and Christian. The most important (because most passionate) of these attacks came from the Christian "apologists" who were then finding their voices. And powerful voices they were. Most of their apologies for Christianity were just as much attacks on pagan doctrines, or else were angry replies to people who denounced Christ as a magician. Usually, the Christians simply turned the tables on their attackers, rejecting necromancy, oracles, liver divination, augury, and astrology, *all* as being inventions of demons.

With most of these Christian writers, their indignant replies to the charge of practicing magic fail to show a return to the rational tone and the clear light of the older Greek tradition. Instead, they anticipate the sin-ridden and fear-ridden world of the Middle Ages. The Christians were not opposed to astrology because it was unscientific, but because it was immoral. They tended to think that science was immoral too.

Not all the Christians as yet were completely opposed to astrology. Many of them, for instance, seem to have accepted the Star of the Nativity as evidence of astrological truth. And the strange apocryphal work known as the *Clementine Recognitions* describes astrology as "the science of mathesis" (the Greek word has the general meaning of the acquisition of knowledge). Abraham, according to the *Recognitions*, "being an astrologer, was able from the rational

Both a first-century A.D. Roman statue of the god Pan (right, teaching a youth to play the pipes) and a 16th-century Swiss drawing of a devil (above) have cloven hoofs and horns. To many early Christians, pagan gods were "demons," and pagan thought (including astrology) the product of demons.

system of the stars to recognize the Creator, while all other men were in error . . . ."

The astrological arguments (and the broader philosophical and theological ones) continued to rage, and gradually the Christians appeared to be winning the day. But paganism did not give up so easily. In the third century, many of the emperors were mystics and Asianizers. Heliogabalus (who became emperor in A.D. 218) took his name from the Syrian Sun-god, who was worshiped in Syria in the form of a conical black stone. This stone was transported to Rome (as Gibbon describes it) "in a solemn procession through the streets of Rome, the way . . . strewed with gold dust; the black stone, set in precious gems, was placed on a chariot drawn by six milk-white horses richly caparisoned . . . ."

Sun worship is not of course to be identified with astrology, but it satisfied some of the same needs. And there is no doubt that some astrologers were Sun worshipers; after all, as astrology developed, the Sun had become increasingly dominant in the heavens. (In early Christian art, Christ is often depicted with some of the attributes of a Sun-god; even as the good shepherd, while he has the lamb on his shoulder, he wears the seven planets around his head.) The later emperor Aurelian (A.D. 270-275) followed Heliogabalus in one respect: He imported an image of the Sun from the East and made Sol Invictus the supreme god in his capital.

The old Roman gods had long ceased to satisfy anyone except the uneducated or simpleminded; the Sun-god from the East fulfilled a spiritual need, and at least was a magnificent symbol. But there was another new god who could beat him on his own ground—or should we say in his own sky?—and fulfill yet more of people's needs.

The last serious persecution of the Christians took place under the emperor Diocletian in A.D. 303. Ten years later, the Edict of Milan assured freedom of worship to men of every religion. Ten years later again, Constantine became sole emperor. Christianity had triumphed; the old pagan gods of Greece and Rome and the comparatively new gods from the East were to fall alike under a shadow, and so were astrology and other "demonic" practices. At the end of the fourth century, the militant Christian fathers came in for the kill: St. Gregory of Nyssa; St. John Chrysostom; St. Ambrose; St. Basil; and especially St. Augustine.

Augustine had an enormous influence on the development of Christianity—which means that he was one of the main founders of the world we live in. It is well known that this scourge of sinners had once cried out: "Lord, make me chaste, but not yet!" It is almost equally striking that this scourge of astrologers (his arguments against them were the best known in the Middle Ages) had as a young man consulted them himself—thereby, as he later put it, sacrificing himself to demons. In his *Confessions* he explains that he was weaned from astrology not by argument but by hearing that a certain wealthy landowner had been born at precisely the same moment as a wretched slave on his estate.

The earliest known portrait of St. Augustine from a sixth-century Roman fresco. Greatest of the Fathers of the Western Church, he attacked astrology on several counts, but mainly on the ground that its claim to influence human destiny challenged the supremacy of God. His arguments discredited astrology for four centuries.

In one of his letters Augustine writes that it is better to reject the errors of the astrologers "than to be forced to condemn and repudiate the divine laws or even the supervision of our own households." An astrologer who sells his silly horoscopes (*fatua fata*) to well-off persons will nevertheless "reprove his wife and even beat her—I won't say if he catches her being improperly playful, but even if she stares too long through the window." But supposing the wife were to say: "Why are you beating *me?* Beat Venus if you can; it's *she* who makes me behave like this." In other words, Augustine is saying, if you throw responsibility for your own actions on Fate, you must be consistent when dealing with other people.

Rome fell in A.D. 410. Augustine's main attack on astrology comes in his last and longest work, *The City of God,* which he wrote after that event and which indeed was inspired by it. Book Five of this work begins, once more, with an attack on the concept of Fate: "Those who hold that stars manage our actions or our passions, good or ill, without God's appointment, are to be silenced and not to be heard . . . for what doth this opinion but flatly exclude all deity?"

Augustine grants that astrological predictions sometimes prove correct. But he ascribes their correctness to "evil spirits (whose care it is to infect . . . and confirm men's minds in this false dangerous opinion of Fate in the stars) and not by any art of discerning of the Horoscope, for such is there none."

For such is there none! Augustine was a doctor of the Church and his words were all but law. What had not been accomplished by arguments was now at last achieved by a gesture of authority. The astrologers were put in their place—outside the pale.

For all that, even in the period of Augustine, astrology had its apologists. The famous Synesius of Cyrene, who began as a country gentleman and ended as a bishop in Alexandria, maintained that astrology can prepare one for the nobler science of theology. He stressed, like so many before him, that the universe is a whole in which the parts are bound together by *sympathy*. (Synesius is also said to have written on alchemy, which again of course is ruled by the principle of sympathy.) One of the reasons he gives for accepting astrology is that history repeats itself because the stars return to their former positions. It is surprising that an early Christian could accept this cyclic view of history; but then the concept has appealed to a certain kind of intellectual (W. B. Yeats for one) down to our own times.

Earlier in the fourth century, there was an aristocratic Roman intellectual— and Christian—who wrote a massive defense of astrology that is still today regarded as an astrological classic. This writer, Julius Firmicus Maternus, held that because the astrologer mediates between human souls and celestial beings, he must lead a pure and austere life. The human soul itself is a spark of that divine mind that exerts its influence through the stars. Therefore astrology is a useful and elevated pursuit; its truth, Firmicus believes (as do its latter-day champions), can be tested experimentally.

Aside from Firmicus, there were some less well known (and less intellectual) writers who appear to be looking backward, but who in fact would have been very much at home in Europe a thousand years later. Solinus (date uncertain but possibly fourth century), wrote a hotchpotch geography that was much used in the Middle Ages and was interested in occult medicine. He sometimes refers to the "discipline of the stars," and repeats from earlier writers a description of the horoscope of the city of Rome itself. This retrospective horoscope apparently revealed that Rome's first foundation stone was laid by Romulus on the 11th day of the Kalends of May between the second and third hours when Jupiter was in Pisces, the Sun in Taurus, the Moon in Libra, and the other four planets in Scorpio.

Horapollo, another diehard (fourth or fifth century), wrote a book called *Hieroglyphics,* to explain the hieroglyphics or written symbols of the ancient Egyptian priests. It is largely concerned with the marvelous behavior of animals (or the behavior of marvelous animals); but what is relevant to our subject is its astrological allusions.

According to Horapollo, the scarab or sacred beetle, so often represented in Egyptian art, rolls its ball of dung from east to west to simulate the Sun and imposes on it the perfect (i.e., spherical) shape of the world. Also, it buries the dung ball for 28 days conformably to the course of the Moon but, to square this with the number of days in the month, is equipped with 30 toes. Another rightly sacred animal is the baboon, who is born circumcised and neither sees nor eats during lunar eclipses. He is understandably kept in the temple, since at the equinoxes he makes water 12 times by day and 12 times by night exactly on the hour; this is why the Egyptians engraved him on practically all of their water clocks.

Pliny, in his *Natural History,* three to four centuries earlier, had been not at all averse to marvels, yet Horapollo belongs to a different world. Though both his astrology and frivolous garrulity would have been frowned upon by the Christian Fathers, his complete lack both of sophistication and of a scientific spirit parallels the Christian mentality that accepted both miracles and demons —a mentality that, combined with the overrunning of Western Europe by the barbarians, among other factors, allowed the so-called Dark Ages to slide over most of Europe.

What happened to astrology in this obscure era? Perhaps to all intents and purposes it vanished. But it is more likely that it continued to flourish (though driven underground) in spite of the Church's disapproval. When we remember how long witches enjoyed a vogue against all the odds, we may guess that astrologers could still get their fees, at least from the less sophisticated or less devout persons. What is an established fact is that astrology eventually made a comeback and was welcomed by the Church herself. But that was some centuries after the fall of Rome, and ahead of our story. Let us go on from where the ancient world left off.

5 The stars on top

In sixth-century Western Europe, most thinkers rejected pagan philosophy, except for its most mystical or anti-scientific branches. So far as the natural sciences were bothered with at all, the attempt to squeeze them into a Christian framework outweighed both observation and reason. Long obsolete cosmologies were revived: A monk named Cosmas attacked the belief that the universe is spherical and claimed instead that it is shaped like the Holy Tabernacle as described in the Book of Exodus. But a spherical heaven is required by astrology; so here a Christian writer shows himself less scientific than the people he condemns for superstition or magical practices.

We have now arrived at the "Dark Ages," or early Middle Ages. A hundred years ago, historians could assume that there were clearly definable borders between one "age" and another. But today, most people tend to think of these "ages" as shading or cross-fading into each other. Old concepts refuse to drop out, while new ones often jump the gun. All the same, after the sixth century, astrological writings in Western Europe were extremely scarce for 400 years. Meanwhile, of course, Byzantium remained civilized, while, far to the west, there was a high degree of culture in Ireland. But for astronomy-astrology we have to wait till the ninth century and then look east to Baghdad.

In that city of Arabian Nights, astronomy and astrology (still playing Siamese twins) regained some of their ancient glory under the patronage of caliphs

Two extracts from a 15th-century fresco illustrating the months of the year, painted by the Italian artist Francesco del Cossa for the Duke of Ferrara. Above, March is represented by the figure of a girl (a personification of spring) over Aries the Ram; below, April is depicted as a man holding the key of spring, seated above Taurus the Bull. The fresco was designed by the duke's court astrologer—a reminder that astrology was in its heyday during the Middle Ages and Renaissance.

like the famous Harun al-Rashid. An observatory (sure proof that these studies were serious) was built in Baghdad, and was used by astrologers like Albumasar, whose book on astrology was one of the first to see print after the invention of the printing press. These protégés of the caliphate, like their predecessors long before in the same part of the world, were also great observers and measurers, as well as makers of astronomical instruments.

In the 10th century the caliphate declined, and by the year 1000 Islamic culture had had its day in Baghdad. It was, however, to flourish for two more centuries in Spain (where an Arabian astronomer published a famous astronomical calendar known as the Toledo Tables), from which country the heritage of paganism was to flow into the rest of Western Europe. By the year 1000 the West was beginning to stir, in astrology as in other things. The 10th century ended with the all-round scholar Gerbert enthroned in Rome as Pope Sylvester.

Though the legend quickly grew that this pope was a magician, in fact he was an intellectual pioneer. At the turn of the millenium, under the aegis of Gerbert, Cosmas's conception of the universe as a tabernacle went out and the spherical universe came in again. The Earth once more sat in the center of things, surrounded by nine concentric spheres—the seven spheres of the planets, that of the fixed stars, and Aristotle's Primum Mobile. This was to become the orthodox medieval picture of the universe. It was wrong, but it was a great advance—or recovery.

In the 11th century, astrology and its peripheral practices were in the air again. There were "Moon books" in circulation and "spheres of life and death" and spheres of "Petosiris" or "Apuleius" and lists of "Egyptian [i.e., unlucky]

days" (about 40 or 50 of them in the year). And by the 12th century, astrology had become thoroughly re-established as a subject of serious study.

The views about astrology of the clerical intelligentsia varied, but they all were concerned with it, and with relating it to other branches of learning. An anonymous 12th-century manuscript, for instance, connects different religions with different planets. Judaism is allotted to Saturn, as it had been by the Roman historian Tacitus. Islam, being a religion both sensual and warlike, falls under both Venus and Mars; its holy day is Friday because that is Venus's day. Christianity under the Roman Empire was related both to the Sun (which stands for honesty, liberality, and victory) and to Jupiter (which stands for peace, equity, and humanity). It is noted by the 12th-century writer that neither Mars nor Saturn is ever in a friendly relationship with Jupiter. Later, the Christian religion became assigned to Mercury; according to Roger Bacon in the 13th century, Mercury's difficult orbit corresponds to the Christian mysteries. Also, Mercury is dominant only when in Virgo, which in this context could be equated with the Virgin Mary.

Astrology by this time covered all fields, from the sublime to the ridiculous: "William of England," who apparently was a citizen of Marseilles, wrote a treatise called *De Urina non Visa* (Of Urine Unseen), explaining "how by astrology to diagnose a case and tell the color and substance of the urine without seeing it."

At this time some astrologers divided their subject into eight branches: the science of judgments (i.e., judicial astrology); medicine; "nigromancy"; agriculture; illusions, or magic; alchemy; the science of images; and the science of

Left, the "sphere of Apuleius" (from an English prayer book written about 970), probably used to predict whether a sick man would live or die. The two figures symbolize life and death. The fate of the sufferer was determined by adding the numbers corresponding to the day of the week and the month to the numbers set against the letters of the sick man's name, and dividing the total by 30. If the result fell below the line marked *sub terra* (underground) the man would die; if above, he would live.

Taking dips into the future still fascinates people today, whatever the method. For instance, in *The Ladies' Oracle* (right), published in Britain in 1962, the reader chooses one of 100 questions about the future, picks a symbol from a chart with her eyes shut, and relates the two to get her answer. Sample question: Shall I be loved long? Answer: As long as you deserve.

mirrors. The inclusion of nigromancy (necromancy) and "illusions" was the cause of astrology's bad name in certain quarters, while it is interesting that alchemy should be treated as a branch of astrology instead of as a parallel science. The mysterious "science of mirrors" was divination by means of polished or reflecting surfaces rubbed with oil, usually in accordance with the astrological hours. Though to a modern reader this practice might seem nearer to optics than to astrology, it provides further proof of some kind of association in the Middle Ages of the natural sciences with the "sciences" of astrology, magic, and fortune telling in general.

In an attempt to find a rational basis for astrology, various spurious works were attributed to Aristotle (who was acquiring an authority almost equal to Holy Writ). Thus we have "the book of Aristotle from 255 volumes of the Indians, containing a digest of all problems, whether pertaining to the sphere or genethlialogy." Aristotle's name (this would have puzzled him) was being linked with that of Hermes. Also attributed to him was a work called *The Secret of Secrets*, which was very popular in the Middle Ages and contained plenty of astrological lore, correlated (in the manner described in Chapter 4) with the virtues of herbs and stones.

Before leaving this century of revivals, we may note that in 1186 the much trusted Toledo Tables foretold a conjunction of the seven planets in Libra, which was bound to cause terrible disasters including hurricanes. The conjunction occurred—but not the hurricanes (unless they took place in some unknown part of the world, like Florida).

In the 13th century the astrological pace became even hotter. In England the center of learning was the new university of Oxford. Learning, of course, included astronomy, and astronomy included astrology. The first recorded chancellor of the university, Robert Grosseteste, accepted astronomy-astrology as the supreme science and held that hardly any human activity, whether it were the planting of vegetables or the practicing of alchemy, could dispense with the astrologer's advice.

Above, an early 18th-century engraving of
Catherine de Médicis (queen of France
1547-89) consulting a magician—possibly
the prophet-astrologer Nostradamus. The
magician (standing in a magic circle of
astrological signs) reveals to the queen
in a mirror the faces of future rulers of
France—an example of prediction by the
''science of mirrors.''

Left, a ninth-century copy of a sixth-
century world map by the Alexandrian monk
Cosmas. The Creator presides over the world
within a universe shaped like the Holy
Tabernacle in the Book of Exodus. This
concept of the universe was widespread in
the Dark Ages, though the spherical universe
came back into favor about 1000.

His pupil, Roger Bacon (who was suspected in his own time of practicing magic, which in fact he condemned), distinguished two kinds of "mathematics," one being magic and the other legitimate judicial astrology. Bacon believed in "elections" (i.e., using astrology to choose the right hour to do something) and also in astrological images and astrological medicine. This last, for Bacon, explained the remarkable case of "the woman of Norwich," who ate nothing for 20 years but retained her health. Also, as a good Franciscan friar, he welcomed the astrological prediction that Islam would endure, from its beginning, for only 693 years. This figure, he says, agrees with the famous "Number of the Beast" in the Apocalypse, which in fact (astrological license?) is 666. Whether the Moslem Era is dated from A.D. 610 or 622, this prediction meant that Islam should have ended near the beginning of the 14th century. Bacon himself died in 1296.

A great academic name on the continent was that of the Dominican Albertus Magnus, the master of Thomas Aquinas. Albertus was a typically medieval figure in that he combined very high intellectual powers with what (to us) seems a naïve credulity. He believed in the magical use of herbs; and he was probably the author of a popular work entitled *The Secrets of Women,* which included the astrological doctrine that a child receives its various qualities from the different heavenly spheres. Also, according to this work, each planet has control for one month over the child in the womb. And it is the constellations that account for monstrous births.

It was Albertus's pupil St. Thomas Aquinas who imposed *system* upon the body of existing knowledge in the Middle Ages, and thereby imposed a "Thomist" world-view upon Western Christendom. Even he allows that the stars have some influence: They serve as media between "the separate intelligences" (such as angels) and our material world. God rules inferior creatures through superior creatures, and so rules our earthly *bodies* through the stars. But Aquinas leaves room for free will, as did the poet Dante, whose whole *Divine Comedy* presupposes a Thomist universe. There are several passages in the *Divine Comedy,* and elsewhere, acknowledging or implying the influence of the stars. In the "Paradiso," referring to the fact that he was born under Gemini, Dante writes (in the Temple Classics translation): "O stars of glory, O light impregnated with mighty power, from which I recognize all, whatso'er it be, my genius . . . ." A striking passage, which looks back to Augustine, is to be found in the "Purgatorio," Canto XVI, where Dante asks one of the suffering spirits about the causes of vice. The spirit replies: "The heavens set your impulses in motion; . . . but . . . a light is given you to know good and evil, and free will [*e libero voler*], which, if it endure the strain in its first battlings with the heavens, at length gains the whole victory. . . . Ye lie subject, in your freedom, to a greater power and to a better nature; and that creates in you mind [*la mente*], which the heavens have not in their charge. Therefore, if the world today goeth astray, in you is the cause, in you be it sought. . . ."

Das ander Buch

Sieben Kreuter deß grossen Alex=
anders deß Keysers/der sieben Planeten
Kreuter genant/folgen hernach.

Alberti Magni. xij

II Wegwart der Sonnen.

j. Golewurtz Saturni.

Ein safft ist gůt dem schmertzen der nieren vnnd schienbeyn/vnd wirt gegeben denē die da schmer tzen leiden.

Die wurtzel ein wenig gekocht/sollen die besessen mē schen/die melancholici tragen in ein schönen tüchlin/ so werden sie entledigt.

Kinder den die zeen koment oder erst wachsent/die sollen sie auch tragē/so koment sie ber für on schmertz. Die wurtzel getragen bei nacht/versichert vor allem vnfall.

WEgwart hat den namē empfangen võ der Sõ nen/dannes ist geyl. Etrlich habens genant/dz hauß der Sonnen/Wañ diß kraut das heylt deß hertzen vñ deß magens wee.Trincket jmant sein safft so macht es jn vast keusch.

Der bei ihm tregt sein wurtzel/so heylt es den weeta gen der augen.

Es hilfft auch den Freneticis/so sie das beisnen tra gen an der brust.

L

Above, two pages from the *Naturalia* (printed in Germany in 1548) by Albertus Magnus, one of the great 13th-century Dominican teachers. Albertus related the magical and medicinal properties of herbs to planetary and Zodiacal influences—another example of the idea of correspondences. Of the two plants shown here, the Martagon lily (left) is "in sympathy" with Saturn, who rules Capricorn and Aquarius, and chicory (right) is "in sympathy" with the Sun, who rules Leo.

Right, a 13th-century seal (probably made for Robert Grosseteste) depicting a chancellor of Oxford surrounded by scholars. Grosseteste was an ardent advocate of astrology, which was studied at Oxford as at most other medieval universities.

141

per chel ueder dinanzi era lor tolto.
Forse p forza gia di parlalia.
si trauolse colli alchun del tutto.
ma io nol uidi ne credo che sia.
Se dio ti lalci lector prender frutto.
di tua lectione or pensa p te stello.
chomio potea tener il rilo alciutto.
Quando la nostra umagine da prello.
uidi si torta chel pianto de glucchi.
le natiche paslaua per lo fello.

Above, an illustration from a 15th-century
Italian manuscript of Dante's "Inferno":
Dante (center, in blue) is led by his
guide Vergil to see the fortune tellers
in hell, whose heads are twisted so they
can only look backward. This is their
punishment for looking into the future
(which is the prerogative of God). Right,
a 15th-century portrayal of Guido Bonatti,
one of the most famous astrologers of the
13th century, who was among the sorcerers
consigned to hell by Dante. In spite of
the Church's opposition to his unorthodox
views, Bonatti escaped the long arm of
the Inquisition.

Thus man's "nature" (subject to the stars) is in opposition to a "better nature" (which must be referred to God). The fact that free will has to *battle* with the stars imputes a very great power to them; neither Dante nor Aquinas would have dreamed of denying this. Repeatedly quoted during this period was a Latin tag: *sapiens dominabitur astris*—the wise man will rule the stars. It was still being quoted in the 17th century, and no doubt was so popular just because people were so frightened. It was both a piece of "wishful thinking" and a gesture, though a cautious one, of defiance.

Among Dante's contemporaries and immediate successors, the huge wings of astrology gave shelter to all types of men, from truth-seeking philosophers to profit-seeking quacks, and to all types of opinion from the profound to the cranky. A 13th-century monk, Ristoro of Arezzo, believed that the northern part of the sky was the nobler and that *therefore* only the northern hemisphere was inhabited; he also was much interested in the horoscopes of horses. One Thomas of Cantimpré held that the brains of wolves and the livers of mice vary in size with the waxing and waning of the Moon. The *Franciscan Chronicles* (by a Franciscan friar named Salimbene) provide an engaging 13th-century example of an astrological quack (translated by G. G. Coulton):

"The Inner Party of Modena [in Northern Italy] had a man of Brescia who called himself an astrologer and diviner, to whom they gave daily ten great pennies of silver, and nightly three great Genoese candles of the purest wax, and he promised them that if they fought a third time they should have the victory. And they answered him: 'We will not fight on a Monday or a Tuesday, for we have been conquered on those two days. Choose us therefore another day; and know that if we gain not this time the promised victory, we will tear out thy remaining evil eye'; for he was one-eyed. So, fearing to be found out in his falsehood, he carried off all that he had gained, and went his way without saluting his hosts."

Italy seems during the Middle Ages to have been the leading country in astrology, which infiltrated not only into the Church but into the new universities. Thus in the school of medicine in Bologna in the 13th century the dictum quoted earlier ran: "A doctor without astrology is like an eye that cannot see." A century later Bologna had a chair of astrology.

Astrology was popular not only among men of learning in the Middle Ages. By the 13th century it had become firmly embedded in the everyday life of the people. The 19th-century Swiss historian Jacob Burckhardt writes: "In all the better families the horoscopes of the children were drawn as a matter of course, and it sometimes happened that for half a lifetime men were haunted by the idle expectation of events that never occurred." There were many instances of astrologers intervening in public affairs, such as the journeys of princes, the laying of foundation stones, or the management of military campaigns. One of the most famous astrologers of the 13th century, Guido Bonatti, assisted the Ghibelline leader Guido da Montefeltro to win a series of battles.

When the constellations were right for victory, Bonatti used to ascend a high church tower with his book and astrolabe and at the exact moment give the signal. The great bell was then rung and there was (presumably) victory.

In Bonatti's influential Latin book the *Liber Astronomicus* (he used the words astronomy and astrology interchangeably), he ranks the astronomer-astrologer above the physician, because human bodies are merely composed of the four elements with the four qualities, whereas the bodies studied by astrologers are composed of a fifth and incorruptible essence. The opposition that Bonatti's teachings met among the clergy was not surprising, seeing that he held that astrologers know more about the stars than theologians do about God. At the same time he reveals that many of the clergy in the 13th century consulted astrologers about their prospects of promotion (which is a good example of an "interrogation").

Bonatti himself claimed to believe that, if you are hesitating to accept an invitation to dinner, the astrologer can help you by predicting the menu. As regards "elections," he held that there was a favorable moment for almost every possible activity, including trimming one's nails. In the field of "revolutions," he thought astrologers could foretell which would be a good year for bishops, monarchs, or cucumbers.

Many other astrologers of the time got into serious difficulties with the Church—like the physician Arnald of Villanova, who wrote a treatise on *Judgments of Infirmities by the Movements of the Planets*. Though Arnald moved in high ecclesiastical circles, the Inquisition (whose attitude to astrology often appears ambiguous) declared some of his writings heretical. Another suspected heretic was Peter of Abano, also called Peter of Padua. Peter was a champion of astrological medicine and of images: He believed that a figure of a scorpion made when the Moon is leaving Scorpio will cure the bite of a scorpion. He also held that the revolution of the eighth sphere (that of the fixed stars), which, he reckoned moved one degree in 70 years, could even turn land into sea; hence the disappearance of Atlantis.

Peter distributed history among the seven planets, each being in charge of 354 years plus four lunar months. Thus Sodom and Gomorrah were destroyed when the Moon was supreme. (Some modern astrologers carve history into much larger slices—of roughly 2000 years each—determined by the *constellations*.) The seven planets, according to Peter, are also associated with seven angels; Mercury is paired with Raphael, the Moon with Gabriel, and so on. What may have involved him with the Church authorities was his discussion of Christ's nativity: It was said that Christ was born when there was a great conjunction of Jupiter and Saturn in the beginning of the first degree of the sign of the Ram (which of course was the very beginning of the Zodiacal system).

The retrospective casting of the nativity of Christ was at this time commonly linked with the prospective casting of that of Antichrist, presumed to depend on a conjunction of Jupiter and the Moon. This also shocked the authorities. But

The original Royal Observatory at
Greenwich, which was built for the first
English Astronomer Royal John Flamsteed.
Flamsteed is said to have chosen the date
for laying the foundation stone by means
of an astrological "election" (erecting a
horoscope to find a favorable time for a
particular project) The date selected
was August 10, 1675.

Peter weathered whatever storm there was. There is a statue to him in Padua, on which he is described as "in astrology indeed so skilled that he incurred suspicion of magic, and, falsely accused of heresy, was acquitted." Less fortunate was Cecco d'Ascoli, who had taught astrology at Bologna and had been court astrologer to the Duke of Florence. He was condemned by the Inquisition and burned at the stake in Florence in 1327; orders were also given to burn his Latin astrological book. One of Cecco's heresies seems to have been that he taught that Christ came to earth in accordance with the will of God *and* with the principles of astrology.

In spite of Cecco's fate (which was most untypical), astrology continued to flourish in the Middle Ages. Italian artists glorified it in frescoes like those in Padua and Ferrara, and in the 15th century those ruthless adventurers the Condottieri each had his own pet astrologer. And Lorenzo de' Medici allowed Marsilio Ficino of Florence to cast all the little Medicis' horoscopes.

Astrology also played a part in the literature of the period—as in the poetry of Geoffrey Chaucer, who was born about 20 years after Dante died and who died himself in 1400. Chaucer is a typical medieval figure. Although most of the astrological references in his *Canterbury Tales* would have been commonplace to his readers, his own astronomical-astrological knowledge was better than commonplace. He pretends modestly in one passage that he knows "no termes of astrology," but he found time and was interested enough to write a treatise on the astrolabe. In the Prologue to the *Canterbury Tales*, he has hardly begun describing his Doctor of Physic before he mentions, high in the list of credentials, the Doctor's astrological knowledge, which includes the use of images. Similarly, that earthy lady the Wife of Bath brings in the stars to explain her own distinctive temperament:

> *Venus me yaf my lust, my likerousnesse [lecherousness],*
> *And Mars yaf me my sturdy hardynesse;*
> *Myn ascendant was Taur and Mars therinne . . . .*

According to Britain's Ingrid Lind, writing today, "Taurus women are good-looking and have solid, well-made bodies [the Wife of Bath had a bold red face and large hips] with a good notion of what such bodies can produce in the way of agreeable sensation."

On the whole, Chaucer seems to have taken his astrology with a grain of salt. (He took plenty of salt, of course, in other spheres, being a typical English empiricist and good-humored iconoclast.) In his longest and most technical astrological passage, in "The Franklin's Tale," he speaks of an astrologer who is setting out "to maken his japes" (i.e., tricks) with his "supersticious cursednesse." Chaucer is obviously no admirer of this astrologer (or "magician"). A lovesick young Englishman has come to consult him, and the magician is about to calculate by astrology the right hour for contriving a monstrous illusion for his client's benefit. Here is some of the description of this operation (from Nevill Coghill's modernized version, for easier reading):

Above, an engraving from an 18th-century edition of Chaucer's *Canterbury Tales*, showing the Wife of Bath as the center of attraction. Though Chaucer was no admirer of astrology, he often referred to it : For example, the Wife of Bath attributes her boldness and earthy vigor to her ascendant sign, Taurus.
Right, a 19th-century astrologer's idea of a Taurus woman, showing the heavy features traditionally ascribed to people influenced by this sign.

His calculating tables were brought out
Newly corrected, he made sure about
The years in series and the single years
To fix the points the planets in their spheres
Were due to reach . . . .
And finding the first mansion of the Moon,
He calculated all the rest in tune
With that. He worked proportionally, knowing
How she would rise and whither she was going
Relative to which planets and their place,
Equal or not, upon the Zodiac face.

Not long after this, in 15th-century France, we find an attack on astrology in the form of an allegory, *The Dream of the Old Pilgrim*, by Philippe de Mézières. The scene is a debate in Paris presided over by Queen Verity. An aged hag enters, wearing a robe embroidered with geometrical figures. She holds a book in one hand and an astrolabe in the other, and wears spectacles because she is nearly blind from stargazing. In her time, we learn, she has been in the employ of King Ptolemy of Egypt, Albumasar, and Neptanebus. Her name is Old Superstition.

Opposing her is a lady delegate from the university of Paris. She is only 18 years old, and wears a close-fitting green dress (which gets greener every moment) and a beautiful green hat with 12 flowers of a ravishing scent around the brim. In one hand she holds a flaming cross, in the other a compendium of theology. Her name is Bonne Foy; and, needless to say, she wins the debate.

Her argument rests on a basic distinction between the two kinds of astronomy (or, as we should now say, between astronomy and astrology). Old Superstition, though discomfited, sweeps off saying she will still find followers among both laity and clergy, not to mention royalty. Bonne Foy returns to the university.

Astrology did find followers elsewhere. Nearly two hundred years later, the Elizabethans still readily accepted the astrological mode. Even a man with such a reputation for free thinking as Sir Walter Raleigh was prepared to concede that there was something in astrology, although (like so many before him) he was careful to leave room for free will. And Raleigh, for all his inherited medieval concepts, was standing on the threshold of the world we know.

The planet Jupiter, with its Zodiac signs Pisces and Sagittarius, from a 15th-century Italian manuscript. The scenes depict three medieval occupations thought to be under Jupiter: An apothecary serves a customer; an alchemist sieves precious metals from sand; a mathematician is consulted by a client. Many astrological texts of the time were illustrated with traditional ideas of the planets and planetary "types."

149

The Renaissance

Newton's *Principia* was published in 1687. The two preceding centuries had been a period of constant, almost unprecedented intellectual ferment and discovery; yet through at least most of the period there are plentiful examples of diehard traditionalism and, even among the innovators, of an ingrained reluctance to go the whole way with themselves. The pioneers of modern astronomy were still hampered by medieval modes of thought. It was only with Newton that men's minds appear to have been finally freed from the medieval shackles (or, depending on your viewpoint, the medieval supports and underpinning).

This is where astrology comes in—or rather stayed in. In 1488 the prominent astrologer Johannes Lichtenberger wrote: "Attention must be paid to the weighty planets Jupiter and Saturn, whose conjunction and coincidence threaten terrible things and announce future calamities . . . and to this terrible conjunction the horrible house of the ill-fated Scorpion has been assigned." And a preface to another of Lichtenberger's books states: "The signs in heaven and in earth are surely not lacking; they are God's and the angels' work, and they warn and threaten the godless lands and countries and have significance." The author of this preface was Martin Luther.

Even while Luther was underwriting the astrologers, the Italian humanist Pico della Mirandola was preparing a massive assault on astrology. Over and over again, Pico makes one basic (and radical) distinction: between astrology and astronomy. This distinction was not observed by 15th-century astronomers like Regiomontanus—or, for that matter, by their more famous successors, such as Kepler. In the mid-15th century, Regiomontanus was an outstanding astronomical observer and inventor of instruments; but he also introduced the particular division of the sky into 12 houses that is used by many astrologers

An illustration from a work by the 15th-century German astrologer Johannes Lichtenberger, showing the "terrible conjunction" that, to Lichtenberger, meant calamity. The sign of Scorpio hovers over personifications of Saturn (right) and Jupiter (with Taurus).

today. To Pico, however, the astronomer (or the true philosopher) does not believe or affirm anything that cannot be demonstrated by evidence or by reason.

Pico also attacked astrology on the evidence of his own experience, this evidence consisting largely- of disasters in his family. Astrologers had promised his brother-in-law a year completely free from danger or misfortune; he died in the course of it. The same thing happened to Pico's nephew-in-law and sister-in-law. The sister-in-law, in fact, while she clasped her husband's hand on her deathbed, had exclaimed: "Look! So much for the predictions of astrologers!" Her husband, on the other hand, had been promised every sort of misfortune and had survived the year unscathed.

At about the same time that Pico was preparing his attack (and when the young Copernicus was studying at Cracow University), an astrologer called Luc Gauric erected the horoscope of the young Giovanni de' Medici and predicted (correctly) that he would become pope. The Italian nobility were by then making a regular practice of employing astrologers. But this does not mean that the "royal" art was not also exceedingly popular among the common people. In the same year (1493) that Gauric made his prediction, a work was published in Paris that has been extensively quoted from in earlier chapters —*The Kalendar and Compost of Shepherds*. The art of printing was barely half a century old, and this was one of the very first books to be printed for the amusement and instruction of the ordinary literate man. It was widely popular and was reprinted in many cities of Europe.

Whoever was the author of this book put his lore into the mouths of shepherds (in accordance with an ancient literary tradition that made shepherds the repositories of wisdom). A good part of the wisdom in this "Compost" is, as we have seen, familiar astrological material. The author accepts the division of the sky into 12 houses (the House of Life, the House of Substance and Riches, and so on) and also the doctrine that each hour is ruled by one of the planets. He slips from prose into verse when he comes to the planets' qualities. To quote from a translation of about 1518:

For to know their natures all
In sooth it is a great conning,
And shows what may befall
When every planet is reigning . . . .
Saturn is highest and coldest, being full bad,
And Mars with his bloody sword ever ready to kill;
Jupiter very good, and Venus maketh lovers glad,
Sol and Luna is half good and half ill . . . .

Immediately preceding the astrological section of the book there is a section entitled "Of Physic and Governance of Health." The first part of this section is captioned: "How shepherds by calculation and speculating knoweth the twelve signs in their course reigning and dominating on the twelve parts of a man's body; and which be good for letting blood, and which be indifferent or

Alter Bauernkalender

evil for the same." There follows a chapter entitled "A picture of the physiognomy of man's body that showeth in what parts the seven planets hath domination in man." The chapter in fact *consists* of a picture. This was the kind of teaching that was most readily acceptable to people in general in the lifetime of Copernicus, the Polish cleric who destroyed the Ptolemaic universe.

Whether Copernicus himself believed in astrology or not, the Austrian professor known as Rheticus (who became his self-appointed impresario) made use of astrology to sell the Copernican revolution. In the middle of a correct account of the new heliocentric system, the *Narratio prima*, Rheticus introduced a digression in which among other things the Second Coming was made dependent on changes in the eccentricity of the Earth's orbit.

Many of the best minds of the age certainly could reconcile astrology with a more "scientific" approach to their own subjects. From the Christian Fathers down, there had always been objections to astrology on *religious* grounds. *Scientific* considerations in the 16th century were just as likely to predispose scientists, or at any rate astronomers, in its favor. A notable example is Tycho Brahe (1546-1601), one of the first great observational astronomers, who spent much of his time casting horoscopes. While he may have done this with his tongue in his cheek (he considered all other astrologers charlatans) or mainly to oblige his friends, he did believe that the stars influenced a man's character and life. He backed up his belief with history. "In 1593," he wrote, "when a

Left, a woodcut from a 1527 edition of *The Kalendar of Shepherds* shows sheep shearing in June attended by the month's Zodiac signs —Gemini (top right) and Cancer (bottom right). Astrological calendars still appear today : Below left, the cover of a 1962 Austrian farmers' calendar, which provides details of weather and Zodiac influences.

Below, a diagram of the heliocentric universe from Copernicus' *De Revolutionibus* (1543). The Sun, at the center, is surrounded by the orbits of the seven planets (in their true order) and the sphere of the fixed stars. This revolutionary concept finally displaced the Ptolemaic, or geocentric, idea of the universe.

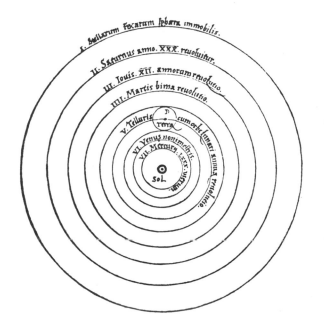

great conjunction of Jupiter and Saturn took place in the first part of the Lion, near to the nebulous stars in Cancer, which Ptolemy calls the smoky and pestilent ones, did not the pestilence which swept over the whole of Europe in the years that followed, and caused innumerable people to perish, confirm the influence of the stars by a very certain fact?"

And Tycho did make one famous prediction. Writing in 1572 on the astrological significance of a comet that had appeared in that year, he predicted that the comet's influence would be greatest in 1592, when a man would be born in Finland "ordained for a great enterprise" in a religious cause. The comet's effect would also be strong in 1632, which, Tycho added, would be the date of the man's death. The career of Gustavus Adolphus of Sweden fitted the prediction almost perfectly. He was born in 1594 (not 1592) in Stockholm (not precisely Finland, though Finland *was* at the time a province of Sweden). But these were the only inconsistencies. Gustavus was one of the greatest champions of Protestantism of the century and led his armies to great victories in the Thirty Years' War (primarily a religious war). And he was killed on the field of his most glorious victory, the battle of Lützen in 1632—a victory over the German imperial forces commanded by Wallenstein.

The irony is that it was Tycho who dealt a serious blow both to Aristotelian cosmology *and* to astrology by proving with his instruments that the famous new star of 1572—the short-lived "nova" that appeared near Cassiopeia—was

Left, an illustration of a sextant from Tycho Brahe's book on astronomical instruments. With the sextant he proved that the new "comet" of 1572 was actually a fixed star, thus shattering the traditional idea of the immutability of the fixed stars. But, though a pioneer of modern astronomy, Brahe remained an astrologer—as did the astronomer Johannes Kepler. In 1624 Kepler cast the horoscope of the famous German general Wallenstein and predicted from it that March 1634 would bring "dreadful disorders over the land." Wallenstein was killed on February 25, 1634 (depicted in a 17th-century print, right).

a genuine "fixed" star belonging to the eighth sphere (which traditionally was assumed to be free from mutability). This astounding phenomenon (at its brightest it could be seen at midday) had, to start with, given astrologers a field day. They treated it as a sinister omen; one theory was that, though lacking a tail, it was a comet, condensed out of human sins and touched off by the wrath of God. Some also thought that it foretold the Second Coming. But to consider it a *fixed* star was astrological and Aristotelian blasphemy. In proving its true status, Tycho unintentionally gave support to the Copernican system (which he did not accept), and also to his young collaborator Kepler (1571-1630), who was one of the great architects of the astronomical revolution.

There is no doubt that Kepler was a genius who, in his own words, "cleansed the Augean stables" of traditional cosmology. At the same time he was a confused and confusing character; his references to astrology often seem ambivalent. Einstein wrote that Kepler's remarks on astrology "show that the inner enemy, conquered and rendered innocuous, was not yet completely dead." In fact this "inner enemy" was probably more alive than Einstein assumed. Like Tycho, Kepler had to practice astrology whether he liked it or not. Also like Tycho, he thought or wanted to think there was something in it somewhere. As a young man he published annual astrological calendars, which no doubt he had to do in order to further his career. Thus for the year 1595 he predicted unrest among the peasants of upper Austria and the flight of the Austrians before a Turkish invasion. Both these predictions came true, though they were probably just shrewd guesses.

In a letter in 1598 to his old tutor Mästlin, Kepler writes of his most recent calendar: "As to all the prognoses, I intend to present to my above-mentioned readers a pleasant enjoyment of the grandeur of nature along with the statements which appear true to me, thus hoping that the readers may be tempted to approve a raise in my salary . . . . If you agree with this you will, I hope, not be angry with me if, as a defender of astrology in word and action, at the same time I try to implant the opinion in the masses that I am not an astrological buffoon." In 1611, writing to a confidant of his patron the Emperor Rudolph (at the time involved in a crisis), he makes a distinction not between astrology and astronomy but between two *kinds* of the former: "Ordinary astrology . . . can easily be used to please both parties. I believe that in such weighty reflections one should not only exclude ordinary astrology but also the one which I have recognized as being *in accordance with nature*" (italics mine).

Kepler knew what was not good for emperors or for the masses; and, whatever truth he may have found in astrology, he obviously loathed the way in which it pandered to human credulity and wishful thinking. Twenty years later, he scoffed at what obviously was one of the sensations of the day: "A girl of eleven living in Kottbus prophesies the end of the world. Her age, her infantile ignorance, and the number of her listeners have provided her with a faithful following."

Some peculiarities of Kepler's views of astrology are discussed (in terms of Jungian psychology) by the physicist W. Pauli, in an essay entitled "The Influence of Archetypal Ideas on the Scientific Theories of Kepler" (translated from the German by Priscilla Silz). Here Kepler appears to be what orthodox astrologers might call a mystical deviationist: Pauli comments that his "peculiar conception of astrology met with no recognition." This conception hinges on the stellar *rays*; Kepler believed that the rays strike the earth at different angles and form harmonious patterns comparable to those of music. The soul, he says, recognizes these patterns *instinctively* and without conscious reflection "because the soul, by virtue of its circular form, is an image of God in Whom these proportions and the geometric truths following thereupon exist from all eternity." And he adds: "If I should express my *own* opinion, it would be that there is no evil star in the heavens . . . chiefly for the following reasons: It is the nature of man as such . . . that *lends to the planetary radiations their effect on itself* [italics mine]; just as the sense of hearing, endowed with the faculty of discerning chords, lends to music such power that it incites him who hears it to dance."

This was a revolutionary idea in astrology: Kepler was, so to speak, transferring the initiative from the stars to man. He goes so far as to say that "the soul bears within itself the idea of the Zodiac." This apparent transposition of the astral and human roles, combined with Kepler's insistence on instinct (which would, for example, invalidate the traditional use of books of ephemerides), makes it not at all surprising that his theories met with no recognition. Neither the astrologers nor the public wanted their astrology blown up into mysticism.

In 1608, when Kepler was in his prime, the telescope was invented. Within two years Galileo had used it to show things contrary to Aristotle; he published his findings in 1610 in a booklet entitled *The Star Messenger*. The messages here delivered were sensational, and not everyone welcomed them. The Moon, for instance, traditionally thought of as a perfect crystalline sphere, was now declared to have a highly irregular surface. And there were vastly more fixed stars than anyone had ever thought. Worse than that, Galileo had discovered four new "planets." (These were, in fact, the satellites of Jupiter, but their discovery was nearly as disturbing to traditional attitudes as the later discoveries of the three planets proper—Uranus, Neptune, and Pluto.) All this hit the astrologers at least as hard as anyone else. Not that this would have worried Galileo. In Kepler the skeptic and the mystic were interlocked, but Galileo was a consistent debunker—though even he (like Kepler) found himself sometimes forced to make astrological predictions. (In 1609 he drew up a horoscope for his patron, the Grand Duke of Tuscany, promising him long life. The Grand Duke died a few weeks later.)

Two pages from Galileo's *The Star Messenger* (1610). Galileo's discoveries of new stars— made with the newly invented telescope— helped to discredit the old cosmology of the astrologers.

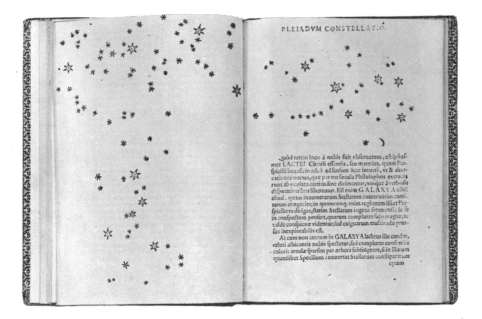

After Kepler and Galileo, and largely because of their own discoveries (which were suspect to the forces of the Counter Reformation), the scene of scientific inquiry shifted to northern Europe and particularly to France, the country of Montaigne and Descartes, and to England, the country of Francis Bacon and Newton. Francis Bacon is generally regarded as the herald of the new era; unlike Galileo, he was not himself a scientific observer and experimenter, but he passionately believed in observation and experiment and made eloquent propaganda on behalf of them. Nevertheless, the mass of works produced by the English astrologers proves that they enjoyed a large public. Early in the 16th century, the famous Dr. John Dee (who also practiced alchemy and crystal gazing) was casting horoscopes for the Tudor royal family. He was later patronized by Queen Elizabeth, but it looks as if his successors made their living on the whole from much humbler clients, who not only believed in astrology but found that it gratified the prevailing taste for the marvelous. On their maps it said "Here be dragons." In the stars it said "Here be your own dragons."

Elizabethan literature makes it obvious that people's forms of expression were conditioned by such long-accepted concepts as those of astrology and of the four humors. We have only to skim through the poets and playwrights to see that it was second nature to them to use astrological terms (though for technical knowledge of the subject they could not have competed with Chaucer). In Christopher Marlowe's *Doctor Faustus*, one of Faustus's friends asserts:

He that is grounded in Astrology,
Enriched with tongues, well seen in minerals,
Hath all the principles Magic doth require.

(Here we have the old linking of astrology and alchemy and the familiar subsumption of both under magic.) In Edmund Spenser's *Faerie Queene*, when the months parade in the so-called "Mutability Cantos," each month either rides upon or is equipped with a Zodiacal emblem. (In fact, of course, the emblems should change about the middle of each month.) Some of their mounts are rather awkward: "Joly June" is carried by a crab "With crooked crawling steps an uncouth pace." And as for February:

And lastly, came cold February, sitting
In an old wagon, for he could not ride;
Drawn of two fishes for the season fitting . . . .

Pisces being traditionally represented by a *pair* of fishes. All this, of course, is mere visual illustration, but it should be remembered that the Crab or the Fishes, even though clichés, meant as much to Spenser's readers as Freudian clichés mean to the average reader in the 20th century.

Shakespeare is full of astrological allusions, which come in very handy when a character wants to comment on the unfairness of it all, as when in *King Lear* the contrast is pointed between the two wicked sisters and Cordelia:

It is the stars,
The stars above us govern our conditions.

Above, a 17th-century English cartoon of an astrologer weighing bags of money taken from clients. In spite of the scientific advances of the period, astrology stayed popular with the majority of people, and continued to be reflected in the literature of the period—for example, in Christopher Marlowe's *Dr. Faustus* (1601), one of many versions of this legendary magician's career. Right, a 17th-century English woodcut showing Faust conjuring up the devil with the aid of a magic Zodiacal circle.

But in the same play the bastard Edmund produces the cynical view of astrology: "This is the excellent foppery of the world, that when we are sick in fortune—often the surfeit of our own behavior—we make guilty of our disasters the Sun, the Moon, and stars. . . ."

Of other Shakespearean characters who draw on this pool of imagery and excuses, Antony complains that he is deserted by his "good stars," while Cassius, in a famous passage in *Julius Caesar*, makes the same point as Edmund but with more dignity:

> *Men at some time are masters of their fates.*
> *The fault, dear Brutus, is not in our stars,*
> *But in ourselves, that we are underlings.*

In Shakespeare's romantic comedies there is Beatrice's remark about herself in *Much Ado about Nothing*: "There was a star danced, and under that was I born"; toward the end of the play her sparring partner, Benedict, says wryly: "I was not born under a rhyming planet, nor can I woo in festival terms." A more brittle example comes from *All's Well that Ends Well*, where the bombastic Parolles is baited by Helena with a play upon words typical of the period and of Shakespeare:

HELENA: Monsieur Parolles, you were born under a charitable star.
PAROLLES: Under Mars, I.
HELENA: I especially think, under Mars.
PAROLLES: Why under Mars?
HELENA: The wars have so kept you under that you must needs be born under Mars.
PAROLLES: When he was predominant.
HELENA: When he was retrograde, I think rather.
PAROLLES: Why think you so?
HELENA: You go so much backward when you fight.

And there is a similar (and perhaps better-known) passage in *Twelfth Night*, involving Sir Toby Belch and Sir Andrew Aguecheek, two titled parasites whose spiritual heirs today would have another drink on the ground that all the bad weather we have been having is due to the nuclear tests:

SIR TOBY: . . . I did think by the excellent constitution of thy leg it was formed under the star of a galliard [an Elizabethan dance].
SIR ANDREW: Aye, 'tis strong, and it does indifferent well in a flame-colored stock. Shall we set about some revels?
SIR TOBY: What shall we do else? Were we not born under Taurus?
SIR ANDREW: Taurus? that's sides and heart.
SIR TOBY: No, sir, it is legs and thighs.

Of many other passages in the Elizabethan playwrights one of the most striking comes toward the end of Webster's grim tragedy *The Duchess of Malfi*. The Machiavellian villain Bosola, who has successfully organized the strangling of the duchess, her children, and her maidservant, overhears the wicked cardinal,

In Shakespeare's *King Lear*, Edmund (here
played by James Booth in the 1963 London
production of the play) ridicules belief
in the influence of the stars. (The
"astrological" instrument he is toying
with bears no resemblance to anything
used by astrologers in real life.)
Unlike Edmund, many of Shakespeare's
characters accept astrology, often
alluding to it in general comments on
the vagaries of fate.

Four human types as seen by the 18th-century Swiss physiognomist Johann Lavater. In the Middle Ages it was believed that individual temperament and physique were determined by the "four humors" (or body liquids)— blood, phlegm, yellow bile, and black bile. For instance, a melancholic nature was thought to result from an excess of black bile.

his employer, planning to have him killed in turn. Bosola, like a good Elizabethan villain, attacks first but stabs the wrong man in the dark:

> *Antonio!*
> *The man I would have saved 'bove mine own life!*
> *We are merely the stars' tennis-balls, struck and bandied*
> *Which way please them.*

Such a view of astral influence is in tune with the stock Elizabethan concept of "blind Fortune" with her wheel.

Typical of the earlier part of the 17th century (in England the Civil War and Protectorate made a great strange gulf in the middle of it) are such peculiar figures as Sir Thomas Browne and Robert Burton. The former, who has one foot in the old world and the other in the new, speaks of astrology without clearly committing himself. Burton (in his *Anatomy of Melancholy*) is also cautious. He uses the famous Latin tag *sapiens dominabitur astris* to make the point that the stars "do incline, but not compel . . . ; and so gently incline, that a wise man may resist them; *sapiens dominabitur astris*: they rule us but God rules them." Yet Burton mainly uses astrology to reinforce his theory of "humors," in particular of melancholy: "The most generous melancholy . . . comes from the conjunction of Saturn and Jupiter in Libra: the bad . . . from the meeting of Saturn and the Moon in Scorpio." Elsewhere he discusses, with a typical massive display of latinity, the astrological causes of love-melancholy.

In the diagram below, each humor (indicated by a color, as in the key, right) is related to its appropriate planetary and Zodiacal symbols : For example, the melancholic (blue) is connected with Mercury (who rules Gemini and Virgo) ; Venus (Taurus and Libra) ; and Saturn (Aquarius and Capricorn).

sanguine

phlegmatic

choleric

melancholic

Burton seems to have been less aware of the new horizons than Browne, but Browne for his part remained a religious man. The Anglican bishop Jeremy Taylor expressed about this time what was probably the orthodox position of the young Church of England: "Let no man let his hopes wander toward future and far-distant events and accidental contingencies"; and quoted St. James on the folly of men who consult "astrologers and witches, oracles and devils."

Astrologers of the people

Taylor was 17 years younger than the French philosopher Descartes, who in this period was, like Galileo in Italy or Thomas Hobbes in England, exploding long-established preconceptions. But this kind of free thinking would have had little appeal to ordinary people, who still found it possible to reconcile both their common sense and their faith with a belief in astrology. This is proved by the great popularity of such astrologers as the Englishman William Lilly (1602-81), who died shortly before Newton published his *Principia*. Lilly's own autobiography is revealing in several respects. He was 30 before he was converted to astrology or saw the prospect of a career in it; when he came to practice, he seems to have been suspect to most groups, even to those to whom he politically adhered. When Cromwell became Protector, one of Lilly's books of predictions "was for a whole week every day in the Parliament House, peeped into by the

Left, a portrait of the astrologer William Lilly. In 1651 Lilly foretold disasters for England, symbolized by his drawing (above) of Gemini falling into flames. Gemini is the sign of the city of London, which suffered the Great Fire of 1666 (shown in an engraving of the time, right).

Presbyterians, one disliking this sentence, another finds another fault, others mis-liked the whole." In the same year, 1653, a violent attack was published by Thomas Gataker, B.D., "Against the Scurrilous Aspersion of that grand Imposter Mr. William Lillie," of whom he writes: "There needs not much skill in his pre-tended Art, to discover the vanity of it."

Two years later Lilly was in trouble again; he writes that he was "indicted . . . by a half-witted young woman . . . for that I had given judgment upon stolen goods, and received 2s. 6d. And this was said to be contrary unto an Act in King James's Time made." For good measure the young woman added "that she had been several times with me, and that afterwards she could not rest a Nights, but was troubled with bears, lions, and tygers etc." There were many other attacks on Lilly; and, though eight years later (in 1663) he was appointed churchwarden of Walton upon Thames, this respectable position did not save him in October 1666 from being summoned before a committee investigating the causes of the Great Fire of London. But this turned out to be an advertisement for his art: "Having found, Sir, that the City of London should be sadly afflicted with a great plague, and not long after with an exorbitant fire, I framed these two hieroglyphics . . . which in effect have proved very true." He records that he was dismissed by the committee with "great civility."

PHILOSOPHIÆ
NATURALIS
PRINCIPIA
MATHEMATICA.

AUCTORE
ISAACO NEWTONO, Eq. Aur.

Editio tertia aucta & emendata.

LONDINI:
Apud Guil. & Joh. Innys, Regiæ Societatis typographos.
MDCCXXVI.

ISAACUS NEWTON EQ. AUR. ÆT. 83.

T. Vanderbank pinxit 1725.   Geo. Vertue Sculpsit 1740.

Above, two pages from an edition printed in 1726 of Isaac Newton's *Principia* (first published in 1687) showing a portrait of the author and the title page. Newton proved that all physical phenomena, stars and planets included, are subject to natural—and rational—laws. In the "Age of Reason," satirists as well as scientists contributed to astrology's disrepute : right, a detail from an 18th-century woodcut of Jonathan Swift (holding a satirical pamphlet) who, under the pseudonym of Isaac Bickerstaff, made a laughing stock of the astrologer John Partridge.

As a *public* astrologer, Lilly had anticipated many astrological journalists of our own day. In 1644 Lilly wrote: "Saturn in the fifth house causeth more abortives than usually have been, the destructions of many men's sons or children, much tergiversation with Ambassadors and foreign Agents, and that they perform not what may be expected from them." It should be noted that the Civil War had *already* broken out.

Of course, Lilly had his rivals. In 1662 one John Gadbury published a *Collectio Geniturarum*, which he describes as "being of Practical Concernment unto Philosophers Physicians Astronomers Astrologers and others that are friends unto Urania" (the muse of astronomy). In his introduction he appears on the defensive, specifying three sorts of people that "seem most of all to oppugn this Noble Art, viz. the *Seeming Religious,* the *Politique,* and the *Ignorant.*" His nativities include Nero, Henry VIII, Queen Elizabeth, James I, Charles I, Luther, Richelieu, Regiomontanus, and Pico della Mirandola. And of Louis XIV (who, unlike the others, was still alive) Gadbury predicted that, if he survives this year (1662) which involves "dangerous Surfeiting, the Stone, and Treachery," then he may enjoy very good health till his 41st year. In fact Louis survived till 1715 and died at the age of 77.

And so it went on through the 17th century—a whole pack of astrologers boasting and backbiting, and most of them, clearly, doing quite well for themselves. Practitioners of related "sciences" were also thriving, like the famous herbalist Nicholas Culpeper, who ascribed the virtues of his herbs to the influence of the planets. But what with Copernicus and Kepler and Galileo's telescope, the writing, so to speak, was on the sky. Just as the ancient Greeks when they stopped asking "How?" declined in astronomy and turned to astrology, so the 17th-century French and English when they stopped asking "Why?" and concentrated on "How?" were inevitably bound to turn their backs on astrology.

It was Newton, of course, who completed the revolution; from then on (at least till recently) the universe has been thought of as *a machine that works.* God could be smuggled in by compromise or presupposed in the wings of the theatre, but this was only because God could neither be seen nor measured. The heavenly bodies, on the other hand, could now be seen and measured better than ever before. Recent astronomy had made sense of the solar system and, both literally and figuratively, put the Earth in its place; this undermined the astrologers' premises, which presupposed the Ptolemaic system.

Recent astronomy had also proved that change and irregularity were not confined to the sublunary sphere. There was Tycho's nova that had flared up, then vanished again; the Moon's surface was full of ups and downs; there were even spots upon the Sun itself. Moreover, instead of a compact and symmetrical universe (as Ptolemaic astronomy and all astrology had presupposed), there was now the dangerous idea of infinite space. In Catholic Italy, Giordano Bruno had been burned for suggesting just this in 1600. Lastly, when Newton explained all the motions of the heavenly bodies by four comparatively simple laws, he explained away the mystery that from the days of ancient Babylon had supplied an incentive, a rationale, and an excuse for astrology.

Newton, by the way, has repeatedly been called by modern astrologers as a witness in their own defense. This rests entirely on the story that the astronomer Edmund Halley, who gave his name to the famous comet, criticized Newton for accepting astrology and that Newton tartly replied to him: "I have studied the subject, Sir, you have not." But there seems to be no historical evidence for this story. The authoritative Ingrid Lind admits: "I do not know if this conversation did in fact take place." And the modern opponent of astrology Robert Eisler takes a very definite stand: "It remains an incontrovertible fact that after the discovery of Kepler's laws and Newton's principles—in other words, ever since the regular movements of the earth and the planets around the sun have been satisfactorily understood and explained—no professional or amateur astronomer of any repute has ever said another word in defense of astrology."

But the astrologers have gone down fighting, even if this fight has largely consisted in ignoring the overwhelming enemy. At the very end of this eye-opening century, well after Newton had worked out his theory of gravity, a typical rearguard action occurred in a book called *The Angelical Guide,* published in 1697. The author, John Case, makes some fascinating assertions, including the statement (quoted in Chapter 1) that the creation of the heavenly bodies took place "on Wednesday, April 22, 18 h.p.m. [6 P.M.] *about* 4002 years before Christ" (italics mine). And Adam (whom Case regards as the first astrologer) "was created in that pleasant place Paradise, *about* [italics mine] the year before Christ 4002, viz. on April 23, at 12 a clock or Midnight."

Later in the same book Case comes down to the practical uses of astrology— ". . . to know by this Angelical Lot or Guide what is to come, Good or Bad." Questions a man (or an unborn child?) may put to an astrologer are answered by consulting different signs of the Zodiac. Examples follow of the kind of questions asked of each sign:

What shape of body shall I have? (Aries)
Whether the thing lost was stolen? (Taurus)
How to know our Brother's Sisters' kindred or relations? (Gemini)
To know when my Grandfather, or my Great-grandfather, or that Old Rogue my Father, will die? (Cancer)
Whether I shall get a good Mistress? (Leo)
To know whether I shall ever keep a pack of Good Hounds, or a parcel of good Hogs or Sheep, or ever to be plagued with Rats or Mice? (Virgo)
Will my Wife be a Whore, or Honest? (Libra)
If I lend my Money, shall I gain? (Scorpio)
Shall I have the Bishopric or Abbey I desire? (Sagittarius)
To know whether I shall ever come to Honour, or be a Justice of the Peace? (Capricorn)

Will Fruits of the Earth be cheap or dear? (Aquarius)

Will any Old Woman chatter against me like a Devil? (Pisces)

Some of these questions might suggest that Case had his tongue in his cheek, but the fact remains that he had a successful practice.

Most of these astrologers must have been as difficult to caricature as, say, advertising men are today. But the wits of the Age of Prose and Reason attempted it. One of the most famous of these satires was directed at an astrologer named John Partridge, who used his almanacs to plug his own prejudices (such as anti-popery), to advance his own political interests, and to become very rich. In the reign of Queen Anne, Partridge was immortalized in print by a hoax that amounted to a practical joke. The joker was Jonathan Swift (writing under the name of Isaac Bickerstaff), who published certain "Predictions for the Year 1708." This was Swift's usual satirical technique: to pretend to believe in the ideas he was attacking, and then to carry them (with a straight face) to absurd extremes. So, as "Bickerstaff," he first states his belief in the art of astrology, while he deplores "those gross impostors who set up to be the artists." He is therefore setting out to provide his own reliable predictions to put imposters like Partridge to shame.

Swift goes straight to his target: "My first prediction is but a trifle; yet I will mention it, to show how ignorant those sottish pretenders to astrology are in their own concerns: It relates to Partridge the almanack-maker. I have consulted the star of his nativity by my own rules; and find he will infallibly die upon the 29th of March next, about eleven at night, of a raging fever: Therefore I advise him to consider of it, and settle his affairs in time."

People bought "Bickerstaff's" predictions and took him seriously. But they may have taken him less seriously when he changed his ground, assumed the name of Partridge himself, and wrote a farcical attack on "Bickerstaff's" predictions. This essay relates what happened on "the 28th of March, anno Dom. 1708, being the night this sham prophet had so impudently fixed for my last." "Partridge" complains of a bell being tolled for him, of the undertaker and then the sexton calling, and many other inconveniences: "I could not stir out of doors for the space of three months after this, but presently one comes up to me in the street, Mr. Partridge, that coffin you was last buried in, I have not yet been paid for . . ."

That Partridge really did suffer from this hoax is obvious. We do not know whether he ever lived it down (the phrase in this context carries more meaning than usual); he died in 1715. It seems that he actually tried to advertise in the papers that he was "not only now alive, but was also alive on the 29th of March in question." As for "Bickerstaff," he suffered too. His "Predictions" was burned by the Inquisition in Portugal, presumably because, besides predicting the death of Partridge, it had also pretended to predict many unfortunate events on the continent, including the death of Louis XIV. So ends a whole era of astrological theory and practice, not with a bang but with a coffee-house giggle.

6 The loss of respectability

In the 16th century a papal astrologer made a mistake in the date when casting Luther's horoscope retrospectively. In the 18th century (the "Age of Enlightenment") this incident was seized upon with delight by the English humorist Laurence Sterne in his novel *The Life and Opinions of Tristram Shandy*. Sterne envisaged a scene in Strasbourg where the two universities, "the Lutheran and the Popish," were "employing the whole depth of their knowledge . . . in determining the point of Martin Luther's damnation."

"The Popish doctors had undertaken to demonstrate, *a priori,* that from the necessary influence of the planets on the twenty-second day of October, 1483,—when the Moon was in the twelfth house, Jupiter, Mars, and Venus in the third; the Sun, Saturn, and Mercury, all got together in the fourth;—that he must in course, and unavoidably, be a damned man; and that his doctrines, by a direct corollary, must be damn'd doctrines too.

"By inspection into his horoscope, where five planets were in coition all at once with Scorpio . . . in the ninth house, which the Arabians allotted to religion, —it appeared that Martin Luther did not care one stiver about the matter;—and that, from the horoscope directed to the conjunction of Mars,—they made it plain likewise he must die cursing and blaspheming; with the blast of which his soul (being steep'd in guilt) sailed before the wind in the lake of Hell-fire." The above horoscope looks pretty odd (one cannot see how there were five

The frontispiece to *Raphael's Witch* or *Oracle of the Future* (published in England in 1831) depicting the mystical wheel of Pythagoras, which is used in a method of numerical divination. The decorative figures include a witch (center) and an astrologer (bottom left)—a typical 19th-century linking of astrology and occultism.

planets to spare for the ninth house) but presumably was meant to be. Sterne was enjoying himself at the expense of a subject that was gradually reaching a stage where it was no longer taken seriously. The late 17th-century English poet John Dryden was probably the last important English writer (at least till nearly our own day) to regard astrology as a serious subject.

Yet Dryden himself also exploited it as a source of rather crude comedy. In a play of his entitled *An Evening's Love* or *The Mock Astrologer* (the plot and title were borrowed from the French dramatist Corneille) a young Englishman in Madrid pretends to be an astrologer because he has designs on a senorita. Unfortunately the heroine's father has studied astrology in his youth and proceeds to test the hero's knowledge by asking him "the best way of rectification for a nativity." The Englishman answers: "Mars rules over the Martial, Jupiter over the Jovial . . . ." "This," says the father indignantly, "every school-boy could have told me." The hero's friend then advises him to be better prepared in future: "If at any time thou ventur'st at particulars, have an evasion ready like Lilly."

Lilly's name is honored again today (and not only by astrologers), but Dryden's successors in the forefront of the Enlightenment had very little respect for him or his kind. A very lean period was beginning for the once proud "queen of the sciences." The modern astrologer Louis de Wohl dates the beginning of the rot from the 16th century with its wars of religion from which "revolution was born and with it that terrible time of gross rationalism" (which, he apparently hopes, is now drawing near its end). But it was in the 18th century that this rationalism became truly free—or gross. Throughout the 16th and much of the 17th century (as we saw in Chapter 5) it was still hampered and complicated by old modes of thought and a residue of superstition.

In England the Royal Society (which was the spearhead of what has been called the "scientific revolution") had been founded in 1662; and yet, on the appearance of the great comet of 1680, we find an educated man like the diarist John Evelyn writing of comets: "They *may* be warnings from God." In Germany, on the same occasion, we find professors and Lutheran ministers stressing the length of the comet's tail and regarding it as a rod of chastisement that God has put in his window—"and all the children fear, but he has in mind only the mischievous." Erhard Weigel, a professor of mathematics whose astrological views admittedly were eccentric, interpreted the vanishing of this comet when about to enter the Milky Way as a warning to parents to feed their children on the milk of true piety. And on the same occasion great attention was paid by serious Germans to the report that a hen in Rome had laid a comet-marked egg; engravings of this hen and her egg were circulated through the country. Many German pamphlets and theses were published about this comet; very few of them were skeptical.

In America the puritanical preacher Increase Mather grabbed at the 1680 comet as the excuse for a hell-fire sermon on "Heaven's Alarm to the World."

Above, a diagram based on the calculations made in 1682 by the English astronomer Edmund Halley, who proved that comets revolve in long elliptical orbits around the Sun (the dot at the center of the planetary orbits). Comets had always been regarded as omens of disaster: Top right, a detail from the 11th-century Bayeux Tapestry records King Harold's dismay when a comet appeared in 1066; center right, a German pamphlet of 1680 depicts a comet-marked egg that was allegedly laid when the comet reappeared that year. This irrational attitude to comets lasted after Halley: It was mocked by an American cartoon of 1910 (right) showing people digging holes in New York's Central Park to escape a comet's "fallout."

Revolution of America

In Holland and France the reactions were less old-fashioned. In the former, the simpler flocks of Calvinists were generally as susceptible as that of Increase Mather, though most of the Dutch elite were contemptuous of the comet as a portent (and of astrology in general). In France the *philosophes* went into action, encouraged by Louis XIV. The famous letter-writer Madame de Sévigné was lightheartedly skeptical. The Protestant professor of philosophy Pierre Bayle delivered a violent attack on the "science" in his *Pensées diverses*—an attack inspired by the comet and by the fact, as he admitted, that France was overrun by astrologers. He seems to have suspected, like many astronomers of the time, that comets might be *periodic;* this hypothesis, which would knock the bottom out of cometary superstition, was proved correct when Halley's comet returned at the end of 1758, as predicted by the followers of Newton. Bayle's book was widely circulated. His equally famous colleague Fontenelle chose the favorite French weapon of mockery. He had a comedy staged in Paris, entitled simply *Le Comète* (see Chapter 9). And in the next generation Voltaire dismissed astrology with contempt in his *Dictionnaire Philosophique.*

As the 18th century's emphasis on reason took firmer hold, European astrology began to lose the ground that it had gained and held during Lilly's time and before. England offers a few isolated examples of astrological writing: For instance, an unorthodox book called *Astro-Theology* by William Derham (who was both a clergyman and a Fellow of the Royal Society) ran through nine editions between 1715 and 1750; but this was really more a work of imaginative astronomy than astrology. And a qualified surgeon, Ebenezer Sibly, who described himself as an "astro-philosopher," wrote a vast book entitled *The Celestial Science of Astrology.* It contained many nativities, including those of Christ and George III, and was illustrated with curious copperplates including a symbolic representation of the American Revolution.

One of the few astrological works that appeared during the 18th-century "Age of Reason" was *The Celestial Science of Astrology* (published in England in 1790) by the self-styled "astro-philosopher" Ebenezer Sibly. Left, one of the book's illustrations symbolizes the American Revolution: The angel in the clouds holds a horoscope cast for the Declaration of Independence in 1776. Right, also from the book, a portrait of the author (within his own horoscope).

Sibly began his book by admitting that he was aware "of the rotted prejudices of the times against the venerable science of Astrology." These prejudices were probably still intact in 1828 when John Varley published his *Treatise on Zodiacal Physiognomy,* which has often been quoted from in earlier chapters. In France, at the end of the century, it was claimed that the revolution had been foretold by Nostradamus in 1555; but the trend of post-revolution France itself was right away from such a "conservative" activity as astrology. In the next hundred years there is far less record of its practice in France and the rest of continental Europe than in England.

In Germany, Goethe is sometimes claimed as an adherent by modern astrologers, but the evidence is not strong. It is true that he starts his autobiography (translation by John Oxenford): "On the 28th of August, 1749, at mid-day, as the clock struck twelve, I came into the world, at Frankfort-on-the-Maine. My horoscope was propitious . . . ." He then gives the details. That he should have bothered to do this does not necessarily prove that he believed in horoscopes; he was a man of vast curiosity who was interested in the sciences of the past as well as those of the present—and future. He did not believe in either magic or Christianity, though both are essential to his story of Faust.

Of course, astrology did not entirely die out in this period. But to find it being practiced and respected with anything like the style it enjoyed in its European heyday, one has to look outside Europe. The Abbé Dubois, a missionary in India toward the end of the 18th century, wrote disapprovingly of the Brahmin *purohitas*: "There is no one in high position who has not one or more official purohitas living in the palace; and these men act, so to speak, like rulers of the universe. They go every morning and with ludicrous gravity announce to the prince, to his state elephant, and to his idols, each in their turn, all that is written in the almanac relating to that particular day."

In 1800 a traveler in Persia, James Morier, was not allowed to leave Basra before the hour decided upon by the astrologers and was also warned to time his arrival at the next place as exactly as possible. The Moslem governor of Basra told Morier that once, when he was about to embark for Calcutta, he "was ordered by these astrologers (as the only means of counteracting the influence of a certain evil star) to go out of his house in a particular aspect; as unfortunately there happened to be no door in that direction, he caused a hole to be made in the wall, and thus made his exit." People often used to say that the East was unchanging: It was mentioned in Chapter 1 that Marco Polo had described central Asian funerals (five centuries before Morier) in which a hole would be broken in the wall so that the corpse might be carried out in the direction ordered by the astrologers.

A British Egyptologist, E. W. Lane, who went to live in Egypt in 1825, wrote: "It was a custom very common in Egypt, as in other Muslim countries, to consult an astrologer previously to giving a name to a child, and to be guided by his choice; but," he adds rather surprisingly, "very few persons now conform

Geomancy is a complicated form of divination
(closely connected with astrology) from rows
of marks in the sand, which were sometimes
interpreted mechanically. This medieval Arab
geomancy machine was operated by knobs,
some representing astrology's 12 houses.

with this old usage." He does stress, however, that astrology was more studied
there than astronomy: "To say that the earth revolves round the Sun, they
consider absolute heresy." Also, though his Egyptians may have become careless
about giving a child a name, whatever name it received remained numerologic-
ally—and therefore astrologically—important. Lane explains that their astrology
was "chiefly employed in casting nativities, and in determining fortunate periods,
etc.; and very commonly, to divine by what sign of the Zodiac a person is influenced; which is usually done by a calculation founded upon the numerical value
of the letters composing his or her name, and that of the mother . . . ." He adds
that the Egyptian brand of geomancy (divination by marks made in the sand,
which is still performed for tourists) is "mainly founded on astrology."

For most of the 19th century, thanks largely to the success of the "scientific
revolution," astrology's disrepute in Europe continued, at least among educated
people. Thus Sir Walter Scott had originally intended his second Waverley
novel, *Guy Mannering,* to have an astrological motivation and framework.
He had got the idea from a story told by an old servant of his father's: A
child is due to be born in a great house when a stranger drops in, who happens
to be an astrologer. He studies the heavens and begs his host "to retard the
birth if practicable, were it but for five minutes"; but, alas, it is not practicable,
so the astrologer warns the father that a terrible crisis will come to his newly

born son about his 21st birthday. When the birthday approaches, the father sends the son to the astrologer, in whose house, as it befalls, he has to face the Devil and fight for his soul and his life.

The more Scott pondered this plot the more he began to suspect that what was good enough for his father's servant was not good enough for the readers of *Waverley*. As he explained himself : "It appeared, on mature consideration, that Astrology, though its influence was once received and admitted by Bacon himself [he means Francis Bacon, not Roger], does not now retain influence over the general mind sufficient even to constitute the mainspring of a romance."

Scott wrote this in 1829. Five years earlier in England the Vagrancy Act had backed up the Witchcraft Act of 1736 in outlawing the astrologers. Astrology's reputation had now reached one of the lowest points in its history, and it was becoming more and more diluted by association with the occult and those other irrational practices that always seem to flourish (as a kind of underground counterpoint) in societies that lay heavy stress on the rational side of human nature. This process was especially obvious on the continent of Europe : For instance, in France about the middle of the century, a man calling himself Eliphas Lévi (real name : Alphonse Louis Constant) gained a measure of fame by pepping up astrology with the occult. In fact, Lévi (who believed in a universal medium called the "Astral Light") seems to have been an occultist first and an astrologer second (a combination that was to become more common as the century progressed). In his *History of Magic* Lévi quotes from an older authority (whom he refers to only as Ballanche) : "Astrology is a synthesis because the Tree of Life is a single tree and because its branches—spread through heaven and bearing flowers of stars—are in correspondence with its roots, which are hidden in earth."

Lévi and his successors in France worked hard to introduce the cabalistic science of numbers into astrology, and the resulting mixture soon made its way from the continent to Britain, where later astrologers were to apply it to horse racing and the stock exchange. The first Zadkiel himself, in his *Handbook of Astrology* (1861), provided fodder for gamblers when he wrote self-righteously of horse racing : "I would not encourage anyone in the pursuit of this pernicious, foolish, and discreditable practice, for the sake of mammon; but if anyone be already engaged therein, and be really anxious about the result"—why, then Zadkiel's book can help him a lot. "If the ninth [the house of honor for the horse] be strong, and the lord of the twelfth be there and not afflicted, then the horse will gain honour by the race and be well placed therein."

Zadkiel (Richard James Morrison) was a typically English figure. Born in 1795, he resigned from the Royal Navy in 1829 and devoted the rest of his life to astrologizing and inventing. His inventions included a bell buoy and a plan for "propelling ships of war in a calm." In 1831 he published *The Herald of Astrology* and followed it with numerous publications including, in particular, the famous annual almanac.

The almanac sold about 60,000 copies annually. The first Zadkiel (the almanac was later continued by others, who also used the pseudonym "Zadkiel") claimed that he had been making correct and unchallenged predictions for over three decades. According to himself this was not only a trade but a crusade: He was devoted to the task of "re-establishing the doctrines of Astrology in the public mind, after being obscured for a season by the spread of *infidelity in religion*" (italics mine). And in *Zadkiel's Legacy* (1842) he brings a high, prophetic tone of voice to his preface: "Many generations shall pass by, many centuries roll away, and this book shall still remain a memento of the sublime powers of astral influence." Like some other modern astrologers, the first Zadkiel also went in for crystal gazing; in 1863 he was described by an indignant rationalist admiral in a letter to the press as "the crystal globe seer who gulled many of our nobility." Zadkiel brought an action against the admiral and was awarded 20 shillings damages and no costs.

Zadkiel did not go out of his way to gloss things over for his public. He was more ruthless than many of his successors in detailing the characteristics of certain signs. He writes of Cancer, for instance: "if a female, prolific, dull, and timid." And of Scorpio: "ill-made feet or bow-legged . . . generally deceitful."

An illustration from *The History of Magic* (1855) by the French occultist Eliphas Lévi. The branches of the "tree of life" contain the seven wonders of the world, which are linked with the seven planets of traditional astrology (indicated by their symbols) and seven metals. For example, the Moon is related to the Temple of Diana (the Roman Moon goddess) at Ephesus, and to silver.

Possibly those of his Victorian public who were dull, deceitful, etc., preferred to be told that the fault was in their stars.

But in spite of Zadkiel's fame, his pronouncements did not go unchallenged. *A Complete Refutation of Astrology* by T. H. Moody, a professor of mathematics, was published in Britain in 1838 by subscription; the subscribers included clergymen, generals, and schoolmistresses. "During the last twenty years," complains Moody, "several new astrological works have appeared, and the high tone of confidence adopted in some of them is truly remarkable." Moody quotes an interesting historical argument from Zadkiel: "We are quite certain that the prejudice against astrology owes its origin chiefly to the cant and hypocrisy of the Puritans in the time of Cromwell." "This is a fine specimen of astrological certainty," says Moody. (But he omits one possible answer: Why, then, did not Charles II, at the Restoration, restore astrology too?) He also sets out to pick holes in some of Zadkiel's horoscopes and in some of the details of his almanacs. When Zadkiel writes of a certain Sunday: "This day is evil till after one o'clock, when you may write letters, commence short journeys, and ask favours," his mathematical opponent makes a sabbatarian choice of weapon: "But God has blessed every Sabbath in the year, and commanded us to rest from all mere worldly occupations."

Moody complained of the "high tone of confidence" employed by the new astrologers. Just as confident as the first Zadkiel was the first "Raphael" (R. C. Smith). While Lieutenant Morrison was still in the Navy, Raphael had published his *Manual of Astrology*. And in the year that Zadkiel published his *Herald*, Raphael came out with his *Witch*, with its strange illustrations like "The Mystical Wheel of Pythagoras" or "The Cabalistical Tablet of the Stars." Typically of its period, this book aspires to be simultaneously awesome and genteel,

Aside from handbooks of the occult, 19th-century astrologers produced a spate of almanacs. Typical examples were the two founded by Britain's Zadkiel and Raphael. Left, the title page of one of Zadkiel's many astrological publications. Right, from *Raphael's Almanac* of 1824, a hieroglyph (a skeleton on the French throne) that was later claimed as a prediction of the death of Louis XVIII. Far right, a drawing from the 1963 edition of the same almanac, which correctly foretold a high proportion of Irish winners in English horse races that year.

Magic Ceremonies.

Such were the mystic rites, ceremonies and incantations, used by the ancient Theurgists to burst asunder the bonds of natural order, and to obtain an awful intercourse with the World of Spirits. Vide page 22.

LONDON.
Published by William Charlton Wright, 65 Paternoster Row.

THE ASTROLOGER, of the Nineteenth Century, OR THE Master Key of Futurity, being a Complete System of ASTROLOGY, GEOMANCY & OCCULT SCIENCE.

I consider the heavens the work of thy fingers, the Moon and the Stars which thou hast ordained. Psal. viii. 3.

They fought from heaven, the Stars in their courses fought against Sisera. Judges v. 20.

Saltis adsit amicum Cicero.

London.
WILLIAM CHARLTON WRIGHT.
Pater Noster Row.
WESTLEY & TYRRELL, DUBLIN. J. ROBERTSON, & Co. EDINBURGH.

Above, the title page and frontispiece from a ''complete system of occult philosophy'' published in 1825. The book includes information on summoning the dead, magic talismans, prophecy—and astrology.

and is described by its author as "adapted to lay about in *drawing rooms*—to be read in *gardens* and *groves*—to ornament a *boudoir*." (All the italics are his.)

These were the sort of people Moody was up against. But it is to be doubted if he converted many of those who had *Raphael's Witch* lying about in their drawing rooms, or any less genteel readers who were ready to lap up the astrological almanacs. Moody uses both scientific and mathematical arguments (he makes play with the precession of the equinoxes as Robert Eisler did; see page 74) and the common-sense appeal to experience (against mundane astrology he gives historical instances of predictions of floods and storms that never happened). But his voice is not the voice of the Enlightenment. One doubts if he would have felt at home with Voltaire or Swift or Hume. In England at least, a new era was beginning; Queen Victoria had ascended the throne a year before Moody's *Refutation* was published. Moody's main approach both reminds us of the early Christian Fathers and anticipates orthodox Victorian Christianity: "Astronomy," he writes, "connects the mind with heaven; but astrology associates it with the daemons of darkness."

One instance of astrological quackery quoted by Moody takes us into the streets and the minds of ordinary people. A certain Charles Paddon had put up the following advertisement (no doubt it was one of hundreds): "The Astrologer of the Nineteenth Century, 32, Grafton Street, Tottenham Court Road. By knowing the time of birth, we are enabled to read in the heavens the story of our whole lives. N.B.—All letters must be post paid. Please to ring the first floor bell." In January 1836, a woman who was a policeman's wife rang the first floor bell and was introduced to Paddon, an impressive gentleman "in a large dressing gown, seated in an immense arm chair," who promptly predicted that her husband, the policeman, would die in the near future. For this she paid him a fee of two shillings and sixpence. As she left the house her husband was waiting outside; he entered and arrested Paddon, presumably on a charge of obtaining money by false pretenses. Moody says that Paddon "appeared almost planet struck and exclaimed 'I am ruined!'" (In Britain, astrologers and fortune tellers had been classed among "rogues and vagabonds" by the two Acts mentioned before. Their legal position remains unaltered today.)

The new planets

Meanwhile, the usurping astronomers continued their ruthless discoveries. The telescope had long since opened up those infinite spaces that horrified Pascal and put paid to the old tidy Aristotelian (or Ptolemaic) universe. From then on the world was to see bigger and bigger telescopes and many more startling advances in the science, the most upsetting for the astrologers being the discovery of the new planets Uranus and Neptune. Some astrologers, admittedly, made these an excuse for the inaccuracies of their predecessors; but others, who wanted to keep the old *septizonium* (the elegant, time-honored, and mystical set-up of seven planetary spheres), argued that these new planets could *not* influence human beings because they could not be seen with the naked eye (an argument that presumed a very narrow and dubious interpretation of the nature of planetary influence).

Uranus, which lies vastly farther out in the solar system than Saturn, was discovered in 1781 by William Herschel. As a gesture to his patron, George III of England, Herschel attempted to call the new planet "Georgium Sidus" (the Georgian Star), while his friends wanted to call it "Herschel." Foreign astronomers prevailed over both and the new planet eventually fell into line with the old ones under the classical name of Uranus. Some 40 years later Uranus was noticed to be behaving strangely (the French astronomer Pierre de Laplace spoke of "some extraneous and unknown influence that has acted upon the planet") and for the next 20 years astronomers in several countries investigated the possibility that there might be yet another unknown planet pulling Uranus out of course.

Finally, in 1846, J. G. Galle, an astronomer in Berlin, prompted by a French colleague, Urbain Leverrier, managed to put his finger (in fact his telescope's refractor) on the very distant planet that was given the name of Neptune. It should be noted that, though these planets were named in an arbitrary manner (see Chapter 2), astrologers ascribed to them influences that seem derived from these names. The same process was repeated when Pluto was discovered in 1930.

"Three new forces to consider should make a great deal of difference," wrote Rupert Gleadow in *Astrology in Everyday Life* (published 1940). "They do," he went on, carrying the war to the enemy, "but it is worth observing that they correspond chiefly to things that have been invented since they were discovered; Uranus, for example, is connected with machinery, and the industrial revolution happened shortly after he was found." In a chapter on the "Aquarian Age" (see Chapter 3) Gleadow attempted to explain contemporary history by picturing it as a conflict between "the old ruler of Aquarius"—Saturn, who represents control, restriction, and slavery—and its new ruler Uranus, who represents "culture, civilization, intelligence," etc. Incidentally, though Gleadow saw Uranus primarily as a good planet, the first Raphael had predicted that "the influence to be expected from this newly discovered star would be eminently evil," its effects being "truly malefic."

Gleadow's description of this conflict, though he may have been merely speaking symbolically, sounds startlingly anthropomorphic: "Saturn does not want to give up his rulership over Aquarius. Uranus began the work of overthrowing him at the end of the eighteenth century. But then in 1846 Neptune was discovered, and Neptune was an ally for Saturn, since his sign *Pisces* [the influence of the name again?] is in sextile [a good aspect] to Saturn's sign Capricorn . . . ." Neptune, he explains, "stands for the absorption of the self into something great and wonderful" and so can be held responsible for the growth of modern dictatorships. But we need not despair since Pluto was discovered in 1930 and "Pluto appears to rule Aries [though Ingrid Lind connects it with Scorpio], which

The new planets

William Herschel **1738-1822**

Urbain Leverrier 1811-77

Percival Lowell 1855-1916

Astrology's traditional seven-planet system was badly shaken when Uranus was discovered in 1781 by the English astronomer William Herschel (far left). Left, the reflector telescope with which he is said to have made the discovery. Gear wheels (right) illustrate astrology's view of Uranus as the patron of machinery. This planet was also declared to be the ruler of Aquarius, here shown with Uranus's symbol.

Astrologers were again disconcerted when calculations made by the French astronomer Urbain Leverrier (far left) led to the discovery of Neptune in 1846. Left, a cartoon by France's Honoré Daumier shows a couple gazing awestruck at the new planet. The "watery" associations with the ocean god Neptune led astrologers to connect the planet with the sea (a connection represented by a submarine, right), and with the sign of Pisces.

America's Percival Lowell (far left) was the first to suspect the existence of the newest planet, Pluto, which was detected in 1930. Left, two photographs taken at a three-day interval show how the changing position of a pinpoint of light (arrowed) confirmed it as a planet. Astrologers still disagree over Pluto's astrological role (though many relate it to Aries). Britain's Margaret Hone connects Pluto's influence with darkness and death, and specifically with the atom bomb (right).

is in sextile to Aquarius and in square [bad relationship] to Capricorn; Pluto is therefore an ally for Uranus and an enemy of Saturn."

This sort of astral battle is complicated by the fact that the opponents can sometimes borrow from each other's armory. Thus, though Uranus is the patron of machines, Gleadow tells us that Pluto in Gemini (which is an airy sign and the sign of transport) produced the airplane. But on the whole modern astrologers employ a certain caution when dealing with the three outer planets. Ingrid Lind explains that, because they take so long to pass through any particular sign of the Zodiac, they are not so relevant to individual horoscopes (this is a let-out for previous horoscopists) but rather must be regarded as "affecting a generation, or as providing background conditions for a period."

Similarly, the American astrologer Grant Lewi (who writes under the name of "Scorpio") attaches historical importance to Uranus being in square (bad relationship) with Neptune: "This position, because of the slow motion of the two planets involved, lasts for many years at a time and consequently influences many people. It is the aspect of the so-called 'younger generation' that ran rampant right after the [first] World War, overturning law, and order, and especially personal morality."

Turning from these debatable planets back to the late 19th century in general: About this time astrological writers began to make very free with tradition, mixing in (to taste) every kind of symbolical significance, especially if it could be drawn from the Bible. This tendency was to develop further toward the end of the century. In 1862 Frances Rolleston published her book *Mazzaroth* (which was mentioned in Chapter 3) in which she not only makes the claim that the astral names and emblems "express the promises and prophecies revealed to Adam, Seth, and Enoch" but commits herself to many fairly exact equations between the Scriptures and the stars. For the Book of Revelation, she finds that its chief revelations are Zodiacal: Thus the 12 precious stones of the Holy City inevitably correspond to the 12 Zodiacal constellations.

A quarter of a century later another lady, Rosa Baughan (women from now on were to take much more part in this once almost entirely masculine mystery), combined astrology with chiromancy. She apportions each finger to a planet and does the same with the lines on the face. Apart from assigning the nose to Mercury, she assigns six lines between the hair and the eyes to the six other planets; in each case, if the line is broken, it indicates something unfortunate. And she explains that Saturn gives you black moles, whether on face or body, and Jupiter purple-brown ones. The appeal of all this detail presumably lay in that age-old principle of correspondences or "sympathy." She herself describes her writings as "Old World lore": "Macrocosm and microcosm must be no longer divorced." She also retains the ancient doctrine of the four humors.

In the U.S.A. about the same time (1892) a curious book was published in Boston called *Astrology of the Old Testament*. Its author, Karl Anderson (who belongs to the same category as Frances Rolleston), described himself as Professor

The 19th-century astrologer Rosa Baughan's version of the wheel of Pythagoras—a method of prediction by numbers that answers questions with "yes" or "no." Here is how it works : A questioner named, say, Tom shuts his eyes and picks a number—say, 9—from the table (right). To this he adds the number that, on the wheel, is opposite his initial T, which is 6, making 15. Next he takes two numbers from the list (right) : One for the day of the week—say, Thursday, which is 31 —and one for Thursday's ruling planet, Jupiter, which is 78. He adds 31 and 78 to 15 making 124, which he then must divide by 30, leaving the remainder 4. If the remainder is among the numbers written in the *lower* half of the inner wheel, the answer is "no." If it is one of the numbers in the *upper* half, the answer is "yes." The answer can be further qualified by the position of the number either on the left side or the right side, which indicate a "long time" and a "short time" respectively. Since Tom's number, 4, is on the upper left side, the answer to his question is "yes, in a long time."

1	11	22	28	29
6	2	12	23	30
15	7	3	13	24
19	16	8	4	14
25	20	17	9	5
27	26	21	18	10

Saturday 45   Saturn 55
Sunday 106   Sun 34
Monday 52   Moon 45
Tuesday 52   Mars 39
Wednesday 102   Mercury 114
Thursday 31   Jupiter 78
Friday 68   Venus 45

of Chaldean, Arabian, and Egyptian Astrology. He also likes a rich, complicated recipe and flavors the soup with the Free Masons, the Great Pyramid, and some odd etymology: The word "angel," he says, is a corruption of the astrological term "angle." This book, like *Mazzaroth,* presupposes a fundamentalist cosmology. But this time the signs of the Zodiac are linked with the 12 tribes of Israel; for example, Taurus with Ephraim and Leo with the Old Testament's "Lion of Judah." And, though Anderson much prefers the Old Testament to the New, he can also explain whatever is valid in the latter: Thus he asserts that when Christ "stooped and wrote upon the ground" he was casting a horoscope or horary question.

These 19th-century writers have been quoted not for their intrinsic merit but because their oddity is a historical phenomenon. As the century wore on, there was in certain circles (in Britain and America especially) a swing away from the rationalist concept of a mechanical universe and a renewed hunger for the irrational. In 1875 the Theosophical Society (with an American, Colonel Olcott, as its president) was founded in the United States by that supercharged eccentric, Madame Blavatsky. This extraordinary woman, whose "lamasery" (i.e., sitting room) was crowded with stuffed snakes and monkeys, specialized in producing psychic phenomena. She always attributed her powers not to herself but to her invisible Himalayan "Masters" (the "White Brotherhood"), chief among whom was "Koot Hoomi." *"Someone who knows all,"* she said, *"dictates to me."*

Repeated attempts were made to discredit her as a charlatan, but at the time of her death in 1891 she numbered over 100,000 followers.

Soon after Theosophy was founded, it recruited a new leader in the equally dynamic but more socially conscious and more intellectual Mrs. Annie Besant. The movement had by this time become linked with India and therefore could not remain untouched by astrology: Indian astrology contained elements that, though suspect to the more intelligent astrologers whether of the Renaissance or the 20th century, had a natural appeal to many theosophists (who preferred their universe to be mystically sensational). Their obsession with a mystical "divine nature" would encourage the acceptance of the early more hermetic view of the stars as divine creatures—and perish the thought that they might be mere "signs," not "causes."

In 1885 there was published in Madras an English translation by N. Chidambaram Aiyar of an alleged astrological classic, the *Brihat Jataka*. The translator explains in his introduction: "The difficulty in conceiving active agency as possessed by the planets when viewed in the light of huge inert balls, will be removed when we suppose that each planet possesses a soul." Not only do they possess souls: They are "rewarding and chastising officers." And that is where we come in, or rather where we never got out. For, according to this Hindu textbook, "the science [of horoscopy] treats of the effects of the good and bad deeds (karma) of men in their previous birth."

Left, Madame Blavatsky, founder of the Theosophical Society in 1875, with two of her disciples. Since the society derived many of its theories from Indian mystical thought, it was inevitably colored by Indian astrology. Below, a monument dedicated to Theosophy at Adyar, India, where Madame Blavatsky established her headquarters in 1879.

THERE IS NO RELIGION HIGHER THAN TRUTH

This involvement of astrology with the doctrine of reincarnation, which would *ipso facto* be unacceptable to any Christian astrologer, would have caused no difficulty to most of the theosophists, who were only too conscious of their "karma." In her often reprinted book *The Secret Doctrine*, Madame Blavatsky, who looked like a gypsy, indulges in what appears to be gypsy-like mystification. Most of her doctrine is highly esoteric and some of the astrological portions would be repugnant to orthodox astrologers. For instance, she has an original view of the Moon, whom she seems to consider primarily evil: "Constantly vampirised by her child [i.e., the earth], she revenges herself on it by soaking it through and through with the nefarious, invisible, and poisoned influence which emanates from the occult side of her nature."

As a double-dyed or multiple-dyed universalizer, Madame Blavatsky will have none of the fixed and specific notations of orthodox Western astrology: "Why see in the Pisces a direct reference to Christ—one of the several world-reformers, a Saviour but for his direct followers, but only a great and glorious Initiate for all the rest—when that constellation shines as a symbol of all the past, present, and future Spiritual Saviours who dispense light and dispel mental darkness?"

Annie Besant was much less extravagant. Though she once wrote of "this ancient and much maligned science," she admitted that she had little knowledge of astrology and in her *Autobiography* makes only moderate, and comparatively conventional, claims for it: "Keeping in view the way in which sun, moon, and planets influence the physical condition of the earth, there is nothing incongruous with the orderly view of nature in the view that they also influence the physical bodies of men. . . . At the most, astrology, as it is now practised, can only calculate the interaction between these physical conditions at any given moment, and the conditions brought to them by a given person whose general constitution and natal conditions are known. *It cannot say what the person will do, nor what will happen to him . . . .*" (italics mine).

Note that in her first sentence Mrs. Besant omits the fixed stars (including the Zodiacal signs), which no one, she says, has ever proved can "influence the physical condition of the earth." And in her second sentence (like a few 20th-century astrologers but unlike the vast majority of their predecessors, who said all they needed was the natal chart) she states that an advance knowledge is required of the "general constitution" of the "given person."

Some popular astrologers

So much for the two great theosophical Amazons. As an example of a theosophist of the time who was also a professional (and highly successful) astrologer, we may take Alan Leo, the son of a soldier in a Scottish regiment. Leo believed he had lived before and also believed, as we saw in Chapter 1, that "every human being belongs to a Father Star in Heaven or Star Angel as did Jesus Christ according to our Scripture." (Most earlier astrologers had denied that

Christ was *influenced* by the Star of Bethlehem.) Leo added: "And I am convinced that every man derives his will power from a Planetary Sphere of Influences which he uses, or abuses, by which we can overcome evil tendencies, and control his animal nature, hence Astrology teaches that Character is Destiny, also [the old cliché] that the Wise man rules his Stars while the fool obeys them."

Leo began his astrological work in the 1880s and soon made friends, or enemies, of other astrologers who gave themselves names like Aphorel, Charubel, Casael, and Sepharial. Together with Aphorel (F. W. Lacey) he launched *The Astrologer's Magazine*. The first number included three horoscopes: those of Jesus Christ, of the then Prince of Wales (Edward VII), and of Stanley, the explorer of Africa.

Leo and Aphorel encountered some antagonism from the editor of *Zadkiel's Almanac*, whose system they did not accept. (The Jacobean situation of quarreling within the fraternity seems to have come around again.) But their paper survived and in 1895 was renamed *Modern Astrology*. They were thus pioneers of the present era of astrological journalism. Leo, who specialized in Uranus (which was very strong in his own horoscope), was an odd person, as was his wife Bessie, who could not agree to any marriage that was not platonic. Bessie received her first lessons in astrology from Leo on the sands of Bournemouth, on which he drew the signs and the planets for her. Later, finding that his Moon and her Sun were in the same degree of Aries, they decided to get married—platonically. Leo agreed because "I have a work to do for the world for which celibacy is

Mrs. Annie Besant, who succeeded Madame Blavatsky as president of the Theosophical Society. Mrs. Besant's views on astrology were less extreme than those of her predecessor: While ascribing some influence to the planets, she denied that astrology alone could provide a true picture of an individual's future.

Britain's Alan Leo (1860-1917)—astrologer,
theosophist, and co-founder of *Modern
Astrology*—depicted in his own horoscope.

essential." Leo died in 1917, after which people began writing to his widow to tell her that he was still teaching them astrology and theosophy "on the astral plane." It seems likely that these people's receptivity was enhanced by their world-war experiences.

But back in the period when Leo was beginning his crusade, a very different type of Englishman lent his weight to the astrological cause by admitting to a qualified belief in the subject. Richard Garnett (1835-1906), Keeper of Printed Books at the British Museum, came of a distinguished family and was not only a well-known author but also a brilliant linguist. And so he can be said to have been one of the first persons in Europe of high intellectual caliber to have taken a serious interest in astrology since the 17th century. Though he himself claimed that his reasoning on the subject was "wholly empirical," he seems to have had a naturally mystical bent that, in reaction against 19th-century materialism and a purely mechanistic cosmology, led him to plump for astral influences. His empiricism consisted in collecting evidence from the horoscopes, for example, of well-known madmen like George III, on the strength of which he claimed to have established "a *prima facie* case." No astrologer at that time had based his defense upon statistics (though modern statisticians would not allow that Garnett had considered nearly enough instances).

Garnett was wary of astrology's "pretension to foretell the *times* of events." What he did attribute to it was the explanation of certain aspects of human character—and therefore the power to estimate the *likelihood* of an individual's behavior. His physics (he assumes the astral influences are transmitted through an "all-pervading aether") would be suspect to modern physicists and astronomers; but his motivation, of course, was not so much scientific as religious. What seems to have appealed to him in astrology is what had appealed to so many before him—the "marvellous harmony" it implies in the universe.

While Richard Garnett was still Keeper of Books in the Museum, another intellectual of vastly greater originality was probing around the fringes of astrology under the influence of a crank. The great man was Sigmund Freud; his mentor was Dr. Wilhelm Fliess, a nose-and-throat specialist with a passion for numerology. Fliess, who within his own field tried to connect the nose with menstruation, was determined to discover a similar periodicity in all the spheres of human and animal life. He was especially obsessed by the numbers 28 (for a woman) and 23 (for a man). Starting with the Moon, which is traditionally linked with menstruation, Fliess seems (in the words of Freud's biographer Ernest Jones) to have been looking for "a deeper connection between astronomical movements and the creation of living organisms. From the nose to the stars, as with Cyrano de Bergerac!"

Fliess's puzzling influence over Freud ceased about the turn of the century and no recognition of numerology, astrology, or related subjects entered the canon of orthodox Freudian psychoanalysis. (Later, as we shall see in Chapter 7, Freud's pupil and rival, C. G. Jung, who looked for something in everything, made an "astrological experiment" in an attempt to relate astrology to his psychological principles.) But, whether or not any professional psychologist has accepted astrology wholly or in part, modern astrologers have attempted to assimilate modern psychology. The ingenious French astrologer André Barbault studied Freud's own horoscope (in which Scorpio was in the ascendant and the Sun, Mercury, Uranus, and Pluto all in Taurus) and comments: "The psychological universe that Freud discovered is that of Taurus (associated with Scorpio)." In a passage quoted in Chapter 3, Barbault sees Taurus as "the meat-safe of the Zodiac . . . and ultimately, through displacement of the oral tendency, the strong-box of the Zodiac." And he continues: "The discovery of the oral *libido* (Taurus) was completed by that of the anal and general *libido* that one meets precisely in Scorpio, Freud's second dominating sign."

In the intervening half-century, which included two world wars, a new school of psychological astrology was to appear in Germany, and K. E. Krafft from Switzerland (see Chapter 7) was to develop what he called "astro-biology," while in the English-speaking countries *traditional* astrology was to flourish in its more popular, and certainly less trustworthy, forms in the annual almanac and the Sunday newspaper. Just before World War I *Zadkiel's Almanac*, now edited by A. J. Pearce, was selling more than 200,000 copies per year.

A typical figure in England was Walter Gorn Old, who called himself "Sepharial" and who, apart from orthodox astrology, went in for fortune telling with cards, crystal gazing, and numerology. Just before World War I he published a "Guide to Speculators" called *The Silver Key.* This book offers an analysis of planetary influence on the turf, partly by names (which are reduced to numbers and then equated with the planets) and partly by colors. He explains that the horoscope for the last Lincoln Handicap race showed "Uranus in the fifth division of the heavens, which is held to rule speculative concerns. This planet indicates grey, or black and white hoops with stripes." The Lincoln Handicap was won by a horse named "Kaffir Chief," whose jockey wore black and white hoops.

In a handicap race, moreover, according to Sepharial, there are also the weights to be considered: You must find out what the Moon's position corresponds with at the time of the race "for inasmuch as the Moon is a proved weight-lifter, we may naturally expect that gravity will be the more readily overcome in that instance, and that the performance of the animal carrying that weight will be proportionately good."

Such were the preoccupations of popular astrologers and their public in 1913. But Sepharial himself, like most of his colleagues, was able to adjust with no trouble to what happened next. In *The Great Devastation* (the foreword is dated October 1914) he bases his preview of the war on a cyclic view of history: "History repeats itself. Substituting Germany for Persia, and France for Greece, you will find the whole history of the war in the eleventh chapter of Daniel." His prose in this booklet has a purple and sometimes semi-biblical quality and the general tone is optimistic: "We are about to enter upon the Aquarian Age wherein Humanity will be its own Dictator, when the public conscience shall be a law unto itself, and the service of Goodwill shall become the sweet slavery of the Soul." In the same year he predicted "a tremendous social upheaval" in Russia; but if he meant the Revolution, he dated it at least a year too early.

In 1915 Sepharial published another booklet: *Why the War Will End in 1917.* (This was sold for a penny by the same publisher who put out, also for a penny, a booklet entitled *The Angel Warriors of Mons,* in which it was argued that this legendary apparition of angels who fought on the Allied side was supported by good evidence.) Sepharial here stresses the sinister horoscope of Kaiser William, whose Moon was "in direct opposition to Uranus, the planet of disruption," and whose mid-heaven was ominously occupied by the malefic planets Mars and Neptune.

Sepharial foretold a German surrender in August 1917. In a section called "The Readjustment" he foresees an "Aquarian Age of a liberated humanity . . . marked by a beneficent Communism." Still, before the millenium comes (in A.D. 2449) the world will have to face "the great climacteric, which lasts from 1991 to 1997, and which ensanguines the whole of the East." But whatever happens in the East the English can be of good heart (Sepharial is always a patriot): "The Anglo-Saxon race will be the paramount power for good in the world during the next sixteen hundred years."

Throughout history all forms of divination have tended to thrive on major wars. World War I was no exception. Alan Leo, who among popular astrologers was far more successful than Sepharial, gave three lectures in 1915 on "Mars; the War Lord." He too is patriotic and looks for historical precedents. "At the time of the Crimean War, the War Lord Mars was in the sign Leo, and it ended in a victory for the British Lion." This astral pattern was repeated in the Boer War. (Leo is careful to point out that Mars is not necessarily malefic.)

As in the Second World War, astrologers were on the whole optimistic. And precise—when they were retrospective. Many accurate horoscopes were produced retrospectively—for example, one was cast for the *Lusitania* for the time of her launching. It seems also clear that astrology emerged from the war stronger than it had been before it. And this in spite of many exploded predictions like Leo's or Sepharial's.

Examples of this aftermath in the 1920s will be given in the next chapter. The most remarkable developments were in Germany; England produced curiosities, like a book published in 1928 entitled *The Brontës and their Stars*, by Maud Margesson. Its publication implies at least that the sort of people who would read the books of the Brontë sisters, or who would be interested in them as personalities, would also be interested in them astrologically. The author

Sigmund Freud (right) with his friend Wilhelm Fliess, a fellow doctor from Austria who postulated a numerical relationship between human physiology and the stars.

admits that her own book can only be approximately correct astrologically, since with all of the Brontës only their birth *days* are known, never their birth *hours*. Thus there is the problem of deciding the rising signs; but this does not deter Miss Margesson. The "only sure and dependable guide to the ascendant," she says, "where the time of birth is unknown, is an intimate knowledge of character and career." Following this topsy-turvy procedure, she finds with Emily, for example, that "there seems to be only one sign that could possibly represent her, and that is the fixed, intense, reserved sign Scorpio." She also stresses the family resemblance in the four Brontë children's horoscopes, pointing out that in each of them "Mercury, the ruler of the mind, is in aspect to the mystic Neptune and the occult Uranus." Unlike the astrologers quoted above, Miss Margesson has no qualms about making these two planets work for individuals.

In the United States (which, with the exception of the theosophists, had been slow to take to the "royal art") the great pioneer was Evangeline Adams (1865-1932), whose married name was Mrs. George E. Jordan and whose philosophy, according to herself, was "a compound of truths of all truths." She was said to be a descendant of John Quincy Adams, sixth president of the United States, which is easy to believe, in respect at least of her drive, courage, and success. According to Irys Vorel, the author of the American *Astrological Handbook,* Miss Adams's career "was truly meteor-like. . . . 'I have Mars conjunct my natal Sun in the 12th House. I will always triumph over my enemies!' she said." Her first arrival in New York City, to set up as a reader of horoscopes, had indeed been meteoric in more senses than one.

Having checked in at the Windsor Hotel on Fifth Avenue she proceeded to inspect the natal chart of its owner, Warren F. Leland. The chart told her that he was threatened immediately with a terrible disaster. Mr. Leland at once thought of a crash on the stock market but then remembered that the next day was a holiday, which meant that stocks couldn't go down at least till after that interval. But what the stars were threatening was not Wall Street but the Windsor, which was burned to the ground next afternoon. Miss Adams lost many of her belongings but had laid the foundation of her future fame as the most popular reader of horoscopes in America.

For all this, in 1914 she was arrested for fortune telling and, instead of buying herself off with a fine, elected to stand trial. She appeared in court loaded with reference books, explained how she made her forecasts, and then capped theory with practice by reading from a birth date of a person unknown to her, who happened to be the judge's son. The judge concluded that: "The defendant raises astrology to the dignity of an exact science." Contemporary astrologers in New York have reason to bless Evangeline Adams for this showdown: Fortune telling there is still illegal but, as is not the case in England, astrology is no longer deemed to be fortune telling. In Washington, D.C., however, as late as November 1959, an astrologer named Katherine Q. Spencer was brought to court on a fortune-telling charge. Still, she too was acquitted.

		Sun	Mon	Tues	Wed	Thurs	Fri	Sat
I	Saturn	4	0	3	0	9	9	9
	Jupiter	5	1	4	1	1	1	1
	Mars	4	0	3	0	9	9	0
	Sun	4	9	3	9	9	9	9
	Venus	8	4	7	4	4	4	4
	Mercury	7	3	6	3	3	3	3
	Moon	2	7	1	7	7	7	7

hours

II			III	Monday					
Sunday	Sun			Moon	1	8	15	22	
Monday	Moon			Saturn	2	9	16	23	
Tuesday	Mars			Jupiter	3	10	17	24	
Wednesday	Mercury			Mars	4	11	18		
Thursday	Jupiter			Sun	5	12	19		
Friday	Venus			Venus	6	13	20		
Saturday	Saturn			Mercury	7	14	21		

IV						V		
AYIQJ	= 1	BKRC	= 2			Alexandra Park	=	5
GLS Sh	= 3	DMT	= 4			last winner	=	2
EN	= 5	WVXU	= 6			planetary hour	=	0
ZO	= 7	PHF	= 8			winning number		7

How to pick the winner in horse racing by a numerological system (evolved by the British astrologer Sepharial) that includes the use of "planetary hours." Take a race run at Alexandra Park at 4 P.M. on Monday, April 22, 1963. First, the name "Alexandra Park" is converted into numbers by relating each letter to the figures in Table IV : A=1, L=3, E=5, and so on. These numbers are added together, and then the figures of the total (41) are added : 4 + 1 = **5**. This process is repeated with the name of the winner of the preceding race ; say the result is **2**. Next, the planetary hour is calculated. Each hour in a day is ruled by a planet (Table III). The race was run on Monday, the Moon's day, so the first hour is the Moon's. So are the eighth hour (since only seven planets are used) and the 15th. As Table III shows, the 16th hour (4 P.M.) is Saturn's. Table I shows that Saturn on Monday has a numerical value of **0**. Now, as shown in Table V, the three numbers that have been calculated are added : 5 + 2 + 0 = **7**. Finally, all the names of the runners on the race card (right) are transposed into figures ; and the one with the value of 7 will win.

Alex. Park   Mon. 22nd Apr.1963

5th Race 4.0   M.& C.(Racing)Ltd.

1		
2		
3	WESTERN QUEEN	7
4	AYLWIN	8
5	ANAHITA	3
6	ESCORT	5
7	FANCY NANCY	5
8	PREPOTENT	6
9	THE TEASE	8

(An earlier astrologer whose fame equaled Miss Adams's had not been so lucky. In 1917 Alan Leo had been prosecuted in London on a charge of "pretending and professing to tell fortunes." Leo's lawyers brought a good defense. They argued that Leo was not an imposter, because he was practicing a science in which he had a *bona fide* belief. They pointed out that free will was an integral part of the science; that astrology merely told "tendencies"; that if a man chose to go out when bombs were falling and get killed, the fault was his own and not in the stars. Leo himself stated that he did not claim to be able to predict the future or the fortunes of others, and tried to emphasize his legitimacy by adding that his clients were mostly of the rich and intellectual classes. But this judge was unimpressed; he fined Leo £5 and £25 costs.)

Having thus made astrology respectable, Miss Adams began to be consulted by the great. In her studio at Carnegie Hall, New York City, she was visited by King Edward VII, Caruso, and Mary Pickford. As for J. P. Morgan, Evangeline Adams wrote: "He was sceptical at first but I convinced him. During the last years of his life I furnished him a regular service. It explained the general effects of the planets on politics, business and the stock market." In *Your Place among the Stars* Miss Adams explained Morgan's success: Among other things in his chart, Jupiter was "tied down very firmly to the material plane, but on that plane he is made very strong." It is probably due to this dynamic lady more than to any other individual that today, according to the American Federation of Astrologers (who admit these figures are merely estimates), the number of horoscopes cast per year runs into millions. The money spent on them would probably run into millions also.

On April 23, 1930, Evangeline Adams began to broadcast three times weekly on her subject. Three months later she announced that she had received 150,000 requests for horoscopes. A year later the letters and requests were coming in at the rate of 4000 a day. It seems clear that she was a "radio personality" and that listeners regarded her as almost a friend. She died on November 10, 1932. Two days later the *New York Times* published some rather pained paragraphs—pained not by her death but by her life: "Radio and astrology dancing to victory hand in hand make a sufficiently odd couple; but that is not all. This incongruous fellowship has flourished in an age of intellectual emancipation . . . ," etc. For the writer of this piece Miss Adams had obviously been both anachronism and arch-enemy.

On November 13 she lay in state in her studio at Carnegie Hall; the public was admitted from noon till 7 P.M. On November 14 her funeral service was thronged with both personal acquaintances and listeners and there were thousands of telegrams of condolence. The preacher commented on Miss Adams's "love and understanding" of her fellow men. To add a posthumous touch of myth, Irys Vorel declared later that Evangeline Adams had predicted her own death and for that reason had politely declined a 21-night lecture tour which had been offered her for the autumn of 1932.

By this time the once royal art had become almost wholly the property of the people, and the mass-communication media were fully aware of its drawing power. In Britain, one of the principal channels for mass astrology was the more "popular" kind of Sunday newspaper such as the *People* and the *Sunday Express*. In the *People* Edward Lyndoe (who claimed to be "the most consulted astrologian of all time") was by the end of 1934 foretelling the immediate decline of Hitler. Also, like so many successful journalists in other spheres, he exploited the good will of his readers by publishing books. A typical example is *Your Next Ten Years and After* (1935), which professed to help anyone, in accordance of course with his stars (no trouble here about *exact* horoscopes), to better himself and his career.

Lyndoe's recommended method is autosuggestion. Size yourself up according to your stars, then make the appropriate suggestions to yourself over and over : "Then go out and win !" All he asks his reader to go by is the *day* of his birth—i.e., what sign the Sun was in at the time (a very rough-and-ready starting-point but the usual one, inevitably, in astrological journalism). Knowing then what sign you belong to, since you know your own birthday, all you need to do is to repeat to yourself a particular set of slogans supplied by Lyndoe, one for each day of the week. Thus on Tuesday, if you are Leo, you will say over and over to yourself when you are alone, as when in bed : "I am more positive today than ever before." If you are Virgo : "One thing at a time, and that one done efficiently" ; if Sagittarius : "As a sportsman I take the rough with the

America's Evangeline Adams helped to make astrology both respectable and popular. Her acquittal in 1914 on a fortune-telling charge improved astrology's status as a profession ; later, her regular radio broadcasts attracted a vast audience and a huge fan mail.

Britain's Prime Minister Neville Chamberlain returns from Munich in 1938. Chamberlain's words "peace in our time" were echoed in predictions by most British astrologers. All were proved wrong by the outbreak of war in the following year.

smooth"; if Aquarius: "I believe passionately in the brotherhood of man." Lyndoe also advises each group what they should concentrate on in each of the next 10 years.

A similar book, *What Your Birthday Stars Foretell* (1933), was written by Lyndoe's rival, R. H. Naylor of the *Sunday Express*. Lyndoe's book had contained no predictions; Naylor, knowing only too well that hardly any of his readers will know what their birthday stars really are or were, is careful to admit in his introduction that his book is by its nature rough-and-ready or, as he calls it, "generalized." And, he goes on, "it has all the faults of a generalization." For all that, it must contain some truth and therefore be some help to the reader. It deals, he explains, with "basic fundamentals of character and fortune. Superficial differences will result from variation in place of birth (horizon), from year of birth, *and even from heredity and environment*" (italics mine). But for truly professional astrologers, as we have seen, the basic fundamentals of character and fortune could not be established without a knowledge of the moment of birth, which gives one the all-important ascendant.

Apart from this catering for stock-type "individuals" (all humanity being divided into 12 groups), this period saw a boom in *mundane* astrology—the foretelling of public events by people who were as often off the target as the politicians themselves. Thus Louis de Wohl wrote in June 1938: "To an astrologer the world picture is perfectly clear." He saw, for instance, that "the dominion of the Mercury types, that is the purely intellectuals [*sic*] of a people, no matter which it may be, *must* have disastrous consequences at the present stage of culture and civilization." Note here the anti-intellectual bias that modern astrologers tend to share with modern politicians (though, to be fair to de Wohl, he was thinking mainly of Hitler and Mussolini).

As we shall see in Chapter 7, de Wohl was to be involved in the coming war in his capacity as astrologer. In the meantime his predictions were, true to type, optimistic—and unfortunately incorrect. He finds his adopted country a model of stability because Chamberlain had an excellent horoscope and because the British Government is a solar system in miniature; so there would be no war in the near future. And (writing in June 1938) he can see that "Autumn 1938, the first three months of 1939 and summer 1940 bring heavy weather for Germany." He adds: "I do not believe that Mahatma Gandhi will survive the first half of 1939." (Gandhi lived till 1948.)

As World War II approached, the astrological journalists (in Britain at least) were almost unanimous in denying that it would happen. In 1939 a peculiar book appears, by one "Leonardo Blake," called *Hitler's Last Year of Power.* Blake is a much lower grade writer than de Wohl, but his statements demonstrate the sort of thing people read and find consoling. The foreword of his book states flatly: "Be reassured: there will be no war."

Blake explains why: The destiny of German was "fixed unalterably by the horoscope of January 18, 1871, when that country was first unified by Bismarck." Though this horoscope is the really important one, it is confirmed by the horoscope of the German Republic for November 9, 1918. As for Hitler's horoscope, it compares very badly with Mr. Chamberlain's: Hitler's power will "ebb away" in September 1939 and in June and July 1940 his "attempts to extend his activities will not succeed." Blake added the prediction that Goebbels "will not survive the crisis of 1940," and that the summer of the same year would see the defeat and downfall of Hitler.

While harnessing the stars to Chamberlain's chariot, Leonardo Blake naturally played down Churchill, though admitting that his horoscope showed profundity, magnanimity, and breadth. He foresaw that "Mr. Churchill's role in affairs during the decisive years to come will not be played at the head of a British Cabinet. Nor will he become a factor in turning the scales of British policy . . . . But when, in 1941, the progressed Sun transits together with the progressed Saturn, a quiet and even a little less happy period breaks for him. He is going to retire more and more from public life . . . ."

It is unnecessary to multiply instances of such popular astrological predictions made on the very eve of the war. We shall see in the next chapter how these astrologers were in no way deterred from continuing such predictions while the war was being waged. And their public were in no way disenchanted with them. At the same time, this was not the whole wartime story of astrology. The whole story was a good deal odder than that.

7 Coming up to date

Just before the Second World War broke out, people like Leonardo Blake were only too ready to foretell that it would not happen. But as soon as it happened they snatched up their pens and were at it again. Thus Blake followed his *Hitler's Last Year of Power* with *The Last Year of War—and After.* For him the last year of war was to coincide with the first year of war: He seems to have written his book in the autumn of 1939. Anyway, it was all to be over by the middle of 1940. Blake was well pleased with himself: He claimed that 10 of his predictions in *Hitler's Last Year of Power* had been verified. As for this new book, here, said Blake, "we are writing history in advance."

The crux of the new book was that in 1940 the German nation would revolt and overthrow the Nazi party. His more particular predictions were as follows:
(1) On March 7, 1940, there will be "brilliant successes" for Chamberlain.
(2) April 20 will be Hitler's last birthday when his Sun will be in conjunction with Saturn and both square to Pluto.
(3) "About May 5, 1940, the transiting Jupiter has to pass over Saturn: a black day for Nazi Germany."
(4) June 1940 will be crucial.
(5) "The July days of 1940 are dark days indeed for Hitler."
Throughout the book Blake keeps threatening Hitler with "universal law." We all know how that law functioned in 1940.

One of the weekly lectures organized by the Astrological Lodge of the Theosophical Society in London. Countless associations and societies—which include every type of astrological enthusiast and cater for every shade of astrological belief—have sprung up all over the modern world.

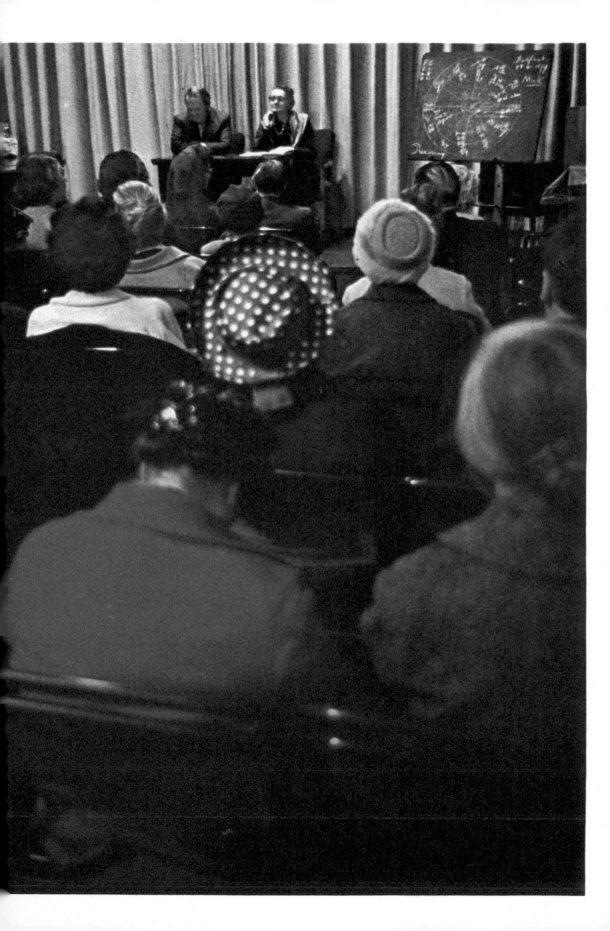

The overwhelming German successes in Europe did not discourage the astrologers of Britain—especially not those of the popular papers like Edward Lyndoe. He came out with the hopeful statement: "The big event of 1941 will be the sudden emergence of a World Leader." This would be the beginning of a new era; but as to the nature of "this coming" (a phrase with a religious sound), Lyndoe wrote: "I reserve my statement." Nor would he commit himself as to the length of the interim period before right triumphed over wrong; he merely hinted that in 1943 investment possibilities would be better than they had been in previous years.

It was this incurable optimism on the part of British astrologers that in June 1942 occasioned that question in Parliament mentioned in Chapter 1. The questioner, who wanted a ban on astrological prediction about the war, got little satisfaction from the Minister of Information. The former had quoted the *People* (Lyndoe's paper) to the effect that a German invasion of England was impossible. The Minister merely commented that astrologers in other papers said England *could* be invaded.

Some 10 months before this, when Britain had been at her most defenseless, the anthropologist Tom Harrisson (founder of Mass Observation) had published an article on "Mass Astrology" in the *New Statesman and Nation* of August 16,

Three British newspaper astrologers, whose astrological predictions on the course of the war were a regular feature of the popular press during the 1940s: left to right, Edward Lyndoe, R. H. Naylor, and Adrienne Arden. All three appeared in a survey by a British magazine in 1941, which analyzed the accuracy of their forecasts. Out of a possible total of 30 marks, Lyndoe scored 9, Naylor 12, and Adrienne Arden 4.

1941. In a cautious footnote to this article Harrisson explains that he is not concerned with "astrological theory, accuracy or intention" but "only with the social effects of contemporary mass astrology." Astrology, he points out, had become "an extensive British interest" since Naylor started in the *Sunday Express* in 1930 and the current war had given it a big additional boost. Mass Observation had accordingly been conducting for the past three months a detailed study of the effect of astrology upon ordinary people. (What this means is that, in accordance with Harrisson's own directives, a large number of researchers—"mass observers"—had gone round with notebooks interviewing people.)

The findings of the observers, as summarized by Harrisson, were roughly as follows: Interest and belief in astrology had "tended steadily to increase since the war," the chief channel being the Sunday press and the chief, addicts being women. Astrology had a complex appeal that included a "constant emphasis on the bright side." Harrisson admitted that, especially among housewives, "the immediate effect is favourable to morale . . . . But the long-term effect is to stress fantasy confidences rather than real ones, and to emphasize the personal interest rather than the common interest."

This article sparked off a couple of others in the illustrated British weekly *Picture Post*. These were more journalistic in tone than Harrisson's. The first

IL VOSTRO DESTINO

Periodo dal 12 al 18 Novembre per ogni tipo zodiacale

LEONE
23 LUGLIO
22 AGOSTO

Non siate pessimisti, ma pratici e realisti, specie se doveste decidere un fidanzamento. Telefonate interessanti.

Divertitevi, lavorate, ma non eccedete in fatiche prolungate.

FRANCESCO WALDNER
horoscope

SEMAINE DU 23 AU 29 NOVEMBRE

Leon Zitrone, né le 25 novembre 1914, Sagittaire.

BELIER
(21 mars-20 avril)
Signe de feu.
Planète : Mars.
Action et lutte.

TAUREAU
(21 avril-21 mai)
Signe de terre.
Planète : Vénus.
Charme et douceur.

GEMEAUX
(22 mai-21 juin)
Signe d'air.
Planète : Mercure.
Intelligence et mouvement.

CANCER
(22 juin-22 juillet)
Signe d'eau.
Planète : Lune.
Rêves et sensibilité.

LION
(23 juillet-23 août)
Signe de feu.
Planète : Soleil.
Eclat et domination.

VIERGE
(24 août-23 septembre)
Signe de terre.
Planète : Mercure.
Intelligence, sens pratique.

PUSHING YOUR LUCK

HOROSCOPE BY CELESTE, AUGUST 14 TO 28, 1963

CAPRICORN (Dec. 23 Jan. 20) You can expect to see all your affairs show a marked improvement during the coming fortnight. This is especially true in regard to conditions in the home. Through an investment of some kind which you made in the past, or through the generosity of a woman, the domestic scene will be much happier. Whether this will be a passing thing or of a more permanent nature remains to be seen. Your great attraction to foreign interests or people continues and it will last for some time to come. This will be most

CANCER (June 22 July 23) There are three important dates for you during the coming fortnight. The first is August 16 and 17 which could raise your personal or professional prestige. This may cause a break with an older partnership or allegiance. The second is August 26 which could take you out of your present home and into an entirely new situation in life. The third is August 29 and 30 when you could fall madly in love, or have some unexpected piece of good luck. All of this, whatever form it may take, will leave you gasping for breath.

began: "The war has brought to millions of minds a new kind of faith, a new kind of stimulus, a new kind of drug or habit . . . . About forty per cent of the people, mainly women, have some belief in astrological prediction." The author again drew heavily on the Sunday newspapers and stressed the way so many of these journalists avoided discussion of the events that really called for it. He noted that many astrologers had predicted that Hitler would invade Sweden, one of the few countries near him that he left alone. As for the German invasion of Russia, Lyndoe had successfully predicted it in the *People,* whereas in the *Sunday Express* for June 22, 1941, Naylor stated defiantly of Germany and Russia: "I still hold to my forecast that they won't quarrel yet." It was on June 22, 1941, that Germany invaded Russia.

In November 1941, *Picture Post* published another article entitled "Astrologers Again," occasioned by a lunch given to astrologers by Miss Christina Foyle, London's biggest bookseller. At the lunch Naylor, irritated by his critics, accused them of having "the immovable idea that astrology postulates that the stars influence mankind. The modern astrologer makes no such absurd statement." In the speech that immediately followed, one Gipsy Petulengro (of the *Sunday Chronicle*) said: "I firmly believe that the stars rule the destiny of

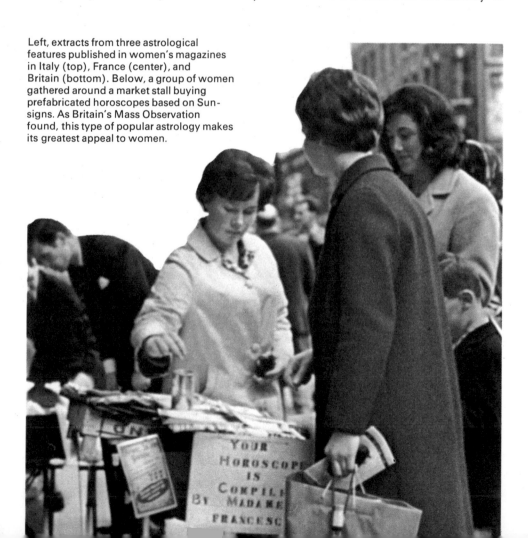

Left, extracts from three astrological features published in women's magazines in Italy (top), France (center), and Britain (bottom). Below, a group of women gathered around a market stall buying prefabricated horoscopes based on Sun-signs. As Britain's Mass Observation found, this type of popular astrology makes its greatest appeal to women.

The well-known British newspaper astrologer
Gipsy Petulengro addressing guests at a
London luncheon held in 1941. At the
luncheon, he and other authors of astrological columns in the popular press made
speeches justifying both their astrological
beliefs and their wartime predictions.

mankind and nations." Petulengro also stated that he had foreseen the fall of France but had kept it dark in case he should be thought defeatist.

Several grades up from the Sunday fortune tellers was the area in which Louis de Wohl operated. Though he claimed Hungary as his fatherland, de Wohl had lived till 1935 in Germany, where he was fairly well known (under the name of Ludwig von Wohl) as a novelist, journalist, and film scriptwriter. He had also been an enthusiastic amateur astrologer; when he came to London he began to turn professional.

Unlike most British astrologers he had the entrée to what would now be called "Establishment" circles and the war gave him the chance to exploit these connections. According to himself, de Wohl met the British Foreign Secretary, Lord Halifax, who asked him for information about Hitler's horoscope. Following this, about September 1940, it seems that he entered the Psychological Research Bureau, after which he was commissioned in the British army with the rank of captain. He had in fact become the British government's official astrologer. (He claimed to have been the sole such official on the Allied side as against six working for the enemy.)

His activities were by their nature secret and for his conduct of this astrological war we must rely mainly on his own account. That he was employed at all does not mean that his distinguished employers believed in astrology. Like a great many other people, they believed that Hitler employed astrologers; de Wohl's job was to check what Hitler might be told by *his* astrological advisers.

In fact, there is no evidence (whatever was the case with the other Nazi leaders) that Hitler himself had any belief or even interest in astrology. Indeed, there is evidence to the contrary. But during the war and even up to the present day many people have chosen to believe that Hitler was as superstitious as some of the Roman emperors and that, like them, he employed his own pet astrologer. De Wohl mentioned six antagonists, but he too seems to have thought that there was one in particular who was Hitler's right-hand star man. In fact, it was owing to the existence of one very original astrologer, who was supposed to be filling this role, that de Wohl himself got his curious job with the British. The name of this bogyman (whom we have met before) was Karl Ernst Krafft.

Krafft was an essentially "modern" astrologer who wished to cut out the dead wood from the ancient art. Shortly before the war he had published in Switzerland a *Treatise of Astro-Biology*, in which he employed the modern statistical method. He was an exponent of "astral heredity," coining the phrase "*astro-hérédonomie*," in an attempt to answer a common objection and to reconcile astrology with the incontestable facts of heredity. He pointed out the coincidences of birth dates within the same family and suggested that members of the same family tend to resemble each other not only in their physical and psychological make-up but also in their natal charts. All this seems rather a far cry from political warfare; but Krafft, who chose to stay in Germany when the war broke out, found himself involved in it—to his cost.

The Swiss astrologer Karl Ernst Krafft. During World War II, Krafft, while a prisoner of the Nazis, was compelled to produce "astrological" propaganda; he finally defied his captors, and died in 1945 on the eve of his transfer to Buchenwald.

(For much of what follows I am indebted to Mr. Felix Nebelmeier of Switzerland, who was himself involved in political warfare—on the Allied side. Since the war Mr. Nebelmeier has made an intensive study of astrology as a social phenomenon and, as part of this, has done some remarkable detective work on the true and sad story of Krafft.)

To appreciate this story we must go back to the days of the Weimar Republic. After Germany's defeat in 1918, astrology had a 15 years' boom in that country: No other country in Europe could show such a large and active astrological movement. This phenomenon was probably occasioned by Germany's economic and social collapse, by the disappearance of the monarchy and the old military caste, by inflation, unemployment, and poverty. As had happened often before in history, people (including very well-educated people) turned in such circumstances to the stars for consolation.

Among the astrologers under the Weimar Republic there was a small but vocal minority of violent nationalists, who published more than their share of books and pamphlets. This minority included four confirmed racialists whose writings were revealingly anti-Semitic. As Mr. Nebelmeier says, "no astrological movement ever produced anything quite like this particular group."

Louis de Wohl refers to one of these nationalist astrologers, whom he (wrongly) calls "Baron Sobottendorf." According to de Wohl, in 1923 the baron warned Hitler against undertaking "anything of importance" in November of that year. "Hitler neglected the warning and undertook his famous beer cellar *Putsch*, which landed him in jail." But de Wohl is wrong on two counts. First, the man's name was not Baron Sobottendorf. He called himself Rudolph Freiherr von S*e*bottendorf, but his real name was Adam Glandeck. Just after the armistice on the Western Front in November 1918 he was a member of the ultra-nationalist Bavarian "Free Corps" movement. He was also a member of the secret *Germanen* order, an anti-Semitic, right-wing, esoteric association.

More important, he bought a small Munich newspaper that later, under the new name of *Völkischer Beobachter,* he sold to the Nazi Party, who made it one of their chief organs of propaganda. As such it survived till 1945. Before he sold this afterward notorious paper, von Sebottendorf was also the editor of the leading German astrological monthly *Astrologische Rundschau.* This paper belonged to a "Dr." Hugo Vollrath, proprietor of the Theosophical Publishing House at Leipzig, who later was to join the Nazi party and try to establish himself as national leader of the German astrological movement.

Furthermore, it was *not* von Sebottendorf (or Baron Sobottendorf or Glandeck) who made the famous prediction in 1923. It was a well-known lady astrologer named Frau Elsbeth Ebertin, who edited a popular annual called *Ein Blick in die Zukunft (A Glimpse into the Future).* In the spring of 1923 someone sent her Hitler's birth date (though not the hour of his birth) and asked for a diagnosis of his character. Some months later she published such a diagnosis together with the warning that it would be unwise for this character to take any precipitate action during the coming November. Hitler is said to have been shown this piece of Frau Ebertin's and to have exclaimed: "What have women and the stars got to do with me?" He made his *Putsch* on November 8; two days later he was arrested and sent to prison, where he wrote the final draft of *Mein Kampf.*

"Sobottendorf" continued to be at least the nominal editor of his astrological paper until about 1930, though it seems that he spent much of his time in Turkey studying old Turkish freemasonry. Having failed to make Frau Ebertin's prediction for her, he now rather disappears from the story. More sinister characters, apart from the Dr. Vollrath mentioned above, were fishing in those troubled waters where the stars were reflected among eddies of racial prejudice.

There was a Munich physician called Dr. Wilhelm Gutberlet who was said to move in Hitler's circle and was credited with "mystic powers." He was an enthusiastic amateur astrologer and also claimed that he could identify people as Jews by the use of a pendulum. Another medical doctor who lived his astrology was Karl Günther Heimsoth, a great friend of Ernst Röhm, the S.A. commander. Dr. Heimsoth, it seems, cast and interpreted Röhm's horoscope in 1929 but was unable to provide a satisfactory reason for Röhm's notorious homosexuality.

It might be expected that these people would have been made welcome when the Nazis got power. But it did not work out like that. When Hitler came to power in 1933 he frowned upon both Gutberlet and Heimsoth, and in the following year they were both liquidated. Dr. Vollrath was still going strong and a Dr. Hugo Korsch (a *legal* doctor this time, who was also President of the Central Astrological Office) joined the Nazi Party just in order to stop Vollrath making a corner in the stars in the name of National Socialism. Yet none of the astrologers who tried could persuade the Nazis to adopt him and grant him a monopoly.

On the contrary, Hitler's assumption of power in 1933 was, to put it mildly, a considerable source of worry to Germany's leading astrologers. Some of them had recently published articles unfavorable to Hitler and his movement, so there was some twisting and covering of tracks. Hitler's official birth hour (and hence his probable ascendant) was well known to astrologers, but juggling attempts were made to provide him with a different birth hour and thereby a different ascendant. (The object was to shift his traditionally disastrous Saturn out of the 10th house, a position associated with an unfortunate end to a public career.) But on the whole, while there had been many references to Hitler's horoscope in the astrological journals during 1931 and 1932, such references began to dwindle. And the fate of Dr. Heimsoth in 1934 showed that Nazi Germany was not altogether safe for astrologers. This moral was to be driven home later.

When Hitler came into power there were half a dozen "serious" astrological periodicals in Germany, including the two conducted respectively by Dr. Korsch and Dr. Vollrath. In five years' time three of these had ceased publication, including those run by Korsch and Vollrath. Vollrath was especially hard hit, since the German branch of the Theosophical Society had also been dissolved. Also, there had been popular astrological weeklies and monthlies crammed with political predictions of the same type as those made by the English Sunday journalists, but after 1933 there were none such in Germany. This particular opium for the masses was under a ban. In the same way every year since 1922 there had been well-attended astrological conferences in Germany; but in 1938 a congress held near Munich was only allowed on condition that no congress report was published. Moreover, the Gestapo was present.

Then came the war and the importance of being Krafft. In 1939 Karl Ernst Krafft was living in a village in the Black Forest not far from the Swiss border. He could easily have returned to Switzerland, but it seems that Germany suited him. He was a great admirer of the Third Reich and was not too worried by the plight of its astrologers; though he was an outstanding authority on astrology, he preferred to call himself a psychological consultant. Also, through a member of Himmler's Head Office for State Security, he was in touch (at least indirectly) with most important people.

His link was a Dr. Fesel. Shortly after the war broke out, Dr. Fesel asked Krafft to write some memoranda for him. These memoranda contained, among other things, economic forecasts based on Krafft's interpretation of planetary cycles and major conjunctions. Fesel presumably intended to circulate them among members of Himmler's organization. (Himmler was apparently one of the Nazi leaders who did have some belief in astrology.) But Krafft did not confine himself to these commissioned memoranda. He had been watching Hitler's horoscope and now issued a prediction that Hitler's life would be in danger during the first 10 days of November 1939. This prediction (just like Frau Ebertin's in 1923) came home to roost in the Munich Beer Cellar. Hitler had

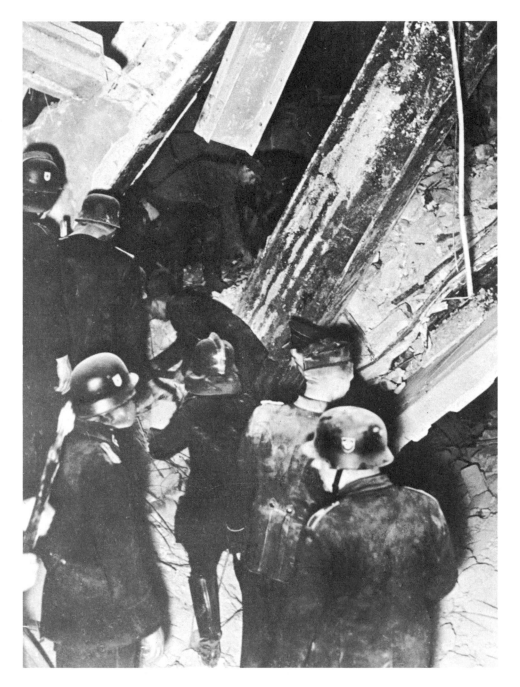

The ruins of the Munich Beer Cellar after
the assassination attempt on Hitler in 1939.
Krafft had earlier predicted a threat to
Hitler's life from his horoscope; though he
was arrested for questioning, there was
no evidence to implicate him in the plot.

been there celebrating the *Putsch* of 1923 but he left before the bomb that was to assassinate him went off. Krafft promptly sent a telegram to Berlin drawing attention to his prediction and adding that Hitler's life would be in danger for a few days longer. Whereupon Krafft was arrested and questioned, only to be released for want of evidence that he had been in any way connected with the bomb. (It reminds one of William Lilly's being questioned—and also dismissed— by the committee that was set up to investigate the causes of the Great Fire of London in 1666.)

After this Krafft moved, or was moved, to Berlin. He may have made himself suspect, but somebody must also have thought him potentially useful. In 1940, keeping closely in touch with various government departments, he was engaged in political warfare, working on the prophecies of Nostradamus. These cryptic and concentrated pieces of apparent nonsense had always come in very handy for political warriors. Krafft did some lengthy and scholarly research on them, which was taken over by the Propaganda Ministry and angled, inevitably, to point to a German victory.

During 1940, Krafft got involved in a curious way with London (and this in its turn had repercussions on Louis de Wohl). The Romanian Minister to London, M. Virgil Tilea, being on leave in Bucharest, took it into his head to write to Krafft asking him for information about coming events. It was not that Tilea believed in astrology as such; but he had met Krafft once in Zurich and decided he had a flair as a prophet. Krafft was flattered by this letter and, being anxious to reply to it, asked his friend Fesel, Himmler's man, how his reply could be forwarded to London. The security high-ups agreed to arrange it, provided they could dictate the general nature of the reply. Once again political warfare was rearing its dubious head. Krafft would have liked to let the whole thing drop, but not so Dr. Fesel and the heads of his department. The letter was drafted and re-drafted seven times. At last M. Tilea received it in London and Krafft handed back his last month's salary to Fesel and said he was finished with that sort of work.

The letter that Tilea read, being by now a pure piece of political warfare writing, made him think that Krafft must be working directly for the Nazis and possibly for Hitler himself. This suspicion was enhanced by the fact that the letter had been sent from Berlin. Tilea showed the letter to various important people in London and suggested that, if Hitler was employing an astrologer (Krafft), it would be sensible of the British to employ another astrologer to tip them off as to what his opposite number would be up to. At first the British high-ups did not respond to this suggestion very eagerly, but finally (on Tilea's suggestion) accepted Louis de Wohl. De Wohl went through the rest of the war imagining he was countering Krafft in Berlin.

But Krafft did not spend the rest of the war in the way de Wohl assumed. On June 12, 1941, he was arrested. Like many other things this was the fault of Rudolf Hess, another Nazi leader who, like Himmler, was generally thought to be under the influence of astrologers. Hess's unauthorized flight into Scotland precipitated a great deal of face-saving and scapegoat-finding in Germany. Among those who suffered, thanks to Hess's reputation, were the astrologers. After all, Hess had had one on his staff at the Brown House in Munich—a certain Ernst Schulte-Strathaus, who was officially an expert on art. Schulte-Strathaus denied that he had ever given Hess any astrological advice or that he had any idea that Hess was going to leave Germany, but the sheer fact of their association provided another weapon against the astrologers. The Gestapo went into action.

The object of this action was twofold: first, to discover whether any astrologer had been connected with Hess; secondly, to destroy the whole astrological movement in Germany. It had been decided that the astrological *Weltanschauung* must by its nature be unsympathetic to National Socialism and that the astrologers as a class were socially undesirable and politically unreliable. The *Aktion Hess* began on June 9, 1941, and continued for several weeks. Amateur and professional astrologers were rounded up left, right, and center and their technical libraries and personal papers confiscated. Also seized were all publishers' and booksellers' stocks of astrological literature.

Most of the people arrested at this time were released fairly soon, after signing an undertaking to cease practicing astrology or even discussing it. But there were two or three of the more serious astrologers who were never released. Among these was Krafft (though this was not known to his opposite number de Wohl). After spending a year in solitary confinement in the Alexanderplatz police prison in Berlin, Krafft was transferred during the summer of 1942 to a Propaganda Ministry building in north Berlin. Here, though still a prisoner, he was once more forced or persuaded into harness for political warfare purposes and for three or four months tried to work his passage to freedom via the stars.

It seems that he had been promised his release provided that over a certain period his work met the requirements of his masters. But there was a proviso that he would have to continue to work for them. Whether his work satisfied the Propaganda Ministry or not (if not, it would be to his credit), he obviously began to suspect that the promise would not be kept. Eventually he refused any further collaboration with his jailers. He was then shut up in the Lehrterstrasse prison from which he was transferred to the Oranienberg concentration camp. He was being transferred again (this time to Buchenwald) when he died on January 8, 1945. (More details about Krafft's astrological theory and practice will be given in the next chapter.)

In spite of the official "extermination" of astrology in Germany, a few practitioners did continue to be employed after the Aktion Hess, presumably because (to save their own skins) they were more willing or able than the perhaps overscrupulous Krafft to divert their art to the needs of political warfare. One such was a well-known Hamburg astrologer called Wulff who specialized in Hindu techniques and who is mentioned in *The Last Days of Hitler* by the British

Benito Mussolini
July 29th 1883
1.54 p.m.
Forli nr. Milan

Below, the Hungarian-born astrologer Louis de Wohl. During World War II the British Government employed de Wohl to anticipate predictions by Hitler's alleged astrological advisers. From Mussolini's horoscope (right), cast in 1941, de Wohl correctly predicted "a violent and sudden end" for the Italian dictator.

historian Hugh Trevor-Roper. But it should be noted that Wulff was to all intents and purposes a prisoner on the estate of Himmler's masseur. It seems he was used by the head of the German secret service Schallenberg to influence Himmler, who toward the end of the war was in a vacillating but suggestible state of mind.

Further evidence that astrology had not completely disappeared is implicit in a letter written by Gerda Bormann to her husband (Martin Bormann, Hess's Chief of Staff and later Hitler's third deputy) on October 26, 1944: "Just as at the end of the last war," she observes, "fortune tellers and prophets have a strong following." On which Bormann has scribbled the comment: "I never even get such rubbish! Don't want to see it either!"

But much more striking than this is another episode recounted in *The Last Days of Hitler*. Hitler himself, as already stated, had little use for astrology and since 1941 the art had been officially condemned by his government. All the same, by the second week of April 1945 it was perhaps a case of any star in a storm. Goebbels in that week sent for two horoscopes—those of Hitler and of the German Reich itself; both had been "carefully kept in one of Himmler's research departments." These he discussed with the Führer in the light of an encouraging historical precedent: When Prussia was on the verge of defeat at the end of the Seven Years War, the tsarina of Russia had unexpectedly died and saved the situation for Frederick the Great. Sure enough, the two more recent horoscopes did hold forth the prospect of a similar "reversal of fortune." For both these horoscopes, according to Professor Trevor-Roper's informant, "had unanimously predicted the outbreak of war in 1939, the victories till 1941, and then the series of defeats culminating in the early months of 1945." The point was that these disasters were to be followed by an overwhelming victory in the second half of April 1945, and by peace in August: Germany would be great again by 1948.

Then followed the death of Roosevelt (compare the tsarina in the other war) and Goebbels at once telephoned to Hitler: "My Führer, I congratulate you. Roosevelt is dead. It is written in the stars that the second half of April will be the turning point for us. This is Friday April the Thirteenth. It is the turning point!" A fortnight later both men were dead.

What was Louis de Wohl doing on the allied side while all this was going on? He himself gives us some of the answers in *The Stars of War and Peace* (published 1952). His initial job, to counter Hitler's (presumed) astrological advisers, simply meant "making the same calculations so as to come to the same interpretative results, which enabled us to know what he ought to be told"—after which it remained only to guess how much they would dare to tell Hitler or how much they would cook their findings.

But some of de Wohl's activities were more positive than this. While he wrote that it was "to the honour of American astrologers" that "many of them had warned their country of the imminent Japanese attack" on Pearl Harbor, he himself claims to have foretold the result of the battle of Alamein after comparing the horoscopes of Montgomery and Rommel, which had been submitted to him without his knowing whose they were. And after 1942, when Hitler lost the initiative, de Wohl claims triumphantly: "Now *we* would time our actions against him . . . . Thus, when we attacked Sicily at the beginning of July 1943 when Jupiter was in 'square,' in an angle of 90 degrees, to the Sun position at Hitler's birth, Hitler knew that 'luck' was against him." De Wohl adds that Hitler also knew that astrology was being used against him: "We had seen to it that he knew." And he spares a word of pity for Mussolini who "had a beautiful horoscope" and who should have had sound astrological advice.

Another activity of de Wohl's during the war is mentioned in *Black Boomerang* by Sefton Delmer (published 1962). Delmer was the chief of British "black" political warfare, which specialized in disseminating lies of every sort for the confusion and undermining of the enemy. At one point it was decided that astrology too was worth a fake. There had been published in Germany up till 1938, when it was stopped, a successful astrological periodical called *Zenit*. Delmer revived *Zenit* for a few issues and de Wohl wrote the texts for him. These contained astrological predictions written *after* the events to which they referred—predictions of a kind, say, that might well put off German submariners from going to sea in their U-boats.

When we now read de Wohl's rather pompous accounts of his own astrological war (the gallant captain with a bandolier full of horoscopes) or think of the ups and downs of the German astrologers, the Second World War starts to resemble one of those galleries of distorting mirrors in a funfair. We saw in Chapter 2 how de Wohl himself attributed the technical inventions of the war to "Uranus running amuck." As for the bomb that ended the war with Japan, he naturally could explain that too. He cast Japan's horoscope retrospectively for July 16, 1945, and found that Mars was in conjunction with the fixed star Algol, known as the Head of the Medusa, "the worst fixed star we know of." (Algol had had an evil reputation through the ages, being called by the Arabs "the Demon." This presumably was because of its fluctuations in brightness. We now know that it is an example of a "binary system"; i.e., Algol is really *two* stars that revolve around, and therefore at intervals eclipse, each other.)

The postwar world

So much for World War II. What of astrology since? In defeated Germany, astrology made the same sort of comeback after its suppression under the Nazis as after the Kaiser's war. And for very much the same reasons. In Hamburg in 1947-48 a popular lecture on astrology could attract an audience of 500 or more. This is not so today, perhaps because Germany has become too prosperous.

Mr. Nebelmeier, who supplied me with the sad tale of Krafft, makes the comment that "if any moral at all can be drawn, it is that astrology cannot flourish under either a totalitarian regime or conditions of almost universal prosperity."

In Germany today, astrology flourishes
again in spite of its wartime suppression.
One of the best-known German astrologers
is Elfriede Keiser, who is said to number
leading politicians among her clientele.

But, if popular astrology is on the wane in Germany, it still remains the country where astrology is treated most seriously, if only by a handful of unusually imaginative scholars.

Among these scholars, Dr. Walter Koch might be selected as representative of the highly academic approach to astrology—an approach that is becoming more and more widespread today. With other German astrological scholars, Koch has been deeply involved in investigating the controversial question of the 12 houses and the mathematical principles involved; and he has published versions of the Regiomontanus and Placidus tables of houses. Koch's other prewar works include numerous articles on Greek and Roman astrology, a book on *Astrological Teachings Concerning Colors* (which grew out of his interest in psychology), and another entitled *The Soul of the Gemstone*, which deals with the occult properties of precious stones.

Koch's career suffered a serious setback during World War II, since he was one of the astrologers imprisoned by the Nazis, and his astrological library was burned by the Gestapo. But after the war, Koch returned to his astrological studies, and was one of the founder members of the Cosmobiological Society in 1946. This society published the first edition of the *Astrological Monthly* in 1949, to which Koch has since been a regular contributor.

In 1959, Koch was appointed scientific adviser to the Association of German Astrologers and that year read a paper on "The Symbolism of Astrological Geometry" to a congress of German astrologers. He has been in the forefront of the modern astrological tendency (which is especially obvious in German astrology) to seek tie-ups between astrology and psychological knowledge. One of the most interesting of this academic scholar's publications, called *Introvert and Extrovert,* is "a study in psychological astrological interpretation."

Introversion and extraversion are, of course, terms given to us by another imaginative scholar who gave astrology the benefit of the doubt—C. G. Jung. Jung also investigated the possibility of links between astrology and psychology; but he was one of a very few who approached the subject from the psychologist's viewpoint, not the astrologer's. He is always being claimed by modern astrologers as a champion of their cause; but, apart from his rather general statement that the moment of a man's birth remains part of his make-up, it would seem that he kept an open mind. He would certainly not have committed himself to the more specific (or arbitrary) assertions so beloved by most astrologers.

In 1950, Jung wrote a treatise called *Synchronicity: an Acausal Connecting Principle.* The word "synchronicity" has since been snapped up by astrologers in their eagerness to find a substitute for the now generally discarded idea (*pace* Gipsy Petulengro and the Hindus) of "astral influence." Thus in 1962 a lady astrologer named Katina Theodossiou declared in a British radio program that cause and effect were out and synchronicity was in: When the planet Mars is active certain things happen on earth (wars, revolutions, etc.) but "the one does not cause the other, they merely coincide."

But what does synchronicity mean? In his treatise Jung starts from the assumption that "the connection of events may in certain circumstances be other than causal." If one could prove, he argues, that "there are genuinely non-causal combinations of events," we should have drastically to revise our view of things, as man has had to before and perhaps is being impelled to now by such

Above right, Reinhold Ebertin, the leading light of the German "cosmobiologists"—a rebel group that has rejected many of astrology's most fundamental theories. Right, the cover of *Kosmobiologie,* which was founded by Ebertin in 1928— today one of Germany's best-selling astrological magazines.

KOSMOBIOLOGIE

Mitteilungsblatt des „Arbeitskreises für kosmobiologische Forschung"
und der „Kosmobiologischen Akademie Aalen, Arbeitsgemeinschaft e. V."

30. Jahrgang   1   Januar 1963

A mandala (or "magic circle") drawn by C. G. Jung in 1928. The mandala form is fundamental to many of the great Eastern religions, such as Taoism or Buddhism. Though it can be seen as a symbol of the soul or psyche, it is also a representation of *totality*—in effect, of the oneness of all things in the universe (whose interrelationships depend more on synchronicity than causality). As Jung points out, this oneness is much the same as the ancient concept of correspondence, or *sympathy*, which was long used to explain and defend astrology.

phenomena as E.S.P. "We should then have to assume that events in general are related to one another on the one hand by causal chains, and on the other hand by a kind of meaningful cross-connection." In other words, events that happen at the same time can be related either because one has *caused* the other or because they each have a similar *meaning* to the mind that perceives them. (Or, of course, they can be chance occurrences, not related at all.)

To give a concrete example of what he means, Jung tells a striking but rather long true story about a recurrent plum pudding. It is easy to invent more brief examples with numbers: A man who had been born at 19.58 hours (7.58 P.M.) might have noticed on his birthday (though not necessarily on his birthday) in A.D. 1958 that his bus ticket was numbered 1958 and then have gone on that evening to score 1958 in some game of chance. That would either be pure chance —a concept that worries Jung as much as the rest of us—or an example of his non-causal principle of meaningful coincidence. There have been many cases where a clock has stopped ("never to go again," as an old song says) at the instant of its owner's death. This, too, would be synchronicity: The clock's stopping would be symbolically (not causally) related to the person's death.

"The primitive mentality," Jung writes, "has always explained synchronicity as magical causality right down to our own day, and on the other hand philosophy assumed a secret correspondence or meaningful connection between natural events until well into the eighteenth century. I prefer the latter hypothesis. . . . ." It will have been noticed that, through the centuries, some astrologers have worked on the former hypothesis and some on the latter. In the concept of synchronicity there are echoes of the idea of "sympathy" (between human life and the universe) that has cropped up so often in our history of astrology.

It was the search for meaningful connections that led Jung to undertake his "astrological experiment." With the usual kinds of check and precaution to avoid foreknowledge or cheating on the part of the investigators, he took as his field of statistical study 483 marriages (i.e., 966 horoscopes). These horoscopes were paired off in different ways, and the object was to establish the differences between the married couples and the non-married. As often happens in such experiments, the first results were the best : In the married couples' horoscopes certain aspects (for example, the woman's Moon in conjunction with the man's Sun) appeared most frequently; and these aspects were the same ones that, according to the long astrological tradition, most favored marriage. But the experiment as a whole was judged by Jung to be inconclusive.

Jung had defined synchronicity as "a psychically conditioned relativity of space and time." To the modern way of thinking, if there is anything at all in astrology, it must involve a rearrangement of our concept of *time*. The Australian astrologer Furze Morrish writes (in a comment on Jung) : "It seems, indeed, as though time . . . is a concrete continuum which contains qualities of basic conditions manifesting simultaneously in various places in a way not to be explained by causal parellelisms." Synchronicity (or, as Morrish calls it, "synchronism") might "help some scientists to understand how astrology could work without any mechanical apparatus linking star and human." On the other hand, he does allow that there may be "astro-causation" between *planets* and persons, possibly by waves through the ether.

This concession of Morrish's about astro-causation resembles a process of thought not uncommon among many modern astrologers. It seems to be assumed that, if proof is given that the planets (or, for that matter, the Sun and Moon) can affect things on earth, then everything else follows, including the significance of the Zodiacal signs—which are for most astrologers not even groups of fixed stars but merely mechanically divided strips of sky. Geophysicists, radio meteorologists, biologists, and others claim to have correlated various terrestrial phenomena (such as electromagnetic storms) with goings on in the solar system. But, assuming these claims are correct, it still seems rather a long jump to the casting and interpretation of horoscopes.

Before leaving Morrish it is worth noting that, unlike the ancients who automatically thought of astrology as a science (and unlike those modern astrologers who lay such stress on observation, experiment, and statistics), Morrish flatly contrasts "science" (as something "strictly inductive") with astrology (which male

	☉	☽	♂	♀	Asc.	Desc.
☉	☌☍	☌☍	☌☍	☍☌	☌	☌
☽	☌☍	☌☍	☍☌	☌☍	☌	☌
♂	☍☌	☌☍	☌☍	☌☍	☌	☌
♀	☌☍	☍☌	☌☍	☍☌	☌	☌
Asc.	☌	☌	☌	☌	☌	☌
Desc.	☌	☌	☌	☌		

female

conjunction ☌   opposition ☍

First Batch		
180 Married Pairs		
Moon	☌ Sun	10.0*
Asc.	☌ Venus	9.4*
Moon	☌ Asc.	7.7*
Moon	☌ Moon	7.2*
Moon	☍ Sun	7.2*
Mars	☌ Moon	7.2
Venus	☍ Moon	7.2*
Mars	☌ Mars	7.2*
Mars	☌ Asc.	6.6
Sun	☌ Mars	6.6*
Venus	☌ Desc.	6.1
Venus	☌ Asc.	6.1
Mars	☌ Desc.	6.1
Sun	☌ Asc.	6.1

deals with "universals"). This was to be expected from his theosophical background: In a chapter entitled "Shadows of Changes in World Thought" he likes to think that he can perceive a swing toward religion. He notes with approval that there is a rapid change going on today from the ethical mode to the aesthetic. The high priests of science were wrong, he proclaims, but so were the high priests of religion. So open the door and let the yogi come in—the yogi who is aware of "the Universal Integrative Factor which turns out to be ONESELF." And Morrish's yogi is, of course, just another name for the astrologer. Tell that to Ptolemy or Firmicus Maternus or Albertus Magnus or even William Lilly!

As regards religion, Ingrid Lind has asked "whether it is possible to believe in astrology and still have a religion." (This, as must have emerged in our historical chapters, is not a new question.) Her answer is that she finds "nothing in it, *if taken at a high enough level* [italics mine], that is incompatible with religion." She falls back on the traditional unity of the world and interdependence of parts. "Is it fantastic," she asks, "to conceive of God, or at any rate of the Solar Logos, as embodying His universe, with the Sun at His heart and the Planets, including Earth, as vital organs of His being?" Still one is tempted to ask: What about Pascal's interstellar spaces? And is the rest of our own galaxy Godless? (Not to mention all those other never-to-be-numbered galaxies.)

Still, many modern astrologers would probably agree with Ingrid Lind that their art has not only a moral but a religious justification. American astrology, at least since the beginning of the theosophical movement, certainly seems to have had a bias in favor of the mystical rather than the scientific. There was,

Second Batch			
220 Married Pairs			
Moon	☌	Moon	10.9%
Mars	☍	Venus	7.7%
Venus	☌	Moon	7.2%
Moon	☍	Sun	6.8%
Moon	☍	Mars	6.8%
Desc.	☌	Mars	6.8%
Desc.	☌	Venus	6.3%
Moon	☍	Venus	6.3%
Venus	☌	Venus	6.3%
Sun	☍	Mars	5.9%
Venus	☌	Desc.	5.4%
Venus	☌	Mars	5.4%
Sun	☌	Moon	5.4%
Sun	☌	Sun	5.4%

Both Batches			
400 Married Pairs			
Moon	☌	Moon	9.2%
Moon	☍	Sun	7.0%
Moon	☌	Sun	7.0%
Mars	☌	Mars	6.2%
Desc.	☌	Venus	6.2%
Moon	☍	Mars	6.2%
Mars	☌	Moon	6.0%
Mars	☍	Venus	5.7%
Moon	☌	Asc.	5.7%
Venus	☌	Desc.	5.7%
Venus	☌	Moon	5.5%
Desc.	☌	Mars	5.2%
Asc.	☌	Venus	5.2%
Sun	☍	Mars	5.2%

Above left, a table setting out the various astrological aspects considered by Jung in his analysis of the horoscopes of 400 married couples. The couples were divided into two groups of 180 and 220 : The middle two tables list the results yielded by each batch of horoscopes ; the last table combines the figures of both. Jung points out that the aspect traditionally most connected with marriage—a conjunction between Sun and Moon—occurred most often in Table 1 and next most often in Table 3. As a famous instance of this aspect, Jung cites the horoscopes of Goethe and his mistress Christiane Vulpius (sketched by Goethe, right).

A crowded gathering of delegates to a
convention held in 1950 by the American
Federation of Astrologers. Federation
members (like those of the British Faculty of
Astrological Studies) must pass examinations
and subscribe to a code of ethics.

for instance, Max Heindel, astrologer and founder of the Rosicrucian Fellowship in San Francisco. And today there is the Presbyterian minister Marc Edmund Jones who issues mimeographed lessons on astrology. As long ago as 1922 Jones founded the "Sabian Society," borrowing the name from an ancient mystical brotherhood in Baghdad. (Some of his "Sabian Symbols" were displayed in Chapter 1.) In 1925 he published in Los Angeles his *Key Truths of Occult Philosophy*: The first key truth is that "Time is Illusion" and the second that "Space is Relationship."

Belonging to the same American school as Jones is Dane Rudhyar; both have contributed to the quarterly astrological magazine *In Search*. For Rudhyar the aim of astrology is a high one: "to transform chaotic human nature into a microcosm." Like Krafft in Europe, he would like to be rid of "European 'classical' astrology" as being "a spiritually lifeless rebirth of Greco-Latin intellectualism." In his best-known book, *The Astrology of Personality*, Rudhyar emphasizes that "Wholeness" is all, a target to be achieved not through the analytical mind but through intuition. Intuition leads to "functional coherency." Rudhyar is another modern astrologer who pays attention to modern (particularly Jungian) psychology. Astrology is the male element (that which gives the formula) while psychology is the female element (that which gives the substantial contents).

True to the theosophical tradition, Rudhyar calls for a "creative aristocracy," being influenced here by his American predecessor Alice Bailey, who had proposed a "New Group of World Servers." He is much concerned with "group personalities" and likes to formulate things in triads—for example, "individual," "collective," "creative." Thus he distinguishes three types of astrology: First, the astrology thought of in terms of the axial motion of the earth (which concerns the *individual* and constitutes natal and horary astrology); second, the type thought of in terms of the earth's orbit around the sun (this is *collective* and constitutes natural or mundane astrology); third, there is occult astrology (which is *creative*). Rudhyar, who also flirts with such things as the number symbolism of the Great Pyramid, would appear to hope that astrology will one day take over from religion.

Whether they make any mystical claims or not, whether they welcome or eschew occult studies, all serious modern astrologers regard themselves as useful members of society. There is a constant lament that universities no longer offer degrees in astrology (as they did in the Middle Ages). But it is interesting that not all universities in the world refuse to acknowledge astrology's existence. Recently one of India's best-known astrologers—Prof. B. V. Raman, scholar and editor of an astrological magazine—gave a series of lectures that prompted the Chancellor of Mysore University to advocate (publicly) the founding of "faculties for astronomical and astrological studies" in Indian universities.

And in 1960 one of the most eminent of America's universities—Harvard itself (specifically, Radcliffe College, an offshoot of Harvard)—permitted a woman student to present a thesis on astrology for her B.A. degree. The student, Marcia Moore, called her thesis "Astrology Today—a Socio-Psychological Survey." Part One of this scrupulous and detailed report summarizes the history of astrology and examines it in relation to modern science—particularly psychology. In his foreword, Charles A. Jayne Jr. (editor of *In Search*) emphasizes the vital distinction between what he calls "the gypsy and fortune-telling element, and those whose interest in astrology is to exploit it commercially, on the one hand, and the quite different element, on the other hand, those for whom it is a serious study."

The second part of the thesis comprises the results obtained from a questionnaire (compiled by a panel that included such big astrological names as Margaret Hone and Marc Edmund Jones) that was designed to discover the collective attitudes and ideas of those most concerned with the validity and practice of astrology—a sort of group analysis. This analysis revealed that only about 20 per cent admitted to earning *any* income from astrology. The questionnaire was sent out to 900 subscribers to *In Search*—mostly members of the American Federation of Astrologers, a highly respectable body with its own code of ethics. (Of the probable 100 or so astrological societies that flourish in America, 25 are affiliated to the A.F.A.)

The magazine *In Search* first appeared in New York in the spring of 1958 and was hailed by astrologers overseas, both in Europe and India. In the first number its editor wrote an article entitled "Toward a New Astrology" in which he suggested that the new astrologer has to reckon with "at least eighteen unknown planets." This is beating the German scientific astrologers at their own game; it looks as if American astrologers are now serious contenders for the heavyweight title. Among others there is Carl Payne Tobey, founder and director of the Institute of Abstract Science (its headquarters are in Arizona) where astrology is taught as "a branch of mathematics." (According to Mr. Tobey himself, his interest in astrology started in the 1920s, when he had lost money in the Florida boom but learned from an acquaintance that "only astrology could explain these things.")

Throughout the world, various kinds of astrological institutes, groups, societies, etc., have been formed to advance the serious study of astrology. Many such organizations offer academic facilities (often in the form of correspondence courses) to would-be astrologers. In London the Faculty of Astrological Studies (founded in 1948, and affiliated with the Astrological Lodge) sets its students examinations: After one year of study you can get a Certificate, after two years a Diploma. If you get a Diploma you have the right to put after your name the letters "D.F. Astrol.S."

While on the subject of serious astrology, it ought to be mentioned that, like the American Federation of Astrologers, the London Faculty of Astrological Studies has a printed code of ethics that is largely intended to counteract any hint of charlatanism attaching to its name. Any student attached to the faculty is

Astrology—always a rich source of allegory and symbolism—provided the British choreographer Frederick Ashton with the theme of the ballet *The Horoscope* (composed by Constant Lambert and first produced in 1938). The ballet tells the story of two lovers (right) who are separated by the contrasting personalities of their Sun-signs Leo and Virgo, but who are finally reconciled by the efforts of Gemini and the Moon (above).

bound by this code to abide by the following rules:

"(a) I will undertake no natal work unless the time and place of birth are stated with reasonable accuracy, or if these are not available, I will explain clearly and unequivocally that any work supplied in such circumstances can only be regarded as inadequate and general.

"(b) In all professional work I will charge a fee commensurate with the dignity of astrological science, except in cases wherein the inquirer, being a genuine seeker after help and not impelled by idle curiosity, is unable to make a payment. In such instances I will give information and advice gratuitously.

"(c) I will in every case make an original and individual study of the case before me and will not use any form of reduplication, nor will I use in my work extracts from others' writings without due acknowledgment.

"(d) In work stated to be astrological I will not insert anything that is not founded upon true astrological science. Should I desire to impart advice for [or?] information derived from other sources I will write this upon a separate sheet with an express statement that it is not based upon Astrology.

"(e) I agree to respect in the strictest manner all confidences reposed in me, unless my duty as a loyal and law-abiding citizen of my country compels me to act otherwise.

"(f) I will use discretion in making any public statements regarding political matters or persons prominent in public life, and will avoid all such as are contrary to good taste and the practice of a decent reticence.

"(g) I undertake to make no improper or unethical use of the Diploma and my status as a Holder thereof and a Member of the Faculty; and as far as in me lies I will conduct all professional astrological work, should I be engaged therein, in accordance with high professional standards.

"(h) I will hold for the general good and not for my private use or advantage any discoveries that I may make or conclusions that I may reach, save only such as might, if divulged in public, conduce to results undesirable in the general interest."

On the other side of the astrological coin, there are a great many practitioners of the ancient art whose interests lie elsewhere than serious scholarship. These are the working professionals: The astrologers who cast horoscopes for clients, write or compile columns in newspapers and magazines, and so on. Of course, this does not mean that there are two distinct camps of "serious" and "popular" astrologers. There are merely different levels, ranging from the academic (who may have a few private clients) to the semi-charlatan who may not subscribe to any code of ethics and who may very likely make a lot of money by selling largely prefabricated horoscopes. (In countries like Britain or America, however, where astrological societies keep an eye out for quackery, clients can be fairly sure that a member of such a society is a reliable practitioner.)

It has been estimated that in the U.S.A. there are over 5000 working astrologers, who cater for about 10,000,000 customers. The charge in America for an individual horoscope can often get as high as $100; in Britain the average fee is about £10 ($28) though it can be as low as £2 or as high as £50. Their clients come from all walks of life: from young girls in search of romance to politicians and financiers. Thus there is little doubt that astrology today is very much alive (perhaps more alive than ever before) and on a popular level as well as a serious one—even if to most people it merely means a surreptitious glance at a horoscope column in the newspaper.

Newspaper horoscopes are astrology's most obvious medium in the modern world. Almost every major popular newspaper in America and Britain features an astrological column, as do many big newspapers in Europe. Even in Belgium, where astrology suffered something of an eclipse immediately after the war, half the daily newspapers run a "What the Stars Say" column. And, apart from the large numbers of magazines devoted exclusively to astrology (in the U.S.A. the most popular, *Horoscope*, has a monthly circulation of 170,000), there are innum-

Ingrid Lind, one of Britain's top astrologers and vice-principal of the London Faculty of Astrological Studies, signs diplomas watched by a fellow tutor. Diplomas are awarded by the Faculty to students who successfully complete a two-year course.

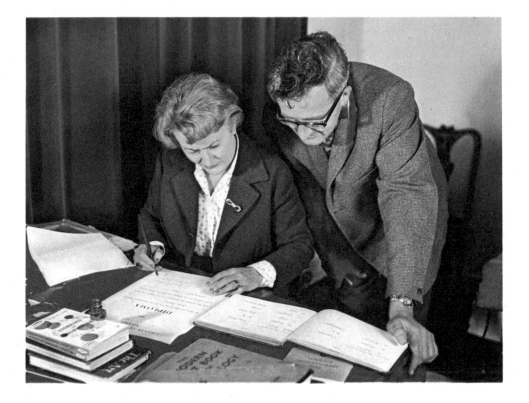

erable periodicals that run a regular horoscope feature. These are usually women's magazines, though evidence shows that men read them too.

Perhaps the best known of these newspaper astrologers is Italy's Francesco Waldner, who produces a syndicated horoscope column that appears in Britain, Italy, and France. Indeed, his feature in the French magazine *Elle* proved so popular that the magazine opened a special horoscope bureau for answering personal questions. And *Elle* (which, incidentally, is read by over half the French adult population) lately ran a feature on the kind of clothes that should be worn by those born under the various Zodiac signs.

As a further sign of astrology's prominence in the 1960s, it should be noticed that advertising people—those knowledgeable takers of the public pulse—often use astrological motifs as eye-catching gimmicks for advertisements. On the assumption, apparently, that the average consumer knows his way around the Zodiac, astrology has been used to sell anything from pre-shrunk shirts to alcoholic drinks. A recent example is a mail-order advertisement in a British women's magazine for a Paris perfume that comes complete with your personal horoscope.

Astrology has also been used in political propaganda, as in the case of a leaflet that was dropped by the French into Austria during World War II. This two-page pamphlet contained stock definitions of Zodiac signs and their effects on individuals; the propagandist part, held back till the last, consisted of the following jingle (entitled "Austrian Groan") bewailing the plight of Austria under the oppression of the Third Reich:

> *Under the banner white and red,*
> *We still had plenty of butter and bread,*
> *Under the Social Democrats*
> *We had lots of roast pork for our lads.*
> *But under your government with Goebbels and Goering,*
> *We only have potatoes and herring.*
> *The Chancellor without spouse,*
> *No bread in the baker's house,*
> *No sow in the butcher's shop:*
> *That's the latest command of the Reich.*

Today, it seems, you can hardly get away from astrology. Israel, for instance, has issued stamps bearing the signs of the Zodiac; and there is an astrological

Many of the institutes and colleges that treat astrology as a serious study hold examinations in order to qualify candidates to practice professionally. Far right, the certificate of proficiency granted by the American Federation of Astrologers; above right, a Belgian certificate issued to students of "scientific astrology"; right, the diploma of the London Faculty of Astrological Studies.

INSTITUT CENTRAL BELGE DE RECHERCHES ASTRO-DYNAMIQUES

ASSOCIATION SANS BUT LUCRATIF, FONDÉE EN 1926

Cours public d'Astrologie Scientifique

DEGRÉ

(1ᵉʳ DEGRÉ — ÉTUDES PRÉLIMINAIRES)
(2ᵉ DEGRÉ — ÉTUDES GÉNÉRALES)
(3ᵉ DEGRÉ — ÉTUDES SPÉCIALES)

CERTIFICAT

Nous attestons que M ——————————

demeurant à ——————— rue ——————— nᵒ ———

a subi avec ———————

l'examen d'études astrologiques du ——————— degré.

Bruxelles, le ———————

LES MEMBRES DU JURY :

VICE-PRÉSIDENT   PRÉSIDENT   PROFESSEUR

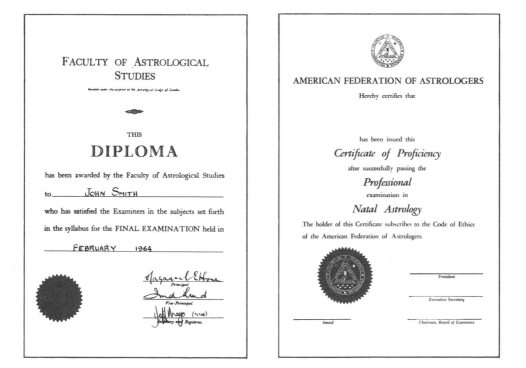

FACULTY OF ASTROLOGICAL STUDIES

founded under the auspices of the Astrological Lodge of London

THIS

DIPLOMA

has been awarded by the Faculty of Astrological Studies

to ___JOHN SMITH___

who has satisfied the Examiners in the subjects set forth

in the syllabus for the FINAL EXAMINATION held in

___FEBRUARY 1964___

Principal
Vice-Principal
(TUTOR)
Secretary and Registrar.

AMERICAN FEDERATION OF ASTROLOGERS

Hereby certifies that

has been issued this

Certificate of Proficiency

after successfully passing the

Professional

examination in

Natal Astrology

The holder of this Certificate subscribes to the Code of Ethics
of the American Federation of Astrologers.

President

Executive Secretary

_____ Issued   Chairman, Board of Examiners

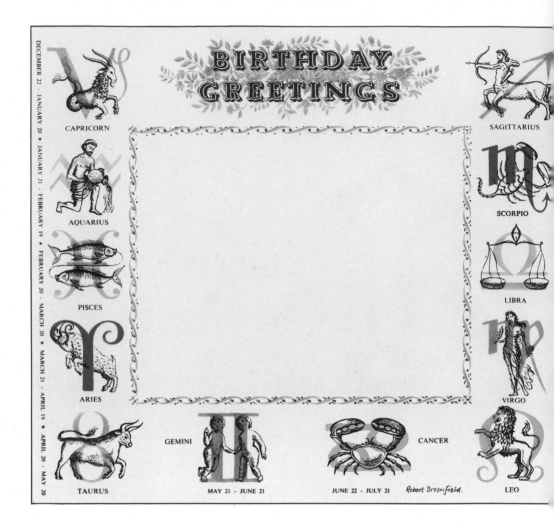

BIRTHDAY GREETINGS

CAPRICORN

AQUARIUS

PISCES

ARIES

TAURUS

GEMINI

MAY 21 - JUNE 21

CANCER

JUNE 22 - JULY 21

Robert Broomfield.

SAGITTARIUS

SCORPIO

LIBRA

VIRGO

LEO

booth in a large Paris department store that gives off-the-cuff predictions to customers.

The different levels of astrology today—from very serious to very popular—are usually well represented at the conventions and conferences that astrologers seem fond of holding. The "International Congress of Astro-Science" (which was held in California from August 29 to September 3, 1963, and which was organized by Dr. Adrian M. Zeigler, President of Astrologers International Ltd.) featured just such a range of interests, from the highly academic to the more light-hearted. On the one hand, there were discussions of astrology and handwriting (or grapho-analysis), of astrology and criminology, and of meteorological astrology; on the other hand, there were talks on subjects like "The Funniest Virgo in Town," and visitors were treated to a "Zodiacal fashion show" and an astrological dance revue.

By way of contrast to this sketch of popular astrology in the Western world today, we can look at its equivalent in Japan: the street-level fortune telling that is carried on from pavement booths in Tokyo. The pavement astrologers,

The familiar figures of the 12 Zodiac signs reappear in an up-to-date form as decoration on Israeli postage stamps (above) and on a British greetings telegram (above left).

FOR ALL THOSE BORN UNDER

Leo (*July 21 - August 22*)
You get a pleasant surprise.
You discover that a new Rolls Rapide
costs only 39 gns cash price because
you buy at straight-from-the-factory cost.

who are known as *Ekisha*, set up their booths at night in shop doorways to attract strollers. Dressed in black kimonos, the Ekisha sit waiting with their books of astrological tables. Forecasts are made from the customer's date and hour of birth, which is then related to the appropriate sign of the Japanese Zodiac. (Incidentally, the Zodiac used by the Japanese has no resemblance to the Western Zodiac. Each of the 12 signs corresponds exactly to one calendar month and all are named after animals: March, for example, falls under the Tiger, and May under the Dragon.) This forecast is tallied with the lines on the customer's palm (read with the aid of a large magnifying glass). The chances of the prediction's being fulfilled are determined by shaking a number of sticks in a shaker, removing a handful, and then counting the remainder. (Different numbers imply different degrees of accuracy.) It is said that most Ekisha are too busy to close their booths much before dawn.

Apparently, in Japan as in the West, demand has created supply. That is, astrology seems to be "what the public wants"; and so they get it. And they get it in a wide variety of forms and, sometimes, from some quite unexpected quarters. Perhaps to end this chapter, we may offer two recent examples—one from India and the other from Britain—that demonstrate how astrology is liable to crop up even today in the most remarkable and unexpected places.

The universal appeal of the Zodiac (as well as its decorative value) has often been exploited as a sales device. Here the signs are featured by two British firms in advertisements for washing machines (left) and non-shrink cottons (right). Below, a display of Zodiac jewelry in a Paris department store.

YOUR HOROSCOPE

TAURUS

The Bull
April 21 – May 22

Taurus subjects can look forward in complete confidence. A year free from the worries of shrinkage is forecast, under the guiding star of "Sanforized". Familiar faces will be unusually welcome. "Sanforized" will continue to give a strong helping hand with cottons.

"Sanforized" Service
20 St. Ann's Square, Manchester 2. BLA 8489/2916

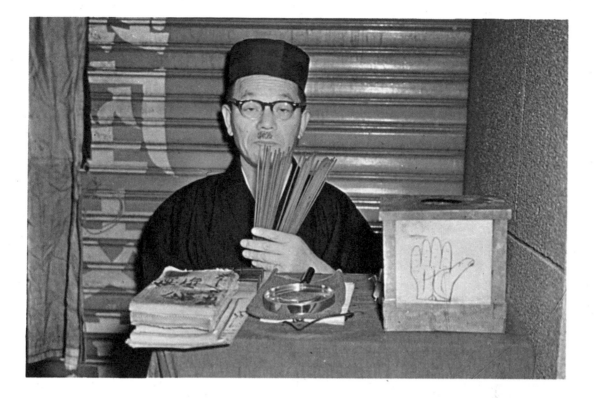

The popular Japanese pavement fortune tellers known as *Ekisha* usually combine astrology with palmistry. Left, an Ekisha examining a client's palm with a magnifying glass; above, he holds the sticks that are used to assess a forecast's chances of fulfillment. Astrologers are regularly consulted in Thailand as well as in Japan: The Thai boxer Pone Kingpetch (left of picture, right) has publicly stated his reluctance to fight on days that are astrologically inauspicious.

DR. A. M. ZIEGLER / CONFERENCE DIRECTOR   AUGUST 29 THRU SEPTEMBER 3, 1963

INTERNATIONAL CONGRESS of ASTRO SCIENCE

THE ZODIAC

MARCH 21

APRIL 20

MAY 21

DEC 22

NOV 23

OCT 23

SEPT. 23

AUG. 24

MIRAMAR HOTEL

PACIFIC OCEAN PARK

MARINELAND

Astrology often makes news, even in the non-specialist press. Above, the British astrologer Edward Whitman, whose comments on the end of the world that was forecast by Indian astrologers for February 5, 1962, were published in a top Sunday newspaper. Left, the cover of a brochure produced for the widely publicized International Congress of Astro-Science held in California in September 1963. Right, a cartoon from a British newspaper that followed a magistrate's suggestion that horoscopes should be cast and interpreted for "juvenile delinquents."

The first was mentioned in Chapter 1 : the end of the world on February 5, 1962, which caused such a stir among the wise men of India. The writer of an article in the British *Sunday Times* for February 4 had taken the trouble to interview a number of people on this prospect. Among others he interviewed Edward Whitman, Secretary of the Federation of British Astrologers. Mr. Whitman was not worried about the morrow : He explained that the Hindus use a fixed Zodiac whereas he, like all good Westerners, uses a moving Zodiac. Moral (apparently) : The world may end for them, but not for us. Over in the U.S.A., however, 22 members of a society called "Understanding Inc." believed the Hindu astrologers and retreated to a small town in the Arizona mountains that they considered, for some reason, to be one place fated to survive the general catastrophe.

Another story reported in the British papers (in December 1962) was that of Charles Legh Shuldham Cornwall-Legh, chairman of the Cheshire Police Authority, and chairman of the Magistrates' Bench at Lymm, Cheshire. This important person came out into the open as saying : "I look forward to the time when it will be standard practice to have available for magistrates an interpreted horoscope of every child charged with a serious offence."

Just how much Mr. Cornwall-Legh was asking will be seen in the next chapter. To *cast* the horoscope of a juvenile delinquent, or anyone else, it would be necessary to know the exact time of his birth (how many people do?). To *interpret* a horoscope, as will be seen, requires a great deal of skill and a good deal of time and trouble.

8   The anatomy of the horoscope

Earlier in this book we looked at some of the basic constituents of a horoscope: the planets, the signs of the Zodiac, and the houses. Some knowledge of these things was necessary before one could move with any sureness through the centuries of astrology's history. Now, having brought that story up to date, we must change our ground and go back to looking at astrological fundamentals —in other words, at the horoscope itself, which is as basic to astrology as, say, the plan of a building is to an architect.

Most of the more technical details in the following pages have been supplied by a very reliable authority on the subject; but, as far as traditional astrology is concerned, there are many textbooks in which the same details are available (though sometimes in an over-simplified or, more often, an over-complicated form). Apart from house division, there is little argument about what the astrologer does when he is casting a horoscope. And in fact anyone can learn to erect a "natal chart" in an hour or two. Just as anyone can learn to draw a building plan. But this doesn't mean he can build the building; or, if he can, that it will stay standing. In the same way, it is the *interpretation* of the horoscope that separates the astrological men from the boys—and that causes the arguments to rage.

But we are first concerned with casting or erecting the chart. To refresh the reader's memory briefly: A horoscope consists of a geocentric map of the solar

A 17th-century Dutch map of astrology's earth-centered universe encircled by the Zodiac band—the system that appears in diagrammatic form on every horoscope chart. The various lines connecting the 12 Zodiac signs illustrate the planetary aspects: The red lines link four planets in "square"; the light blue lines, six planets in "sextile"; other lines forming equilateral triangles join three planets in "trine."

system at a given moment of time. On this map the positions of the Sun, Moon, and the other eight planets are calculated in relation to the signs of the Zodiac. The Zodiac is an imaginary band of sky representing the Sun's annual path through the fixed stars. (The Sun's apparent "movement" along this path is, of course, produced by the earth's own annual orbit around the Sun.) With the exception of Pluto, all the planets also appear to move around the earth within about 8° of the center of this band of sky.

Most modern astrologers are primarily interested in "natal" or "genethliacal" horoscopy—that is, they are interested in the individual horoscope, which is erected for a specific *time* (if possible, to the nearest minute) and takes into account the exact *geographical position* (latitude and longitude) of the individual's birthplace. (The individual for whom a horoscope is cast is usually called the "native.") These, then, are the essential data that the astrologer must have to cast a horoscope: date of birth, accurate time of birth, place of birth. With these, the astrologer sets out to compute the native's *ascendant* and its related *medium coeli* (M.C. or mid-heaven).

He makes his computations with the aid of two reference books (which are not difficult to find in libraries or bookshops). One is called an *ephemeris* (we have inherited the name and the thing from the Greeks), which tells you what was where in the solar system at any particular time. The other book is called a *table of houses* by which the astrologer makes corrections with regard to the position of the individual's birthplace. (Some ephemerides include tables of houses for particular latitudes.)

The astrologer's first step is to find out (from his ephemeris) what the *sidereal time* was at noon on the day of birth in question. Sidereal time is measured by the stars and not (like ordinary clock time) by the Sun. In a sidereal day the stars appear to have made one complete circuit of the sky; but the Sun hasn't quite completed its apparent circuit. So the sidereal day is a few minutes (of clock time) shorter than the ordinary day. This discrepancy, known as the "acceleration on interval," must be allowed for when calculating the sidereal time at birth.

Astrology uses sidereal time (usually written as just S.T.) as a means of indicating the positions of the stars as seen at a given time and place. To put it briefly, the astrologer must translate his information (birth time and birthplace) into S.T. so that he can use his tables—since these give the positions of the stars and planets in terms of S.T. The S.T. is found by simple arithmetic.

The ephemeris obviously cannot give the S.T. that corresponds with every minute of every day; so all it gives is the corresponding S.T. to noon on the day in question. Then the astrologer must work out the S.T. of the moment of birth. He works this out by *adding* the necessary number of hours and minutes for births after noon, and *subtracting* them for births before noon. For example:

Assume that the birth date in question is July 5, 1960, and that the time of birth is 7.20 P.M. (We will also assume, to avoid questions of longitude for the moment, that this is the birth date of someone born near the meridian of Greenwich. Thus that time of birth—7.20 P.M.—will be in Greenwich Mean Time, or G.M.T.) The ephemeris tells us that, on that date, the S.T. at noon was six hours, 53 minutes, and 56 seconds. Now, since the time of the birth in question was *after* noon, to find the S.T. for the precise moment of birth we must add seven hours 20 minutes (known as the "interval") to the S.T. at noon. We must also allow for the "acceleration on interval" by adding 10 seconds for each hour—which works out at one minute 13 seconds. We get the following total :

$$6^h\ 53^m\ 56^s$$
$$+\ 7^h\ 20^m\ \ \ 0^s$$
$$+\ \ \ \ \ \ \ 1^m\ 13^s$$
$$\overline{14^h\ 15^m\ \ \ 9^s}$$

Most of the commonly used ephemerides use G.M.T. as a standard. So, for natives not born on the Greenwich meridian, the time of birth must be converted into G.M.T. before the above addition can be performed. For instance, Central European Time is one hour fast by comparison with G.M.T. while Eastern Standard Time (U.S.A.) is five hours slow. So for a birth at New York at 9 P.M. the G.M.T. is 4 P.M.; for a birth at Munich at 1 P.M. C.E.T., the equivalent G.M.T. is noon.

Now we have established the S.T. that corresponds to the time of birth in Greenwich time. We must next convert this into *local* S.T. for people born in places other than on the Greenwich meridian. This involves *longitude* : We must

A world map shows the earth divided into 24 different time zones. (The international date line marks the point where one weekday becomes the next.) The figures at the bottom show the time in each zone corresponding to noon in Greenwich Mean Time.

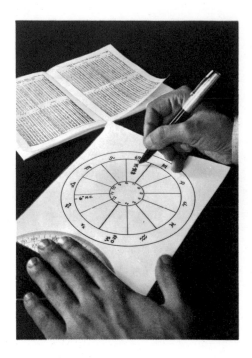

An astrologer casting a horoscope: His equipment consists of a protractor to plot the exact positions of the various elements of the horoscope; an ephemeris (a book containing the tables necessary for his calculations); and a blank horoscope chart on which he writes the specific details of the "native's" horoscope. Here he is writing in the planet Venus (having already filled in the ascendant, Zodiac signs, and M.C.).

convert degrees and minutes of longitude (east or west of the Greenwich meridian) into minutes and seconds of time. This, too, is a simple process. Longitude is transformed into time simply by multiplying by four. For instance:

Vienna is 16° 22′ 54″ east of Greenwich. Multiply this by four, and the result is 65 minutes 32 seconds (of time). Now, because Vienna is east of Greenwich, this 65ᵐ 32ˢ would be added to the s.t. at Greenwich. (Subtract for all points west.)

Here we might pause and review these manipulations of time. The astrologer first takes the moment of birth as it is expressed in *local time* (Central European, Eastern Standard, or whatever) and translates it into Greenwich Mean Time. Then, using the ephemeris, he translates that into sidereal time *for Greenwich*. Finally, using longitude, he arrives at the moment of birth expressed in sidereal time *for the birthplace*.

Next, *latitude* (north or south of the equator) comes in. The astrologer looks into his tables of houses and finds that, at the already-established sidereal time of birth and at the given latitude of the birthplace, a certain degree of the Zodiac was "rising" over the eastern horizon. This is the ascendant. And now the job of calculating the horoscope is nearly done.

(The astrologer must know the exact latitude—for the same sidereal time will give different ascendants for different latitudes. For example, an s.t. of 13ʰ 2ᵐ 40ˢ gives an ascendant of 20° 19′ Sagittarius at the latitude of 46° North, but gives an ascendant of 10° 26′ Sagittarius at 56° North.)

When the ascendant has been calculated, it is marked on the blank circle of the horoscope chart. A line is drawn connecting the degree of the ascendant with a point exactly opposite on the other side of the chart—which is the descendant. The table of houses also gives the related *mid-heaven* or M.C., and so the astrologer draws a line bisecting the ascendant-descendant line connecting the M.C. and the *imum coeli*. And there he has the four angles of the chart and its quadrants.

During any period of 24 hours there are 360 possible ascendants, each with its related mid-heaven. A different (succeeding) degree of the ecliptic (and therefore of the Zodiac) "rises" above the horizon every four minutes. So if Smith was born five minutes after Jones (even if they were both born in the same place), Smith will have a different degree of the Zodiac for his ascendant. And if Jones's ascendant was, say, 30° Scorpio, Smith will also have a different ascendant *sign*—1° Sagittarius.

Unfortunately, with the vast majority of people it is not so easy to establish the ascendant and mid-heaven with the proper accuracy. You are lucky if the ascendant is accurate to within even three or four degrees—i.e., 12 to 16 minutes of time. This might make a very serious difference, since the sign on the ascendant may have changed in that time; and, as we have seen, adjacent signs (like Aries and Taurus) tend to be very unlike each other. Both ancient and modern astrologers have stressed the deplorable results of such vagueness about the time of one's birth. But the same vagueness does, of course, supply the astrologer with a ready-made excuse for an inaccurate prediction.

Assuming that the ascendant and mid-heaven *have* been accurately established, the astrologer then proceeds to fill in the so-called "house" boundaries. (The data for these is obtained from tables of houses for the latitude in question.) Commencing at the ascendant, which is the "cusp" or beginning of the first house, the horoscope is then divided into 12 sectors or houses.

Incidentally, very few astrologers understand the various mathematical theories of house division, since an expert knowledge of spherical trigonometry is required. Most people use Placidus tables (named after Placidus de Tito, the 17th-century Italian astronomer and astrologer), not because they are necessarily the best but because they are most readily available. Regiomontanus and Campanus tables can also be found, as well as the new *Geburtsorthäuser* (birthplace) tables recently calculated by Dr. W. A. Koch of Germany, who is one of the world's greatest experts in this very difficult field. But in all the latter cases the degree values of the intermediate cusps (i.e., for houses 2, 3, 5, 6, 8, 9, 11, and 12) will be different from the Placidean cusps. Thus four different astrologers, each using a different house division system, will produce four different horoscopes as far as the intermediate houses are concerned, although the ascendant and mid-heaven will be the same in each case.

Enemies of astrology like the late Robert Eisler have found in these disagreements about house division some very nice fuel for their polemics. Eisler

D M	D W	Sidereal Time.	☉ Long.	☉ Dec.	☽ Long.	☽ Lat.	☽ Dec.	MIDNIGHT ☽Long.	MIDNIGHT ☽Dec.	Ψ Long.	♅ Long.	L
		H. M. S.	° ′ ″	° ′	° ′ ″	° ′	° ′	° ′ ″	° ′ ″	° ′	° ′	°
1	F	6 38 9	9♋37 48	23 N 6	1♎43 14	1 N13	0 N26	8♎11 7	1 S 38	6♏26	18♌51	15
2	S	6 42 6	10 35 0	23 1	14 44 55	2 18	3 S 42	21 25 5	5 45	6 ℞26	18 54	15
3	☉	6 46 3	11 32 11	22 56	28 12 1	3 17	7 46	5♏ 5 59	9 43	6 25	18 58	15
4	M	6 49 59	12 29 22	22 51	12♏ 7 7	4 7	11 33	19 15 21	13 15 6	6 25	19 1	15
5	Tu	6 53 56	13 26 34	22 46	26 30 28	4 43	14 47	3 ♐52 0	16 6	6 24	19 4	15

How to cast the horoscope of a "native" born in London on July 5, 1960, at 7.20 P.M. The first step is to calculate the sidereal time at birth. The time of birth and the "acceleration on interval" (which is worked out as explained on p. 245) are added to the S.T. for noon on July 5 (found on Table I). The result of this addition (far right) is the S.T. at birth. The next step : The S.T. at birth is related to Table II, which gives 0° 29′ Capricorn as the ascendant and 6° Scorpio as the M.C. These are plotted on the horoscope and the other Zodiac signs written in.

Next, the positions of the faster-moving planets must be found—for example, Venus. Find the *motion* of Venus on Table III (1°14′). Then find on Table IV the log of 1°14′ (12891) and the log of the interval of 7h 20m (5149) ; add these and convert the total (18040) into degrees (23′) in the way explained on p. 250. Add this figure to the position of Venus at noon, found on Table 1—16°59′ in Cancer— and you have Venus's position at the birth time (17°22′ Cancer). The process is repeated for the other fast-moving planets. The positions of the slower planets (in red on Table I) are transferred straight onto the chart. (The position of Pluto is found on Table V.) The chart is now complete.

II TABLES OF HOUSES FOR LONDON

Sidereal Time.	10 ♏	11 ♏	12 ♐	Ascen ♐		2 ♒	3 ♓
H. M. S.	°	°	°	°	′	°	°
13 51 37	0	22	10	25	20	10	27
13 55 27	1	23	11	26	10	11	28
13 59 17	2	24	11	27	2	12	♈
14 3 8	3	25	12	27	53	14	1
14 6 59	4	26	13	28	45	15	2
14 10 51	5	26	14	29	36	16	4
14 14 44	6	27	15	0♑29		18	5
14 18 37	7	28	15	1	23	19	6
14 22 31	8	29	16	2	18	20	8
14 26 25	9	♐	17	3	14	22	9

III   JULY

D	☉	☽	♂	♀	☿	☽ dec.
	° ′ ″	° ′ ″	° ′	° ′	° ′	° ′
1	0 57 12	13 1 41	42	1 14	0 7	4 8
2	0 57 11	13 27 6	43	1 14	0 3	4 4
3	0 57 11	13 55 6	43	1 13	0 3	3 47
4	0 57 12	14 23 21	43	1 14	0 6	3 14
5	0 57 10	14 48 48	42	1 14	0 12	2 22

IV   ⚹ PROPORTIONAL LOGARITHMS FOR FINDING THE PLANETS' PLACES

Min.	DEGREES OR HOURS																Min.
	0	1	2	3	4	5	6	7	8	9	10	11	12	13	14	15	
0	3.1584	1.3802	1.0792	9031	7781	6812	6021	5351	4771	4260	3802	3388	3010	2663	2341	2041	0
1	3.1584	1.3730	1.0756	9007	7763	6798	6009	5341	4762	4252	3795	3382	3004	2657	2336	2036	1
2	2.8573	1,3660	1.0720	8983	7745	6784	5997	5330	4753	4244	3788	3375	2998	2652	2330	2032	2
3	2.6812	1.3590	1.0685	8959	7728	6769	5985	5320	4744	4236	3780	3368	2992	2646	2325	2027	3
4	2.5563	1.3522	1.0649	8935	7710	6755	5973	5310	4735	4228	3773	3362	2986	2640	2320	2022	4
5	2.4594	1.3454	1.0614	8912	7692	6741	5961	5300	4726	4220	3766	3355	2980	2635	2315	2017	5
6	2.3802	1.3388	1.0580	8888	7674	6726	5949	5289	4717	4212	3759	3349	2974	2629	2310	2012	6
7	2.3133	1.3323	1.0546	8865	7657	6712	5937	5279	4708	4204	3752	3342	2968	2624	2305	2008	7
8	2.2553	1.3258	1.0511	8842	7639	6698	5925	5269	4699	4196	3745	3336	2962	2618	2300	2003	8
9	2.2041	1.3195	1.0478	8819	7622	6684	5913	5259	4690	4188	3737	3329	2956	2613	2295	1998	9
10	2.1584	1.3133	1.0444	8796	7604	6670	5902	5249	4682	4180	3730	3323	2950	2607	2289	1993	10
11	2.1170	1.3071	1.0411	8773	7587	6656	5890	5239	4673	4172	3723	3316	2944	2602	2284	1988	11
12	2.0792	1.3010	1.0378	8751	7570	6642	5878	5229	4664	4164	3716	3310	2938	2596	2279	1984	12
13	2.0444	1.2950	1.0345	8728	7552	6628	5866	5219	4655	4156	3709	3303	2933	2591	2274	1979	13
14	2.0122	1.2891	1.0313	8706	7535	6614	5855	5209	4646	4148	3702	3297	2927	2585	2269	1974	14
15	1.9823	1.2833	1.0280	8683	7518	6600	5843	5199	4638	4141	3695	3291	2921	2580	2264	1969	15
16	1.9542	1.2775	1.0248	8661	7501	6587	5832	5189	4629	4133	3688	3284	2915	2574	2259	1965	16
17	1.9279	1.2719	1.0216	8639	7484	6573	5820	5179	4620	4125	3681	3278	2909	2569	2254	1960	17
18	1.9031	1.2663	1.0185	8617	7467	6559	5809	5169	4611	4117	3674	3271	2903	2564	2249	1955	18
19	1.8796	1.2607	1.0153	8595	7451	6546	5797	5159	4603	4109	3667	3265	2897	2558	2244	1950	19
20	1.8573	1.2553	1.0122	8573	7434	6532	5786	5149	4594	4102	3660	3258	2891	2553	2239	1946	20
21	1.8361	1.2499	1.0091	8552	7417	6519	5774	5139	4585	4094	3653	3252	2885	2547	2234	1941	21
22	1.8159	1.2445	1.0061	8530	7401	6505	5763	5129	4577	4086	3646	3246	2880	2542	2229	1936	22
23	1.7966	1.2393	1.0030	8509	7384	6492	5752	5120	4568	4079	3639	3239	2874	2536	2223	1932	23

♃	♂	♀	☿	Lunar Aspects.								
Long.	Long.	Long.	Long.	⊙	♇	♆	♅	♄	♃	♂	♀	☿
♐18	8♉ 4	12♋ 4	0♌ 5	∠	∨	∠		□				✳
℞10	8 46	13 18	0 12	□	∠	✳	□					
3	9 29	14 32	0 15	✳				✳				□
56	10 12	15 45	0 ℞12	△	☌	□	✳	∠	☍	△		
49	10 55	16 59	0 6	⊡			∠	∨		⊡		△

V   THE POSITION OF PLUTO (♇) IN 1960.

Date.	Long.	Lat.	Dec.
	° ′	° ′	° ′
May 10	3♍36	12 N 30	21 N 48
20	3 D 36	12 27	21 45
30	3 39	12 24	21 41
June 9	3 45	12 21	21 36
19	3 54	12 18	21 30
29	4 5	12 16	21 24
July 9		12 14	21 16
19	4 35	12 12	21 9
29	4 53	12 11	21 1
Aug. 8	5 12	12 10	20 53
18	5 31	12 10	20 46

date of birth	July 5, 1960
place	London
latitude	51° 30′
time of birth	19hrs. 20mins.

time of birth	19	20	0
−noon	12	0	0
interval	7	20	0
+sidereal time	6	53	56
	14	13	56
+acceleration on interval		1	13
sidereal time at birth	14	15	9
motion of ♀ on July 5	1°	14′	
log of 1° 14′	1.2891		
+constant log	5149		
	1.8040		

position of ♀ on July 5	16°	59′ in ♋
+converted result of log=		
movement of ♀ in 7° 20′		23′
position of ♀ at birth	17°	22′ in ♋

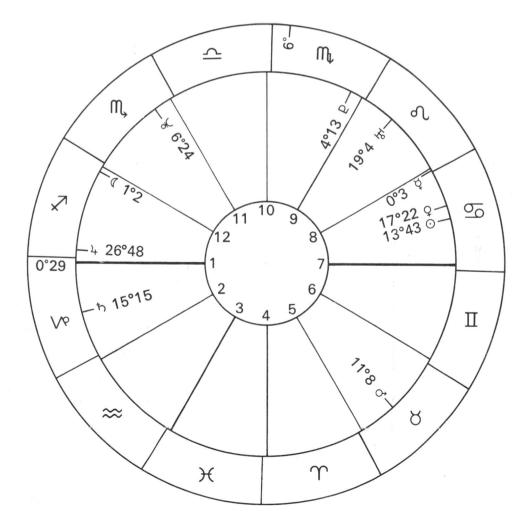

maintains that in the ancient world the original division was into *eight* houses, arrived at simply by halving each quarter of the heaven. The division of 12, he argues, has nothing to do with the divisions of the horizon "but rests originally on the division of the day into twelve hours of *variable* seasonal length" (italics mine).

But to get back to our horoscope: The astrologer now fills in the position of the Sun, Moon, and planets. In the case of the *slower*-moving planets (Saturn, Uranus, Neptune, Jupiter, and Pluto), this is a simple matter of referring to the ephemeris, finding the positions for noon on the day of birth, and transferring these straight onto the chart. But for the *faster*-moving planets (Venus, Mercury, the Sun and Moon), the positions must be adjusted to allow for planetary movement between noon and the time of birth. To clarify the calculations involved, refer to the sample horoscope on p. 249 and find the position of Venus.

First, since we are dealing with time after noon, we look up in the ephemeris the planet's motion at noon on the day of birth. (For before-noon time, look up the planetary motion for the previous day.) We then turn to the log tables at the back of the ephemeris and find the log of this motion; to this we add the log of seven hours 20 minutes (the interval) and convert the total back into degrees. This gives us the difference in Venus's position between noon and 7.20 P.M. We add this figure to the noon position of Venus (given in the ephemeris) and we have the position of Venus at 7.20 P.M. Incidentally, for a planet that is retrograde (marked by R in the tables), the whole process would be reversed; that is, we subtract the movement on interval from the planet's position at noon.

A word of reminder about aspects is necessary here. Obviously, among the slower-moving planets, such important aspects as conjunctions, squares, and oppositions can occur only at rare intervals. During a period of five years Saturn moves only about 60°, Uranus 20°, Neptune 10°, and Pluto 8°. But during the same five-year period the Sun will have circled the Zodiac five times (5 × 360°

Campanus   Regiomontanus

250

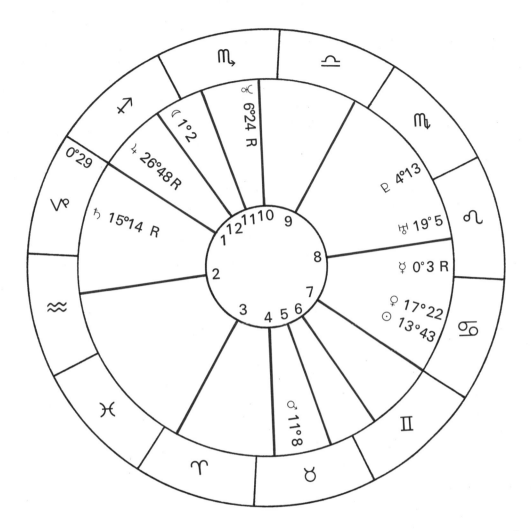

Above, a chart showing "unequal" house division according to the system evolved by Regiomontanus. Left, a diagram of Regiomontanus's "space" system shows six of the 12 circles that represent the houses (like segments of an orange) marked off along the celestial equator (C). The houses' divisions, or cusps (which must be calculated by trigonometry), are the points on the ecliptic (B) cut by the circles. Far left, a diagram of Campanus's method of house division, which also results in their unequal size. In this case, the houses are divided along the "prime vertical"—the line joining the zenith and the nadir (A).

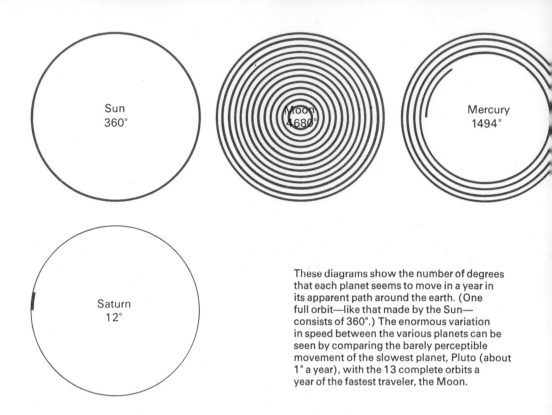

Sun
360°

Moon
4680°

Mercury
1494°

Saturn
12°

These diagrams show the number of degrees that each planet seems to move in a year in its apparent path around the earth. (One full orbit—like that made by the Sun—consists of 360°.) The enormous variation in speed between the various planets can be seen by comparing the barely perceptible movement of the slowest planet, Pluto (about 1° a year), with the 13 complete orbits a year of the fastest traveler, the Moon.

= 1800°) and the Moon will have circled it about 60 times. Thus while a Saturn-Jupiter conjunction, for instance, will occur only once every 19,859 years, Sun-Moon conjunctions occur monthly, and the faster planets (including the Sun and Moon) are constantly forming new aspects with each other and with all the slower planets.

It thus follows that everybody born during a given month of any year will have four of the eight planets in very much the same positions in their horoscope charts. Again, if one ignores the Moon (which moves about 12° during 24 hours and will therefore pass from one Zodiacal sign to another every two or three days), there is no marked change during the course of a week as far as the aspects are concerned, although one or more planets may have passed into a fresh sign of the Zodiac.

Here, finally, is a quick summary of the entire procedure:
1.   Find out the native's date of birth, exact time of birth, and place of birth. Also the longitude and latitude of place of birth.
2.   Find out from the ephemeris the sidereal time at noon (G.M.T.) for the given day of birth.
3.   By simple addition or subtraction, find the equivalent S.T. for the moment of birth (making sure that the moment is expressed in G.M.T.).
4.   Convert the longitude of the native's place of birth into hours, minutes, and seconds by multiplying by four.
5.   Find the *local* S.T. for the place of birth by adding or subtracting the longitude to or from the Greenwich S.T.

6. Look up the local s.t. in a table of houses to find the ascendant and the mid-heaven.

7. Fill in the ascendant, descendant, mid-heaven, and *imum coeli* on the blank horoscope chart.

8. Fill in the positions of the houses, according to the tables.

9. Fill in the positions of the planets, also according to the tables (remembering again to convert Greenwich s.t. into local s.t.).

10. Interpret the completed horoscope.

The problem of interpretation

Anyone can soon memorize and master the first nine steps of the astrologer's procedure. The stumbling block is number 10. How (and from where) can a beginner learn what the chart itself "means"?

For most astrologers, the conventional basis for interpretation is "the tradition"—essentially a literary tradition, based upon a long succession of astrological manuscripts (for the centuries prior to the invention of printing in 1440) and upon the many hundreds of books and manuals published after that date. The tradition is immense, varied, and still growing. To read the entirety would require an incredible effort of scholarship on the part of a would-be astrologer. What actually happens instead is that every new generation of astrologers, in its own manuals, rewrites the fundamental principles of astrology in a contemporary idiom. Even A. J. Pearce's once immensely popular *The Text-Book of Astrology* (two volumes, 1879-89) now seems fairly outdated.

air: ♊ ♒ ♎   water: ♋ ♏ ♓

The majority of astrologers learn interpretation from such books. Margaret E. Hone, for instance, advises the student of astrology that he "will *never* become fluent and quick in interpretation until he so thoroughly grasps the nature of each *planet, sign, house* and *aspect,* that he can apply them as related in any chart, without constant reference to books." But, she adds, the beginner "needs the help of books in his work, at first."

The heavy weight of the tradition thus prevents the astrologer from bringing very much originality into his interpretative work. The meanings of the various parts of the horoscope were settled long ago; and most astrologers accept them. This acceptance can be seen in practically any set of excerpts, dealing with the same subject, from the astrological textbooks. For example, the following is a set of quotations concerning the first house of the horoscope (which begins at the point of the all-important ascendant). To lead off, here is the meaning of the first house according to John Gadbury's *The Doctrine of Nativities* (1658), which corresponds in most respects with similar examples from 16th- and 17th-century French manuals:

"This House hath proper Signification of the Life of the Native; his Stature, Form and Shape; the Temperature and Accidents of the Body; the Qualities of the Minde; the Visage, its Fashion, Complexion and Colour, and all the Parts thereof . . . Sun in the first [House] makes the native honoured among his brethren . . . he will rule over others; will acquire Authority, Honour, and Dignity from Princes; he will have a great increase of Riches; he will be of long life and powerful."

Sepharial, one of the British astrological writers whom we have met before, closely follows Gadbury in his *A New Manual of Astrology* (1898):

"The first House denotes the body of the native, his physical condition and appearance. . . ." And further: "Sun in First House gives honour and success. A proud disposition; frank, outspoken, generous; despising cliques and coteries; independent and firm. It also gives a love of display and publicity, accompanied by high motives."

fire: ♈ ♌ ♐

earth: ♉ ♍ ♑

As well as ascribing individual qualities to the signs and houses, astrology also classes them into various groups, whose meanings must also be considered when a horoscope is interpreted. The medieval German paintings (above) illustrate the four "elements" of air, water, fire, and earth. The four "triplicities," each comprising three signs, are as follows: *airy* signs indicating "intellectual and articulate" character; *watery*, "emotional and unstable"; *fiery*, "ardent and keen"; *earthy*, "practical and cautious."

Right, a diagram representing the "quadruplicities"—a division of the signs into three groups of four: The *cardinal* signs are linked by the blue lines; the *fixed* by the red; the *mutable* by the black.

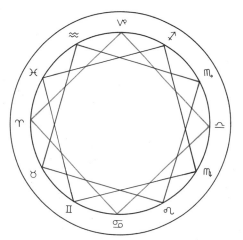

Right, a diagram shows the 12 houses colored to show their classification into *angular* (light blue), implying initiative; *succedent* (white), steadiness of purpose; *cadent* (dark blue), widespread activity.

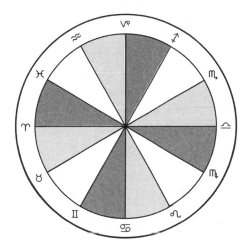

255

A sample interpretation based on the horoscope on p. 249

1 General view of the chart	No marked tendency for harmony or disharmony, though the influence of Saturn is strong (see below, 11 and 14).
2 The quadruplicities	These are well balanced : three planets in cardinal signs, three in mutable, and four in fixed. The slight edge toward fixed is offset by the fact that neither the ascendant nor the Sun is in the fixed quadruplicity.
3 The elements	There are four planets in fiery signs, three (and the ascendant) in earthy, three (and the M.C.) in watery, but none in airy. The absence of "airiness" might result in a lack of intellect, though the native is strong in common sense ("earthy") and intuition ("watery").
4 Rising and setting planets	Saturn in the first house and Jupiter above the horizon in the 12th (both rising) may produce a conflict between restraint and expansiveness. Sun and Venus setting indicate an orientation toward others.
5 Position of the planets above or below the horizon	More planets are above the horizon, adding to the "outward" orientation of the personality.
6 Planetary occupation of the four quadrants	The accent is on the third quadrant (five planets from the seventh house to the M.C.), emphasizing the importance of the seventh, eighth, and ninth houses.
7 The decanates	Since the ascendant is in the first decanate of Capricorn, the native's personality will be almost entirely Capricornian.
8 The Sun's position in relation to the Zodiac	The Sun is in Cancer, which gives Cancerian qualities to the "deeper self."
9 The Moon's position in relation to the Zodiac	The Moon is in Sagittarius, whose qualities will affect automatic reactions and manner. The strong difference between Sagittarius and Cancer will create some deep-seated conflict.
10 The ascendant's position in relation to the Zodiac	Capricorn as the rising sign or ascendant will affect physical appearance.
11 The ascendant's ruler	Saturn, ruler of Capricorn, is in Capricorn, and in the first house, which gives the planet an immense influence in the horoscope. The native must try to overcome his excess of "Saturnine" coldness, caution, meanness, etc.
12 Planets in relation to the houses	Sun, Mercury, and Venus in the seventh house help to orient the native toward others, offsetting Saturn's selfishness. Mars in the fifth gives physical energy and magnetism. Neptune in the 11th—in conjunction with the M.C., the "career point"—lends ambition and creativity to the personality. Uranus in the eighth gives an interest in mysticism, counteracting Saturn's "heaviness."

13	Planets in relation to the Zodiac signs	Jupiter and Saturn are (as we have seen) in their own signs, increasing the strength of each. Mars in Taurus adds to sensuality.
14	Planetary aspects	The Sun is in conjunction with Venus, in good aspect to Mars and Neptune, and in bad aspect to Saturn. Some effects of these aspects we have seen. The Sun's good aspect to Mars adds to the strength of personality, and the Moon's good aspect to Mercury gives emotional stability. Mercury's bad aspect to Neptune might add to the tendency to escapism. Venus's bad aspects to the Moon, Saturn, Pluto, and Uranus indicate difficulties in love and marriage. Mars's good aspect to Saturn balances energy with caution. Mars's bad aspect to Uranus could mean an explosive nature under the surface.

A generation later V. E. Robson, in his *A Beginner's Guide to Practical Astrology* (1931), wrote:

"[The first house indicates] the Native, or subject of the Horoscope himself; his appearance, habits, characteristics, health, temperament and the general way in which he looks on the world. . . . Sun in 1st: generous, dignified, proud, ambitious, confident, boastful, fond of display, independent. Honour and success. Good vitality. Few brothers."

The modern German "cosmobiologer" Reinhold Ebertin is one of the mavericks who prefer to bring in their own interpretative meanings, breaking entirely with the traditional formulations of the Gadbury-Sepharial-Robson school. In his book *The Combination of Stellar Influences* (1950) Ebertin defines the ascendant as "Personality (Environment)," adding that the individual's psychological characteristics would then depend upon the Zodiacal sign in which the ascendant happened to be. He also relates the ascendant to "reactions to the external world, the 'I' in relation to other people, especially those in the native's environment."

But even with all the reference books at his elbow the beginner still will not find interpretation a simple process. The horoscope contains a great many factors, some quite complex, all of which (if the job is to be done properly) must be taken into consideration. To underline some "ingredients":

There are the quadruplicities—i.e., the number of planets respectively in cardinal, fixed, and mutable signs of the Zodiac. (Aries is cardinal, Taurus fixed, and Gemini mutable, and the succession runs cardinal, fixed, mutable throughout the remaining signs. An excess of planets of one "quality" is said to make the native psychologically one-sided.) And there are the triplicities—the number of planets in fiery, earthy, airy, and watery signs. (Aries is fiery, Taurus earthy, Gemini airy, Cancer watery, and so on in the fire-earth-air-water succession throughout the remaining signs. A person with many planets in *fixed* and *earthy* signs, for instance, might be considered potentially phlegmatic.)

Also important are the number of planets in the east and west respectively (it is thought that if the majority of planets are in the western half of the chart, their effects would be especially noticeable in the second half of the native's life); and the number of planets above and below the horizon—the line joining the ascendant and descendant (planets below the horizon are considered less "effective" than those above it).

These are only a few of the separate elements of an individual horoscope—quite a long way from the "if you were born with your Sun in Taurus" kind of astrology popularized by the newspapers. What is required is the ability to grasp and interpret all these combinations and then, from the available "evidence," to arrive at a reasonable synthesis of what it all means or is supposed to mean.

Whatever else they may have invented, the early astrologers were responsible for the first known attempt at a complete system of human typology. Nearly all astrologers classify people by their *Zodiacal* types; but for one "pure" type there are many mixed, where more than one Zodiacal sign has a say in the native's constitution. Oddly enough, we are assured, the pure types are often quite evident and a skilled astrologer will be able to hit upon a person's Sun-sign and/or ascendant with remarkable accuracy without knowing the birth month. This can often be done on the basis of only a casual encounter and a few minutes of conversation, during which the subject will give himself away quite unconsciously.

There are "planetary" types as well: The man with the "sunny" disposition, the "lunatic," the mercurial, martial, jovial (Jupiter), and saturnine characters. The basic meaning of any planet, when it is in a given Zodiacal sign, will of course be modified by the interpretative meaning ascribed to that sign. And the traditional interpretations accorded to the houses (outlined briefly in Chapter 3), especially if occupied by planets, should also assist the astrologer to pinpoint a number of important factors concerning the native's "type."

As for the meanings of the *aspects,* there is sometimes a lack of unanimity among the various authorities, but some general statements can be made. The interpretation of conjunctions will obviously depend upon the planets in question, since Sun conjunction Jupiter will obviously be "better" than Sun conjunction Saturn. Oppositions can be taken to indicate a "stress" of some kind. Sextiles and especially trines are supposed to be "good" or favorable aspects, while the square (90°) is considered "bad." Hans Genuit holds the view that a multiplicity of aspects in a chart indicates a complicated personality, but he is careful to add that it is difficult to decide how the aspects will work out. Ingrid Lind stresses that the strength of the planets, as indicated by the aspects, gives the key to the native's personality—in her words, to his "power to make use of his qualities."

It is just possible, though, that all these complex considerations to be included in the interpretation of a horoscope may serve to blind people by science. No matter how many factors must be considered in determining the meaning of a horoscope, the interpretations offered by the majority of astrologers seem to be simply collections of conventional statements culled from the vast number of astrological cookbooks.

Too often, interpretations are produced by what is called "blind diagnosis," which means that the astrologer does not meet his client but simply provides a written interpretation that has been made with little or no knowledge of the native's social background, education, and psychological temperament. (This is just the kind of interpretation that Margaret Hone dismisses contemptuously as "astrology by post." It is "astrology by interview" that she insists on.) The written statements offered in this way usually fall into the lowest category of astrological interpretation: the "character analysis" that is vague and obscure

A "telefortune" machine at a British holiday resort represents prediction by astrology in its simplest (and most suspect) form. The girl has set the right-hand dial (marked "female") at her Sun-sign, and is listening to a recorded forecast of her future.

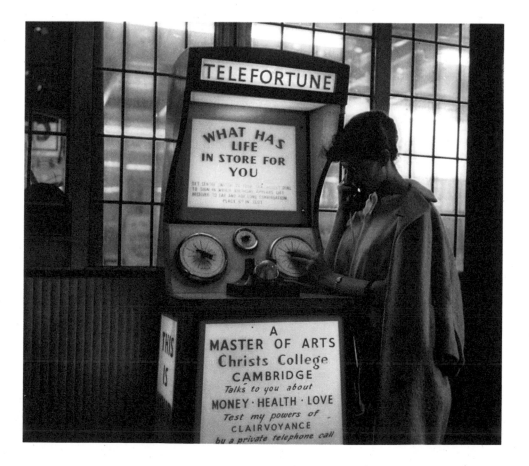

enough to allow almost anyone to recognize himself or herself (especially if the vagueness seems complimentary). Statements like these crop up continually in such interpretations:

"This is a strong chart."

"There is a promise of eventual success."

"You are approaching a time of change."

"The horoscope indicates that you dislike being 'trapped in a rut.'"

"You possess many neglected or little-used abilities."

"Romantic feelings are strong."

Some of the more sophisticated astrologers might argue in favor of blind diagnosis, believing that prior knowledge of the native is quite unnecessary to a talented and perceptive interpreter. But most others look down on the popular type of blind diagnosis as a piece of inferior and cut-price magic. K. E. Krafft, for instance, always refused to provide any kind of interpretation without first having a personal interview with the client. Or, in the absence of an interview, he invariably demanded specimens of handwriting executed at different periods of the native's life, and photographs as well. It might seem that Krafft wanted things made easy for him; but we should remember that he called himself a "psychological consultant." Any kind of psychologist must know who he is dealing with; yet in a truly blind diagnosis the subject is completely unspecified. It might be a man or a woman—it might be a white mouse. All the astrologer is given is the time and place of birth.

For all this, and in spite of all the arguments against astrology (and there are many), the fact remains that some accomplished astrologers (and there are a few) have the unexplained ability to analyze accurately a person's character and personality as it is revealed in the horoscope's cosmic symbolism. Later in this book we will look at some examples of interpretative (and predictive) successes, and they will make one thing certain: When such positive results occur, they are not obtained on the basis of mechanical or rule-of-thumb interpretation of the chart's various combinations. Nor can they be explained in terms of coincidence. The odds are usually too heavy against "lucky guesses."

Then how are the successes achieved? There is no ready-made answer, but *intuition* obviously plays an important part. C. G. Jung (who included astrology among what he called the "various intuitive methods of interpreting fate") once drew an interesting analogy that can help to explain what is meant by intuition here. Jung pointed out that "whatever happens in a given moment has inevitably the quality peculiar to that moment." (Paraphrased into less precise terms, this implies that the qualities of the moment of one's birth—the time of year, etc.—leave a lasting mark upon one.) Jung continues:

"There are certain connoisseurs who can tell you merely from the appearance, taste, and behavior of a wine the site of its vineyard and the year of its origin. There are antiquarians who with almost uncanny accuracy will name the time and place of origin and the maker of an *objet d'art* or piece of furniture on merely looking at it. And there are even astrologers who can tell you, without any previous knowledge of your nativity, what the position of the sun and moon was and what zodiacal sign rose above the horizon at the moment of your birth."

Turning the analogy round, we can say that there are the rare few astrologers who can look at a map of the heavens as they supposedly were at the moment of your birth and tell you what kind of person you are, and even what seems to be in store for you in the future. This, then, must be intuition, combined with experience and with a highly developed ability to assess people's characters (these rare astrologers seldom stoop to blind diagnosis). In such cases the horoscope seems to function as merely a kind of "focusing point" for the intuition. A clairvoyant's crystal ball (for an exceptional clairvoyant) serves a similar purpose; and, it might be suggested, so do dreams or various association tests in psychiatry.

But leaving this rarefied atmosphere and getting back to the ordinary astrologer (the majority) whose interpretations derive more from the tradition than intuition: If the recipient of a chart has some astrological knowledge, he can usually disentangle or analyze (and thus compensate for) the reasoning that lies behind the interpretation. But he will find this much more difficult in relation to *predictive* statements. Here we are no longer concerned with a fairly well-defined tradition but with the choice of one of a number of rather speculative procedures. Yet prediction is what most people who go to astrologers want—prediction dealing with their problems (usually rather obvious problems involving things like love or money).

This is asking a lot. The natal horoscope itself is at least an expression of certain astronomical *facts* that have been wedded to a symbolic system. But this is not the case with the so-called "progressed" horoscope, in which the various factors (planets, ascendant, etc.) are advanced or "progressed" in accordance with given keys to give a reading for the native's future.

"A day for a year" is the phrase used to describe one system of progression, which is based on the assumption that one day's movements of the planets after birth corresponds to a year in the native's life. The astrologer decides which day in the ephemeris of the birth year corresponds to the year that he wishes to assess. Thus to cast a progressed horoscope for a person approaching his 50th birthday, the astrologer would erect and interpret a chart corresponding to the 50th *day* following his birth.

The so-called *primary system* is based not on the orbital movements of the planets but on the rotation of the earth. To avoid getting bogged down in this system's mathematical and astronomical complications, it need only be mentioned that this system involves difficult calculations, and at the same time can be wrecked by the smallest error. For instance, an error of only four minutes for the birth time would result in a further error that would be equivalent to 12 months for the "prediction."

There are other complex and symbolic keys for progressing the planetary positions, but the "day for a year" is most widely used. Any of these systems seems arbitrary enough to give ammunition to a dozen enemies of astrology. Even astrology's friends have pointed out their weaknesses. For fun K. E. Krafft once invented a legendary personality to whom he ascribed a birth date, time, and place selected at random. Then, before erecting a natal chart or calculating any progressions, he wrote down a score of imaginary events supposedly experienced by this native during his fictitious lifetime. When he investigated the native's progressions he was amused (but not surprised) to find that he could almost invariably see something in the progressed horoscope that logically seemed to fit the case.

Much predictive work is done on the basis of the so-called "transits"; and the mechanics of this system are not quite as speculative as they are in the case of directions according to hypothetical keys or rates of progression. A transit is defined as the actual passage of a planet over the position of any planet or point in the birth chart. Thus, if one has an ephemeris for any particular year (past, present, or future), it is easy enough to check the transits. And according to the nature of the transiting planet the transit itself may be interpreted as favorable or unfavorable in nature. For example, a person born on January 23, 1898, would have had his natal Sun in 3° 34' of Aquarius. Saturn exactly transited this position at about midnight on February 2-3, 1962. Transiting Saturn conjunction Sun would not be considered favorable.

Many of the best modern astrologers prefer to avoid any kind of predictive work—perhaps in the light of its associations with cheap fortune telling, but also because predictions can be dangerous. It is very likely that certain kinds of prediction (such as the "beware of accidents during the first three days of February" variety) are often fulfilled because the native is unconsciously impelled —by what is popularly called "the power of suggestion"—to make them come true. K. E. Krafft, for instance, always refused to undertake predictive work for individual clients, partly because of the uncertain techniques (of "progressing" horoscopes) but also because of the moral and psychological dangers.

Science or mystery?

Krafft's own astrological career (before he fell into the Nazis' hands) itself represents the two camps into which many modern astrologers are divided. First of all, many are insistent that astrology itself should be recognized as a *science*. No field of inquiry would appear so unsuitable for serious scientific investigation. Nevertheless, the full strength of modern statistical analysis has been turned on astrology: Krafft himself spent nearly a decade collecting and analyzing statistics to prove astrology's validity.

He began his huge and gallant undertaking while he was still a natural-sciences student at the University of Geneva in 1921. He produced detailed statistical studies (mentioned in Chapter 1) of the planetary factors and angles in the charts of more than 2000 musicians; also, on the basis of data from the official registers at Geneva, he completed studies relating to hereditary factors (of a planetary nature) in the horoscopes of members of several generations in the same family. His preliminary findings were presented at a Statistical Congress at Geneva in 1923, and caused a certain amount of interest in academic circles (the more so because Professor L. Hersch, who had taught Krafft statistical methods, vouched for the scientific nature of his procedures).

But in spite of Professor Hersch's recommendations, the authorities refused to allow Krafft to present a thesis on "Cosmic Influences on Human Life" for a doctorate. Krafft thereupon left Geneva without a diploma of any kind and removed himself to London, where he spent six months of 1924 studying advanced statistical techniques at the University of London before returning to Switzerland in July 1924.

During the next three or four years Krafft combined a successful career in a large Zurich printing and publishing firm with the continuation of the statistical enquiry that he had begun in 1921. By 1929 he had assembled a body of material consisting of more than a million individually numbered observations. He published a preliminary synthesis of his findings in several articles published between 1926-29 in the more respectable German astrological journals; and he himself had no doubt whatever that he had succeeded in providing sound scientific evidence for the existence of "cosmic influences."

Official science (foreseeably) ignored his work. But, surprisingly, even in German astrological circles Krafft's work apparently failed to stimulate more

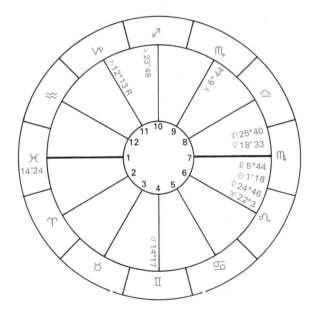

Here the chart interpreted on p. 256 has been "progressed" by 50 years (one day for each year)—which, when related to the natal chart may reveal possible future trends in the native's life. The Sun is now in Virgo, which favors practical work. Saturn, who dominated the natal chart, comes into exact opposition with the Sun when the native is 21—perhaps marking the removal of conflicts and frustrations. The ascendant, now in Pisces and in trine with the natal Sun and in sextile with Saturn, emphasizes the Sun-Saturn opposition, indicating that the native may now reap the reward of his former hard work. Another important aspect is Mercury in trine to the natal Jupiter, implying mental stimulation. All progressed charts, most astrologers agree, must be studied in relation to the birth chart.

than a mild interest. (These circles had also initiated their own statistical project at much the same time but did little or nothing with the material that they assembled.) So Krafft was let down, so to speak, by both the sheep and the goats. In any case, very few people were qualified to follow his mathematical arguments. Poisson's Law (of probabilities) might be all very well in its way, but what most of these people wanted were comprehensible and moderately foolproof methods by which they could demonstrate that astrology "works."

Nor are the requirements any different in astrological circles today. During the past 60 years there have been many isolated attempts other than Krafft's to prove the validity of astrology upon an objectively statistical basis. There were the investigations made early in this century by the French amateur astrologer Paul Choisnard (mentioned in Chapter 1); and the experiments in blind diagnosis made in the last few years by Professor Hans Bender of the Institute of Parapsychology of the University of Freiburg (Breisgau, Germany); and many more. But perhaps one of the most striking of all modern statistical examinations of astrology was made in the early 1950s by Michel Gauquelin, a Parisian academic psychologist who had a first-class knowledge of modern statistical techniques. Gauquelin read Krafft's *Traité* and, although completely uninterested in the astrological tradition as such, decided to try to reconstruct some of Krafft's major experiments. He soon discovered that it would not be possible even to check them on the basis of the material presented in the *Traité*, and also came to the conclusion that even Krafft's statistical methods were in themselves highly suspect. He thereupon resolved to mount a full-scale experiment of his own.

Whereas Krafft had to a very large extent worked without birth-hour data, Gauquelin laboriously collected such material from official registers in France, Italy, Germany, Belgium, and Holland and eventually erected and analyzed about 24,000 horoscopes, which must have contained a total of about a quarter of a million factors. These horoscopes were then filed under "professional" categories—i.e., for scientists, sporting champions, soldiers, politicians, actors, painters, musicians, men of letters, journalists, and industrial magnates.

Much to Gauquelin's surprise (and, it seems, not without a certain embarrassment) he ultimately arrived at the conclusion that certain propositions contained in the astrological tradition *could* be substantiated to some extent. For example, he found that a dominant Jupiter *does* particularly concern ecclesiastics and a dominant Mars does link up with sportsmen. His work met with a mixed reception: The scientific critics were more disapproving than approving and, again, even the astrologers were not as interested as they might have been.

Both before and after the Second World War various groups of astrologers or individual astrologers have attempted fairly ambitious statistical investigations, although never on the same scale as either Krafft's or Gauquelin's. Furthermore, it would appear that the majority of them were initiated without a detailed

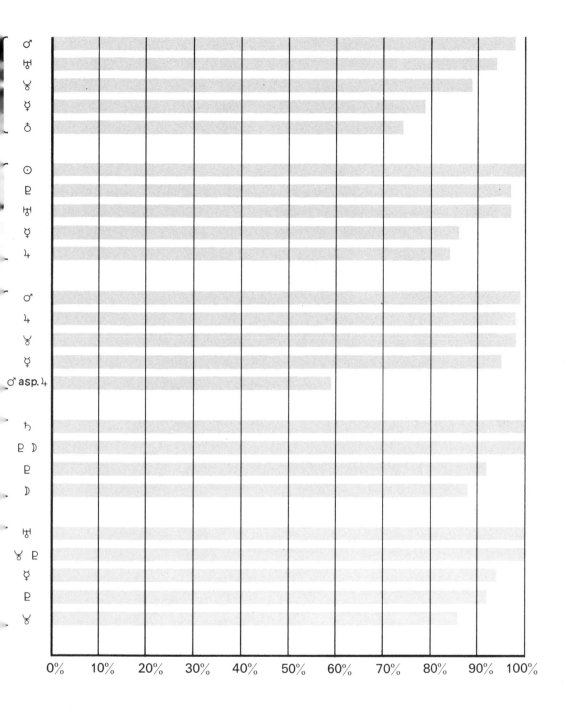

An immense statistical examination of
astrology was begun in 1924 by the Church
of Light, Los Angeles, U.S.A. Thousands of
horoscopes were erected, progressed, and
tabulated ; among the findings were statistics
that seem to indicate what planet governs a
given job or profession. Here, simplified
charts show the dominant planets of film
stars, politicans, athletes, farmers—
and astrologers.

knowledge of what had been attempted in the past by men like Choisnard or Krafft, or even of what was being done by contemporaries. If one characteristic of a science is the free and ready pooling of information, then astrology is not a science. And the astrologers who, like Krafft, have attempted in a scientific manner and for scientific ends to base their beliefs upon statistics have failed to interest more than a tiny minority of their colleagues.

Incidentally, along with all these batteries of statistics, some modern adherents of astrology point to other "evidence" of its rational (i.e. scientific) basis. In fact, such people go much further than most modern astrological writers (who, as we have seen, believe that the stars are merely "signs"); they claim that the heavenly bodies actually have a *causal* effect on people. This hypothesis is presented in objective detail by C. G. Jung (who, like a good scientist, wished to examine every possible view of astrology before presenting his own view in terms of synchronicity). Jung writes:

"In the light of the most recent astrophysical research, astrological correspondence is probably not a matter of synchronicity but, very largely, a causal rela-

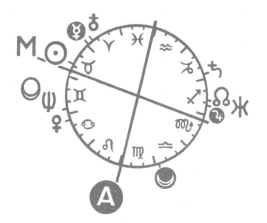

The horoscopes of a mother (top left), a father (top right), and a son (left)—three of many charts studied by K. E. Krafft in an attempt to trace an inherited resemblance between the natal charts of members of the same family. Though there is little similarity between the charts of mother and son, those of father and son have several factors in common: Both have Jupiter in Sagittarius, Moon in Libra, and adjacent ascendants (though these are in different signs).

tionship. As Professor Max Knoll has demonstrated, the solar proton radiation is influenced to such a degree by planetary conjunctions, opposition, and quartile aspects that the appearance of magnetic storms can be predicted with a fair amount of probability."

Therefore, on the basis of new scientific knowledge, Jung suggests that "it is just conceivable that there is a causal connection between the planetary aspects and the psycho-physiological disposition."

But Jung's cautious words "just conceivable" are just a scientist's way of saying that one should not dismiss any possibility before investigating it. And his own investigation (the astrological experiment discussed in Chapter 7) proved to his own satisfaction at least that, if there was anything in astrology, it was due to the operation of the *non*-causal principle of synchronicity. He concludes: "Although I was obliged to express doubt, earlier, about the mantic [i.e., divinatory, irrational] character of astrology, I am now forced as a result of my astrological experiment to recognize it again."

K. E. Krafft also came to recognize the irrational nature of astrology. When at the end of the 1920s he had been disappointed by the reception of his statistics, he tired of the statistics themselves and turned in the opposite direction. He had always had something of a mystical bent; this tendency flowered in the development of his complicated astro-psychological symbolical system, which he called *Typocosmy*.

If in the final analysis we agree with Krafft and Jung (and of course many others) that astrology is an irrational phenomenon, then the door is opened to a great many of these eccentric, "breakaway" systems of horoscopic interpretation. Obviously, the mechanical application of the tradition's stereotyped meanings has in many cases served to reduce modern astrology to the level of a parlor game. In an attempt to counteract this tendency, many modern astrologers are working to replace the tradition with a more up-to-date brand of irrationalism—for example, Furze Morrish's mystical "psycho-evolutionary" system (which was described in Chapter 3), or the German "cosmobiologists" of the Reinhold Ebertin school. Ebertin's astrological rebels completely ignore house division and do not even appear to bother overmuch about the signs of the Zodiac. They work almost solely with "complexes" of planets on a common axis. Faithful traditionalists regard Ebertin and his followers as dangerous heretics; on the other hand, Ebertin believes that the sooner the astrologers throw overboard what he calls astrology's "medieval ballast," the better.

It seems that Germany is the home of a great many modern astrological heresies. There is also the so-called Hamburg School, founded by Alfred Witte some 40 years ago, which uses eight completely hypothetical trans-Neptunian planets and, furthermore, has produced ephemerides showing their movements. This system, it is claimed, can yield excellent interpretations of horoscopes. Even traditionalist astrologers, who look askance at the Hamburg school's interpretative methods, have been known to fall back on them when all else fails.

The success of any form of divination—whether from palms or horoscopes—may depend on an incalculable element of intuition. A tea-cup fortune teller might see among the tea leaves (left) the shapes of a lion (meaning influence), of Libra the Scales (meaning marriage), of the letter M (the initial of a loved one). But his final interpretation would depend on several factors, including position and clarity of outline. Similarly, in the interpretation of Tarot cards (which are usually set out as in the diagram above right), the stock meaning of a card varies according to its position in relation to the "significator" card (marked 1), which represents the person whose fortune is being told. The Tarot cards depicted here are (from left to right) the Lovers, the one of Cups, the Wheel of Fortune, the one of Clubs, the Knight of Wands, and Death.

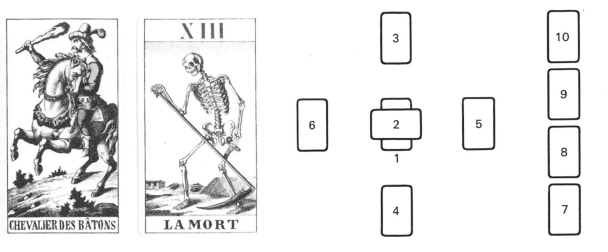

In Vienna, a member of this school (signing himself simply Herr Stuiber) has in the last few years written several short monographs entitled "Some Remarkable Astrological Experiments." These indicate that the Hamburg School astrologers can on occasion give precise and surprising answers to even improbable questions. For instance, one of these astrologers was told the time and place of birth of a woman whose identity was quite unknown to him; and he was asked what happened to the woman on March 4, 1954, at 4 P.M. in Vienna. His answer was correct: The woman had been shot in the back.

Such systems, like the tradition, could presumably be taught; but whether they could then be applied by the students with any success seems more than doubtful. It would be as impossible to create (by whatever system) a new race of astrological *virtuosi* as to create a hundred violinists or painters of genius. The short answer would be that gifted astrologers are "born, not made" with the necessary qualities—though, apart from the general idea of intuition, these qualities are apparently quite inexplicable.

It is perhaps just this irrationalism, this intuitive and mysterious basis of astrology, that is (and has always been) the sole source of its appeal—and one of the main reasons why scientific investigations of astrology seem to lack appeal even for astrologers. Most people who think about it all would *like* there to be some validity in astrology—something, it would seem, that cannot be scientifically proved but has to be taken on trust and perhaps with a catch in the breath. Such people will point to successful interpretations or predictions as indications that "there's something in it." And then they will be shaken by interpretations that failed, predictions that never came true. The next chapter will include a few of each kind of prediction; but what, if anything, will be proved by such occurrences must remain dependent on the individual reader, and which side of the fence he finds himself on.

9 Predictions and pronouncements

This chapter is simply a short anthology, containing examples from the past and present of two kinds of astrological statement. First, there are statements of opinion, setting forth the attitudes to astrology held by various authors (many of whom are well known outside the astrological realm). Some of the authors approve, others disapprove. A few of them more or less reserve their opinion (as Plutarch does); others take astrology's value for granted and merely describe some specific application (as Culpeper does). Also, some of these quotations are taken from works of literature—plays, poems, novels—and, whether for or against, reflect the interest taken by literary men of all ages in astrology as a social phenomenon.

Interspersed throughout the opinions are samples of *predictive* statements. Astrology has always taken upon itself the double function of providing a key to character and personality and of providing glimpses of the future. (More recent astrologers, however, have turned away from divination, and consider astrology to be more a form of psychology than of fortune telling.) Throughout previous chapters we have occasionally looked at examples of prediction; and we have seen that astrology's friends often use successful predictions as proof of the art's validity, while its enemies often use unsuccessful predictions to prove the contrary. The examples that follow are not put forward to prove anything: Included are some predictions that came true and some others that didn't.

A prophetic vision of a bad harvest (from
a German woodcut of 1627) based on
"celestial signs" that allegedly appeared
in the sky at the time.

Planets and shepherds

My son thou shalt understand
That, to avoid all idleness,
This matter oft thou shalt take in hand
To read of shepherd's business;
And special of the planets seven,
Of Mars and Saturn that is full high
Also of Sol, the middle heaven,
And under him Venus, Luna, and Mercury.
For to know their natures all
In sooth it is a great conning,
And show what may befall
When every planet is reigning;
By their working oft we be moved
To look lusty and plays of jollity,
And by some of them as clerks have proved
They steer us to theft, murder, and vility.
Some be good, some be bad verily,
Some be not comfortable to man nor beast;
Some hot, some cold, some wet, some dry,
If three be good, four be worse at the least;
Saturn is highest, and coldest being full bad,
And Mars with his bloody sword, ever ready to kill;
Jupiter very good, and Venus maketh lovers glad,
Sol and Luna is half good and half ill,
Mercury is good, and evil verily.
And hereafter thou shalt know
Which of the seven most worthy be,
And who reigneth high and who a-low;
Of every planet's property—
Which is the best among them all
That causeth wealth, sorrow, or sin.
Tarry and here, son thou shall
Speak soft, for now I begin.

—from *The Kalendar and Compost of Shepherds*,
published in Paris 1493, translated about 1518

A woodcut of an idealized medieval shepherd
from the frontispiece to a French edition of
The Kalendar of Shepherds.

Organs of providence

"And if we cannot deny but that God hath given virtues to springs and fountains, to cold earth, to plants and stones, minerals, and to the excremental parts of the basest living creatures, why should we rob the beautiful stars of their working powers? For, seeing they are many in number and of eminent beauty and magnitude, we may not think that in the treasury of his wisdom who is infinite there can be wanting, even for every star, a peculiar virtue and operation; as every herb, plant, fruit, and flower adorning the face of the earth hath the like. For as these were not created to beautify the earth alone and to cover and shadow her dusty face but otherwise for the use of man and beast to feed them and cure them; so were not those uncountable glorious bodies set in the firmament to no other end than to adorn it but for instruments and organs of his divine providence, so far as it hath pleased his just will to determine."
—Sir Walter Raleigh, *History of the World,* 1614

One of Europe's greatest calamities—the Black Death of 1348—was foreseen by two medieval astrologers. John of Bassigney, an English scholar writing in the 1340s, proclaimed that in the year 1352 (a few years late), a pestilence would cover the whole world that would kill about two thirds of the population. His prediction, he said, rested partly on information that he had obtained from other scholars on his travels, and partly on his study of the stars. (It should be mentioned that almost all of John's predictions concerned disasters, devastations, scourges, wars, and the like.)

Another 14th-century scholar, England's John of Eschenden, is supposed to have predicted the Black Death from an eclipse of the Moon and certain planetary conjunctions that occurred in 1345. He stated that the effects of the eclipse would last for eight years and six months, during which time "men and beasts will suffer long diseases and there will be death and many wars and flight; . . . great corruption in the air, and great scarcity of crops from excessive cold and rains and worms."

The beginnings of Rome

"Likewise in the time of Marcus Varro (as a man learned, and one that had read as much of ancient stories as any Roman) there was a friend of his called Tarrutius, a great philosopher and mathematician, who being given to the calculation of astronomy for the delight of speculation only, wherein he was thought most excellent: it did fall out that Varro gave him this question, to search out what hour and day the nativity of Romulus was, who gathered it out by certain accidents, as they do in the resolutions of certain geometrical questions. For they say, that by the self same science, one may tell before of things to come, and to happen to a man in his life, knowing certainly the hour of his nativity: and how one may tell also the hour of his nativity, when by accidents they know what hath happened to him all his life.

"Tarrutius did the question that Varro gave him. And having thoroughly considered the adventures, deeds, and gests of Romulus, how long he lived, and how he died: all which being gathered and conferred together, he did boldly judge for a certainty, that he was conceived in his mother's womb, in the first year of the second Olympiad, the three and twentieth day of the month which the Egyptians call Choeac, and now is called December, about three of the clock in the morning, in which hour there was a whole eclipse of the sun: and that he was born into the world, in the month Thouth which is the month of September, about the rising of the sun. And that Rome was begun by him on the ninth day of the month which the Egyptians call Pharmuthi, and answereth now to the month of April, between two and three of the clock in the morning. For they will say that a city hath his revolution and his time of continuance appointed, as well as the life of a man: and that they knew by the situation of the stars, the day of her beginning and foundation.

"These things and such other like, peradventure will please the readers better for their strangeness and curiosity, than offend or mislike them for their falsehood."

—Plutarch, *Life of Romulus,* Englished by Sir Thomas North, 1603

Women to avoid
> *Beware the Woman, too, and shun her Sight,*
> *Who, in these Studies, does her self Delight.*
> *By whom a greasie Almanack is born,*
> *With often handling, like chaste Amber, worn:*
> *Not now consulting, but consulted, she*
> *Of the Twelve Houses, and their Lords, is free,*
> *She, if the Scheme a fatal Journey show,*
> *Stays safe at Home, but lets her Husband go.*
> *If but a Mile she Travel out of Town,*
> *The Planetary House must first be known:*
> *And lucky moment; if her Eye but akes*
> *Or itches, its Decumbiture she takes.*
> *No Nourishment receives in her Disease,*
> *But what the Stars, and Ptolemy shall please.*

> —Juvenal, from *The Sixth Satire,*
> translated by John Dryden (1693)

According to the "English Chronicles" of 1186, all Europe panicked at one time in that century because of a prediction by astrologers of an approaching conjunction of planets in the constellation Libra. The fact that the conjunction was to take place in an "airy" or "windy" sign was interpreted as signifying (in addition to other horrors) a terrific wind-storm. In many parts of Europe people built themselves caves underground and special services were held in many churches. Aside from earthquakes and hurricanes, it was prophesied that cities in sandy regions were to be completely buried and that Egypt and Ethiopia were to become uninhabitable. Storms apparently did occur, but nothing of the magnitude indicated in the predictions.

Aphorisms of Cardan

When the Moon is in Scorpio in square of Saturn in Leo, or in his opposition when he is in Taurus partilely, the Native rarely has either Wife or Children, but if Saturn be in Aquarius, he will be a mere Woman hater.

Mercury, mixing his Beams with Mars, is a great argument of a violent death.

When Venus is with Saturn, and beholds the Lord of the Ascendant, the Native is inclinable to Sodomy, or at least shall love old hard-favoured Women, or poor dirty Wenches.

The Moon, full of Light in Conjunction with Mars, makes the Native be counted a Fool, but if she be void of light and with Saturn, he is so indeed.

A Woman that has Mars with the Moon is *Right,* I'll warrant her.

The Moon in Aquarius or Pisces, makes the Native not at all acceptable amongst Princes or Grandees.

In Purging, 'tis best that both the Moon and Lord of the Ascendant descend and be under the Earth, in vomiting that they Ascend.

In the past women were often seen as the dupes of superstition (and astrology). In this satirical engraving (1792) a corrupt fortune teller exploits an innocent maiden.

Make no new Clothes, nor first put them on when the Moon is in Scorpio, especially if she be full of light and beheld of Mars, for they will be apt to be torn and quickly worn out.

If a Comet appear whilst a Woman goes with Child, if it be either in the fourth, fifth, or eighth month, such Child will prove very prone to anger and quarrels, and if he be of quality, to sedition.

Saturn in fixed signs causes scarcity of Corn, dear years, and the Death of many Men.

When Saturn is in Libra and Jupiter in Cancer, great Changes and Alterations shall happen in the world.

—Jerome Cardan, *Seven Segments,*
1547, translated by William Lilly, 1676

Calvin condemns

"There hath been of long time a foolish curiosity to judge by the stars of all things what should chance unto men : and thence to enquire and take counsel as touching those matters which are to be done. But we will by and by God willing declare that it is nothing but a devilish superstition. Yea, and it hath been rejected by a common consent as pernicious to mankind. And yet at this day it hath got the upper hand in such sort that many which think themselves witty men, yea and have been so judged, are as it were bewitched therewith."

—John Calvin (1509-63)

A page from *The Ravens Almanack*—a parody
of the astrological almanacs that were
popular in England during the 17th century.

Rauens Almanacke.

The Dommion of the Moone in Mans body.

Aries The head and face

Taurus Necke and Throate
Cancer Breſt ſtomacke and Lungs
Uirgo Guts and Belly
Scorpio Secrets & bladder
Capricornus. Knees

Gemini Armes and ſhoulders

Leo Hart & backe.

Sagitarius the Thighes

Aquarius Legges.

Pisces The teete

Louis XI of France (1423-83) often consulted a famous astrologer named d'Almonsor. Others consulted him as well : According to one story that attached itself to this astrologer's name, he was visited late one night by two knights and their armed retainers. The knights ordered d'Almonsor to read their fates.

D'Almonsor cast their horoscopes and predicted that one knight would die violently—but heroically, and for a good cause. As for the second knight, d'Almonsor also foretold death, adding that this knight was menaced by a powerful man and that death would probably come through a poisoned drink.

The first knight was the Duke of Burgundy, who was killed in battle shortly after the prediction. The second knight, the Duke of Berry, also died shortly afterward : His death was widely thought to have been due to poison given to him on the orders of Louis XI.

A 17th-century manuscript records a prediction that is supposed to have been made of the death of Henry IV of France in 1610. According to this story, an Italian astrologer named Francisco Corvino was working quietly in Florence when, suddenly, he announced to his companions that "tomorrow, one of the greatest monarchs in Christendom will be slain." And, the manuscript says, the very next day in Paris Henry IV was stabbed to death by an assassin.

A mock almanac

"To the Lyons of the Wood (the young Courtiers), to the wild Buck of the Forrest (the gallants and younger Brothers), to the Harts of the field, and to all the whole Countrie that are brought up wisely, yet prove Gulls and are borne rich yet die beggars : the new English astrologer dedicateth his Ravens Almanack.

"Amongst Gentlemen that have full purses, and those that cry 'tillil, let the world slide,' the week shall run out so quickly and so merrily, that on the Saturday morning it shall be hard for them to tell whether the day that went before were Friday.

"The same losse of memorie will fall upon many that shall go drunk to bed.

"O you common Fiddlers likewise that scrape out a poor living out of dryed Cats guts : I prophesy that many of you shall this year be troubled with abominable noises and singing in your heads, in so much that a great part of you shall dye beggars."

—*The Ravens Almanack,* 1609

In medieval and Renaissance times, astrologers seem to have predicted the end of the world more frequently than anything else. Here are a few examples :

In 1500 an Italian astrologer, Agostino Nifo, asserted that the starry portents of a flood were undeniable, adding that this disaster was due to the sins of man, which cried out for divine punishment. In 1520 Johann Virdung, an Austrian astrologer, declared some meteors seen at Vienna to be warnings of a flood to take place at the time of some important planetary conjunctions in 1524.

The "floods in 1524" cry was taken up by scores of astrologers and almanacs. From Rome in 1521 one Sebastian Constantinus announced that he had seen a solar eclipse in the house of death, a most ominous position. And then a famous German astrologer, Johann Stoeffler, forecast in February 1524 that 20 conjunctions would take place that year, of which 16 would occupy "a watery sign." This signified, he said, floods of such an extent that the world would be destroyed.

These predictions set off a continent-wide panic. People apparently built arks, boats, and rafts to save themselves. Whole communities packed and left home for higher ground. It was said that even Charles V, emperor of Spain and Germany, had men mark out places that would be less exposed to flood waters, in the hope that the floods would be only partial.

To keep the record straight, it should be added that during that year there *were* abnormally heavy rains, and considerable flooding, in many parts of Europe.

Edmund disagrees

"This is the excellent foppery of the world, that, when we are sick in fortune—often the surfeit of our own behavior—we make guilty of our disasters the sun, the moon, and the stars; as if we were villains by necessity, fools by heavenly compulsion, knaves, thieves and treachers by spherical predominance, drunkards, liars and adulterers by an enforced obedience of planetary influence; and all that we are evil in, by a divine thrusting on: an admirable evasion of whoremaster man, to lay his goatish disposition to the charge of a star! My father compounded with my mother under the dragon's tail, and my nativity was under *ursa major*; so that it follows I am rough and lecherous. 'Sfoot! I should have been that I am had the maidenliest star in the firmament twinkled on my bastardizing."

—Shakespeare, *King Lear*, I, ii

When Marie Thérèse of Spain (daughter of Philip IV) was a child, the court astrologer told her that she would some day marry the greatest king in all Europe and that this marriage would avert a war. In June 1660 she married Louis XIV of France and the marriage prevented a war between France and Spain over a territorial disagreement.

Fate of an astrologer

"Nectanebus, King of Egypt, was driven into Macedonia by fourteen nations in rebellion and later he wished to teach astrology to King Alexander who, they say, was his son. Alexander gave him a push and knocked him into a pit where he broke his neck. So it would have served him better to have watched the earth than the heavens."

—Nicole Oresme, from *Livre de Divinacions*, 1361-65

Fate of an anti-astrologer

"[Sir Christopher Heydon] the author of that incomparable *Defence of Judicial Astrology,* written in answer to a book against Astrology, by Mr. John Chambers; in which Defence, this learned Knight was so exact in his Responses, so satisfactory and full in his Arguments, so strenuous in his Proofs thereof, that when once Mr. Chambers (who no question was a great Scholar) had seen and perused it, and found the same unanswerable, and his own Arguments so fully refuted and retorted, he for very grief died."

—John Gadbury, *Collectio Geniturarum,* 1662

A grain of salt

"[The astrologer sat] before a Square Table, covered with a green Carpet, on which lay a huge book in *Folio,* wide open, full of Strange Characters, such as the *Aegyptians* and *Chaldaeans* were never guilty of; not far from that, a silver Wand, a Surplus, a Watering Pot, with all the superstitions or rather fayned Instruments of his cousening Art. And to put a fairer colour on his black and foul Science, on his head he had a four-cornered Cap, on his backe a fair Gown (but made of a strange fashion) in his right hand he held an Astrolabe, in his left a Mathematical Glass. . . ."

A fraudulent astrologer (from the title page of *Astrologaster*), equipped with astrolabe and "mathematical glass," receives a client.

"He was as well acquainted with the Twelve Signs in Heaven, as any Trades-man with those in Cheape-side, and run over the Nature of the Seven Planets as nimbly as the French Vaulter over the Ropes. And I myself . . . could dis-course to you what a sullen fellow *Saturn* is (on whom the permanent continua-tion of all things depend), what a jovial fellow *Jupiter* (on whom the fecundity of Agent Causes rely), what a quarrelling Swash-buckler *Mars* (on whom the swift expedition of any thing to the effect doth hang), what a hot fellow *Sol* (whom all Agent Causes follow), what a wanton wench *Venus* (on whom the fecundity of all Material Causes look after), what a merry fellow *Mercury* (in whom a manifold virtue doth flourish), and what a mad Lass *Luna* (on whom the increase and decrease of Human things consist)."

—John Melton, *Astrologaster,* or the *Figure Caster,* 1620

Heaven's alarm to the world

"The Great God, when he made the world, placed the stars in heaven, to be for signs as to events that in the ordinary course of nature should come to pass. (Gen. I : 14.)

"There are also extraordinary stars sometimes appearing in the heavens . . . blazing stars called comets, from the streamlike long hair which attends them. Such a star is prodigious and a fearful sight. . . . As for the sign in heaven now appearing, what calamities may be portended thereby? . . . In general we have cause to fear that sweeping judgments are thereby signified; that the Lord is coming down from Heaven with a long beesom of destruction which shall sweep away a world of sinners before it.

"Judgments, which are God's sharp razors on mankind whereby he doth shear down multitudes of sinful people, draw near. . . . God by the blazing star is speaking to other places, and not to New England only. And it may be He is declaring to that generation of hairy scalps who go on still in their trespasses that the day of the Calamity is at hand.

". . . I am persuaded that the floods of great water are coming. I am per-suaded that God is about to open the windows of heaven and to pour down the cataracts of his wrath ere this generation is passed away. Let us then prepare for trouble, for the Lord has fired his beacon in the heavens. Let everyone that is godly pray unto the Lord before the Floods of great waters come nigh unto us."

—The American religious leader Increase Mather, from a sermon
on the comet of 1680

An astrologer recants

"I also being a boy learned this Art of my Father, afterward I lost much time and labour therein; at length I learned that altogether it was built upon no other foundation but upon mere trifles, and feignings of imaginations. . . ."

—Henry Cornelius Agrippa, *Of the Vanitie and Uncertaintie of
Artes and Sciences,* translated by James Sanford, 1569

In 1583 the English astrologer Richard Harvey (along with many other astrologers) predicted a conjunction of Saturn and Jupiter for high noon on April 28 of that year. He pointed out that these two planets had been in conjunction in the watery sign of Cancer just prior to the Biblical deluge in Noah's time. This time they would be together in the fiery sign of Aries: The result, he said, would be burnings, strife, and other fiery calamities (including the appearance of a great comet). "The very frame of the world cannot endure long after," he added, and "the same Jesus Christ shall come again in unspeakable majestie!"

An attack on Lilly

"Mr. Lillie in all these dreadful Eclipses and malignant Aspects, finds much matter of bad, dismal and disastrous concernement, to Princes, Potentates, Priests, Lawyers, Husbandmen, Graziers, etc. but none at all ever to Wizards, Witches, Conjurers, Fortune-tellers, Sorcerers, Stargazers, Astrologers, etc. No malignity of any Aspect belike is able to reach them."

—Thomas Gataker, *Against the Scurrilous Aspersion of that grand Imposter, Mr. William Lillie,* 1653

The astrologer-astronomer William Whiston (who succeeded Isaac Newton at Cambridge in 1703) gave a lecture in 1736 predicting an eclipse of the Moon, accompanied by the appearance of a great comet, for precisely five A.M. on the following Thursday. These portents, Whiston told his audience, would herald the return of the Messiah to earth; the world would end on the next Friday, by fire and earthquake.

In fact, a comet did appear at about the appointed time. The prediction had been fairly widely publicized, and the city of London was briefly thrown into panic. Thousands of people fled the city.

Planets and plants

(The Stars' own Vegetable Garden and Medicine Chest)

Celandine: This is an herb of the Sun, and under the celestial Lion: it is one of the best cures for the eyes; for the eyes are subject to the luminaries: let it then be gathered when the Sun is in Leo, and the Moon in Aries.

Cucumbers: There is no dispute to be made, but that they are under the dominion of the Moon, though they are so much cried out against for their coldness, and if they were but one degree colder they would be poison.

Fennel: One good old fashion is not yet left off, viz. to boil Fennel with fish; for it consumes that phlegmatic humour, which fish most plentifully afford and annoy the body with, though few that use it know wherefore they do it; I suppose the reason of its benefit this way is, because it is an herb of Mercury, and under Virgo, and therefore bears antipathy to Pisces.

Peach-tree: Lady Venus owns this tree, and by it opposes the ill effects of Mars; and indeed for children and young people, nothing is better to purge cholera and the jaundice, than the leaves and flowers of this tree, being made into a syrup or conserve: let such as delight to please their lust, regard the fruit; but such as have lost their health, and their children's, let them regard what I say, they may safely give two spoonfuls of the syrup at a time; it is as gentle as Venus herself.

Nettle (*Urtica Vulgaris*): This is an herb Mars claims dominion over. You know Mars is hot and dry, and you know as well that winter is cold and moist; then you may know as well the reason why Nettle Tops, eaten in the spring, consume the phlegmatic superfluities in the body of man, that the coldness and moistness of winter has left behind.

Wild carrots: Wild Carrots belong to Mercury, and therefore break wind, and remove stitches in the sides, provoke urine and women's courses, and help to break and expel the stone; the seed also of the same works the like effect, and is good for the dropsy, and those whose bellies are swollen with wind.

Houseleek: It is an herb of Jupiter; and it is reported by Mezaldus, to preserve what it grows upon from fire and lightning.

Lettuce (*Common Garden*): The Moon owns it, and that is the reason it cools and moistens what heat and dryness Mars causes, because Mars has his full in Cancer; and it cools the heat because the Sun rules it, between whom and the Moon is a reception in the generation of men.

Hellebore: It is an herb of Saturn, and therefore no marvel if it has some sullen conditions with it, and would be far safer, being purified by the art of the alchymist than given raw.

Saffron: It is an herb of the Sun, and under the Lion, and therefore you need not demand a reason why it strengthens the heart so exceedingly.

Lily of the Valley: It is under the dominion of Mercury, and therefore it strengthens the brain, recruiting a weak memory, and makes it strong again.

Artichokes: They are under the dominion of Venus, and therefore it is not wonderful if they excite lust."

—Nicholas Culpeper, *The English Physician Enlarged*, 1653,
(revised and amplified by G. A. Gordon)

Postscript:—In the same work some other plants of interest are assigned as follows:

To the Sun: The olive, peony, vine, and walnut.

To the Moon: Water-cress and water lily, pumpkin and turnip, sea holly, willow, and white rose.

Mercury: Mushrooms, lavender, and parsley.

Venus: Apple and cherry, gooseberry, raspberry and strawberry, primrose, sorrels, wild thyme, and violet.

Mars: Chives, onion, mustard, radish and horse-radish, hops and peppers, tobacco, honeysuckle, wormwood.

Jupiter: The oak and the orange, peas and dandelion.

Saturn: Holly and ivy, hemlock and nightshade, poplar, quince, and yew.

Two 17th-century English doctors who successfully practiced both medicine and astrology: Left, Nicholas Culpeper (depicted within his own horoscope) above his house in London; above, a portrait of John Case from his book *The Angelical Guide.*

The star-doomed infant

No sooner does he peep into
The world, but he has done his do . . . .
Married his punctual dose of wives,
Is cuckolded, and breaks, or thrives, . . .
As if men from the stars did suck
Old-age, diseases, and ill-luck,
Wit, folly, honor, virtue, vice,
Trade, travel, women, claps, and dice;
And draw with the first air they breath,
Battle, and murther, sudden death.
Are not these fine commodities
To be imported from the skies?

—Samuel Butler, *Hudibras,* 1664

An astrologer's advertisement

Within this place
Lives Doctor Case.
He is said to have got more by this distich, than did Mr. Dryden by all his works.
—Joseph Addison in *The Tatler,* October 21, 1710

The star-struck valet

(Scene: House of an Astrologer)

The Valet: Lord, save us, Françoise, there's a career for one—Astrology! I'm trying to learn it on the side. I'm carefully collecting notes of everything our master says, and to show you how far I've progressed, you're now going to be completely astonished. Look, I'm working on an almanac for the year Sixteen Eightyone that we're just about to enter. . . . I've already done a good part of it. I've filled in all the days of all the months and I've almost this moment polished off December. But I'm left with one little difficulty, about which I want to consult you. I don't know if at the end of my almanac (for I must fill it out a little) I ought to put in 'Some Lives of Notable Persons' or 'The Methods of Planting Cabbages.'

[*Later in the play the action is affected by the great new comet of 1680; the Astrologer has received a letter from Rome.*]

The Countess: Monsieur, I observe strong signs of astonishment on your features.

The Astrologer: Ah, Madame, what a prodigy!

The Countess: Explain yourself immediately.

The Astrologer: Here's certainly something no one can have seen before.

The Countess: What's happened at Rome that's more terrible than here?

The Astrologer: A comet—

The Countess: Yet *another* comet! You terrify me.

The Astrologer: But you'd never guess what *kind* of comet!

The Countess: What is it this time?

The Astrologer: A comet in an egg.

The Countess: A comet in an egg! I'll never eat eggs again.

The Valet: Nor me either! Suppose I were to turn up a whole omelette of comets?

—Bernard Fontenelle, *La Comète,* 1681

A British astrological writer using the pseudonym "Astrologus" stated in 1793 that, from eclipses (especially of the Sun), astrologers can safely predict "notable events concerning the rise or fall of governments; the foundation or fall of cities, towns or fortifications—the breach of leagues among princes, the captivity, sorrow, or sickness of their miserable subjects; wars, quarrels, and tempests; inundations, duels, and litigations—religious controversies, and irreligious persecutions among mankind—the death or destruction of cattle, the infidelity of servants and the treachery of friends—the decay of navigation and the loss of shipping."

He offered the following instances as proof:

On April 30, A.D. 59, an eclipse of the Sun was followed by the murder of Agrippina by Nero. In A.D. 463, an eclipse was followed by a war in Persia. On March 20, 1140, after a total eclipse of the Sun, King Stephen lost a battle with

William II, the German kaiser, reviewing
troops in 1918. A British almanac forecast
war from the kaiser's horoscope in 1908.

the Earl of Gloucester and was taken prisoner. In 1536 an eclipse was followed
by the separation of England from the Church of Rome and the death of Queen
Catherine. Two eclipses in 1781 (one in April and the other in October), which
were total eclipses as seen from the West Indies, were accompanied by "terrible
storms and tempests that almost desolated the West India Islands, sunk the
Ville de Paris, many other ships . . . and a great number of merchant men."

We can add to this list two examples (from other sources) of events that coincided with eclipses of the Moon: In 1870, three days after a total eclipse of the
Moon, the Emperor Napoleon III declared war on Prussia. And in 1897 the
catastrophic collapse of the Tay Bridge in Scotland while a passenger train was
crossing it took place during a partial eclipse of the Moon.

In 1908 the British periodical *Old Moore's Monthly Messenger* analyzed the
chart of the kaiser of Germany as follows:

"The Kaiser's Ascendant is nearly opposite the Mars of King Edward of
England, while Mercury is on Mars in the latter, a certain indication of disputes
and quarrels, and that natural action of the latter is likely to militate against
the former's colonial policy. We call special attention to the point,
because in view of the coming planetary influences and especially eclipses there
is no doubt that the dogs of war cannot be held in the leash much longer. . . ."

Betting by the stars

"Most of Priscilla's days were spent casting the horoscopes of horses, and she invested her money scientifically, as the Stars dictated. She betted on football too, and had a large notebook in which she registered the horoscopes of all the players in all the teams of the League. The process of balancing the horoscopes of two elevens one against the other was a very delicate and difficult one. A match between the Spurs and the Villa entailed a conflict in the heavens so vast and so complicated that it was not to be wondered at if she sometimes made a mistake about the outcome."

—Aldous Huxley, *Crome Yellow*, 1921

In 1946 a popular British astrological magazine stated: "Because of the astrological portents in his horoscope, rumours of Stalin's ill-health may be taken seriously." The writer went on to say that Stalin's disappearance from the international scene within the next 18 months was almost a certainty, and then there would be an astonishing reorientation in U.S.S.R. internal and foreign policies. (Stalin lived and remained in power until 1953.)

A recent "end-of-the-world" forecast was the catastrophe predicted by Indian astrologers in 1962. In Britain, a mountain-side prayer meeting was held to avert this disaster.

In January, 1910, *Old Moore's Monthly Messenger,* dealing with the chart of King Edward VII, warned against "accidents and indisposition." In April 1910 the magazine considered the new Moon and drew from it an indication of future "illness and death in Royal circles." In the same issue, an article devoted to the king's son, the Prince of Wales, stated: "It is not pleasing to note that Sun is directed to square Saturn, an influence which operates from 1908 to 1910. . . . Saturn rules MC, which denotes the father. It is therefore clear that a family loss is foreshadowed in the near future." (King Edward VII died in May 1910.)

Mr. Nehru writes
(Referring to the birth of his first grandson in 1944): "In my letter to Indu I suggested to her to ask you to get a proper horoscope made by a competent person. Such permanent records of the date and time of birth are desirable. As for the time I suppose the proper solar time should be mentioned and not the artificial time which is being used outside now. War time is at least an hour ahead of the normal time."

—Prime Minister Nehru, *Letters to his Sister,* 1963

A German astrologer, Herr Troinski, wrote in the December 1958 issue of the *Berliner Auskunftsbogen:* "In the year 1963, Pope John XXIII will come under very dangerous tertiary directions, both primary and secondary. . . ." He alluded to certain aspects that would occur—specifically Mars in opposition to Saturn and the Sun in square to Mars, Uranus, and Pluto. And he concluded with the prophecy: "This could mean the death of the Pope."

A superstitious residue
"They [modern defenders of astrology] will not acknowledge honestly the decisive fact that their futile practices have been investigated with the greatest care and impartiality by the foremost scholars of the leading Western nations for now almost three centuries, and that not one of these has failed to condemn them as the stale, superstitious residue of what was once a great, pantheistic religion and a glorious philosophical attempt to understand and rationally to explain the universe, a bold enterprise to which we owe not only the whole of our astronomical knowledge, but the most essential part of all our physical science."

—Robert Eisler, *The Royal Art of Astrology,* 1946

A British astrological publication in 1959 predicted trouble for the year 1962. An eclipse of the Sun would be accompanied with a conjunction of the malefics Mars and Saturn, Neptune in square to Mars and Saturn, and other similarly calamitous portents. Many sudden and violent events would occur, the article said, among which would be a period of great hardship for the British royal family. Also, during this period Britain itself would go through terrible turmoil: The existing form of government would be overthrown with much bloodshed.

A science of relating

"Astrology does not offer an explanation of the laws of the universe, nor why the universe exists. What it does, to put it in simplest terms, is to show us that there is a correspondence between macrocosm and microcosm. In short, that there is a rhythm to the universe, and that man's own life partakes of this rhythm. For centuries men have observed and studied the nature of this correspondence. Whether astrology be a science or a pseudo-science, the fact remains that the oldest and the greatest civilizations we know of had for centuries upon centuries used it as a basis for thought and action. That it degenerated into mere fortune-telling, and why, is another story.

"It is not to discover what is going to 'happen' to us, it is not to forestall the blows of fate, that we should look to our horoscopes. A chart when properly read should enable one to understand the overall pattern of one's life. It should make a man more aware of the fact that his own life obeys the same rhythmical, cyclical laws as do other natural phenomena. It should prepare him to welcome change, constant change, and to understand that there is no good or bad, but always the two together in changing degrees, and that out of what is seemingly bad can come good and vice versa. Astrology might indeed be called a science of relating, whose first fruit is the dictum that fate is character."

—Henry Miller, from the foreword to *Henry Miller: His World of Urania,*
by Sydney Omarr, 1960

As for the future, the famed 16th-century astrologer and seer Nostradamus perhaps deserves the last vaguely ominous and cryptic word. The following quatrains are from the *Complete Prophecies* of Nostradamus, translated in 1951 by Henry Robert:

> *In the year 1999 and seven months*
> *From the skies shall come an alarmingly powerful king,*
> *To raise again the great king of the Jacquerie,*
> *Before and after, Mars shall reign at will.*
>
> . . . .
>
> *The year seven of the great number being past*
> *There shall be seen the sports of the ghostly sacrifice*
> *Not far from the great age of the millennium,*
> *That the buried shall come out of their graves.*

The translator in his notes on the quatrains states that the first of these apparently means that a tremendous world revolution is predicted for the year 1999, which is to bring about a complete upheaval of existing social orders, and that this revolution is to be preceded by world war. And the second of the quoted quatrains, the translator says, means simply that in the year 7000 judgment day will be pronounced, the dead will rise from their graves, and the world will come to an end.

Appendices

The 10 planets

Here in capsule form are the planets, signs, and houses with their hieroglyphs, their interrelationships in the horoscope, and some of the qualities assigned to them. This last information has (in the case of the planets and signs) been based on the meanings detailed in the German astrologer Reinhold Ebertin's book *The Combination of Stellar Influences*. The meanings of the houses have been adapted from those suggested by the British astrologer Sepharial.

Spheres of Influence	Related Signs
Sun The masculine principle; spirit, mind, the living being; the will to live, vitality, will-power, determination; health and the heart; the man, the father, authority.	Leo
Moon The feminine principle; the soul, the psyche; the mother, fecundity, adaptation; the wife, the family, the nation; hereditary qualities.	Cancer
Mercury Intellect, mediation, transmission of knowledge; judgment, critical ability, analysis.	Gemini Virgo
Venus Love and art; physical attraction; feeling, sense of harmony and beauty; girl or maiden, sweetheart or mistress.	Taurus Libra
Mars Energy and action; courage and determination; impulsiveness, ruthlessness, brutality; soldiers, sportsmen, technicians, craftsmen, surgeons.	Aries Scorpio

Related Signs	Spheres of Influence

Jupiter

Sagittarius
Pisces

Harmony, law, and religion; expansion and enlargement; ownership; moral and religious aspirations; judges, high ecclesiastics, bankers, wealthy people, fortune hunters.

Saturn

Capricorn
Aquarius

Inhibition and concentration; consolidation, perseverance. seriousness, caution, and economy; melancholy, reserve, and taciturnity; segregation and seclusion; calcification, old age; agriculture, mining, and real estate.

Uranus

(Aquarius)

Suddenness, revolution, transmutation; independence, excitability, and impulsiveness; innovators, reformers, inventors, and technicians; magicians, occultists, and astrologers (the "paranormal").

Neptune

(Pisces)

Impressionability; fantasy and imagination; inclination to mysticism; vagueness, confusion, deception; people of doubtful character, confidence men.

Pluto

(Scorpio)

Higher power or providence; invisible forces or powers; the will to exercise power, to influence the masses; propagandists and politicians, actors and orators.

291

The 12 signs of the Zodiac

	Spheres of Influence	Related Planets
	Aries Will, the urge to act, the spirit of enterprise, leadership, passion, ambition, impatience, rashness.	Mars
	Taurus Perseverance, consolidation, endurance, sense of form.	Venus
	Gemini Vicariousness, adaptability, mobility, superficiality.	Mercury
	Cancer Wealth of feeling, parenthood, the quality of "attachment."	Moon
	Leo The will to create, self-confidence, self-reliance, action, the sex urge.	Sun
	Virgo Diligence and care, tidiness, correct behavior, the critical faculty.	Mercury

Related Planets	Spheres of Influence	
	Libra	
Venus	Sense of justice, desire for harmony, sociability.	
	Scorpio	
Mars (Pluto)	Tenacity, endurance, perseverance, overestimation of self, passion, the struggle for survival.	
	Sagittarius	
Jupiter	Cultivation of inner or spiritual side of life; planning, striving, action, expansion.	
	Capricorn	
Saturn	Concentration on personal self; conservatism, zeal, and industry; a sense of reality.	
	Aquarius	
Saturn (Uranus)	Expectancy, powers of observation, adaptability, planning, helpfulness.	
	Pisces	
Jupiter (Neptune)	Vagueness, sensitivity, emotionalism, intuition; self-sacrifice.	

The 12 houses

	Spheres of Influence	**Related Signs**
	First The body of the native, his physical condition and appearance.	Aries Mars
	Second Money, possessions of value; trade; gain or loss.	Taurus Venus
	Third Letters, papers, writings; all means of communication and transportation; brothers and sisters, near relations, neighbors.	Gemini Mercury
	Fourth The residence; the place of birth; houses, landed property, grounds, mines, underground places; the mother in a man's chart, the father in a woman's.	Cancer Moon
	Fifth Pleasures, love affairs, non-marital sex ties; children, schools, theatres, education; places of amusement and all sensual enjoyments.	Leo Sun
	Sixth Health, servants, food, clothing, physical comforts; employees, small animals, and domestic creatures; climatic and other conditions affecting health.	Virgo Mercury

Seventh

Libra
Venus

The husband in a woman's chart, the wife in a man's; partners, contracts, agreements; litigation, open enemies.

Eighth

Scorpio
Mars

Death, dissolution, loss; the wife's or husband's wealth and possessions; the partner's property; legacies, bequests, and wills.

Ninth

Sagittarius
Jupiter

Religion and philosophy; publications; sea voyages, foreign countries; dreams, spiritual occurrences; the clergy and church affairs; relatives by marriage.

Tenth

Capricorn
Saturn

The occupation; credit, honor, and rank; employer, superior, or master; business affairs, government.

Eleventh

Aquarius
Saturn
(Uranus)

Friends, counselors, companions, society; wishes and hopes; financial affairs of employers or others in command of the native.

Twelfth

Pisces
Jupiter
(Neptune)

Confinement, restraint, prison, exile; secret enemies, plots; large animals.

The major aspects

No hard-and-fast meanings can be ascribed to the planetary aspects, which (more than any other horoscopic element) must be judged in relation to the chart as a whole. This list merely explains their general tendencies. Aspects have always been classified as "good" or "bad," though today they are often labeled "easy" or "difficult." (Conjunction falls into neither category, since its influence depends entirely on the qualities of the two planets involved.)

	Name	Meaning
☌	Conjunction	In a conjunction, the planets' natures must be considered in relation to each other; in some cases they will harmonize and in others, conflict. For example: Saturn (traditionally cold) in conjunction with Venus (naturally loving) will tend to limit or chill the affections. Mars and Venus in conjunction will enforce each other's sensuality and will lead to happy love relationships.
☍	Opposition	Traditionally a "difficult" aspect, implying tension that may lead to an aggravation or a conflict of the planets' influences: On the other hand, this "bad" effect may sometimes be modified: For example, Jupiter and the Sun in opposition, which could produce conceit and extravagance, might be offset by the caution of a well-placed Saturn.
△	Trine	An "easy" aspect, indicating a harmonious relationship of the planets involved. Some astrologers regard, say, Venus trine Jupiter as a mark of too easy-going a nature; but Mars and Saturn in trine might well imply practical ability and courage.

Meaning	Name	

A "difficult" aspect showing an uneasy struggle between the various planetary principles. Moon square Venus (both planets concerned with the home) might show a lack of domestic harmony. With Mars square Saturn, Mars's fierceness might aggravate the coldness of Saturn to produce brutality.

Square □

Like trine, a favorable aspect (though not so strong), but more usually applied to mental rather than physical characteristics. Mercury (traditionally connected with the intellect) in sextile with Mars would give strength of mind; Mercury in sextile with Jupiter would show a witty and cheerful mentality.

Sextile ✳

Some other less important aspects (to which most astrologers today tend to give little weight in horoscopes) are briefly as follows:

Like square, a difficult aspect.

Semi-square ∟

An "unnatural" aspect, implying strain.

Quincunx ⊼

Traditionally considered, like sextile, to be a favorable aspect. Today both semi-sextile and quincunx are treated by most astrologers as "stressful" relationships.

Semi-sextile ⊻

Appendix 3

National horoscopes

Italy

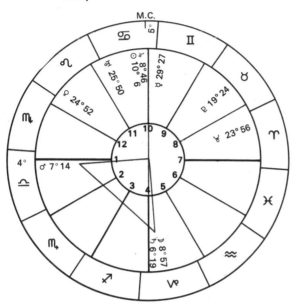

In this chart (cast for July 2, 1871, the date of King Victor Emmanuel's triumphal entry into Rome) heavy "afflictions" are apparent across the "angles" formed by the ascendant-descendant and the M.C.-I.C. These imply that, despite good intentions, the consolidation of the new unified nation could be a long and difficult process. Under Mussolini's regime, Mars's aggressive and ambitious elements (in conjunction with the ascendant, Libra) were in full play. For example, the invasion of Abyssinia on October 3, 1935, took place when the Sun was in conjunction with Mars and in square with Italy's Jupiter, Saturn, and Moon. The failure of Mussolini's later policies is suggested by Saturn square Mars; and on July 25, 1943, Uranus trine Italy's Mars coincided with the fall of Fascism.

England

A horoscope cast for the coronation of William I, the first king of England, on Christmas Day, 1066. The emphasis on the ninth house considered together with the nature of the fiery sign Aries (the ascendant) adds up to the conventional picture of England as an adventurous, pioneering, and empire-building nation. At the outbreak of World War II, the Sun was exactly trine the position of the Sun in this horoscope, whereas Saturn was placed exactly over Hitler's Sun. The determined resistance offered by the English during the Battle of Britain is reflected in the protective position of Saturn, in trine to England's Sun.

Israel

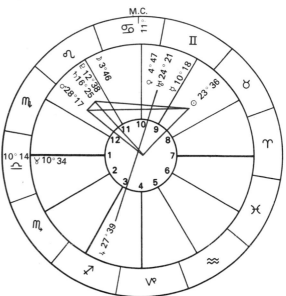

Traditionally, the Taurus-Scorpio polarity is associated with the Jews, but in this chart (cast for the proclamation of the State of Israel on May 14, 1948) the Sun in Taurus and the Cancerian mid-heaven can be said to imply the Jewish people's centuries-old longing for a national home. Neptune rising suggests that the high aspirations of Zionism may be achieved only at the expense of strife and bloodshed, since the Sun is in square with Mars and Saturn. So-called "friends" of Israel could provoke conflict, and internal political feuds could hamper the State's development. The opposition of Jupiter (which, due to its position in the third house, could be associated with the Arabs) to Uranus is a warning of sudden and explosive outbreaks whenever major transits "activate" these points on the chart.

France

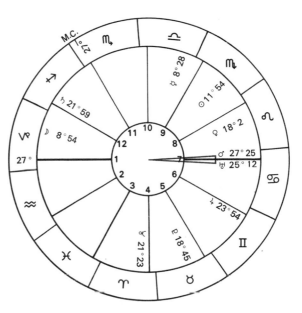

A horoscope cast for September 4, 1870, when the Third French Republic was proclaimed. Disrupting and dangerous aspects of Mars and Uranus (here in opposition to the ascendant) and an unsettling tension across the chart have been persistent features of many of the crises in recent French history. For example, when war broke out on August 4, 1914, the Moon was in conjunction with the ascendant and in opposition to Uranus and Mars, which was square Saturn and Jupiter. Similarly, when the cease-fire in Algeria came into force on March 19, 1961, Saturn was in opposition to Mars-Uranus—an aspect that cannot be said to promise peace.

West Germany

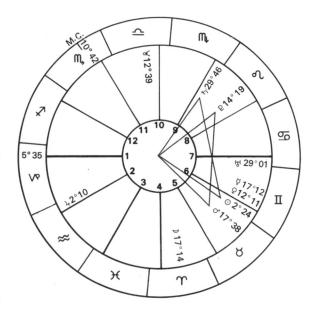

A horoscope cast for the formation of the West German Republic on May 23, 1949, reflects the pattern of Germany's prosperity and progress since the war. A capacity for hard work and discipline and a sense of national duty are apparent from the positions of Capricorn in the ascendant, the Moon in Aries, Scorpio at the mid-heaven, and Mars in Taurus. The aspects of Mars square Pluto and the Sun square Saturn might prove ominous, if Germany's interests should ever conflict with the present balance of world power. This unfortunate possibility is further emphasized by the difficult relations of Mars and Pluto to Russia's fateful Saturn-Sun-Mercury-Uranus T-square formation.

U.S.S.R.

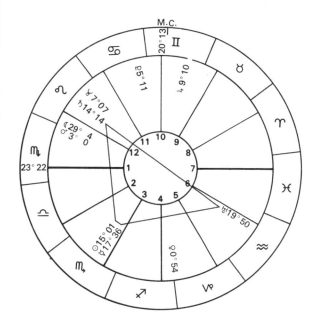

The most significant feature of this chart (cast for November 8, 1917) is the difficult "T-square" pattern formed by the opposition between Saturn and Uranus, both of which are in square to the Sun and Mercury. This configuration of planets suggests the underlying conflict and disagreements between the supreme authority (the Sun), scientists (Uranus), and the state administrators and police (Saturn), which could periodically bring about drastic changes in internal policy. Nazi Germany's preparations for invading Russia (April-May 1941) took place when Germany's Saturn was transiting the U.S.S.R.'s Sun-Saturn-Uranus. When the invasion began on June 22, 1941, Neptune (treachery and fanaticism) and Mars (aggression) were in opposition on Germany's chart and were bisecting the "polarity" formed by Russia's ascendant and descendant.

U.S.A.

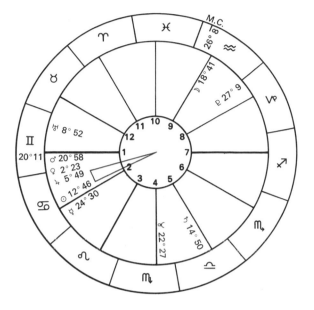

The chart has been cast for the Declaration of Independence on July 4, 1776. It shows Gemini (traditionally the sign of America) in the ascendant, the Sun in conjunction with Jupiter, and the Moon at the mid-heaven in Aquarius—all of which reflect the self-confidence, patriotism, and enthusiasm that are often associated with America. The positions of the ascendant, the mid-heaven, and the Moon are always considered to indicate events of national importance. For example, on November 22, 1963, the day of President Kennedy's assassination, Saturn was in conjunction with America's Moon, and Mars was in opposition to its position in the U.S.A.'s original chart.

The Atomic Age

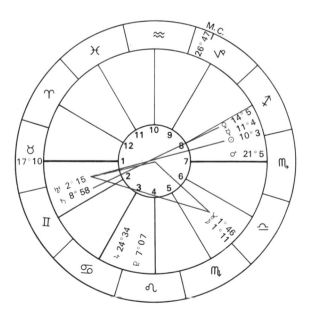

The positions of Uranus and Pluto—the planets associated with atomic power—are the most significant factors in this chart cast for the first controlled atomic chain reaction on December 2, 1942. Fortunately, Pluto receives strong beneficial aspects, and is favorably linked with both Uranus and Saturn. The friction between the planets grouped in the first and seventh houses underlines nuclear power's possible threat to world peace, but Saturn's key position gives hope of its eventual limitation to purely peaceful and domestic purposes (Saturn-Uranus trine Moon-Neptune). A world crisis threatens from October 1965 to June 1966, when Uranus and Pluto will be in conjunction in Virgo. But since the planets will be trine to the ascendant, it seems that this crisis will give way to a new era of constructive use of atomic energy.

Appendix 2

Tables of sidereal time

Everyone knows his Sun-sign—the sign he was "born under"—but few people know their ascendant, which is far more important in deciding one's astrological "type." The following tables list the sidereal time at noon at Greenwich for every day since January 1, 1901; and from them anyone born anywhere in the Northen Hemisphere can calculate the S.T. of his birth time. (For the Southern Hemisphere, see p. 326.) Once the S.T. has been worked out, finding the ascendant is a simple matter of reference to the appropriate table.

1901

	Jan.	Feb.	Mar.	April	May	June	July	Aug.	Sept.	Oct.	Nov.	Dec.
1	18 41 46	20 43 59	22 34 23	0 36 36	2 34 53	4 37 6	6 35 22	8 37 36	10 39 49	12 38 5	14 40 19	16 38 35
2	18 45 43	20 47 56	22 38 19	0 40 32	2 38 49	4 41 2	6 39 19	8 41 32	10 43 45	12 42 2	14 44 15	16 42 32
3	18 49 39	20 51 52	22 42 16	0 44 29	2 42 46	4 44 59	6 43 16	8 45 29	10 47 42	12 45 59	14 48 12	16 46 28
4	18 53 36	20 55 49	22 46 12	0 48 26	2 46 42	4 48 55	6 47 12	8 49 25	10 51 39	12 49 55	14 52 8	16 50 25
5	18 57 32	20 59 46	22 50 9	0 52 22	2 50 39	4 52 52	6 51 9	8 53 22	10 55 35	12 53 52	14 56 5	16 54 21
6	19 1 29	21 3 42	22 54 6	0 56 19	2 54 35	4 56 49	6 55 5	8 57 18	10 59 32	12 57 48	15 0 1	16 58 18
7	19 5 25	21 7 39	22 58 2	1 0 15	2 58 32	5 0 45	6 59 2	9 1 15	11 3 28	13 1 45	15 3 58	17 2 15
8	19 9 22	21 11 35	23 1 59	1 4 12	3 2 28	5 4 42	7 2 58	9 5 12	11 7 25	13 5 41	15 7 54	17 6 11
9	19 13 19	21 15 32	23 5 55	1 8 8	3 6 25	5 8 38	7 6 55	9 9 8	11 11 21	13 9 38	15 11 51	17 10 8
10	19 17 15	21 19 28	23 9 52	1 12 5	3 10 22	5 12 35	7 10 51	9 13 5	11 15 18	13 13 34	15 15 48	17 14 4
11	19 21 12	21 23 25	23 13 48	1 16 1	3 14 18	5 16 31	7 14 48	9 17 1	11 19 14	13 17 31	15 19 44	17 18 1
12	19 25 8	21 27 21	23 17 45	1 19 58	3 18 15	5 20 28	7 18 45	9 20 58	11 23 11	13 21 28	15 23 41	17 21 57
13	19 29 5	21 31 18	23 21 41	1 23 55	3 22 11	5 24 24	7 22 41	9 24 54	11 27 8	13 25 24	15 27 37	17 25 54
14	19 33 1	21 35 15	23 25 38	1 27 51	3 26 8	5 28 21	7 26 38	9 28 51	11 31 4	13 29 21	15 31 34	17 29 50
15	19 36 58	21 39 11	23 29 35	1 31 48	3 30 4	5 32 18	7 30 34	9 32 47	11 35 1	13 33 17	15 35 30	17 33 47
16	19 40 54	21 43 8	23 33 31	1 35 44	3 34 1	5 36 14	7 34 31	9 36 44	11 38 57	13 37 14	15 39 27	17 37 44
17	19 44 51	21 47 4	23 37 28	1 39 41	3 37 57	5 40 11	7 38 27	9 40 41	11 42 54	13 41 10	15 43 23	17 41 40
18	19 48 48	21 51 1	23 41 24	1 43 37	3 41 54	5 44 7	7 42 24	9 44 37	11 46 50	13 45 7	15 47 20	17 45 37
19	19 52 44	21 54 57	23 45 21	1 47 34	3 45 51	5 48 4	7 46 20	9 48 34	11 50 47	13 49 3	15 51 17	17 49 33
20	19 56 41	21 58 54	23 49 17	1 51 30	3 49 47	5 52 0	7 50 17	9 52 30	11 54 43	13 53 0	15 55 13	17 53 30
21	20 0 37	22 2 50	23 53 14	1 55 27	3 53 44	5 55 57	7 54 14	9 56 27	11 58 40	13 56 57	15 59 10	17 57 26
22	20 4 34	22 6 47	23 57 10	1 59 24	3 57 40	5 59 53	7 58 10	10 0 23	12 2 36	14 0 53	16 3 6	18 1 23
23	20 8 30	22 10 43	0 1 7	2 3 20	4 1 37	6 3 50	8 2 7	10 4 20	12 6 33	14 4 50	16 7 3	18 5 20
24	20 12 27	22 14 40	0 5 4	2 7 17	4 5 33	6 7 47	8 6 3	10 8 16	12 10 30	14 8 46	16 10 59	18 9 16
25	20 16 23	22 18 37	0 9 0	2 11 13	4 9 30	6 11 43	8 10 0	10 12 13	12 14 26	14 12 43	16 14 56	18 13 13
26	20 20 20	22 22 33	0 12 57	2 15 10	4 13 26	6 15 40	8 13 56	10 16 10	12 18 23	14 16 39	16 18 52	18 17 9
27	20 24 17	22 26 30	0 16 53	2 19 6	4 17 23	6 19 36	8 17 53	10 20 6	12 22 19	14 20 36	16 22 49	18 21 6
28	20 28 13	22 30 26	0 20 50	2 23 3	4 21 20	6 23 33	8 21 49	10 24 3	12 26 16	14 24 32	16 26 46	18 25 2
29	20 32 10		0 24 46	2 26 59	4 25 16	6 27 29	8 25 46	10 27 59	12 30 12	14 28 29	16 30 42	18 28 59
30	20 36 6		0 28 43	2 30 56	4 29 13	6 31 26	8 29 43	10 31 56	12 34 9	14 32 25	16 34 39	18 32 55
31	20 40 3		0 32 39		4 33 9		8 33 39	10 35 52		14 36 22		18 36 52

1902

	Jan.	Feb.	Mar.	April	May	June	July	Aug.	Sept.	Oct.	Nov.	Dec.
1	18 40 49	20 43 2	22 33 25	0 35 38	2 33 55	4 36 8	6 34 25	8 36 38	10 38 51	12 37 8	14 39 21	16 37 38
2	18 44 45	20 46 58	22 37 22	0 39 35	2 37 52	4 40 5	6 38 21	8 40 35	10 42 48	12 41 4	14 43 18	16 41 34
3	18 48 42	20 50 55	22 41 18	0 43 32	2 41 48	4 44 1	6 42 18	8 44 31	10 46 44	12 45 1	14 47 14	16 45 31
4	18 52 38	20 54 51	22 45 15	0 47 28	2 45 45	4 47 58	6 46 15	8 48 28	10 50 41	12 48 58	14 51 11	16 49 27
5	18 56 35	20 58 48	22 49 11	0 51 25	2 49 41	4 51 54	6 50 11	8 52 24	10 54 38	12 52 54	14 55 7	16 53 24
6	19 0 31	21 2 45	22 53 8	0 55 21	2 53 38	4 55 51	6 54 8	8 56 21	10 58 34	12 56 51	14 59 4	16 57 20
7	19 4 28	21 6 41	22 57 5	0 59 18	2 57 34	4 59 48	6 58 4	9 0 17	11 2 31	13 0 47	15 3 0	17 1 17
8	19 8 24	21 10 38	23 1 1	1 3 14	3 1 31	5 3 44	7 2 1	9 4 14	11 6 27	13 4 44	15 6 57	17 5 14
9	19 12 21	21 14 34	23 4 58	1 7 11	3 5 27	5 7 41	7 5 57	9 8 11	11 10 24	13 8 40	15 10 53	17 9 10
10	19 16 18	21 18 31	23 8 54	1 11 7	3 9 24	5 11 37	7 9 54	9 12 7	11 14 20	13 12 37	15 14 50	17 13 7
11	19 20 14	21 22 27	23 12 51	1 15 4	3 13 21	5 15 34	7 13 50	9 16 4	11 18 17	13 16 33	15 18 47	17 17 3
12	19 24 11	21 26 24	23 16 47	1 19 0	3 17 17	5 19 30	7 17 47	9 20 0	11 22 13	13 20 30	15 22 43	17 21 0
13	19 28 7	21 30 20	23 20 44	1 22 57	3 21 14	5 23 27	7 21 44	9 23 57	11 26 10	13 24 26	15 26 40	17 24 56
14	19 32 4	21 34 17	23 24 40	1 26 54	3 25 10	5 27 23	7 25 40	9 27 53	11 30 6	13 28 23	15 30 36	17 28 53
15	19 36 0	21 38 14	23 28 37	1 30 50	3 29 7	5 31 20	7 29 37	9 31 50	11 34 3	13 32 20	15 34 33	17 32 49
16	19 39 57	21 42 10	23 32 34	1 34 47	3 33 3	5 35 17	7 33 33	9 35 46	11 38 0	13 36 16	15 38 29	17 36 46
17	19 43 53	21 46 7	23 36 30	1 38 43	3 37 0	5 39 13	7 37 30	9 39 43	11 41 56	13 40 13	15 42 26	17 40 43
18	19 47 50	21 50 3	23 40 27	1 42 40	3 40 56	5 43 10	7 41 26	9 43 40	11 45 53	13 44 9	15 46 22	17 44 39
19	19 51 47	21 54 0	23 44 23	1 46 36	3 44 53	5 47 6	7 45 23	9 47 36	11 49 49	13 48 6	15 50 19	17 48 36
20	19 55 43	21 57 56	23 48 20	1 50 33	3 48 50	5 51 3	7 49 19	9 51 33	11 53 46	13 52 2	15 54 16	17 52 32
21	19 59 40	22 1 53	23 52 16	1 54 29	3 52 46	5 54 59	7 53 16	9 55 29	11 57 42	13 55 59	15 58 12	17 56 29
22	20 3 36	22 5 49	23 56 13	1 58 26	3 56 43	5 58 56	7 57 13	9 59 26	12 1 39	13 59 56	16 2 9	18 0 25
23	20 7 33	22 9 46	0 0 9	2 2 23	4 0 39	6 2 52	8 1 9	10 3 22	12 5 35	14 3 52	16 6 5	18 4 22
24	20 11 29	22 13 43	0 4 6	2 6 19	4 4 36	6 6 49	8 5 6	10 7 19	12 9 32	14 7 49	16 10 2	18 8 18
25	20 15 26	22 17 39	0 8 3	2 10 16	4 8 32	6 10 46	8 9 2	10 11 15	12 13 28	14 11 45	16 13 58	18 12 15
26	20 19 22	22 21 36	0 11 59	2 14 12	4 12 29	6 14 42	8 12 59	10 15 12	12 17 25	14 15 42	16 17 55	18 16 12
27	20 23 19	22 25 32	0 15 56	2 18 9	4 16 25	6 18 39	8 16 55	10 19 9	12 21 22	14 19 38	16 21 51	18 20 8
28	20 27 16	22 29 29	0 19 52	2 22 5	4 20 22	6 22 35	8 20 52	10 23 5	12 25 18	14 23 35	16 25 48	18 24 5
29	20 31 12		0 23 49	2 26 2	4 24 19	6 26 32	8 24 48	10 27 2	12 29 15	14 27 31	16 29 45	18 28 1
30	20 35 9		0 27 45	2 29 58	4 28 15	6 30 28	8 28 45	10 30 58	12 33 11	14 31 28	16 33 41	18 31 58
31	20 39 5		0 31 42		4 32 12		8 32 42	10 34 55		14 35 24		18 35 54

First, refer to the map of time zones on p. 245 and translate your own time into Greenwich Mean Time. Then find the S.T. at noon on your birthday in the following tables. Add to this figure the number of hours you were born after noon, plus 10 seconds for every hour. (Subtract in both cases if you were born before noon.) Next, if you were not born on the Greenwich meridian, you convert this S.T. into the S.T. for your birthplace. Find in an atlas the longitude of your birthplace; multiply this figure by four to convert the total into minutes and seconds of time. Add this total (if born east of Greenwich) to the S.T. (or subtract if west) and you have your S.T. at birth. Now you can find your ascendant in a table of houses for your specific latitude.

1903

Jan.	Feb.	Mar.	April	May	June	July	Aug.	Sept.	Oct.	Nov.	Dec.	
18 39 51	20 42 4	22 32 28	0 34 41	2 32 57	4 35 11	6 33 27	8 35 40	10 37 54	12 36 10	14 38 23	16 36 40	1
18 43 47	20 46 1	22 36 24	0 38 37	2 36 54	4 39 7	6 37 24	8 39 37	10 41 50	12 40 7	14 42 20	16 40 37	2
18 47 44	20 49 57	22 40 21	0 42 34	2 40 50	4 43 4	6 41 20	8 43 34	10 45 47	12 44 3	14 46 16	16 44 33	3
18 51 41	20 53 54	22 44 17	0 46 30	2 44 47	4 47 0	6 45 17	8 47 30	10 49 43	12 48 0	14 50 13	16 48 30	4
18 55 37	20 57 50	22 48 14	0 50 27	2 48 44	4 50 57	6 49 14	8 51 27	10 53 40	12 51 56	14 54 10	16 52 26	5
18 59 34	21 1 47	22 52 10	0 54 24	2 52 40	4 54 53	6 53 10	8 55 23	10 57 36	12 55 53	14 58 6	16 56 23	6
19 3 30	21 5 43	22 56 7	0 58 20	2 56 37	4 58 50	6 57 7	8 59 20	11 1 33	12 59 50	15 2 3	17 0 19	7
19 7 27	21 9 40	23 0 4	1 2 17	3 0 33	5 2 46	7 1 3	9 3 16	11 5 30	13 3 46	15 5 59	17 4 16	8
19 11 23	21 13 37	23 4 0	1 6 13	3 4 30	5 6 43	7 5 0	9 7 13	11 9 26	13 7 43	15 9 56	17 8 12	9
19 15 20	21 17 33	23 7 57	1 10 10	3 8 26	5 10 40	7 8 56	9 11 9	11 13 23	13 11 39	15 13 52	17 12 9	10
19 19 17	21 21 30	23 11 53	1 14 6	3 12 23	5 14 36	7 12 53	9 15 6	11 17 19	13 15 36	15 17 49	17 16 6	11
19 23 13	21 25 26	23 15 50	1 18 3	3 16 19	5 18 33	7 16 49	9 19 3	11 21 16	13 19 32	15 21 45	17 20 2	12
19 27 10	21 29 23	23 19 46	1 21 59	3 20 16	5 22 29	7 20 46	9 22 59	11 25 12	13 23 29	15 25 42	17 23 59	13
19 31 6	21 33 19	23 23 43	1 25 56	3 24 13	5 26 26	7 24 43	9 26 56	11 29 9	13 27 25	15 29 39	17 27 55	14
19 35 3	21 37 16	23 27 39	1 29 53	3 28 9	5 30 22	7 28 39	9 30 52	11 33 5	13 31 22	15 33 35	17 31 52	15
19 38 59	21 41 12	23 31 36	1 33 49	3 32 6	5 34 19	7 32 36	9 34 49	11 37 2	13 35 19	15 37 32	17 35 48	16
19 42 56	21 45 9	23 35 33	1 37 46	3 36 2	5 38 15	7 36 32	9 38 45	11 40 59	13 39 15	15 41 28	17 39 45	17
19 46 53	21 49 6	23 39 29	1 41 42	3 39 59	5 42 12	7 40 29	9 42 42	11 44 55	13 43 12	15 45 25	17 43 41	18
19 50 49	21 53 2	23 43 26	1 45 39	3 43 55	5 46 9	7 44 25	9 46 38	11 48 52	13 47 8	15 49 21	17 47 38	19
19 54 45	21 56 59	23 47 22	1 49 35	3 47 52	5 50 5	7 48 22	9 50 35	11 52 48	13 51 5	15 53 18	17 51 35	20
19 58 42	22 0 55	23 51 19	1 53 32	3 51 48	5 54 2	7 52 18	9 54 32	11 56 45	13 55 1	15 57 14	17 55 31	21
20 2 39	22 4 52	23 55 15	1 57 28	3 55 45	5 57 58	7 56 15	9 58 28	12 0 41	13 58 58	16 1 11	17 59 28	22
20 6 35	22 8 48	23 59 12	2 1 25	3 59 42	6 1 55	8 0 12	10 2 25	12 4 38	14 2 54	16 5 8	18 3 24	23
20 10 32	22 12 45	0 3 8	2 5 21	4 3 38	6 5 51	8 4 8	10 6 21	12 8 34	14 6 51	16 9 4	18 7 21	24
20 14 28	22 16 41	0 7 5	2 9 18	4 7 35	6 9 48	8 8 5	10 10 18	12 12 31	14 10 47	16 13 1	18 11 17	25
20 18 25	22 20 38	0 11 1	2 13 15	4 11 31	6 13 44	8 12 1	10 14 14	12 16 27	14 14 44	16 16 57	18 15 14	26
20 22 21	22 24 35	0 14 58	2 17 11	4 15 28	6 17 41	8 15 58	10 18 11	12 20 24	14 18 41	16 20 54	18 19 10	27
20 26 18	22 28 31	0 18 55	2 21 8	4 19 24	6 21 38	8 19 54	10 22 7	12 24 21	14 22 37	16 24 50	18 23 7	28
20 30 15		0 22 51	2 25 4	4 23 21	6 25 34	8 23 51	10 26 4	12 28 17	14 26 34	16 28 47	18 27 4	29
20 34 11		0 26 48	2 29 1	4 27 17	6 29 31	8 27 47	10 30 1	12 32 14	14 30 30	16 32 43	18 31 0	30
20 38 8		0 30 44		4 31 14		8 31 44	10 33 57		14 34 27		18 34 57	31

1904

Jan.	Feb.	Mar.	April	May	June	July	Aug.	Sept.	Oct.	Nov.	Dec.	
18 38 53	20 41 7	22 35 27	0 37 40	2 35 56	4 38 9	6 36 26	8 38 39	10 40 53	12 39 9	14 41 22	16 39 39	1
18 42 50	20 45 3	22 39 23	0 41 36	2 39 53	4 42 6	6 40 23	8 42 36	10 44 49	12 43 6	14 45 19	16 43 35	2
18 46 46	20 49 0	22 43 20	0 45 33	2 43 49	4 46 3	6 44 19	8 46 33	10 48 46	12 47 2	14 49 15	16 47 32	3
18 50 43	20 52 56	22 47 16	0 49 29	2 47 46	4 49 59	6 48 16	8 50 29	10 52 42	12 50 59	14 53 12	16 51 29	4
18 54 40	20 56 53	22 51 13	0 53 26	2 51 42	4 53 56	6 52 12	8 54 26	10 56 39	12 54 55	14 57 8	16 55 25	5
18 58 36	21 0 49	22 55 9	0 57 22	2 55 39	4 57 52	6 56 9	8 58 22	11 0 35	12 58 52	15 1 5	16 59 22	6
19 2 33	21 4 46	22 59 6	1 1 19	2 59 36	5 1 49	7 0 6	9 2 19	11 4 32	13 2 48	15 5 2	17 3 18	7
19 6 29	21 8 42	23 3 2	1 5 16	3 3 32	5 5 45	7 4 2	9 6 15	11 8 28	13 6 45	15 8 58	17 7 15	8
19 10 26	21 12 39	23 6 59	1 9 12	3 7 29	5 9 42	7 7 59	9 10 12	11 12 25	13 10 42	15 12 55	17 11 11	9
19 14 22	21 16 36	23 10 56	1 13 9	3 11 25	5 13 38	7 11 55	9 14 8	11 16 22	13 14 38	15 16 51	17 15 8	10
19 18 19	21 20 32	23 14 52	1 17 5	3 15 22	5 17 35	7 15 52	9 18 5	11 20 18	13 18 35	15 20 48	17 19 4	11
19 22 15	21 24 29	23 18 49	1 21 2	3 19 18	5 21 32	7 19 48	9 22 1	11 24 15	13 22 31	15 24 44	17 23 1	12
19 26 12	21 28 25	23 22 45	1 24 58	3 23 15	5 25 28	7 23 45	9 25 58	11 28 11	13 26 28	15 28 41	17 26 58	13
19 30 9	21 32 22	23 26 42	1 28 55	3 27 11	5 29 25	7 27 41	9 29 55	11 32 8	13 30 24	15 32 37	17 30 54	14
19 34 5	21 36 18	23 30 38	1 32 51	3 31 8	5 33 21	7 31 38	9 33 51	11 36 4	13 34 21	15 36 34	17 34 51	15
19 38 2	21 40 15	23 34 35	1 36 48	3 35 5	5 37 18	7 35 35	9 37 48	11 40 1	13 38 17	15 40 31	17 38 47	16
19 41 58	21 44 11	23 38 31	1 40 45	3 39 1	5 41 14	7 39 31	9 41 44	11 43 57	13 42 14	15 44 27	17 42 44	17
19 45 55	21 48 8	23 42 28	1 44 41	3 42 58	5 45 11	7 43 28	9 45 41	11 47 54	13 46 11	15 48 24	17 46 40	18
19 49 51	21 52 4	23 46 24	1 48 38	3 46 54	5 49 7	7 47 24	9 49 37	11 51 51	13 50 7	15 52 20	17 50 37	19
19 53 48	21 56 1	23 50 21	1 52 34	3 50 51	5 53 4	7 51 21	9 53 34	11 55 47	13 54 4	15 56 17	17 54 34	20
19 57 44	21 59 58	23 54 18	1 56 31	3 54 47	5 57 1	7 55 17	9 57 30	11 59 44	13 58 0	16 0 13	17 58 30	21
20 1 41	22 3 54	23 58 14	2 0 27	3 58 44	6 0 57	7 59 14	10 1 27	12 3 40	14 1 57	16 4 10	18 2 27	22
20 5 38	22 7 51	0 2 11	2 4 24	4 2 40	6 4 54	8 3 10	10 5 24	12 7 37	14 5 53	16 8 6	18 6 23	23
20 9 34	22 11 47	0 6 7	2 8 20	4 6 37	6 8 50	8 7 7	10 9 20	12 11 33	14 9 50	16 12 3	18 10 20	24
20 13 31	22 15 44	0 10 4	2 12 17	4 10 34	6 12 47	8 11 4	10 13 17	12 15 30	14 13 46	16 16 0	18 14 16	25
20 17 27	22 19 40	0 14 0	2 16 13	4 14 30	6 16 43	8 15 0	10 17 13	12 19 26	14 17 43	16 19 56	18 18 13	26
20 21 24	22 23 37	0 17 57	2 20 10	4 18 27	6 20 40	8 18 57	10 21 10	12 23 23	14 21 39	16 23 53	18 22 9	27
20 25 20	22 27 33	0 21 53	2 24 7	4 22 23	6 24 36	8 22 53	10 25 6	12 27 19	14 25 36	16 27 49	18 26 6	28
20 29 17	22 31 30	0 25 50	2 28 3	4 26 20	6 28 33	8 26 50	10 29 3	12 31 16	14 29 33	16 31 46	18 30 3	29
20 33 13		0 29 47	2 32 0	4 30 16	6 32 30	8 30 46	10 32 59	12 35 13	14 33 29	16 35 42	18 33 59	30
20 37 10		0 33 43		4 34 13		8 34 43	10 36 56		14 37 26		18 37 56	31

1905

	Jan.	Feb.	Mar.	April	May	June	July	Aug.	Sept.	Oct.	Nov.	Dec.
1	18 41 52	20 44 5	22 34 29	0 36 42	2 34 59	4 37 12	6 35 29	8 37 42	10 39 55	12 38 11	14 40 25	16 38 41
2	18 45 49	20 48 2	22 38 25	0 40 39	2 38 55	4 41 8	6 39 25	8 41 38	10 43 51	12 42 8	14 44 21	16 42 38
3	18 49 45	20 51 59	22 42 22	0 44 35	2 42 52	4 45 5	6 43 22	8 45 35	10 47 48	12 46 5	14 48 18	16 46 34
4	18 53 42	20 55 55	22 46 19	0 48 32	2 46 48	4 49 2	6 47 18	8 49 31	10 51 45	12 50 1	14 52 14	16 50 31
5	18 57 38	20 59 52	22 50 15	0 52 28	2 50 45	4 52 58	6 51 15	8 53 28	10 55 41	12 53 58	14 56 11	16 54 28
6	19 1 35	21 3 48	22 54 12	0 56 25	2 54 41	4 56 55	6 55 11	8 57 25	10 59 38	12 57 54	15 0 7	16 58 24
7	19 5 32	21 7 45	22 58 8	1 0 21	2 58 38	5 0 51	6 59 8	9 1 21	11 3 34	13 1 51	15 4 4	17 2 21
8	19 9 28	21 11 41	23 2 5	1 4 18	3 2 35	5 4 48	7 3 4	9 5 18	11 7 31	13 5 47	15 8 1	17 6 17
9	19 13 25	21 15 38	23 6 1	1 8 14	3 6 31	5 8 44	7 7 1	9 9 14	11 11 27	13 9 44	15 11 57	17 10 14
10	19 17 21	21 19 34	23 9 58	1 12 11	3 10 28	5 12 41	7 10 58	9 13 11	11 15 24	13 13 40	15 15 54	17 14 10
11	19 21 18	21 23 31	23 13 54	1 16 8	3 14 24	5 16 37	7 14 54	9 17 7	11 19 20	13 17 37	15 19 50	17 18 7
12	19 25 14	21 27 28	23 17 51	1 20 4	3 18 21	5 20 34	7 18 51	9 21 4	11 23 17	13 21 34	15 23 47	17 22 3
13	19 29 11	21 31 24	23 21 48	1 24 1	3 22 17	5 24 31	7 22 47	9 25 0	11 27 14	13 25 30	15 27 43	17 26 0
14	19 33 7	21 35 21	23 25 44	1 27 57	3 26 14	5 28 27	7 26 44	9 28 57	11 31 10	13 29 27	15 31 40	17 29 57
15	19 37 4	21 39 17	23 29 41	1 31 54	3 30 10	5 32 24	7 30 40	9 32 54	11 35 7	13 33 23	15 35 36	17 33 53
16	19 41 1	21 43 14	23 33 37	1 35 50	3 34 7	5 36 20	7 34 37	9 36 50	11 39 3	13 37 20	15 39 33	17 37 50
17	19 44 57	21 47 10	23 37 34	1 39 47	3 38 3	5 40 17	7 38 33	9 40 47	11 43 0	13 41 16	15 43 30	17 41 46
18	19 48 54	21 51 7	23 41 30	1 43 43	3 42 0	5 44 13	7 42 30	9 44 43	11 46 56	13 45 13	15 47 26	17 45 43
19	19 52 50	21 55 3	23 45 27	1 47 40	3 45 57	5 48 10	7 46 27	9 48 40	11 50 53	13 49 9	15 51 23	17 49 39
20	19 56 47	21 59 0	23 49 23	1 51 37	3 49 53	5 52 6	7 50 23	9 52 36	11 54 49	13 53 6	15 55 19	17 53 36
21	20 0 43	22 2 56	23 53 20	1 55 33	3 53 50	5 56 3	7 54 20	9 56 33	11 58 46	13 57 3	15 59 16	17 57 32
22	20 4 40	22 6 53	23 57 17	1 59 30	3 57 46	6 0 0	7 58 16	10 0 29	12 2 43	14 0 59	16 3 12	18 1 29
23	20 8 36	22 10 50	0 1 13	2 3 26	4 1 43	6 3 56	8 2 13	10 4 26	12 6 39	14 4 56	16 7 9	18 5 26
24	20 12 33	22 14 46	0 5 10	2 7 23	4 5 39	6 7 53	8 6 9	10 8 23	12 10 36	14 8 52	16 11 5	18 9 22
25	20 16 30	22 18 43	0 9 6	2 11 19	4 9 36	6 11 49	8 10 6	10 12 19	12 14 32	14 12 49	16 15 2	18 13 19
26	20 20 26	22 22 39	0 13 3	2 15 16	4 13 33	6 15 46	8 14 2	10 16 16	12 18 29	14 16 45	16 18 59	18 17 15
27	20 24 23	22 26 36	0 16 59	2 19 12	4 17 29	6 19 42	8 17 59	10 20 12	12 22 25	14 20 42	16 22 55	18 21 12
28	20 28 19	22 30 32	0 20 56	2 23 9	4 21 26	6 23 39	8 21 56	10 24 9	12 26 22	14 24 38	16 26 52	18 25 8
29	20 32 16		0 24 52	2 27 6	4 25 22	6 27 35	8 25 52	10 28 5	12 30 18	14 28 35	16 30 48	18 29 5
30	20 36 12		0 28 49	2 31 2	4 29 19	6 31 32	8 29 49	10 32 2	12 34 15	14 32 32	16 34 45	18 33 1
31	20 40 9		0 32 45		4 33 15		8 33 45	10 35 58		14 36 28		18 36 58

1906

	Jan.	Feb.	Mar.	April	May	June	July	Aug.	Sept.	Oct.	Nov.	Dec.
1	18 40 55	20 43 8	22 33 31	0 35 44	2 34 1	4 36 14	6 34 31	8 36 44	10 38 57	12 37 14	14 39 27	16 37 44
2	18 44 51	20 47 4	22 37 28	0 39 41	2 37 58	4 40 11	6 38 28	8 40 41	10 42 54	12 41 10	14 43 24	16 41 40
3	18 48 48	20 51 1	22 41 24	0 43 38	2 41 54	4 44 7	6 42 24	8 44 37	10 46 50	12 45 7	14 47 20	16 45 37
4	18 52 44	20 54 57	22 45 21	0 47 34	2 45 51	4 48 4	6 46 21	8 48 34	10 50 47	12 49 4	14 51 17	16 49 33
5	18 56 41	20 58 54	22 49 18	0 51 31	2 49 47	4 52 0	6 50 17	8 52 30	10 54 44	12 53 0	14 55 13	16 53 30
6	19 0 37	21 2 51	22 53 14	0 55 27	2 53 44	4 55 57	6 54 14	8 56 27	10 58 40	12 56 57	14 59 10	16 57 27
7	19 4 34	21 6 47	22 57 11	0 59 24	2 57 40	4 59 54	6 58 10	9 0 24	11 2 37	13 0 53	15 3 6	17 1 23
8	19 8 30	21 10 44	23 1 7	1 3 20	3 1 37	5 3 50	7 2 7	9 4 20	11 6 33	13 4 50	15 7 3	17 5 20
9	19 12 27	21 14 40	23 5 4	1 7 17	3 5 33	5 7 47	7 6 3	9 8 17	11 10 30	13 8 46	15 11 0	17 9 16
10	19 16 24	21 18 37	23 9 0	1 11 13	3 9 30	5 11 43	7 10 0	9 12 13	11 14 26	13 12 43	15 14 56	17 13 13
11	19 20 20	21 22 33	23 12 57	1 15 10	3 13 27	5 15 40	7 13 57	9 16 10	11 18 23	13 16 39	15 18 53	17 17 9
12	19 24 17	21 26 30	23 16 53	1 19 7	3 17 23	5 19 36	7 17 53	9 20 6	11 22 19	13 20 36	15 22 49	17 21 6
13	19 28 13	21 30 26	23 20 50	1 23 3	3 21 20	5 23 33	7 21 50	9 24 3	11 26 16	13 24 33	15 26 46	17 25 2
14	19 32 10	21 34 23	23 24 47	1 27 0	3 25 16	5 27 29	7 25 46	9 27 59	11 30 13	13 28 29	15 30 42	17 28 59
15	19 36 6	21 38 20	23 28 43	1 30 56	3 29 13	5 31 26	7 29 43	9 31 56	11 34 9	13 32 26	15 34 39	17 32 56
16	19 40 3	21 42 16	23 32 40	1 34 53	3 33 9	5 35 23	7 33 39	9 35 53	11 38 6	13 36 22	15 38 35	17 36 52
17	19 43 59	21 46 13	23 36 36	1 38 49	3 37 6	5 39 19	7 37 36	9 39 49	11 42 2	13 40 19	15 42 32	17 40 49
18	19 47 56	21 50 9	23 40 33	1 42 46	3 41 2	5 43 16	7 41 32	9 43 46	11 45 59	13 44 15	15 46 29	17 44 45
19	19 51 53	21 54 6	23 44 29	1 46 42	3 44 59	5 47 12	7 45 29	9 47 42	11 49 55	13 48 12	15 50 25	17 48 42
20	19 55 49	21 58 2	23 48 26	1 50 39	3 48 56	5 51 9	7 49 26	9 51 39	11 53 52	13 52 8	15 54 22	17 52 38
21	19 59 46	22 1 59	23 52 22	1 54 35	3 52 52	5 55 5	7 53 22	9 55 35	11 57 48	13 56 5	15 58 18	17 56 35
22	20 3 42	22 5 55	23 56 19	1 58 32	3 56 49	5 59 2	7 57 19	9 59 32	12 1 45	14 0 2	16 2 15	18 0 31
23	20 7 39	22 9 52	0 0 15	2 2 29	4 0 45	6 2 59	8 1 15	10 3 28	12 5 42	14 3 58	16 6 11	18 4 28
24	20 11 35	22 13 49	0 4 12	2 6 25	4 4 42	6 6 55	8 5 12	10 7 25	12 9 38	14 7 55	16 10 8	18 8 25
25	20 15 32	22 17 45	0 8 9	2 10 22	4 8 38	6 10 52	8 9 8	10 11 22	12 13 35	14 11 51	16 14 4	18 12 21
26	20 19 28	22 21 42	0 12 5	2 14 18	4 12 35	6 14 48	8 13 5	10 15 18	12 17 31	14 15 48	16 18 1	18 16 18
27	20 23 25	22 25 38	0 16 2	2 18 15	4 16 31	6 18 45	8 17 1	10 19 15	12 21 28	14 19 44	16 21 58	18 20 14
28	20 27 22	22 29 35	0 19 58	2 22 11	4 20 28	6 22 41	8 20 58	10 23 11	12 25 24	14 23 41	16 25 54	18 24 11
29	20 31 18		0 23 55	2 26 8	4 24 25	6 26 38	8 24 55	10 27 8	12 29 21	14 27 37	16 29 51	18 28 7
30	20 35 15		0 27 51	2 30 4	4 28 21	6 30 34	8 28 51	10 31 4	12 33 17	14 31 34	16 33 47	18 32 4
31	20 39 11		0 31 48		4 32 18		8 32 48	10 35 1		14 35 31		18 36 0

1907

	Jan.	Feb.	Mar.	April	May	June	July	Aug.	Sept.	Oct.	Nov.	Dec.
1	18 39 57	20 42 10	22 32 34	0 34 47	2 33 4	4 35 17	6 33 33	8 35 47	10 38 0	12 36 16	14 38 30	16 36 46
2	18 43 54	20 46 7	22 36 30	0 38 43	2 37 0	4 39 13	6 37 30	8 39 43	10 41 56	12 40 13	14 42 26	16 40 43
3	18 47 50	20 50 3	22 40 27	0 42 40	2 40 57	4 43 10	6 41 27	8 43 40	10 45 53	12 44 9	14 46 23	16 44 39
4	18 51 47	20 54 0	22 44 23	0 46 37	2 44 53	4 47 6	6 45 23	8 47 36	10 49 50	12 48 6	14 50 19	16 48 36
5	18 55 43	20 57 57	22 48 20	0 50 33	2 48 50	4 51 3	6 49 20	8 51 33	10 53 46	12 52 3	14 54 16	16 52 33
6	18 59 40	21 1 53	22 52 17	0 54 30	2 52 46	4 55 0	6 53 16	8 55 29	10 57 43	12 55 59	14 58 12	16 56 29
7	19 3 36	21 5 50	22 56 13	0 58 26	2 56 43	4 58 56	6 57 13	8 59 26	11 1 39	12 59 56	15 2 9	17 0 26
8	19 7 33	21 9 46	23 0 10	1 2 23	3 0 39	5 2 53	7 1 9	9 3 23	11 5 36	13 3 52	15 6 6	17 4 22
9	19 11 29	21 13 43	23 4 6	1 6 19	3 4 36	5 6 49	7 5 6	9 7 19	11 9 32	13 7 49	15 10 2	17 8 19
10	19 15 26	21 17 39	23 8 3	1 10 16	3 8 33	5 10 46	7 9 2	9 11 16	11 13 29	13 11 45	15 13 59	17 12 15
11	19 19 23	21 21 36	23 11 59	1 14 12	3 12 29	5 14 42	7 12 59	9 15 12	11 17 25	13 15 42	15 17 55	17 16 12
12	19 23 19	21 25 32	23 15 56	1 18 9	3 16 26	5 18 39	7 16 55	9 19 9	11 21 22	13 19 38	15 21 52	17 20 8
13	19 27 16	21 29 29	23 19 52	1 22 6	3 20 22	5 22 35	7 20 52	9 23 5	11 25 19	13 23 35	15 25 48	17 24 5
14	19 31 12	21 33 26	23 23 49	1 26 2	3 24 19	5 26 32	7 24 49	9 27 2	11 29 15	13 27 32	15 29 45	17 28 2
15	19 35 9	21 37 22	23 27 46	1 29 59	3 28 15	5 30 29	7 28 45	9 30 58	11 33 12	13 31 28	15 33 41	17 31 58
16	19 39 5	21 41 19	23 31 42	1 33 55	3 32 12	5 34 25	7 32 42	9 34 55	11 37 8	13 35 25	15 37 38	17 35 55
17	19 43 2	21 45 15	23 35 39	1 37 52	3 36 8	5 38 22	7 36 38	9 38 52	11 41 5	13 39 21	15 41 35	17 39 51
18	19 46 59	21 49 12	23 39 35	1 41 48	3 40 5	5 42 18	7 40 35	9 42 48	11 45 1	13 43 18	15 45 31	17 43 48
19	19 50 55	21 53 8	23 43 32	1 45 45	3 44 2	5 46 15	7 44 32	9 46 45	11 48 58	13 47 14	15 49 28	17 47 44
20	19 54 52	21 57 5	23 47 28	1 49 41	3 47 58	5 50 11	7 48 28	9 50 41	11 52 54	13 51 11	15 53 24	17 51 41
21	19 58 48	22 1 1	23 51 25	1 53 38	3 51 55	5 54 8	7 52 25	9 54 38	11 56 51	13 55 8	15 57 21	17 55 37
22	20 2 45	22 4 58	23 55 21	1 57 35	3 55 51	5 58 4	7 56 21	9 58 34	12 0 48	13 59 4	16 1 17	17 59 34
23	20 6 41	22 8 54	23 59 18	2 1 31	3 59 48	6 2 1	8 0 18	10 2 31	12 4 44	14 3 1	16 5 14	18 3 31
24	20 10 38	22 12 51	0 3 15	2 5 28	4 3 44	6 5 58	8 4 14	10 6 27	12 8 41	14 6 57	16 9 10	18 7 27
25	20 14 34	22 16 48	0 7 11	2 9 24	4 7 41	6 9 54	8 8 11	10 10 24	12 12 37	14 10 54	16 13 7	18 11 24
26	20 18 31	22 20 44	0 11 8	2 13 21	4 11 37	6 13 51	8 12 7	10 14 21	12 16 34	14 14 50	16 17 4	18 15 20
27	20 22 28	22 24 41	0 15 4	2 17 17	4 15 34	6 17 47	8 16 4	10 18 17	12 20 30	14 18 47	16 21 0	18 19 17
28	20 26 24	22 28 37	0 19 1	2 21 14	4 19 31	6 21 44	8 20 1	10 22 14	12 24 27	14 22 43	16 24 57	18 23 13
29	20 30 21		0 22 57	2 25 10	4 23 27	6 25 40	8 23 57	10 26 10	12 28 23	14 26 40	16 28 53	18 27 10
30	20 34 17		0 26 54	2 29 7	4 27 24	6 29 37	8 27 54	10 30 7	12 32 20	14 30 37	16 32 50	18 31 6
31	20 38 14		0 30 50		4 31 20		8 31 50	10 34 3		14 34 33		18 35 3

Day	Jan.	Feb.	Mar.	April	May	June	July	Aug.	Sept.	Oct.	Nov.	Dec.
1	18 39 0	20 41 13	22 35 33	0 37 46	2 36 3	4 38 16	6 36 33	8 38 46	10 40 59	12 39 16	14 41 29	16 39 46
2	18 42 56	20 45 9	22 39 29	0 41 43	2 39 59	4 42 12	6 40 29	8 42 42	10 44 56	12 43 12	14 45 25	16 43 42
3	18 46 53	20 49 6	22 43 26	0 45 39	2 43 56	4 46 9	6 44 26	8 46 39	10 48 52	12 47 9	14 49 22	16 47 39
4	18 50 49	20 53 3	22 47 23	0 49 36	2 47 52	4 50 6	6 48 22	8 50 36	10 52 49	12 51 5	14 53 19	16 51 35
5	18 54 46	20 56 59	22 51 19	0 53 32	2 51 49	4 54 2	6 52 19	8 54 32	10 56 45	12 55 2	14 57 15	16 55 32
6	18 58 42	21 0 56	22 55 16	0 57 29	2 55 45	4 57 59	6 56 15	8 58 29	11 0 42	12 58 58	15 1 12	16 59 28
7	19 2 39	21 4 52	22 59 12	1 1 25	2 59 42	5 1 55	7 0 12	9 2 25	11 4 38	13 2 55	15 5 8	17 3 25
8	19 6 36	21 8 49	23 3 0	1 5 22	3 3 39	5 5 52	7 4 9	9 6 22	11 8 35	13 6 52	15 9 5	17 7 21
9	19 10 32	21 12 45	23 7 5	1 9 19	3 7 35	5 9 48	7 8 5	9 10 18	11 12 32	13 10 48	15 13 1	17 11 18
10	19 14 29	21 16 42	23 11 2	1 13 15	3 11 32	5 13 45	7 12 2	9 14 15	11 16 28	13 14 45	15 16 58	17 15 15
11	19 18 25	21 20 38	23 14 58	1 17 12	3 15 28	5 17 42	7 15 58	9 18 11	11 20 25	13 18 41	15 20 54	17 19 11
12	19 22 22	21 24 35	23 18 55	1 21 8	3 19 25	5 21 38	7 19 55	9 22 8	11 24 21	13 22 38	15 24 51	17 23 8
13	19 26 18	21 28 32	23 22 52	1 25 5	3 23 21	5 25 35	7 23 51	9 26 5	11 28 18	13 26 34	15 28 48	17 27 4
14	19 30 15	21 32 28	23 26 48	1 29 1	3 27 18	5 29 31	7 27 48	9 30 1	11 32 14	13 30 31	15 32 44	17 31 1
15	19 34 11	21 36 25	23 30 45	1 32 58	3 31 14	5 33 28	7 31 44	9 33 58	11 36 11	13 34 27	15 36 41	17 34 57
16	19 38 8	21 40 21	23 34 41	1 36 54	3 35 11	5 37 24	7 35 41	9 37 54	11 40 7	13 38 23	15 40 37	17 38 54
17	19 42 5	21 44 18	23 38 38	1 40 51	3 39 8	5 41 21	7 39 38	9 41 51	11 44 4	13 42 21	15 44 34	17 42 50
18	19 46 1	21 48 14	23 42 34	1 44 47	3 43 4	5 45 17	7 43 34	9 45 47	11 48 0	13 46 17	15 48 30	17 46 47
19	19 49 58	21 52 11	23 46 31	1 48 44	3 47 1	5 49 14	7 47 31	9 49 44	11 51 57	13 50 14	15 52 27	17 50 44
20	19 53 54	21 56 7	23 50 27	1 52 41	3 50 57	5 53 11	7 51 27	9 53 40	11 55 54	13 54 10	15 56 23	17 54 40
21	19 57 51	22 0 4	23 54 24	1 56 37	3 54 54	5 57 7	7 55 24	9 57 37	11 59 50	13 58 7	16 0 20	17 58 37
22	20 1 47	22 4 1	23 58 21	2 0 34	3 58 50	6 1 4	7 59 20	10 1 34	12 3 47	14 2 3	16 4 17	18 2 33
23	20 5 44	22 7 57	0 2 17	2 4 30	4 2 47	6 5 0	8 3 17	10 5 30	12 7 43	14 6 0	16 8 13	18 6 30
24	20 9 40	22 11 54	0 6 14	2 8 27	4 6 43	6 8 57	8 7 13	10 9 27	12 11 40	14 9 56	16 12 10	18 10 26
25	20 13 37	22 15 50	0 10 10	2 12 23	4 10 40	6 12 53	8 11 10	10 13 23	12 15 36	14 13 53	16 16 6	18 14 23
26	20 17 34	22 19 47	0 14 7	2 16 20	4 14 37	6 16 50	8 15 7	10 17 20	12 19 33	14 17 50	16 20 3	18 18 19
27	20 21 30	22 23 43	0 18 3	2 20 17	4 18 33	6 20 46	8 19 3	10 21 16	12 23 29	14 21 46	16 23 59	18 22 16
28	20 25 27	22 27 40	0 22 0	2 24 13	4 22 30	6 24 43	8 23 0	10 25 13	12 27 26	14 25 43	16 27 56	18 26 13
29	20 29 23		0 25 56	2 28 10	4 26 26	6 28 40	8 26 56	10 29 9	12 31 23	14 29 39	16 31 52	18 30 9
30	20 33 20		0 29 53	2 32 6	4 30 23	6 32 36	8 30 53	10 33 6	12 35 19	14 33 36	16 35 49	18 34 6
31	20 37 16		0 33 50		4 34 19		8 34 49	10 37 3		14 37 32		18 38 2

Day	Jan.	Feb.	Mar.	April	May	June	July	Aug.	Sept.	Oct.	Nov.	Dec.
1	18 41 59	20 44 12	22 34 36	0 36 49	2 35 5	4 37 19	6 35 35	8 37 49	10 40 2	12 38 18	14 40 32	16 38 48
2	18 45 55	20 48 9	22 38 32	0 40 45	2 39 2	4 41 15	6 39 32	8 41 45	10 43 58	12 42 15	14 44 28	16 42 45
3	18 49 52	20 52 5	22 42 29	0 44 42	2 42 58	4 45 12	6 43 29	8 45 42	10 47 55	12 46 12	14 48 25	16 46 41
4	18 53 49	20 56 2	22 46 25	0 48 38	2 46 55	4 49 8	6 47 25	8 49 38	10 51 52	12 50 8	14 52 21	16 50 38
5	18 57 45	20 59 58	22 50 22	0 52 35	2 50 52	4 53 5	6 51 22	8 53 35	10 55 48	12 54 5	14 56 18	16 54 35
6	19 1 42	21 3 55	22 54 18	0 56 32	2 54 48	4 57 1	6 55 18	8 57 31	10 59 45	12 58 1	15 0 14	16 58 31
7	19 5 38	21 7 51	22 58 15	1 0 28	2 58 45	5 0 58	6 59 15	9 1 28	11 3 41	13 1 58	15 4 11	17 2 28
8	19 9 35	21 11 48	23 2 12	1 4 25	3 2 41	5 4 55	7 3 11	9 5 25	11 7 38	13 5 54	15 8 8	17 6 24
9	19 13 31	21 15 45	23 6 8	1 8 21	3 6 38	5 8 51	7 7 8	9 9 21	11 11 34	13 9 51	15 12 4	17 10 21
10	19 17 28	21 19 41	23 10 5	1 12 18	3 10 34	5 12 48	7 11 4	9 13 18	11 15 31	13 13 47	15 16 1	17 14 17
11	19 21 24	21 23 38	23 14 1	1 16 14	3 14 31	5 16 44	7 15 1	9 17 14	11 19 27	13 17 44	15 19 57	17 18 14
12	19 25 21	21 27 34	23 17 58	1 20 11	3 18 28	5 20 41	7 18 58	9 21 11	11 23 24	13 21 40	15 23 54	17 22 10
13	19 29 18	21 31 31	23 21 54	1 24 7	3 22 24	5 24 37	7 22 54	9 25 7	11 27 21	13 25 37	15 27 50	17 26 7
14	19 33 14	21 35 27	23 25 51	1 28 4	3 26 21	5 28 34	7 26 51	9 29 4	11 31 17	13 29 34	15 31 47	17 30 4
15	19 37 11	21 39 24	23 29 47	1 32 1	3 30 17	5 32 30	7 30 47	9 33 0	11 35 14	13 33 30	15 35 43	17 34 0
16	19 41 7	21 43 20	23 33 44	1 35 57	3 34 14	5 36 27	7 34 44	9 36 57	11 39 10	13 37 27	15 39 40	17 37 57
17	19 45 4	21 47 17	23 37 40	1 39 54	3 38 10	5 40 24	7 38 40	9 40 54	11 43 7	13 41 23	15 43 37	17 41 53
18	19 49 0	21 51 14	23 41 37	1 43 50	3 42 7	5 44 20	7 42 37	9 44 50	11 47 3	13 45 20	15 47 33	17 45 50
19	19 52 57	21 55 10	23 45 34	1 47 47	3 46 3	5 48 17	7 46 33	9 48 47	11 51 0	13 49 16	15 51 30	17 49 46
20	19 56 53	21 59 7	23 49 30	1 51 43	3 50 0	5 52 13	7 50 30	9 52 43	11 54 56	13 53 13	15 55 26	17 53 43
21	20 0 50	22 3 3	23 53 27	1 55 40	3 53 57	5 56 10	7 54 27	9 56 40	11 58 53	13 57 10	15 59 23	17 57 40
22	20 4 47	22 7 0	23 57 23	1 59 36	3 57 53	6 0 6	7 58 23	10 0 36	12 2 49	14 1 6	16 3 19	18 1 36
23	20 8 43	22 10 56	0 1 20	2 3 33	4 1 50	6 4 3	8 2 20	10 4 33	12 6 46	14 5 3	16 7 16	18 5 33
24	20 12 40	22 14 53	0 5 16	2 7 30	4 5 46	6 8 0	8 6 16	10 8 29	12 10 43	14 8 59	16 11 12	18 9 29
25	20 16 36	22 18 49	0 9 13	2 11 26	4 9 43	6 11 56	8 10 13	10 12 26	12 14 39	14 12 56	16 15 9	18 13 26
26	20 20 33	22 22 46	0 13 9	2 15 23	4 13 39	6 15 53	8 14 9	10 16 22	12 18 32	14 16 52	16 19 5	18 17 22
27	20 24 29	22 26 43	0 17 6	2 19 19	4 17 36	6 19 49	8 18 6	10 20 19	12 22 32	14 20 49	16 23 2	18 21 19
28	20 28 26	22 30 39	0 21 3	2 23 16	4 21 32	6 23 46	8 22 2	10 24 16	12 26 29	14 24 45	16 26 59	18 25 15
29	20 32 22		0 24 59	2 27 12	4 25 29	6 27 42	8 25 59	10 28 12	12 30 25	14 28 42	16 30 55	18 29 12
30	20 36 19		0 28 56	2 31 9	4 29 26	6 31 39	8 29 56	10 32 9	12 34 22	14 32 39	16 34 52	18 33 9
31	20 40 16		0 32 52		4 33 22		8 33 52	10 36 5		14 36 35		18 37 5

Day	Jan.	Feb.	Mar.	April	May	June	July	Aug.	Sept.	Oct.	Nov.	Dec.
1	18 41 2	20 43 15	22 33 38	0 35 52	2 34 8	4 36 22	6 34 38	8 36 52	10 39 5	12 37 21	14 39 35	16 37 51
2	18 44 58	20 47 11	22 37 35	0 39 48	2 38 5	4 40 18	6 38 35	8 40 48	10 43 1	12 41 18	14 43 31	16 41 48
3	18 48 55	20 51 8	22 41 32	0 43 45	2 42 1	4 44 15	6 42 31	8 44 45	10 46 58	12 45 14	14 47 28	16 45 44
4	18 52 51	20 55 5	22 45 28	0 47 41	2 45 58	4 48 11	6 46 28	8 48 41	10 50 54	12 49 11	14 51 24	16 49 41
5	18 56 48	20 59 1	22 49 25	0 51 38	2 49 54	4 52 8	6 50 24	8 52 38	10 54 51	12 53 8	14 55 21	16 53 37
6	19 0 44	21 2 58	22 53 21	0 55 34	2 53 51	4 56 4	6 54 21	8 56 34	10 58 48	12 57 4	14 59 17	16 57 34
7	19 4 41	21 6 54	22 57 18	0 59 31	2 57 47	5 0 1	6 58 18	9 0 31	11 2 44	13 1 1	15 3 14	17 1 31
8	19 8 38	21 10 51	23 1 14	1 3 27	3 1 44	5 3 57	7 2 14	9 4 27	11 6 41	13 4 57	15 7 10	17 5 27
9	19 12 34	21 14 47	23 5 11	1 7 24	3 5 41	5 7 54	7 6 11	9 8 24	11 10 37	13 8 54	15 11 7	17 9 24
10	19 16 31	21 18 44	23 9 7	1 11 21	3 9 37	5 11 50	7 10 7	9 12 21	11 14 34	13 12 50	15 15 4	17 13 20
11	19 20 27	21 22 40	23 13 4	1 15 17	3 13 34	5 15 47	7 14 4	9 16 17	11 18 30	13 16 47	15 19 0	17 17 17
12	19 24 24	21 26 37	23 17 1	1 19 14	3 17 30	5 19 44	7 18 0	9 20 14	11 22 27	13 20 43	15 22 57	17 21 13
13	19 28 20	21 30 34	23 20 57	1 23 10	3 21 27	5 23 40	7 21 57	9 24 10	11 26 23	13 24 40	15 26 53	17 25 10
14	19 32 17	21 34 30	23 24 54	1 27 7	3 25 23	5 27 37	7 25 54	9 28 7	11 30 20	13 28 37	15 30 50	17 29 6
15	19 36 13	21 38 27	23 28 50	1 31 3	3 29 20	5 31 33	7 29 50	9 32 3	11 34 16	13 32 33	15 34 46	17 33 3
16	19 40 10	21 42 23	23 32 47	1 35 0	3 33 17	5 35 30	7 33 47	9 36 0	11 38 13	13 36 30	15 38 43	17 37 0
17	19 44 7	21 46 20	23 36 43	1 38 56	3 37 13	5 39 26	7 37 43	9 39 56	11 42 9	13 40 26	15 42 39	17 40 56
18	19 48 3	21 50 16	23 40 40	1 42 53	3 41 10	5 43 23	7 41 40	9 43 53	11 46 6	13 44 23	15 46 36	17 44 53
19	19 52 0	21 54 13	23 44 36	1 46 50	3 45 7	5 47 20	7 45 36	9 47 50	11 50 3	13 48 19	15 50 33	17 48 49
20	19 55 56	21 58 9	23 48 33	1 50 46	3 49 3	5 51 16	7 49 33	9 51 46	11 53 59	13 52 16	15 54 29	17 52 46
21	19 59 53	22 2 6	23 52 29	1 54 43	3 53 0	5 55 13	7 53 29	9 55 43	11 57 56	13 56 12	15 58 26	17 56 42
22	20 3 49	22 6 3	23 56 26	1 58 39	3 56 56	5 59 9	7 57 26	9 59 39	12 1 52	14 0 9	16 2 22	18 0 39
23	20 7 46	22 9 59	0 0 23	2 2 36	4 0 52	6 3 6	8 1 23	10 3 36	12 5 49	14 4 6	16 6 19	18 4 36
24	20 11 42	22 13 56	0 4 19	2 6 32	4 4 49	6 7 2	8 5 19	10 7 32	12 9 45	14 8 2	16 10 15	18 8 32
25	20 15 39	22 17 52	0 8 16	2 10 29	4 8 46	6 10 59	8 9 16	10 11 29	12 13 42	14 11 59	16 14 12	18 12 29
26	20 19 36	22 21 49	0 12 12	2 14 25	4 12 42	6 14 55	8 13 12	10 15 25	12 17 39	14 15 55	16 18 8	18 16 25
27	20 23 32	22 25 45	0 16 9	2 18 22	4 16 39	6 18 52	8 17 9	10 19 22	12 21 35	14 19 52	16 22 5	18 20 22
28	20 27 29	22 29 42	0 20 5	2 22 19	4 20 35	6 22 49	8 21 5	10 23 18	12 25 32	14 23 48	16 26 2	18 24 18
29	20 31 25		0 24 2	2 26 15	4 24 32	6 26 45	8 25 2	10 27 15	12 29 28	14 27 45	16 29 58	18 28 15
30	20 35 22		0 27 59	2 30 12	4 28 28	6 30 42	8 28 58	10 31 12	12 33 25	14 31 41	16 33 55	18 32 11
31	20 39 18		0 31 55		4 32 25		8 32 55	10 35 8		14 35 38		18 36 8

1911

	Jan.	Feb.	Mar.	April	May	June	July	Aug.	Sept.	Oct.	Nov.	Dec.
1	18 40 5	20 42 18	22 32 41	0 34 55	2 33 11	4 35 24	6 33 41	8 35 54	10 38 8	12 36 24	14 38 37	16 36 54
2	18 44 1	20 46 14	22 36 38	0 38 51	2 37 8	4 39 21	6 37 38	8 39 51	10 42 4	12 40 21	14 42 34	16 40 51
3	18 47 58	20 50 11	22 40 34	0 42 48	2 41 4	4 43 18	6 41 34	8 43 48	10 46 1	12 44 17	14 46 31	16 44 47
4	18 51 54	20 54 8	22 44 31	0 46 44	2 45 1	4 47 14	6 45 31	8 47 44	10 49 57	12 48 14	14 50 27	16 48 44
5	18 55 51	20 58 4	22 48 28	0 50 41	2 48 57	4 51 11	6 49 27	8 51 41	10 53 54	12 52 11	14 54 24	16 52 40
6	18 59 47	21 2 1	22 52 24	0 54 37	2 52 54	4 55 7	6 53 24	8 55 37	10 57 50	12 56 7	14 58 20	16 56 37
7	19 3 44	21 5 57	22 56 21	0 58 34	2 56 51	4 59 4	6 57 21	8 59 34	11 1 47	13 0 4	15 2 17	17 0 34
8	19 7 40	21 9 54	23 0 17	1 2 30	3 0 47	5 3 0	7 1 17	9 3 30	11 5 44	13 4 0	15 6 13	17 4 30
9	19 11 37	21 13 50	23 4 14	1 6 27	3 4 44	5 6 57	7 5 14	9 7 27	11 9 40	13 7 57	15 10 10	17 8 27
10	19 15 34	21 17 47	23 8 10	1 10 24	3 8 40	5 10 53	7 9 10	9 11 23	11 13 37	13 11 53	15 14 7	17 12 23
11	19 19 30	21 21 43	23 12 7	1 14 20	3 12 37	5 14 50	7 13 7	9 15 20	11 17 33	13 15 50	15 18 3	17 16 20
12	19 23 27	21 25 40	23 16 3	1 18 17	3 16 33	5 18 47	7 17 3	9 19 17	11 21 30	13 19 46	15 22 0	17 20 16
13	19 27 23	21 29 37	23 20 0	1 22 13	3 20 30	5 22 43	7 21 0	9 23 13	11 25 26	13 23 43	15 25 56	17 24 13
14	19 31 20	21 33 33	23 23 57	1 26 10	3 24 26	5 26 40	7 24 56	9 27 10	11 29 23	13 27 40	15 29 53	17 28 9
15	19 35 16	21 37 30	23 27 53	1 30 6	3 28 23	5 30 36	7 28 53	9 31 6	11 33 19	13 31 36	15 33 49	17 32 6
16	19 39 13	21 41 26	23 31 50	1 34 3	3 32 20	5 34 33	7 32 50	9 35 3	11 37 16	13 35 33	15 37 46	17 36 3
17	19 43 9	21 45 23	23 35 46	1 37 59	3 36 16	5 38 29	7 36 46	9 38 59	11 41 13	13 39 29	15 41 42	17 39 59
18	19 47 6	21 49 19	23 39 43	1 41 56	3 40 13	5 42 26	7 40 43	9 42 56	11 45 9	13 43 26	15 45 39	17 43 56
19	19 51 3	21 53 16	23 43 39	1 45 53	3 44 9	5 46 23	7 44 39	9 46 52	11 49 6	13 47 22	15 49 36	17 47 52
20	19 54 59	21 57 12	23 47 36	1 49 49	3 48 6	5 50 19	7 48 36	9 50 49	11 53 2	13 51 19	15 53 32	17 51 49
21	19 58 56	22 1 9	23 51 32	1 53 46	3 52 2	5 54 16	7 52 32	9 54 46	11 56 59	13 55 15	15 57 29	17 55 45
22	20 2 52	22 5 6	23 55 29	1 57 42	3 55 59	5 58 12	7 56 29	9 58 42	12 0 55	13 59 12	16 1 25	17 59 42
23	20 6 49	22 9 2	23 59 26	2 1 39	3 59 55	6 2 9	8 0 25	10 2 39	12 4 52	14 3 9	16 5 22	18 3 39
24	20 10 45	22 12 59	0 3 22	2 5 35	4 3 52	6 6 5	8 4 22	10 6 35	12 8 48	14 7 5	16 9 18	18 7 35
25	20 14 42	22 16 55	0 7 19	2 9 32	4 7 49	6 10 2	8 8 19	10 10 32	12 12 45	14 11 2	16 13 15	18 11 32
26	20 18 39	22 20 52	0 11 15	2 13 28	4 11 45	6 13 58	8 12 15	10 14 28	12 16 42	14 14 58	16 17 11	18 15 28
27	20 22 35	22 24 48	0 15 12	2 17 25	4 15 42	6 17 55	8 16 12	10 18 25	12 20 38	14 18 55	16 21 8	18 19 25
28	20 26 32	22 28 45	0 19 8	2 21 22	4 19 38	6 21 52	8 20 8	10 22 21	12 24 35	14 22 51	16 25 5	18 23 21
29	20 30 28		0 23 5	2 25 18	4 23 35	6 25 48	8 24 5	10 26 18	12 28 31	14 26 48	16 29 1	18 27 18
30	20 34 25		0 27 1	2 29 15	4 27 31	6 29 45	8 28 1	10 30 15	12 32 28	14 30 44	16 32 58	18 31 14
31	20 38 21		0 30 58		4 31 28		8 31 58	10 34 11		14 34 41		18 35 11

1912

	Jan.	Feb.	Mar.	April	May	June	July	Aug.	Sept.	Oct.	Nov.	Dec.
1	18 39 8	20 41 21	22 35 41	0 37 54	2 36 11	4 38 24	6 36 41	8 38 54	10 41 7	12 39 24	14 41 37	16 39 54
2	18 43 4	20 45 17	22 39 38	0 41 51	2 40 7	4 42 21	6 40 37	8 42 51	10 45 4	12 43 20	14 45 34	16 43 50
3	18 47 1	20 49 14	22 43 34	0 45 47	2 44 4	4 46 17	6 44 34	8 46 47	10 49 0	12 47 17	14 49 30	16 47 47
4	18 50 57	20 53 11	22 47 31	0 49 44	2 48 0	4 50 14	6 48 30	8 50 44	10 52 57	12 51 14	14 53 27	16 51 43
5	18 54 54	20 57 7	22 51 27	0 53 40	2 51 57	4 54 10	6 52 27	8 54 40	10 56 53	12 55 10	14 57 23	16 55 40
6	18 58 50	21 1 4	22 55 24	0 57 37	2 55 54	4 58 7	6 56 24	8 58 37	11 0 50	12 59 7	15 1 20	16 59 37
7	19 2 47	21 5 0	22 59 20	1 1 33	2 59 50	5 2 3	7 0 20	9 2 33	11 4 47	13 3 3	15 5 16	17 3 33
8	19 6 43	21 8 57	23 3 17	1 5 30	3 3 47	5 6 0	7 4 17	9 6 30	11 8 43	13 7 0	15 9 13	17 7 30
9	19 10 40	21 12 53	23 7 13	1 9 27	3 7 43	5 9 56	7 8 13	9 10 27	11 12 40	13 10 56	15 13 10	17 11 26
10	19 14 37	21 16 50	23 11 10	1 13 23	3 11 40	5 13 53	7 12 10	9 14 23	11 16 36	13 14 53	15 17 6	17 15 23
11	19 18 33	21 20 46	23 15 6	1 17 20	3 15 36	5 17 50	7 16 6	9 18 20	11 20 33	13 18 49	15 21 3	17 19 19
12	19 22 30	21 24 43	23 19 3	1 21 16	3 19 33	5 21 46	7 20 3	9 22 16	11 24 29	13 22 46	15 24 59	17 23 16
13	19 26 26	21 28 40	23 23 0	1 25 13	3 23 29	5 25 43	7 23 59	9 26 13	11 28 26	13 26 43	15 28 56	17 27 13
14	19 30 23	21 32 36	23 26 56	1 29 9	3 27 26	5 29 39	7 27 56	9 30 9	11 32 22	13 30 39	15 32 52	17 31 9
15	19 34 19	21 36 33	23 30 53	1 33 6	3 31 23	5 33 36	7 31 53	9 34 6	11 36 19	13 34 36	15 36 49	17 35 6
16	19 38 16	21 40 29	23 34 49	1 37 2	3 35 19	5 37 32	7 35 49	9 38 2	11 40 16	13 38 32	15 40 45	17 39 2
17	19 42 12	21 44 26	23 38 46	1 40 59	3 39 16	5 41 29	7 39 46	9 41 59	11 44 12	13 42 29	15 44 42	17 42 59
18	19 46 9	21 48 22	23 42 42	1 44 56	3 43 12	5 45 26	7 43 42	9 45 56	11 48 9	13 46 25	15 48 39	17 46 55
19	19 50 6	21 52 19	23 46 39	1 48 52	3 47 9	5 49 22	7 47 39	9 49 52	11 52 5	13 50 22	15 52 35	17 50 52
20	19 54 2	21 56 15	23 50 35	1 52 49	3 51 5	5 53 19	7 51 35	9 53 49	11 56 2	13 54 18	15 56 32	17 54 48
21	19 57 59	22 0 12	23 54 32	1 56 45	3 55 2	5 57 15	7 55 32	9 57 45	11 59 58	13 58 15	16 0 28	17 58 45
22	20 1 55	22 4 9	23 58 29	2 0 42	3 58 58	6 1 12	7 59 29	10 1 42	12 3 55	14 2 12	16 4 25	18 2 42
23	20 5 52	22 8 5	0 2 25	2 4 38	4 2 55	6 5 8	8 3 25	10 5 38	12 7 51	14 6 8	16 8 21	18 6 38
24	20 9 48	22 12 2	0 6 22	2 8 35	4 6 52	6 9 5	8 7 22	10 9 35	12 11 48	14 10 5	16 12 18	18 10 35
25	20 13 45	22 15 58	0 10 18	2 12 31	4 10 48	6 13 1	8 11 18	10 13 31	12 15 45	14 14 1	16 16 14	18 14 31
26	20 17 41	22 19 55	0 14 15	2 16 28	4 14 45	6 16 58	8 15 15	10 17 28	12 19 41	14 17 58	16 20 11	18 18 28
27	20 21 38	22 23 51	0 18 11	2 20 25	4 18 41	6 20 55	8 19 11	10 21 25	12 23 38	14 21 54	16 24 8	18 22 24
28	20 25 35	22 27 48	0 22 8	2 24 21	4 22 38	6 24 51	8 23 8	10 25 21	12 27 34	14 25 51	16 28 4	18 26 21
29	20 29 31	22 31 44	0 26 4	2 28 18	4 26 34	6 28 48	8 27 4	10 29 18	12 31 31	14 29 47	16 32 1	18 30 17
30	20 33 28		0 30 1	2 32 14	4 30 31	6 32 44	8 31 1	10 33 14	12 35 27	14 33 44	16 35 57	18 34 14
31	20 37 24		0 33 58		4 34 27		8 34 58	10 37 11		14 37 41		18 38 11

1913

	Jan.	Feb.	Mar.	April	May	June	July	Aug.	Sept.	Oct.	Nov.	Dec.
1	18 42 7	20 44 20	22 34 44	0 36 57	2 35 14	4 37 27	6 35 44	8 37 57	10 40 10	12 38 27	14 40 40	16 38 57
2	18 46 4	20 48 17	22 38 41	0 40 54	2 39 10	4 41 24	6 39 40	8 41 54	10 44 7	12 42 24	14 44 37	16 42 53
3	18 50 0	20 52 14	22 42 37	0 44 50	2 43 7	4 45 20	6 43 37	8 45 50	10 48 3	12 46 20	14 48 33	16 46 50
4	18 53 57	20 56 10	22 46 34	0 48 47	2 47 3	4 49 17	6 47 34	8 49 47	10 52 0	12 50 17	14 52 30	16 50 47
5	18 57 53	21 0 7	22 50 30	0 52 43	2 51 0	4 53 13	6 51 30	8 53 43	10 55 57	12 54 13	14 56 26	16 54 43
6	19 1 50	21 4 3	22 54 27	0 56 40	2 54 57	4 57 10	6 55 27	8 57 40	10 59 53	12 58 10	15 0 23	16 58 40
7	19 5 46	21 8 0	22 58 23	1 0 36	2 58 53	5 1 6	6 59 23	9 1 36	11 3 50	13 2 6	15 4 19	17 2 36
8	19 9 43	21 11 56	23 2 20	1 4 33	3 2 50	5 5 3	7 3 20	9 5 33	11 7 46	13 6 3	15 8 16	17 6 33
9	19 13 40	21 15 53	23 6 16	1 8 30	3 6 46	5 9 0	7 7 16	9 9 30	11 11 43	13 9 59	15 12 13	17 10 29
10	19 17 36	21 19 49	23 10 13	1 12 26	3 10 43	5 12 56	7 11 13	9 13 26	11 15 39	13 13 56	15 16 9	17 14 26
11	19 21 33	21 23 46	23 14 10	1 16 23	3 14 39	5 16 53	7 15 9	9 17 23	11 19 36	13 17 52	15 20 6	17 18 22
12	19 25 29	21 27 43	23 18 6	1 20 19	3 18 36	5 20 49	7 19 6	9 21 19	11 23 32	13 21 49	15 24 2	17 22 19
13	19 29 26	21 31 39	23 22 3	1 24 16	3 22 32	5 24 46	7 23 2	9 25 16	11 27 29	13 25 45	15 27 59	17 26 16
14	19 33 22	21 35 36	23 25 59	1 28 12	3 26 29	5 28 42	7 26 59	9 29 12	11 31 26	13 29 42	15 31 55	17 30 12
15	19 37 19	21 39 32	23 29 56	1 32 9	3 30 26	5 32 39	7 30 56	9 33 9	11 35 22	13 33 39	15 35 52	17 34 9
16	19 41 16	21 43 29	23 33 52	1 36 5	3 34 22	5 36 35	7 34 52	9 37 5	11 39 19	13 37 35	15 39 48	17 38 5
17	19 45 12	21 47 25	23 37 49	1 40 2	3 38 19	5 40 32	7 38 49	9 41 2	11 43 15	13 41 32	15 43 45	17 42 2
18	19 49 9	21 51 22	23 41 45	1 43 59	3 42 15	5 44 29	7 42 45	9 44 59	11 47 12	13 45 28	15 47 42	17 45 58
19	19 53 5	21 55 18	23 45 42	1 47 55	3 46 12	5 48 25	7 46 42	9 48 55	11 51 8	13 49 25	15 51 38	17 49 55
20	19 57 2	21 59 15	23 49 39	1 51 52	3 50 8	5 52 22	7 50 38	9 52 52	11 55 5	13 53 21	15 55 35	17 53 51
21	20 0 58	22 3 12	23 53 35	1 55 48	3 54 5	5 56 18	7 54 35	9 56 48	11 59 1	13 57 18	15 59 31	17 57 48
22	20 4 55	22 7 8	23 57 32	1 59 45	3 58 1	6 0 15	7 58 32	10 0 45	12 2 58	14 1 15	16 3 28	18 1 45
23	20 8 51	22 11 5	0 1 28	2 3 41	4 1 58	6 4 11	8 2 28	10 4 41	12 6 55	14 5 11	16 7 24	18 5 41
24	20 12 48	22 15 1	0 5 25	2 7 38	4 5 55	6 8 8	8 6 25	10 8 38	12 10 51	14 9 8	16 11 21	18 9 38
25	20 16 45	22 18 58	0 9 21	2 11 34	4 9 51	6 12 4	8 10 21	10 12 34	12 14 48	14 13 4	16 15 18	18 13 34
26	20 20 41	22 22 54	0 13 18	2 15 31	4 13 48	6 16 1	8 14 18	10 16 31	12 18 44	14 17 1	16 19 14	18 17 31
27	20 24 38	22 26 51	0 17 14	2 19 28	4 17 44	6 19 58	8 18 14	10 20 28	12 22 41	14 20 57	16 23 11	18 21 27
28	20 28 34	22 30 47	0 21 11	2 23 24	4 21 41	6 23 54	8 22 11	10 24 24	12 26 37	14 24 54	16 27 7	18 25 24
29	20 32 31		0 25 7	2 27 21	4 25 37	6 27 51	8 26 7	10 28 21	12 30 34	14 28 50	16 31 4	18 29 20
30	20 36 27		0 29 4	2 31 17	4 29 34	6 31 47	8 30 4	10 32 17	12 34 30	14 32 47	16 35 0	18 33 17
31	20 40 24		0 33 1		4 33 31		8 34 1	10 36 14		14 36 44		18 37 14

1914

Jan.	Feb.	Mar.	April	May	June	July	Aug.	Sept.	Oct.	Nov.	Dec.	
18 41 10	20 43 23	22 33 47	0 36 0	2 34 17	4 36 30	6 34 47	8 37 0	10 39 13	12 37 30	14 39 43	16 38 0	1
18 45 7	20 47 20	22 37 44	0 39 57	2 38 13	4 40 27	6 38 43	8 40 57	10 43 10	12 41 27	14 43 40	16 41 56	2
18 49 3	20 51 17	22 41 40	0 43 53	2 42 10	4 44 23	6 42 40	8 44 53	10 47 6	12 45 23	14 47 36	16 45 53	3
18 53 0	20 55 13	22 45 37	0 47 50	2 46 7	4 48 20	6 46 37	8 48 50	10 51 3	12 49 20	14 51 33	16 49 50	4
18 56 56	20 59 10	22 49 33	0 51 46	2 50 3	4 52 16	6 50 33	8 52 46	10 55 0	12 53 16	14 55 29	16 53 46	5
19 0 53	21 3 6	22 53 30	0 55 43	2 54 0	4 56 13	6 54 30	8 56 43	10 58 56	12 57 13	14 59 26	16 57 43	6
19 4 50	21 7 3	22 57 26	0 59 40	2 57 56	5 0 9	6 58 26	9 0 39	11 2 53	13 1 9	15 3 23	17 1 39	7
19 8 46	21 10 59	23 1 23	1 3 36	3 1 53	5 4 6	7 2 23	9 4 36	11 6 49	13 5 6	15 7 19	17 5 36	8
19 12 43	21 14 56	23 5 19	1 7 33	3 5 49	5 8 3	7 6 19	9 8 33	11 10 46	13 9 2	15 11 16	17 9 32	9
19 16 39	21 18 52	23 9 16	1 11 29	3 9 46	5 11 59	7 10 16	9 12 29	11 14 42	13 12 59	15 15 12	17 13 29	10
19 20 36	21 22 49	23 13 13	1 15 26	3 13 42	5 15 56	7 14 12	9 16 26	11 18 39	13 16 56	15 19 9	17 17 25	11
19 24 32	21 26 46	23 17 9	1 19 22	3 17 39	5 19 52	7 18 9	9 20 22	11 22 35	13 20 52	15 23 5	17 21 22	12
19 28 29	21 30 42	23 21 6	1 23 19	3 21 36	5 23 49	7 22 6	9 24 19	11 26 32	13 24 49	15 27 2	17 25 19	13
19 32 25	21 34 39	23 25 2	1 27 15	3 25 32	5 27 45	7 26 2	9 28 15	11 30 29	13 28 45	15 30 58	17 29 15	14
19 36 22	21 38 35	23 28 59	1 31 12	3 29 29	5 31 42	7 29 59	9 32 12	11 34 25	13 32 42	15 34 55	17 33 12	15
19 40 19	21 42 32	23 32 55	1 35 9	3 33 25	5 35 38	7 33 55	9 36 9	11 38 22	13 36 38	15 38 52	17 37 8	16
19 44 15	21 46 28	23 36 52	1 39 5	3 37 22	5 39 35	7 37 52	9 40 5	11 42 18	13 40 35	15 42 48	17 41 5	17
19 48 12	21 50 25	23 40 48	1 43 2	3 41 18	5 43 32	7 41 48	9 44 2	11 46 15	13 44 31	15 46 45	17 45 1	18
19 52 8	21 54 21	23 44 45	1 46 58	3 45 15	5 47 28	7 45 45	9 47 58	11 50 11	13 48 28	15 50 41	17 48 58	19
19 56 5	21 58 18	23 48 42	1 50 55	3 49 11	5 51 25	7 49 41	9 51 55	11 54 8	13 52 25	15 54 38	17 52 55	20
20 0 1	22 2 15	23 52 38	1 54 51	3 53 8	5 55 21	7 53 38	9 55 51	11 58 4	13 56 21	15 58 34	17 56 51	21
20 3 58	22 6 11	23 56 35	1 58 48	3 57 5	5 59 18	7 57 35	9 59 48	12 2 1	14 0 18	16 2 31	18 0 48	22
20 7 54	22 10 8	0 0 31	2 2 44	4 1 1	6 3 14	8 1 31	10 3 44	12 5 58	14 4 14	16 6 27	18 4 44	23
20 11 51	22 14 4	0 4 28	2 6 41	4 4 58	6 7 11	8 5 28	10 7 41	12 9 54	14 8 11	16 10 24	18 8 41	24
20 15 48	22 18 1	0 8 24	2 10 38	4 8 54	6 11 8	8 9 24	10 11 37	12 13 51	14 12 7	16 14 21	18 12 37	25
20 19 44	22 21 57	0 12 21	2 14 34	4 12 51	6 15 4	8 13 21	10 15 34	12 17 47	14 16 4	16 18 17	18 16 34	26
20 23 41	22 25 54	0 16 17	2 18 31	4 16 47	6 19 1	8 17 17	10 19 31	12 21 44	14 20 0	16 22 14	18 20 30	27
20 27 37	22 29 50	0 20 14	2 22 27	4 20 44	6 22 57	8 21 14	10 23 27	12 25 40	14 23 57	16 26 10	18 24 27	28
20 31 34		0 24 11	2 26 24	4 24 40	6 26 54	8 25 10	10 27 24	12 29 37	14 27 54	16 30 7	18 28 24	29
20 35 30		0 28 7	2 30 20	4 28 37	6 30 50	8 29 7	10 31 20	12 33 33	14 31 50	16 34 3	18 32 20	30
20 39 27		0 32 4		4 32 34		8 33 4	10 35 17		14 35 47		18 36 17	31

1915

Jan.	Feb.	Mar.	April	May	June	July	Aug.	Sept.	Oct.	Nov.	Dec.	
18 40 13	20 42 27	22 32 50	0 35 3	2 33 20	4 35 33	6 33 50	8 36 3	10 38 16	12 36 33	14 38 46	16 37 3	1
18 44 10	20 46 23	22 36 47	0 39 0	2 37 16	4 39 30	6 37 46	8 40 0	10 42 13	12 40 30	14 42 43	16 40 59	2
18 48 6	20 50 20	22 40 43	0 42 56	2 41 13	4 43 26	6 41 43	8 43 56	10 46 9	12 44 26	14 46 39	16 44 56	3
18 52 3	20 54 16	22 44 40	0 46 53	2 45 10	4 47 23	6 45 40	8 47 53	10 50 6	12 48 23	14 50 36	16 48 53	4
18 55 59	20 58 13	22 48 36	0 50 49	2 49 6	4 51 19	6 49 36	8 51 49	10 54 3	12 52 19	14 54 32	16 52 49	5
18 59 56	21 2 9	22 52 33	0 54 46	2 53 2	4 55 16	6 53 33	8 55 46	10 57 59	12 56 16	14 58 29	16 56 46	6
19 3 53	21 6 6	22 56 29	0 58 43	2 56 59	4 59 12	6 57 29	8 59 42	11 1 56	13 0 12	15 2 26	17 0 42	7
19 7 49	21 10 2	23 0 26	1 2 39	3 0 56	5 3 9	7 1 26	9 3 39	11 5 52	13 4 9	15 6 22	17 4 39	8
19 11 46	21 13 59	23 4 22	1 6 36	3 4 52	5 7 6	7 5 22	9 7 36	11 9 49	13 8 5	15 10 19	17 8 35	9
19 15 42	21 17 56	23 8 19	1 10 32	3 8 49	5 11 2	7 9 19	9 11 32	11 13 45	13 12 2	15 14 15	17 12 32	10
19 19 39	21 21 52	23 12 16	1 14 29	3 12 45	5 14 59	7 13 15	9 15 29	11 17 42	13 15 59	15 18 12	17 16 28	11
19 23 35	21 25 49	23 16 12	1 18 25	3 16 42	5 18 55	7 17 12	9 19 25	11 21 38	13 19 55	15 22 8	17 20 25	12
19 27 32	21 29 45	23 20 9	1 22 22	3 20 39	5 22 52	7 21 9	9 23 22	11 25 35	13 23 52	15 26 5	17 24 22	13
19 31 28	21 33 42	23 24 5	1 26 18	3 24 35	5 26 48	7 25 5	9 27 18	11 29 32	13 27 48	15 30 1	17 28 18	14
19 35 25	21 37 38	23 28 2	1 30 15	3 28 32	5 30 45	7 29 2	9 31 15	11 33 28	13 31 45	15 33 58	17 32 15	15
19 39 22	21 41 35	23 31 58	1 34 12	3 32 28	5 34 42	7 32 58	9 35 12	11 37 25	13 35 41	15 37 55	17 36 11	16
19 43 18	21 45 31	23 35 55	1 38 8	3 36 25	5 38 38	7 36 55	9 39 8	11 41 21	13 39 38	15 41 51	17 40 8	17
19 47 15	21 49 28	23 39 51	1 42 5	3 40 21	5 42 35	7 40 51	9 43 5	11 45 18	13 43 34	15 45 48	17 44 4	18
19 51 11	21 53 25	23 43 48	1 46 1	3 44 18	5 46 31	7 44 48	9 47 1	11 49 14	13 47 31	15 49 44	17 48 1	19
19 55 8	21 57 21	23 47 45	1 49 58	3 48 14	5 50 28	7 48 44	9 50 58	11 53 11	13 51 28	15 53 41	17 51 57	20
19 59 4	22 1 18	23 51 41	1 53 54	3 52 11	5 54 24	7 52 41	9 54 54	11 57 7	13 55 24	15 57 37	17 55 54	21
20 3 1	22 5 14	23 55 38	1 57 51	3 56 8	5 58 21	7 56 38	9 58 51	12 1 4	13 59 21	16 1 34	17 59 51	22
20 6 58	22 9 11	23 59 34	2 1 47	4 0 4	6 2 17	8 0 34	10 2 47	12 5 1	14 3 17	16 5 30	18 3 47	23
20 10 54	22 13 7	0 3 31	2 5 44	4 4 1	6 6 14	8 4 31	10 6 44	12 8 57	14 7 14	16 9 27	18 7 44	24
20 14 51	22 17 4	0 7 27	2 9 41	4 7 57	6 10 11	8 8 27	10 10 40	12 12 54	14 11 10	16 13 24	18 11 40	25
20 18 47	22 21 0	0 11 24	2 13 37	4 11 54	6 14 7	8 12 24	10 14 37	12 16 50	14 15 7	16 17 20	18 15 37	26
20 22 44	22 24 57	0 15 21	2 17 34	4 15 50	6 18 4	8 16 20	10 18 33	12 20 47	14 19 3	16 21 17	18 19 33	27
20 26 40	22 28 54	0 19 17	2 21 30	4 19 47	6 22 0	8 20 17	10 22 30	12 24 43	14 23 0	16 25 13	18 23 30	28
20 30 37		0 23 14	2 25 27	4 23 43	6 25 57	8 24 13	10 26 27	12 28 40	14 26 57	16 29 10	18 27 27	29
20 34 33		0 27 10	2 29 23	4 27 40	6 29 53	8 28 10	10 30 23	12 32 36	14 30 53	16 33 6	18 31 23	30
20 38 30		0 31 7		4 31 37		8 32 7	10 34 20		14 34 50		18 35 20	31

1916

Jan.	Feb.	Mar.	April	May	June	July	Aug.	Sept.	Oct.	Nov.	Dec.	
18 39 16	20 41 29	22 35 50	0 38 3	2 36 19	4 38 33	6 36 49	8 39 3	10 41 16	12 39 32	14 41 46	16 40 2	1
18 43 13	20 45 26	22 39 46	0 41 59	2 40 16	4 42 29	6 40 46	8 42 59	10 45 12	12 43 29	14 45 42	16 43 59	2
18 47 9	20 49 23	22 43 43	0 45 56	2 44 12	4 46 26	6 44 42	8 46 56	10 49 9	12 47 26	14 49 39	16 47 55	3
18 51 6	20 53 19	22 47 39	0 49 52	2 48 9	4 50 22	6 48 39	8 50 52	10 53 6	12 51 22	14 53 35	16 51 52	4
18 55 2	20 57 16	22 51 36	0 53 49	2 52 6	4 54 19	6 52 36	8 54 49	10 57 2	12 55 19	14 57 32	16 55 49	5
18 58 59	21 1 12	22 55 32	0 57 46	2 56 2	4 58 15	6 56 32	8 58 45	11 0 59	12 59 15	15 1 28	16 59 45	6
19 2 56	21 5 9	22 59 29	1 1 42	2 59 59	5 2 12	7 0 29	9 2 42	11 4 55	13 3 12	15 5 25	17 3 42	7
19 6 52	21 9 5	23 3 25	1 5 39	3 3 55	5 6 9	7 4 25	9 6 38	11 8 52	13 7 8	15 9 22	17 7 38	8
19 10 49	21 13 2	23 7 22	1 9 35	3 7 52	5 10 5	7 8 22	9 10 35	11 12 48	13 11 5	15 13 18	17 11 35	9
19 14 45	21 16 58	23 11 19	1 13 32	3 11 48	5 14 2	7 12 18	9 14 32	11 16 45	13 15 1	15 17 15	17 15 31	10
19 18 42	21 20 55	23 15 15	1 17 28	3 15 45	5 17 58	7 16 15	9 18 28	11 20 41	13 18 58	15 21 11	17 19 28	11
19 22 38	21 24 52	23 19 12	1 21 25	3 19 41	5 21 55	7 20 12	9 22 25	11 24 38	13 22 55	15 25 8	17 23 24	12
19 26 35	21 28 48	23 23 8	1 25 21	3 23 38	5 25 51	7 24 8	9 26 21	11 28 34	13 26 51	15 29 4	17 27 21	13
19 30 31	21 32 45	23 27 5	1 29 18	3 27 35	5 29 48	7 28 5	9 30 18	11 32 31	13 30 48	15 33 1	17 31 18	14
19 34 28	21 36 41	23 31 1	1 33 14	3 31 31	5 33 44	7 32 1	9 34 14	11 36 28	13 34 44	15 36 57	17 35 14	15
19 38 25	21 40 38	23 34 58	1 37 11	3 35 28	5 37 41	7 35 58	9 38 11	11 40 24	13 38 41	15 40 54	17 39 11	16
19 42 21	21 44 34	23 38 54	1 41 8	3 39 24	5 41 38	7 39 54	9 42 8	11 44 21	13 42 37	15 44 51	17 43 7	17
19 46 18	21 48 31	23 42 51	1 45 4	3 43 21	5 45 34	7 43 51	9 46 4	11 48 17	13 46 34	15 48 47	17 47 4	18
19 50 14	21 52 27	23 46 48	1 49 1	3 47 17	5 49 31	7 47 47	9 50 1	11 52 14	13 50 30	15 52 44	17 51 0	19
19 54 11	21 56 24	23 50 44	1 52 57	3 51 14	5 53 27	7 51 44	9 53 57	11 56 10	13 54 27	15 56 40	17 54 57	20
19 58 7	22 0 21	23 54 41	1 56 54	3 55 10	5 57 24	7 55 41	9 57 54	12 0 7	13 58 24	16 0 37	17 58 53	21
20 2 4	22 4 17	23 58 37	2 0 50	3 59 7	6 1 20	7 59 37	10 1 50	12 4 3	14 2 20	16 4 33	18 2 50	22
20 6 0	22 8 14	0 2 34	2 4 47	4 3 4	6 5 17	8 3 34	10 5 47	12 8 0	14 6 17	16 8 30	18 6 47	23
20 9 57	22 12 10	0 6 30	2 8 43	4 7 0	6 9 13	8 7 30	10 9 43	12 11 57	14 10 13	16 12 26	18 10 43	24
20 13 54	22 16 7	0 10 27	2 12 40	4 10 57	6 13 10	8 11 27	10 13 40	12 15 53	14 14 10	16 16 23	18 14 40	25
20 17 50	22 20 3	0 14 23	2 16 37	4 14 53	6 17 7	8 15 23	10 17 36	12 19 50	14 18 6	16 20 20	18 18 36	26
20 21 47	22 24 0	0 18 20	2 20 33	4 18 50	6 21 3	8 19 20	10 21 33	12 23 46	14 22 3	16 24 16	18 22 33	27
20 25 43	22 27 56	0 22 17	2 24 30	4 22 46	6 25 0	8 23 16	10 25 30	12 27 43	14 25 59	16 28 13	18 26 29	28
20 29 40	22 31 53	0 26 13	2 28 26	4 26 43	6 28 56	8 27 13	10 29 26	12 31 39	14 29 56	16 32 9	18 30 26	29
20 33 36		0 30 10	2 32 23	4 30 40	6 32 53	8 31 10	10 33 23	12 35 36	14 33 53	16 36 6	18 34 23	30
20 37 33		0 34 6		4 34 36		8 35 6	10 37 19		14 37 49		18 38 19	31

1917

	Jan.	Feb.	Mar.	April	May	June	July	Aug.	Sept.	Oct.	Nov.	Dec.
1	18 42 16	20 44 29	22 34 52	0 37 6	2 35 22	4 37 35	6 35 52	8 38 5	10 40 19	12 38 35	14 40 48	16 39 5
2	18 46 12	20 48 25	22 38 49	0 41 2	2 39 19	4 41 32	6 39 49	8 42 2	10 44 15	12 42 32	14 44 45	16 43 2
3	18 50 9	20 52 22	22 42 46	0 44 59	2 43 15	4 45 29	6 43 45	8 45 59	10 48 12	12 46 28	14 48 42	16 46 58
4	18 54 5	20 56 19	22 46 42	0 48 55	2 47 12	4 49 25	6 47 42	8 49 55	10 52 8	12 50 25	14 52 38	16 50 55
5	18 58 2	21 0 15	22 50 39	0 52 52	2 51 8	4 53 22	6 51 38	8 53 52	10 56 5	12 54 21	14 56 35	16 54 51
6	19 1 58	21 4 12	22 54 35	0 56 48	2 55 5	4 57 18	6 55 35	8 57 48	11 0 1	12 58 18	15 0 31	16 58 48
7	19 5 55	21 8 8	22 58 32	1 0 45	2 59 2	5 1 15	6 59 32	9 1 45	11 3 58	13 2 15	15 4 28	17 2 44
8	19 9 52	21 12 5	23 2 28	1 4 41	3 2 58	5 5 11	7 3 28	9 5 41	11 7 55	13 6 11	15 8 24	17 6 41
9	19 13 48	21 16 1	23 6 25	1 8 38	3 6 55	5 9 8	7 7 25	9 9 38	11 11 51	13 10 8	15 12 21	17 10 38
10	19 17 45	21 19 58	23 10 21	1 12 35	3 10 51	5 13 4	7 11 21	9 13 34	11 15 48	13 14 4	15 16 17	17 14 34
11	19 21 41	21 23 54	23 14 18	1 16 31	3 14 48	5 17 1	7 15 18	9 17 31	11 19 44	13 18 1	15 20 14	17 18 31
12	19 25 38	21 27 51	23 18 15	1 20 28	3 18 44	5 20 58	7 19 14	9 21 28	11 23 41	13 21 57	15 24 11	17 22 27
13	19 29 34	21 31 48	23 22 11	1 24 24	3 22 41	5 24 54	7 23 11	9 25 24	11 27 37	13 25 54	15 28 7	17 26 24
14	19 33 31	21 35 44	23 26 8	1 28 21	3 26 37	5 28 51	7 27 7	9 29 21	11 31 34	13 29 50	15 32 4	17 30 20
15	19 37 27	21 39 41	23 30 4	1 32 17	3 30 34	5 32 47	7 31 4	9 33 17	11 35 30	13 33 47	15 36 0	17 34 17
16	19 41 24	21 43 37	23 34 1	1 36 14	3 34 31	5 36 44	7 35 1	9 37 14	11 39 27	13 37 44	15 39 57	17 38 13
17	19 45 21	21 47 34	23 37 57	1 40 10	3 38 27	5 40 40	7 38 57	9 41 10	11 43 24	13 41 40	15 43 53	17 42 10
18	19 49 17	21 51 30	23 41 54	1 44 7	3 42 24	5 44 37	7 42 54	9 45 7	11 47 20	13 45 37	15 47 50	17 46 7
19	19 53 14	21 55 27	23 45 50	1 48 4	3 46 20	5 48 34	7 46 50	9 49 3	11 51 17	13 49 33	15 51 46	17 50 3
20	19 57 10	21 59 23	23 49 47	1 52 0	3 50 17	5 52 30	7 50 47	9 53 0	11 55 13	13 53 30	15 55 43	17 54 0
21	20 1 7	22 3 20	23 53 44	1 55 57	3 54 13	5 56 27	7 54 43	9 56 57	11 59 10	13 57 26	15 59 39	17 57 56
22	20 5 3	22 7 17	23 57 40	1 59 53	3 58 10	6 0 23	7 58 40	10 0 53	12 3 6	14 1 23	16 3 36	18 1 53
23	20 9 0	22 11 13	0 1 37	2 3 50	4 2 6	6 4 20	8 2 36	10 4 50	12 7 3	14 5 19	16 7 33	18 5 49
24	20 12 56	22 15 10	0 5 33	2 7 46	4 6 3	6 8 16	8 6 33	10 8 46	12 10 59	14 9 16	16 11 29	18 9 46
25	20 16 53	22 19 6	0 9 30	2 11 43	4 10 0	6 12 13	8 10 30	10 12 43	12 14 56	14 13 13	16 15 26	18 13 43
26	20 20 50	22 23 3	0 13 26	2 15 39	4 13 56	6 16 ·9	8 14 26	10 16 39	12 18 53	14 17 9	16 19 22	18 17 39
27	20 24 46	22 26 59	0 17 23	2 19 36	4 17 53	6 20 6	8 18 23	10 20 36	12 22 49	14 21 6	16 23 19	18 21 36
28	20 28 43	22 30 56	0 21 19	2 23 33	4 21 49	6 24 3	8 22 19	10 24 32	12 26 46	14 25 2	16 27 15	18 25 32
29	20 32 39		0 25 16	2 27 29	4 25 46	6 27 59	8 26 16	10 28 29	12 30 42	14 28 59	16 31 12	18 29 29
30	20 36 36		0 29 12	2 31 26	4 29 42	6 31 56	8 30 12	10 32 26	12 34 39	14 32 55	16 35 9	18 33 25
31	20 40 32		0 33 9		4 33 39		8 34 9	10 36 22		14 36 52		18 37 22

1918

	Jan.	Feb.	Mar.	April	May	June	July	Aug.	Sept.	Oct.	Nov.	Dec.
1	18 41 18	20 43 32	22 33 55	0 36 8	2 34 25	4 36 38	6 34 55	8 37 8	10 39 21	12 37 38	14 39 51	16 38 8
2	18 45 15	20 47 28	22 37 52	0 40 5	2 38 22	4 40 35	6 38 51	8 41 5	10 43 18	12 41 35	14 43 48	16 42 4
3	18 49 12	20 51 25	22 41 48	0 44 1	2 42 18	4 44 31	6 42 48	8 45 1	10 47 14	12 45 31	14 47 44	16 46 1
4	18 53 8	20 55 21	22 45 45	0 47 58	2 46 15	4 48 28	6 46 45	8 48 58	10 51 11	12 49 28	14 51 41	16 49 57
5	18 57 5	20 59 18	22 49 41	0 51 55	2 50 11	4 52 24	6 50 41	8 52 54	10 55 8	12 53 24	14 55 37	16 53 54
6	19 1 1	21 3 15	22 53 38	0 55 51	2 54 8	4 56 21	6 54 38	8 56 51	10 59 4	12 57 21	14 59 34	16 57 51
7	19 4 58	21 7 11	22 57 35	0 59 48	2 58 4	5 0 18	6 58 34	9 0 48	11 3 1	13 1 17	15 3 30	17 1 47
8	19 8 54	21 11 8	23 1 31	1 3 44	3 2 1	5 4 14	7 2 31	9 4 44	11 6 57	13 5 14	15 7 27	17 5 44
9	19 12 51	21 15 4	23 5 28	1 7 41	3 5 57	5 8 11	7 6 27	9 8 41	11 10 54	13 9 10	15 11 24	17 9 40
10	19 16 47	21 19 1	23 9 24	1 11 37	3 9 54	5 12 7	7 10 24	9 12 37	11 14 50	13 13 7	15 15 20	17 13 37
11	19 20 44	21 22 57	23 13 21	1 15 34	3 13 51	5 16 4	7 14 20	9 16 34	11 18 47	13 17 3	15 19 17	17 17 33
12	19 24 41	21 26 54	23 17 17	1 19 30	3 17 47	5 20 0	7 18 17	9 20 30	11 22 43	13 21 0	15 23 13	17 21 30
13	19 28 37	21 30 50	23 21 14	1 23 27	3 21 44	5 23 57	7 22 14	9 24 27	11 26 40	13 24 57	15 27 10	17 25 26
14	19 32 34	21 34 47	23 25 10	1 27 24	3 25 40	5 27 53	7 26 10	9 28 23	11 30 37	13 28 53	15 31 6	17 29 23
15	19 36 30	21 38 43	23 29 7	1 31 20	3 29 37	5 31 50	7 30 7	9 32 20	11 34 33	13 32 50	15 35 3	17 33 20
16	19 40 27	21 42 40	23 33 4	1 35 17	3 33 33	5 35 47	7 34 3	9 36 17	11 38 30	13 36 46	15 38 59	17 37 16
17	19 44 23	21 46 37	23 37 0	1 39 13	3 37 30	5 39 43	7 38 0	9 40 13	11 42 26	13 40 43	15 42 56	17 41 13
18	19 48 20	21 50 33	23 40 57	1 43 10	3 41 26	5 43 40	7 41 56	9 44 10	11 46 23	13 44 39	15 46 53	17 45 9
19	19 52 16	21 54 30	23 44 53	1 47 6	3 45 23	5 47 36	7 45 53	9 48 6	11 50 19	13 48 36	15 50 49	17 49 6
20	19 56 13	21 58 26	23 48 50	1 51 3	3 49 20	5 51 33	7 49 50	9 52 3	11 54 16	13 52 32	15 54 46	17 53 2
21	20 0 10	22 2 23	23 52 46	1 54 59	3 53 16	5 55 29	7 53 46	9 55 59	11 58 12	13 56 29	15 58 42	17 56 59
22	20 4 6	22 6 19	23 56 43	1 58 56	3 57 13	5 59 26	7 57 43	9 59 56	12 2 9	14 0 26	16 2 39	18 0 56
23	20 8 3	22 10 16	0 0 39	2 2 53	4 1 9	6 3 22	8 1 39	10 3 52	12 6 6	14 4 22	16 6 35	18 4 52
24	20 11 59	22 14 12	0 4 36	2 6 49	4 5 6	6 7 19	8 5 36	10 7 49	12 10 2	14 8 19	16 10 32	18 8 49
25	20 15 56	22 18 9	0 8 32	2 10 46	4 9 2	6 11 16	8 9 32	10 11 45	12 13 59	14 12 15	16 14 28	18 12 45
26	20 19 52	22 22 6	0 12 29	2 14 42	4 12 59	6 15 12	8 13 29	10 15 42	12 17 55	14 16 12	16 18 25	18 16 42
27	20 23 49	22 26 2	0 16 26	2 18 39	4 16 55	6 19 9	8 17 25	10 19 39	12 21 52	14 20 8	16 22 22	18 20 38
28	20 27 45	22 29 59	0 20 22	2 22 35	4 20 52	6 23 5	8 21 22	10 23 35	12 25 48	14 24 5	16 26 18	18 24 35
29	20 31 42		0 24 19	2 26 32	4 24 49	6 27 2	8 25 19	10 27 32	12 29 45	14 28 1	16 30 15	18 28 31
30	20 35 39		0 28 15	2 30 28	4 28 45	6 30 58	8 29 15	10 31 28	12 33 41	14 31 58	16 34 11	18 32 28
31	20 39 35		0 32 12		4 32 42		8 33 12	10 35 25		14 35 55		18 36 25

1919

	Jan.	Feb.	Mar.	April	May	June	July	Aug.	Sept.	Oct.	Nov.	Dec.
1	18 40 21	20 42 34	22 32 58	0 35 11	2 33 28	4 35 41	6 33 58	8 36 11	10 38 24	12 36 41	14 38 54	16 37 10
2	18 44 18	20 46 31	22 36 54	0 39 8	2 37 24	4 39 37	6 37 54	8 40 7	10 42 21	12 40 37	14 42 50	16 41 7
3	18 48 14	20 50 27	22 40 51	0 43 4	2 41 21	4 43 34	6 41 51	8 44 4	10 46 17	12 44 34	14 46 47	16 45 3
4	18 52 11	20 54 24	22 44 48	0 47 1	2 45 17	4 47 30	6 45 47	8 48 0	10 50 14	12 48 30	14 50 43	16 49 0
5	18 56 7	20 58 21	22 48 44	0 50 57	2 49 14	4 51 27	6 49 44	8 51 57	10 54 10	12 52 27	14 54 40	16 52 57
6	19 0 4	21 2 17	22 52 41	0 54 54	2 53 10	4 55 24	6 53 40	8 55 54	10 58 7	12 56 23	14 58 36	16 56 53
7	19 4 0	21 6 14	22 56 37	0 58 50	2 57 7	4 59 20	6 57 37	8 59 50	11 2 3	13 0 20	15 2 33	17 0 50
8	19 7 57	21 10 10	23 0 34	1 2 47	3 1 3	5 3 17	7 1 33	9 3 47	11 6 0	13 4 16	15 6 30	17 4 46
9	19 11 54	21 14 7	23 4 30	1 6 43	3 5 0	5 7 13	7 5 30	9 7 43	11 9 56	13 8 13	15 10 26	17 8 43
10	19 15 50	21 18 3	23 8 27	1 10 40	3 8 57	5 11 10	7 9 27	9 11 40	11 13 53	13 12 10	15 14 23	17 12 39
11	19 19 47	21 22 0	23 12 23	1 14 37	3 12 53	5 15 6	7 13 23	9 15 36	11 17 49	13 16 6	15 18 19	17 16 36
12	19 23 43	21 25 56	23 16 20	1 18 33	3 16 50	5 19 3	7 17 20	9 19 33	11 21 46	13 20 3	15 22 16	17 20 32
13	19 27 40	21 29 53	23 20 16	1 22 30	3 20 46	5 22 59	7 21 16	9 23 29	11 25 42	13 23 59	15 26 12	17 24 29
14	19 31 36	21 33 50	23 24 13	1 26 26	3 24 43	5 26 56	7 25 13	9 27 26	11 29 39	13 27 56	15 30 9	17 28 26
15	19 35 33	21 37 46	23 28 10	1 30 23	3 28 39	5 30 53	7 29 9	9 31 23	11 33 36	13 31 52	15 34 5	17 32 22
16	19 39 29	21 41 43	23 32 6	1 34 19	3 32 36	5 34 49	7 33 6	9 35 19	11 37 32	13 35 49	15 38 2	17 36 19
17	19 43 26	21 45 39	23 36 3	1 38 16	3 36 32	5 38 46	7 37 2	9 39 16	11 41 29	13 39 45	15 41 59	17 40 15
18	19 47 23	21 49 36	23 39 59	1 42 12	3 40 29	5 42 42	7 40 59	9 43 12	11 45 25	13 43 42	15 45 55	17 44 12
19	19 51 19	21 53 32	23 43 56	1 46 9	3 44 26	5 46 39	7 44 56	9 47 9	11 49 22	13 47 38	15 49 52	17 48 8
20	19 55 16	21 57 29	23 47 52	1 50 5	3 48 22	5 50 35	7 48 52	9 51 5	11 53 18	13 51 35	15 53 48	17 52 5
21	19 59 12	22 1 25	23 51 49	1 54 2	3 52 19	5 54 32	7 52 49	9 55 2	11 57 15	13 55 32	15 57 45	17 56 1
22	20 3 9	22 5 22	23 55 45	1 57 59	3 56 15	5 58 28	7 56 45	9 58 58	12 1 12	13 59 28	16 1 41	17 59 58
23	20 7 5	22 9 19	23 59 42	2 1 55	4 0 12	6 2 25	8 0 42	10 2 55	12 5 8	14 3 25	16 5 38	18 3 55
24	20 11 2	22 13 15	0 3 39	2 5 52	4 4 8	6 6 22	8 4 38	10 6 52	12 9 5	14 7 21	16 9 34	18 7 51
25	20 14 58	22 17 12	0 7 35	2 9 48	4 8 5	6 10 18	8 8 35	10 10 48	12 13 1	14 11 18	16 13 31	18 11 48
26	20 18 55	22 21 8	0 11 32	2 13 45	4 12 1	6 14 15	8 12 31	10 14 45	12 16 58	14 15 14	16 17 28	18 15 44
27	20 22 52	22 25 5	0 15 28	2 17 41	4 15 58	6 18 11	8 16 28	10 18 41	12 20 54	14 19 11	16 21 24	18 19 41
28	20 26 48	22 29 1	0 19 25	2 21 38	4 19 55	6 22 8	8 20 25	10 22 38	12 24 51	14 23 7	16 25 21	18 23 37
29	20 30 45		0 23 21	2 25 34	4 23 51	6 26 4	8 24 21	10 26 34	12 28 47	14 27 4	16 29 17	18 27 34
30	20 34 41		0 27 18	2 29 31	4 27 48	6 30 1	8 28 18	10 30 31	12 32 44	14 31 1	16 33 14	18 31 31
31	20 38 38		0 31 14		4 31 44		8 32 14	10 34 27		14 34 57		18 35 27

	Jan.	Feb.	Mar.	April	May	June	July	Aug.	Sept.	Oct.	Nov.	Dec.	
1	18 39 24	20 41 37	22 35 57	0 38 10	2 36 27	4 38 40	6 36 57	8 39 10	10 41 23	12 39 40	14 41 53	16 40 9	1
2	18 43 20	20 45 33	22 39 53	0 42 7	2 40 23	4 42 36	6 40 53	8 43 6	10 45 20	12 43 36	14 45 49	16 44 6	2
3	18 47 17	20 49 30	22 43 50	0 46 3	2 44 20	4 46 33	6 44 50	8 47 3	10 49 16	12 47 33	14 49 46	16 48 2	3
4	18 51 13	20 53 27	22 47 47	0 50 0	2 48 16	4 50 30	6 48 46	8 50 59	10 53 13	12 51 29	14 53 42	16 51 59	4
5	18 55 10	20 57 23	22 51 43	0 53 56	2 52 13	4 54 26	6 52 43	8 54 56	10 57 9	12 55 26	14 57 39	16 55 56	5
6	18 59 6	21 1 20	22 55 40	0 57 53	2 56 9	4 58 23	6 56 39	8 58 53	11 1 6	12 59 22	15 1 35	16 59 52	6
7	19 3 3	21 5 16	22 59 36	1 1 49	3 0 6	5 2 19	7 0 36	9 2 49	11 5 2	13 3 19	15 5 32	17 3 49	7
8	19 7 0	21 9 13	23 3 33	1 5 46	3 4 3	5 6 16	7 4 32	9 6 46	11 8 59	13 7 15	15 9 29	17 7 45	8
9	19 10 56	21 13 9	23 7 29	1 9 42	3 7 59	5 10 12	7 8 29	9 10 42	11 12 56	13 11 12	15 13 25	17 11 42	9
10	19 14 53	21 17 6	23 11 26	1 13 39	3 11 56	5 14 9	7 12 26	9 14 39	11 16 52	13 15 9	15 17 22	17 15 38	10
11	19 18 49	21 21 2	23 15 22	1 17 36	3 15 52	5 18 5	7 16 22	9 18 35	11 20 49	13 19 5	15 21 18	17 19 35	11
12	19 22 46	21 24 59	23 19 19	1 21 32	3 19 49	5 22 2	7 20 19	9 22 32	11 24 45	13 23 2	15 25 15	17 23 31	12
13	19 26 42	21 28 56	23 23 16	1 25 29	3 23 45	5 25 59	7 24 15	9 26 28	11 28 42	13 26 58	15 29 11	17 27 28	13
14	19 30 39	21 32 52	23 27 12	1 29 25	3 27 42	5 29 55	7 28 12	9 30 25	11 32 38	13 30 55	15 33 8	17 31 25	14
15	19 34 35	21 36 49	23 31 9	1 33 22	3 31 38	5 33 52	7 32 8	9 34 22	11 36 35	13 34 51	15 37 4	17 35 21	15
16	19 38 32	21 40 45	23 35 5	1 37 18	3 35 35	5 37 48	7 36 5	9 38 18	11 40 31	13 38 48	15 41 1	17 39 18	16
17	19 42 29	21 44 42	23 39 2	1 41 15	3 39 32	5 41 45	7 40 1	9 42 15	11 44 28	13 42 44	15 44 58	17 43 14	17
18	19 46 25	21 48 38	23 42 58	1 45 11	3 43 28	5 45 41	7 43 58	9 46 11	11 48 24	13 46 41	15 48 54	17 47 11	18
19	19 50 22	21 52 35	23 46 55	1 49 8	3 47 25	5 49 38	7 47 55	9 50 8	11 52 21	13 50 37	15 52 51	17 51 7	19
20	19 54 18	21 56 31	23 50 51	1 53 5	3 51 21	5 53 34	7 51 51	9 54 4	11 56 17	13 54 34	15 56 47	17 55 4	20
21	19 58 15	22 0 28	23 54 48	1 57 1	3 55 18	5 57 31	7 55 48	9 58 1	12 0 14	13 58 31	16 0 44	17 59 0	21
22	20 2 11	22 4 25	23 58 45	2 0 58	3 59 14	6 1 28	7 59 44	10 1 57	12 4 11	14 2 27	16 4 40	18 2 57	22
23	20 6 8	22 8 21	0 2 41	2 4 54	4 3 11	6 5 24	8 3 41	10 5 54	12 8 7	14 6 24	16 8 37	18 6 54	23
24	20 10 4	22 12 18	0 6 38	2 8 51	4 7 7	6 9 21	8 7 37	10 9 51	12 12 4	14 10 20	16 12 33	18 10 50	24
25	20 14 1	22 16 14	0 10 34	2 12 47	4 11 4	6 13 17	8 11 34	10 13 47	12 16 0	14 14 17	16 16 30	18 14 47	25
26	20 17 58	22 20 11	0 14 31	2 16 44	4 15 1	6 17 14	8 15 30	10 17 44	12 19 57	14 18 13	16 20 27	18 18 43	26
27	20 21 54	22 24 7	0 18 27	2 20 40	4 18 57	6 21 10	8 19 27	10 21 40	12 23 53	14 22 10	16 24 23	18 22 40	27
28	20 25 51	22 28 4	0 22 24	2 24 37	4 22 54	6 25 7	8 23 24	10 25 37	12 27 50	14 26 6	16 28 20	18 26 36	28
29	20 29 47	22 32 0	0 26 20	2 28 34	4 26 50	6 29 3	8 27 20	10 29 33	12 31 46	14 30 3	16 32 16	18 30 33	29
30	20 33 44		0 30 17	2 32 30	4 30 47	6 33 0	8 31 17	10 33 30	12 35 43	14 34 0	16 36 13	18 34 30	30
31	20 37 40		0 34 14		4 34 43		8 35 13	10 37 26		14 37 56		18 38 26	31

	Jan.	Feb.	Mar.	April	May	June	July	Aug.	Sept.	Oct.	Nov.	Dec.	
1	18 42 23	20 44 36	22 34 59	0 37 12	2 35 29	4 37 42	6 35 59	8 38 12	10 40 25	12 38 42	14 40 55	16 39 12	1
2	18 46 19	20 48 32	22 38 56	0 41 9	2 39 26	4 41 39	6 39 56	8 42 9	10 44 22	12 42 38	14 44 52	16 43 8	2
3	18 50 16	20 52 29	22 42 52	0 45 6	2 43 22	4 45 35	6 43 52	8 46 5	10 48 18	12 46 35	14 48 48	16 47 5	3
4	18 54 12	20 56 26	22 46 49	0 49 2	2 47 19	4 49 32	6 47 49	8 50 2	10 52 15	12 50 32	14 52 45	16 51 1	4
5	18 58 9	21 0 22	22 50 46	0 52 59	2 51 15	4 53 29	6 51 45	8 53 58	10 56 12	12 54 28	14 56 41	16 54 58	5
6	19 2 5	21 4 19	22 54 42	0 56 55	2 55 12	4 57 25	6 55 42	8 57 55	11 0 8	12 58 25	15 0 38	16 58 55	6
7	19 6 2	21 8 15	22 58 39	1 0 52	2 59 8	5 1 22	6 59 38	9 1 52	11 4 5	13 2 21	15 4 34	17 2 51	7
8	19 9 59	21 12 12	23 2 35	1 4 48	3 3 5	5 5 18	7 3 35	9 5 48	11 8 1	13 6 18	15 8 31	17 6 48	8
9	19 13 55	21 16 8	23 6 32	1 8 45	3 7 1	5 9 15	7 7 31	9 9 45	11 11 58	13 10 14	15 12 28	17 10 44	9
10	19 17 52	21 20 5	23 10 28	1 12 41	3 10 58	5 13 11	7 11 28	9 13 41	11 15 54	13 14 11	15 16 24	17 14 41	10
11	19 21 48	21 24 1	23 14 25	1 16 38	3 14 55	5 17 8	7 15 25	9 17 38	11 19 51	13 18 7	15 20 21	17 18 37	11
12	19 25 45	21 27 58	23 18 21	1 20 35	3 18 51	5 21 4	7 19 21	9 21 34	11 23 47	13 22 4	15 24 17	17 22 34	12
13	19 29 41	21 31 55	23 22 18	1 24 31	3 22 48	5 25 1	7 23 18	9 25 31	11 27 44	13 26 1	15 28 14	17 26 30	13
14	19 33 38	21 35 51	23 26 15	1 28 28	3 26 44	5 28 58	7 27 14	9 29 27	11 31 41	13 29 57	15 32 10	17 30 27	14
15	19 37 34	21 39 48	23 30 11	1 32 24	3 30 41	5 32 54	7 31 11	9 33 24	11 35 37	13 33 54	15 36 7	17 34 24	15
16	19 41 31	21 43 44	23 34 8	1 36 21	3 34 37	5 36 51	7 35 7	9 37 21	11 39 34	13 37 50	15 40 3	17 38 20	16
17	19 45 28	21 47 41	23 38 4	1 40 17	3 38 34	5 40 47	7 39 4	9 41 17	11 43 30	13 41 47	15 44 0	17 42 17	17
18	19 49 24	21 51 37	23 42 1	1 44 14	3 42 30	5 44 44	7 43 0	9 45 14	11 47 27	13 45 43	15 47 57	17 46 13	18
19	19 53 21	21 55 34	23 45 57	1 48 10	3 46 27	5 48 40	7 46 57	9 49 10	11 51 23	13 49 40	15 51 53	17 50 10	19
20	19 57 17	21 59 30	23 49 54	1 52 7	3 50 23	5 52 37	7 50 54	9 53 7	11 55 20	13 53 36	15 55 50	17 54 6	20
21	20 1 14	22 3 27	23 53 50	1 56 4	3 54 20	5 56 33	7 54 50	9 57 3	11 59 16	13 57 33	15 59 46	17 58 3	21
22	20 5 10	22 7 24	23 57 47	2 0 0	3 58 17	6 0 30	7 58 47	10 1 0	12 3 13	14 1 30	16 3 43	18 1 59	22
23	20 9 7	22 11 20	0 1 44	2 3 57	4 2 13	6 4 27	8 2 43	10 4 56	12 7 10	14 5 26	16 7 39	18 5 56	23
24	20 13 3	22 15 17	0 5 40	2 7 53	4 6 10	6 8 23	8 6 40	10 8 53	12 11 6	14 9 23	16 11 36	18 9 53	24
25	20 17 0	22 19 13	0 9 37	2 11 50	4 10 6	6 12 20	8 10 36	10 12 50	12 15 3	14 13 19	16 15 32	18 13 49	25
26	20 20 57	22 23 10	0 13 33	2 15 46	4 14 3	6 16 16	8 14 33	10 16 46	12 18 59	14 17 16	16 19 29	18 17 46	26
27	20 24 53	22 27 6	0 17 30	2 19 43	4 17 59	6 20 13	8 18 29	10 20 43	12 22 56	14 21 12	16 23 26	18 21 42	27
28	20 28 50	22 31 3	0 21 26	2 23 39	4 21 56	6 24 9	8 22 26	10 24 39	12 26 52	14 25 9	16 27 22	18 25 39	28
29	20 32 46		0 25 23	2 27 36	4 25 52	6 28 6	8 26 23	10 28 36	12 30 49	14 29 5	16 31 19	18 29 35	29
30	20 36 43		0 29 19	2 31 33	4 29 49	6 32 2	8 30 19	10 32 32	12 34 45	14 33 2	16 35 15	18 33 32	30
31	20 40 39		0 33 16		4 33 46		8 34 16	10 36 29		14 36 59		18 37 28	31

	Jan.	Feb.	Mar.	April	May	June	July	Aug.	Sept.	Oct.	Nov.	Dec.	
1	18 41 25	20 43 38	22 34 2	0 36 15	2 34 31	4 36 45	6 35 1	8 37 15	10 39 28	12 37 44	14 39 57	16 38 14	1
2	18 45 22	20 47 35	22 37 58	0 40 11	2 38 28	4 40 41	6 38 58	8 41 11	10 43 24	12 41 41	14 43 54	16 42 11	2
3	18 49 18	20 51 31	22 41 55	0 44 8	2 42 24	4 44 38	6 42 54	8 45 8	10 47 21	12 45 37	14 47 51	16 46 7	3
4	18 53 15	20 55 28	22 45 51	0 48 5	2 46 21	4 48 34	6 46 51	8 49 4	10 51 17	12 49 34	14 51 44	16 50 4	4
5	18 57 11	20 59 24	22 49 48	0 52 1	2 50 18	4 52 31	6 50 48	8 53 1	10 55 14	12 53 30	14 55 44	16 54 0	5
6	19 1 8	21 3 21	22 53 45	0 55 58	2 54 14	4 56 27	6 54 44	8 56 57	10 59 10	12 57 27	14 59 40	16 57 57	6
7	19 5 4	21 7 18	22 57 41	0 59 54	2 58 11	5 0 24	6 58 41	9 0 54	11 3 7	13 1 24	15 3 37	17 1 53	7
8	19 9 1	21 11 14	23 1 38	1 3 51	3 2 7	5 4 21	7 2 37	9 4 50	11 7 3	13 5 20	15 7 33	17 5 50	8
9	19 12 57	21 15 11	23 5 34	1 7 47	3 6 4	5 8 17	7 6 34	9 8 47	11 11 0	13 9 17	15 11 30	17 9 47	9
10	19 16 54	21 19 7	23 9 31	1 11 44	3 10 0	5 12 14	7 10 30	9 12 44	11 14 57	13 13 13	15 15 26	17 13 43	10
11	19 20 51	21 23 4	23 13 27	1 15 40	3 13 57	5 16 10	7 14 27	9 16 40	11 18 53	13 17 10	15 19 23	17 17 40	11
12	19 24 47	21 27 0	23 17 24	1 19 37	3 17 53	5 20 7	7 18 23	9 20 37	11 22 50	13 21 6	15 23 16	17 21 36	12
13	19 28 44	21 30 57	23 21 20	1 23 33	3 21 50	5 24 3	7 22 20	9 24 33	11 26 46	13 25 3	15 27 16	17 25 33	13
14	19 32 40	21 34 53	23 25 17	1 27 30	3 25 47	5 28 0	7 26 17	9 28 30	11 30 43	13 28 59	15 31 13	17 29 29	14
15	19 36 37	21 38 50	23 29 13	1 31 27	3 29 43	5 31 56	7 30 13	9 32 26	11 34 39	13 32 56	15 35 9	17 33 26	15
16	19 40 33	21 42 47	23 33 10	1 35 23	3 33 40	5 35 53	7 34 10	9 36 23	11 38 36	13 36 53	15 39 6	17 37 22	16
17	19 44 30	21 46 43	23 37 7	1 39 20	3 37 36	5 39 50	7 38 6	9 40 19	11 42 33	13 40 49	15 43 2	17 41 19	17
18	19 48 26	21 50 40	23 41 3	1 43 16	3 41 33	5 43 46	7 42 3	9 44 16	11 46 29	13 44 46	15 46 59	17 45 16	18
19	19 52 23	21 54 36	23 45 0	1 47 13	3 45 29	5 47 43	7 45 59	9 48 13	11 50 26	13 48 42	15 50 55	17 49 12	19
20	19 56 20	21 58 33	23 48 56	1 51 9	3 49 26	5 51 39	7 49 56	9 52 9	11 54 22	13 52 39	15 54 52	17 53 9	20
21	20 0 16	22 2 29	23 52 53	1 55 6	3 53 23	5 55 36	7 53 52	9 56 6	11 58 19	13 56 35	15 58 49	17 57 5	21
22	20 4 13	22 6 26	23 56 49	1 59 2	3 57 19	5 59 32	7 57 49	10 0 2	12 2 15	14 0 32	16 2 45	18 1 2	22
23	20 8 9	22 10 22	0 0 46	2 2 59	4 1 16	6 3 29	8 1 46	10 3 59	12 6 12	14 4 28	16 6 42	18 4 58	23
24	20 12 6	22 14 19	0 4 42	2 6 56	4 5 12	6 7 25	8 5 42	10 7 55	12 10 8	14 8 25	16 10 38	18 8 55	24
25	20 16 2	22 18 16	0 8 39	2 10 52	4 9 9	6 11 22	8 9 39	10 11 52	12 14 5	14 12 22	16 14 35	18 12 51	25
26	20 19 59	22 22 12	0 12 36	2 14 49	4 13 5	6 15 19	8 13 35	10 15 48	12 18 2	14 16 18	16 18 31	18 16 48	26
27	20 23 55	22 26 9	0 16 32	2 18 45	4 17 2	6 19 15	8 17 32	10 19 45	12 21 58	14 20 15	16 22 28	18 20 45	27
28	20 27 52	22 30 5	0 20 29	2 22 42	4 20 58	6 23 12	8 21 28	10 23 42	12 25 55	14 24 11	16 26 24	18 24 41	28
29	20 31 49		0 24 25	2 26 38	4 24 55	6 27 8	8 25 25	10 27 38	12 29 51	14 28 8	16 30 21	18 28 38	29
30	20 35 45		0 28 22	2 30 35	4 28 52	6 31 5	8 29 21	10 31 35	12 33 48	14 32 4	16 34 18	18 32 34	30
31	20 39 42		0 32 18		4 32 48		8 33 18	10 35 31		14 36 1		18 36 31	31

1923

	Jan.	Feb.	Mar.	April	May	June	July	Aug.	Sept.	Oct.	Nov.	Dec.
1	18 40 27	20 42 41	22 33 4	0 35 17	2 33 34	4 35 47	6 34 4	8 36 17	10 38 30	12 36 47	14 39 0	16 37 16
2	18 44 24	20 46 37	22 37 1	0 39 14	2 37 30	4 39 44	6 38 0	8 40 13	10 42 27	12 40 43	14 42 56	16 41 13
3	18 48 20	20 50 34	22 40 57	0 43 10	2 41 27	4 43 40	6 41 57	8 44 10	10 46 23	12 44 40	14 46 53	16 45 10
4	18 52 17	20 54 30	22 44 54	0 47 7	2 45 23	4 47 37	6 45 53	8 48 7	10 50 20	12 48 36	14 50 49	16 49 6
5	18 56 14	20 58 27	22 48 50	0 51 3	2 49 20	4 51 33	6 49 50	8 52 3	10 54 16	12 52 33	14 54 46	16 53 3
6	19 0 10	21 2 23	22 52 47	0 55 0	2 53 17	4 55 30	6 53 46	8 56 0	10 58 13	12 56 29	14 58 43	16 56 59
7	19 4 7	21 6 20	22 56 43	0 58 57	2 57 13	4 59 26	6 57 43	8 59 56	11 2 9	13 0 26	15 2 39	17 0 56
8	19 8 3	21 10 16	23 0 40	1 2 53	3 1 10	5 3 23	7 1 40	9 3 53	11 6 6	13 4 23	15 6 36	17 4 52
9	19 12 0	21 14 13	23 4 37	1 6 50	3 5 6	5 7 19	7 5 36	9 7 49	11 10 3	13 8 19	15 10 32	17 8 49
10	19 15 56	21 18 10	23 8 33	1 10 46	3 9 3	5 11 16	7 9 33	9 11 46	11 13 59	13 12 16	15 14 29	17 12 45
11	19 19 53	21 22 6	23 12 30	1 14 43	3 12 59	5 15 13	7 13 29	9 15 42	11 17 56	13 16 12	15 18 25	17 16 42
12	19 23 49	21 26 3	23 16 26	1 18 39	3 16 56	5 19 9	7 17 26	9 19 39	11 21 52	13 20 9	15 22 22	17 20 39
13	19 27 46	21 29 59	23 20 23	1 22 36	3 20 52	5 23 6	7 21 22	9 23 36	11 25 49	13 24 5	15 26 18	17 24 35
14	19 31 43	21 33 56	23 24 19	1 26 32	3 24 49	5 27 2	7 25 19	9 27 32	11 29 45	13 28 2	15 30 15	17 28 32
15	19 35 39	21 37 52	23 28 16	1 30 29	3 28 46	5 30 59	7 29 15	9 31 29	11 33 42	13 31 58	15 34 12	17 32 28
16	19 39 36	21 41 49	23 32 12	1 34 25	3 32 42	5 34 55	7 33 12	9 35 25	11 37 38	13 35 55	15 38 8	17 36 25
17	19 43 32	21 45 45	23 36 9	1 38 22	3 36 39	5 38 52	7 37 9	9 39 22	11 41 35	13 39 51	15 42 5	17 40 21
18	19 47 29	21 49 42	23 40 5	1 42 19	3 40 35	5 42 48	7 41 5	9 43 18	11 45 31	13 43 48	15 46 1	17 44 18
19	19 51 25	21 53 39	23 44 2	1 46 15	3 44 32	5 46 45	7 45 2	9 47 15	11 49 28	13 47 45	15 49 58	17 48 14
20	19 55 22	21 57 35	23 47 59	1 50 12	3 48 28	5 50 42	7 48 58	9 51 11	11 53 25	13 51 41	15 53 54	17 52 11
21	19 59 18	22 1 32	23 51 55	1 54 8	3 52 25	5 54 38	7 52 55	9 55 8	11 57 21	13 55 38	15 57 51	17 56 8
22	20 3 15	22 5 28	23 55 52	1 58 5	3 56 21	5 58 35	7 56 51	9 59 5	12 1 18	13 59 34	16 1 47	18 0 4
23	20 7 12	22 9 25	23 59 48	2 2 1	4 0 18	6 2 31	8 0 48	10 3 1	12 5 14	14 3 31	16 5 44	18 4 1
24	20 11 8	22 13 21	0 3 45	2 5 58	4 4 15	6 6 28	8 4 44	10 6 58	12 9 11	14 7 27	16 9 41	18 7 57
25	20 15 5	22 17 18	0 7 41	2 9 54	4 8 11	6 10 24	8 8 41	10 10 54	12 13 7	14 11 24	16 13 37	18 11 54
26	20 19 1	22 21 14	0 11 38	2 13 51	4 12 8	6 14 21	8 12 38	10 14 51	12 17 4	14 15 20	16 17 34	18 15 50
27	20 22 58	22 25 11	0 15 34	2 17 48	4 16 4	6 18 17	8 16 34	10 18 47	12 21 0	14 19 17	16 21 30	18 19 47
28	20 26 54	22 29 8	0 19 31	2 21 44	4 20 1	6 22 14	8 20 31	10 22 44	12 24 57	14 23 14	16 25 27	18 23 43
29	20 30 51		0 23 28	2 25 41	4 23 57	6 26 11	8 24 27	10 26 40	12 28 54	14 27 10	16 29 23	18 27 40
30	20 34 47		0 27 24	2 29 37	4 27 54	6 30 7	8 28 24	10 30 37	12 32 50	14 31 7	16 33 20	18 31 37
31	20 38 44		0 31 21		4 31 50		8 32 20	10 34 34		14 35 3		18 35 33

1924

	Jan.	Feb.	Mar.	April	May	June	July	Aug.	Sept.	Oct.	Nov.	Dec.
1	18 39 30	20 41 43	22 36 3	0 38 16	2 36 33	4 38 46	6 37 3	8 39 16	10 41 29	12 39 46	14 41 59	16 40 15
2	18 43 26	20 45 40	22 40 0	0 42 13	2 40 29	4 42 42	6 40 59	8 43 12	10 45 26	12 43 42	14 45 55	16 44 12
3	18 47 23	20 49 36	22 43 56	0 46 9	2 44 26	4 46 39	6 44 56	8 47 9	10 49 22	12 47 39	14 49 52	16 48 9
4	18 51 19	20 53 33	22 47 53	0 50 6	2 48 22	4 50 36	6 48 52	8 51 6	10 53 19	12 51 35	14 53 48	16 52 5
5	18 55 16	20 57 29	22 51 49	0 54 2	2 52 19	4 54 32	6 52 49	8 55 2	10 57 15	12 55 32	14 57 45	16 56 2
6	18 59 12	21 1 26	22 55 46	0 57 59	2 56 15	4 58 29	6 56 45	8 58 59	11 1 12	12 59 28	15 1 42	16 59 58
7	19 3 9	21 5 22	22 59 42	1 1 55	3 0 12	5 2 25	7 0 42	9 2 55	11 5 8	13 3 25	15 5 38	17 3 55
8	19 7 6	21 9 19	23 3 39	1 5 52	3 4 9	5 6 22	7 4 39	9 6 52	11 9 5	13 7 21	15 9 35	17 7 51
9	19 11 2	21 13 15	23 7 35	1 9 49	3 8 5	5 10 18	7 8 35	9 10 48	11 13 1	13 11 18	15 13 31	17 11 48
10	19 14 59	21 17 12	23 11 32	1 13 45	3 12 2	5 14 15	7 12 32	9 14 45	11 16 58	13 15 15	15 17 28	17 15 44
11	19 18 55	21 21 8	23 15 29	1 17 42	3 15 58	5 18 11	7 16 28	9 18 41	11 20 55	13 19 11	15 21 24	17 19 41
12	19 22 52	21 25 5	23 19 25	1 21 38	3 19 55	5 22 8	7 20 25	9 22 38	11 24 51	13 23 8	15 25 21	17 23 38
13	19 26 48	21 29 2	23 23 22	1 25 35	3 23 51	5 26 5	7 24 21	9 26 35	11 28 48	13 27 4	15 29 17	17 27 34
14	19 30 45	21 32 58	23 27 18	1 29 31	3 27 48	5 30 1	7 28 18	9 30 31	11 32 44	13 31 1	15 33 14	17 31 31
15	19 34 42	21 36 55	23 31 15	1 33 28	3 31 44	5 33 58	7 32 14	9 34 28	11 36 41	13 34 57	15 37 10	17 35 27
16	19 38 38	21 40 51	23 35 11	1 37 24	3 35 41	5 37 54	7 36 11	9 38 24	11 40 37	13 38 54	15 41 7	17 39 24
17	19 42 35	21 44 48	23 39 8	1 41 21	3 39 38	5 41 51	7 40 8	9 42 21	11 44 34	13 42 50	15 45 4	17 43 20
18	19 46 31	21 48 44	23 43 4	1 45 18	3 43 34	5 45 47	7 44 4	9 46 17	11 48 30	13 46 47	15 49 0	17 47 17
19	19 50 28	21 52 41	23 47 1	1 49 14	3 47 31	5 49 44	7 48 1	9 50 14	11 52 27	13 50 44	15 52 57	17 51 13
20	19 54 24	21 56 37	23 50 57	1 53 11	3 51 27	5 53 40	7 51 57	9 54 10	11 56 24	13 54 40	15 56 53	17 55 10
21	19 58 21	22 0 34	23 54 54	1 57 7	3 55 24	5 57 37	7 55 54	9 58 7	12 0 20	13 58 37	16 0 50	17 59 7
22	20 2 17	22 4 31	23 58 51	2 1 4	3 59 20	6 1 34	7 59 50	10 2 4	12 4 17	14 2 33	16 4 46	18 3 3
23	20 6 14	22 8 27	0 2 47	2 5 0	4 3 17	6 5 30	8 3 47	10 6 0	12 8 13	14 6 30	16 8 43	18 7 0
24	20 10 11	22 12 24	0 6 44	2 8 57	4 7 13	6 9 27	8 7 43	10 9 57	12 12 10	14 10 26	16 12 40	18 10 56
25	20 14 7	22 16 20	0 10 40	2 12 53	4 11 10	6 13 23	8 11 40	10 13 53	12 16 6	14 14 23	16 16 36	18 14 53
26	20 18 4	22 20 17	0 14 37	2 16 50	4 15 7	6 17 20	8 15 37	10 17 50	12 20 3	14 18 19	16 20 33	18 18 49
27	20 22 0	22 24 13	0 18 33	2 20 46	4 19 3	6 21 16	8 19 33	10 21 46	12 23 59	14 22 16	16 24 29	18 22 46
28	20 25 57	22 28 10	0 22 30	2 24 43	4 23 0	6 25 13	8 23 30	10 25 43	12 27 56	14 26 13	16 28 26	18 26 42
29	20 29 53	22 32 6	0 26 26	2 28 40	4 26 56	6 29 10	8 27 26	10 29 39	12 31 52	14 30 9	16 32 22	18 30 39
30	20 33 50		0 30 23	2 32 36	4 30 53	6 33 6	8 31 23	10 33 36	12 35 49	14 34 6	16 36 19	18 34 36
31	20 37 46		0 34 20		4 34 49		8 35 19	10 37 32		14 38 2		18 38 32

1925

	Jan.	Feb.	Mar.	April	May	June	July	Aug.	Sept.	Oct.	Nov.	Dec.
1	18 42 29	20 44 42	22 35 5	0 37 19	2 35 35	4 37 48	6 36 5	8 38 18	10 40 31	12 38 48	14 41 1	16 39 18
2	18 46 25	20 48 38	22 39 2	0 41 15	2 39 32	4 41 45	6 40 2	8 42 15	10 44 28	12 42 45	14 44 58	16 43 14
3	18 50 22	20 52 35	22 42 59	0 45 12	2 43 28	4 45 41	6 43 58	8 46 11	10 48 25	12 46 41	14 48 54	16 47 11
4	18 54 18	20 56 32	22 46 55	0 49 8	2 47 25	4 49 38	6 47 55	8 50 8	10 52 21	12 50 38	14 52 51	16 51 8
5	18 58 15	21 0 28	22 50 52	0 53 5	2 51 22	4 53 35	6 51 51	8 54 5	10 56 18	12 54 34	14 56 47	16 55 4
6	19 2 11	21 4 25	22 54 48	0 57 1	2 55 18	4 57 31	6 55 48	8 58 1	11 0 14	12 58 31	15 0 44	16 59 1
7	19 6 8	21 8 21	22 58 45	1 0 58	2 59 14	5 1 28	6 59 44	9 1 58	11 4 11	13 2 27	15 4 41	17 2 57
8	19 10 5	21 12 18	23 2 41	1 4 54	3 3 11	5 5 24	7 3 41	9 5 54	11 8 7	13 6 24	15 8 37	17 6 54
9	19 14 1	21 16 14	23 6 38	1 8 51	3 7 8	5 9 21	7 7 38	9 9 51	11 12 4	13 10 20	15 12 34	17 10 50
10	19 17 58	21 20 11	23 10 34	1 12 48	3 11 4	5 13 17	7 11 34	9 13 47	11 16 0	13 14 17	15 16 30	17 14 47
11	19 21 54	21 24 7	23 14 31	1 16 44	3 15 1	5 17 14	7 15 31	9 17 44	11 19 57	13 18 14	15 20 27	17 18 43
12	19 25 51	21 28 4	23 18 28	1 20 41	3 18 57	5 21 10	7 19 27	9 21 40	11 23 54	13 22 10	15 24 23	17 22 40
13	19 29 47	21 32 1	23 22 24	1 24 37	3 22 54	5 25 7	7 23 24	9 25 37	11 27 50	13 26 7	15 28 20	17 26 37
14	19 33 44	21 35 57	23 26 21	1 28 34	3 26 50	5 29 4	7 27 20	9 29 34	11 31 47	13 30 3	15 32 16	17 30 33
15	19 37 40	21 39 54	23 30 17	1 32 30	3 30 47	5 33 0	7 31 17	9 33 30	11 35 43	13 34 0	15 36 13	17 34 30
16	19 41 37	21 43 50	23 34 14	1 36 27	3 34 43	5 36 57	7 35 13	9 37 27	11 39 40	13 37 56	15 40 10	17 38 26
17	19 45 34	21 47 47	23 38 10	1 40 23	3 38 40	5 40 53	7 39 10	9 41 23	11 43 36	13 41 53	15 44 6	17 42 23
18	19 49 30	21 51 43	23 42 7	1 44 20	3 42 37	5 44 50	7 43 7	9 45 20	11 47 33	13 45 49	15 48 3	17 46 19
19	19 53 27	21 55 40	23 46 3	1 48 16	3 46 33	5 48 46	7 47 3	9 49 16	11 51 29	13 49 46	15 51 59	17 50 16
20	19 57 23	21 59 36	23 50 0	1 52 13	3 50 30	5 52 43	7 51 0	9 53 13	11 55 26	13 53 43	15 55 56	17 54 12
21	20 1 20	22 3 33	23 53 56	1 56 10	3 54 26	5 56 40	7 54 56	9 57 9	11 59 23	13 57 39	15 59 52	17 58 9
22	20 5 16	22 7 30	23 57 53	2 0 6	3 58 23	6 0 36	7 58 53	10 1 6	12 3 19	14 1 36	16 3 49	18 2 6
23	20 9 13	22 11 26	0 1 50	2 4 3	4 2 19	6 4 33	8 2 49	10 5 3	12 7 16	14 5 32	16 7 45	18 6 2
24	20 13 9	22 15 23	0 5 46	2 7 59	4 6 16	6 8 29	8 6 46	10 8 59	12 11 12	14 9 29	16 11 42	18 9 59
25	20 17 6	22 19 19	0 9 43	2 11 56	4 10 12	6 12 26	8 10 42	10 12 55	12 15 9	14 13 25	16 15 39	18 13 55
26	20 21 3	22 23 16	0 13 39	2 15 52	4 14 9	6 16 22	8 14 39	10 16 52	12 19 5	14 17 22	16 19 35	18 17 52
27	20 24 59	22 27 12	0 17 36	2 19 49	4 18 6	6 20 19	8 18 36	10 20 49	12 23 2	14 21 18	16 23 32	18 21 48
28	20 28 56	22 31 9	0 21 32	2 23 45	4 22 2	6 24 15	8 22 32	10 24 45	12 26 58	14 25 15	16 27 28	18 25 45
29	20 32 52		0 25 29	2 27 42	4 25 59	6 28 12	8 26 29	10 28 42	12 30 55	14 29 11	16 31 25	18 29 42
30	20 36 49		0 29 25	2 31 39	4 29 55	6 32 9	8 30 25	10 32 38	12 34 52	14 33 8	16 35 21	18 33 38
31	20 40 45		0 33 22		4 33 52		8 34 22	10 36 35		14 37 5		18 37 35

Day	Jan.	Feb.	Mar.	April	May	June	July	Aug.	Sept.	Oct.	Nov.	Dec.
1	18 41 31	20 43 44	22 34 8	0 36 21	2 34 38	4 36 51	6 35 8	8 37 21	10 39 34	12 37 51	14 40 4	16 38 20
2	18 45 28	20 47 41	22 38 5	0 40 18	2 38 34	4 40 47	6 39 4	8 41 17	10 43 31	12 41 47	14 44 0	16 42 17
3	18 49 24	20 51 38	22 42 1	0 44 14	2 42 31	4 44 44	6 43 1	8 45 14	10 47 27	12 45 44	14 47 57	16 46 14
4	18 53 21	30 55 34	22 45 58	0 48 11	2 46 27	4 48 41	6 46 57	8 49 11	10 51 24	12 49 40	14 51 53	16 50 10
5	18 57 17	20 59 31	22 49 54	0 52 7	2 50 24	4 52 37	6 50 54	8 53 7	10 55 20	12 53 37	14 55 50	16 54 7
6	19 1 14	21 3 27	22 53 51	0 56 4	2 54 20	4 56 34	6 54 50	8 57 4	10 59 17	12 57 33	14 59 47	16 58 3
7	19 5 11	21 7 24	22 57 47	1 0 0	2 58 17	5 0 30	6 58 47	9 1 0	11 3 13	13 1 30	15 3 43	17 2 0
8	19 9 7	21 11 20	23 1 44	1 3 57	3 2 14	5 4 27	7 2 44	9 4 57	11 7 10	13 5 27	15 7 40	17 5 56
9	19 13 4	21 15 17	23 5 40	1 7 53	3 6 10	5 8 23	7 6 40	9 8 53	11 11 6	13 9 23	15 11 36	17 9 53
10	19 17 0	21 19 13	23 9 37	1 11 50	3 10 7	5 12 20	7 10 37	9 12 50	11 15 3	13 13 20	15 15 33	17 13 50
11	19 20 57	21 23 10	23 13 33	1 15 47	3 14 3	5 16 16	7 14 33	9 16 46	11 19 0	13 17 16	15 19 29	17 17 46
12	19 24 53	21 27 7	23 17 30	1 19 43	3 18 0	5 20 13	7 18 30	9 20 43	11 22 56	13 21 13	15 23 26	17 21 43
13	19 28 50	21 31 3	23 21 27	1 23 40	3 21 56	5 24 10	7 22 26	9 24 40	11 26 53	13 25 9	15 27 22	17 25 39
14	19 32 46	21 35 0	23 25 23	1 27 36	3 25 53	5 28 6	7 26 23	9 28 36	11 30 49	13 29 6	15 31 19	17 29 36
15	19 36 43	21 38 56	23 29 20	1 31 33	3 29 49	5 32 3	7 30 19	9 32 33	11 34 46	13 33 2	15 35 16	17 33 32
16	19 40 40	21 42 53	23 33 16	1 35 29	3 33 46	5 35 59	7 34 16	9 36 29	11 38 42	13 36 59	15 39 12	17 37 29
17	19 44 36	21 46 49	23 37 13	1 39 26	3 37 43	5 39 56	7 38 13	9 40 26	11 42 39	13 40 56	15 43 9	17 41 25
18	19 48 33	21 50 46	23 41 9	1 43 22	3 41 39	5 43 52	7 42 9	9 44 22	11 46 35	13 44 52	15 47 5	17 45 22
19	19 52 29	21 54 42	23 45 6	1 47 19	3 45 36	5 47 49	7 46 6	9 48 19	11 50 32	13 48 49	15 51 2	17 49 19
20	19 56 26	21 58 39	23 49 2	1 51 16	3 49 32	5 51 46	7 50 2	9 52 15	11 54 29	13 52 45	15 54 58	17 53 15
21	20 0 22	22 2 36	23 52 59	1 55 12	3 53 29	5 55 42	7 53 59	9 56 12	11 58 25	13 56 42	15 58 55	17 57 12
22	20 4 19	22 6 32	23 56 56	1 59 9	3 57 25	5 59 39	7 57 55	10 0 9	12 2 22	14 0 38	16 2 51	18 1 8
23	20 8 15	22 10 29	0 0 52	2 3 5	4 1 22	6 3 35	8 1 52	10 4 5	12 6 18	14 4 35	16 6 48	18 5 5
24	20 12 12	22 14 25	0 4 49	2 7 2	4 5 18	6 7 32	8 5 48	10 8 2	12 10 15	14 8 31	16 10 45	18 9 1
25	20 16 9	22 18 22	0 8 45	2 10 58	4 9 15	6 11 28	8 9 45	10 11 58	12 14 11	14 12 28	16 14 41	18 12 58
26	20 20 5	22 22 18	0 12 42	2 14 55	4 13 12	6 15 25	8 13 42	10 15 55	12 18 8	14 16 24	16 18 38	18 16 54
27	20 24 2	22 26 15	0 16 38	2 18 51	4 17 8	6 19 21	8 17 38	10 19 51	12 22 4	14 20 21	16 22 34	18 20 51
28	20 27 58	22 30 11	0 20 35	2 22 48	4 21 5	6 23 18	8 21 35	10 23 48	12 26 1	14 24 18	16 26 31	18 24 48
29	20 31 55		0 24 31	2 26 45	4 25 1	6 27 15	8 25 31	10 27 44	12 29 58	14 28 14	16 30 27	18 28 44
30	20 35 51		0 28 28	2 30 41	4 28 58	6 31 11	8 29 28	10 31 41	12 33 54	14 32 11	16 34 24	18 32 41
31	20 39 48		0 32 25		4 32 54		8 33 24	10 35 38		14 36 7		18 36 37

Day	Jan.	Feb.	Mar.	April	May	June	July	Aug.	Sept.	Oct.	Nov.	Dec.
1	18 40 34	20 42 47	22 33 11	0 35 24	2 33 40	4 35 54	6 34 10	8 36 24	10 38 37	12 36 53	14 39 7	16 37 23
2	18 44 30	20 46 44	22 37 7	0 39 20	2 37 37	4 39 50	6 38 7	8 40 20	10 42 33	12 40 50	14 43 3	16 41 20
3	18 48 27	20 50 40	22 41 4	0 43 17	2 41 33	4 43 47	6 42 3	8 44 17	10 46 30	12 44 46	14 47 0	16 45 16
4	18 52 23	20 54 37	22 45 0	0 47 13	2 45 30	4 47 43	6 46 0	8 48 13	10 50 26	12 48 43	14 50 56	16 49 13
5	18 56 20	20 58 33	22 48 57	0 51 10	2 49 27	4 51 40	6 49 57	8 52 10	10 54 23	12 52 40	14 54 53	16 53 9
6	19 0 17	21 2 30	22 52 53	0 55 6	2 53 23	4 55 36	6 53 53	8 56 6	10 58 20	12 56 36	14 58 49	16 57 6
7	19 4 13	21 6 26	22 56 50	0 59 3	2 57 20	4 59 33	6 57 50	9 0 3	11 2 16	13 0 33	15 2 46	17 1 3
8	19 8 10	21 10 23	23 0 46	1 3 0	3 1 16	5 3 29	7 1 46	9 3 59	11 6 13	13 4 29	15 6 42	17 4 59
9	19 12 6	21 14 20	23 4 43	1 6 56	3 5 13	5 7 26	7 5 43	9 7 56	11 10 9	13 8 26	15 10 39	17 8 56
10	19 16 3	21 18 16	23 8 40	1 10 53	3 9 9	5 11 23	7 9 39	9 11 53	11 14 6	13 12 22	15 14 36	17 12 52
11	19 19 59	21 22 13	23 12 36	1 14 49	3 13 6	5 15 19	7 13 36	9 15 49	11 18 2	13 16 19	15 18 32	17 16 49
12	19 23 56	21 26 9	23 16 33	1 18 46	3 17 2	5 19 16	7 17 32	9 19 46	11 21 59	13 20 15	15 22 29	17 20 45
13	19 27 52	21 30 6	23 20 29	1 22 42	3 20 59	5 23 12	7 21 29	9 23 42	11 25 55	13 24 12	15 26 25	17 24 42
14	19 31 49	21 34 2	23 24 26	1 26 39	3 24 56	5 27 9	7 25 26	9 27 39	11 29 52	13 28 9	15 30 22	17 28 38
15	19 35 46	21 37 59	23 28 22	1 30 35	3 28 52	5 31 5	7 29 22	9 31 35	11 33 49	13 32 5	15 34 18	17 32 35
16	19 39 42	21 41 55	23 32 19	1 34 32	3 32 49	5 35 2	7 33 19	9 35 32	11 37 45	13 36 2	15 38 15	17 36 32
17	19 43 39	21 45 52	23 36 15	1 38 29	3 36 45	5 38 58	7 37 15	9 39 28	11 41 42	13 39 58	15 42 11	17 40 28
18	19 47 35	21 49 48	23 40 12	1 42 25	3 40 42	5 42 55	7 41 12	9 43 25	11 45 38	13 43 55	15 46 8	17 44 25
19	19 51 32	21 53 45	23 44 9	1 46 22	3 44 38	5 46 52	7 45 8	9 47 22	11 49 35	13 47 51	15 50 5	17 48 21
20	19 55 28	21 57 42	23 48 5	1 50 18	3 48 35	5 50 48	7 49 5	9 51 18	11 53 31	13 51 48	15 54 1	17 52 18
21	19 59 25	22 1 38	23 52 2	1 54 15	3 52 31	5 54 45	7 53 1	9 55 15	11 57 28	13 55 44	15 57 58	17 56 14
22	20 3 21	22 5 35	23 55 58	1 58 11	3 56 28	5 58 41	7 56 58	9 59 11	12 1 24	13 59 41	16 1 54	18 0 11
23	20 7 18	22 9 31	23 59 55	2 2 8	4 0 25	6 2 38	8 0 55	10 3 8	12 5 21	14 3 38	16 5 51	18 4 7
24	20 11 15	22 13 28	0 3 51	2 6 4	4 4 21	6 6 34	8 4 51	10 7 4	12 9 17	14 7 34	16 9 47	18 8 4
25	20 15 11	22 17 24	0 7 48	2 10 1	4 8 18	6 10 31	8 8 48	10 11 1	12 13 14	14 11 31	16 13 44	18 12 1
26	20 19 8	22 21 21	0 11 44	2 13 58	4 12 14	6 14 28	8 12 44	10 14 57	12 17 11	14 15 27	16 17 40	18 15 57
27	20 23 4	22 25 17	0 15 41	2 17 54	4 16 11	6 18 24	8 16 41	10 18 54	12 21 7	14 19 24	16 21 37	18 19 54
28	20 27 1	22 29 14	0 19 38	2 21 51	4 20 7	6 22 21	8 20 37	10 22 51	12 25 4	14 23 20	16 25 34	18 23 50
29	20 30 57		0 23 34	2 25 47	4 24 4	6 26 17	8 24 34	10 26 47	12 29 0	14 27 17	16 29 30	18 27 47
30	20 34 54		0 27 31	2 29 44	4 28 0	6 30 14	8 28 30	10 30 44	12 32 57	14 31 13	16 33 27	18 31 43
31	20 38 51		0 31 27		4 31 57		8 32 27	10 34 40		14 35 10		18 35 40

Day	Jan.	Feb.	Mar.	April	May	June	July	Aug.	Sept.	Oct.	Nov.	Dec.
1	18 39 37	20 41 50	22 36 10	0 38 23	2 36 40	4 38 53	6 37 10	8 39 23	10 41 36	12 39 53	14 42 6	16 40 23
2	18 43 33	20 45 46	22 40 6	0 42 20	2 40 36	4 42 49	6 41 6	8 43 19	10 45 33	12 43 49	14 46 2	16 44 19
3	18 47 30	20 49 43	22 44 3	0 46 16	2 44 33	4 46 46	6 45 3	8 47 16	10 49 29	12 47 46	14 49 59	16 48 16
4	18 51 26	20 53 39	22 48 0	0 50 13	2 48 30	4 50 43	6 48 59	8 51 13	10 53 26	12 51 42	14 53 56	16 52 12
5	18 55 23	20 57 36	22 51 56	0 54 9	2 52 26	4 54 39	6 52 56	8 55 9	10 57 22	12 55 39	14 57 52	16 56 9
6	18 59 19	21 1 33	22 55 53	0 58 6	2 56 23	4 58 36	6 56 52	8 59 6	11 1 19	12 59 35	15 1 49	17 0 5
7	19 3 16	21 5 29	22 59 49	1 2 2	3 0 19	5 2 32	7 0 49	9 3 2	11 5 15	13 3 32	15 5 45	17 4 2
8	19 7 12	21 9 26	23 3 46	1 5 59	3 4 16	5 6 29	7 4 46	9 6 59	11 9 12	13 7 29	15 9 42	17 7 59
9	19 11 9	21 13 22	23 7 42	1 9 55	3 8 12	5 10 25	7 8 42	9 10 55	11 13 9	13 11 25	15 13 38	17 11 55
10	19 15 6	21 17 19	23 11 39	1 13 52	3 12 9	5 14 22	7 12 39	9 14 52	11 17 5	13 15 22	15 17 35	17 15 52
11	19 19 2	21 21 15	23 15 35	1 17 49	3 16 5	5 18 18	7 16 35	9 18 48	11 21 2	13 19 18	15 21 31	17 19 48
12	19 22 59	21 25 12	23 19 32	1 21 45	3 20 2	5 22 15	7 20 32	9 22 45	11 24 58	13 23 15	15 25 28	17 23 45
13	19 26 55	21 29 8	23 23 29	1 25 42	3 23 58	5 26 12	7 24 28	9 26 42	11 28 55	13 27 11	15 29 25	17 27 41
14	19 30 52	21 33 5	23 27 25	1 29 38	3 27 55	5 30 8	7 28 25	9 30 38	11 32 51	13 31 8	15 33 21	17 31 38
15	19 34 48	21 37 2	23 31 22	1 33 35	3 31 51	5 34 5	7 32 21	9 34 35	11 36 48	13 35 4	15 37 18	17 35 34
16	19 38 45	21 40 58	23 35 18	1 37 31	3 35 48	5 38 1	7 36 18	9 38 31	11 40 44	13 39 1	15 41 14	17 39 31
17	19 42 41	21 44 55	23 39 15	1 41 28	3 39 45	5 41 58	7 40 15	9 42 28	11 44 41	13 42 58	15 45 11	17 43 28
18	19 46 38	21 48 51	23 43 11	1 45 24	3 43 41	5 45 54	7 44 11	9 46 24	11 48 38	13 46 54	15 49 7	17 47 24
19	19 50 35	21 52 48	23 47 8	1 49 21	3 47 38	5 49 51	7 48 8	9 50 21	11 52 34	13 50 51	15 53 4	17 51 21
20	19 54 31	21 56 44	23 51 1	1 53 18	3 51 34	5 53 48	7 52 1	9 54 18	11 56 31	13 54 47	15 57 0	17 55 17
21	19 58 28	22 0 41	23 55 1	1 57 14	3 55 31	5 57 44	7 56 1	9 58 14	12 0 27	13 58 44	16 0 57	17 59 14
22	20 2 24	22 4 37	23 58 58	2 1 11	3 59 27	6 1 11	7 59 57	10 2 11	12 4 24	14 2 40	16 4 54	18 3 10
23	20 6 21	22 8 34	0 2 54	2 5 7	4 3 24	6 5 37	8 3 54	10 6 7	12 8 20	14 6 37	16 8 50	18 7 7
24	20 10 17	22 12 31	0 6 51	2 9 4	4 7 20	6 9 34	8 7 50	10 10 4	12 12 17	14 10 33	16 12 47	18 11 3
25	20 14 14	22 16 27	0 10 47	2 13 0	4 11 17	6 13 30	8 11 47	10 14 0	12 16 13	14 14 30	16 16 43	18 15 0
26	20 18 10	22 20 24	0 14 44	2 16 57	4 15 14	6 17 27	8 15 44	10 17 57	12 20 10	14 18 27	16 20 40	18 18 57
27	20 22 7	22 24 20	0 18 40	2 20 53	4 19 10	6 21 23	8 19 40	10 21 53	12 24 7	14 22 23	16 24 36	18 22 53
28	20 26 4	22 28 17	0 22 37	2 24 50	4 23 7	6 25 20	8 23 37	10 25 50	12 28 3	14 26 20	16 28 33	18 26 50
29	20 30 0	22 32 13	0 26 33	2 28 47	4 27 3	6 29 17	8 27 33	10 29 46	12 32 0	14 30 16	16 32 29	18 30 46
30	20 33 57		0 30 30	2 32 43	4 31 0	6 33 13	8 31 30	10 33 43	12 35 56	14 34 13	16 36 26	18 34 43
31	20 37 53		0 34 26		4 34 56		8 35 26	10 37 40		14 38 9		18 38 39

1929

	Jan.	Feb.	Mar.	April	May	June	July	Aug.	Sept.	Oct.	Nov.	Dec.
1	18 42 36	20 44 49	22 35 13	0 37 26	2 35 43	4 37 56	6 36 13	8 38 26	10 40 39	12 38 56	14 41 9	16 39 26
2	18 46 32	20 48 46	22 39 9	0 41 22	2 39 39	4 41 52	6 40 9	8 42 22	10 44 36	12 42 52	14 45 5	16 43 22
3	18 50 29	20 52 42	22 43 6	0 45 19	2 43 36	4 45 49	6 44 6	8 46 19	10 48 32	12 46 49	14 49 2	16 47 19
4	18 54 26	20 56 39	22 47 2	0 49 16	2 47 32	4 49 45	6 48 2	8 50 15	10 52 29	12 50 45	14 52 59	16 51 15
5	18 58 22	21 0 35	22 50 59	0 53 12	2 51 29	4 53 42	6 51 59	8 54 12	10 56 25	12 54 42	14 56 55	16 55 12
6	19 2 19	21 4 32	22 54 56	0 57 9	2 55 25	4 57 39	6 55 55	8 58 9	11 0 22	12 58 38	15 0 52	16 59 8
7	19 6 15	21 8 29	22 58 52	1 1 5	2 59 22	5 1 35	6 59 52	9 2 5	11 4 18	13 2 35	15 4 48	17 3 5
8	19 10 12	21 12 25	23 2 49	1 5 2	3 3 18	5 5 32	7 3 48	9 6 2	11 8 15	13 6 32	15 8 45	17 7 1
9	19 14 8	21 16 22	23 6 45	1 8 58	3 7 15	5 9 28	7 7 45	9 9 58	11 12 11	13 10 28	15 12 41	17 10 58
10	19 18 5	21 20 18	23 10 42	1 12 55	3 11 12	5 13 25	7 11 42	9 13 55	11 16 8	13 14 25	15 16 38	17 14 55
11	19 22 2	21 24 15	23 14 38	1 16 51	3 15 8	5 17 21	7 15 38	9 17 51	11 20 5	13 18 21	15 20 34	17 18 51
12	19 25 58	21 28 11	23 18 35	1 20 48	3 19 5	5 21 18	7 19 35	9 21 48	11 24 1	13 22 18	15 24 31	17 22 48
13	19 29 55	21 32 8	23 22 31	1 24 45	3 23 1	5 25 14	7 23 31	9 25 44	11 27 58	13 26 14	15 28 28	17 26 44
14	19 33 51	21 36 4	23 26 28	1 28 41	3 26 58	5 29 11	7 27 28	9 29 41	11 31 54	13 30 11	15 32 24	17 30 41
15	19 37 48	21 40 1	23 30 24	1 32 38	3 30 54	5 33 8	7 31 24	9 33 38	11 35 51	13 34 7	15 36 21	17 34 37
16	19 41 44	21 43 58	23 34 21	1 36 34	3 34 51	5 37 4	7 35 21	9 37 34	11 39 47	13 38 4	15 40 17	17 38 34
17	19 45 41	21 47 54	23 38 18	1 40 31	3 38 47	5 41 1	7 39 17	9 41 31	11 43 44	13 42 1	15 44 14	17 42 30
18	19 49 37	21 51 51	23 42 14	1 44 27	3 42 44	5 44 57	7 43 14	9 45 27	11 47 40	13 45 57	15 48 10	17 46 27
19	19 53 34	21 55 47	23 46 11	1 48 24	3 46 41	5 48 54	7 47 11	9 49 24	11 51 37	13 49 54	15 52 7	17 50 24
20	19 57 31	21 59 44	23 50 7	1 52 20	3 50 37	5 52 50	7 51 7	9 53 20	11 55 34	13 53 50	15 56 3	17 54 20
21	20 1 27	22 3 40	23 54 4	1 56 17	3 54 34	5 56 47	7 55 4	9 57 17	11 59 30	13 57 47	16 0 0	17 58 17
22	20 5 24	22 7 37	23 58 0	2 0 14	3 58 30	6 0 44	7 59 0	10 1 13	12 3 27	14 1 43	16 3 57	18 2 13
23	20 9 20	22 11 33	0 1 57	2 4 10	4 2 27	6 4 40	8 2 57	10 5 10	12 7 23	14 5 40	16 7 53	18 6 10
24	20 13 17	22 15 30	0 5 53	2 8 7	4 6 23	6 8 37	8 6 53	10 9 7	12 11 20	14 9 36	16 11 50	18 10 6
25	20 17 13	22 19 27	0 9 50	2 12 3	4 10 20	6 12 33	8 10 50	10 13 3	12 15 16	14 13 33	16 15 46	18 14 3
26	20 21 10	22 23 23	0 13 47	2 16 0	4 14 16	6 16 30	8 14 46	10 17 0	12 19 13	14 17 30	16 19 43	18 18 0
27	20 25 6	22 27 20	0 17 43	2 19 56	4 18 13	6 20 26	8 18 43	10 20 56	12 23 9	14 21 26	16 23 39	18 21 56
28	20 29 3	22 31 16	0 21 40	2 23 53	4 22 10	6 24 23	8 22 40	10 24 53	12 27 6	14 25 23	16 27 36	18 25 53
29	20 33 0		0 25 36	2 27 49	4 26 6	6 28 19	8 26 36	10 28 49	12 31 3	14 29 19	16 31 32	18 29 49
30	20 36 56		0 29 33	2 31 46	4 30 3	6 32 16	8 30 33	10 32 46	12 34 59	14 33 16	16 35 29	18 33 46
31	20 40 53		0 33 29		4 33 59		8 34 29	10 36 42		14 37 12		18 37 42

1930

	Jan.	Feb.	Mar.	April	May	June	July	Aug.	Sept.	Oct.	Nov.	Dec.
1	18 41 39	20 43 52	22 34 16	0 36 29	2 34 46	4 36 59	6 35 16	8 37 29	10 39 42	12 37 59	14 40 12	16 38 29
2	18 45 35	20 47 49	22 38 12	0 40 25	2 38 42	4 40 55	6 39 12	8 41 25	10 43 39	12 41 55	14 44 8	16 42 25
3	18 49 32	20 51 45	22 42 9	0 44 22	2 42 39	4 44 52	6 43 9	8 45 22	10 47 35	12 45 52	14 48 5	16 46 22
4	18 53 29	20 55 42	22 46 5	0 48 19	2 46 35	4 48 48	6 47 5	8 49 18	10 51 32	12 49 48	14 52 2	16 50 18
5	18 57 25	20 59 38	22 50 2	0 52 15	2 50 32	4 52 45	6 51 2	8 53 15	10 55 28	12 53 45	14 55 58	16 54 15
6	19 1 22	21 3 35	22 53 58	0 56 12	2 54 28	4 56 42	6 54 58	8 57 12	10 59 25	12 57 41	14 59 55	16 58 11
7	19 5 18	21 7 31	22 57 55	1 0 8	2 58 25	5 0 38	6 58 55	9 1 8	11 3 21	13 1 38	15 3 51	17 2 8
8	19 9 15	21 11 28	23 1 52	1 4 5	3 2 22	5 4 35	7 2 51	9 5 5	11 7 18	13 5 35	15 7 48	17 6 4
9	19 13 11	21 15 25	23 5 48	1 8 1	3 6 18	5 8 31	7 6 48	9 9 1	11 11 14	13 9 31	15 11 44	17 10 1
10	19 17 8	21 19 21	23 9 45	1 11 58	3 10 15	5 12 28	7 10 45	9 12 58	11 15 11	13 13 28	15 15 41	17 13 58
11	19 21 4	21 23 18	23 13 41	1 15 54	3 14 11	5 16 24	7 14 41	9 16 54	11 19 8	13 17 24	15 19 37	17 17 54
12	19 25 1	21 27 14	23 17 38	1 19 51	3 18 8	5 20 21	7 18 38	9 20 51	11 23 4	13 21 21	15 23 34	17 21 51
13	19 28 58	21 31 11	23 21 34	1 23 48	3 22 4	5 24 17	7 22 34	9 24 47	11 27 1	13 25 17	15 27 31	17 25 47
14	19 32 54	21 35 7	23 25 31	1 27 44	3 26 1	5 28 14	7 26 31	9 28 44	11 30 57	13 29 14	15 31 27	17 29 44
15	19 36 51	21 39 4	23 29 27	1 31 41	3 29 57	5 32 11	7 30 27	9 32 41	11 34 54	13 33 10	15 35 24	17 33 40
16	19 40 47	21 43 0	23 33 24	1 35 37	3 33 54	5 36 7	7 34 24	9 36 37	11 38 50	13 37 7	15 39 20	17 37 37
17	19 44 44	21 46 57	23 37 21	1 39 34	3 37 50	5 40 4	7 38 20	9 40 34	11 42 47	13 41 4	15 43 17	17 41 33
18	19 48 40	21 50 54	23 41 17	1 43 30	3 41 47	5 44 0	7 42 17	9 44 30	11 46 43	13 45 0	15 47 13	17 45 30
19	19 52 37	21 54 50	23 45 14	1 47 27	3 45 44	5 47 57	7 46 14	9 48 27	11 50 40	13 48 57	15 51 10	17 49 27
20	19 56 33	21 58 47	23 49 10	1 51 23	3 49 40	5 51 53	7 50 10	9 52 23	11 54 37	13 52 53	15 55 6	17 53 23
21	20 0 30	22 2 43	23 53 7	1 55 20	3 53 37	5 55 50	7 54 7	9 56 20	11 58 33	13 56 50	15 59 3	17 57 20
22	20 4 27	22 6 40	23 57 3	1 59 17	3 57 33	5 59 47	7 58 3	10 0 16	12 2 30	14 0 46	16 3 0	18 1 16
23	20 8 23	22 10 36	0 1 0	2 3 13	4 1 30	6 3 43	8 2 0	10 4 13	12 6 26	14 4 43	16 6 56	18 5 13
24	20 12 20	22 14 33	0 4 56	2 7 10	4 5 26	6 7 40	8 5 56	10 8 10	12 10 23	14 8 39	16 10 53	18 9 9
25	20 16 16	22 18 29	0 8 53	2 11 6	4 9 23	6 11 36	8 9 53	10 12 6	12 14 19	14 12 36	16 14 49	18 13 6
26	20 20 13	22 22 26	0 12 50	2 15 3	4 13 19	6 15 33	8 13 49	10 16 3	12 18 16	14 16 33	16 18 46	18 17 3
27	20 24 9	22 26 22	0 16 46	2 18 59	4 17 16	6 19 29	8 17 46	10 19 59	12 22 12	14 20 29	16 22 42	18 20 59
28	20 28 6	22 30 19	0 20 43	2 22 56	4 21 13	6 23 26	8 21 43	10 23 56	12 26 9	14 24 26	16 26 39	18 24 56
29	20 32 2		0 24 39	2 26 52	4 25 9	6 27 22	8 25 39	10 27 52	12 30 6	14 28 22	16 30 35	18 28 52
30	20 35 59		0 28 36	2 30 49	4 29 6	6 31 19	8 29 36	10 31 49	12 34 2	14 32 19	16 34 32	18 32 49
31	20 39 56		0 32 32		4 33 2		8 33 32	10 35 45		14 36 15		18 36 45

1931

	Jan.	Feb.	Mar.	April	May	June	July	Aug.	Sept.	Oct.	Nov.	Dec.
1	18 40 42	20 42 55	22 33 19	0 35 32	2 33 48	4 36 2	6 34 18	8 36 32	10 38 45	12 37 1	14 39 15	16 37 31
2	18 44 38	20 46 51	22 37 15	0 39 28	2 37 45	4 39 58	6 38 15	8 40 28	10 42 41	12 40 58	14 43 11	16 41 28
3	18 48 35	20 50 48	22 41 12	0 43 25	2 41 41	4 43 55	6 42 11	8 44 25	10 46 38	12 44 55	14 47 8	16 45 24
4	18 52 31	20 54 45	22 45 8	0 47 21	2 45 38	4 47 51	6 46 8	8 48 21	10 50 34	12 48 51	14 51 4	16 49 21
5	18 56 28	20 58 41	22 49 5	0 51 18	2 49 34	4 51 48	6 50 4	8 52 18	10 54 31	12 52 48	14 55 1	16 53 18
6	19 0 24	21 2 38	22 53 1	0 55 14	2 53 31	4 55 44	6 54 1	8 56 14	10 58 28	12 56 44	14 58 57	16 57 14
7	19 4 21	21 6 35	22 56 58	0 59 11	2 57 28	4 59 41	6 57 58	9 0 11	11 2 24	13 0 41	15 2 54	17 1 11
8	19 8 18	21 10 31	23 0 54	1 3 7	3 1 24	5 3 37	7 1 54	9 4 7	11 6 21	13 4 37	15 6 50	17 5 7
9	19 12 14	21 14 27	23 4 51	1 7 4	3 5 21	5 7 34	7 5 51	9 8 4	11 10 17	13 8 34	15 10 47	17 9 4
10	19 16 11	21 18 24	23 8 47	1 11 1	3 9 17	5 11 31	7 9 47	9 12 1	11 14 14	13 12 30	15 14 44	17 13 0
11	19 20 7	21 22 20	23 12 44	1 14 57	3 13 14	5 15 27	7 13 44	9 15 57	11 18 10	13 16 27	15 18 40	17 16 57
12	19 24 4	21 26 17	23 16 40	1 18 54	3 17 10	5 19 24	7 17 40	9 19 54	11 22 7	13 20 24	15 22 37	17 20 53
13	19 28 0	21 30 14	23 20 37	1 22 50	3 21 7	5 23 20	7 21 37	9 23 50	11 26 3	13 24 20	15 26 33	17 24 50
14	19 31 57	21 34 10	23 24 34	1 26 47	3 25 3	5 27 17	7 25 34	9 27 47	11 30 0	13 28 17	15 30 30	17 28 47
15	19 35 53	21 38 7	23 28 30	1 30 43	3 29 0	5 31 13	7 29 30	9 31 43	11 33 57	13 32 13	15 34 26	17 32 43
16	19 39 50	21 42 3	23 32 27	1 34 40	3 32 57	5 35 10	7 33 27	9 35 40	11 37 53	13 36 10	15 38 23	17 36 40
17	19 43 47	21 46 0	23 36 23	1 38 36	3 36 53	5 39 6	7 37 23	9 39 37	11 41 50	13 40 6	15 42 20	17 40 36
18	19 47 43	21 49 56	23 40 20	1 42 33	3 40 50	5 43 3	7 41 20	9 43 33	11 45 46	13 44 3	15 46 16	17 44 33
19	19 51 40	21 53 53	23 44 16	1 46 30	3 44 46	5 47 0	7 45 16	9 47 30	11 49 43	13 47 59	15 50 13	17 48 29
20	19 55 36	21 57 49	23 48 13	1 50 26	3 48 43	5 50 56	7 49 13	9 51 26	11 53 39	13 51 56	15 54 9	17 52 26
21	19 59 33	22 1 46	23 52 10	1 54 23	3 52 39	5 54 53	7 53 9	9 55 23	11 57 36	13 55 52	15 58 6	17 56 22
22	20 3 29	22 5 43	23 56 6	1 58 19	3 56 36	5 58 49	7 57 6	9 59 19	12 1 32	13 59 49	16 2 8	18 0 19
23	20 7 26	22 9 39	0 0 3	2 2 16	4 0 33	6 2 46	8 1 3	10 3 16	12 5 29	14 3 46	16 5 59	18 4 16
24	20 11 22	22 13 36	0 3 59	2 6 12	4 4 29	6 6 42	8 4 59	10 7 12	12 9 26	14 7 42	16 9 55	18 8 12
25	20 15 19	22 17 32	0 7 55	2 10 9	4 8 26	6 10 39	8 8 56	10 11 9	12 13 22	14 11 39	16 13 52	18 12 9
26	20 19 16	22 21 29	0 11 53	2 14 5	4 12 22	6 14 36	8 12 52	10 15 5	12 17 19	14 15 35	16 17 49	18 16 5
27	20 23 12	22 25 25	0 15 49	2 18 2	4 16 19	6 18 32	8 16 49	10 19 2	12 21 15	14 19 32	16 21 45	18 20 2
28	20 27 9	22 29 22	0 19 45	2 21 59	4 20 15	6 22 29	8 20 45	10 22 59	12 25 12	14 23 28	16 25 42	18 23 58
29	20 31 5		0 23 42	2 25 55	4 24 12	6 26 25	8 24 42	10 26 55	12 29 8	14 27 25	16 29 38	18 27 55
30	20 35 2		0 27 39	2 29 52	4 28 8	6 30 22	8 28 38	10 30 52	12 33 5	14 31 21	16 33 35	18 31 52
31	20 38 58		0 31 35		4 32 5		8 32 35	10 34 48		14 35 18		18 35 48

1932

Day	Jan.	Feb.	Mar.	April	May	June	July	Aug.	Sept.	Oct.	Nov.	Dec.
1	18 39 45	20 41 58	22 36 18	0 38 31	2 36 48	4 39 1	6 37 18	8 39 31	10 41 44	12 40 1	14 42 14	16 40 31
2	18 43 41	20 45 55	22 40 15	0 42 28	2 40 44	4 42 58	6 41 14	8 43 28	10 45 41	12 43 58	14 46 11	16 44 27
3	18 47 38	20 49 51	22 44 11	0 46 24	2 44 41	4 46 54	6 45 11	8 47 24	10 49 38	12 47 54	14 50 7	16 48 24
4	18 51 34	20 53 44	22 48 8	0 50 21	2 48 37	4 50 51	6 49 8	8 51 21	10 53 34	12 51 51	14 54 4	16 52 21
5	18 55 31	20 57 44	22 52 4	0 54 17	2 52 34	4 54 47	6 53 4	8 55 17	10 57 31	12 55 47	14 58 0	16 56 17
6	18 59 27	21 1 41	22 56 1	0 58 14	2 56 31	4 58 44	6 57 1	8 59 14	11 1 27	12 59 44	15 1 57	17 0 14
7	19 3 24	21 5 37	22 59 57	1 2 10	3 0 27	5 2 40	7 0 57	9 3 10	11 5 24	13 3 40	15 5 54	17 4 10
8	19 7 21	21 9 34	23 3 54	1 6 7	3 4 24	5 6 37	7 4 54	9 7 7	11 9 20	13 7 37	15 9 50	17 8 7
9	19 11 17	21 13 30	23 7 50	1 10 4	3 8 20	5 10 34	7 8 50	9 11 4	11 13 17	13 11 33	15 13 47	17 12 3
10	19 15 14	21 17 27	23 11 47	1 14 0	3 12 17	5 14 30	7 12 47	9 15 0	11 17 13	13 15 30	15 17 43	17 16 0
11	19 19 10	21 21 24	23 15 44	1 17 57	3 16 13	5 18 27	7 16 43	9 18 57	11 21 10	13 19 27	15 21 40	17 19 57
12	19 23 7	21 25 20	23 19 40	1 21 53	3 20 10	5 22 23	7 20 40	9 22 53	11 25 6	13 23 23	15 25 36	17 23 53
13	19 27 3	21 29 17	23 23 37	1 25 50	3 24 7	5 26 20	7 24 37	9 26 50	11 29 3	13 27 20	15 29 33	17 27 49
14	19 31 0	21 33 13	23 27 33	1 29 46	3 28 3	5 30 16	7 28 33	9 30 46	11 33 0	13 31 16	15 33 29	17 31 46
15	19 34 56	21 37 10	23 31 30	1 33 43	3 32 0	5 34 13	7 32 30	9 34 43	11 36 56	13 35 13	15 37 26	17 35 43
16	19 38 53	21 41 6	23 35 26	1 37 40	3 35 56	5 38 10	7 36 26	9 38 40	11 40 53	13 39 9	15 41 23	17 39 39
17	19 42 50	21 45 3	23 39 23	1 41 36	3 39 53	5 42 6	7 40 23	9 42 36	11 44 49	13 43 6	15 45 19	17 43 36
18	19 46 46	21 48 59	23 43 19	1 45 33	3 43 49	5 46 3	7 44 19	9 46 33	11 48 46	13 47 2	15 49 16	17 47 32
19	19 50 43	21 52 56	23 47 16	1 49 29	3 47 46	5 49 59	7 48 16	9 50 29	11 52 42	13 50 59	15 53 12	17 51 29
20	19 54 39	21 56 53	23 51 13	1 53 26	3 51 42	5 53 56	7 52 12	9 54 26	11 56 39	13 54 56	15 57 9	17 55 26
21	19 58 36	22 0 49	23 55 9	1 57 22	3 55 39	5 57 52	7 56 9	9 58 22	12 0 35	13 58 52	16 1 5	17 59 22
22	20 2 32	22 4 46	23 59 6	2 1 19	3 59 36	6 1 49	8 0 6	10 2 19	12 4 32	14 2 49	16 5 2	18 3 19
23	20 6 29	22 8 42	0 3 2	2 5 15	4 3 32	6 5 45	8 4 2	10 6 15	12 8 29	14 6 45	16 8 58	18 7 15
24	20 10 25	22 12 39	0 6 59	2 9 12	4 7 29	6 9 42	8 7 59	10 10 12	12 12 25	14 10 42	16 12 55	18 11 12
25	20 14 22	22 16 35	0 10 55	2 13 9	4 11 25	6 13 39	8 11 55	10 14 9	12 16 22	14 14 38	16 16 52	18 15 8
26	20 18 19	22 20 32	0 14 52	2 17 5	4 15 22	6 17 35	8 15 52	10 18 5	12 20 18	14 18 35	16 20 48	18 19 5
27	20 22 15	22 24 28	0 18 48	2 21 2	4 19 18	6 21 32	8 19 48	10 22 2	12 24 15	14 22 31	16 24 45	18 23 1
28	20 26 12	22 28 25	0 22 45	2 24 58	4 23 15	6 25 28	8 23 45	10 25 58	12 28 11	14 26 28	16 28 41	18 26 58
29	20 30 8	22 32 22	0 26 42	2 28 55	4 27 11	6 29 25	8 27 42	10 29 55	12 32 8	14 30 25	16 32 38	18 30 55
30	20 34 5		0 30 38	2 32 51	4 31 8	6 33 21	8 31 38	10 33 51	12 36 4	14 34 21	16 36 34	18 34 51
31	20 38 1		0 34 35		4 35 5		8 35 35	10 37 48		14 38 18		18 38 47

1933

Day	Jan.	Feb.	Mar.	April	May	June	July	Aug.	Sept.	Oct.	Nov.	Dec.
1	18 42 44	20 44 58	22 35 21	0 37 34	2 35 51	4 38 4	6 36 21	8 38 34	10 40 47	12 39 4	14 41 17	16 39 34
2	18 46 41	20 48 54	22 39 18	0 41 31	2 39 47	4 42 1	6 40 17	8 42 31	10 44 44	12 43 1	14 45 14	16 43 30
3	18 50 37	20 52 51	22 43 14	0 45 27	2 43 44	4 45 57	6 44 14	8 46 27	10 48 41	12 46 57	14 49 10	16 47 27
4	18 54 34	20 56 47	22 47 11	0 49 24	2 47 41	4 49 54	6 48 11	8 50 24	10 52 37	12 50 54	14 53 7	16 51 24
5	18 58 30	21 0 44	22 51 7	0 53 20	2 51 37	4 53 50	6 52 7	8 54 20	10 56 34	12 54 50	14 57 3	16 55 20
6	19 2 27	21 4 40	22 55 4	0 57 17	2 55 34	4 57 47	6 56 4	8 58 17	11 0 30	12 58 47	15 1 0	16 59 17
7	19 6 24	21 8 37	22 59 0	1 1 14	2 59 30	5 1 44	7 0 0	9 2 14	11 4 27	13 2 43	15 4 57	17 3 13
8	19 10 20	21 12 33	23 2 57	1 5 10	3 3 27	5 5 40	7 3 57	9 6 10	11 8 23	13 6 40	15 8 53	17 7 10
9	19 14 17	21 16 30	23 6 54	1 9 7	3 7 23	5 9 37	7 7 53	9 10 7	11 12 20	13 10 36	15 12 50	17 11 6
10	19 18 13	21 20 27	23 10 50	1 13 3	3 11 20	5 13 33	7 11 50	9 14 3	11 16 16	13 14 33	15 16 46	17 15 3
11	19 22 10	21 24 23	23 14 47	1 17 0	3 15 16	5 17 30	7 15 47	9 18 0	11 20 13	13 18 30	15 20 43	17 19 0
12	19 26 6	21 28 20	23 18 43	1 20 56	3 19 13	5 21 26	7 19 43	9 21 56	11 24 10	13 22 26	15 24 39	17 22 56
13	19 30 3	21 32 16	23 22 40	1 24 53	3 23 10	5 25 23	7 23 40	9 25 53	11 28 6	13 26 23	15 28 36	17 26 53
14	19 34 0	21 36 13	23 26 36	1 28 49	3 27 6	5 29 19	7 27 36	9 29 49	11 32 3	13 30 19	15 32 32	17 30 49
15	19 37 56	21 40 9	23 30 33	1 32 46	3 31 3	5 33 16	7 31 33	9 33 46	11 35 59	13 34 16	15 36 29	17 34 46
16	19 41 53	21 44 6	23 34 29	1 36 43	3 34 59	5 37 13	7 35 29	9 37 43	11 39 56	13 38 12	15 40 26	17 38 42
17	19 45 49	21 48 2	23 38 26	1 40 39	3 38 56	5 41 9	7 39 26	9 41 39	11 43 52	13 42 9	15 44 22	17 42 39
18	19 49 45	21 51 59	23 42 23	1 44 36	3 42 52	5 45 6	7 43 22	9 45 36	11 47 49	13 46 5	15 48 19	17 46 35
19	19 53 42	21 55 56	23 46 19	1 48 32	3 46 49	5 49 2	7 47 19	9 49 32	11 51 45	13 50 2	15 52 15	17 50 32
20	19 57 39	21 59 52	23 50 16	1 52 29	3 50 45	5 52 59	7 51 16	9 53 29	11 55 42	13 53 59	15 56 12	17 54 29
21	20 1 35	22 3 49	23 54 12	1 56 25	3 54 42	5 56 55	7 55 12	9 57 25	11 59 38	13 57 55	16 0 8	17 58 25
22	20 5 32	22 7 45	23 58 9	2 0 22	3 58 39	6 0 52	7 59 9	10 1 22	12 3 35	14 1 52	16 4 5	18 2 22
23	20 9 29	22 11 42	0 2 5	2 4 18	4 2 35	6 4 48	8 3 5	10 5 18	12 7 32	14 5 48	16 8 1	18 6 18
24	20 13 25	22 15 38	0 6 2	2 8 15	4 6 32	6 8 45	8 7 2	10 9 15	12 11 28	14 9 45	16 11 58	18 10 15
25	20 17 22	22 19 35	0 9 58	2 12 12	4 10 28	6 12 42	8 10 58	10 13 12	12 15 25	14 13 41	16 15 55	18 14 11
26	20 21 18	22 23 31	0 13 55	2 16 8	4 14 25	6 16 38	8 14 55	10 17 8	12 19 21	14 17 38	16 19 51	18 18 8
27	20 25 15	22 27 28	0 17 51	2 20 5	4 18 21	6 20 35	8 18 51	10 21 5	12 23 18	14 21 34	16 23 48	18 22 4
28	20 29 11	22 31 25	0 21 48	2 24 1	4 22 18	6 24 31	8 22 48	10 25 1	12 27 14	14 25 31	16 27 44	18 26 1
29	20 33 8		0 25 45	2 27 58	4 26 15	6 28 28	8 26 45	10 28 58	12 31 11	14 29 28	16 31 41	18 29 58
30	20 37 4		0 29 41	2 31 54	4 30 11	6 32 24	8 30 41	10 32 54	12 35 8	14 33 24	16 35 37	18 33 54
31	20 41 1		0 33 38		4 34 8		8 34 38	10 36 51		14 37 21		18 37 51

1934

Day	Jan.	Feb.	Mar.	April	May	June	July	Aug.	Sept.	Oct.	Nov.	Dec.
1	18 41 47	20 44 1	22 34 24	0 36 37	2 34 54	4 37 7	6 35 24	8 37 37	10 39 50	12 38 7	14 40 20	16 38 37
2	18 45 44	20 47 57	22 38 21	0 40 34	2 38 50	4 41 4	6 39 20	8 41 34	10 43 47	12 42 4	14 44 17	16 42 33
3	18 49 40	20 51 54	22 42 17	0 44 30	2 42 47	4 45 0	6 43 17	8 45 30	10 47 44	12 46 0	14 48 13	16 46 30
4	18 53 37	20 55 50	22 46 14	0 48 27	2 46 44	4 48 57	6 47 14	8 49 27	10 51 40	12 49 57	14 52 10	16 50 27
5	18 57 33	20 59 47	22 50 10	0 52 23	2 50 40	4 52 53	6 51 10	8 53 23	10 55 37	12 53 53	14 56 6	16 54 23
6	19 1 30	21 3 43	22 54 7	0 56 20	2 54 37	4 56 50	6 55 7	8 57 20	10 59 33	12 57 50	15 0 3	16 58 20
7	19 5 27	21 7 40	22 58 3	1 0 17	2 58 33	5 0 47	6 59 3	9 1 17	11 3 30	13 1 46	15 4 0	17 2 16
8	19 9 23	21 11 36	23 2 0	1 4 13	3 2 30	5 4 43	7 3 0	9 5 13	11 7 26	13 5 43	15 7 56	17 6 13
9	19 13 20	21 15 33	23 5 57	1 8 10	3 6 26	5 8 40	7 6 56	9 9 10	11 11 23	13 9 39	15 11 53	17 10 9
10	19 17 16	21 19 30	23 9 53	1 12 6	3 10 23	5 12 36	7 10 53	9 13 6	11 15 19	13 13 36	15 15 49	17 14 6
11	19 21 13	21 23 26	23 13 50	1 16 3	3 14 19	5 16 33	7 14 49	9 17 3	11 19 16	13 17 33	15 19 46	17 18 2
12	19 25 9	21 27 23	23 17 46	1 19 59	3 18 16	5 20 29	7 18 46	9 20 59	11 23 12	13 21 29	15 23 42	17 21 59
13	19 29 6	21 31 19	23 21 43	1 23 56	3 22 13	5 24 26	7 22 42	9 24 56	11 27 9	13 25 26	15 27 39	17 25 56
14	19 33 3	21 35 16	23 25 39	1 27 52	3 26 9	5 28 22	7 26 39	9 28 52	11 31 6	13 29 22	15 31 35	17 29 52
15	19 36 59	21 39 12	23 29 36	1 31 49	3 30 6	5 32 19	7 30 36	9 32 49	11 35 2	13 33 19	15 35 32	17 33 49
16	19 40 56	21 43 9	23 33 32	1 35 46	3 34 2	5 36 16	7 34 32	9 36 46	11 38 59	13 37 15	15 39 29	17 37 45
17	19 44 52	21 47 5	23 37 29	1 39 42	3 37 59	5 40 12	7 38 29	9 40 42	11 42 55	13 41 12	15 43 25	17 41 42
18	19 48 49	21 51 2	23 41 26	1 43 39	3 41 55	5 44 9	7 42 25	9 44 39	11 46 52	13 45 8	15 47 22	17 45 38
19	19 52 45	21 54 59	23 45 22	1 47 35	3 45 52	5 48 5	7 46 22	9 48 35	11 50 48	13 49 5	15 51 18	17 49 35
20	19 56 42	21 58 55	23 49 19	1 51 32	3 49 48	5 52 2	7 50 18	9 52 32	11 54 45	13 53 1	15 55 15	17 53 31
21	20 0 38	22 2 52	23 53 15	1 55 28	3 53 45	5 55 58	7 54 15	9 56 28	11 58 41	13 56 58	15 59 11	17 57 28
22	20 4 35	22 6 48	23 57 12	1 59 25	3 57 42	5 59 55	7 58 12	10 0 25	12 2 38	14 0 55	16 3 8	18 1 25
23	20 8 32	22 10 45	0 1 8	2 3 21	4 1 38	6 3 51	8 2 8	10 4 21	12 6 35	14 4 51	16 7 4	18 5 21
24	20 12 28	22 14 41	0 5 5	2 7 18	4 5 35	6 7 48	8 6 5	10 8 18	12 10 31	14 8 48	16 11 1	18 9 18
25	20 16 25	22 18 38	0 9 1	2 11 15	4 9 31	6 11 45	8 10 1	10 12 14	12 14 28	14 12 44	16 14 58	18 13 14
26	20 20 21	22 22 34	0 12 58	2 15 11	4 13 28	6 15 41	8 13 58	10 16 11	12 18 24	14 16 41	16 18 54	18 17 11
27	20 24 18	22 26 31	0 16 55	2 19 8	4 17 24	6 19 38	8 17 54	10 20 7	12 22 21	14 20 37	16 22 51	18 21 7
28	20 28 14	22 30 28	0 20 51	2 23 4	4 21 21	6 23 34	8 21 51	10 24 4	12 26 17	14 24 34	16 26 47	18 25 4
29	20 32 11		0 24 48	2 27 1	4 25 17	6 27 31	8 25 48	10 28 1	12 30 14	14 28 30	16 30 44	18 29 1
30	20 36 7		0 28 44	2 30 57	4 29 14	6 31 27	8 29 44	10 31 57	12 34 10	14 32 27	16 34 40	18 32 57
31	20 40 4		0 32 41		4 33 11		8 33 41	10 35 54		14 36 24		18 36 54

1935

	Jan.	Feb.	Mar.	April	May	June	July	Aug.	Sept.	Oct.	Nov.	Dec.
1	18 40 50	20 43 3	22 33 27	0 35 40	2 33 57	4 36 10	6 34 27	8 36 40	10 38 53	12 37 10	14 39 23	16 37 40
2	18 44 47	20 47 0	22 37 24	0 39 37	2 37 53	4 40 7	6 38 23	8 40 37	10 42 50	12 41 6	14 43 20	16 41 36
3	18 48 43	20 50 57	22 41 20	0 43 33	2 41 50	4 44 3	6 42 20	8 44 33	10 46 46	12 45 3	14 47 16	16 45 33
4	18 52 40	20 54 53	22 45 17	0 47 30	2 45 46	4 48 0	6 46 16	8 48 30	10 50 43	12 49 0	14 51 13	16 49 29
5	18 56 36	20 58 50	22 49 13	0 51 26	2 49 43	4 51 56	6 50 13	8 52 26	10 54 39	12 52 56	14 55 9	16 53 26
6	19 0 33	21 2 46	22 53 10	0 55 23	2 53 40	4 55 53	6 54 10	8 56 23	10 58 36	12 56 53	14 59 6	16 57 23
7	19 4 30	21 6 43	22 57 6	0 59 20	2 57 36	4 59 49	6 58 6	9 0 20	11 2 33	13 0 49	15 3 2	17 1 19
8	19 8 26	21 10 39	23 1 3	1 3 16	3 1 33	5 3 46	7 2 3	9 4 16	11 6 29	13 4 46	15 6 59	17 5 16
9	19 12 23	21 14 26	23 4 59	1 7 13	3 5 30	5 7 43	7 6 0	9 8 13	11 10 26	13 8 42	15 10 55	17 9 12
10	19 16 19	21 18 32	23 8 56	1 11 9	3 9 26	5 11 39	7 9 56	9 12 9	11 14 22	13 12 39	15 14 52	17 13 9
11	19 20 16	21 22 29	23 12 53	1 15 6	3 13 22	5 15 36	7 13 52	9 16 6	11 18 19	13 16 35	15 18 49	17 17 5
12	19 24 12	21 26 26	23 16 49	1 19 2	3 17 19	5 19 32	7 17 49	9 20 2	11 22 15	13 20 32	15 22 45	17 21 2
13	19 28 9	21 30 22	23 20 46	1 22 59	3 21 16	5 23 29	7 21 45	9 23 59	11 26 12	13 24 29	15 26 42	17 24 58
14	19 32 5	21 34 19	23 24 42	1 26 55	3 25 12	5 27 25	7 25 42	9 27 55	11 30 8	13 28 25	15 30 38	17 28 55
15	19 36 2	21 38 15	23 28 39	1 30 52	3 29 9	5 31 22	7 29 39	9 31 52	11 34 5	13 32 22	15 34 35	17 32 52
16	19 39 59	21 42 12	23 32 35	1 34 48	3 33 5	5 35 18	7 33 35	9 35 48	11 38 2	13 36 18	15 38 31	17 36 48
17	19 43 55	21 46 8	23 36 32	1 38 45	3 37 2	5 39 15	7 37 32	9 39 45	11 41 58	13 40 15	15 42 28	17 40 45
18	19 47 52	21 50 5	23 40 28	1 42 42	3 40 58	5 43 12	7 41 28	9 43 42	11 45 55	13 44 11	15 46 25	17 44 41
19	19 51 48	21 54 1	23 44 25	1 46 38	3 44 55	5 47 8	7 45 25	9 47 38	11 49 51	13 48 8	15 50 21	17 48 38
20	19 55 45	21 57 58	23 48 22	1 50 35	3 48 51	5 51 5	7 49 21	9 51 35	11 53 48	13 52 4	15 54 18	17 52 34
21	19 59 41	22 1 55	23 52 18	1 54 31	3 52 48	5 55 1	7 53 18	9 55 31	11 57 44	13 56 1	15 58 14	17 56 31
22	20 3 38	22 5 51	23 56 15	1 58 28	3 56 44	5 58 58	7 57 15	9 59 28	12 1 41	13 59 58	16 2 11	18 0 27
23	20 7 34	22 9 48	0 0 11	2 2 25	4 0 41	6 2 54	8 1 11	10 3 24	12 5 37	14 3 54	16 6 7	18 4 24
24	20 11 31	22 13 44	0 4 8	2 6 21	4 4 38	6 6 51	8 5 8	10 7 21	12 9 34	14 7 51	16 10 4	18 8 21
25	20 15 28	22 17 41	0 8 4	2 10 17	4 8 34	6 10 47	8 9 4	10 11 17	12 13 31	14 11 47	16 14 0	18 12 17
26	20 19 24	22 21 37	0 12 1	2 14 14	4 12 31	6 14 44	8 13 1	10 15 14	12 17 27	14 15 44	16 17 57	18 16 14
27	20 23 21	22 25 34	0 15 57	2 18 11	4 16 27	6 18 41	8 16 57	10 19 11	12 21 24	14 19 40	16 21 54	18 20 10
28	20 27 17	22 29 30	0 19 54	2 22 7	4 20 24	6 22 37	8 20 54	10 23 7	12 25 20	14 23 37	16 25 50	18 24 7
29	20 31 14		0 23 51	2 26 4	4 24 20	6 26 34	8 24 50	10 27 4	12 29 17	14 27 33	16 29 47	18 28 3
30	20 35 10		0 27 47	2 30 0	4 28 17	6 30 30	8 28 47	10 31 0	12 33 13	14 31 30	16 33 43	18 32 0
31	20 39 7		0 31 44		4 32 13		8 32 44	10 34 57		14 35 26		18 35 56

1936

	Jan.	Feb.	Mar.	April	May	June	July	Aug.	Sept.	Oct.	Nov.	Dec.
1	18 39 53	20 42 6	22 36 26	0 38 40	2 36 56	4 39 9	6 37 26	8 39 39	10 41 53	12 40 9	14 42 22	16 40 39
2	18 43 50	20 46 3	22 40 23	0 42 36	2 40 53	4 43 6	6 41 23	8 43 36	10 45 49	12 44 6	14 46 19	16 44 36
3	18 47 46	20 49 59	22 44 20	0 46 33	2 44 49	4 47 3	6 45 19	8 47 32	10 49 46	12 48 2	14 50 15	16 48 32
4	18 51 43	20 53 56	22 48 16	0 50 29	2 48 46	4 50 59	6 49 16	8 51 29	10 53 42	12 51 59	14 54 12	16 52 29
5	18 55 39	20 57 53	22 52 13	0 54 26	2 52 42	4 54 56	6 53 12	8 55 26	10 57 39	12 55 55	14 58 9	16 56 25
6	18 59 36	21 1 49	22 56 9	0 58 22	2 56 39	4 58 52	6 57 9	8 59 22	11 1 35	12 59 52	15 2 5	17 0 22
7	19 3 32	21 5 46	23 0 6	1 2 19	3 0 35	5 2 49	7 1 6	9 3 19	11 5 32	13 3 49	15 6 2	17 4 18
8	19 7 29	21 9 42	23 4 2	1 6 15	3 4 32	5 6 45	7 5 2	9 7 15	11 9 28	13 7 45	15 9 58	17 8 15
9	19 11 26	21 13 39	23 7 59	1 10 12	3 8 29	5 10 42	7 8 59	9 11 12	11 13 25	13 11 42	15 13 55	17 12 12
10	19 15 22	21 17 35	23 11 55	1 14 9	3 12 25	5 14 39	7 12 55	9 15 8	11 17 22	13 15 38	15 17 51	17 16 8
11	19 19 19	21 21 32	23 15 52	1 18 5	3 16 22	5 18 35	7 16 52	9 19 5	11 21 18	13 19 35	15 21 48	17 20 5
12	19 23 15	21 25 28	23 19 48	1 22 2	3 20 18	5 22 32	7 20 48	9 23 2	11 25 15	13 23 31	15 25 44	17 24 1
13	19 27 12	21 29 25	23 23 45	1 25 58	3 24 15	5 26 28	7 24 45	9 26 58	11 29 11	13 27 28	15 29 41	17 27 58
14	19 31 8	21 33 22	23 27 42	1 29 55	3 28 11	5 30 25	7 28 41	9 30 55	11 33 8	13 31 24	15 33 38	17 31 54
15	19 35 5	21 37 18	23 31 38	1 33 51	3 32 8	5 34 21	7 32 38	9 34 51	11 37 4	13 35 21	15 37 34	17 35 51
16	19 39 1	21 41 15	23 35 35	1 37 48	3 36 5	5 38 18	7 36 35	9 38 48	11 41 1	13 39 17	15 41 31	17 39 47
17	19 42 58	21 45 11	23 39 31	1 41 44	3 40 1	5 42 14	7 40 31	9 42 44	11 44 57	13 43 14	15 45 27	17 43 44
18	19 46 55	21 49 8	23 43 28	1 45 41	3 43 58	5 46 11	7 44 28	9 46 41	11 48 54	13 47 11	15 49 24	17 47 41
19	19 50 50	21 53 4	23 47 24	1 49 38	3 47 54	5 50 7	7 48 24	9 50 37	11 52 51	13 51 7	15 53 20	17 51 37
20	19 54 48	21 57 0	23 51 21	1 53 34	3 51 51	5 54 4	7 52 21	9 54 34	11 56 47	13 55 4	15 57 17	17 55 34
21	19 58 44	22 0 57	23 55 17	1 57 31	3 55 47	5 58 1	7 56 17	9 58 31	12 0 44	13 59 0	16 1 13	17 59 30
22	20 2 41	22 4 54	23 59 14	2 1 27	3 59 44	6 1 57	8 0 14	10 2 27	12 4 40	14 2 57	16 5 10	18 3 27
23	20 6 38	22 8 51	0 3 11	2 5 24	4 3 40	6 5 54	8 4 10	10 6 24	12 8 37	14 6 54	16 9 7	18 7 23
24	20 10 34	22 12 47	0 7 7	2 9 20	4 7 37	6 9 50	8 8 7	10 10 20	12 12 33	14 10 50	16 13 3	18 11 20
25	20 14 30	22 16 44	0 11 4	2 13 17	4 11 34	6 13 47	8 12 4	10 14 16	12 16 30	14 14 46	16 17 0	18 15 16
26	20 18 27	22 20 40	0 15 0	2 17 13	4 15 30	6 17 43	8 16 0	10 18 13	12 20 26	14 18 43	16 20 56	18 19 13
27	20 22 24	22 24 37	0 18 57	2 21 10	4 19 27	6 21 40	8 19 57	10 22 10	12 24 23	14 22 40	16 24 53	18 23 10
28	20 26 20	22 28 33	0 22 53	2 25 7	4 23 23	6 25 36	8 23 53	10 26 6	12 28 20	14 26 36	16 28 49	18 27 6
29	20 30 17	22 32 31	0 26 50	2 29 3	4 27 20	6 29 33	8 27 50	10 30 3	12 32 16	14 30 33	16 32 46	18 31 3
30	20 34 13		0 30 46	2 33 0	4 31 16	6 33 30	8 31 46	10 34 0	12 36 13	14 34 29	16 36 42	18 34 59
31	20 38 10		'0 34 43		4 35 13		8 35 43	10 37 56		14 38 26		18 38 56

1937

	Jan.	Feb.	Mar.	April	May	June	July	Aug.	Sept.	Oct.	Nov.	Dec.
1	18 42 52	20 45 6	22 35 29	0 37 42	2 35 59	4 38 12	6 36 29	8 38 42	10 40 55	12 39 12	14 41 25	16 39 42
2	18 46 49	20 49 2	22 39 26	0 41 39	2 39 55	4 42 9	6 40 25	8 42 39	10 44 52	12 43 8	14 45 22	16 43 38
3	18 50 45	20 52 59	22 43 22	0 45 35	2 43 52	4 46 5	6 44 22	8 46 35	10 48 48	12 47 5	14 49 18	16 47 35
4	18 54 42	20 56 55	22 47 19	0 49 32	2 47 49	4 50 2	6 48 18	8 50 32	10 52 45	12 51 1	14 53 15	16 51 31
5	18 58 39	21 0 52	22 51 15	0 53 28	2 51 45	4 53 58	6 52 15	8 54 28	10 56 41	12 54 58	14 57 11	16 55 28
6	19 2 35	21 4 48	22 55 12	0 57 25	2 55 42	4 57 55	6 56 12	8 58 25	11 0 38	12 58 55	15 1 8	16 59 24
7	19 6 32	21 8 45	22 59 8	1 1 22	2 59 38	5 1 51	7 0 8	9 2 21	11 4 35	13 2 51	15 5 4	17 3 21
8	19 10 28	21 12 42	23 3 5	1 5 18	3 3 35	5 5 48	7 4 5	9 6 18	11 8 31	13 6 48	15 9 1	17 7 18
9	19 14 25	21 16 38	23 7 2	1 9 15	3 7 31	5 9 45	7 8 1	9 10 15	11 12 28	13 10 44	15 12 57	17 11 14
10	19 18 21	21 20 35	23 10 58	1 13 11	3 11 28	5 13 41	7 11 58	9 14 11	11 16 24	13 14 41	15 16 54	17 15 11
11	19 22 18	21 24 31	23 14 55	1 17 8	3 15 24	5 17 38	7 15 54	9 18 8	11 20 21	13 18 37	15 20 51	17 19 7
12	19 26 14	21 28 28	23 18 51	1 21 4	3 19 21	5 21 34	7 19 51	9 22 4	11 24 17	13 22 34	15 24 47	17 23 4
13	19 30 11	21 32 24	23 22 48	1 25 1	3 23 18	5 25 31	7 23 48	9 26 1	11 28 14	13 26 30	15 28 44	17 27 0
14	19 34 8	21 36 21	23 26 44	1 28 57	3 27 14	5 29 27	7 27 44	9 29 57	11 32 10	13 30 27	15 32 40	17 30 57
15	19 38 4	21 40 17	23 30 41	1 32 54	3 31 11	5 33 24	7 31 41	9 33 54	11 36 7	13 34 24	15 36 37	17 34 53
16	19 42 1	21 44 14	23 34 37	1 36 51	3 35 7	5 37 20	7 35 37	9 37 50	11 40 4	13 38 20	15 40 33	17 38 50
17	19 45 57	21 48 10	23 38 34	1 40 47	3 39 4	5 41 17	7 39 34	9 41 47	11 44 0	13 42 17	15 44 30	17 42 47
18	19 49 54	21 52 7	23 42 31	1 44 44	3 43 0	5 45 14	7 43 30	9 45 44	11 47 57	13 46 14	15 48 26	17 46 43
19	19 53 50	21 56 4	23 46 27	1 48 40	3 46 57	5 49 10	7 47 27	9 49 40	11 51 53	13 50 10	15 52 23	17 50 40
20	19 57 47	22 0 0	23 50 24	1 52 37	3 50 53	5 53 7	7 51 23	9 53 37	11 55 50	13 54 6	15 56 20	17 54 36
21	20 1 43	22 3 57	23 54 20	1 56 33	3 54 50	5 57 3	7 55 20	9 57 33	11 59 46	13 58 3	16 0 16	17 58 33
22	20 5 40	22 7 53	23 58 17	2 0 30	3 58 47	6 1 0	7 59 17	10 1 30	12 3 43	14 2 0	16 4 13	18 2 29
23	20 9 37	22 11 50	0 2 13	2 4 26	4 2 43	6 4 56	8 3 13	10 5 26	12 7 39	14 5 56	16 8 9	18 6 26
24	20 13 33	22 15 46	0 6 10	2 8 23	4 6 40	6 8 53	8 7 10	10 9 23	12 11 36	14 9 53	16 12 6	18 10 23
25	20 17 30	22 19 43	0 10 6	2 12 20	4 10 36	6 12 49	8 11 6	10 13 19	12 15 33	14 13 49	16 16 2	18 14 19
26	20 21 26	22 23 39	0 14 3	2 16 16	4 14 33	6 16 46	8 15 3	10 17 16	12 19 29	14 17 46	16 19 59	18 18 16
27	20 25 23	22 27 36	0 18 0	2 20 13	4 18 29	6 20 43	8 18 59	10 21 12	12 23 26	14 21 42	16 23 55	18 22 12
28	20 29 19	22 31 33	0 21 56	2 24 9	4 22 26	6 24 39	8 22 56	10 25 9	12 27 22	14 25 39	16 27 52	18 26 9
29	20 33 16		0 25 53	2 28 6	4 26 22	6 28 36	8 26 52	10 29 5	12 31 19	14 29 35	16 31 49	18 30 5
30	20 37 13		0 29 49	2 32 2	4 30 19	6 32 32	8 30 49	10 33 2	12 35 15	14 33 32	16 35 45	18 34 2
31	20 41 9		0 33 46		4 34 16		8 34 46	10 36 59		14 37 28		18 37 58

1938

	Jan.	Feb.	Mar.	April	May	June	July	Aug.	Sept.	Oct.	Nov.	Dec.	
1	18 41 55	20 44 8	22 34 32	0 36 45	2 35 1	4 37 15	6 35 32	8 37 45	10 39 58	12 38 14	14 40 28	16 38 44	1
2	18 45 52	20 48 5	22 38 28	0 40 41	2 38 58	4 41 11	6 39 28	8 41 41	10 43 54	12 42 11	14 44 24	16 42 41	2
3	18 49 48	20 52 1	22 42 25	0 44 38	2 42 55	4 45 8	6 43 25	8 45 38	10 47 51	12 46 7	14 48 21	16 46 37	3
4	18 53 45	20 55 58	22 46 22	0 48 35	2 46 51	4 49 4	6 47 21	8 49 34	10 51 47	12 50 4	14 52 17	16 50 34	4
5	18 57 41	20 59 54	22 50 18	0 52 31	2 50 48	4 53 1	6 51 18	8 53 31	10 55 44	12 54 1	14 56 14	16 54 30	5
6	19 1 38	21 3 51	22 54 14	0 56 28	2 54 44	4 56 57	6 55 14	8 57 27	10 59 41	12 57 57	15 0 10	16 58 27	6
7	19 5 34	21 7 48	22 58 11	1 0 24	2 58 41	5 0 54	6 59 11	9 1 24	11 3 37	13 1 54	15 4 7	17 2 24	7
8	19 9 31	21 11 44	23 2 8	1 4 21	3 2 37	5 4 51	7 3 7	9 5 21	11 7 34	13 5 50	15 8 3	17 6 20	8
9	19 13 27	21 15 41	23 6 4	1 8 17	3 6 34	5 8 47	7 7 4	9 9 17	11 11 30	13 9 47	15 12 0	17 10 17	9
10	19 17 24	21 19 37	23 10 1	1 12 14	3 10 30	5 12 44	7 11 0	9 13 14	11 15 27	13 13 43	15 15 57	17 14 13	10
11	19 21 21	21 23 34	23 13 57	1 16 10	3 14 27	5 16 40	7 14 57	9 17 10	11 19 23	13 17 40	15 19 53	17 18 10	11
12	19 25 17	21 27 31	23 17 54	1 20 7	3 18 24	5 20 37	7 18 54	9 21 7	11 23 20	13 21 36	15 23 50	17 22 6	12
13	19 29 14	21 31 27	23 21 50	1 24 3	3 22 20	5 24 33	7 22 50	9 25 3	11 27 16	13 25 33	15 27 46	17 26 3	13
14	19 33 10	21 35 23	23 25 47	1 28 0	3 26 17	5 28 30	7 26 47	9 29 0	11 31 13	13 29 30	15 31 43	17 29 59	14
15	19 37 7	21 39 20	23 29 43	1 31 57	3 30 13	5 32 26	7 30 43	9 32 56	11 35 10	13 33 26	15 35 39	17 33 56	15
16	19 41 3	21 43 17	23 33 40	1 35 53	3 34 10	5 36 23	7 34 40	9 36 52	11 39 6	13 37 22	15 39 36	17 37 53	16
17	19 45 0	21 47 13	23 37 37	1 39 50	3 38 6	5 40 20	7 38 36	9 40 49	11 43 3	13 41 19	15 43 32	17 41 49	17
18	19 48 56	21 51 10	23 41 33	1 43 46	3 42 3	5 44 16	7 42 33	9 44 46	11 46 59	13 45 16	15 47 29	17 45 46	18
19	19 52 53	21 55 6	23 45 30	1 47 43	3 45 59	5 48 13	7 46 29	9 48 43	11 50 56	13 49 12	15 51 26	17 49 42	19
20	19 56 50	21 59 3	23 49 26	1 51 39	3 49 56	5 52 9	7 50 26	9 52 39	11 54 52	13 53 9	15 55 22	17 53 39	20
21	20 0 46	22 3 0	23 53 23	1 55 36	3 53 53	5 56 6	7 54 23	9 56 36	11 58 49	13 57 5	15 59 19	17 57 35	21
22	20 4 43	22 6 56	23 57 19	1 59 32	3 57 49	6 0 2	7 58 19	10 0 32	12 2 46	14 1 2	16 3 15	18 1 32	22
23	20 8 39	22 10 52	0 1 16	2 3 29	4 1 46	6 3 59	8 2 16	10 4 29	12 6 42	14 4 59	16 7 12	18 5 28	23
24	20 12 36	22 14 49	0 5 12	2 7 26	4 5 42	6 7 55	8 6 12	10 8 25	12 10 39	14 8 55	16 11 8	18 9 25	24
25	20 16 32	22 18 45	0 9 9	2 11 22	4 9 39	6 11 52	8 10 9	10 12 22	12 14 35	14 12 52	16 15 5	18 13 22	25
26	20 20 29	22 22 42	0 13 6	2 15 19	4 13 35	6 15 49	8 14 5	10 16 19	12 18 32	14 16 48	16 19 1	18 17 18	26
27	20 24 25	22 26 39	0 17 2	2 19 15	4 17 32	6 19 45	8 18 2	10 20 15	12 22 28	14 20 45	16 22 58	18 21 15	27
28	20 28 22	22 30 35	0 20 59	2 23 12	4 21 28	6 23 42	8 21 58	10 24 12	12 26 25	14 24 41	16 26 55	18 25 11	28
29	20 32 19		0 24 55	2 27 8	4 25 25	6 27 38	8 25 55	10 28 8	12 30 22	14 28 38	16 30 51	18 29 8	29
30	20 36 15		0 28 52	2 31 5	4 29 22	6 31 35	8 29 52	10 32 5	12 34 18	14 32 34	16 34 48	18 33 4	30
31	20 40 12		0 32 48		4 33 18		8 33 48	10 36 1		14 36 31		18 37 1	31

1939

	Jan.	Feb.	Mar.	April	May	June	July	Aug.	Sept.	Oct.	Nov.	Dec.	
1	18 40 57	20 43 11	22 33 34	0 35 47	2 34 4	4 36 17	6 34 34	8 36 47	10 39 0	12 37 17	14 39 30	16 37 47	1
2	18 44 54	20 47 7	22 37 31	0 39 44	2 38 0	4 40 14	6 38 30	8 40 44	10 42 57	12 41 13	14 43 27	16 41 43	2
3	18 48 51	20 51 4	22 41 27	0 43 40	2 41 57	4 44 10	6 42 27	8 44 40	10 46 53	12 45 10	14 47 23	16 45 40	3
4	18 52 47	20 55 0	22 45 24	0 47 37	2 45 53	4 48 7	6 46 24	8 48 37	10 50 50	12 49 6	14 51 20	16 49 36	4
5	18 56 44	20 58 57	22 49 20	0 51 34	2 49 50	4 52 3	6 50 20	8 52 33	10 54 46	12 53 3	14 55 16	16 53 33	5
6	19 0 40	21 2 54	22 53 17	0 55 30	2 53 47	4 56 0	6 54 17	8 56 30	10 58 43	12 57 0	14 59 13	16 57 29	6
7	19 4 37	21 6 50	22 57 14	0 59 27	2 57 43	4 59 56	6 58 13	9 0 26	11 2 40	13 0 56	15 3 9	17 1 26	7
8	19 8 33	21 10 47	23 1 10	1 3 23	3 1 40	5 3 53	7 2 10	9 4 23	11 6 36	13 4 53	15 7 5	17 5 22	8
9	19 12 30	21 14 44	23 5 7	1 7 20	3 5 36	5 7 50	7 6 6	9 8 20	11 10 33	13 8 49	15 11 2	17 9 19	9
10	19 16 26	21 18 40	23 9 3	1 11 16	3 9 33	5 11 46	7 10 3	9 12 16	11 14 29	13 12 46	15 14 59	17 13 16	10
11	19 20 23	21 22 36	23 13 0	1 15 13	3 13 29	5 15 43	7 13 59	9 16 13	11 18 26	13 16 42	15 18 55	17 17 12	11
12	19 24 20	21 26 33	23 16 56	1 19 9	3 17 26	5 19 39	7 17 56	9 20 9	11 22 22	13 20 39	15 22 52	17 21 9	12
13	19 28 16	21 30 29	23 20 53	1 23 6	3 21 23	5 23 36	7 21 53	9 24 6	11 26 19	13 24 35	15 26 49	17 25 5	13
14	19 32 13	21 34 26	23 24 49	1 27 3	3 25 19	5 27 32	7 25 49	9 28 2	11 30 15	13 28 32	15 30 45	17 29 2	14
15	19 36 9	21 38 22	23 28 46	1 30 59	3 29 16	5 31 29	7 29 46	9 31 59	11 34 12	13 32 29	15 34 42	17 32 58	15
16	19 40 6	21 42 19	23 32 43	1 34 56	3 33 12	5 35 25	7 33 42	9 35 55	11 38 9	13 36 25	15 38 38	17 36 55	16
17	19 44 2	21 46 16	23 36 39	1 38 52	3 37 9	5 39 22	7 37 39	9 39 52	11 42 5	13 40 22	15 42 35	17 40 52	17
18	19 47 59	21 50 12	23 40 36	1 42 49	3 41 5	5 43 19	7 41 35	9 43 49	11 46 2	13 44 18	15 46 31	17 44 48	18
19	19 51 55	21 54 9	23 44 32	1 46 45	3 45 2	5 47 15	7 45 32	9 47 45	11 49 58	13 48 15	15 50 28	17 48 45	19
20	19 55 52	21 58 5	23 48 29	1 50 42	3 48 58	5 51 12	7 49 28	9 51 42	11 53 55	13 52 11	15 54 24	17 52 41	20
21	19 59 49	22 2 2	23 52 25	1 54 38	3 52 55	5 55 8	7 53 25	9 55 38	11 57 51	13 56 8	15 58 21	17 56 38	21
22	20 3 45	22 5 59	23 56 22	1 58 35	3 56 52	5 59 5	7 57 22	9 59 35	12 1 48	14 0 4	16 2 18	18 0 34	22
23	20 7 42	22 9 55	0 0 18	2 2 31	4 0 48	6 3 1	8 1 18	10 3 31	12 5 44	14 4 1	16 6 14	18 4 31	23
24	20 11 38	22 13 51	0 4 15	2 6 28	4 4 45	6 6 58	8 5 15	10 7 28	12 9 41	14 7 58	16 10 11	18 8 27	24
25	20 15 35	22 17 48	0 8 11	2 10 25	4 8 41	6 10 55	8 9 11	10 11 24	12 13 38	14 11 54	16 14 7	18 12 24	25
26	20 19 31	22 21 45	0 12 8	2 14 21	4 12 38	6 14 51	8 13 8	10 15 21	12 17 34	14 15 51	16 18 4	18 16 21	26
27	20 23 28	22 25 41	0 16 5	2 18 18	4 16 34	6 18 48	8 17 4	10 19 18	12 21 31	14 19 47	16 22 0	18 20 17	27
28	20 27 24	22 29 38	0 20 1	2 22 14	4 20 31	6 22 44	8 21 1	10 23 14	12 25 27	14 23 44	16 25 57	18 24 14	28
29	20 31 21		0 23 58	2 26 11	4 24 27	6 26 41	8 24 57	10 27 11	12 29 24	14 27 40	16 29 53	18 28 10	29
30	20 35 18		0 27 54	2 30 7	4 28 24	6 30 37	8 28 54	10 31 7	12 33 20	14 31 37	16 33 50	18 32 7	30
31	20 39 14		0 31 51		4 32 21		8 32 51	10 35 4		14 35 33		18 36 3	31

1940

	Jan.	Feb.	Mar.	April	May	June	July	Aug.	Sept.	Oct.	Nov.	Dec.	
1	18 40 0	20 42 13	22 36 33	0 38 46	2 37 3	4 39 16	6 37 33	8 39 46	10 41 59	12 40 16	14 42 29	16 40 46	1
2	18 43 56	20 46 10	22 40 30	0 42 43	2 40 59	4 43 13	6 41 29	8 43 43	10 45 56	12 44 12	14 46 25	16 44 42	2
3	18 47 53	20 50 6	22 44 26	0 46 39	2 44 56	4 47 9	6 45 26	8 47 39	10 49 52	12 48 9	14 50 22	16 48 39	3
4	18 51 50	20 54 3	22 48 23	0 50 36	2 48 53	4 51 6	6 49 22	8 51 36	10 53 49	12 52 5	14 54 19	16 52 35	4
5	18 55 46	20 57 59	22 52 19	0 54 33	2 52 49	4 55 2	6 53 19	8 55 32	10 57 45	12 56 2	14 58 15	16 56 32	5
6	18 59 43	21 1 56	22 56 16	0 58 29	2 56 46	4 58 59	6 57 16	8 59 29	11 1 42	12 59 58	15 2 12	17 0 28	6
7	19 3 39	21 5 52	23 0 13	1 2 26	3 0 42	5 2 55	7 1 12	9 3 25	11 5 38	13 3 55	15 6 8	17 4 25	7
8	19 7 36	21 9 49	23 4 9	1 6 22	3 4 39	5 6 52	7 5 9	9 7 22	11 9 35	13 7 52	15 10 5	17 8 21	8
9	19 11 32	21 13 46	23 8 6	1 10 19	3 8 35	5 10 49	7 9 5	9 11 18	11 13 32	13 11 48	15 14 1	17 12 18	9
10	19 15 29	21 17 42	23 12 2	1 14 15	3 12 32	5 14 45	7 13 2	9 15 15	11 17 28	13 15 45	15 17 58	17 16 14	10
11	19 19 25	21 21 39	23 15 59	1 18 12	3 16 28	5 18 42	7 16 58	9 19 12	11 21 25	13 19 41	15 21 54	17 20 11	11
12	19 23 22	21 25 35	23 19 55	1 22 8	3 20 25	5 22 38	7 20 55	9 23 8	11 25 21	13 23 38	15 25 51	17 24 8	12
13	19 27 19	21 29 32	23 23 52	1 26 5	3 24 22	5 26 35	7 24 51	9 27 5	11 29 18	13 27 34	15 29 48	17 28 4	13
14	19 31 15	21 33 28	23 27 48	1 30 1	3 28 18	5 30 31	7 28 48	9 31 1	11 33 14	13 31 31	15 33 44	17 32 1	14
15	19 35 12	21 37 25	23 31 45	1 33 58	3 32 15	5 34 28	7 32 45	9 34 58	11 37 11	13 35 27	15 37 41	17 35 57	15
16	19 39 8	21 41 21	23 35 41	1 37 55	3 36 11	5 38 24	7 36 41	9 38 54	11 41 7	13 39 24	15 41 37	17 39 54	16
17	19 43 5	21 45 18	23 39 38	1 41 51	3 40 8	5 42 21	7 40 38	9 42 51	11 45 4	13 43 21	15 45 34	17 43 50	17
18	19 47 1	21 49 15	23 43 35	1 45 48	3 44 4	5 46 18	7 44 34	9 46 47	11 49 1	13 47 17	15 49 30	17 47 47	18
19	19 50 58	21 53 11	23 47 31	1 49 44	3 48 1	5 50 14	7 48 31	9 50 44	11 52 57	13 51 14	15 53 27	17 51 44	19
20	19 54 54	21 57 8	23 51 28	1 53 41	3 51 57	5 54 11	7 52 27	9 54 41	11 56 54	13 55 10	15 57 23	17 55 40	20
21	19 58 51	22 1 4	23 55 24	1 57 37	3 55 54	5 58 7	7 56 24	9 58 37	12 0 50	13 59 7	16 1 20	17 59 37	21
22	20 2 48	22 5 1	23 59 21	2 1 34	3 59 51	6 2 4	8 0 20	10 2 34	12 4 47	14 3 3	16 5 17	18 3 33	22
23	20 6 44	22 8 57	0 3 17	2 5 30	4 3 47	6 6 0	8 4 17	10 6 30	12 8 43	14 7 0	16 9 13	18 7 30	23
24	20 10 41	22 12 54	0 7 14	2 9 27	4 7 44	6 9 57	8 8 14	10 10 27	12 12 40	14 10 56	16 13 10	18 11 26	24
25	20 14 37	22 16 50	0 11 10	2 13 24	4 11 40	6 13 53	8 12 10	10 14 23	12 16 36	14 14 53	16 17 6	18 15 23	25
26	20 18 34	22 20 47	0 15 7	2 17 20	4 15 37	6 17 50	8 16 7	10 18 20	12 20 33	14 18 50	16 21 3	18 19 19	26
27	20 22 30	22 24 44	0 19 4	2 21 17	4 19 33	6 21 47	8 20 3	10 22 16	12 24 30	14 22 46	16 24 59	18 23 16	27
28	20 26 27	22 28 40	0 23 0	2 25 13	4 23 30	6 25 43	8 24 0	10 26 13	12 28 26	14 26 43	16 28 56	18 27 13	28
29	20 30 23	22 32 37	0 26 57	2 29 10	4 27 26	6 29 40	8 27 56	10 30 10	12 32 23	14 30 39	16 32 52	18 31 9	29
30	20 34 20		0 30 53	2 33 6	4 31 23	6 33 36	8 31 53	10 34 6	12 36 19	14 34 36	16 36 49	18 35 6	30
31	20 38 17		0 34 50		4 35 20		8 35 49	10 38 3		14 38 32		18 39 2	31

1941

	Jan.	Feb.	Mar.	April	May	June	July	Aug.	Sept.	Oct.	Nov.	Dec.
1	18 42 59	20 45 12	22 35 36	0 37 49	2 36 5	4 38 18	6 36 35	8 38 48	10 41 2	12 39 18	14 41 31	16 39 48
2	18 46 55	20 49 9	22 39 32	0 41 45	2 40 2	4 42 15	6 40 32	8 42 45	10 44 58	12 43 15	14 45 28	16 43 44
3	18 50 52	20 53 5	22 43 29	0 45 42	2 43 58	4 46 12	6 44 28	8 46 41	10 48 55	12 47 11	14 49 24	16 47 41
4	18 54 48	20 57 2	22 47 25	0 49 38	2 47 55	4 50 8	6 48 25	8 50 38	10 52 51	12 51 8	14 53 21	16 51 38
5	18 58 45	21 0 58	22 51 22	0 53 35	2 51 51	4 54 5	6 52 21	8 54 35	10 56 48	12 55 4	14 57 17	16 55 34
6	19 2 42	21 4 55	22 55 18	0 57 31	2 55 48	4 58 1	6 56 18	8 58 31	11 0 44	12 59 1	15 1 14	16 59 31
7	19 6 38	21 8 51	22 59 15	1 1 28	2 59 45	5 1 58	7 0 14	9 2 28	11 4 41	13 2 57	15 5 11	17 3 27
8	19 10 35	21 12 48	23 3 11	1 5 25	3 3 41	5 5 54	7 4 11	9 6 24	11 8 37	13 6 54	15 9 7	17 7 24
9	19 14 31	21 16 44	23 7 8	1 9 21	3 7 38	5 9 51	7 8 8	9 10 21	11 12 34	13 10 50	15 13 4	17 11 20
10	19 18 28	21 20 41	23 11 5	1 13 18	3 11 34	5 13 47	7 12 4	9 14 17	11 16 30	13 14 47	15 17 0	17 15 17
11	19 22 24	21 24 38	23 15 1	1 17 14	3 15 31	5 17 44	7 16 1	9 18 14	11 20 27	13 18 44	15 20 57	17 19 13
12	19 26 21	21 28 34	23 18 58	1 21 11	3 19 27	5 21 41	7 19 57	9 22 10	11 24 24	13 22 40	15 24 53	17 23 10
13	19 30 17	21 32 31	23 22 54	1 25 7	3 23 24	5 25 37	7 23 54	9 26 7	11 28 20	13 26 37	15 28 50	17 27 7
14	19 34 14	21 36 27	23 26 51	1 29 4	3 27 20	5 29 34	7 27 50	9 30 4	11 32 17	13 30 33	15 32 46	17 31 3
15	19 38 11	21 40 24	23 30 47	1 33 0	3 31 17	5 33 30	7 31 47	9 34 0	11 36 13	13 34 30	15 36 43	17 35 0
16	19 42 7	21 44 20	23 34 44	1 36 57	3 35 14	5 37 27	7 35 43	9 37 57	11 40 10	13 38 26	15 40 40	17 38 56
17	19 46 4	21 48 17	23 38 40	1 40 53	3 39 10	5 41 23	7 39 40	9 41 53	11 44 6	13 42 23	15 44 36	17 42 53
18	19 50 0	21 52 13	23 42 37	1 44 50	3 43 7	5 45 20	7 43 37	9 45 50	11 48 3	13 46 19	15 48 33	17 46 49
19	19 53 57	21 56 10	23 46 33	1 48 47	3 47 3	5 49 16	7 47 33	9 49 46	11 51 59	13 50 16	15 52 29	17 50 46
20	19 57 54	22 0 7	23 50 30	1 52 43	3 51 0	5 53 13	7 51 30	9 53 43	11 55 56	13 54 13	15 56 26	17 54 42
21	20 1 50	22 4 3	23 54 27	1 56 40	3 54 56	5 57 10	7 55 26	9 57 39	11 59 53	13 58 9	16 0 22	17 58 39
22	20 5 47	22 8 0	23 58 23	2 0 36	3 58 53	6 1 6	7 59 23	10 1 36	12 3 49	14 2 6	16 4 19	18 2 36
23	20 9 43	22 11 56	0 2 20	2 4 33	4 2 49	6 5 3	8 3 19	10 5 33	12 7 46	14 6 2	16 8 15	18 6 32
24	20 13 40	22 15 53	0 6 16	2 8 29	4 6 46	6 8 59	8 7 16	10 9 29	12 11 42	14 9 59	16 12 12	18 10 29
25	20 17 36	22 19 49	0 10 13	2 12 26	4 10 43	6 12 56	8 11 12	10 13 26	12 15 39	14 13 55	16 16 9	18 14 25
26	20 21 33	22 23 46	0 14 9	2 16 22	4 14 39	6 16 52	8 15 9	10 17 22	12 19 35	14 17 52	16 20 5	18 18 22
27	20 25 29	22 27 42	0 18 6	2 20 19	4 18 36	6 20 49	8 19 6	10 21 19	12 23 32	14 21 48	16 24 2	18 22 18
28	20 29 26	22 31 39	0 22 2	2 24 16	4 22 32	6 24 45	8 23 2	10 25 15	12 27 28	14 25 45	16 27 58	18 26 15
29	20 33 22		0 25 59	2 28 12	4 26 29	6 28 42	8 26 59	10 29 12	12 31 25	14 29 42	16 31 55	18 30 11
30	20 37 19		0 29 56	2 32 9	4 30 25	6 32 39	8 30 55	10 33 8	12 35 22	14 33 38	16 35 51	18 34 8
31	20 41 15		0 33 52		4 34 22		8 34 52	10 37 5		14 37 35		18 38 5

1942

	Jan.	Feb.	Mar.	April	May	June	July	Aug.	Sept.	Oct.	Nov.	Dec.
1	18 42 1	20 44 14	22 34 38	0 36 51	2 35 8	4 37 21	6 35 38	8 37 51	10 40 4	12 38 20	14 40 34	16 38 50
2	18 45 58	20 48 11	22 38 34	0 40 48	2 39 4	4 41 17	6 39 34	8 41 47	10 44 0	12 42 17	14 44 30	16 42 47
3	18 49 54	20 52 8	22 42 31	0 44 44	2 43 1	4 45 14	6 43 31	8 45 44	10 47 57	12 46 14	14 48 27	16 46 43
4	18 53 51	20 56 4	22 46 28	0 48 41	2 46 57	4 49 10	6 47 27	8 49 40	10 51 54	12 50 10	14 52 23	16 50 40
5	18 57 47	21 0 1	22 50 24	0 52 37	2 50 54	4 53 7	6 51 24	8 53 37	10 55 50	12 54 7	14 56 20	16 54 36
6	19 1 44	21 3 57	22 54 21	0 56 34	2 54 50	4 57 4	6 55 20	8 57 33	10 59 47	12 58 3	15 0 16	16 58 33
7	19 5 40	21 7 54	22 58 17	1 0 30	2 58 47	5 1 0	6 59 17	9 1 30	11 3 43	13 2 0	15 4 13	17 2 30
8	19 9 37	21 11 50	23 2 14	1 4 27	3 2 43	5 4 57	7 3 13	9 5 27	11 7 40	13 5 56	15 8 9	17 6 26
9	19 13 34	21 15 47	23 6 10	1 8 23	3 6 40	5 8 53	7 7 10	9 9 23	11 11 36	13 9 53	15 12 6	17 10 23
10	19 17 30	21 19 43	23 10 7	1 12 20	3 10 37	5 12 50	7 11 6	9 13 20	11 15 33	13 13 49	15 16 3	17 14 19
11	19 21 27	21 23 40	23 14 3	1 16 17	3 14 33	5 16 46	7 15 3	9 17 16	11 19 29	13 17 46	15 19 59	17 18 16
12	91 25 23	21 27 36	23 18 0	1 20 13	3 18 30	5 20 43	7 19 0	9 21 13	11 23 26	13 21 43	15 23 56	17 22 12
13	19 29 20	21 31 33	23 21 57	1 24 10	3 22 26	5 24 39	7 22 56	9 25 9	11 27 23	13 25 39	15 27 52	17 26 9
14	19 33 16	21 35 30	23 25 53	1 28 6	3 26 23	5 28 36	7 26 53	9 29 6	11 31 19	13 29 36	15 31 49	17 30 5
15	19 37 13	21 39 26	23 29 50	1 32 3	3 30 19	5 32 33	7 30 49	9 33 2	11 35 16	13 33 32	15 35 45	17 34 2
16	19 41 9	21 43 23	23 33 46	1 35 59	3 34 16	5 36 29	7 34 46	9 36 59	11 39 12	13 37 29	15 39 42	17 37 59
17	19 45 6	21 47 19	23 37 43	1 39 56	3 38 12	5 40 26	7 38 42	9 40 56	11 43 9	13 41 25	15 43 38	17 41 55
18	19 49 3	21 51 16	23 41 39	1 43 52	3 42 9	5 44 22	7 42 39	9 44 52	11 47 5	13 45 22	15 47 35	17 45 52
19	19 52 59	21 55 12	23 45 36	1 47 49	3 46 6	5 48 19	7 46 36	9 48 49	11 51 2	13 49 18	15 51 32	17 49 48
20	19 56 56	21 59 9	23 49 32	1 51 45	3 50 2	5 52 15	7 50 32	9 52 45	11 54 58	13 53 15	15 55 28	17 53 45
21	20 0 52	22 3 5	23 53 29	1 55 42	3 53 59	5 56 12	7 54 29	9 56 42	11 58 55	13 57 11	15 59 25	17 57 41
22	20 4 49	22 7 2	23 57 25	1 59 39	3 57 55	6 0 8	7 58 25	10 0 38	12 2 51	14 1 8	16 3 21	18 1 38
23	20 8 45	22 10 59	0 1 22	2 3 35	4 1 52	6 4 5	8 2 22	10 4 35	12 6 48	14 5 5	16 7 18	18 5 35
24	20 12 42	22 14 55	0 5 19	2 7 32	4 5 48	6 8 2	8 6 18	10 8 31	12 10 45	14 9 1	16 11 14	18 9 31
25	20 16 38	22 18 52	0 9 15	2 11 28	4 9 45	6 11 58	8 10 15	10 12 28	12 14 41	14 12 58	16 15 11	18 13 28
26	20 20 35	22 22 48	0 13 12	2 15 25	4 13 41	6 15 55	8 14 11	10 16 25	12 18 38	14 16 54	16 19 7	18 17 24
27	20 24 32	22 26 45	0 17 8	2 19 21	4 17 38	6 19 51	8 18 8	10 20 21	12 22 34	14 20 51	16 23 4	18 21 21
28	20 28 28	22 30 41	0 21 5	2 23 18	4 21 35	6 23 48	8 22 5	10 24 18	12 26 31	14 24 47	16 27 1	18 25 17
29	20 32 25		0 25 1	2 27 14	4 25 31	6 27 44	8 26 1	10 28 14	12 30 27	14 28 44	16 30 57	18 29 14
30	20 36 21		0 28 58	2 31 11	4 29 28	6 31 41	8 29 58	10 32 11	12 34 24	14 32 40	16 34 54	18 33 10
31	20 40 18		0 32 54		4 33 24		8 33 54	10 36 7		14 36 37		18 37 7

1943

	Jan.	Feb.	Mar.	April	May	June	July	Aug.	Sept.	Oct.	Nov.	Dec.
1	18 41 4	20 43 17	22 33 40	0 35 53	2 34 10	4 36 23	6 34 40	8 36 53	10 39 6	12 37 23	14 39 36	16 37 53
2	18 45 0	20 47 13	22 37 37	0 39 50	2 38 7	4 40 20	6 38 36	8 40 50	10 43 3	12 41 19	14 43 33	16 41 49
3	18 48 57	20 51 10	22 41 33	0 43 46	2 42 3	4 44 16	6 42 33	8 44 46	10 46 59	12 45 16	14 47 29	16 45 46
4	18 52 53	20 55 6	22 45 30	0 47 43	2 46 0	4 48 13	6 46 30	8 48 43	10 50 56	12 49 13	14 51 26	16 49 42
5	18 56 50	20 59 3	22 49 26	0 51 40	2 49 56	4 52 9	6 50 26	8 52 39	10 54 53	12 53 9	14 55 22	16 53 39
6	19 0 46	21 3 0	22 53 23	0 55 36	2 53 53	4 56 6	6 54 23	8 56 36	10 58 49	12 57 6	14 59 19	16 57 35
7	19 4 43	21 6 56	22 57 20	0 59 33	2 57 49	5 0 3	6 58 19	9 0 32	11 2 46	13 1 2	15 3 15	17 1 33
8	19 8 39	21 10 53	23 1 16	1 3 29	3 1 46	5 3 59	7 2 16	9 4 29	11 6 42	13 4 59	15 7 12	17 5 29
9	19 12 36	21 14 49	23 5 13	1 7 26	3 5 42	5 7 56	7 6 12	9 8 26	11 10 39	13 8 55	15 11 8	17 9 25
10	19 16 33	21 18 46	23 9 9	1 11 22	3 9 39	5 11 52	7 10 9	9 12 22	11 14 36	13 12 52	15 15 5	17 13 22
11	19 20 29	21 22 42	23 13 6	1 15 19	3 13 36	5 15 49	7 14 5	9 16 19	11 18 32	13 16 48	15 19 2	17 17 18
12	19 24 26	21 26 39	23 17 2	1 19 15	3 17 32	5 19 45	7 18 2	9 20 15	11 22 28	13 20 45	15 22 58	17 21 15
13	19 28 22	21 30 35	23 20 59	1 23 12	3 21 29	5 23 42	7 21 59	9 24 12	11 26 25	13 24 41	15 26 55	17 25 11
14	19 32 19	21 34 32	23 24 55	1 27 9	3 25 25	5 27 38	7 25 55	9 28 8	11 30 21	13 28 38	15 30 51	17 29 8
15	19 36 15	21 38 29	23 28 52	1 31 5	3 29 22	5 31 35	7 29 52	9 32 5	11 34 18	13 32 35	15 34 48	17 33 4
16	19 40 12	21 42 25	23 32 49	1 35 2	3 33 18	5 35 32	7 33 48	9 36 1	11 38 15	13 36 31	15 38 44	17 37 1
17	19 44 8	21 46 22	23 36 45	1 38 58	3 37 15	5 39 28	7 37 45	9 39 58	11 42 11	13 40 28	15 42 41	17 40 58
18	19 48 5	21 50 18	23 40 42	1 42 55	3 41 11	5 43 25	7 41 41	9 43 55	11 46 8	13 44 24	15 46 37	17 44 54
19	19 52 2	21 54 15	23 44 38	1 46 51	3 45 8	5 47 21	7 45 38	9 47 51	11 50 4	13 48 21	15 50 34	17 48 51
20	19 55 58	21 58 11	23 48 35	1 50 48	3 49 4	5 51 18	7 49 34	9 51 48	11 54 1	13 52 17	15 54 31	17 52 47
21	19 59 55	22 2 8	23 52 31	1 54 44	3 53 1	5 55 14	7 53 31	9 55 44	11 57 57	13 56 14	15 58 27	17 56 44
22	20 3 51	22 6 4	23 56 28	1 58 41	3 56 58	5 59 11	7 57 28	9 59 41	12 1 54	14 0 10	16 2 24	18 0 40
23	20 7 48	22 10 1	0 0 24	2 2 38	4 0 54	6 3 7	8 1 24	10 3 37	12 5 50	14 4 7	16 6 20	18 4 37
24	20 11 44	22 13 57	0 4 21	2 6 34	4 4 51	6 7 4	8 5 21	10 7 34	12 9 47	14 8 4	16 10 17	18 8 33
25	20 15 41	22 17 54	0 8 18	2 10 31	4 8 47	6 11 1	8 9 17	10 11 30	12 13 44	14 12 0	16 14 13	18 12 30
26	20 19 37	22 21 51	0 12 14	2 14 27	4 12 44	6 14 57	8 13 14	10 15 27	12 17 40	14 15 57	16 18 10	18 16 27
27	20 23 34	22 25 47	0 16 11	2 18 24	4 16 40	6 18 54	8 17 10	10 19 24	12 21 37	14 19 53	16 22 6	18 20 24
28	20 27 31	22 29 44	0 20 7	2 22 20	4 20 37	6 22 50	8 21 7	10 23 20	12 25 33	14 23 50	16 26 3	18 24 20
29	20 31 27		0 24 4	2 26 17	4 24 34	6 26 47	8 25 3	10 27 17	12 29 30	14 27 46	16 30 0	18 28 16
30	20 35 24		0 28 0	2 30 13	4 28 30	6 30 43	8 29 0	10 31 14	12 33 26	14 31 43	16 33 56	18 32 13
31	20 39 20		0 31 57		4 32 27		8 32 57	10 35 10		14 35 39		18 36 9

	Jan.	Feb.	Mar.	April	May	June	July	Aug.	Sept.	Oct.	Nov.	Dec.
1	18 40 6	20 42 20	22 36 39	0 38 52	2 37 9	4 39 22	6 37 39	8 39 52	10 42 5	12 40 22	14 42 35	16 40 52
2	18 44 3	20 46 13	22 40 36	0 42 49	2 41 6	4 43 19	6 41 35	8 43 49	10 46 2	12 44 18	14 46 32	16 44 48
3	18 47 59	20 50 12	22 44 32	0 46 46	2 45 2	4 47 15	6 45 32	8 47 45	10 49 58	12 48 15	14 50 28	16 48 45
4	18 51 56	20 54 9	22 48 29	0 50 42	2 48 59	4 51 12	6 49 29	8 51 42	10 53 55	12 52 12	14 54 25	16 52 41
5	18 55 52	20 58 5	22 52 25	0 54 39	2 52 55	4 55 8	6 53 25	8 55 38	10 57 52	12 56 8	14 58 21	16 56 38
6	18 59 49	21 2 2	22 56 22	0 58 35	2 56 52	4 59 5	6 57 22	8 59 35	11 1 48	13 0 5	15 2 18	17 0 35
7	19 3 45	21 5 59	23 0 19	1 2 32	3 0 48	5 3 2	7 1 18	9 3 32	11 5 45	13 4 1	15 6 14	17 4 31
8	19 7 42	21 9 55	23 4 16	1 6 28	3 4 45	5 6 58	7 5 15	9 7 28	11 9 41	13 7 58	15 10 11	17 8 28
9	19 11 38	21 13 52	23 8 12	1 10 25	3 8 41	5 10 55	7 9 11	9 11 25	11 13 38	13 11 54	15 14 8	17 12 24
10	19 15 35	21 17 48	23 12 8	1 14 21	3 12 38	5 14 51	7 13 8	9 15 21	11 17 34	13 15 51	15 18 4	17 16 21
11	19 19 32	21 21 45	23 16 5	1 18 18	3 16 35	5 18 48	7 17 5	9 19 18	11 21 31	13 19 47	15 22 1	17 20 17
12	19 23 28	21 25 41	23 20 1	1 22 14	3 20 31	5 22 44	7 21 1	9 23 14	11 25 27	13 23 44	15 25 57	17 24 14
13	19 27 25	21 29 38	23 23 58	1 26 11	3 24 28	5 26 41	7 24 58	9 27 11.	11 29 24	13 27 41	15 29 54	17 28 10
14	19 31 21	21 33 34	23 27 54	1 30 8	3 28 24	5 30 37	7 28 54	9 31 7	11 33 21	13 31 37	15 33 50	17 32 7
15	19 35 18	21 37 31	23 31 51	1 34 4	3 32 21	5 34 34	7 32 51	9 35 4	11 37 17	13 35 34	15 37 47	17 36 4
16	19 39 14	21 41 28	23 35 48	1 38 1	3 36 17	5 38 31	7 36 47	9 39 1	11 41 14	13 39 30	15 41 43	17 40 0
17	19 43 11	21 45 24	23 39 44	1 41 57	3 40 14	5 42 27	7 40 44	9 42 57	11 45 10	13 43 27	15 45 40	17 43 57
18	19 47 7	21 49 21	23 43 41	1 45 54	3 44 10	5 46 24	7 44 40	9 46 54	11 49 7	13 47 23	15 49 37	17 47 53
19	19 51 4	21 53 18	23 47 37	1 49 50	3 48 7	5 50 20	7 48 37	9 50 50	11 53 3	13 51 20	15 53 33	17 51 50
20	19 55 0	21 57 14	23 51 34	1 53 47	3 52 4	5 54 17	7 52 34	9 54 47	11 57 0	13 55 16	15 57 30	17 55 46
21	19 58 57	22 1 10	23 55 30	1 57 43	3 56 0	5 58 13	7 56 30	9 58 43	12 0 56	13 59 13	16 1 26	17 59 43
22	20 2 51	22 5 7	23 59 27	2 1 40	3 59 57	6 2 10	8 0 27	10 2 40	12 4 53	14 3 10	16 5 23	18 3 39
23	20 6 50	22 9 3	0 3 23	2 5 37	4 3 53	6 6 6	8 4 23	10 6 36	12 8 50	14 7 6	16 9 19	18 7 36
24	20 10 47	22 13 0	0 7 20	2 9 33	4 7 50	6 10 3	8 8 20	10 10 33	12 12 46	14 11 3	16 13 16	18 11 33
25	20 14 43	22 16 57	0 11 17	2 13 30	4 11 46	6 14 0	8 12 16	10 14 29	12 16 43	14 14 59	16 17 12	18 15 29
26	20 18 40	22 20 53	0 15 13	2 17 26	4 15 43	6 17 56	8 16 13	10 18 26	12 20 39	14 18 56	16 21 9	18 19 26
27	20 22 36	22 24 50	0 19 10	2 21 23	4 19 39	6 21 53	8 20 9	10 22 23	12 24 36	14 22 52	16 25 6	18 23 22
28	20 26 33	22 28 46	0 23 6	2 25 19	4 23 36	6 25 49	8 24 6	10 26 19	12 28 32	14 26 49	16 29 2	18 27 19
29	20 30 30	22 32 43	0 27 3	2 29 16	4 27 33	6 29 46	8 28 3	10 30 16	12 32 29	14 30 45	16 32 59	18 31 15
30	20 34 26		0 30 59	2 33 12	4 31 29	6 33 42	8 31 59	10 34 12	12 36 25	14 34 42	16 36 55	18 35 12
31	20 38 23		0 34 56		4 35 26		8 35 56	10 38 9		14 38 39		18 39 9

	Jan.	Feb.	Mar.	April	May	June	July	Aug.	Sept.	Oct.	Nov.	Dec.
1	18 43 5	20 45 18	22 35 42	0 37 55	2 36 12	4 38 25	6 36 42	8 38 55	10 41 8	12 39 25	14 41 38	16 39 54
2	18 47 2	20 49 15	22 39 38	0 41 52	2 40 8	4 42 21	6 40 38	8 42 51	10 45 5	12 43 21	14 45 34	16 43 51
3	18 50 58	20 53 11	22 43 35	0 45 48	2 44 5	4 46 18	6 44 35	8 46 48	10 49 1	12 47 18	14 49 31	16 47 48
4	18 54 55	20 57 8	22 47 31	0 49 45	2 48 1	4 50 14	6 48 31	8 50 44	10 52 58	12 51 14	14 53 27	16 51 44
5	18 58 51	21 1 5	22 51 28	0 53 41	2 51 58	4 54 11	6 52 28	8 54 41	10 56 54	12 55 11	14 57 24	16 55 41
6	19 2 48	21 5 1	22 55 25	0 57 38	2 55 54	4 58 8	6 56 24	8 58 38	11 0 51	12 59 7	15 1 20	16 59 38
7	19 6 44	21 8 58	22 59 21	1 1 34	2 59 51	5 2 4	7 0 21	9 2 34	11 4 47	13 3 4	15 5 17	17 3 34
8	19 10 41	21 12 54	23 3 18	1 5 31	3 3 47	5 6 1	7 4 17	9 6 31	11 8 44	13 7 0	15 9 14	17 7 30
9	19 14 38	21 16 51	23 7 14	1 9 27	3 7 44	5 9 57	7 8 14	9 10 27	11 12 40	13 10 57	15 13 10	17 11 27
10	19 18 34	21 20 47	23 11 11	1 13 24	3 11 40	5 13 54	7 12 11	9 14 24	11 16 37	13 14 54	15 17 7	17 15 23
11	19 22 31	21 24 44	23 15 7	1 17 21	3 15 37	5 17 50	7 16 7	9 18 20	11 20 34	13 18 50	15 21 3	17 19 20
12	19 26 28	21 28 40	23 19 4	1 21 17	3 19 33	5 21 47	7 20 4	9 22 17	11 24 30	13 22 47	15 25 0	17 23 17
13	19 30 24	21 32 37	23 23 0	1 25 14	3 23 30	5 25 44	7 24 0	9 26 13	11 28 27	13 26 44	15 28 56	17 27 13
14	19 34 20	21 36 34	23 26 57	1 29 10	3 27 27	5 29 40	7 27 57	9 30 10	11 32 24	13 30 40	15 32 53	17 31 10
15	19 38 17	21 40 30	23 30 54	1 33 7	3 31 23	5 33 37	7 31 53	9 34 7	11 36 20	13 34 36	15 36 50	17 35 6
16	19 42 13	21 44 27	23 34 50	1 37 3	3 35 20	5 37 33	7 35 50	9 38 3	11 40 16	13 38 33	15 40 46	17 39 3
17	19 46 10	21 48 24	23 38 47	1 41 0	3 39 16	5 41 30	7 39 47	9 42 0	11 44 13	13 42 29	15 44 43	17 42 59
18	19 50 7	21 52 20	23 42 43	1 44 56	3 43 13	5 45 26	7 43 43	9 45 56	11 48 9	13 46 26	15 48 40	17 46 56
19	19 54 3	21 56 16	23 46 40	1 48 53	3 47 10	5 49 23	7 47 40	9 49 53	11 52 6	13 50 23	15 52 36	17 50 52
20	19 58 0	22 0 13	23 50 36	1 52 49	3 51 6	5 53 19	7 51 36	9 53 49	11 56 2	13 54 19	15 56 33	17 54 49
21	20 1 56	22 4 9	23 54 33	1 56 46	3 55 3	5 57 16	7 55 33	9 57 46	11 59 59	13 58 16	16 0 29	17 58 46
22	20 5 53	22 8 6	23 58 29	2 0 43	3 58 59	6 1 13	7 59 29	10 1 42	12 3 56	14 2 12	16 4 25	18 2 42
23	20 9 49	22 12 3	0 2 26	2 4 39	4 2 56	6 5 9	8 3 26	10 5 39	12 7 52	14 6 9	16 8 22	18 6 39
24	20 13 46	22 15 59	0 6 23	2 8 36	4 6 52	6 9 6	8 7 22	10 9 36	12 11 49	14 10 5	16 12 19	18 10 35
25	20 17 42	22 19 56	0 10 19	2 12 32	4 10 49	6 13 2	8 11 19	10 13 32	12 15 45	14 14 2	16 16 15	18 14 32
26	20 21 39	22 23 52	0 14 16	2 16 29	4 14 45	6 16 59	8 15 15	10 17 29	12 19 42	14 17 58	16 20 12	18 18 28
27	20 25 36	22 27 49	0 18 12	2 20 25	4 18 42	6 20 55	8 19 12	10 21 25	12 23 38	14 21 55	16 24 8	18 22 25
28	20 29 32	22 31 45	0 22 9	2 24 22	4 22 39	6 24 52	8 23 9	10 25 22	12 27 35	14 25 52	16 28 5	18 26 21
29	20 33 29		0 26 5	2 28 18	4 26 35	6 28 48	8 27 5	10 29 18	12 31 31	14 29 48	16 32 1	18 30 18
30	20 37 25		0 30 2	2 32 15	4 30 32	6 32 45	8 31 2	10 33 15	12 35 28	14 33 45	16 35 58	18 34 15
31	20 41 22		0 33 58		4 34 28		8 34 58	10 37 11		14 37 42		18 38 11

	Jan.	Feb.	Mar.	April	May	June	July	Aug.	Sept.	Oct.	Nov.	Dec.
1	18 42 8	20 44 21	22 34 45	0 36 58	2 35 14	4 37 28	6 35 44	8 37 58	10 40 11	12 38 27	14 40 40	16 38 57
2	18 46 4	20 48 18	22 38 41	0 40 54	2 39 11	4 41 24	6 39 41	8 41 54	10 44 7	12 42 24	14 44 37	16 42 54
3	18 50 1	20 52 14	22 42 38	0 44 51	2 43 7	4 45 17	6 43 37	8 45 51	10 48 4	12 46 20	14 48 34	16 46 50
4	18 53 57	20 56 11	22 46 34	0 48 47	2 47 4	4 49 17	6 47 34	8 49 47	10 52 0	12 50 17	14 52 30	16 50 47
5	18 57 54	21 0 7	22 50 31	0 52 44	2 51 0	4 53 14	6 51 30	8 53 44	10 55 57	12 54 14	14 56 27	16 54 43
6	19 1 51	21 4 4	22 54 27	0 56 40	2 54 57	4 57 10	6 55 27	8 57 40	10 59 53	12 58 10	15 0 23	16 58 40
7	19 5 47	21 8 0	22 58 24	1 0 37	2 58 54	5 1 7	6 59 24	9 1 37	11 3 50	13 2 7	15 4 20	17 2 37
8	19 9 44	21 11 57	23 2 20	1 4 34	3 2 50	5 5 3	7 3 20	9 5 33	11 7 47	13 6 3	15 8 16	17 6 33
9	19 13 40	21 15 53	23 6 17	1 8 30	3 6 47	5 9 0	7 7 17	9 9 30	11 11 43	13 10 0	15 12 13	17 10 30
10	19 17 37	21 19 50	23 10 13	1 12 27	3 10 43	5 12 57	7 11 13	9 13 27	11 15 40	13 13 56	15 16 9	17 14 26
11	19 21 33	21 23 47	23 14 10	1 16 23	3 14 40	5 16 53	7 15 10	9 17 23	11 19 36	13 17 53	15 20 6	17 18 23
12	19 25 30	21 27 43	23 18 7	1 20 20	3 18 36	5 20 50	7 19 6	9 21 20	11 23 33	13 21 49	15 24 3	17 22 19
13	19 29 26	21 31 40	23 22 3	1 24 16	3 22 33	5 24 46	7 23 3	9 25 16	11 27 29	13 25 46	15 27 59	17 26 16
14	19 33 23	21 35 36	23 26 0	1 28 13	3 26 29	5 28 43	7 27 0	9 29 13	11 31 26	13 29 42	15 31 56	17 30 12
15	19 37 20	21 39 33	23 29 56	1 32 9	3 30 26	5 32 39	7 30 56	9 33 9	11 35 22	13 33 39	15 35 52	17 34 9
16	19 41 16	21 43 29	23 33 53	1 36 6	3 34 23	5 36 36	7 34 53	9 37 6	11 39 19	13 37 36	15 39 49	17 38 6
17	19 45 13	21 47 26	23 37 49	1 40 3	3 38 19	5 40 32	7 38 49	9 41 2	11 43 16	13 41 32	15 43 45	17 42 2
18	19 49 9	21 51 22	23 41 46	1 43 59	3 42 16	5 44 29	7 42 46	9 44 59	11 47 12	13 45 29	15 47 42	17 45 59
19	19 53 6	21 55 19	23 45 42	1 47 56	3 46 12	5 48 25	7 46 42	9 48 56	11 51 9	13 49 25	15 51 39	17 49 55
20	19 57 2	21 59 16	23 49 39	1 51 52	3 50 9	5 52 22	7 50 39	9 52 52	11 55 5	13 53 22	15 55 35	17 53 52
21	20 0 59	22 3 12	23 53 36	1 55 49	3 54 5	5 56 19	7 54 35	9 56 49	11 59 2	13 57 18	15 59 32	17 57 49
22	20 4 55	22 7 9	23 57 32	1 59 45	3 58 2	6 0 15	7 58 32	10 0 45	12 2 58	14 1 15	16 3 28	18 1 45
23	20 8 52	22 11 5	0 1 29	2 3 42	4 1 59	6 4 12	8 2 29	10 4 42	12 6 55	14 5 12	16 7 25	18 5 42
24	20 12 48	22 15 2	0 5 25	2 7 38	4 5 55	6 8 8	8 6 25	10 8 38	12 10 51	14 9 8	16 11 21	18 9 38
25	20 16 45	22 18 58	0 9 22	2 11 35	4 9 52	6 12 5	8 10 22	10 12 35	12 14 48	14 13 5	16 15 18	18 13 35
26	20 20 42	22 22 55	0 13 18	2 15 32	4 13 48	6 16 1	8 14 18	10 16 31	12 18 45	14 17 1	16 19 14	18 17 31
27	20 24 38	22 26 51	0 17 15	2 19 28	4 17 45	6 19 58	8 18 15	10 20 28	12 22 41	14 20 58	16 23 11	18 21 28
28	20 28 35	22 30 48	0 21 11	2 23 25	4 21 41	6 23 55	8 22 11	10 24 25	12 26 38	14 24 54	16 27 8	18 25 24
29	20 32 31		0 25 8	2 27 21	4 25 38	6 27 51	8 26 8	10 28 21	12 30 35	14 28 51	16 31 4	18 29 21
30	20 36 28		0 29 5	2 31 18	4 29 34	6 31 48	8 30 5	10 32 18	12 34 31	14 32 47	16 35 1	18 33 17
31	20 40 24		0 33 1		4 33 31		8 34 1	10 36 14		14 36 44		18 37 14

1947

	Jan.	Feb.	Mar.	April	May	June	July	Aug.	Sept.	Oct.	Nov.	Dec.
1	18 41 10	20 43 24	22 33 47	0 36 0	2 34 17	4 36 30	6 34 47	8 37 0	10 39 14	12 37 30	14 39 43	16 38 0
2	18 45 7	20 47 20	22 37 44	0 39 57	2 38 14	4 40 27	6 38 44	8 40 57	10 43 10	12 41 27	14 43 40	16 41 57
3	18 49 4	20 51 17	22 41 40	0 43 54	2 42 10	4 44 23	6 42 40	8 44 53	10 47 7	12 45 24	14 47 38	16 45 53
4	18 53 0	20 55 13	22 45 37	0 47 50	2 46 7	4 48 20	6 46 37	8 48 50	10 51 3	12 49 20	14 51 33	16 49 50
5	18 56 57	20 59 10	22 49 34	0 51 47	2 50 3	4 52 17	6 50 33	8 52 47	10 55 0	12 53 16	14 55 30	16 53 46
6	19 0 53	21 3 7	22 53 30	0 55 43	2 54 0	4 56 13	6 54 30	8 56 43	10 58 56	12 57 13	14 59 26	16 57 43
7	19 4 50	21 7 3	22 57 27	0 59 40	2 57 56	5 0 10	6 58 26	9 0 40	11 2 53	13 1 10	15 3 23	17 1 39
8	19 8 46	21 11 0	23 1 23	1 3 36	3 1 53	5 4 6	7 2 23	9 4 36	11 6 49	13 5 6	15 7 19	17 5 36
9	19 12 43	21 14 56	23 5 20	1 7 33	3 5 50	5 8 3	7 6 20	9 8 33	11 10 46	13 9 3	15 11 16	17 9 33
10	19 16 40	21 18 53	23 9 16	1 11 29	3 9 46	5 11 59	7 10 16	9 12 30	11 14 43	13 12 59	15 15 12	17 13 29
11	19 20 36	21 22 49	23 13 13	1 15 26	3 13 43	5 15 56	7 14 13	9 16 26	11 18 39	13 16 56	15 19 9	17 17 26
12	19 24 33	21 26 46	23 17 9	1 19 23	3 17 39	5 19 52	7 18 9	9 20 22	11 22 36	13 20 52	15 23 5	17 21 22
13	19 28 29	21 30 42	23 21 6	1 23 19	3 21 36	5 23 49	7 22 6	9 24 19	11 26 32	13 24 49	15 27 2	17 25 19
14	19 32 26	21 34 39	23 25 3	1 27 16	3 25 32	5 27 46	7 26 2	9 28 16	11 30 29	13 28 45	15 30 59	17 29 15
15	19 36 22	21 38 36	23 28 59	1 31 12	3 29 29	5 31 42	7 29 59	9 32 12	11 34 25	13 32 42	15 34 55	17 33 12
16	19 40 19	21 42 32	23 32 56	1 35 9	3 33 25	5 35 39	7 33 55	9 36 9	11 38 22	13 36 38	15 38 52	17 37 8
17	19 44 15	21 46 29	23 36 52	1 39 5	3 37 22	5 39 35	7 37 52	9 40 5	11 42 18	13 40 35	15 42 48	17 41 5
18	19 48 12	21 50 25	23 40 49	1 43 2	3 41 19	5 43 32	7 41 49	9 44 2	11 46 15	13 44 32	15 46 45	17 45 2
19	19 52 9	21 54 22	23 44 45	1 46 59	3 45 15	5 47 28	7 45 45	9 47 59	11 50 12	13 48 28	15 50 41	17 48 58
20	19 56 5	21 58 18	23 48 42	1 50 55	3 49 12	5 51 25	7 49 42	9 51 55	11 54 8	13 52 25	15 54 38	17 52 55
21	20 0 2	22 2 15	23 52 38	1 54 52	3 53 8	5 55 22	7 53 38	9 55 51	11 58 5	13 56 21	15 58 34	17 56 51
22	20 3 58	22 6 11	23 56 35	1 58 48	3 57 5	5 59 18	7 57 35	9 59 48	12 2 1	14 0 18	16 2 31	18 0 48
23	20 7 55	22 10 8	0 0 31	2 2 45	4 1 1	6 3 15	8 1 31	10 3 45	12 5 58	14 4 14	16 6 28	18 4 44
24	20 11 51	22 14 5	0 4 28	2 6 41	4 4 58	6 7 11	8 5 28	10 7 41	12 9 54	14 8 11	16 10 24	18 8 41
25	20 15 48	22 18 1	0 8 25	2 10 38	4 8 54	6 11 8	8 9 24	10 11 38	12 13 51	14 12 7	16 14 21	18 12 37
26	20 19 44	22 21 58	0 12 21	2 14 34	4 12 51	6 15 4	8 13 21	10 15 34	12 17 47	14 16 4	16 18 17	18 16 34
27	20 23 41	22 25 54	0 16 18	2 18 31	4 16 48	6 19 1	8 17 18	10 19 31	12 21 44	14 20 1	16 22 14	18 20 31
28	20 27 38	22 29 51	0 20 14	2 22 27	4 20 44	6 22 57	8 21 14	10 23 27	12 25 41	14 23 57	16 26 10	18 24 27
29	20 31 34		0 24 11	2 26 24	4 24 41	6 26 54	8 25 11	10 27 24	12 29 37	14 27 54	16 30 7	18 28 24
30	20 35 31		0 28 7	2 30 21	4 28 37	6 30 51	8 29 7	10 31 20	12 33 34	14 31 51	16 34 3	18 32 20
31	20 39 27		0 32 4		4 32 34		8 33 4	10 35 17		14 35 47		18 36 17

1948

	Jan.	Feb.	Mar.	April	May	June	July	Aug.	Sept.	Oct.	Nov.	Dec.
1	18 40 13	20 42 27	22 36 47	0 39 0	2 37 17	4 39 30	6 37 47	8 40 0	10 42 13	12 40 30	14 42 43	16 41 0
2	18 44 10	20 46 23	22 40 43	0 42 56	2 41 13	4 43 26	6 41 43	8 43 56	10 46 10	12 44 26	14 46 39	16 44 56
3	18 48 7	20 50 20	22 44 40	0 46 53	2 45 10	4 47 23	6 45 40	8 47 53	10 50 6	12 48 23	14 50 36	16 48 53
4	18 52 3	20 54 16	22 48 36	0 50 50	2 49 6	4 51 19	6 49 36	8 51 50	10 54 3	12 52 19	14 54 33	16 52 49
5	18 56 0	20 58 13	22 52 33	0 54 46	2 53 3	4 55 16	6 53 33	8 55 46	10 57 59	12 56 16	14 58 29	16 56 46
6	18 59 56	21 2 9	22 56 30	0 58 43	2 56 59	4 59 13	6 57 29	8 59 43	11 1 56	13 0 12	15 2 26	17 0 42
7	19 3 53	21 6 6	23 0 26	1 2 39	3 0 56	5 3 9	7 1 26	9 3 39	11 5 52	13 4 9	15 6 22	17 4 39
8	19 7 49	21 10 3	23 4 23	1 6 36	3 4 52	5 7 6	7 5 22	9 7 36	11 9 49	13 8 6	15 10 19	17 8 36
9	19 11 46	21 13 59	23 8 19	1 10 32	3 8 49	5 11 2	7 9 19	9 11 32	11 13 46	13 12 2	15 14 15	17 12 32
10	19 15 42	21 17 56	23 12 16	1 14 29	3 12 46	5 14 59	7 13 16	9 15 29	11 17 42	13 15 59	15 18 12	17 16 29
11	19 19 39	21 21 53	23 16 12	1 18 25	3 16 42	5 18 55	7 17 12	9 19 26	11 21 39	13 19 55	15 22 8	17 20 25
12	19 23 36	21 25 49	23 20 9	1 22 22	3 20 39	5 22 52	7 21 9	9 23 22	11 25 35	13 23 52	15 26 5	17 24 22
13	19 27 32	21 29 46	23 24 5	1 26 19	3 24 35	5 26 49	7 25 5	9 27 19	11 29 32	13 27 48	15 30 2	17 28 18
14	19 31 29	21 33 42	23 28 2	1 30 15	3 28 32	5 30 45	7 29 2	9 31 15	11 33 28	13 31 45	15 33 58	17 32 15
15	19 35 25	21 37 38	23 31 59	1 34 12	3 32 28	5 34 42	7 32 59	9 35 12	11 37 25	13 35 41	15 37 55	17 36 11
16	19 39 22	21 41 35	23 35 55	1 38 8	3 36 25	5 38 38	7 36 55	9 39 8	11 41 21	13 39 38	15 41 51	17 40 8
17	19 43 18	21 45 32	23 39 52	1 42 5	3 40 21	5 42 35	7 40 52	9 43 5	11 45 18	13 43 35	15 45 48	17 44 5
18	19 47 15	21 49 28	23 43 48	1 46 1	3 44 18	5 46 32	7 44 48	9 47 1	11 49 14	13 47 31	15 49 44	17 48 1
19	19 51 11	21 53 25	23 47 45	1 49 58	3 48 15	5 50 28	7 48 45	9 50 58	11 53 11	13 51 28	15 53 41	17 51 58
20	19 55 8	21 57 21	23 51 41	1 53 54	3 52 11	5 54 24	7 52 41	9 54 54	11 57 8	13 55 24	15 57 37	17 55 54
21	19 59 5	22 1 18	23 55 38	1 57 51	3 56 8	5 58 21	7 56 38	9 58 51	12 1 4	13 59 21	16 1 34	17 59 51
22	20 3 1	22 5 14	23 59 34	2 1 48	4 0 4	6 2 18	8 0 34	10 2 48	12 5 1	14 3 17	16 5 31	18 3 47
23	20 6 58	22 9 11	0 3 31	2 5 44	4 4 1	6 6 14	8 4 31	10 6 44	12 8 57	14 7 14	16 9 27	18 7 44
24	20 10 54	22 13 7	0 7 28	2 9 41	4 7 58	6 10 11	8 8 27	10 10 41	12 12 54	14 11 10	16 13 24	18 11 40
25	20 14 51	22 17 4	0 11 24	2 13 37	4 11 54	6 14 7	8 12 24	10 14 37	12 16 50	14 15 7	16 17 20	18 15 37
26	20 18 47	22 21 1	0 15 21	2 17 34	4 15 50	6 18 4	8 16 21	10 18 34	12 20 47	14 19 4	16 21 17	18 19 34
27	20 22 44	22 24 57	0 19 17	2 21 30	4 19 47	6 22 0	8 20 17	10 22 30	12 24 43	14 23 0	16 25 13	18 23 30
28	20 26 40	22 28 54	0 23 14	2 25 27	4 23 44	6 25 57	8 24 14	10 26 27	12 28 40	14 26 57	16 29 10	18 27 27
29	20 30 37	22 32 50	0 27 10	2 29 23	4 27 40	6 29 53	8 28 10	10 30 23	12 32 37	14 30 53	16 33 6	18 31 23
30	20 34 34		0 31 7	2 33 20	4 31 37	6 33 50	8 32 7	10 34 20	12 36 33	14 34 50	16 37 3	18 35 20
31	20 38 30		0 35 3		4 35 33		8 36 3	10 38 17		14 38 46		18 39 16

1949

	Jan.	Feb.	Mar.	April	May	June	July	Aug.	Sept.	Oct.	Nov.	Dec.
1	18 43 13	20 45 26	22 35 50	0 38 3	2 36 20	4 38 33	6 36 50	8 39 3	10 41 16	12 39 33	14 41 46	16 40 3
2	18 47 9	20 49 23	22 39 46	0 41 59	2 40 16	4 42 29	6 40 46	8 42 59	10 45 13	12 43 29	14 45 42	16 43 59
3	18 51 6	20 53 19	22 43 43	0 45 56	2 44 13	4 46 26	6 44 43	8 46 56	10 49 9	12 47 26	14 49 39	16 47 56
4	18 55 3	20 57 16	22 47 39	0 49 53	2 48 9	4 50 23	6 48 39	8 50 53	10 53 6	12 51 22	14 53 36	16 51 52
5	18 58 59	21 1 12	22 51 36	0 53 49	2 52 6	4 54 19	6 52 36	8 54 49	10 57 2	12 55 19	14 57 32	16 55 49
6	19 2 56	21 5 9	22 55 33	0 57 46	2 56 2	4 58 16	6 56 32	8 58 46	11 0 59	12 59 15	15 1 29	16 59 45
7	19 6 52	21 9 6	22 59 29	1 1 42	2 59 59	5 2 12	7 0 29	9 2 42	11 4 55	13 3 12	15 5 25	17 3 42
8	19 10 49	21 13 2	23 3 26	1 5 39	3 3 55	5 6 9	7 4 25	9 6 39	11 8 52	13 7 9	15 9 22	17 7 39
9	19 14 45	21 16 59	23 7 22	1 9 35	3 7 52	5 10 5	7 8 22	9 10 35	11 12 49	13 11 5	15 13 18	17 11 35
10	19 18 42	21 20 55	23 11 19	1 13 32	3 11 49	5 14 2	7 12 19	9 14 32	11 16 45	13 15 2	15 17 15	17 15 32
11	19 22 38	21 24 52	23 15 15	1 17 28	3 15 45	5 17 58	7 16 15	9 18 28	11 20 42	13 18 58	15 21 11	17 19 28
12	19 26 35	21 28 48	23 19 12	1 21 25	3 19 42	5 21 55	7 20 12	9 22 25	11 24 38	13 22 55	15 25 8	17 23 25
13	19 30 32	21 32 45	23 23 8	1 25 22	3 23 38	5 25 52	7 24 8	9 26 22	11 28 35	13 26 51	15 29 5	17 27 21
14	19 34 28	21 36 41	23 27 5	1 29 18	3 27 35	5 29 48	7 28 5	9 30 18	11 32 31	13 30 48	15 33 1	17 31 18
15	19 38 25	21 40 38	23 31 2	1 33 15	3 31 31	5 33 45	7 32 1	9 34 15	11 36 28	13 34 44	15 36 58	17 35 14
16	19 42 21	21 44 35	23 34 58	1 37 11	3 35 28	5 37 41	7 35 58	9 38 11	11 40 24	13 38 41	15 40 54	17 39 11
17	19 46 18	21 48 31	23 38 55	1 41 8	3 39 24	5 41 38	7 39 55	9 42 8	11 44 21	13 42 38	15 44 51	17 43 8
18	19 50 14	21 52 28	23 42 51	1 45 4	3 43 21	5 45 34	7 43 51	9 46 4	11 48 18	13 46 34	15 48 47	17 47 4
19	19 54 11	21 56 24	23 46 48	1 49 1	3 47 18	5 49 31	7 47 48	9 50 1	11 52 14	13 50 31	15 52 44	17 51 1
20	19 58 8	22 0 21	23 50 44	1 52 57	3 51 14	5 53 27	7 51 44	9 53 57	11 56 11	13 54 27	15 56 40	17 54 57
21	20 2 4	22 4 17	23 54 41	1 56 54	3 55 11	5 57 24	7 55 41	9 57 54	12 0 7	13 58 24	16 0 37	17 58 54
22	20 6 1	22 8 14	23 58 37	2 0 51	3 59 7	6 1 21	7 59 37	10 1 51	12 4 4	14 2 20	16 4 34	18 2 50
23	20 9 57	22 12 10	0 2 34	2 4 47	4 3 4	6 5 17	8 3 34	10 5 47	12 8 0	14 6 17	16 8 30	18 6 47
24	20 13 54	22 16 7	0 6 31	2 8 44	4 7 0	6 9 14	8 7 30	10 9 44	12 11 57	14 10 13	16 12 27	18 10 43
25	20 17 50	22 20 4	0 10 27	2 12 40	4 10 57	6 13 10	8 11 27	10 13 40	12 15 53	14 14 10	16 16 23	18 14 40
26	20 21 47	22 24 0	0 14 24	2 16 37	4 14 53	6 17 7	8 15 24	10 17 37	12 19 50	14 18 7	16 20 20	18 18 37
27	20 25 43	22 27 57	0 18 20	2 20 33	4 18 50	6 21 3	8 19 20	10 21 33	12 23 46	14 22 3	16 24 16	18 22 33
28	20 29 40	22 31 53	0 22 17	2 24 30	4 22 47	6 25 0	8 23 17	10 25 30	12 27 43	14 26 0	16 28 13	18 26 30
29	20 33 37		0 26 13	2 28 26	4 26 43	6 28 56	8 27 13	10 29 26	12 31 40	14 29 56	16 32 10	18 30 26
30	20 37 33		0 30 10	2 32 23	4 30 40	6 32 53	8 31 10	10 33 23	12 35 36	14 33 53	16 36 6	18 34 23
31	20 41 30		0 34 6		4 34 36		8 35 6	10 37 20		14 37 49		18 38 19

Jan.	Feb.	Mar.	April	May	June	July	Aug.	Sept.	Oct.	Nov.	Dec.	
18 42 16	20 44 29	22 34 53	0 37 6	2 35 23	4 37 36	6 35 53	8 38 6	10 40 19	12 38 36	14 40 49	16 39 6	1
18 46 12	20 48 26	22 38 49	0 41 3	2 39 19	4 41 32	6 39 49	8 42 2	10 44 16	12 42 32	14 44 46	16 43 2	2
18 50 9	20 52 22	22 42 46	0 44 59	2 43 16	4 45 29	6 43 46	8 45 59	10 48 12	12 46 29	14 48 42	16 46 59	3
18 54 6	20 56 19	22 46 42	0 48 56	2 47 12	4 49 26	6 47 42	8 49 56	10 52 9	12 50 25	14 52 39	16 50 55	4
18 58 2	21 0 15	22 50 39	0 52 52	2 51 9	4 53 22	6 51 39	8 53 52	10 56 5	12 54 22	14 56 35	16 54 52	5
19 1 59	21 4 12	22 54 36	0 56 49	2 55 5	4 57 19	6 55 35	8 57 49	11 0 2	12 58 19	15 0 32	16 58 48	6
19 5 55	21 8 9	22 58 32	1 0 45	2 59 2	5 1 15	6 59 32	9 1 45	11 3 58	13 2 15	15 4 28	17 2 45	7
19 9 52	21 12 5	23 2 29	1 4 42	3 2 59	5 5 12	7 3 29	9 5 42	11 7 55	13 6 12	15 8 25	17 6 42	8
19 13 48	21 16 2	23 6 25	1 8 38	3 6 55	5 9 8	7 7 25	9 9 38	11 11 52	13 10 8	15 12 21	17 10 38	9
19 17 45	21 19 58	23 10 22	1 12 35	3 10 52	5 13 5	7 11 22	9 13 35	11 15 48	13 14 5	15 16 18	17 14 35	10
19 21 42	21 23 55	23 14 18	1 16 32	3 14 48	5 17 1	7 15 18	9 17 31	11 19 45	13 18 1	15 20 14	17 18 31	11
19 25 38	21 27 51	23 18 15	1 20 28	3 18 45	5 20 58	7 19 15	9 21 28	11 23 41	13 21 58	15 24 11	17 22 28	12
19 29 35	21 31 48	23 22 11	1 24 25	3 22 41	5 24 55	7 23 11	9 25 25	11 27 38	13 25 54	15 28 8	17 26 24	13
19 33 31	21 35 44	23 26 8	1 28 21	3 26 38	5 28 51	7 27 8	9 29 21	11 31 34	13 29 51	15 32 4	17 30 21	14
19 37 28	21 39 41	23 30 5	1 32 18	3 30 34	5 32 48	7 31 4	9 33 18	11 35 31	13 33 48	15 36 1	17 34 18	15
19 41 24	21 43 38	23 34 1	1 36 14	3 34 31	5 36 44	7 35 1	9 37 14	11 39 27	13 37 44	15 39 57	17 38 14	16
19 45 21	21 47 34	23 37 58	1 40 11	3 38 27	5 40 41	7 38 58	9 41 11	11 43 24	13 41 41	15 43 54	17 42 11	17
19 49 17	21 51 31	23 41 54	1 44 7	3 42 24	5 44 37	7 42 54	9 45 7	11 47 21	13 45 37	15 47 50	17 46 7	18
19 53 14	21 55 27	23 45 51	1 48 4	3 46 21	5 48 34	7 46 51	9 49 4	11 51 17	13 49 34	15 51 47	17 50 4	19
19 57 11	21 59 24	23 49 47	1 52 0	3 50 17	5 52 30	7 50 47	9 53 0	11 55 14	13 53 30	15 55 44	17 54 0	20
20 1 7	22 3 20	23 53 44	1 55 57	3 54 14	5 56 27	7 54 44	9 56 57	11 59 10	13 57 27	15 59 40	17 57 57	21
20 5 4	22 7 17	23 57 40	1 59 54	3 58 10	6 0 24	7 58 40	10 0 54	12 3 7	14 1 23	16 3 37	18 1 53	22
20 9 0	22 11 13	0 1 37	2 3 50	4 2 7	6 4 20	8 2 37	10 4 50	12 7 3	14 5 20	16 7 33	18 5 50	23
20 12 57	22 15 10	0 5 34	2 7 47	4 6 3	6 8 17	8 6 33	10 8 47	12 11 0	14 9 17	16 11 30	18 9 47	24
20 16 53	22 19 7	0 9 30	2 11 43	4 10 0	6 12 13	8 10 30	10 12 43	12 14 56	14 13 13	16 15 26	18 13 43	25
20 20 50	22 23 3	0 13 27	2 15 40	4 13 57	6 16 10	8 14 27	10 16 40	12 18 53	14 17 10	16 19 23	18 17 40	26
20 24 46	22 27 0	0 17 23	2 19 36	4 17 53	6 20 6	8 18 23	10 20 36	12 22 50	14 21 6	16 23 19	18 21 36	27
20 28 43	22 30 56	0 21 20	2 23 33	4 21 50	6 24 3	8 22 20	10 24 33	12 26 46	14 25 3	16 27 16	18 25 33	28
20 32 40		0 25 16	2 27 29	4 25 46	6 28 0	8 26 16	10 28 29	12 30 43	14 28 59	16 31 13	18 29 29	29
20 36 36		0 29 13	2 31 26	4 29 43	6 31 56	8 30 13	10 32 26	12 34 39	14 32 56	16 35 9	18 33 26	30
20 40 33		0 33 9		4 33 39		8 34 9	10 36 23		14 36 52		18 37 22	31

Jan.	Feb.	Mar.	April	May	June	July	Aug.	Sept.	Oct.	Nov.	Dec.	
18 41 19	20 43 32	22 33 56	0 36 9	2 34 26	4 36 39	6 34 56	8 37 9	10 39 22	12 37 39	14 39 52	16 38 9	1
18 45 16	20 47 29	22 37 52	0 40 6	2 38 22	4 40 35	6 38 52	8 41 6	10 43 19	12 41 35	14 43 49	16 42 5	2
18 49 12	20 51 25	22 41 49	0 44 2	2 42 19	4 44 32	6 42 49	8 45 2	10 47 15	12 45 32	14 47 45	16 46 2	3
18 53 9	20 55 22	22 45 46	0 47 59	2 46 15	4 48 29	6 46 45	8 48 59	10 51 12	12 49 28	14 51 42	16 49 58	4
18 57 5	20 59 19	22 49 42	0 51 55	2 50 12	4 52 25	6 50 42	8 52 55	10 55 8	12 53 25	14 55 38	16 53 55	5
19 1 2	21 3 15	22 53 39	0 55 52	2 54 8	4 56 22	6 54 38	8 56 52	10 59 5	12 57 22	14 59 35	16 57 52	6
19 4 58	21 7 12	22 57 35	0 59 49	2 58 5	5 0 18	6 58 35	9 0 48	11 3 1	13 1 18	15 3 31	17 1 48	7
19 8 55	21 11 8	23 1 32	1 3 45	3 2 2	5 4 15	7 2 32	9 4 45	11 6 58	13 5 15	15 7 28	17 5 45	8
19 12 51	21 15 5	23 5 28	1 7 41	3 5 58	5 8 11	7 6 28	9 8 41	11 10 55	13 9 11	15 11 24	17 9 41	9
19 16 48	21 19 1	23 9 25	1 11 38	3 9 55	5 12 8	7 10 25	9 12 38	11 14 51	13 13 8	15 15 21	17 13 38	10
19 20 45	21 22 58	23 13 21	1 15 35	3 13 51	5 16 5	7 14 21	9 16 35	11 18 48	13 17 4	15 19 18	17 17 34	11
19 24 41	21 26 54	23 17 18	1 19 31	3 17 48	5 20 1	7 18 18	9 20 31	11 22 44	13 21 1	15 23 14	17 21 31	12
19 28 38	21 30 51	23 21 14	1 23 28	3 21 44	5 23 58	7 22 14	9 24 28	11 26 41	13 24 57	15 27 11	17 25 27	13
19 32 34	21 34 48	23 25 11	1 27 24	3 25 41	5 27 54	7 26 11	9 28 24	11 30 37	13 28 54	15 31 7	17 29 24	14
19 36 31	21 38 44	23 29 8	1 31 21	3 29 37	5 31 51	7 30 7	9 32 21	11 34 34	13 32 51	15 35 4	17 33 21	15
19 40 27	21 42 41	23 33 4	1 35 17	3 33 34	5 35 47	7 34 4	9 36 17	11 38 31	13 36 47	15 39 0	17 37 17	16
19 44 24	21 46 37	23 37 1	1 39 14	3 37 31	5 39 44	7 38 1	9 40 14	11 42 27	13 40 44	15 42 57	17 41 14	17
19 48 20	21 50 34	23 40 57	1 43 11	3 41 27	5 43 40	7 41 57	9 44 10	11 46 24	13 44 40	15 46 53	17 45 10	18
19 52 17	21 54 30	23 44 54	1 47 7	3 45 24	5 47 37	7 45 54	9 48 7	11 50 20	13 48 37	15 50 50	17 49 7	19
19 56 14	21 58 27	23 48 50	1 51 4	3 49 20	5 51 34	7 49 50	9 52 4	11 54 17	13 52 33	15 54 47	17 53 3	20
20 0 10	22 2 23	23 52 47	1 55 0	3 53 17	5 55 30	7 53 47	9 56 0	11 58 13	13 56 30	15 58 43	17 57 0	21
20 4 7	22 6 20	23 56 43	1 58 57	3 57 13	5 59 27	7 57 43	9 59 57	12 2 10	14 0 26	16 2 40	18 0 56	22
20 8 3	22 10 17	0 0 40	2 2 53	4 1 10	6 3 23	8 1 40	10 3 53	12 6 6	14 4 23	16 6 36	18 4 53	23
20 12 0	22 14 13	0 4 37	2 6 50	4 5 6	6 7 20	8 5 37	10 7 50	12 10 3	14 8 20	16 10 33	18 8 50	24
20 15 56	22 18 10	0 8 33	2 10 46	4 9 3	6 11 16	8 9 33	10 11 46	12 13 59	14 12 16	16 14 29	18 12 46	25
20 19 53	22 22 6	0 12 30	2 14 43	4 13 0	6 15 13	8 13 30	10 15 43	12 17 56	14 16 13	16 18 26	18 16 43	26
20 23 50	22 26 3	0 16 26	2 18 39	4 16 56	6 19 9	8 17 26	10 19 39	12 21 53	14 20 9	16 22 22	18 20 39	27
20 27 46	22 29 59	0 20 23	2 22 36	4 20 53	6 23 6	8 21 23	10 23 36	12 25 49	14 24 6	16 26 19	18 24 36	28
20 31 43		0 24 19	2 26 33	4 24 49	6 27 3	8 25 19	10 27 33	12 29 46	14 28 2	16 30 16	18 28 32	29
20 35 39		0 28 16	2 30 29	4 28 46	6 30 59	8 29 16	10 31 29	12 33 42	14 31 59	16 34 12	18 32 29	30
20 39 36		0 32 12		4 32 42		8 33 12	10 35 26		14 35 55		18 36 25	31

Jan.	Feb.	Mar.	April	May	June	July	Aug.	Sept.	Oct.	Nov.	Dec.	
18 40 22	20 42 35	22 36 57	0 39 9	2 37 25	4 39 39	6 37 55	8 40 9	10 42 22	12 40 38	14 42 52	16 41 8	1
18 44 19	20 46 32	22 40 52	0 43 5	2 41 22	4 43 35	6 41 52	8 44 5	10 46 18	12 44 35	14 46 48	16 45 5	2
18 48 15	20 50 28	22 44 49	0 47 2	2 45 18	4 47 32	6 45 48	8 48 2	10 50 15	12 48 31	14 50 45	16 49 1	3
18 52 12	20 54 25	22 48 45	0 50 58	2 49 15	4 51 28	6 49 45	8 51 58	10 54 11	12 52 28	14 54 41	16 52 58	4
18 56 8	20 58 22	22 52 42	0 54 55	2 53 11	4 55 25	6 53 41	8 55 55	10 58 8	12 56 25	14 58 38	16 56 55	5
19 0 5	21 2 18	22 56 38	0 58 51	2 57 8	4 59 21	6 57 38	8 59 51	11 2 5	13 0 21	15 2 34	17 0 51	6
19 4 1	21 6 15	23 0 35	1 2 48	3 1 5	5 3 18	7 1 35	9 3 48	11 6 1	13 4 18	15 6 31	17 4 48	7
19 7 58	21 10 11	23 4 31	1 6 44	3 5 1	5 7 14	7 5 31	9 7 44	11 9 58	13 8 14	15 10 27	17 8 44	8
19 11 54	21 14 8	23 8 28	1 10 41	3 8 58	5 11 11	7 9 28	9 11 41	11 13 54	13 12 11	15 14 24	17 12 41	9
19 15 51	21 18 4	23 12 24	1 14 38	3 12 54	5 15 8	7 13 24	9 15 38	11 17 51	13 16 7	15 18 21	17 16 37	10
19 19 48	21 22 1	23 16 21	1 18 34	3 16 51	5 19 4	7 17 21	9 19 34	11 21 47	13 20 4	15 22 17	17 20 34	11
19 23 44	21 25 57	23 20 18	1 22 31	3 20 47	5 23 1	7 21 17	9 23 31	11 25 44	13 24 0	15 26 14	17 24 30	12
19 27 41	21 29 54	23 24 14	1 26 27	3 24 44	5 26 57	7 25 14	9 27 27	11 29 40	13 27 57	15 30 10	17 28 27	13
19 31 37	21 33 51	23 28 11	1 30 24	3 28 40	5 30 54	7 29 11	9 31 24	11 33 37	13 31 54	15 34 7	17 32 24	14
19 35 34	21 37 47	23 32 7	1 34 20	3 32 37	5 34 50	7 33 7	9 35 20	11 37 34	13 35 50	15 38 3	17 36 20	15
19 39 30	21 41 44	23 36 4	1 38 17	3 36 34	5 38 47	7 37 4	9 39 17	11 41 30	13 39 47	15 42 0	17 40 17	16
19 43 27	21 45 40	23 40 0	1 42 13	3 40 30	5 42 43	7 41 0	9 43 13	11 45 27	13 43 43	15 45 56	17 44 13	17
19 47 24	21 49 37	23 43 57	1 46 10	3 44 27	5 46 40	7 44 57	9 47 10	11 49 23	13 47 40	15 49 53	17 48 10	18
19 51 20	21 53 33	23 47 53	1 50 7	3 48 23	5 50 37	7 48 53	9 51 7	11 53 20	13 51 36	15 53 50	17 52 6	19
19 55 17	21 57 30	23 51 50	1 54 3	3 52 20	5 54 33	7 52 50	9 55 3	11 57 16	13 55 33	15 57 46	17 56 3	20
19 59 13	22 1 26	23 55 47	1 58 0	3 56 16	5 58 30	7 56 46	9 59 0	12 1 13	13 59 29	16 1 43	17 59 59	21
20 3 10	22 5 23	23 59 43	2 1 56	4 0 13	6 2 26	8 0 43	10 2 56	12 5 9	14 3 26	16 5 39	18 3 56	22
20 7 6	22 9 20	0 3 40	2 5 53	4 4 9	6 6 23	8 4 40	10 6 53	12 9 6	14 7 23	16 9 36	18 7 53	23
20 11 3	22 13 16	0 7 36	2 9 49	4 8 6	6 10 19	8 8 36	10 10 49	12 13 2	14 11 19	16 13 32	18 11 49	24
20 14 59	22 17 13	0 11 33	2 13 46	4 12 3	6 14 16	8 12 33	10 14 46	12 16 59	14 15 16	16 17 29	18 15 46	25
20 18 56	22 21 9	0 15 29	2 17 42	4 15 59	6 18 12	8 16 29	10 18 42	12 20 56	14 19 12	16 21 25	18 19 42	26
20 22 53	22 25 6	0 19 26	2 21 39	4 19 56	6 22 9	8 20 26	10 22 39	12 24 52	14 23 9	16 25 22	18 23 39	27
20 26 49	22 29 2	0 23 22	2 25 36	4 23 52	6 26 6	8 24 22	10 26 36	12 28 49	14 27 5	16 29 19	18 27 35	28
20 30 46	22 32 59	0 27 19	2 29 32	4 27 49	6 30 2	8 28 19	10 30 32	12 32 45	14 31 2	16 33 15	18 31 32	29
20 34 42		0 31 15	2 33 29	4 31 45	6 33 59	8 32 15	10 34 29	12 36 42	14 34 58	16 37 12	18 35 28	30
20 38 39		0 35 12		4 35 42		8 36 12	10 38 25		14 38 55		18 39 25	31

1953

	Jan.	Feb.	Mar.	April	May	June	July	Aug.	Sept.	Oct.	Nov.	Dec.
1	18 43 22	20 45 35	22 35 58	0 38 12	2 36 28	4 38 41	6 36 58	8 39 11	10 41 25	12 39 41	14 41 55	16 40 11
2	18 47 18	20 49 31	22 39 55	0 42 8	2 40 25	4 42 38	6 40 55	8 43 8	10 45 21	12 43 38	14 45 51	16 44 8
3	18 51 15	20 53 28	22 43 52	0 46 5	2 44 21	4 46 35	6 44 51	8 47 5	10 49 18	12 47 34	14 49 48	16 48 4
4	18 55 11	20 57 25	22 47 48	0 50 1	2 48 18	4 50 31	6 48 48	8 51 1	10 53 14	12 51 31	14 53 44	16 52 1
5	18 59 8	21 1 21	22 51 45	0 53 58	2 52 14	4 54 28	6 52 44	8 54 58	10 57 11	12 55 28	14 57 41	16 55 57
6	19 3 4	21 5 18	22 55 41	0 57 54	2 56 11	4 58 24	6 56 41	8 58 54	11 1 7	12 59 24	15 1 37	16 59 54
7	19 7 1	21 9 14	22 59 38	1 1 51	3 0 8	5 2 21	7 0 38	9 2 51	11 5 4	13 3 21	15 5 34	17 3 51
8	19 10 57	21 13 11	23 3 34	1 5 47	3 4 4	5 6 17	7 4 34	9 6 47	11 9 1	13 7 17	15 9 30	17 7 47
9	19 14 54	21 17 7	23 7 31	1 9 44	3 8 1	5 10 14	7 8 31	9 10 44	11 12 57	13 11 14	15 13 27	17 11 44
10	19 18 51	21 21 4	23 11 27	1 13 41	3 11 57	5 14 10	7 12 27	9 14 41	11 16 54	13 15 10	15 17 23	17 15 40
11	19 22 47	21 25 0	23 15 24	1 17 37	3 15 54	5 18 7	7 16 24	9 18 37	11 20 50	13 19 7	15 21 20	17 19 37
12	19 26 44	21 28 57	23 19 21	1 21 34	3 19 50	5 22 4	7 20 20	9 22 34	11 24 47	13 23 3	15 25 17	17 23 33
13	19 30 40	21 32 54	23 23 17	1 25 30	3 23 47	5 26 0	7 24 17	9 26 30	11 28 43	13 27 0	15 29 13	17 27 30
14	19 34 37	21 36 50	23 27 14	1 29 27	3 27 43	5 29 57	7 28 13	9 30 27	11 32 40	13 30 56	15 33 10	17 31 26
15	19 38 33	21 40 47	23 31 10	1 33 23	3 31 40	5 33 53	7 32 10	9 34 23	11 36 36	13 34 53	15 37 6	17 35 23
16	19 42 30	21 44 43	23 35 7	1 37 20	3 35 37	5 37 50	7 36 7	9 38 20	11 40 33	13 38 50	15 41 3	17 39 20
17	19 46 27	21 48 40	23 39 3	1 41 16	3 39 33	5 41 46	7 40 3	9 42 16	11 44 30	13 42 46	15 44 59	17 43 16
18	19 50 23	21 52 36	23 43 0	1 45 13	3 43 30	5 45 43	7 44 0	9 46 13	11 48 26	13 46 43	15 48 56	17 47 13
19	19 54 20	21 56 33	23 46 56	1 49 10	3 47 26	5 49 40	7 47 56	9 50 9	11 52 23	13 50 39	15 52 52	17 51 9
20	19 58 16	22 0 29	23 50 53	1 53 6	3 51 23	5 53 36	7 51 53	9 54 6	11 56 19	13 54 36	15 56 49	17 55 6
21	20 2 13	22 4 26	23 54 49	1 57 3	3 55 19	5 57 33	7 55 49	9 58 3	12 0 16	13 58 32	16 0 46	17 59 2
22	20 6 9	22 8 23	23 58 46	2 0 59	3 59 16	6 1 29	7 59 46	10 1 59	12 4 12	14 2 29	16 4 42	18 2 59
23	20 10 6	22 12 19	0 2 43	2 4 56	4 3 12	6 5 26	8 3 43	10 5 56	12 8 9	14 6 25	16 8 39	18 6 55
24	20 14 2	22 16 16	0 6 39	2 8 52	4 7 9	6 9 22	8 7 39	10 9 52	12 12 5	14 10 22	16 12 35	18 10 52
25	20 17 59	22 20 12	0 10 36	2 12 49	4 11 6	6 13 19	8 11 36	10 13 49	12 16 2	14 14 19	16 16 32	18 14 49
26	20 21 56	22 24 9	0 14 32	2 16 45	4 15 2	6 17 15	8 15 32	10 17 45	12 19 59	14 18 15	16 20 28	18 18 45
27	20 25 52	22 28 5	0 18 29	2 20 42	4 18 59	6 21 12	8 19 29	10 21 42	12 23 55	14 22 12	16 24 25	18 22 42
28	20 29 49	22 32 2	0 22 25	2 24 39	4 22 55	6 25 9	8 23 25	10 25 38	12 27 52	14 26 8	16 28 22	18 26 38
29	20 33 45		0 26 22	2 28 35	4 26 52	6 29 5	8 27 22	10 29 35	12 31 48	14 30 5	16 32 18	18 30 35
30	20 37 42		0 30 18	2 32 32	4 30 48	6 33 2	8 31 18	10 33 32	12 35 45	14 34 1	16 36 15	18 34 31
31	20 41 38		0 34 15		4 34 45		8 35 15	10 37 28		14 37 58		18 38 28

1954

	Jan.	Feb.	Mar.	April	May	June	July	Aug.	Sept.	Oct.	Nov.	Dec.
1	18 42 24	20 44 38	22 35 1	0 37 14	2 35 31	4 37 44	6 36 1	8 38 14	10 40 28	12 38 44	14 40 57	16 39 14
2	18 46 21	20 48 34	22 38 58	0 41 11	2 39 28	4 41 41	6 39 58	8 42 11	10 44 24	12 42 41	14 44 54	16 43 11
3	18 50 18	20 52 31	22 42 54	0 45 8	2 43 24	4 45 37	6 43 54	8 46 7	10 48 21	12 46 37	14 48 50	16 47 7
4	18 54 14	20 56 27	22 46 51	0 49 4	2 47 21	4 49 34	6 47 51	8 50 4	10 52 17	12 50 34	14 52 47	16 51 4
5	18 58 11	21 0 24	22 50 48	0 53 1	2 51 17	4 53 31	6 51 47	8 54 1	10 56 14	12 54 30	14 56 44	16 55 0
6	19 2 7	21 4 21	22 54 44	0 56 57	2 55 14	4 57 27	6 55 44	8 57 57	11 0 10	12 58 27	15 0 40	16 58 57
7	19 6 4	21 8 17	22 58 41	1 0 54	2 59 10	5 1 24	6 59 40	9 1 54	11 4 7	13 2 23	15 4 37	17 2 53
8	19 10 0	21 12 14	23 2 37	1 4 50	3 3 7	5 5 20	7 3 37	9 5 50	11 8 3	13 6 20	15 8 33	17 6 50
9	19 13 57	21 16 10	23 6 34	1 8 47	3 7 4	5 9 17	7 7 34	9 9 47	11 12 0	13 10 17	15 12 30	17 10 46
10	19 17 54	21 20 7	23 10 30	1 12 43	3 11 0	5 13 13	7 11 30	9 13 43	11 15 57	13 14 13	15 16 26	17 14 43
11	19 21 50	21 24 3	23 14 27	1 16 40	3 14 57	5 17 10	7 15 27	9 17 40	11 19 53	13 18 10	15 20 23	17 18 40
12	19 25 47	21 28 0	23 18 23	1 20 37	3 18 53	5 21 6	7 19 23	9 21 36	11 23 50	13 22 6	15 24 19	17 22 36
13	19 29 43	21 31 56	23 22 20	1 24 33	3 22 50	5 25 3	7 23 20	9 25 33	11 27 46	13 26 3	15 28 16	17 26 33
14	19 33 40	21 35 53	23 26 17	1 28 30	3 26 46	5 29 0	7 27 16	9 29 30	11 31 43	13 29 59	15 32 13	17 30 29
15	19 37 36	21 39 50	23 30 13	1 32 26	3 30 43	5 32 56	7 31 13	9 33 26	11 35 39	13 33 56	15 36 9	17 34 26
16	19 41 33	21 43 46	23 34 10	1 36 23	3 34 39	5 36 53	7 35 9	9 37 23	11 39 36	13 37 52	15 40 6	17 38 22
17	10 45 29	21 47 43	23 38 6	1 40 19	3 38 36	5 40 49	7 39 6	9 41 19	11 43 32	13 41 49	15 44 2	17 42 19
18	19 49 26	21 51 39	23 42 3	1 44 16	3 42 33	5 44 46	7 43 3	9 45 16	11 47 29	13 45 46	15 47 59	17 46 15
19	19 53 23	21 55 36	23 45 59	1 48 12	3 46 29	5 48 42	7 46 59	9 49 12	11 51 26	13 49 42	15 51 55	17 50 12
20	19 57 19	21 59 32	23 49 56	1 52 9	3 50 26	5 52 39	7 50 56	9 53 9	11 55 22	13 53 39	15 55 52	17 54 9
21	20 1 16	22 3 29	23 53 52	1 56 6	3 54 22	5 56 35	7 54 52	9 57 5	11 59 19	13 57 35	15 59 48	17 58 5
22	20 5 12	22 7 25	23 57 49	2 0 2	3 58 19	6 0 32	7 58 49	10 1 2	12 3 15	14 1 32	16 3 45	18 2 2
23	20 9 9	22 11 22	0 1 45	2 3 59	4 2 15	6 4 29	8 2 45	10 4 59	12 7 12	14 5 28	16 7 42	18 5 58
24	20 13 5	22 15 19	0 5 42	2 7 55	4 6 12	6 8 25	8 6 42	10 8 55	12 11 8	14 9 25	16 11 38	18 9 55
25	20 17 2	22 19 15	0 9 39	2 11 52	4 10 8	6 12 22	8 10 38	10 12 52	12 15 5	14 13 21	16 15 35	18 13 51
26	20 20 58	22 23 12	0 13 35	2 15 48	4 14 5	6 16 18	8 14 35	10 16 48	12 19 1	14 17 18	16 19 31	18 17 47
27	20 24 55	22 27 8	0 17 32	2 19 45	4 18 2	6 20 15	8 18 32	10 20 45	12 22 58	14 21 15	16 23 28	18 21 45
28	20 28 52	22 31 5	0 21 28	2 23 41	4 21 58	6 24 11	8 22 28	10 24 41	12 26 54	14 25 11	16 27 24	18 25 41
29	20 32 48		0 25 25	2 27 38	4 25 55	6 28 8	8 26 25	10 28 38	12 30 51	14 29 8	16 31 21	18 29 38
30	20 36 45		0 29 21	2 31 35	4 29 51	6 32 5	8 30 21	10 32 34	12 34 48	14 33 4	16 35 17	18 33 34
31	20 40 41		0 33 18		4 33 48		8 34 18	10 36 31		14 37 1		18 37 31

1955

	Jan.	Feb.	Mar.	April	May	June	July	Aug.	Sept.	Oct.	Nov.	Dec.
1	18 41 27	20 43 41	22 34 4	0 36 17	2 34 34	4 36 47	6 35 4	8 37 17	10 39 30	12 37 47	14 40 0	16 38 17
2	18 45 24	20 47 37	22 38 1	0 40 14	2 38 30	4 40 44	6 39 0	8 41 14	10 43 27	12 41 43	14 43 57	16 42 13
3	18 49 20	20 51 34	22 41 57	0 44 10	2 42 27	4 44 40	6 42 57	8 45 10	10 47 23	12 45 40	14 47 53	16 46 10
4	18 53 17	20 55 30	22 45 54	0 48 7	2 46 24	4 48 37	6 46 53	8 49 7	10 51 20	12 49 36	14 51 50	16 50 6
5	18 57 14	20 59 27	22 49 50	0 52 3	2 50 20	4 52 33	6 50 50	8 53 3	10 55 16	12 53 33	14 55 46	16 54 3
6	19 1 10	21 3 23	22 53 47	0 56 0	2 54 17	4 56 30	6 54 47	8 57 0	10 59 13	12 57 30	14 59 43	16 57 59
7	19 5 7	21 7 20	22 57 43	0 59 57	2 58 13	5 0 26	6 58 43	9 0 56	11 3 10	13 1 26	15 3 39	17 1 56
8	19 9 3	21 11 16	23 1 40	1 3 53	3 2 10	5 4 23	7 2 40	9 4 53	11 7 6	13 5 23	15 7 36	17 5 53
9	19 13 0	21 15 13	23 5 37	1 7 50	3 6 6	5 8 20	7 6 36	9 8 50	11 11 3	13 9 19	15 11 32	17 9 49
10	19 16 56	21 19 10	23 9 33	1 11 46	3 10 3	5 12 16	7 10 33	9 12 46	11 14 59	13 13 16	15 15 29	17 13 46
11	19 20 53	21 23 6	23 13 30	1 15 43	3 13 59	5 16 13	7 14 29	9 16 43	11 18 56	13 17 12	15 19 26	17 17 42
12	19 24 49	21 27 3	23 17 26	1 19 39	3 17 56	5 20 9	7 18 26	9 20 39	11 22 52	13 21 9	15 23 22	17 21 39
13	19 28 46	21 30 59	23 21 23	1 23 36	3 21 53	5 24 6	7 22 22	9 24 36	11 26 49	13 25 5	15 27 19	17 25 35
14	19 32 43	21 34 56	23 25 19	1 27 32	3 25 49	5 28 2	7 26 19	9 28 32	11 30 45	13 29 2	15 31 15	17 29 32
15	19 36 39	21 38 52	23 29 16	1 31 29	3 29 46	5 31 59	7 30 16	9 32 29	11 34 42	13 32 59	15 35 12	17 33 29
16	19 40 36	21 42 49	23 33 12	1 35 26	3 33 42	5 35 55	7 34 12	9 36 25	11 38 39	13 36 55	15 39 8	17 37 25
17	19 44 32	21 46 45	23 37 9	1 39 22	3 37 39	5 39 52	7 38 9	9 40 22	11 42 35	13 40 52	15 43 5	17 41 22
18	19 48 29	21 50 42	23 41 6	1 43 19	3 41 35	5 43 49	7 42 5	9 44 19	11 46 32	13 44 48	15 47 1	17 45 18
19	19 52 25	21 54 39	23 45 2	1 47 15	3 45 32	5 47 45	7 46 2	9 48 15	11 50 28	13 48 45	15 50 58	17 49 15
20	19 56 22	21 58 35	23 48 59	1 51 12	3 49 28	5 51 42	7 49 58	9 52 12	11 54 25	13 52 41	15 54 55	17 53 11
21	20 0 18	22 2 32	23 52 55	1 55 8	3 53 25	5 55 38	7 53 55	9 56 8	11 58 21	13 56 38	15 58 51	17 57 8
22	20 4 15	22 6 28	23 56 52	1 59 5	3 57 22	5 59 35	7 57 52	10 0 5	12 2 18	14 0 34	16 2 48	18 1 4
23	20 8 12	22 10 25	0 0 48	2 3 1	4 1 18	6 3 31	8 1 48	10 4 1	12 6 14	14 4 31	16 6 44	18 5 1
24	20 12 8	22 14 21	0 4 45	2 6 58	4 5 15	6 7 28	8 5 45	10 7 58	12 10 11	14 8 28	16 10 41	18 8 58
25	20 16 5	22 18 18	0 8 41	2 10 55	4 9 11	6 11 24	8 9 41	10 11 54	12 14 8	14 12 24	16 14 37	18 12 54
26	20 20 1	22 22 14	0 12 38	2 14 51	4 13 8	6 15 21	8 13 38	10 15 51	12 18 4	14 16 21	16 18 34	18 16 51
27	20 23 58	22 26 11	0 16 34	2 18 48	4 17 4	6 19 18	8 17 34	10 19 48	12 22 1	14 20 17	16 22 30	18 20 47
28	20 27 54	22 30 8	0 20 31	2 22 44	4 21 1	6 23 14	8 21 31	10 23 44	12 25 57	14 24 14	16 26 27	18 24 44
29	20 31 51		0 24 28	2 26 41	4 24 57	6 27 11	8 25 27	10 27 41	12 29 54	14 28 10	16 30 24	18 28 40
30	20 35 47		0 28 24	2 30 37	4 28 54	6 31 7	8 29 24	10 31 37	12 33 50	14 32 7	16 34 20	18 32 37
31	20 39 44		0 32 21		4 32 51		8 33 21	10 35 34		41 36 3		18 36 33

1956

	Jan.	Feb.	Mar.	April	May	June	July	Aug.	Sept.	Oct.	Nov.	Dec.
1	18 40 30	20 42 43	22 37 3	0 39 16	2 37 33	4 39 46	6 38 3	8 40 16	10 42 29	12 40 46	14 42 59	16 41 16
2	18 44 27	20 46 40	22 41 0	0 43 13	2 41 30	4 43 43	6 42 0	8 44 13	10 46 26	12 44 43	14 46 56	16 45 12
3	18 48 23	20 50 36	22 44 56	0 47 10	2 45 26	4 47 39	6 45 56	8 48 9	10 50 23	12 48 39	14 50 52	16 49 9
4	18 52 20	20 54 33	22 48 53	0 51 6	2 49 23	4 51 36	6 49 53	8 52 6	10 54 19	12 52 36	14 54 49	16 53 6
5	18 56 16	20 58 29	22 52 50	0 55 3	2 53 19	4 55 33	6 53 49	8 56 2	10 58 16	12 56 32	14 58 45	16 57 2
6	19 0 13	21 2 26	22 56 46	0 58 59	2 57 16	4 59 29	6 57 46	8 59 59	11 2 12	13 0 29	15 2 42	17 0 59
7	19 4 9	21 6 23	23 0 43	1 2 56	3 1 12	5 3 26	7 1 42	9 3 56	11 6 9	13 4 25	15 6 38	17 4 55
8	19 8 6	21 10 19	23 4 39	1 6 52	3 5 9	5 7 22	7 5 39	9 7 52	11 10 5	13 8 22	15 10 35	17 8 52
9	19 12 2	21 14 16	23 8 36	1 10 49	3 9 5	5 11 19	7 9 35	9 11 49	11 14 2	13 12 18	15 14 32	17 12 48
10	19 15 59	21 18 12	23 12 32	1 14 45	3 13 2	5 15 15	7 13 32	9 15 45	11 17 58	13 16 15	15 18 28	17 16 45
11	19 19 56	21 22 9	23 16 29	1 18 42	3 16 59	5 19 12	7 17 29	9 19 42	11 21 55	13 20 12	15 22 25	17 20 41
12	19 23 52	21 26 5	23 20 25	1 22 39	3 20 55	5 23 8	7 21 25	9 23 38	11 25 52	13 24 8	15 26 21	17 24 38
13	19 27 49	21 30 2	23 24 22	1 26 35	3 24 52	5 27 5	7 25 22	9 27 35	11 29 48	13 28 5	15 30 18	17 28 35
14	19 31 45	21 33 58	23 28 19	1 30 32	3 28 48	5 31 2	7 29 18	9 31 31	11 33 45	13 32 1	15 34 14	17 32 31
15	19 35 42	21 37 55	23 32 15	1 34 28	3 32 45	5 34 58	7 33 15	9 35 28	11 37 41	13 35 58	15 38 11	17 36 28
16	19 39 38	21 41 52	23 36 12	1 38 25	3 36 41	5 38 55	7 37 11	9 39 25	11 41 38	13 39 54	15 42 7	17 40 24
17	19 43 35	21 45 48	23 40 8	1 42 21	3 40 38	5 42 51	7 41 8	9 43 21	11 45 34	13 43 51	15 46 4	17 44 21
18	19 47 31	21 49 45	23 44 5	1 46 18	3 44 35	5 46 48	7 45 4	9 47 18	11 49 31	13 47 47	15 50 1	17 48 17
19	19 51 28	21 53 41	23 48 1	1 50 14	3 48 31	5 50 44	7 49 1	9 51 14	11 53 27	13 51 44	15 53 57	17 52 14
20	19 55 25	21 57 38	23 51 58	1 54 11	3 52 28	5 54 41	7 52 58	9 55 11	11 57 24	13 55 40	15 57 54	17 56 10
21	19 59 21	22 1 34	23 55 54	1 58 8	3 56 24	5 58 37	7 56 54	9 59 7	12 1 20	13 59 37	16 1 50	18 0 7
22	20 3 18	22 5 31	23 59 51	2 2 4	4 0 21	6 2 34	8 0 51	10 3 4	12 5 17	14 3 34	16 5 47	18 4 4
23	20 7 14	22 9 27	0 3 47	2 6 1	4 4 17	6 6 31	8 4 47	10 7 0	12 9 14	14 7 30	16 9 43	18 8 0
24	20 11 11	22 13 24	0 7 44	2 9 57	4 8 14	6 10 27	8 8 44	10 10 57	12 13 10	14 11 27	16 13 40	18 11 57
25	20 15 7	22 17 21	0 11 41	2 13 54	4 12 10	6 14 24	8 12 40	10 14 54	12 17 7	14 15 23	16 17 36	18 15 53
26	20 19 4	22 21 17	0 15 37	2 17 50	4 16 7	6 18 20	8 16 37	10 18 50	12 21 3	14 19 20	16 21 33	18 19 50
27	20 23 0	22 25 14	0 19 34	2 21 47	4 20 4	6 22 17	8 20 33	10 22 47	12 25 0	14 23 16	16 25 30	18 23 46
28	20 26 57	22 29 10	0 23 30	2 25 43	4 24 0	6 26 13	8 24 30	10 26 43	12 28 56	14 27 13	16 29 26	18 27 43
29	20 30 54	22 33 7	0 27 27	2 29 40	4 27 57	6 30 10	8 28 27	10 30 40	12 32 53	14 31 10	16 33 23	18 31 39
30	20 34 50		0 31 23	2 33 37	4 31 53	6 34 6	8 32 23	10 34 36	12 36 49	14 35 6	16 37 19	18 35 36
31	20 38 47		0 35 20		4 35 50		8 36 20	10 38 33		14 39 3		18 39 33

1957

	Jan.	Feb.	Mar.	April	May	June	July	Aug.	Sept.	Oct.	Nov.	Dec.
1	18 43 29	20 45 42	22 36 6	0 38 19	2 36 36	4 38 49	6 37 6	8 39 19	10 41 32	12 39 49	14 42 2	16 40 18
2	18 47 26	20 49 39	22 40 2	0 42 16	2 40 32	4 42 45	6 41 2	8 43 15	10 45 28	12 43 45	14 45 58	16 44 15
3	18 51 22	20 53 35	22 43 59	0 46 12	2 44 29	4 46 42	6 44 59	8 47 12	10 49 25	12 47 42	14 49 55	16 48 11
4	18 55 19	20 57 32	22 47 56	0 50 9	2 48 25	4 50 38	6 48 55	8 51 8	10 53 22	12 51 38	14 53 51	16 52 8
5	18 59 15	21 1 29	22 51 52	0 54 5	2 52 22	4 54 35	6 52 52	8 55 5	10 57 18	12 55 35	14 57 48	16 56 5
6	19 3 12	21 5 25	22 55 49	0 58 2	2 56 18	4 58 32	6 56 48	8 59 2	11 1 15	12 59 31	15 1 44	17 0 1
7	19 7 8	21 9 22	22 59 45	1 1 58	3 0 15	5 2 28	7 0 45	9 2 58	11 5 11	13 3 28	15 5 41	17 3 58
8	19 11 5	21 13 18	23 3 42	1 5 55	3 4 11	5 6 25	7 4 41	9 6 55	11 9 8	13 7 24	15 9 38	17 7 54
9	19 15 2	21 17 15	23 7 38	1 9 51	3 8 8	5 10 21	7 8 38	9 10 51	11 13 4	13 11 21	15 13 34	17 11 51
10	19 18 58	21 21 11	23 11 35	1 13 48	3 12 5	5 14 18	7 12 35	9 14 48	11 17 1	13 15 17	15 17 31	17 15 47
11	19 22 55	21 25 8	23 15 31	1 17 45	3 16 1	5 18 14	7 16 31	9 18 44	11 20 57	13 19 14	15 21 27	17 19 44
12	19 26 51	21 29 4	23 19 28	1 21 41	3 19 58	5 22 11	7 20 28	9 22 41	11 24 54	13 23 11	15 25 24	17 23 40
13	19 30 48	21 33 1	23 23 25	1 25 38	3 23 54	5 26 8	7 24 24	9 26 37	11 28 51	13 27 7	15 29 20	17 27 37
14	19 34 44	21 36 58	23 27 21	1 29 34	3 27 51	5 30 4	7 28 21	9 30 34	11 32 47	13 31 4	15 33 17	17 31 34
15	19 38 41	21 40 54	23 31 18	1 33 31	3 31 47	5 34 1	7 32 17	9 34 31	11 36 44	13 35 0	15 37 13	17 35 30
16	19 42 37	21 44 51	23 35 14	1 37 27	3 35 44	5 37 57	7 36 14	9 38 27	11 40 40	13 38 57	15 41 10	17 39 27
17	19 46 34	21 48 47	23 39 11	1 41 24	3 39 40	5 41 54	7 40 10	9 42 24	11 44 37	13 42 53	15 45 7	17 43 23
18	19 50 31	21 52 44	23 43 7	1 45 20	3 43 37	5 45 50	7 44 7	9 46 20	11 48 33	13 46 50	15 49 3	17 47 20
19	19 54 27	21 56 40	23 47 4	1 49 17	3 47 34	5 49 47	7 48 4	9 50 17	11 52 30	13 50 46	15 53 0	17 51 16
20	19 58 24	22 0 37	23 51 0	1 53 14	3 51 30	5 53 43	7 52 0	9 54 13	11 56 26	13 54 43	15 56 56	17 55 13
21	20 2 20	22 4 33	23 54 57	1 57 10	3 55 27	5 57 40	7 55 57	9 58 10	12 0 23	13 58 40	16 0 53	17 59 9
22	20 6 17	22 8 30	23 58 53	2 1 7	3 59 23	6 1 36	7 59 53	10 2 6	12 4 20	14 2 36	16 4 49	18 3 6
23	20 10 13	22 12 27	0 2 50	2 5 3	4 3 20	6 5 33	8 3 50	10 6 3	12 8 16	14 6 33	16 8 46	18 7 3
24	20 14 10	22 16 23	0 6 47	2 9 0	4 7 16	6 9 30	8 7 46	10 10 0	12 12 13	14 10 29	16 12 42	18 10 59
25	20 18 6	22 20 20	0 10 43	2 12 56	4 11 13	6 13 26	8 11 43	10 13 56	12 16 9	14 14 26	16 16 39	18 14 56
26	20 22 3	22 24 16	0 14 40	2 16 53	4 15 9	6 17 23	8 15 39	10 17 53	12 20 6	14 18 22	16 20 36	18 18 52
27	20 26 0	22 28 13	0 18 36	2 20 49	4 19 6	6 21 19	8 19 36	10 21 49	12 24 2	14 22 19	16 24 32	18 22 49
28	20 29 56	22 32 9	0 22 33	2 24 46	4 23 3	6 25 16	8 23 33	10 25 46	12 27 59	14 26 15	16 28 29	18 26 45
29	20 33 53		0 26 29	2 28 42	4 26 59	6 29 12	8 27 29	10 29 42	12 31 55	14 30 12	16 32 25	18 30 42
30	20 37 49		0 30 26	2 32 39	4 30 56	6 33 9	8 31 26	10 33 39	12 35 52	14 34 9	16 36 22	18 34 38
31	20 41 46		0 34 22		4 34 52		8 35 22	10 37 35		14 38 5		18 38 35

1958

	Jan.	Feb.	Mar.	April	May	June	July	Aug.	Sept.	Oct.	Nov.	Dec.
1	18 42 32	20 44 45	22 35 8	0 37 21	2 35 38	4 37 51	6 36 8	8 38 21	10 40 34	12 38 51	14 41 4	16 39 21
2	18 46 28	20 48 41	22 39 5	0 41 18	2 39 35	4 41 48	6 40 5	8 42 18	10 44 31	12 42 48	14 45 1	16 43 17
3	18 50 25	20 52 38	22 43 1	0 45 15	2 43 31	4 45 45	6 44 1	8 46 14	10 48 27	12 46 44	14 48 57	16 47 14
4	18 54 21	20 56 35	22 46 58	0 49 11	2 47 28	4 49 41	6 47 58	8 50 11	10 52 24	12 50 41	14 52 54	16 51 10
5	18 58 18	21 0 31	22 50 55	0 53 8	2 51 24	4 53 37	6 51 54	8 54 7	10 56 21	12 54 37	14 56 50	16 55 7
6	19 2 14	21 4 28	22 54 51	0 57 4	2 55 21	4 57 34	6 55 51	8 58 4	11 0 17	12 58 34	15 0 47	16 59 3
7	19 6 11	21 8 24	22 58 48	1 1 1	2 59 17	5 1 31	6 59 47	9 2 1	11 4 14	13 2 30	15 4 43	17 3 0
8	19 10 7	21 12 21	23 2 44	1 4 57	3 3 14	5 5 27	7 3 44	9 5 57	11 8 10	13 6 27	15 8 40	17 6 57
9	19 14 4	21 16 17	23 6 41	1 8 54	3 7 10	5 9 24	7 7 40	9 9 54	11 12 7	13 10 24	15 12 36	17 10 53
10	19 18 1	21 20 14	23 10 37	1 12 50	3 11 7	5 13 20	7 11 37	9 13 50	11 16 3	13 14 20	15 16 33	17 14 50
11	19 21 57	21 24 10	23 14 34	1 16 47	3 15 4	5 17 17	7 15 34	9 17 47	11 20 0	13 18 16	15 20 30	17 18 46
12	19 25 54	21 28 7	23 18 30	1 20 44	3 19 0	5 21 13	7 19 30	9 21 43	11 23 56	13 22 13	15 24 26	17 22 43
13	19 29 50	21 32 3	23 22 27	1 24 40	3 22 57	5 25 10	7 23 27	9 25 40	11 27 53	13 26 10	15 28 23	17 26 39
14	19 33 47	21 36 0	23 26 24	1 28 37	3 26 53	5 29 6	7 27 23	9 29 36	11 31 50	13 30 6	15 32 19	17 30 36
15	19 37 43	21 39 57	23 30 20	1 32 33	3 30 50	5 33 3	7 31 20	9 33 33	11 35 46	13 34 3	15 36 16	17 34 33
16	19 41 40	21 43 53	23 34 17	1 36 30	3 34 46	5 37 0	7 35 16	9 37 30	11 39 43	13 37 59	15 40 12	17 38 29
17	19 45 36	21 47 50	23 38 13	1 40 26	3 38 43	5 40 56	7 39 13	9 41 26	11 43 39	13 41 56	15 44 9	17 42 26
18	19 49 33	21 51 46	23 42 10	1 44 23	3 42 39	5 44 53	7 43 9	9 45 23	11 47 36	13 45 52	15 48 5	17 46 22
19	19 53 30	21 55 43	23 46 6	1 48 19	3 46 36	5 48 49	7 47 6	9 49 19	11 51 32	13 49 49	15 52 2	17 50 19
20	19 57 26	21 59 39	23 50 3	1 52 16	3 50 33	5 52 46	7 51 3	9 53 16	11 55 29	13 53 45	15 55 59	17 54 15
21	20 1 23	22 3 36	23 53 59	1 56 12	3 54 29	5 56 42	7 54 59	9 57 12	11 59 25	13 57 42	15 59 55	17 58 12
22	20 5 19	22 7 32	23 57 56	2 0 9	3 58 26	6 0 39	7 58 56	10 1 9	12 3 22	14 1 39	16 3 52	18 2 8
23	20 9 16	22 11 29	0 1 53	2 4 6	4 2 23	6 4 35	8 2 52	10 5 5	12 7 19	14 5 35	16 7 48	18 6 5
24	20 13 12	22 15 26	0 5 49	2 8 2	4 6 19	6 8 32	8 6 49	10 9 2	12 11 15	14 9 32	16 11 45	18 10 2
25	20 17 9	22 19 22	0 9 46	2 11 59	4 10 15	6 12 29	8 10 45	10 12 59	12 15 12	14 13 28	16 15 41	18 13 58
26	20 21 5	22 23 19	0 13 42	2 15 55	4 14 12	6 16 25	8 14 42	10 16 55	12 19 8	14 17 25	16 19 38	18 17 55
27	20 25 2	22 27 15	0 17 39	2 19 52	4 18 8	6 20 22	8 18 38	10 20 52	12 23 5	14 21 22	16 23 34	18 21 51
28	20 28 58	22 31 12	0 21 35	2 23 48	4 22 5	6 24 18	8 22 35	10 24 48	12 27 1	14 25 18	16 27 31	18 25 48
29	20 32 55		0 25 32	2 27 45	4 26 2	6 28 15	8 26 32	10 28 45	12 30 58	14 29 14	16 31 27	18 29 44
30	20 36 52		0 29 28	2 31 41	4 29 58	6 32 11	8 30 28	10 32 41	12 34 54	14 33 11	16 35 24	18 33 41
31	20 40 48		0 33 25		4 33 55		8 34 25	10 36 38		14 37 7		18 37 37

1959

	Jan.	Feb.	Mar.	April	May	June	July	Aug.	Sept.	Oct.	Nov.	Dec.
1	18 41 34	20 43 47	22 34 11	0 36 24	2 34 40	4 36 54	6 35 10	8 37 24	10 39 37	12 37 53	14 40 6	16 38 23
2	18 45 31	20 47 44	22 38 7	0 40 20	2 38 37	4 40 50	6 39 7	8 41 20	10 43 33	12 41 50	14 44 3	16 42 20
3	18 49 27	20 51 40	22 42 4	0 44 17	2 42 34	4 44 47	6 43 3	8 45 17	10 47 30	12 45 46	14 47 59	16 46 16
4	18 53 24	20 55 37	22 46 0	0 48 13	2 46 30	4 48 43	6 47 0	8 49 13	10 51 26	12 49 43	14 51 56	16 50 13
5	18 57 20	20 59 33	22 49 57	0 52 10	2 50 27	4 52 40	6 50 57	8 53 10	10 55 23	12 53 39	14 55 53	16 54 9
6	19 1 17	21 3 30	22 53 53	0 56 7	2 54 23	4 56 36	6 54 53	8 57 6	10 59 19	12 57 36	14 59 49	16 58 6
7	19 5 13	21 7 27	22 57 50	1 0 3	2 58 20	5 0 33	6 58 50	9 1 3	11 3 16	13 1 33	15 3 46	17 2 2
8	19 9 10	21 11 23	23 1 47	1 4 0	3 2 16	5 4 30	7 2 46	9 4 59	11 7 13	13 5 29	15 7 42	17 5 59
9	19 13 6	21 15 20	23 5 43	1 7 56	3 6 13	5 8 26	7 6 43	9 8 56	11 11 9	13 9 26	15 11 39	17 9 56
10	19 17 3	21 19 16	23 9 40	1 11 53	3 10 9	5 12 23	7 10 39	9 12 53	11 15 6	13 13 22	15 15 35	17 13 52
11	19 21 0	21 23 13	23 13 36	1 15 49	3 14 6	5 16 19	7 14 36	9 16 49	11 19 2	13 17 19	15 19 32	17 17 49
12	19 24 56	21 27 9	23 17 33	1 19 46	3 18 2	5 20 16	7 18 32	9 20 46	11 22 59	13 21 15	15 23 28	17 21 45
13	19 28 53	21 31 6	23 21 29	1 23 42	3 21 59	5 24 12	7 22 29	9 24 42	11 26 55	13 25 12	15 27 25	17 25 42
14	19 32 49	21 35 2	23 25 26	1 27 39	3 25 56	5 28 9	7 26 26	9 28 39	11 30 52	13 29 8	15 31 22	17 29 38
15	19 36 46	21 38 59	23 29 22	1 31 36	3 29 52	5 32 5	7 30 22	9 32 35	11 34 48	13 33 5	15 35 18	17 33 35
16	19 40 42	21 42 56	23 33 19	1 35 32	3 33 49	5 36 2	7 34 19	9 36 32	11 38 45	13 37 2	15 39 15	17 37 31
17	19 44 39	21 46 52	23 37 16	1 39 29	3 37 45	5 39 59	7 38 15	9 40 28	11 42 42	13 40 58	15 43 11	17 41 28
18	19 48 35	21 50 49	23 41 12	1 43 25	3 41 42	5 43 55	7 42 12	9 44 25	11 46 38	13 44 55	15 47 8	17 45 25
19	19 52 32	21 54 45	23 45 9	1 47 22	3 45 38	5 47 52	7 46 8	9 48 22	11 50 35	13 48 51	15 51 4	17 49 21
20	19 56 29	21 58 42	23 49 5	1 51 18	3 49 35	5 51 48	7 50 5	9 52 18	11 54 31	13 52 48	15 55 1	17 53 18
21	20 0 25	22 2 38	23 53 2	1 55 15	3 53 31	5 55 45	7 54 1	9 56 15	11 58 28	13 56 44	15 58 57	17 57 14
22	20 4 22	22 6 35	23 56 58	1 59 11	3 57 28	5 59 41	7 57 58	10 0 11	12 2 24	14 0 41	16 2 54	18 1 11
23	20 8 18	22 10 31	0 0 55	2 3 8	4 1 25	6 3 38	8 1 55	10 4 8	12 6 21	14 4 37	16 6 51	18 5 7
24	20 12 15	22 14 28	0 4 51	2 7 5	4 5 21	6 7 34	8 5 51	10 8 4	12 10 17	14 8 34	16 10 47	18 9 4
25	20 16 11	22 18 25	0 8 48	2 11 1	4 9 18	6 11 31	8 9 48	10 12 1	12 14 14	14 12 31	16 14 44	18 13 0
26	20 20 8	22 22 21	0 12 45	2 14 58	4 13 14	6 15 28	8 13 44	10 15 57	12 18 11	14 16 27	16 18 40	18 16 57
27	20 24 4	22 26 18	0 16 41	2 18 54	4 17 11	6 19 24	8 17 41	10 19 54	12 22 7	14 20 24	16 22 37	18 20 54
28	20 28 1	22 30 14	0 20 38	2 22 51	4 21 7	6 23 21	8 21 37	10 23 50	12 26 4	14 24 20	16 26 33	18 24 50
29	20 31 58		0 24 34	2 26 47	4 25 4	6 27 17	8 25 34	10 27 47	12 30 0	14 28 17	16 30 30	18 28 47
30	20 35 54		0 28 31	2 30 44	4 29 1	6 31 14	8 29 30	10 31 44	12 33 57	14 32 13	16 34 26	18 32 43
31	20 39 51		0 32 27		4 32 57		8 33 27	10 35 40		14 36 10		18 36 40

1960

	Jan.	Feb.	Mar.	April	May	June	July	Aug.	Sept.	Oct.	Nov.	Dec.
1	18 40 36	20 42 50	22 37 10	0 39 23	2 37 39	4 39 53	6 38 9	8 40 22	10 42 36	12 40 52	14 43 5	16 41 22
2	18 44 33	20 46 46	22 41 6	0 43 19	2 41 36	4 43 49	6 42 6	8 44 19	10 46 32	12 44 49	14 47 2	16 45 19
3	18 48 29	20 50 43	22 45 3	0 47 16	2 45 32	4 47 46	6 46 2	8 48 16	10 50 29	12 48 45	14 50 58	16 49 15
4	18 52 26	20 54 39	22 48 59	0 51 12	2 49 29	4 51 42	6 49 59	8 52 12	10 54 25	12 52 42	14 54 55	16 53 12
5	18 56 23	20 58 36	22 52 56	0 55 9	2 53 25	4 55 39	6 53 55	8 56 9	10 58 22	12 56 38	14 58 52	16 57 8
6	19 0 19	21 2 32	22 56 52	0 59 5	2 57 22	4 59 35	6 57 52	9 0 5	11 2 18	13 0 35	15 2 48	17 1 5
7	19 4 16	21 6 29	23 0 49	1 3 2	3 1 19	5 3 32	7 1 49	9 4 2	11 6 15	13 4 31	15 6 45	17 5 1
8	19 8 12	21 10 25	23 4 45	1 6 59	3 5 15	5 7 28	7 5 45	9 7 58	11 10 11	13 8 28	15 10 41	17 8 58
9	19 12 9	21 14 22	23 8 42	1 10 55	3 9 12	5 11 25	7 9 42	9 11 55	11 14 8	13 12 25	15 14 38	17 12 54
10	19 16 5	21 18 19	23 12 39	1 14 52	3 13 8	5 15 22	7 13 38	9 15 51	11 18 5	13 16 21	15 18 34	17 16 51
11	19 20 2	21 22 15	23 16 35	1 18 48	3 17 5	5 19 18	7 17 35	9 19 48	11 22 1	13 20 18	15 22 31	17 20 48
12	19 23 58	21 26 12	23 20 32	1 22 45	3 21 1	5 23 15	7 21 31	9 23 45	11 25 58	13 24 14	15 26 27	17 24 44
13	19 27 55	21 30 8	23 24 28	1 26 41	3 24 58	5 27 11	7 25 28	9 27 41	11 29 54	13 28 11	15 30 24	17 28 41
14	19 31 52	21 34 5	23 28 25	1 30 38	3 28 55	5 31 8	7 29 24	9 31 38	11 33 51	13 32 7	15 34 21	17 32 37
15	19 35 48	21 38 1	23 32 21	1 34 34	3 32 51	5 35 4	7 33 21	9 35 34	11 37 47	13 36 4	15 38 17	17 36 34
16	19 39 45	21 41 58	23 36 18	1 38 31	3 36 48	5 39 1	7 37 18	9 39 31	11 41 44	13 40 0	15 42 14	17 40 30
17	19 43 41	21 45 54	23 40 14	1 42 28	3 40 44	5 42 57	7 41 14	9 43 27	11 45 40	13 43 57	15 46 10	17 44 27
18	19 47 38	21 49 51	23 44 11	1 46 24	3 44 41	5 46 54	7 45 11	9 47 24	11 49 37	13 47 54	15 50 7	17 48 23
19	19 51 34	21 53 48	23 48 8	1 50 21	3 48 37	5 50 51	7 49 8	9 51 20	11 53 34	13 51 50	15 54 3	17 52 20
20	19 55 31	21 57 44	23 52 4	1 54 17	3 52 34	5 54 47	7 53 4	9 55 17	11 57 30	13 55 47	15 58 0	17 56 17
21	19 59 27	22 1 41	23 56 1	1 58 14	3 56 30	5 58 44	7 57 0	9 59 14	12 1 27	13 59 43	16 1 56	18 0 13
22	20 3 24	22 5 37	23 59 57	2 2 10	4 0 27	6 2 40	8 0 57	10 3 10	12 5 23	14 3 40	16 5 53	18 4 10
23	20 7 21	22 9 34	0 3 54	2 6 7	4 4 24	6 6 37	8 4 53	10 7 7	12 9 20	14 7 36	16 9 50	18 8 6
24	20 11 17	22 13 30	0 7 50	2 10 3	4 8 20	6 10 33	8 8 50	10 11 3	12 13 16	14 11 33	16 13 46	18 12 3
25	20 15 14	22 17 27	0 11 47	2 14 0	4 12 17	6 14 30	8 12 47	10 15 0	12 17 13	14 15 29	16 17 43	18 15 59
26	20 19 10	22 21 23	0 15 43	2 17 57	4 16 13	6 18 26	8 16 43	10 18 56	12 21 9	14 19 26	16 21 39	18 19 56
27	20 23 7	22 25 20	0 19 40	2 21 53	4 20 10	6 22 23	8 20 40	10 22 53	12 25 6	14 23 23	16 25 36	18 23 52
28	20 27 3	22 29 17	0 23 37	2 25 50	4 24 6	6 26 20	8 24 36	10 26 49	12 29 3	14 27 19	16 29 32	18 27 49
29	20 31 0	22 33 13	0 27 33	2 29 47	4 28 3	6 30 16	8 28 33	10 30 46	12 32 59	14 31 16	16 33 29	18 31 46
30	20 34 56		0 31 30	2 33 43	4 31 59	6 34 13	8 32 29	10 34 42	12 36 56	14 35 12	16 37 25	18 35 42
31	20 38 53		0 35 26		4 35 56		8 36 26	10 38 39		14 39 9		18 39 39

1961

	Jan.	Feb.	Mar.	April	May	June	July	Aug.	Sept.	Oct.	Nov.	Dec.
1	18 43 35	20 45 48	22 36 12	0 38 25	2 36 42	4 38 55	6 37 12	8 39 25	10 41 38	12 39 55	14 42 8	16 40 24
2	18 47 32	20 49 45	22 40 9	0 42 22	2 40 38	4 42 51	6 41 8	8 43 21	10 45 35	12 43 51	14 46 4	16 44 21
3	18 51 28	20 53 42	22 44 5	0 46 18	2 44 35	4 46 48	6 45 5	8 47 18	10 49 31	12 47 48	14 50 1	16 48 17
4	18 55 25	20 57 38	22 48 2	0 50 15	2 48 31	4 50 45	6 49 1	8 51 14	10 53 28	12 51 44	14 53 57	16 52 14
5	18 59 21	21 1 35	22 51 58	0 54 11	2 52 28	4 54 41	6 52 58	8 55 11	10 57 24	12 55 41	14 57 54	16 56 11
6	19 3 18	21 5 31	22 55 55	0 58 8	2 56 24	4 58 38	6 56 54	8 59 8	11 1 21	12 59 37	15 1 50	17 0 7
7	19 7 15	21 9 28	22 59 51	1 2 4	3 0 21	5 2 34	7 0 51	9 3 4	11 5 17	13 3 34	15 5 47	17 4 4
8	19 11 11	21 13 24	23 3 48	1 6 1	3 4 18	5 6 31	7 4 47	9 7 1	11 9 14	13 7 30	15 9 44	17 8 0
9	19 15 8	21 17 21	23 7 44	1 9 58	3 8 14	5 10 27	7 8 44	9 10 57	11 13 10	13 11 27	15 13 40	17 11 57
10	19 19 4	21 21 17	23 11 41	1 13 54	3 12 11	5 14 24	7 12 41	9 14 54	11 17 7	13 15 23	15 17 37	17 15 53
11	19 23 1	21 25 14	23 15 37	1 17 51	3 16 7	5 18 20	7 16 37	9 18 50	11 21 4	13 19 20	15 21 33	17 19 50
12	19 26 57	21 29 11	23 19 34	1 21 47	3 20 4	5 22 17	7 20 34	9 22 47	11 25 0	13 23 17	15 25 30	17 23 46
13	19 30 54	21 33 7	23 23 31	1 25 44	3 24 0	5 26 14	7 24 30	9 26 43	11 28 57	13 27 13	15 29 26	17 27 43
14	19 34 50	21 37 4	23 27 27	1 29 40	3 27 57	5 30 10	7 28 27	9 30 40	11 32 53	13 31 10	15 33 23	17 31 40
15	19 38 47	21 41 0	23 31 24	1 33 37	3 31 53	5 34 7	7 32 23	9 34 37	11 36 50	13 35 6	15 37 19	17 35 36
16	19 42 44	21 44 57	23 35 20	1 37 33	3 35 50	5 38 3	7 36 20	9 38 33	11 40 46	13 39 3	15 41 16	17 39 33
17	19 46 40	21 48 53	23 39 17	1 41 30	3 39 47	5 42 0	7 40 16	9 42 30	11 44 43	13 42 59	15 45 13	17 43 29
18	19 50 37	21 52 50	23 43 13	1 45 26	3 43 43	5 45 56	7 44 13	9 46 26	11 48 39	13 46 56	15 49 9	17 47 26
19	19 54 33	21 56 46	23 47 10	1 49 23	3 47 40	5 49 53	7 48 10	9 50 23	11 52 36	13 50 52	15 53 6	17 51 22
20	19 58 30	22 0 43	23 51 6	1 53 20	3 51 36	5 53 49	7 52 6	9 54 19	11 56 32	13 54 49	15 57 2	17 55 19
21	20 2 26	22 4 40	23 55 3	1 57 16	3 55 33	5 57 46	7 56 3	9 58 16	12 0 29	13 58 46	16 0 59	17 59 15
22	20 6 23	22 8 36	23 59 0	2 1 13	3 59 29	6 1 43	7 59 59	10 2 12	12 4 26	14 2 42	16 4 55	18 3 12
23	20 10 19	22 12 33	0 2 56	2 5 9	4 3 26	6 5 39	8 3 56	10 6 9	12 8 22	14 6 39	16 8 52	18 7 9
24	20 14 16	22 16 29	0 6 53	2 9 6	4 7 22	6 9 36	8 7 52	10 10 6	12 12 19	14 10 35	16 12 48	18 11 5
25	20 18 13	22 20 26	0 10 49	2 13 2	4 11 19	6 13 32	8 11 49	10 14 2	12 16 15	14 14 32	16 16 45	18 15 2
26	20 22 9	22 24 22	0 14 46	2 16 59	4 15 16	6 17 29	8 15 45	10 17 59	12 20 12	14 18 28	16 20 42	18 18 58
27	20 26 6	22 28 19	0 18 42	2 20 55	4 19 12	6 21 25	8 19 42	10 21 55	12 24 8	14 22 25	16 24 38	18 22 55
28	20 30 2	22 32 15	0 22 39	2 24 52	4 23 9	6 25 22	8 23 39	10 25 52	12 28 5	14 26 21	16 28 35	18 26 51
29	20 33 59		0 26 35	2 28 49	4 27 5	6 29 18	8 27 35	10 29 48	12 32 1	14 30 18	16 32 31	18 30 48
30	20 37 55		0 30 32	2 32 45	4 31 2	6 33 15	8 31 32	10 33 45	12 35 58	14 34 15	16 36 28	18 34 45
31	20 41 52		0 34 29		4 34 58		8 35 28	10 37 41		14 38 11		18 38 41

1962

Day	Jan.	Feb.	Mar.	April	May	June	July	Aug.	Sept.	Oct.	Nov.	Dec.
1	18 42 38	20 44 51	22 35 14	0 37 28	2 35 44	4 37 57	6 36 14	8 38 27	10 40 40	12 38 57	14 41 10	16 39 27
2	18 46 34	20 48 47	22 39 11	0 41 24	2 39 41	4 41 54	6 40 11	8 42 24	10 44 37	12 42 54	14 45 7	16 43 23
3	18 50 31	20 52 44	22 43 7	0 45 21	2 43 37	4 45 50	6 44 7	8 46 20	10 48 34	12 46 50	14 49 3	16 47 20
4	18 54 27	20 56 41	22 47 4	0 49 17	2 47 34	4 49 47	6 48 4	8 50 17	10 52 30	12 50 47	14 53 0	16 51 16
5	18 58 24	21 0 37	22 51 1	0 53 14	2 51 30	4 53 44	6 52 0	8 54 13	10 56 27	12 54 43	14 56 56	16 55 13
6	19 2 20	21 4 34	22 54 57	0 57 10	2 55 27	4 57 40	6 55 57	8 58 10	11 0 23	12 58 40	15 0 53	16 59 10
7	19 6 17	21 8 30	22 58 54	1 1 7	2 59 23	5 1 37	6 59 53	9 2 7	11 4 20	13 2 36	15 4 49	17 3 6
8	19 10 14	21 12 27	23 2 50	1 5 3	3 3 20	5 5 33	7 3 50	9 6 3	11 8 16	13 6 33	15 8 46	17 7 3
9	19 14 10	21 16 23	23 6 47	1 9 0	3 7 17	5 9 30	7 7 46	9 10 0	11 12 13	13 10 29	15 12 43	17 10 59
10	19 18 7	21 20 20	23 10 43	1 12 56	3 11 13	5 13 26	7 11 43	9 13 56	11 16 9	13 14 26	15 16 39	17 14 56
11	19 22 3	21 24 16	23 14 40	1 16 53	3 15 10	5 17 23	7 15 40	9 17 53	11 20 6	13 18 23	15 20 36	17 18 52
12	19 26 0	21 28 13	23 18 36	1 20 50	3 19 6	5 21 19	7 19 36	9 21 49	11 24 3	13 22 19	15 24 32	17 22 49
13	19 29 56	21 32 10	23 22 33	1 24 46	3 23 3	5 25 16	7 23 33	9 25 46	11 27 59	13 26 16	15 28 29	17 26 46
14	19 33 53	21 36 6	23 26 30	1 28 43	3 26 59	5 29 13	7 27 29	9 29 42	11 31 56	13 30 12	15 32 25	17 30 42
15	19 37 49	21 40 3	23 30 26	1 32 39	3 30 56	5 33 9	7 31 26	9 33 39	11 35 52	13 34 9	15 36 22	17 34 39
16	19 41 46	21 43 59	23 34 23	1 36 36	3 34 52	5 37 6	7 35 22	9 37 36	11 39 49	13 38 5	15 40 18	17 38 35
17	19 45 43	21 47 56	23 38 19	1 40 32	3 38 49	5 41 2	7 39 19	9 41 32	11 43 45	13 42 2	15 44 15	17 42 32
18	19 49 39	21 51 52	23 42 16	1 44 29	3 42 46	5 44 59	7 43 15	9 45 29	11 47 42	13 45 58	15 48 12	17 46 28
19	19 53 36	21 55 49	23 46 12	1 48 25	3 46 42	5 48 55	7 47 12	9 49 25	11 51 38	13 49 55	15 52 8	17 50 25
20	19 57 32	21 59 45	23 50 9	1 52 22	3 50 39	5 52 52	7 51 9	9 53 22	11 55 35	13 53 52	15 56 5	17 54 21
21	20 1 29	22 3 42	23 54 5	1 56 19	3 54 35	5 56 48	7 55 5	9 57 18	11 59 31	13 57 48	16 0 1	17 58 18
22	20 5 25	22 7 39	23 58 2	2 0 15	3 58 32	6 0 45	7 59 2	10 1 15	12 3 28	14 1 45	16 3 58	18 2 15
23	20 9 22	22 11 35	0 1 59	2 4 12	4 2 28	6 4 42	8 2 58	10 5 11	12 7 25	14 5 41	16 7 54	18 6 11
24	20 13 18	22 15 32	0 5 55	2 8 8	4 6 25	6 8 38	8 6 55	10 9 8	12 11 21	14 9 38	16 11 51	18 10 8
25	20 17 15	22 19 28	0 9 52	2 12 5	4 10 21	6 12 35	8 10 51	10 13 5	12 15 18	14 13 34	16 15 47	18 14 4
26	20 21 12	22 23 25	0 13 48	2 16 1	4 14 18	6 16 31	8 14 48	10 17 1	12 19 14	14 17 31	16 19 44	18 18 1
27	20 25 8	22 27 21	0 17 45	2 19 58	4 18 15	6 20 28	8 18 44	10 20 58	12 23 11	14 21 27	16 23 41	18 21 57
28	20 29 5	22 31 18	0 21 41	2 23 54	4 22 11	6 24 24	8 22 41	10 24 54	12 27 7	14 25 24	16 27 37	18 25 54
29	20 33 1		0 25 38	2 27 51	4 26 8	6 28 21	8 26 38	10 28 51	12 31 4	14 29 20	16 31 34	18 29 50
30	20 36 58		0 29 34	2 31 48	4 30 4	6 32 17	8 30 34	10 32 47	12 35 0	14 33 17	16 35 30	18 33 47
31	20 40 54		0 33 31		4 34 1		8 34 31	10 36 44		14 37 14		18 37 44

1963

Day	Jan.	Feb.	Mar.	April	May	June	July	Aug.	Sept.	Oct.	Nov.	Dec.
1	18 41 40	20 43 53	22 34 17	0 36 30	2 34 47	4 37 0	6 35 17	8 37 30	10 39 43	12 38 0	14 40 13	16 38 29
2	18 45 37	20 47 50	22 38 13	0 40 27	2 38 43	4 40 56	6 39 13	8 41 26	10 43 40	12 41 56	14 44 9	16 42 26
3	18 49 33	20 51 46	22 42 10	0 44 23	2 42 40	4 44 53	6 43 10	8 45 23	10 47 36	12 45 53	14 48 6	16 46 23
4	18 53 30	20 55 43	22 46 7	0 48 20	2 46 36	4 48 49	6 47 6	8 49 19	10 51 33	12 49 49	14 52 2	16 50 19
5	18 57 26	20 59 40	22 50 3	0 52 16	2 50 33	4 52 46	6 51 3	8 53 16	10 55 29	12 53 46	14 55 59	16 54 16
6	19 1 23	21 3 36	22 54 0	0 56 13	2 54 29	4 56 43	6 54 59	8 57 13	10 59 26	12 57 42	14 59 55	16 58 12
7	19 5 19	21 7 33	22 57 56	1 0 9	2 58 26	5 0 39	6 58 56	9 1 9	11 3 22	13 1 39	15 3 52	17 2 9
8	19 9 16	21 11 29	23 1 53	1 4 6	3 2 22	5 4 36	7 2 52	9 5 6	11 7 19	13 5 35	15 7 49	17 6 5
9	19 13 13	21 15 26	23 5 49	1 8 2	3 6 19	5 8 32	7 6 49	9 9 2	11 11 15	13 9 32	15 11 45	17 10 2
10	19 17 9	21 19 22	23 9 46	1 11 59	3 10 16	5 12 29	7 10 46	9 12 59	11 15 12	13 13 29	15 15 42	17 13 58
11	19 21 6	21 23 19	23 13 42	1 15 56	3 14 12	5 16 25	7 14 42	9 16 55	11 19 9	13 17 25	15 19 38	17 17 55
12	19 25 2	21 27 15	23 17 39	1 19 52	3 18 9	5 20 22	7 18 39	9 20 52	11 23 5	13 21 22	15 23 35	17 21 52
13	19 28 59	21 31 12	23 21 35	1 23 49	3 22 5	5 24 19	7 22 35	9 24 48	11 27 2	13 25 18	15 27 31	17 25 48
14	19 32 55	21 35 9	23 25 32	1 27 45	3 26 2	5 28 15	7 26 32	9 28 45	11 30 58	13 29 15	15 31 28	17 29 45
15	19 36 52	21 39 5	23 29 29	1 31 42	3 29 58	5 32 12	7 30 28	9 32 42	11 34 55	13 33 11	15 35 24	17 33 41
16	19 40 48	21 43 2	23 33 25	1 35 38	3 33 55	5 36 8	7 34 25	9 36 38	11 38 51	13 37 8	15 39 21	17 37 38
17	19 44 45	21 46 58	23 37 22	1 39 35	3 37 51	5 40 5	7 38 21	9 40 35	11 42 48	13 41 4	15 43 18	17 41 34
18	19 48 42	21 50 55	23 41 18	1 43 31	3 41 48	5 44 1	7 42 18	9 44 31	11 46 44	13 45 1	15 47 14	17 45 31
19	19 52 38	21 54 51	23 45 15	1 47 28	3 45 45	5 47 58	7 46 15	9 48 28	11 50 41	13 48 58	15 51 11	17 49 27
20	19 56 35	21 58 48	23 49 11	1 51 25	3 49 41	5 51 54	7 50 11	9 52 24	11 54 37	13 52 54	15 55 7	17 53 24
21	20 0 31	22 2 44	23 53 8	1 55 21	3 53 38	5 55 51	7 54 8	9 56 21	11 58 34	13 56 51	15 59 4	17 57 21
22	20 4 28	22 6 41	23 57 4	1 59 18	3 57 34	5 59 48	7 58 4	10 0 17	12 2 31	14 0 47	16 3 0	18 1 17
23	20 8 24	22 10 38	0 1 1	2 3 14	4 1 31	6 3 44	8 2 1	10 4 14	12 6 27	14 4 44	16 6 57	18 5 14
24	20 12 21	22 14 34	0 4 58	2 7 11	4 5 27	6 7 41	8 5 57	10 8 11	12 10 24	14 8 40	16 10 54	18 9 10
25	20 16 17	22 18 31	0 8 54	2 11 7	4 9 24	6 11 37	8 9 54	10 12 7	12 14 20	14 12 37	16 14 50	18 13 7
26	20 20 14	22 22 27	0 12 51	2 15 4	4 13 20	6 15 34	8 13 50	10 16 4	12 18 17	14 16 33	16 18 47	18 17 3
27	20 24 11	22 26 24	0 16 47	2 19 0	4 17 17	6 19 30	8 17 47	10 20 0	12 22 13	14 20 30	16 22 43	18 21 0
28	20 28 7	22 30 20	0 20 44	2 22 57	4 21 14	6 23 27	8 21 44	10 23 57	12 26 10	14 24 27	16 26 40	18 24 56
29	20 32 4		0 24 40	2 26 54	4 25 10	6 27 23	8 25 40	10 27 53	12 30 6	14 28 23	16 30 36	18 28 53
30	20 36 0		0 28 37	2 30 50	4 29 7	6 31 20	8 29 37	10 31 50	12 34 3	14 32 20	16 34 33	18 32 50
31	20 39 57		0 32 33		4 33 3		8 33 33	10 35 46		14 36 16		18 36 46

1964

Day	Jan.	Feb.	Mar.	April	May	June	July	Aug.	Sept.	Oct.	Nov.	Dec.
1	18 40 43	20 42 56	22 37 16	0 39 29	2 37 46	4 39 59	6 38 16	8 40 19	10 42 42	12 40 59	14 43 12	16 41 29
2	18 44 39	20 46 53	22 41 13	0 43 26	2 41 42	4 43 56	6 42 12	8 44 26	10 46 39	12 44 55	14 47 9	16 45 25
3	18 48 36	20 50 49	22 45 9	0 47 22	2 45 39	4 47 52	6 46 9	8 48 22	10 50 35	12 48 52	14 51 5	16 49 22
4	18 52 32	20 54 46	22 49 6	0 51 19	2 49 36	4 51 49	6 50 5	8 52 19	10 54 32	12 52 48	14 55 2	16 53 18
5	18 56 29	20 58 42	22 53 2	0 55 15	2 53 32	4 55 45	6 54 2	8 56 15	10 58 28	12 56 45	14 58 58	16 57 15
6	19 0 26	21 2 39	22 56 59	0 59 12	2 57 29	4 59 42	6 57 59	9 0 12	11 2 25	13 0 42	15 2 55	17 1 11
7	19 4 22	21 6 35	23 0 55	1 3 8	3 1 25	5 3 38	7 1 55	9 4 8	11 6 22	13 4 38	15 6 51	17 5 8
8	19 8 19	21 10 32	23 4 52	1 7 5	3 5 22	5 7 35	7 5 52	9 8 5	11 10 18	13 8 35	15 10 48	17 9 5
9	19 12 15	21 14 28	23 8 48	1 11 2	3 9 18	5 11 31	7 9 48	9 12 1	11 14 15	13 12 31	15 14 44	17 13 1
10	19 16 12	21 18 25	23 12 45	1 14 58	3 13 15	5 15 28	7 13 45	9 15 58	11 18 11	13 16 28	15 18 41	17 16 58
11	19 20 8	21 22 22	23 16 42	1 18 55	3 17 11	5 19 25	7 17 41	9 19 55	11 22 8	13 20 24	15 22 38	17 20 54
12	19 24 5	21 26 18	23 20 38	1 22 51	3 21 8	5 23 21	7 21 38	9 23 51	11 26 4	13 24 21	15 26 34	17 24 51
13	19 28 1	21 30 15	23 24 35	1 26 48	3 25 4	5 27 18	7 25 35	9 27 48	11 30 1	13 28 17	15 30 31	17 28 47
14	19 31 58	21 34 11	23 28 31	1 30 44	3 29 1	5 31 14	7 29 31	9 31 44	11 33 57	13 32 14	15 34 27	17 32 44
15	19 35 55	21 38 8	23 32 28	1 34 41	3 32 58	5 35 11	7 33 28	9 35 41	11 37 54	13 36 11	15 38 24	17 36 40
16	19 39 51	21 42 4	23 36 24	1 38 37	3 36 54	5 39 7	7 37 24	9 39 37	11 41 51	13 40 7	15 42 20	17 40 37
17	19 43 48	21 46 1	23 40 21	1 42 34	3 40 51	5 43 4	7 41 21	9 43 34	11 45 47	13 44 4	15 46 17	17 44 34
18	19 47 44	21 49 57	23 44 17	1 46 31	3 44 47	5 47 1	7 45 17	9 47 30	11 49 44	13 48 0	15 50 13	17 48 30
19	19 51 41	21 53 54	23 48 14	1 50 27	3 48 44	5 50 57	7 49 14	9 51 27	11 53 40	13 51 57	15 54 10	17 52 27
20	19 55 37	21 57 50	23 52 11	1 54 24	3 52 40	5 54 53	7 53 10	9 55 23	11 57 37	13 55 53	15 58 7	17 56 23
21	19 59 34	22 1 47	23 56 7	1 58 20	3 56 37	5 58 50	7 57 7	9 59 20	12 1 33	13 59 50	16 2 3	18 0 20
22	20 3 30	22 5 44	0 0 4	2 2 17	4 0 33	6 2 47	8 1 3	10 3 17	12 5 30	14 3 46	16 6 0	18 4 16
23	20 7 27	22 9 40	0 4 0	2 6 13	4 4 30	6 6 43	8 5 0	10 7 13	12 9 27	14 7 43	16 9 56	18 8 13
24	20 11 23	22 13 37	0 7 57	2 10 10	4 8 27	6 10 40	8 8 57	10 11 10	12 13 23	14 11 40	16 13 53	18 12 10
25	20 15 20	22 17 33	0 11 53	2 14 6	4 12 23	6 14 36	8 12 53	10 15 6	12 17 19	14 15 36	16 17 49	18 16 6
26	20 19 17	22 21 30	0 15 50	2 18 3	4 16 20	6 18 33	8 16 50	10 19 3	12 21 16	14 19 33	16 21 46	18 20 3
27	20 23 13	22 25 26	0 19 46	2 22 0	4 20 16	6 22 30	8 20 46	10 22 59	12 25 13	14 23 29	16 25 42	18 23 59
28	20 27 10	22 29 23	0 23 43	2 25 56	4 24 13	6 26 26	8 24 43	10 26 56	12 29 9	14 27 26	16 29 39	18 27 56
29	20 31 6	22 33 19	0 27 40	2 29 53	4 28 9	6 30 23	8 28 40	10 30 53	12 33 6	14 31 22	16 33 36	18 31 52
30	20 35 3		0 31 36	2 33 49	4 32 6	6 34 19	8 32 36	10 34 49	12 37 2	14 35 19	16 37 33	18 35 49
31	20 38 59		0 35 33		4 36 2		8 36 32	10 38 46		14 39 15		18 39 45

Tables of houses

Since it is impossible here to give tables of houses for every degree of latitude, the following are examples of tables giving ascendants for anyone born at any time on or near the latitudes of London and New York. You look up in the S.T. column the figure nearest to your S.T. at birth, and find its corresponding ascendant in the next column.

Table of Houses for London. Latitude 51° 32′ N

Sidereal Time (H. M. S.)	Ascen (° ♋ ′)	Sidereal Time (H. M. S.)	Ascen (° ♍ ′)	Sidereal Time (H. M. S.)	Ascen (° ♎ ′)	Sidereal Time (H. M. S.)	Ascen (° ♐ ′)	Sidereal Time (H. M. S.)	Ascen (° ♑ ′)	Sidereal Time (H. M. S.)	Ascen (° ♊ ′)
0 0 0	26 36	3 51 15	7 21	8 8 45	22 40	12 0 0	3 23	15 51 15	27 15	20 8 45	2 45
0 3 40	27 17	3 55 25	8 5	8 12 54	23 24	12 3 40	4 4	15 55 25	28 42	20 12 54	4 9
0 7 20	27 56	3 59 36	8 49	8 17 3	24 7	12 7 20	4 45	15 59 36	0♒11	20 17 3	5 32
0 11 0	28 42	4 3 48	9 33	8 21 11	24 50	12 11 0	5 26	16 3 48	1 42	20 21 11	6 53
0 14 41	29 17	4 8 0	10 17	8 25 19	25 34	12 14 41	6 7	16 8 0	3 16	20 25 19	8 12
0 18 21	29 55	4 12 13	11 2	8 29 26	26 18	12 18 21	6 48	16 12 13	4 53	20 29 26	9 27
0 22 2	0♌34	4 16 26	11 46	8 33 31	27 1	12 22 2	7 29	16 16 26	6 32	20 33 31	10 43
0 25 42	1 14	4 20 40	12 30	8 37 37	27 44	12 25 42	8 10	16 20 40	8 12	20 37 37	11 58
0 29 23	1 55	4 24 55	13 15	8 41 41	28 26	12 29 23	8 51	16 24 55	9 57	20 41 41	13 9
0 33 4	2 33	4 29 10	14 0	8 45 45	29 8	12 33 4	9 33	16 29 10	11 44	20 45 45	14 18
0 36 45	3 14	4 33 26	14 45	8 49 48	29 50	12 36 45	10 15	16 33 26	13 34	20 49 48	15 25
0 40 26	3 54	4 37 42	15 30	8 53 51	0♏32	12 40 26	10 57	16 37 42	15 26	20 53 51	16 32
0 44 8	4 33	4 41 59	16 15	8 57 52	1 15	12 44 8	11 40	16 41 59	17 20	20 57 52	17 39
0 47 50	5 12	4 46 16	17 0	9 1 53	1 58	12 47 50	12 22	16 46 16	19 18	21 1 53	18 44
0 51 32	5 52	4 50 34	17 45	9 5 53	2 39	12 51 32	13 4	16 50 34	21 22	21 5 53	19 48
0 55 14	6 30	4 54 52	18 30	9 9 53	3 21	12 55 14	13 47	16 54 52	23 29	21 9 53	20 51
0 58 57	7 9	4 59 10	19 16	9 13 52	4 3	12 58 57	14 30	16 59 10	25 36	21 13 52	21 53
1 2 40	7 50	5 3 29	20 3	9 17 50	4 44	13 2 40	15 14	17 3 29	27 46	21 17 50	22 53
1 6 23	8 30	5 7 49	20 49	9 21 47	5 26	13 6 23	15 59	17 7 49	0♓0	21 21 47	23 52
1 10 7	9 9	5 12 9	21 35	9 25 44	6 7	13 10 7	16 44	17 12 9	2 19	21 25 44	24 51
1 13 51	9 48	5 16 29	22 20	9 29 40	6 48	13 13 51	17 29	17 16 29	4 40	21 29 40	25 48
1 17 35	10 28	5 20 49	23 6	9 33 35	7 29	13 17 35	18 14	17 20 49	7 2	21 33 35	26 44
1 21 20	11 8	5 25 9	23 51	9 37 29	8 9	13 21 20	19 0	17 25 9	9 26	21 37 29	27 40
1 25 6	11 48	5 29 30	24 37	9 41 23	8 50	13 25 6	19 45	17 29 30	11 54	21 41 23	28 34
1 28 52	12 28	5 33 51	25 23	9 45 16	9 31	13 28 52	20 31	17 33 51	14 24	21 45 16	29 29
1 32 38	13 8	5 38 12	26 9	9 49 9	10 11	13 32 38	21 18	17 38 12	17 0	21 49 9	0♋22
1 36 25	13 48	5 42 34	26 55	9 53 1	10 51	13 36 25	22 6	17 42 34	19 33	21 53 1	1 15
1 40 12	14 28	5 46 55	27 41	9 56 52	11 32	13 40 12	22 54	17 46 55	22 6	21 56 52	2 7
1 44 0	15 8	5 51 17	28 27	10 0 43	12 12	13 44 0	23 42	17 51 17	24 40	22 0 43	2 57
1 47 48	15 48	5 55 38	29 13	10 4 33	12 53	13 47 48	24 31	17 55 38	27 40	22 4 33	3 48
1 51 37	16 28	6 0 0	30 0	10 8 23	13 33	13 51 37	25 20	18 0 0	30 0	22 8 23	4 38
1 55 27	17 8	6 4 22	0♎47	10 12 12	14 13	13 55 27	26 10	18 4 22	2♈39	22 12 12	5 28
1 59 17	17 48	6 8 43	1 33	10 16 0	14 53	13 59 17	27 2	18 8 43	5 19	22 16 0	6 17
2 3 8	18 28	6 13 5	2 19	10 19 48	15 33	14 3 8	27 53	18 13 5	7 55	22 19 48	7 5
2 6 59	19 9	6 17 26	3 5	10 23 35	16 13	14 6 59	28 45	18 17 26	10 29	22 23 35	7 53
2 10 51	19 49	6 21 48	3 51	10 27 22	16 52	14 10 51	29 36	18 21 48	13 2	22 27 22	8 42
2 14 44	20 29	6 26 9	4 37	10 31 8	17 32	14 14 44	0♑29	18 26 9	15 36	22 31 8	9 29
2 18 37	21 10	6 30 30	5 23	10 34 54	18 13	14 18 37	1 23	18 30 30	18 6	22 34 54	10 16
2 22 31	21 51	6 34 51	6 9	10 38 40	18 52	14 22 31	2 18	18 34 51	20 34	22 38 40	11 2
2 26 25	22 32	6 39 11	6 55	10 42 25	19 31	14 26 25	3 14	18 39 11	22 59	22 42 25	11 47
2 30 20	23 14	6 43 31	7 40	10 46 9	20 11	14 30 20	4 11	18 43 31	25 22	22 46 9	12 31
2 34 16	23 55	6 47 51	8 26	10 49 53	20 50	14 34 16	5 9	18 47 51	27 42	22 49 53	13 16
2 38 13	24 36	6 52 11	9 12	10 53 37	21 30	14 38 13	6 7	18 52 11	29 58	22 53 37	14 1
2 42 10	25 17	6 56 31	9 58	10 57 20	22 9	14 42 10	7 6	18 56 31	2♉13	22 57 20	14 45
2 46 8	25 58	7 0 50	10 43	11 1 3	22 49	14 46 8	8 6	19 0 50	4 24	23 1 3	15 28
2 50 7	26 40	7 5 8	11 28	11 4 46	23 28	14 50 7	9 8	19 5 8	6 30	23 4 46	16 11
2 54 7	27 22	7 9 26	12 14	11 8 28	24 8	14 54 7	10 11	19 9 26	8 36	23 8 28	16 54
2 58 7	28 4	7 13 44	12 59	11 12 10	24 47	14 58 7	11 15	19 13 44	10 40	23 12 10	17 39
3 2 8	28 46	7 18 1	13 45	11 15 52	25 27	15 2 8	12 20	19 18 1	12 39	23 15 52	18 20
3 6 9	29 28	7 22 18	14 30	11 19 34	26 6	15 6 9	13 27	19 22 18	14 35	23 19 34	19 3
3 10 12	0♍12	7 26 34	15 15	11 23 15	26 45	15 10 12	14 35	19 26 34	16 28	23 23 15	19 45
3 14 15	0 54	7 30 50	16 0	11 26 56	27 25	15 14 15	15 43	19 30 50	18 17	23 26 56	20 26
3 18 19	1 36	7 35 5	16 45	11 30 37	28 5	15 18 19	16 52	19 35 5	20 3	23 30 37	21 8
3 22 23	2 20	7 39 20	17 30	11 34 18	28 44	15 22 23	18 3	19 39 20	21 48	23 34 18	21 50
3 26 29	3 2	7 43 34	18 15	11 37 58	29 24	15 26 29	19 16	19 43 34	23 29	23 37 58	22 31
3 30 35	3 45	7 47 47	18 59	11 41 39	0♐3	15 30 35	20 32	19 47 47	25 9	23 41 39	23 12
3 34 41	4 28	7 52 0	19 43	11 45 19	0 43	15 34 41	21 48	19 52 0	26 45	23 45 19	23 53
3 38 49	5 11	7 56 12	20 27	11 49 0	1 23	15 38 49	23 8	19 56 12	28 18	23 49 0	24 32
3 42 57	5 54	8 0 24	21 11	11 52 40	2 3	15 42 57	24 29	20 0 24	29 49	23 52 40	25 15
3 47 6	6 38	8 4 35	21 56	11 56 20	2 43	15 47 6	25 51	20 4 35	1♊19	23 56 20	25 56
3 51 15	7 21	8 8 45	22 40	12 0 0	3 23	15 51 15	27 15	20 8 45	2 45	24 0 0	26 36

51° 32

40° 43

Table of Houses for New York. Latitude 40° 43′ N

Sidereal Time H. M. S.	Ascen ° ♋ ′	Sidereal Time H. M. S.	Ascen ° ♍ ′	Sidereal Time H. M. S.	Ascen ° ♎ ′	Sidereal Time H. M. S.	Ascen ° ♐ ′	Sidereal Time H. M. S.	Ascen ° ♒ ′	Sidereal Time H. M. S.	Ascen ° ♉ ′
0 0 0	18 53	3 51 15	4 32	8 8 45	25 28	12 0 0	11 7	15 51 15	9 8	20 8 45	20 52
0 3 40	19 38	3 55 25	5 22	8 12 54	26 17	12 3 40	11 52	15 55 25	10 31	20 12 54	22 14
0 7 20	20 23	3 59 36	6 10	8 17 3	27 5	12 7 20	12 37	15 59 36	11 56	20 17 3	23 35
0 11 0	21 12	4 3 48	7 0	8 21 11	27 54	12 11 0	13 19	16 3 48	13 23	20 21 11	24 55
0 14 41	21 55	4 8 0	7 49	8 25 19	28 43	12 14 41	14 7	16 7 0	14 50	20 25 19	26 14
0 18 21	22 40	4 12 13	8 40	8 29 26	29 31	12 18 21	14 52	16 12 13	16 19	20 29 26	27 32
0 22 2	23 24	4 16 26	9 30	8 33 31	0 ♏ 20	12 22 2	15 38	16 16 26	17 50	20 33 31	28 46
0 25 42	24 8	4 20 40	10 19	8 37 37	1 8	12 25 42	16 23	16 20 40	19 22	20 37 37	0 ♊ 3
0 29 23	24 54	4 24 55	11 10	8 41 41	1 56	12 29 23	17 11	16 24 55	20 56	20 41 41	1 17
0 33 4	25 37	4 29 10	12 0	8 45 45	2 43	12 33 4	17 58	16 29 10	22 30	20 45 45	2 29
0 36 45	26 22	4 33 26	12 51	8 49 48	3 31	12 36 45	18 45	16 33 26	24 7	20 49 48	3 41
0 40 26	27 5	4 37 42	13 41	8 53 51	4 18	12 40 26	19 32	16 37 42	25 44	20 53 51	4 51
0 44 8	27 50	4 41 59	14 32	8 57 52	5 6	12 44 8	20 20	16 41 59	27 23	20 57 52	6 1
0 47 50	28 33	4 46 16	15 23	9 1 53	5 53	12 47 50	21 8	16 46 16	29 4	21 1 53	7 9
0 51 32	29 18	4 50 34	16 14	9 5 53	6 40	12 51 32	21 57	16 50 34	0 ♓ 45	21 5 53	8 16
0 55 14	0 ♌ 3	4 54 52	17 5	9 9 53	7 27	12 55 14	22 43	16 54 52	2 27	21 9 53	9 23
0 58 57	0 46	4 59 10	17 56	9 13 52	8 13	12 58 57	23 31	16 59 10	4 11	21 13 52	10 30
1 2 40	1 31	5 3 29	18 47	9 17 50	9 0	13 2 40	24 22	17 3 29	5 56	21 17 50	11 33
1 6 23	2 14	5 7 49	19 39	9 21 47	9 46	13 6 23	25 11	17 7 49	7 43	21 21 47	12 37
1 10 7	2 58	5 12 9	20 30	9 25 44	10 33	13 10 7	26 1	17 12 9	9 30	21 25 44	13 41
1 13 51	3 43	5 16 29	21 22	9 29 40	11 19	13 13 51	26 51	17 16 29	11 18	21 29 40	14 43
1 17 35	4 27	5 20 49	22 13	9 33 35	12 4	13 17 35	27 40	17 20 49	13 8	21 33 35	15 44
1 21 20	5 12	5 25 9	23 5	9 37 29	12 50	13 21 20	28 32	17 25 9	14 57	21 37 29	16 45
1 25 6	5 56	5 29 30	23 57	9 41 23	13 36	13 25 6	29 23	17 29 30	16 48	21 41 23	17 45
1 28 52	6 40	5 33 51	24 49	9 45 16	14 21	13 28 52	0 ♑ 14	17 33 51	18 41	21 45 16	18 44
1 32 38	7 25	5 38 12	25 40	9 49 9	15 7	13 32 38	1 7	17 38 12	20 33	21 49 9	19 42
1 36 25	8 9	5 42 34	26 32	9 53 1	15 52	13 36 25	2 0	17 42 34	22 25	21 53 1	20 40
1 40 12	8 53	5 46 55	27 25	9 56 52	16 38	13 40 12	2 52	17 46 55	24 19	21 56 52	21 37
1 44 0	9 38	5 51 17	28 16	10 0 43	17 22	13 44 0	3 46	17 51 17	26 12	22 0 43	22 33
1 47 48	10 24	5 55 38	29 8	10 4 33	18 7	13 47 48	4 41	17 55 38	28 7	22 4 33	23 30
1 51 37	11 8	6 0 0	30 0	10 8 23	18 52	13 51 37	5 35	18 0 0	30 0	22 8 23	24 25
1 55 27	11 53	6 4 22	0 ♎ 52	10 12 12	19 36	13 55 27	6 30	18 4 22	1 ♈ 53	22 12 12	25 19
1 59 17	12 38	6 8 43	1 44	10 16 0	20 22	13 59 17	7 27	18 8 43	3 48	22 16 0	26 14
2 3 8	13 22	6 13 5	2 35	10 19 48	21 7	14 3 8	8 23	18 13 5	5 41	22 19 48	27 8
2 6 59	14 8	6 17 26	3 28	10 23 35	21 51	14 6 59	9 20	18 17 26	7 35	22 23 35	28 0
2 10 51	14 53	6 21 48	4 20	10 27 22	22 35	14 10 51	10 18	18 21 48	9 27	22 27 22	28 53
2 14 44	15 39	6 26 9	5 11	10 31 8	23 20	14 14 44	11 16	18 26 9	11 19	22 31 8	29 46
2 18 37	16 24	6 30 30	6 3	10 34 54	24 4	14 18 37	12 15	18 30 30	13 12	22 34 54	0 ♋ 37
2 22 31	17 10	6 34 51	6 55	10 38 40	24 48	14 22 31	13 15	18 34 51	15 3	22 38 40	1 28
2 26 25	17 56	6 39 11	7 47	10 42 25	25 33	14 26 25	14 16	18 39 11	16 52	22 42 25	2 20
2 30 20	18 41	6 43 31	8 38	10 46 9	26 17	14 30 20	15 17	18 43 31	18 42	22 46 9	3 9
2 34 16	19 27	6 47 51	9 30	10 49 53	27 2	14 34 16	16 19	18 47 51	20 30	22 49 53	3 59
2 38 13	20 14	6 52 11	10 21	10 53 37	27 46	14 38 13	17 23	18 52 11	22 17	22 53 37	4 49
2 42 10	21 0	6 56 31	11 13	10 57 20	28 29	14 42 10	18 27	18 56 31	24 4	22 57 20	5 38
2 46 8	21 47	7 0 50	12 4	11 1 3	29 14	14 46 8	19 30	19 0 50	25 49	23 1 3	6 27
2 50 7	22 33	7 5 8	12 55	11 4 46	29 57	14 50 7	20 37	19 5 8	27 33	23 4 46	7 17
2 54 7	23 20	7 9 26	13 46	11 8 28	0 ♐ 42	14 54 7	21 44	19 9 20	29 15	23 8 28	8 3
2 58 7	24 7	7 13 44	14 37	11 12 10	1 27	14 58 7	22 51	19 13 44	0 ♉ 56	23 12 10	8 52
3 2 8	24 54	7 18 1	15 28	11 15 52	2 10	15 2 8	23 59	19 18 1	2 37	23 15 52	9 40
3 6 9	25 42	7 22 18	16 19	11 19 34	2 55	15 6 9	25 9	19 22 18	4 16	23 19 34	10 28
3 10 12	26 29	7 26 34	17 9	11 23 15	3 38	15 10 12	26 19	19 26 34	5 53	23 23 15	11 15
3 14 15	27 17	7 30 50	18 0	11 26 56	4 23	15 14 15	27 31	19 30 50	7 30	23 26 56	12 2
3 18 19	28 4	7 35 5	18 50	11 30 37	5 7	15 18 19	28 43	19 35 5	9 4	23 30 37	12 49
3 22 23	28 52	7 39 20	19 41	11 34 18	5 52	15 22 23	29 57	19 39 20	10 38	23 34 18	13 37
3 26 29	29 40	7 43 34	20 30	11 38 0	6 36	15 26 29	1 ♒ 14	19 43 34	12 10	23 37 58	14 22
3 30 35	0 ♍ 29	7 47 47	21 20	11 41 39	7 20	15 30 35	2 28	19 47 47	13 51	23 41 39	15 8
3 34 41	1 17	7 52 0	22 11	11 45 19	8 5	15 34 41	3 46	19 52 0	15 10	23 45 19	15 55
3 38 49	2 6	7 56 12	23 0	11 49 0	8 50	15 38 49	5 5	19 56 12	16 37	23 49 0	16 41
3 42 57	2 55	8 0 24	23 50	11 52 40	9 37	15 42 57	6 25	20 0 24	18 4	23 52 40	17 23
3 47 6	3 43	8 4 35	24 38	11 56 20	10 22	15 47 6	7 46	20 4 35	19 29	23 56 20	18 8
3 51 15	4 32	8 8 45	25 28	12 0 0	11 7	15 51 15	9 8	20 8 45	20 52	24 0 0	18 53

325

A Southern Hemisphere horoscope

Horoscopes of natives born south of the equator are calculated by the same method as that used for northerners—with only two differences:

1. To compensate for the difference in sidereal time in southern latitudes, 12 hours must be added to the s.t. calculated for the time of birth.

2. Since no tables of houses are available for the Southern Hemisphere, the native's ascendant sign will be sign of the Zodiac directly *opposite* to that given in the tables compiled for the corresponding northern latitude. For example, 15° Scorpio would be reversed to 15° Taurus.

Steps for calculation

Date of birth	January 10, 1939
Place	Melbourne, Australia
Latitude	37° 58′ S.
Longitude	145° 0′ E.
Local time	7 A.M.
G.M.T.	5 P.M.

S.T. at Greenwich at noon on January 10	19	16	27
+ interval from noon	5		
+ acceleration on interval at the rate of 10 seconds per hour			50
	24	17	17
Longitude 145° x 4	9	40	
Local S.T. at birth	33	57	17
Add 12 hours for latitude 37° 58′ S.	12		
	45	57	17
Subtract 24 (to bring the figure within the 24-hour span of a sidereal day)	24		
	21	57	17

Look this figure up in the table of houses and find the ascendant, 22° Gemini; reverse sign to 22° Sagittarius

Appendix 4

Simplified ephemerides of the planets

After the ascendant and the Sun-sign, the most important astrological factors are the positions of the planets in relation to the Zodiac. For example, five planets in a sign give that sign great emphasis; or a planet occupying its "own" sign strengthens the sign's importance. By using the following simplified ephemerides, you can find the approximate positions on your birthday of most planets; the tables list the Zodiac signs occupied by each of seven planets during the different months of every year from 1901 to 1964. When a planet moved out of a sign during the month, the date of the change is given. For example, in January 1902, Mercury moved out of Capricorn into Aquarius on the 12th. (Sometimes planets appear to move backward through the Zodiac and are called *retrograde*.) The tables cannot take into consideration specific degrees of positions; nor, for reasons of space, do they list the positions of the Moon (which moves into a different sign every two or three days) or of Pluto, which moves very slowly and has little influence on individuals.

1901

Month	Mercury ☿	Venus ♀	Mars ♂	Jupiter ♃	Saturn ♄	Uranus ♅	Neptune ♆
Jan.	1 ♐ / 2 ♑ / 20 ♒	1 ♐ / 16 ♑	1 ♏	1 ♐ / 18 ♑	1 ♑	1 ♐	1 ♊
Feb.	6 ♓ / 16 ♈	20 ♒	♏	♑	♑	♐	♊
March	9 ♓	3 ♓ / 29 ♈	♏	♑	♑	♐	♊
April	1 ♈	24 ♉	♏	♑	♑	♐	♊
May	4 ♉ / 19 ♊	19 ♊	♏	♑	♑	♐	♊
June	2 ♋	11 ♋	♏	♑	♑	♐	♊
July	♋	3 ♌ / 27 ♍	14 ♎	♑	♑	♐ / 20 ♋	♊
Aug.	9 ♌ / 25 ♍	23 ♎	♎	♑	♑	♐	♋
Sept.	11 ♎	19 ♏	14 ♏	♑	♑	♐	♋
Oct.	3 ♏	15 ♐	17 ♐	♑	♑	♐	♋
Nov.	♏	8 ♑	24 ♑	♑	♑	♐	♋
Dec.	8 ♐ / 26 ♑	3 ♒	30 ♒	♑	♑	♐	♋

1902

Month	Mercury ☿	Venus ♀	Mars ♂	Jupiter ♃	Saturn ♄	Uranus ♅	Neptune ♆
Jan.	1 ♑ / 12 ♒ / 31 ♓	1 ♒ / 8 ♓	1 ♒	1 ♑ / 28 ♒	1 ♒	1 ♐	1 ♊
Feb.	19 ♒	7 ♒	5 ♓	♒	♒	♐	♊
March	16 ♓	♒	18 ♈	♒	♒	♐	♊
April	9 ♈ / 26 ♉	3 ♓	30 ♉	♒	♒	♐	♊
May	11 ♊ / 29 ♋	7 ♈	♉	♒	♒	♐	♊
June	♋	5 ♉	10 ♊	♒	♒	♐	♊
July	♋	24 ♊ / 26 ♋	20 ♋	♒	♒	♐	♊
Aug.	12 ♌ / 16 ♍	18 ♌	♋	♒	♒	♐	♊
Sept.	4 ♎	11 ♍	1 ♌	♒	♒	♐	♊
Oct.	3 ♏ / 12 ♎	7 ♎	19 ♍	♒	♒	♐	♊
Nov.	11 ♏	2 ♏ / 26 ♐	♏	♒	♒	♐	♊
Dec.	1 ♐ / 19 ♑	18 ♑	17 ♎	♒	♒	♐	♊

1903

	Mercury ☿	Venus ♀	Mars ♂	Jupiter ♃	Saturn ♄	Uranus ♅	Neptune ♆
Jan.	1 ♑ / 5 ♒	1 ♑ / 9 ♒	1 ♎	1 ♒	1 ♒	1 ♐	1 ♋
Feb.	♒	2 ♓ / 29 ♈	♎	9 ♓	♒	♐	♋
March	13 ♓	26 ♉	♎	♓	♒	♐	♋
April	1 ♈ / 18 ♉	20 ♊	24 ♏	♓	♒	♐	♋
May	4 ♊	14 ♋	29 ♎	♓	♒	♐	♋
June	♊	7 ♌	♎	♓	♒	♐	♋
July	10 ♋ / 24 ♌	5 ♏	♎	♓	♒	♐	♋
Aug.	8 ♍ / 30 ♎	♏	11 ♏	♓	♒	♐	♋
Sept.	♎	♏	26 ♐	♓	♒	♐	♋
Oct.	♎	♏	♐	♓	♒	♐	♋
Nov.	5 ♏ / 24 ♐	8 ♎	3 ♑	♓	♒	♐	♋
Dec.	12 ♑ / 31 ♒	11 ♏	9 ♒	♓	♒	♐	♋

1904

	Mercury ☿	Venus ♀	Mars ♂	Jupiter ♃	Saturn ♄	Uranus ♅	Neptune ♆
Jan.	1 ♒ / 16 ♑	1 ♏ / 6 ♐ / 30 ♑	1 ♒ / 16 ♓	1 ♓	1 ♒	1 ♐	1 ♋
Feb.	14 ♒	22 ♒	27 ♈	28 ♈	♈	♐	♋
March	5 ♓ / 24 ♈	18 ♓	♈	♈	♈	♐	♋
April	9 ♉	12 ♈	10 ♉	♈	♈	♐	♋
May	♉	9 ♉	21 ♊	♈	♈	♐	♋
June	15 ♊	3 ♊ / 25 ♋	30 ♋	♈	♈	♐	♋
July	2 ♋ / 15 ♌ / 31 ♍	18 ♌	♋	♈	♈	♐	♋
Aug.	♍	11 ♏	11 ♌	♈	♈	♐	♋
Sept.	♍	6 ♎	27 ♏	♈	♈	♐	♋
Oct.	8 ♎ / 28 ♏	2 ♏ / 27 ♐	♏	♈	♈	♐	♋
Nov.	16 ♐	19 ♑	19 ♎	♈	♈	♐	♋
Dec.	5 ♑	11 ♒	♎	♈	♈	19 ♑	♋

1905

	Mercury ☿	Venus ♀	Mars ♂	Jupiter ♃	Saturn ♄	Uranus ♅	Neptune ♆
Jan.	1 ♑	1 ♒ / 5 ♓	1 ♎ / 17 ♏	1 ♈	1 ♒	1 ♑	1 ♋
Feb.	8 ♒ / 26 ♓	3 ♈	♏	♈	♒	♑	♋
March	16 ♈	11 ♉	♏	16 ♉	17 ♓	♑	♋
April	4 ♉ / 25 ♈	♉	♏	♉	♓	♑	♋
May	17 ♉	2 ♈	♏	♉	♓	♑	♋
June	10 ♊ / 23 ♋	1 ♉	♏	♉	♓	♑	♋
July	7 ♌ / 25 ♍	10 ♊	♏	♉	♓	♑	♋
Aug.	♍	6 ♋ / 31 ♌	26 ♐	1 ♊	♓	♑	♋
Sept.	♍	25 ♍	♐	♊	29 ♒	♑	♋
Oct.	1 ♎ / 21 ♏	21 ♎	8 ♑	♊	♒	♑	♋
Nov.	9 ♐	16 ♏	15 ♒	22 ♉	♒	♑	♋
Dec.	2 ♑ / 10 ♐	10 ♐	24 ♓	♉	3 ♓	♑	♋

1906

	Mercury ☿	Venus ♀	Mars ♂	Jupiter ♃	Saturn ♄	Uranus ♅	Neptune ♆
Jan.	1 ♐ / 13 ♑	1 ♐ / 2 ♑ / 24 ♒	1 ♓	1 ♉	1 ♓	1 ♑	1 ♋
Feb.	1 ♒ / 18 ♓	16 ♓	5 ♈	♉	♓	♑	♋
March	8 ♈	14 ♈	20 ♉	22 ♊	♓	♑	♋
April	♈	9 ♉	♉	♊	♓	♑	♋
May	16 ♉	4 ♊ / 27 ♋	2 ♊	♊	♓	♑	♋
June	2 ♊ / 15 ♋ / 29 ♌	19 ♌	12 ♋	♊	♓	♑	♋
July	♌	14 ♏	24 ♌	30 ♋	♓	♑	♋
Aug.	♌	11 ♎	♌	♋	♓	♑	♋
Sept.	6 ♍ / 24 ♎	10 ♏	8 ♏	♋	♓	♑	♋
Oct.	13 ♏	13 ♐	29 ♎	♋	♓	♑	♋
Nov.	4 ♐	♐	♎	♋	♓	♑	♋
Dec.	5 ♏ / 15 ♐	10 ♏ / 30 ♐	20 ♏	♋	♓	♑	♋

1907

Mercury ☿	Venus ♀	Mars ♂	Jupiter ♃	Saturn ♄	Uranus ♅	Neptune ♆	
1 ♐ / 7 ♑ / 25 ♒	1 ♐	1 ♏	1 ♋	1 ♓	1 ♑	1 ♋	Jan.
11 ♓	7 ♑	9 ♐	♋	♓	♑	♋	Feb.
5 ♈	5 ♒ / 31 ♓	♐	♋	♓	♑	♋	March
♈	27 ♈	2 ♑	♋	♓	♑	♋	April
9 ♉ / 24 ♊	24 ♉	♑	♋	♓	♑	♋	May
7 ♋ / 25 ♌	18 ♊	♑	♋	♓	♑	♋	June
29 ♋	11 ♋	♑	♋	♓	♑	♋	July
10 ♌ / 30 ♍	3 ♌ / 27 ♍	♑	8 ♌	♓	♑	♋	Aug.
16 ♎	22 ♎	♑	♌	♓	♑	♋	Sept.
7 ♏	18 ♏	9 ♒	♌	♓	♑	♋	Oct.
♏	11 ♐	♒	♌	♓	♑	♋	Nov.
12 ♐ / 31 ♑	3 ♑ / 25 ♒	♒	♌	♓	♑	♋	Dec.

1908

Mercury ☿	Venus ♀	Mars ♂	Jupiter ♃	Saturn ♄	Uranus ♅	Neptune ♆	
1 ♑ / 17 ♒	1 ♒ / 18 ♓	1 ♓ / 11 ♈	1 ♌	1 ♓	1 ♑	1 ♋	Jan.
4 ♓	14 ♈	26 ♉	♌	♓	♑	♋	Feb.
♓	12 ♉	♉	♌	11 ♈	♑	♋	March
12 ♈	8 ♊	10 ♊	♌	♈	♑	♋	April
1 ♉ / 15 ♊ / 30 ♊	6 ♋	22 ♋	♌	♈	♑	♋	May
♋	♋	♋	♌	♈	♑	♋	June
♋	♋	4 ♌	♌	♈	♑	♋	July
6 ♌ / 21 ♍	♋	20 ♍	31 ♏	♈	♑	♋	Aug.
8 ♎	7 ♌	♍	♏	♈	♑	♋	Sept.
1 ♏ / 31 ♎	6 ♍	9 ♎	♏	♈	♑	♋	Oct.
13 ♏	3 ♎ / 30 ♏	28 ♏	♏	♈	♑	♋	Nov.
5 ♐ / 23 ♑	24 ♐	♏	♏	♈	♑	♋	Dec.

1909

Mercury ☿	Venus ♀	Mars ♂	Jupiter ♃	Saturn ♄	Uranus ♅	Neptune ♆	
1 ♑ / 9 ♒	1 ♐ / 16 ♑	1 ♏ / 13 ♐	1 ♏	1 ♈	1 ♑	1 ♌	Jan.
♒	7 ♒	24 ♐	♏	♈	♑	♌	Feb.
15 ♓	3 ♓ / 29 ♈	♑	♏	♈	♑	♌	March
5 ♈ / 22 ♉	24 ♉	6 ♒	♏	♈	♑	♌	April
7 ♊	18 ♊	21 ♓	♏	♈	♑	♌	May
♊	10 ♋	♓	♏	♈	♑	♌	June
13 ♋ / 29 ♌	3 ♌ / 27 ♍	16 ♈	♏	♈	♑	♌	July
12 ♍	23 ♎	♈	♏	♈	♑	♌	Aug.
1 ♎	19 ♏	♈	♏	♈	♑	♌	Sept.
♎	14 ♐	4 ♓	9 ♎	♈	♑	♌	Oct.
9 ♏ / 28 ♐	7 ♑	19 ♈	♎	♈	♑	♌	Nov.
16 ♑	3 ♒	♈	♎	♈	♑	♌	Dec.

1910

Mercury ☿	Venus ♀	Mars ♂	Jupiter ♃	Saturn ♄	Uranus ♅	Neptune ♆	
1 ♑ / 2 ♒	1 ♒ / 11 ♓ / 30 ♒	1 ♈ / 27 ♉	1 ♎	1 ♈	1 ♒	1 ♋	Jan.
2 ♑ / 13 ♒	♒	♉	♎	♈	♒	♋	Feb.
10 ♓ / 29 ♈	♒	18 ♊	♎	♈	♒	♋	March
14 ♉	4 ♓	♊	♎	♈	♒	♋	April
3 ♊ / 30 ♉	7 ♈	2 ♋	♎	28 ♉	♒	♋	May
15 ♊	5 ♉	15 ♌	♎	♉'	♒	♋	June
6 ♋ / 20 ♌	1 ♊ / 25 ♋	♌	♎	♉	♒	♋	July
6 ♍ / 28 ♎	17 ♌	2 ♍	♎	♉	♒	♋	Aug.
28 ♏	11 ♏	21 ♎	♎	♉	♒	♋	Sept.
12 ♎	6 ♎	♎	♎	♉	♒	♋	Oct.
2 ♏ / 21 ♐	1 ♏ / 25 ♐	9 ♏	20 ♏	24 ♈	♒	♋	Nov.
9 ♑	18 ♑	23 ♐	♏	♈	♒	♋	Dec.

1911

	Mercury ☿	Venus ♀	Mars ♂	Jupiter ♃	Saturn ♄	Uranus ♅	Neptune ♆
Jan.	1 ♑	1 ♑ / 9 ♒	1 ♐	1 ♏	1 ♈	1 ♑	1 ♋
Feb.	11 ♒	1 ♓ / 27 ♈	1 ♑	♏	12 ♉	♑	♋
March	3 ♓ / ♈	26 ♉	11 ♒	♏	♉	4 ♒	♋
April	7 ♉	20 ♊	20 ♓	♏	♉	♒	♋
May	♉	13 ♋	♓	♏	♉	♒	♋
June	14 ♊ / 29 ♋	6 ♌	2 ♈	♏	♉	♒	♋
July	12 ♌ / 29 ♍	5 ♍	18 ♉	♏	♉	14 ♑	♋
Aug.	♍	♍	♉	♏	♉	♑	♋
Sept.	♍	♍	9 ♊	♏	♉	♑	♋
Oct.	6 ♎ / 25 ♏	♍	♊	♏	♉	♑	♋
Nov.	14 ♐	9 ♎	24 ♉	♏	♉	♑	♋
Dec.	3 ♑ / 28 ♐	10 ♏	♉	19 ♐	♉	25 ♒	♋

1912

	Mercury ☿	Venus ♀	Mars ♂	Jupiter ♃	Saturn ♄	Uranus ♅	Neptune ♆
Jan.	1 ♐ / 15 ♑	1 ♏ / 6 ♐ / 30 ♑	1 ♉	1 ♐	1 ♉	1 ♒	1 ♋
Feb.	5 ♒ / 24 ♓	22 ♒	7 ♊	♐	♉	♒	♋
March	12 ♈	17 ♓	♊	♐	♉	♒	♋
April	♈	12 ♈	5 ♋	♐	♉	♒	♋
May	18 ♉	8 ♉	24 ♌	♐	♉	♒	♋
June	6 ♊	2 ♊ / 25 ♋	♌	♐	♉	♒	♋
July	3 ♌ / 24 ♍	17 ♌	13 ♏	♐	24 ♊	♒	♋
Aug.	21 ♌	10 ♍	♏	♐	♊	♒	♋
Sept.	9 ♍ / 28 ♎	6 ♎	2 ♎	♐	♊	♒	♋
Oct.	17 ♏	2 ♏ / 26 ♐	21 ♏	♐	♊	♒	♋
Nov.	6 ♐	18 ♑	♏	♐	12 ♉	♒	♋
Dec.	♐	11 ♒	3 ♐	♐	♉	♒	♋

1913

	Mercury ☿	Venus ♀	Mars ♂	Jupiter ♃	Saturn ♄	Uranus ♅	Neptune ♆
Jan.	1 ♐ / 10 ♑ / 28 ♒	1 ♒ / 5 ♓	1 ♐ / 10 ♑	1 ♐ / 2 ♑	1 ♉	1 ♒ / ♒	1 ♋ / ♋
Feb.	15 ♓	3 ♈	16 ♒	♑	♉	♒	♋
March	5 ♈	12 ♉	27 ♓	♑	♉	♒	♋
April	7 ♓ / 12 ♈	25 ♈	♓	♑	12 ♊	♒	♋
May	13 ♉ / 29 ♊	♈	7 ♈	♑	♊	♒	♋
June	11 ♋ / 26 ♌	3 ♉	19 ♉	♑	♊	♒	♋
July	♌	10 ♊	♉	♑	♊	♒	♋
Aug.	♌	6 ♋ / 31 ♌	1 ♊	♑	♊	♒	♋
Sept.	3 ♍ / 20 ♎	25 ♍	16 ♋	♑	♊	♒	29 ♌
Oct.	10 ♏	21 ♎	♋	♑	♊	♒	♌
Nov.	2 ♐	16 ♏	♋	♑	♊	♒	♌
Dec.	♐	10 ♐	♋	♑	♊	♒	♌

1914

	Mercury ☿	Venus ♀	Mars ♂	Jupiter ♃	Saturn ♄	Uranus ♅	Neptune ♆
Jan.	1 ♐ / 4 ♑ / 21 ♒	1 ♑ / 23 ♒	1 ♋	1 ♑ / 12 ♒	1 ♊	1 ♒	1 ♋
Feb.	7 ♓	16 ♓	♋	♒	♊	♒	♋
March	♓	13 ♈	♋	♒	♊	♒	♋
April	16 ♈	9 ♉	26 ♌	♒	♊	♒	♋
May	6 ♉ / 20 ♊	3 ♊ / 26 ♋	♌	♒	♊	♒	♋
June	3 ♋ / 28 ♌	18 ♌	21 ♍	♒	♊	♒	♋
July	7 ♋	13 ♍	♏	♒	♊	♒	19 ♌
Aug.	10 ♌ / 26 ♍	11 ♎	14 ♎	♒	23 ♋	♒	♌
Sept.	12 ♎	10 ♏	♎	♒	♋	♒	♌
Oct.	4 ♏	14 ♐	2 ♏	♒	♋	♒	♌
Nov.	♏	♐	14 ♐	♒	♋	♒	♌
Dec.	9 ♐ / 28 ♑	2 ♏	22 ♑	♒	9 ♊	♒	♌

1915

	Mercury ☿		Venus ♀		Mars ♂		Jupiter ♃		Saturn ♄	Uranus ♅	Neptune ♆	
	1	♑	1	♏	1	♑	1	♒	1 ♊	1 ♒	1 ♌	Jan.
	14	♒	2	♐	27	♒	24	♓				
	1	♓	7	♑		♒		♓	♊	♒	♌	Feb.
	25	♒										
	17	♓	5	♒	6	♓		♓	♊	♒	12 ♋	March
			31	♓								
	10	♈	26	♈	16	♈		♓	♊	♒	♋	April
	28	♉										
	12	♊	23	♉	28	♉		♓	11 ♋	♒	10 ♌	May
	29	♋										
		♋	17	♊		♉		♓	♋	♒	♌	June
		♋	11	♋	9	♊		♓	♋	♒	♌	July
	3	♌	2	♌	19	♋		♓	♋	♒	♌	Aug.
	18	♍	26	♍								
	5	♎	21	♎		♋		♓	♋	♒	♌	Sept.
	2	♏	17	♏	4	♌		♓	♋	♒	♌	Oct.
	19	♎										
	13	♏	10	♐		♌		♓	♋	♒	♌	Nov.
	3	♐	3	♑	9	♏		♓	♋	♒	♌	Dec.
	20	♑	25	♒								

1916

	Mercury ☿		Venus ♀		Mars ♂		Jupiter ♃		Saturn ♄	Uranus ♅	Neptune ♆	
	1	♑	1	♏	1	♏	1	♓	1 ♋	1 ♒	1 ♌	Jan.
	6	♒	18	♓	25	♌						
		♒	13	♈		♌	9	♈	♋	♒	♌	Feb.
	13	♓	12	♉		♌		♈	♋	♒	♌	March
	2	♈	8	♊		♌		♈	♋	♒	♌	April
	18	♉										
	4	♊	6	♋	23	♏		♈	♋	♒	♌	May
		♊		♋		♏		♈	♋	♒	♌	June
	11	♋		♋	23	♎	6	♉	♋	♒	♌	July
	25	♌										
	9	♏		♋		♎		♉	♋	♒	♌	Aug.
	29	♎										
		♎	7	♌	12	♏		♉	16 ♌	♒	♌	Sept.
		♎	6	♏	25	♐	16	♈	♌	♒	♌	Oct.
	5	♏	2	♎		♐		♈	♌	♒	♌	Nov.
	24	♐	29	♏								
	12	♑	24	♐	2	♑		♈	♌	♒	♌	Dec.
	31	♒										

1917

	Mercury ☿		Venus ♀		Mars ♂		Jupiter ♃		Saturn ♄	Uranus ♅	Neptune ♆	
	1	♒	1	♐	1	♑	1	♈	1 ♌	1 ♒	1 ♌	Jan.
	19	♑	15	♑	6	♒			10 ♋			
	13	♒	7	♒	13	♓	23	♉	♋	♒	♌	Feb.
	7	♓	2	♓	26	♈		♈	♋	♒	♌	March
	25	♈	28	♈								
	10	♉	23	♉		♈		♉	♋	♒	♌	April
		♉	18	♊	7	♉		♉	♋	♒	♌	May
	16	♊	10	♋	18	♊		♉	4 ♌	♒	♌	June
	3	♋	2	♌	28	♋	9	♊	♌	♒	♌	July
	16	♌	26	♍								
	1	♏	22	♎		♋		♊	♌	♒	♌	Aug.
	29	♎										
	12	♏	18	♏	9	♌		♊	♌	♒	♌	Sept.
	10	♎	14	♐	28	♍		♊	♌	♒	♌	Oct.
	29	♏										
	17	♐	7	♑		♏		♊	♌	♒	♌	Nov.
	6	♑	3	♒		♏		♊	♌	♒	♌	Dec.

1918

	Mercury ☿		Venus ♀		Mars ♂		Jupiter ♃		Saturn ♄	Uranus ♅	Neptune ♆	
	1	♑	1	♒	1	♏	1	♊	1 ♌	1 ♒	1 ♌	Jan.
					6	♎	10	♉				
	9	♒		♒		♎	12	♊	♌	♒	♌	Feb.
	28	♓										
	17	♈		♒	3	♏		♊	♌	♒	♌	March
	5	♉	4	♓		♏		♊	♌	♒	♌	April
	4	♈	6	♈		♏		♊	♌	11 ♓	♌	May
	14	♉										
	11	♊	4	♉	12	♎		♊	♌	27 ♒	♌	June
	25	♋										
	8	♌	1	♊	21	♏	13	♋	♌	♒	♌	July
	26	♏	25	♋								
		♏	17	♌		♏		♋	♌	♒	♌	Aug.
		♏	10	♏		♏		♋	♌	♒	♌	Sept.
	3	♎	6	♎	4	♐		♋	♌	♒	♌	Oct.
	22	♏										
	11	♐	1	♏	11	♑		♋	8 ♏	♒	♌	Nov.
			25	♐								
	2	♑	17	♑	17	♒		♋	♏	♒	♌	Dec.
	16	♐										

1919

	Mercury ☿	Venus ♀	Mars ♂	Jupiter ♃	Saturn ♄	Uranus ♅	Neptune ♆
Jan.	1 ♐ / 14 ♑	1 ♑ / 8 ♒	1 ♒ / 24 ♓	1 ♋	1 ♏ / 11 ♌	1 ♒	1 ♌
Feb.	2 ♒ / 20 ♓	1 ♓ / 27 ♈	♓	♋	♌	14 ♓	♌
March	9 ♈	25 ♉	6 ♈	♋	♌	♓	♌
April	♈	19 ♊	18 ♉	♋	♌	♓	♌
May	17 ♉	13 ♋	29 ♊	♋	♌	♓	♌
June	3 ♊ / 16 ♋	6 ♌	♊	♋	♌	♓	♌
July	1 ♌	5 ♍	9 ♋	23 ♌	20 ♏	♓	♌
Aug.	♌	♍	20 ♌	♌	♏	♓	♌
Sept.	7 ♍ / 25 ♎	♍	♌	♌	♏	♓	♌
Oct.	15 ♏	♍	6 ♍	♌	♏	♓	♌
Nov.	5 ♐	9 ♎	29 ♎	♌	♏	♓	♌
Dec.	♐	10 ♏	♎	♌	♏	♓	♌

1920

	Mercury ☿	Venus ♀	Mars ♂	Jupiter ♃	Saturn ♄	Uranus ♅	Neptune ♆
Jan.	1 ♐ / 8 ♑ / 26 ♒	1 ♏ / 6 ♐ / 24 ♑	1 ♎	1 ♌	1 ♏	1 ♓	1 ♌
Feb.	12 ♓	21 ♒	4 ♏	♌	♏	♓	♌
March	3 ♈ / 18 ♓	16 ♓	♏	♌	♏	♓	♌
April	17 ♈	11 ♈	20 ♐	♌	♏	♓	♌
May	11 ♉ / 25 ♊	8 ♉	♎	♌	♏	♓	♌
June	7 ♋ / 24 ♌	2 ♊ / 24 ♋	♎	♌	♏	♓	♌
July	♌	17 ♌	17 ♏	♌	♏	♓	♌
Aug.	30 ♍	10 ♍	♏	15 ♏	♏	♓	♌
Sept.	16 ♎	5 ♎	8 ♐	♏	♏	♓	♌
Oct.	7 ♏	1 ♏ / 26 ♐	18 ♑	♏	♏	♓	♌
Nov.	♏	18 ♑	24 ♒	♏	♏	♓	♌
Dec.	12 ♐ / ,31 ♑	10 ♒	♒	♏	♏	♓	♌

1921

	Mercury ☿	Venus ♀	Mars ♂	Jupiter ♃	Saturn ♄	Uranus ♅	Neptune ♆
Jan.	1 ♑ / 18 ♒	1 ♒ / 4 ♓	1 ♒ / 2 ♓	1 ♏	1 ♏	1 ♓	1 ♌
Feb.	4 ♓	3 ♈	13 ♈	♏	♏	♓	♌
March	♓	13 ♉	28 ♉	♏	♏	♓	♌
April	13 ♈	18 ♈	♉	♏	♏	♓	♌
May	2 ♉ / 16 ♊ / 31 ♋	♈	9 ♊	♏	♏	♓	♌
June	♋	5 ♉	19 ♋	♏	♏	♓	♌
July	♋	10 ♊	31 ♌	♏	♏	♓	♌
Aug.	7 ♌ / 22 ♍	6 ♋ / 30 ♌	♌	♏	♏	♓	♌
Sept.	9 ♎	24 ♍	15 ♏	24 ♎	29 ♎	♓	♌
Oct.	2 ♏	20 ♎	♏	♎	♎	♓	♌
Nov.	6 ♎ / 13 ♏	15 ♏	6 ♎	♎	♎	♓	♌
Dec.	6 ♐ / 24 ♑	9 ♐	29 ♏	♎	♎	♓	♌

1922

	Mercury ☿	Venus ♀	Mars ♂	Jupiter ♃	Saturn ♄	Uranus ♅	Neptune ♆
Jan.	1 ♑ / 10 ♒ / 30 ♓	1 ♑ / 23 ♒	1 ♏	1 ♎	1 ♎	1 ♓	1 ♌
Feb.	11 ♒	15 ♓	22 ♐	♎	♎	♓	♌
March	16 ♓	13 ♈	♐	♎	♎	♓	♌
April	7 ♈ / 24 ♉	8 ♉	♐	♎	♎	♓	♌
May	9 ♊	3 ♊ / 26 ♋	♐	♎	♎	♓	♌
June	1 ♋ / 11 ♊	18 ♌	♐	♎	♎	♓	♌
July	14 ♋ / 30 ♌	13 ♍	♐	♎	♎	♓	♌
Aug.	14 ♏	10 ♎	♐	♎	♎	♓	♌
Sept.	2 ♎	10 ♏	13 ♑	♎	♎	♓	♌
Oct.	♎	16 ♐	27 ♒	♎	♎	♓	♌
Nov.	10 ♏ / 29 ♐	25 ♏	♒	3 ♏	♎	♓	♌
Dec.	17 ♑	♏	8 ♓	♏	♎	♓	♌

1923

Mercury ☿	Venus ♀	Mars ♂	Jupiter ♃	Saturn ♄	Uranus ♅	Neptune ♆	
1 ♑ / 3 ♒	1 ♏ / 4 ♐	1 ♓ / 21 ♈	1 ♏	1 ♎	1 ♓	1 ♌	Jan.
♒	6 ♑	♈	♏	♎	♓	♌	Feb.
11 ♓ / 30 ♈	5 ♒ / 30 ♓	7 ♉	♏	♎	♓	♌	March
17 ♉	26 ♈	19 ♊	♏	♎	♓	♌	April
3 ♊	23 ♉	31 ♋	♏	♎	♓	♌	May
♊	17 ♊	♋	♏	♎	♓	♌	June
8 ♋ / 22 ♌	10 ♋	12 ♌	♏	♎	♓	♌	July
6 ♍ / 28 ♎	2 ♌ / 26 ♍	28 ♏	♏	♎	♓	♌	Aug.
♎	21 ♎	♏	♏	♎	♓	♌	Sept.
4 ♏ / 11 ♎	17 ♏	17 ♎	♏	♎	♓	♌	Oct.
3 ♏ / 22 ♐	10 ♐	♎	♏	♎	♓	♌	Nov.
10 ♑ / 31 ♒	2 ♑ / 24 ♒	7 ♏	3 ♐	♎	♓	♌	Dec.

1924

Mercury ☿	Venus ♀	Mars ♂	Jupiter ♃	Saturn ♄	Uranus ♅	Neptune ♆	
1 ♒ / 7 ♑	1 ♒ / 17 ♓	1 ♏ / 23 ♐	1 ♐	1 ♎ / 6 ♏	1 ♓	1 ♌	Jan.
12 ♒	13 ♈	♐	♐	♏	♓	♌	Feb.
3 ♓ / 21 ♈	12 ♉	7 ♑	♐	20 ♎	♓	♌	March
7 ♉	8 ♊	21 ♒	♐	♎	♓	♌	April
♉	6 ♋	♒	♐	♎	♓	♌	May
14 ♊ / 30 ♋	♋	15 ♓	♐	♎	♓	♌	June
12 ♌ / 29 ♍	♋	♓	♐	♎	♓	♌	July
♍	♋	♓	♐	♎	♓	♌	Aug.
♍	7 ♌	♓	♐	25 ♏	♓	♌	Sept.
7 ♎ / 26 ♏	6 ♍	♓	♐	♏	♓	♌	Oct.
14 ♐	2 ♎ / 29 ♏	♓	♐	♏	♓	♌	Nov.
3 ♑	23 ♐	19 ♈	18 ♑	♏	♓	♌	Dec.

1925

Mercury ☿	Venus ♀	Mars ♂	Jupiter ♃	Saturn ♄	Uranus ♅	Neptune ♆	
1 ♐ / 14 ♑	1 ♐ / 15 ♑	1 ♈	1 ♑	1 ♏	1 ♓	1 ♌	Jan.
6 ♒ / 24 ♓	6 ♒	2 ♉	♑	♏	♓	♌	Feb.
13 ♈	2 ♓ / 28 ♈	27 ♊	♑	♏	♓	♌	March
♈	23 ♉	♊	♑	♏	♓	♌	April
18 ♉	17 ♊	10 ♋	♑	♏	♓	♌	May
8 ♊	9 ♋	22 ♌	♑	♏	♓	♌	June
4 ♋ / 25 ♍	2 ♌ / 26 ♍	♌	♑	♏	♓	♌	July
♍	22 ♎	9 ♍	♑	♏	♓	♌	Aug.
29 ♎	18 ♏	28 ♎	♑	♏	♓	♌	Sept.
18 ♏	14 ♐	♎	♑	♏	♓	♌	Oct.
7 ♐	7 ♑	16 ♏	♑	♏	♓	♌	Nov.
♐	3 ♒	31 ♐	27 ♒	♏	♓	♌	Dec.

1926

Mercury ☿	Venus ♀	Mars ♂	Jupiter ♃	Saturn ♄	Uranus ♅	Neptune ♆	
1 ♐ / 11 ♑ / 30 ♒	1 ♒	1 ♐	1 ♒	1 ♏	1 ♓	1 ♌	Jan.
16 ♓	♒	9 ♑	♒	♏	♓	♌	Feb.
6 ♈	♒	20 ♒	♒	♏	♓	♌	March
♈	4 ♓	30 ♓	♒	♏	♓	♌	April
14 ♉ / 30 ♊	6 ♈	♓	♒	♏	♓	♌	May
12 ♋ / 28 ♌	4 ♉ / 30 ♊	13 ♈	♒	♏	♓	♌	June
♌	24 ♋	♈	♒	♏	♓	♌	July
♌	16 ♌	3 ♉	♒	♏	♓	♌	Aug.
4 ♍ / 21 ♎	9 ♍	♉	♒	♏	♓	♌	Sept.
11 ♍	5 ♎ / 31 ♏	♉	♒	♏	♓	♌	Oct.
3 ♐ / 27 ♏	24 ♐	♉	♒	♏	♓	♌	Nov.
15 ♐	17 ♑	♉	♒	17 ♐	♓	♌	Dec.

1927

	Mercury ☿	Venus ♀	Mars ♂	Jupiter ♃	Saturn ♄	Uranus ♅	Neptune ♆
Jan.	1 ♐, 5 ♑, 22 ♒	1 ♑, 8 ♒, 31 ♓	1 ♉	1 ♒, 6 ♓	1 ♐	1 ♓	1 ♌
Feb.	9 ♓	26 ♈	27 ♊	♓	♐	♓	♌
March	♓	25 ♉	♊	♓	♐	24 ♈	♌
April	17 ♈	19 ♊	17 ♋	♓	♐	♈	♌
May	7 ♉, 22 ♊	12 ♋		♓	♐	♈	♌
June	5 ♋, 26 ♌	6 ♌	2 ♌	2 ♈	♐	♈	♌
July	16 ♋	5 ♍	21 ♏	♈	10 ♏	♈	♌
Aug.	10 ♌, 27 ♍	♍	♏	♈	♏	♈	♌
Sept.	14 ♎	♍	10 ♎	18 ♓	2 ♐	♈	12 ♍
Oct.	5 ♏	♏	29 ♏	♓	♐	♈	♍
Nov.	♏	9 ♎	♏	♓	♐	♈	♏
Dec.	11 ♐, 29 ♑	10 ♏	11 ♐	♓	♐	1 ♓, 21 ♈	♏

1928

	Mercury ☿	Venus ♀	Mars ♂	Jupiter ♃	Saturn ♄	Uranus ♅	Neptune ♆
Jan.	1 ♑, 15 ♒	1 ♏, 5 ♐, 29 ♑	1 ♐, 19 ♑	1 ♓, 19 ♈	1 ♐	1 ♈	1 ♏
Feb.	2 ♓	21 ♒	25 ♒	♈	♐	♈	29 ♌
March	2 ♒, 15 ♓	16 ♓	♒	♈	♐	♈	♌
April	10 ♈, 28 ♉	11 ♈	4 ♓	♈	♐	♈	♌
May	13 ♊, 29 ♋	7 ♉	16 ♈	♈	♐	♈	♌
June	♋	1 ♊, 24 ♋	28 ♉	12 ♉	♐	♈	♌
July	♋	18 ♌	♉	♉	♐	♈	13 ♏
Aug.	4 ♌, 18 ♍	9 ♍	12 ♊	♉	♐	♈	♏
Sept.	6 ♎	4 ♎	♊	♉	♐	♈	♏
Oct.	1 ♏, 23 ♎	1 ♏, 25 ♐	3 ♋	♉	♐	♈	♏
Nov.	12 ♏	17 ♑	♋	30 ♈	♐	♈	♏
Dec.	3 ♐, 21 ♑	10 ♒	21 ♊	♈	♐	♈	♏

1929

	Mercury ☿	Venus ♀	Mars ♂	Jupiter ♃	Saturn ♄	Uranus ♅	Neptune ♆
Jan.	1 ♑, 7 ♒	1 ♒, 4 ♓	1 ♊	1 ♈, 22 ♉	1 ♐	1 ♈	1 ♏
Feb.	♒	3 ♈	♊	♉	♐	♈	♏
March	14 ♓	15 ♉	11 ♋	♉	13 ♑	♈	♏
April	3 ♈, 20 ♉	12 ♈	♋	♉	♑	♈	♏
May	5 ♊	♈	8 ♌	♉	8 ♐	♈	♏
June	♊	5 ♉	30 ♌	21 ♊	♐	♈	♏
July	12 ♋, 26 ♌	9 ♊	♏	♊	♐	♈	♏
Aug.	10 ♍, 30 ♎	5 ♋, 30 ♌	21 ♎	♊	♐	♈	♏
Sept.	♎	24 ♍	♎	♊	♐	♈	♏
Oct.	♎	20 ♎	9 ♏	♊	♐	♈	♏
Nov.	7 ♏, 26 ♐	15 ♏	21 ♐	♊	29 ♑	♈	♏
Dec.	14 ♑	9 ♐, 31 ♑	29 ♑	♊	♑	♈	♏

1930

	Mercury ☿	Venus ♀	Mars ♂	Jupiter ♃	Saturn ♄	Uranus ♅	Neptune ♆
Jan.	1 ♒, 24 ♑	1 ♑, 22 ♒	1 ♑	1 ♊	1 ♑	1 ♈	1 ♏
Feb.	13 ♒	15 ♓	4 ♒	♊	♑	♈	♏
March	8 ♓, 27 ♈	12 ♈	14 ♓	♊	♑	♈	♏
April	12 ♉	8 ♉	24 ♈	♊	♑	♈	♏
May	♉	2 ♊, 25 ♋	♈	♊	♑	♈	♏
June	16 ♊	17 ♌	5 ♉	26 ♋	♑	♈	♏
July	5 ♋, 18 ♌	12 ♍	17 ♊	♋	♑	♈	♏
Aug.	2 ♍, 28 ♎	10 ♎	28 ♋	♋	♑	♈	♏
Sept.	19 ♍	10 ♏	♋	♋	♑	♈	♏
Oct.	11 ♎, 31 ♏	18 ♐	16 ♌	♋	♑	♈	♏
Nov.	19 ♐	17 ♏	♌	♋	♑	♈	♏
Dec.	7 ♑	♏	♌	♋	♑	♈	♏

1931

Mercury ☿	Venus ♀	Mars ♂	Jupiter ♃	Saturn ♄	Uranus ♅	Neptune ♆	
1 ♑	1 ♏ / 6 ♐	1 ♌	1 ♋	1 ♑	1 ♈	1 ♏	Jan.
10 ♒	7 ♑	♌	♋	♑	♈	♏	Feb.
1 ♓ / 19 ♈	5 ♒ / 30 ♓	♌	♋	♑	♈	♏	March
6 ♉	26 ♈	♌	♋	♑	♈	♏	April
♉	23 ♉	♌	♋	♑	♈	♏	May
13 ♊ / 27 ♋	17 ♊	6 ♍	♋	♑	♈	♏	June
10 ♌ / 28 ♍	10 ♋	♍	7 ♌	♑	♈	♏	July
♍	2 ♌ / 26 ♍	2 ♎	♌	♑	♈	♏	Aug.
♍	21 ♎	21 ♏	♌	♑	♈	♏	Sept.
5 ♎ / 24 ♏	17 ♏	♏	♌	♑	♈	♏	Oct.
12 ♐	10 ♐	3 ♐	♌	♑	♈	♏	Nov.
2 ♑ / 21 ♐	2 ♑ / 24 ♒	10 ♑	♌	♑	♈	♏	Dec.

1932

Mercury ☿	Venus ♀	Mars ♂	Jupiter ♃	Saturn ♄	Uranus ♅	Neptune ♆	
1 ♐ / 15 ♑	1 ♒ / 17 ♓	1 ♑ / 15 ♒	1 ♌	1 ♑	1 ♈	1 ♏	Jan.
4 ♒ / 22 ♓	13 ♈	22 ♓	♌	5 ♒	♈	♏	Feb.
10 ♈	12 ♉	♓	♌	♒	♈	♏	March
♈	8 ♊	3 ♈	♌	♒	♈	♏	April
17 ♉	7 ♋	16 ♉	♌	♒	♈	♏	May
4 ♊ / 17 ♋	♋	26 ♊	♌	♒	♈	♏	June
1 ♌ / 26 ♍	14 ♊ / 29 ♋	♊	30 ♏	♒	♈	♏	July
12 ♌	♋	5 ♋	♏	♒	♈	♏	Aug.
8 ♍ / 26 ♎	8 ♌	18 ♌	♏	♒	♈	♏	Sept.
16 ♏	6 ♏	♌	♏	♒	♈	♏	Oct.
5 ♐	2 ♎ / 29 ♏	9 ♏	♏	♒	♈	♏	Nov.
♐	23 ♐	♏	♏	♒	♈	♏	Dec.

1933

Mercury ☿	Venus ♀	Mars ♂	Jupiter ♃	Saturn ♄	Uranus ♅	Neptune ♆	
1 ♐ / 9 ♑ / 27 ♒	1 ♐ / 15 ♑	1 ♏	1 ♏	1 ♒	1 ♈	1 ♏	Jan.
12 ♓	6 ♒	♏	♏	♒	♈	♏	Feb.
4 ♈ / 25 ♓	2 ♓ / 27 ♈	♏	♏	♒	♈	♏	March
17 ♈	23 ♉	♏	♏	♒	♈	♏	April
12 ♉ / 27 ♊	17 ♊	♏	♏	♒	♈	♏	May
9 ♋ / 26 ♌	9 ♋	♏	♏	♒	♈	♏	June
♌	2 ♌ / 26 ♍	7 ♎	♏	♒	♈	♏	July
♌	22 ♎	30 ♏	♏	♒	♈	♏	Aug.
1 ♍ / 18 ♎	18 ♏	♏	8 ♎	♒	♈	♏	Sept.
9 ♏	14 ♐	13 ♐	♎	♒	♈	♏	Oct.
3 ♐ / 14 ♏	7 ♑	20 ♑	♎	♒	♈	♏	Nov.
14 ♐	3 ♒	26 ♒	♎	♒	♈	♏	Dec.

1934

Mercury ☿	Venus ♀	Mars ♂	Jupiter ♃	Saturn ♄	Uranus ♅	Neptune ♆	
1 ♐ / 2 ♑ / 19 ♒	1 ♒	1 ♒	1 ♎	1 ♒	1 ♈	1 ♏	Jan.
6 ♓	♒	1 ♓	♎	♒	♈	♏	Feb.
♓	♒	14 ♈	♎	♒	♈	♏	March
15 ♈	5 ♓	26 ♉	♎	♒	♈	♏	April
4 ♉ / 18 ♊	6 ♈	♉	♎	6 ♓	♈	♏	May
2 ♋	4 ♉ / 30 ♊	6 ♊	♎	♓	♈	♏	June
♋	24 ♋	16 ♋	♎	15 ♒	♈	♏	July
9 ♌ / 24 ♍	16 ♌	27 ♌	♎	♒	♈	♏	Aug.
11 ♎	9 ♍	♌	♎	♒	♈	♏	Sept.
3 ♏	5 ♎ / 31 ♏	14 ♏	19 ♏	♒	♈	♏	Oct.
♏	24 ♐	♏	♏	♒	♈	♏	Nov.
8 ♐ / 26 ♑	16 ♑	10 ♎	♏	♒	♈	♏	Dec.

1935

	Mercury ☿	Venus ♀	Mars ♂	Jupiter ♃	Saturn ♄	Uranus ♅	Neptune ♆
Jan.	1 ♑ / 12 ♒ / 31 ♓	1 ♑ / 7 ♒ / 31 ♓	1 ♎	1 ♏	1 ♒ / 22 ♓	1 ♈	1 ♏
Feb.	17 ♒	26 ♈	♎	♏	♓	♈	♏
March	17 ♓	25 ♉	♎	♏	♓	♈	♏
April	9 ♈ / 26 ♉	19 ♊	♎	♏	♓	♈	♏
May	10 ♊ / 30 ♋	12 ♋	♎	♏	1 ♓	1 ♉	♏
June	21 ♊	6 ♌	♎	♏	♓	♉	♏
July	14 ♋	5 ♍	♎	♏	♓	♉	♏
Aug.	1 ♌ / 16 ♍	♍	4 ♏	♏	♓	♉	♏
Sept.	4 ♎	♍	20 ♐	♏	♓	♉	♏
Oct.	♎	♍	29 ♑	♏	♓	♉	♏
Nov.	11 ♏	10 ♎	♑	18 ♐	♓	♉	♏
Dec.	1 ♐ / 19 ♑	10 ♏	4 ♒	♐	♓	15 ♈	♏

1936

	Mercury ☿	Venus ♀	Mars ♂	Jupiter ♃	Saturn ♄	Uranus ♅	Neptune ♆
Jan.	1 ♑ / 5 ♒	1 ♏ / 5 ♐ / 29 ♑	1 ♒	1 ♐	1 ♓	1 ♈	1 ♏
Feb.	♒	21 ♒	22 ♈	♐	♓	8 ♉	♏
March	12 ♓ / 31 ♈	16 ♓	♈	♐	♓	♉	♏
April	17 ♉	11 ♈	5 ♉	♐	♓	♉	♏
May	3 ♊	7 ♉	17 ♊	♐	♓	♉	♏
June	♊	1 ♊ / 24 ♋	26 ♋	♐	♓	♉	♏
July	9 ♋ / 23 ♌	16 ♌	♋	♐	♓	♉	♏
Aug.	7 ♍ / 29 ♎	9 ♍	7 ♌	♐	♓	♉	♏
Sept.	♎	4 ♎	23 ♍	♐	♓	♉	♏
Oct.	♎	1 ♏ / 25 ♐	♍	♐	♓	♉	♏
Nov.	4 ♏ / 23 ♐	17 ♑	14 ♎	♐	♓	♉	♏
Dec.	11 ♑ / 30 ♒	10 ♒	♎	2 ♑	♓	♉	♏

1937

	Mercury ☿	Venus ♀	Mars ♂	Jupiter ♃	Saturn ♄	Uranus ♅	Neptune ♆
Jan.	1 ♒ / 12 ♑	1 ♒ / 4 ♓	1 ♎ / 9 ♏	1 ♑	1 ♓	1 ♉	1 ♏
Feb.	13 ♒	3 ♈	♏	♑	♓	♉	♏
March	5 ♓ / 23 ♈	19 ♉	20 ♐	♑	♓	♉	♏
April	9 ♉	4 ♈	♐	♑	17 ♈	♉	♏
May	♉	♈	9 ♏	♑	♈	♉	♏
June	15 ♊	6 ♉	♏	♑	♈	♉	♏
July	2 ♋ / 14 ♌ / 31 ♍	10 ♊	♏	♑	♈	♉	♏
Aug.	♍	5 ♋ / 30 ♌	15 ♐	♑	♈	♉	♏
Sept.	♍	24 ♍	♐	♑	♈	♉	♏
Oct.	8 ♎ / 28 ♏	20 ♎	1 ♑	♑	♈	♉	♏
Nov.	16 ♐	15 ♏	9 ♒	♑	11 ♓	♉	♏
Dec.	4 ♑	9 ♐ / 31 ♑	19 ♓	10 ♒	26 ♈	♉	♏

1938

	Mercury ☿	Venus ♀	Mars ♂	Jupiter ♃	Saturn ♄	Uranus ♅	Neptune ♆
Jan.	1 ♑ / 8 ♐ / 13 ♑	1 ♑ / 22 ♒	1 ♓ / 31 ♈	1 ♒	1 ♈	1 ♉	1 ♏
Feb.	7 ♒ / 26 ♓	15 ♓	♈	♒	♈	♉	♏
March	15 ♈	12 ♈	16 ♉	♒	♈	♉	♏
April	5 ♉ / 20 ♈	8 ♉	27 ♊	26 ♓	♈	♉	♏
May	18 ♉	2 ♊ / 25 ♋	♊	♓	♈	♉	♏
June	9 ♊ / 23 ♋	17 ♌	7 ♋	♓	♈	♉	♏
July	6 ♌ / 26 ♍	12 ♍	20 ♌	♓	♈	♉	♏
Aug.	♍	10 ♎	♌	22 ♒	♈	♉	♏
Sept.	♍	11 ♏	4 ♍	♒	♈	♉	♏
Oct.	1 ♎ / 20 ♏	21 ♐	25 ♎	♒	♈	♉	♏
Nov.	9 ♐	10 ♏	♎	♒	♈	♉	♏
Dec.	♐	♏	15 ♏	15 ♓	♈	♉	♏

1939

Mercury ☿	Venus ♀	Mars ♂	Jupiter ♃	Saturn ♄	Uranus ♅	Neptune ♆	
1 ♐, 13 ♑	1 ♏, 7 ♐	1 ♏	1 ♓	1 ♈	1 ♉	1 ♏	Jan.
1 ♒, 18 ♓	7 ♑	2 ♐	♓	♈	♉	♏	Feb.
8 ♈	4 ♒, 30 ♓	22 ♑	♓	♈	♉	♏	March
♈	25 ♈	♑	♓	♈	♉	♏	April
16 ♉	22 ♉	18 ♒	9 ♈	♈	♉	♏	May
2 ♊, 14 ♋	16 ♊	♒	♈	♈	♉	♏	June
29 ♌	10 ♋	♒	♈	♈	♉	♏	July
♌	1 ♌, 25 ♍	5 ♑	♈	1 ♉, 30 ♈	♉	♏	Aug.
6 ♍, 23 ♎	20 ♎	15 ♒	♈	♈	♉	♏	Sept.
13 ♏	16 ♏	♒	♈	♈	♉	♏	Oct.
4 ♐	9 ♐	15 ♓	12 ♓	♈	♉	♏	Nov.
2 ♏, 16 ♐	2 ♑, 24 ♒	♓	10 ♈	♈	♉	♏	Dec.

1940

Mercury ☿	Venus ♀	Mars ♂	Jupiter ♃	Saturn ♄	Uranus ♅	Neptune ♆	
1 ♐, 7 ♑, 24 ♒	1 ♒, 17 ♓	1 ♓, 4 ♈	1 ♈	1 ♈	1 ♉	1 ♏	Jan.
10 ♓	12 ♈	21 ♉	♈	♈	♉	♏	Feb.
♓	11 ♉	♉	♈	31 ♉	♉	♏	March
17 ♈	8 ♊	6 ♊	♈	♉	♉	♏	April
8 ♉, 23 ♊	7 ♋	18 ♋	24 ♉	♉	♉	♏	May
5 ♋, 25 ♌	♋	30 ♌	♉	♉	♉	♏	June
23 ♋	6 ♊	♌	♉	♉	♉	♏	July
10 ♌, 28 ♍	1 ♋	16 ♏	♉	♉	♉	♏	Aug.
15 ♎	7 ♌	♏	♉	♉	♉	♏	Sept.
6 ♏	5 ♏	5 ♎	♉	♉	♉	♏	Oct.
♏, 28 ♏	2 ♎, 28 ♏	24 ♏	♉	♉	♉	♏	Nov.
11 ♐, 30 ♑	23 ♐	♏	♉	♉	♉	♏	Dec.

1941

Mercury ☿	Venus ♀	Mars ♂	Jupiter ♃	Saturn ♄	Uranus ♅	Neptune ♆	
1 ♑, 16 ♒	1 ♐, 14 ♑	1 ♏, 8 ♐	1 ♉	1 ♉	1 ♉	1 ♏	Jan.
2 ♓	6 ♒	18 ♑	♉	♉	♉	♏	Feb.
♓	1 ♓, 27 ♈	31 ♑	♉	♉	♉	♏	March
12 ♈, 30 ♉	22 ♉	♑	♉	♉	♉	♏	April
15 ♊, 30 ♋	17 ♊	12 ♓	♉	♉	♉	♏	May
♋	8 ♋	30 ♈	4 ♊	♉	♉	♏	June
♋	1 ♌, 25 ♍	♈	♊	♉	♉	♏	July
6 ♌, 20 ♍	21 ♎	♈	♊	♉	♉	♏	Aug.
7 ♎	18 ♏	♈	♊	♉	♉	♏	Sept.
2 ♏, 28 ♎	13 ♐	♈	♊	♉	♉	♏	Oct.
14 ♏	7 ♑	♈	♊	♉	♉	23 ♎	Nov.
5 ♐, 23 ♑	4 ♒	♈	♊	♉	♉	♎	Dec.

1942

Mercury ☿	Venus ♀	Mars ♂	Jupiter ♃	Saturn ♄	Uranus ♅	Neptune ♆	
1 ♑, 9 ♒	1 ♒	1 ♈, 17 ♉	1 ♊	1 ♉	1 ♉	1 ♎	Jan.
♒	♒	♉	♊	♉	♉	12 ♏	Feb.
15 ♓	♒	12 ♊	♊	♉	♉	♏	March
5 ♈, 22 ♉	5 ♓	27 ♋	♊	♉	♉	♏	April
7 ♊	6 ♈	♋	♊	22 ♊	♉	♏	May
♊	2 ♉, 30 ♊	11 ♌	10 ♋	♊	20 ♊	♏	June
13 ♋, 29 ♌	24 ♋	29 ♍	♋	♊	♊	♏	July
12 ♍	16 ♌	♍	♋	♊	♊	♏	Aug.
1 ♎	9 ♍	17 ♎	♋	♊	♊	18 ♎	Sept.
♎	5 ♎, 31 ♏	♎	♋	♊	♊	♎	Oct.
8 ♏, 28 ♐	24 ♐	5 ♏	♋	♊	♊	♎	Nov.
15 ♑	16 ♑	19 ♐	♋	♊	8 ♉	♎	Dec.

1943

	Mercury ☿		Venus ♀		Mars ♂		Jupiter ♃		Saturn ♄		Uranus ♅		Neptune ♆	
Jan.	1	♑	1	♑	1	♐	1	♋	1	♊	1	♉	1	♎
	2	♒	7	♒	27	♑								
	30	♑	31	♓										
Feb.	14	♒	26	♈		♑		♋		♊		♉		♎
March	10	♓	24	♉	6	♒		♋		♊		♉		♎
	29	♈												
April	14	♉	18	♊	14	♓		♋		♊	9	♊		♎
May	4	♊	12	♋	27	♈		♋		♊		♊	21	♏
	24	♉												
June	16	♊	6	♌		♈	20	♌		♊		♊		♏
July	7	♋	6	♍	10	♉		♌		♊		♊	3	♎
	20	♌												
Aug.	4	♍		♍	27	♊		♌		♊		♊		♎
	28	♎												
Sept.	25	♍		♍		♊		♌		♊		♊		♎
Oct.	12	♎		♍		♊		♌		♊		♊		♎
Nov.	1	♏	10	♎		♊		♌		♊		♊		♎
	20	♐												
Dec.	8	♑	10	♏		♊		♌		♊		♊		♎

1944

	Mercury ☿		Venus ♀		Mars ♂		Jupiter ♃		Saturn ♄		Uranus ♅		Neptune ♆	
Jan.	1	♑	1	♏	1	♊	1	♌	1	♊	1	♊	1	♎
			5	♐										
			29	♑										
Feb.	11	♒	20	♒		♊		♌		♊		♊		♎
March	2	♓	16	♓	29	♋		♌		♊		♊		♎
	20	♈												
April	6	♉	10	♈		♋		♌		♊		♊		♎
May		♉	7	♉	19	♌		♌		♊		♊		♎
			31	♊										
June	13	♊	23	♋		♌		♌	20	♋		♊		♎
	28	♋												
July	11	♌	16	♌	8	♍	13	♏		♋		♊		♎
	28	♍												
Aug.		♍	9	♍	29	♎		♏		♋		♊		♎
Sept.		♍	4	♎		♎		♏		♋		♊		♎
			30	♏										
Oct.	5	♎	25	♐	17	♏		♏		♋		♊		♎
	24	♏												
Nov.	12	♐	17	♑	29	♐		♏		♋		♊		♎
Dec.	2	♑	9	♒		♐		♏		♋		♊		♎
	24	♐												

1945

	Mercury ☿		Venus ♀		Mars ♂		Jupiter ♃		Saturn ♄		Uranus ♅		Neptune ♆	
Jan.	1	♐	1	♒	1	♐	1	♏	1	♋	1	♊	1	♎
	15	♑	4	♓	6	♑								
Feb.	4	♒	3	♈	12	♒		♏		♋		♊		♎
	22	♓												
March	12	♈		♈	22	♓		♏		♋		♊		♎
April		♈		♈		♓		♏		♋		♊		♎
May	18	♉		♈	3	♈		♏		♋		♊		♎
June	6	♊	7	♉	14	♉		♏		♋		♊		♎
	19	♑												
July	3	♌	9	♊	27	♊		♏		♋		♊		♎
	25	♍												
Aug.	18	♌	5	♋		♊	23	♎		♋		♊		♎
			29	♌										
Sept.	9	♍	23	♍	8	♋		♎		♋		♊		♎
	28	♎												
Oct.	17	♏	19	♎		♋		♎		♋		♊		♎
Nov.	6	♐	14	♏	4	♌		♎		♋		♊		♎
Dec.		♐	8	♐		♌		♎		♋		♊		♎
			30	♑										

1946

	Mercury ☿		Venus ♀		Mars ♂		Jupiter ♃		Saturn ♄		Uranus ♅		Neptune ♆	
Jan.	1	♐	1	♑	1	♌	1	♎	1	♋	1	♊	1	♎
	10	♑	22	♒	5	♋								
	28	♒												
Feb.	15	♓	14	♓		♋		♎		♋		♊		♎
March	5	♈	12	♈		♋		♎		♋		♊		♎
April	1	♓	7	♉	17	♌		♎		♋		♊		♎
	16	♈												
May	13	♉	2	♊		♌		♎		♋		♊		♎
	29	♊	25	♋										
June	11	♋	17	♌	16	♍		♎		♋		♊		♎
	26	♌												
July		♌	12	♍		♍		♎	17	♌		♊		♎
Aug.		♌	10	♎	9	♎		♎		♌		♊		♎
Sept.	3	♍	11	♏	28	♏		♎		♌		♊		♎
	20	♎												
Oct.	10	♏		♏		♏	4	♏		♌		♊		♎
Nov.	3	♐		♏	10	♐		♏		♌		♊		♎
	20	♏												
Dec.	15	♐		♏	18	♑		♏		♌		♊		♎

1947

	Mercury ☿	Venus ♀	Mars ♂	Jupiter ♃	Saturn ♄	Uranus ♅	Neptune ♆
Jan.	1 ♐ / 3 ♑ / 21 ♒	1 ♏ / 8 ♐	1 ♑ / 23 ♒	1 ♏	1 ♌	1 ♊	1 ♎
Feb.	7 ♓	7 ♑	♒	♏	♌	♊	♎
March	♓	4 ♒ / 29 ♓	2 ♓	♏	♌	♊	♎
April	16 ♈	25 ♈	12 ♈	♏	♌	♊	♎
May	6 ♉ / 20 ♊	22 ♉	24 ♉	♏	♌	♊	♎
June	3 ♋	16 ♊	♉	♏	♌	♊	♎
July	♋	9 ♋	4 ♊	♏	♌	♊	♎
Aug.	10 ♌ / 26 ♍	1 ♌ / 25 ♍	14 ♋	♏	♌	♊	♎
Sept.	12 ♎	19 ♎	28 ♌	♏	♌	♊	♎
Oct.	4 ♏	16 ♏	♌	♏	♌	♊	♎
Nov.	♏	9 ♐	24 ♍	2 ♐	♌	♊	♎
Dec.	9 ♐ / 27 ♑	1 ♑ / 23 ♒	♏	♐	♌	♊	♎

1948

	Mercury ☿	Venus ♀	Mars ♂	Jupiter ♃	Saturn ♄	Uranus ♅	Neptune ♆
Jan.	1 ♑ / 13 ♒	1 ♒ / 16 ♓	1 ♏	1 ♐	1 ♌	1 ♊	1 ♎
Feb.	1 ♓ / 22 ♒	12 ♈	23 ♌	♐	♌	♊	♎
March	16 ♓	11 ♉	♌	♐	♌	♊	♎
April	9 ♈ / 26 ♉	8 ♊	♌	♐	♌	♊	♎
May	11 ♊ / 29 ♋	8 ♋	12 ♍	♐	♌	♊	♎
June	30 ♊	30 ♊	♍	♐	♌	♊	♎
July	12 ♋	♊	17 ♍	♐	♌	♊	♎
Aug.	2 ♌ / 16 ♍	3 ♋	♎	♐	28 ♍	28 ♋	♎
Sept.	4 ♎	7 ♌	7 ♏	♐	♍	♋	♎
Oct.	2 ♏ / 14 ♎	5 ♍	21 ♐	♐	♍	♋	♎
Nov.	12 ♏	1 ♎ / 28 ♏	27 ♑	15 ♑	♍	17 ♊	♎
Dec.	1 ♐ / 19 ♑	22 ♐	♑	♑	♍	♊	♎

1949

	Mercury ☿	Venus ♀	Mars ♂	Jupiter ♃	Saturn ♄	Uranus ♅	Neptune ♆
Jan.	♑ / 5 ♒	1 ♐ / 14 ♑	1 ♑ / 2 ♒	1 ♑	1 ♍	1 ♊	1 ♎
Feb.	♒	5 ♒	9 ♓	♑	♍	♊	♎
March	13 ♓	1 ♓ / 26 ♈	22 ♈	27 ♒	♍	♊	♎
April	2 ♈ / 18 ♉	22 ♉	♈	♒	♍	♊	♎
May	4 ♊	16 ♊	3 ♉	♒	♍	♊	♎
June	♊	8 ♋ / 30 ♌	13 ♊	♒	♍	9 ♋	♎
July	11 ♋ / 25 ♌ / 8 ♍	25 ♍	24 ♋	17 ♑	♍	♋	♎
Aug.	29 ♎	21 ♎	♋	♑	♍	♋	♎
Sept.	♎	17 ♏	4 ♌	♑	♍	♋	♎
Oct.	♎	13 ♐	23 ♍	♑	♍	♋	♎
Nov.	5 ♏ / 24 ♐	7 ♑	♍	18 ♒	♍	♋	♎
Dec.	12 ♑ / 31 ♒	4 ♒	24 ♎	♒	♍	♋	♎

1950

	Mercury ☿	Venus ♀	Mars ♂	Jupiter ♃	Saturn ♄	Uranus ♅	Neptune ♆
Jan.	1 ♒ / 17 ♑	1 ♒	1 ♎	1 ♒	1 ♍	1 ♋	1 ♎
Feb.	13 ♑	♒	♎	♒	♍	♋	♎
March	7 ♓ / 25 ♈	♒	♎	♒	♍	♋	♎
April	10 ♉	5 ♓	2 ♏	3 ♓	♍	♋	♎
May	♉	6 ♈	♏	♓	♍	♋	♎
June	16 ♊	3 ♉ / 29 ♊	11 ♎	♓	♍	♋	♎
July	3 ♋ / 16 ♌	23 ♋	♎	♓	♍	♋	♎
Aug.	1 ♏ / 31 ♎	15 ♌	15 ♏	♓	♍	♋	♎
Sept.	8 ♏	8 ♏	30 ♐	♓	♍	♋	♎
Oct.	9 ♎ / 29 ♏	4 ♎ / 30 ♏	♐	♓	♍	♋	♎
Nov.	17 ♐	23 ♐	7 ♑	♓	10 ♎	♋	♎
Dec.	6 ♑	15 ♑	13 ♒	♓	♎	♋	♎

1951

	Mercury ☿	Venus ♀	Mars ♂	Jupiter ♃	Saturn ♄	Uranus ♅	Neptune ♆
Jan.	1 ♑	1 ♑ / 6 ♒ / 30 ♓	1 ♒ / 20 ♓	1 ♓	1 ♎	1 ♋	1 ♎
Feb.	9 ♒ / 27 ♓	25 ♈	♓	♓	♏	♋	♎
March	17 ♈	24 ♉	2 ♈	♓	24 ♏	♋	♎
April	5 ♉ / 29 ♈	18 ♊	14 ♉	19 ♈	♏	♋	♎
May	17 ♉	11 ♋	25 ♊	♈	♏	♋	♎
June	11 ♊ / 25 ♋	5 ♌	♊	♈	♏	♋	♎
July	8 ♌ / 26 ♏	6 ♏	4 ♋	♈	♏	♋	♎
Aug.	♏	♏	15 ♌	♈	3 ♎	♋	♎
Sept.	♏	♏	♌	♈	♎	♋	♎
Oct.	3 ♎ / 22 ♏	♏	1 ♏	♈	♎	♋	♎
Nov.	10 ♐	10 ♎	23 ♎	♈	♎	♋	♎
Dec.	2 ♑ / 13 ♐	10 ♏	♎	♈	♎	♋	♎

1952

	Mercury ☿	Venus ♀	Mars ♂	Jupiter ♃	Saturn ♄	Uranus ♅	Neptune ♆
Jan.	1 ♐ / 14 ♑	1 ♏ / 3 ♐ / 28 ♑	1 ♎ / 24 ♏	1 ♈	1 ♎	1 ♋	1 ♎
Feb.	2 ♒ / 20 ♓	20 ♒	♏	♈	♎	♋	♎
March	8 ♈	15 ♓	♏	♈	♎	♋	♎
April	♈	11 ♈	♏	♈	♎	♋	♎
May	16 ♉	6 ♉ / 31 ♊	28 ♎	6 ♉	♎	♋	♎
June	2 ♊ / 15 ♋ / 29 ♌	23 ♋	25 ♏	♉	♎	♋	♎
July	♌	15 ♌	♏	♉	♎	♋	♎
Aug.	♌	8 ♍	♏	♉	♎	♋	♎
Sept.	6 ♏ / 24 ♎	3 ♎ / 30 ♏	1 ♐	♉	♎	♋	♎
Oct.	13 ♏	24 ♐	13 ♑	♉	♎	♋	♎
Nov.	4 ♐	16 ♑	19 ♒ / 28 ♓	♉	♎	♋	♎
Dec.	7 ♏ / 14 ♐	9 ♒	♓	♉	♎	♋	♎

1953

	Mercury ☿	Venus ♀	Mars ♂	Jupiter ♃	Saturn ♄	Uranus ♅	Neptune ♆
Jan.	1 ♐ / 7 ♑ / 25 ♒	1 ♒ / 4 ♓	1 ♓	1 ♉	1 ♎	1 ♋	1 ♎
Feb.	11 ♓	3 ♈	8 ♈	♉	♎	♋	♎
March	4 ♈ / 14 ♓	♈	24 ♉	♉	♎	♋	♎
April	17 ♈	♈	♉	♉	♎	♋	♎
May	10 ♉ / 25 ♊	♈	5 ♊	18 ♊	♎	♋	♎
June	7 ♋ / 25 ♌	8 ♉	14 ♋	♊	♎	♋	♎
July	31 ♋	9 ♊	27 ♌	♊	♎	♋	♎
Aug.	9 ♌ / 30 ♍	4 ♋ / 29 ♌	♌	♊	♎	♋	♎
Sept.	16 ♎	23 ♍	11 ♏	♊	♎	♋	♎
Oct.	7 ♏	19 ♎	♏	♊	♎	♋	♎
Nov.	♏	13 ♏	1 ♎	♊	2 ♏	♋	♎
Dec.	12 ♐ / 31 ♑	8 ♐ / 30 ♑	24 ♏	♊	♏	♋	♎

1954

	Mercury ☿	Venus ♀	Mars ♂	Jupiter ♃	Saturn ♄	Uranus ♅	Neptune ♆
Jan.	1 ♑ / 17 ♒	1 ♑ / 21 ♒	1 ♏	1 ♊	1 ♏	1 ♋	1 ♎
Feb.	4 ♓	14 ♓	14 ♐	♊	♏	♋	♎
March	♓	11 ♈	♐	♊	♏	♋	♎
April	13 ♈	7 ♉	13 ♑	♊	♏	♋	♎
May	2 ♉ / 16 ♊ / 31 ♋	1 ♊ / 24 ♋	♑	24 ♋	♏	♋	♎
June	♋	16 ♌	♑	♋	♏	♋	♎
July	♋	11 ♍	4 ♐	♋	♏	♋	♎
Aug.	7 ♌ / 22 ♍	9 ♎	25 ♑	♋	♏	♋	♎
Sept.	9 ♎	11 ♏	♑	♋	♏	♋	♎
Oct.	2 ♏	♏	18 ♒	12 ♌	♏	♋	♎
Nov.	3 ♎ / 14 ♏	♏	♒	♌	♏	♋	♎
Dec.	6 ♐ / 24 ♑	♏	1 ♓	24 ♋	♏	♋	♎

1955

	Mercury ☿	Venus ♀	Mars ♂	Jupiter ♃	Saturn ♄	Uranus ♅	Neptune ♆
Jan.	1 ♑, 10 ♒, 31 ♓	1 ♏, 8 ♐	1 ♓, 15 ♈	1 ♋	1 ♏	1 ♋	1 ♎
Feb.	7 ♒	6 ♑	♈	♋	♏	♋	♎
March	16 ♓	4 ♒, 29 ♓	2 ♉	♋	♏	♋	♎
April	7 ♈, 24 ♉	25 ♈	15 ♊	♋	♏	♋	♎
May	8 ♊	21 ♉	26 ♋	♋	♏	♋	♎
June	♊	15 ♊		1 ♋	♏	♋	♎
July	14 ♋, 30 ♌	8 ♋, 31 ♌	8 ♌	♌	♏	19 ♌	♎
Aug.	14 ♍	24 ♍	24 ♍	♌	♏	♌	♎
Sept.	2 ♎	19 ♎	♍	♌	♏	♌	♎
Oct.	♎	15 ♏	13 ♎	27 ♏	♏	♌	♎
Nov.	10 ♏, 29 ♐	8 ♐	♎	♏	♏	♌	♎
Dec.	17 ♑	1 ♑, 23 ♒	2 ♏	♏	♏	♌	♎

1956

	Mercury ☿	Venus ♀	Mars ♂	Jupiter ♃	Saturn ♄	Uranus ♅	Neptune ♆
Jan.	1 ♑, 3 ♒	1 ♒, 16 ♓	1 ♏, 17 ♐	1 ♏	1 ♏	1 ♌	1 ♎
Feb.	5 ♑, 13 ♒	11 ♈	29 ♑	10 ♌	4 ♐	♌	♎
March	10 ♓, 29 ♈	11 ♉	♑	♌	♐	♌	♎
April	14 ♉	7 ♊	12 ♒	♌	20 ♏	♌	♎
May	3 ♊	9 ♋	29 ♓	♌	♏	♌	♎
June	2 ♉, 13 ♊	24 ♊	♓	♌	23 ♏	♌	♎
July	7 ♋, 21 ♌	♊	♓	♌	♏	♌	♎
Aug.	5 ♍, 28 ♎	5 ♋	♓	♌	♏	♌	♎
Sept.	30 ♍	7 ♌	♓	♌	♏	♌	♎
Oct.	11 ♎	5 ♏	♓	♌	27 ♐	♌	♎
Nov.	♏, 21 ♐	1 ♎, 27 ♏	♓	♌	♐	♌	♎
Dec.	9 ♑	22 ♐	6 ♈	8 ♍	♐	♌	3 ♏

1957

	Mercury ☿	Venus ♀	Mars ♂	Jupiter ♃	Saturn ♄	Uranus ♅	Neptune ♆
Jan.	1 ♑	1 ♐, 13 ♑	1 ♈	1 ♎	1 ♐	1 ♌	1 ♏
Feb.	11 ♒	5 ♒, 28 ♓	2 ♉	28 ♏	♐	♌	♏
March	3 ♓, 21 ♈	26 ♈	22 ♊	♏	♐	♌	♏
April	7 ♉	21 ♉	♊	♏	♐	17 ♌	♎
May	♉	16 ♊	5 ♋	♏	♐	♌	♎
June	14 ♊, 29 ♋	7 ♋, 30 ♌	18 ♌	♏	♐	♌	♎
July	12 ♌, 29 ♍	24 ♍	♌	♏	♐	♌	♎
Aug.	♍	20 ♎	4 ♍	4 ♎	♐	♌	♎
Sept.	♏	17 ♏	24 ♎	♎	♐	♌	♎
Oct.	6 ♎, 25 ♏	13 ♐	♎	♎	♐	♌, 2 ♏	♏
Nov.	14 ♐	6 ♑	12 ♏	♎	♐	♌	♏
Dec.	3 ♑, 29 ♐	4 ♒	26 ♐	♎	♐	♌	♏

1958

	Mercury ☿	Venus ♀	Mars ♂	Jupiter ♃	Saturn ♄	Uranus ♅	Neptune ♆
Jan.	1 ♐, 15 ♑	1 ♒	1 ♐	1 ♎	1 ♐	1 ♌	1 ♏
Feb.	6 ♒, 24 ♓	♒	4 ♑	8 ♏, 26 ♎	♐	♌	♏
March	13 ♈	♒	15 ♒	♎	♐	♌	♏
April	♈	5 ♓	24 ♓	♎	♐	♌	♏
May	18 ♉	5 ♈	♈	♎	♐	♌	♏
June	♊, 21 ♋	3 ♉, 29 ♊	6 ♈	♎	♐	♌	♏
July	4 ♌, 25 ♍	23 ♋	24 ♉	♎	♐	♌	♏
Aug.	25 ♌	15 ♌	♉	♎	♐	♌	♏
Sept.	9 ♍, 29 ♎	8 ♏	30 ♊	17 ♏	♐	♌	♏
Oct.	18 ♏	4 ♎, 30 ♏	21 ♉	♏	♐	♌	♏
Nov.	7 ♐	23 ♐	♉	♏	♐	♌	♏
Dec.	♐	15 ♑	♉	♏	♐	♌	♏

1959

	Mercury ☿	Venus ♀	Mars ♂	Jupiter ♃	Saturn ♄	Uranus ♅	Neptune ♆
Jan.	1 ♐ / 11 ♑ / 30 ♒	1 ♑ / 6 ♒ / 30 ♓	1 ♉	1 ♏	1 ♐ / 5 ♑	1 ♌	1 ♏
Feb.	16 ♓	24 ♈	16 ♊	♏	♑	♌	♏
March	6 ♈	23 ♉	♊	7 ♐	♑	♌	♏
April	♈	17 ♊	11 ♋	♏	♑	♌	♏
May	14 ♉ / 30 ♊	11 ♋	28 ♌	♏	♑	♌	♏
June	12 ♋ / 27 ♌	5 ♌	♌	♏	♑	♌	♏
July	♌	6 ♍	17 ♏	♏	♑	♌	♏
Aug.	♌	♍	♏	♏	♑	♌	♏
Sept.	4 ♍ / 21 ♎	18 ♌ / 25 ♍	6 ♎	♏	♑	♌	♏
Oct.	11 ♏	♏	25 ♏	16 ♐	♑	♎	♏
Nov.	3 ♐ / 25 ♏	10 ♎	♏	♐	♑	♎	♏
Dec.	16 ♐	9 ♏	7 ♐	♐	♑	♎	♏

1960

	Mercury ☿	Venus ♀	Mars ♂	Jupiter ♃	Saturn ♄	Uranus ♅	Neptune ♆
Jan.	1 ♐ / 5 ♑ / 22 ♒	1 ♏ / 4 ♐ / 28 ♑	15 ♑	1 ♐	1 ♑	1 ♌	1 ♏
Feb.	8 ♓	19 ♒	21 ♒	♐	♑	♌	♏
March	♓	14 ♓	30 ♓	1 ♑	♑	♌	♏
April	16 ♈	9 ♈	♓	♑	♑	♌	♏
May	6 ♉ / 21 ♊	6 ♉ / 30 ♊	11 ♈	♑	♑	♌	♏
June	3 ♋ / 26 ♌	22 ♋	23 ♉	12 ♐	♑	♌	♏
July	11 ♋	15 ♌	♉	♐	♑	♌	♏
Aug.	10 ♌ / 26 ♍	8 ♍	5 ♊	♐	♑	♌	♏
Sept.	12 ♎	3 ♎ / 29 ♏	21 ♋	♐	♑	♌	♏
Oct.	4 ♏	24 ♐	♋	26 ♑	♑	♌	♏
Nov.	♏	16 ♑	♋	♑	♑	♌	♏
Dec.	9 ♐ / 28 ♑	9 ♒	♋	♑	♑	♌	♏

1961

	Mercury ☿	Venus ♀	Mars ♂	Jupiter ♃	Saturn ♄	Uranus ♅	Neptune ♆
Jan.	1 ♑ / 14 ♒	1 ♒ / 3 ♓	1 ♋	1 ♑	1 ♑	1 ♌	1 ♏
Feb.	1 ♓ / 26 ♒	3 ♈	♋	♑	♑	♌	♏
March	16 ♓	♈	♋	4 ♒	21 ♒	♌	♏
April	10 ♈ / 28 ♉	♈	♋	♒	♒	♌	♏
May	12 ♊ / 29 ♋	♈	2 ♌	♒	♒	♌	♏
June	♋	8 ♉	25 ♏	♒	♒	♌	♏
July	♋	9 ♊	♏	♒	1 ♑	♌	♏
Aug.	3 ♌ / 18 ♍	4 ♋ / 28 ♌	17 ♎	♒	♑	♌	♏
Sept.	5 ♎	22 ♍	♎	7 ♑	♑	11 ♏	♏
Oct.	1 ♏ / 20 ♎	18 ♎	6 ♏	11 ♒	♑	♏	♏
Nov.	12 ♏	13 ♏	17 ♐	♒	♑	♏	♏
Dec.	3 ♐ / 20 ♑	7 ♐ / 30 ♑	25 ♑	♒	15 ♒	♏	♏

1962

	Mercury ☿	Venus ♀	Mars ♂	Jupiter ♃	Saturn ♄	Uranus ♅	Neptune ♆
Jan.	1 ♑ / 7 ♒	1 ♑ / 20 ♒	1 ♑ / 30 ♒	1 ♒	1 ♒	1 ♏	1 ♏
Feb.	♒	13 ♓	♒	♒	♒	♏	♏
March	14 ♓	11 ♈	9 ♓	15 ♓	♓	16 ♌	♏
April	3 ♈ / 20 ♉	6 ♉	19 ♈	♓	♓	♌	♏
May	5 ♊	1 ♊ / 24 ♋	♈	♓	♓	♌	♏
June	♊	16 ♌	1 ♉	♓	♓	23 ♏	♏
July	12 ♋ / 26 ♌	11 ♍	12 ♊	♓	♓	♏	♏
Aug.	10 ♍ / 30 ♎	9 ♎	23 ♋	♓	♓	♏	♏
Sept.	♎	11 ♏	♋	♓	♓	♏	♏
Oct.	♎	♏	8 ♌	♓	♓	♏	♏
Nov.	7 ♏ / 26 ♐	♏	♌	♓	♓	♏	♏
Dec.	13 ♑	♏	♌	♓	♓	♏	♏

1963

	Mercury ☿	Venus ♀	Mars ♂	Jupiter ♃	Saturn ♄	Uranus ♅	Neptune ♆	
	1 ♒, 22 ♑	1 ♏, 9 ♐	1 ♌	1 ♓	1 ♒	1 ♍	1 ♏	Jan.
	14 ♒	6 ♑	♌	♓	♒	♍	♏	Feb.
	8 ♓, 26 ♈	3 ♒, 28 ♓	♌	♓	♒	♍	♏	March
	12 ♉	24 ♈	♌	3 ♈	♒	♍	♏	April
	♉	21 ♉	29 ♍	♈	♒	♍	♏	May
	17 ♊	15 ♊	♍	♈	♒	♍	♏	June
	5 ♋, 18 ♌	8 ♋, 31 ♌	27 ♎	♈	♒	♍	♏	July
	2 ♍, 29 ♎	23 ♍	♎	♈	♒	♍	♏	Aug.
	15 ♍	18 ♎	16 ♏	♈	♒	♍	♏	Sept.
	11 ♎, 30 ♏	15 ♏	29 ♐	♈	♒	♍	♏	Oct.
	18 ♐	8 ♐, 30 ♑	♐	♈	♒	♍	♏	Nov.
	7 ♑	22 ♒	6 ♑	♈	♒	♍	♏	Dec.

1964

	Mercury ☿	Venus ♀	Mars ♂	Jupiter ♃	Saturn ♄	Uranus ♅	Neptune ♆	
	1 ♑	1 ♒, 15 ♓	1 ♑, 11 ♒	1 ♈	1 ♒	1 ♍	1 ♏	Jan.
	10 ♒, 29 ♓	11 ♈	17 ♓	♈	♒	♍	♏	Feb.
	17 ♈	10 ♉	24 ♈	♈	1 ♓	♍	♏	March
	5 ♉	7 ♊	♈	20 ♉	♓	♍	♏	April
	♉	10 ♋	11 ♉	♉	♓	♍	♏	May
	11 ♊, 25 ♋	18 ♊	21 ♊	♉	♓	♍	♏	June
	8 ♌, 26 ♍	♊	31 ♋	♉	♓	♍	♏	July
	♍	6 ♋	♋	♉	♓	♍	♏	Aug.
	♍	7 ♌	12 ♌	♉	♓	♍	♏	Sept.
	3 ♎, 22 ♏	4 ♍, 31 ♎	♌	♉	♓	♍	♏	Oct.
	11 ♐	27 ♏	1 ♍	♉	♓	♍	♏	Nov.
	1 ♑, 17 ♐	21 ♐	♍	♉	♓	♍	♏	Dec.

1965

	Mercury ☿	Venus ♀	Mars ♂	Jupiter ♃	Saturn ♄	Uranus ♅	Neptune ♆	
	1 ♐, 13 ♑	1 ♐, 12 ♑	1 ♍	1 ♉	1 ♓	1 ♍	1 ♏	Jan.
	3 ♒, 21 ♓	5 ♒	♍	♉	♓	♍	♏	Feb.
	9 ♈	25 ♈	♍	♉	♓	♍	♏	March
	♈	19 ♉	♍	23 ♊	♓	♍	♏	April
	16 ♉	13 ♊	♍	♊	♓	♍	♏	May
	2 ♊, 16 ♋	6 ♋	29 ♎	♊	♓	♍	♏	June
	2 ♌, 31 ♍	26 ♌	♎	♊	♓	♍	♏	July
	3 ♌	20 ♍	20 ♏	♊	♓	♍	♏	Aug.
	9 ♍, 25 ♎	14 ♎	♏	21 ♋	♓	♍	♏	Sept.
	13 ♏	10 ♏	4 ♐	♋	♓	♍	♏	Oct.
	2 ♐	6 ♐	14 ♑	17 ♊	♓	♍	♏	Nov.
	♐	7 ♒	23 ♒	♊	♓	♍	♏	Dec.

1966

	Mercury ☿	Venus ♀	Mars ♂	Jupiter ♃	Saturn ♄	Uranus ♅	Neptune ♆	
	1 ♐, 8 ♑, 27 ♒	1 ♒	30 ♓	1 ♊	1 ♓	1 ♍	1 ♏	Jan.
	13 ♓	7 ♑, 25 ♒	♓	♊	♓	♍	♏	Feb.
	3 ♓, 22 ♈	♒	10 ♈	♊	♓	♍	♏	March
	18 ♈	7 ♓	18 ♉	♊	♓	♍	♏	April
	10 ♉, 25 ♊	5 ♈	29 ♊	6 ♋	♓	♍	♏	May
	8 ♋, 27 ♌	1 ♉, 28 ♊	♊	♋	♓	♍	♏	June
	♌	22 ♋	11 ♋	♋	♓	♍	♏	July
	♌	16 ♌	26 ♌	♋	♓	♍	♏	Aug.
	17 ♎	9 ♍	♌	27 ♌	♓	♍	♏	Sept.
	6 ♏, 30 ♐	3 ♎, 27 ♏	13 ♍	♌	♓	♍	♏	Oct.
	21 ♏	22 ♐	♍	♌	♓	♍	♏	Nov.
	12 ♐	14 ♑	4 ♎	♌	♓	♍	♏	Dec.

Index

France, 10, 88, 175, 176, 232, 299
Franco, General Francisco, 95
free will, 140-3, 148, 198
French Revolution, 53 ; predicted, 15, *15*, 176
Freud, Sigmund, 83, 193, *195*
Fuscus, Arellius, 35

Gabriel (Hingson), 15, 35
Gadbury, John, 165-7, 254, 279
Gagarin, Yuri, *65*
Galilei, Galileo, 100, 157, *157*, 164
Galle, J. G., 183
gambling, 194, *197*
Gandhi, Mohandas, *13*, 93, 201
Garibaldi, Giuseppe, 88
Garnett, Richard, 86, 192-3
Gataker, Thomas, 165, 281
Gauquelin, Michel, 264
Gauric, Luc, 151
Gemini, 49, 51, 63, 85-6, *117*, *164*, 292
genethliacal astrology, 18, *19*, 116, 244
Genuit, Hans, 258
geomancy, 177, *177*
George III, king of England, 86, 89
Gerbert, see Pope Sylvester
Germany, 8-10, 68, 172, 176, 209-10,
    218-20, 300 ; see also Nazis
Gladstone, William Ewart, 64
Gleadow, Rupert, 13, 21, 32, 34, 38, 47, 51,
    66, 67, 68, 76, 77, 85, 88, 91, 98, 100,
    101, 183, 186
Goebbels, Dr., 95, 117
Goering, Hermann, 58, 95
Goethe, Johann Wolfgang, 95, 176, *225*
Greenwich Mean Time, 242-6, *248* ; time
    zones, *245* ; see also sidereal time
Greenwich Royal Observatory, *145*
Grosseteste, Robert, 138, *141*
Gustavus Adolphus, king of Sweden, 154
Gutberlet, Dr. Wilhelm, 211

Halley, 168-9 ; comet, *173*, 175
Hamburg School, 267-9
Hari, Mata, *94*
Harrisson, Tom, 34, 204-5 ; see also Mass
    Observation
Harvard University, 227
Harvey, Richard, 281
Heimsoth, Karl Günther, 211
Heindel, Max, 49, 68, 77, 227
Heliogabalus, Roman emperor, 130
Henry IV, king of France, 277
herbals, *141*, 167, 281-2
Hermetic writings, 42, 49, 62, 80, 126-8, 138
Hermes Trismegistus, 35, 126-8, 138
Hersch, Prof. L., 263
Herschel, Sir William, 64, 183, *183*
Hess, Rudolf, 214, 215
Heydon, Sir Christopher, 279
Himmler, 214, 217

Hindu astrology, 20, 30, *33*, 42, 47, 62, 106,
    109, 176, 189, 221, 236 ; see also India
history of astrology : Mesopotamia, 106-11 ;
    Greece, 112-16 ; Egypt, 110-11 ; Rome,
    116-28 ; early Christian, 128-33 ; Dark
    Ages, 134-6 ; Middle Ages, 42, 62, 136-48 ;
    Renaissance, 62, 150-62 ; 17th-18th
    centuries, 162-76 ; 19th century, 176-90 ;
    20th century, 195-237 ; World War II,
    201-18 ; postwar, 218-41
Hitler, Adolf, 16, 58, 66, 201, 209, 211, *213*,
    214, 298 ; see also World War II, Nazis
Hobbes, Thomas, 164
Hölderlin, Johann Christian, 103
Holmes, Sherlock, *84*, 86
Holst, Gustav, *11*
Homer, 49, 52, 53, 56
Hone, Margaret, 38, 42, 47, 57, 66, 68, 185,
    228, 254, 259
Horapollo, 133
horary astrology, *19*, 20
horoscope : definition, 242-4 ; casting, 242-
    53, *246*, *248* ; interpretation, 253-61 ;
    progressed, 261-2, *263* ; Southern
    hemisphere, 326
horse racing, *197*
house division. 247-50, *251*
houses, 22, *22*, *104*, 105, 219, 247, 250
    251, *255*, 294
houses, tables of, *248*, 324-5
Hugo, Victor, 95
humors, 162, *163*
Huxley, Aldous, 286

imum coeli (I.C.), 23, *23*, 41, 247
In Search, 14, 227, 228
India, 10, *13*, 20, 30, *109*, 176, *189*, *240*,
    241, *286*
Inquisition, *142*, 144, 146, 169
Institute of Abstract Science, 228
Institute of Parapsychology, 264
International Congress of Astro-Science,
    234, *240*
Israel, *43*, *235*, 299
Italy, 143, 167, 232, 298
Ivan the Terrible, 91

James VI of Scotland and I of England, 76
Japanese astrology, 30, 236, *239*
Jayne, Charles A., Jr., 228
Jerusalem, 17, *17*
Jesus Christ, 128, 130, 146, 186, 190-1
Joffre, Marshal Joseph, 99
John of Bassigney, 273
John of Eschenden, 273
Jones, Ernest, 193
Jones, Marc Edmund, 21-2, 227, 228
judicial astrology, 18, *19*, 157
Jung, Carl Gustav, 26, 35, 74, 193, 220-3,
    222, *224*, 260-1, 266-7

Jupiter, 58-60, 96, 103, 137, *149*, *253*, 291
Justinian, Byzantine emperor, 49
Juvenal, 125, 274
juvenile delinquency, 240

Kalendar and Compost of Shepherds, 38,
  40, 42, 46, 50-1, 55, 56, 58-9, 60-1, 91,
  151, *153*, 272
Kant, Immanuel, 99
Kepler, Johannes, 34, 62-3, 86, 99, 150,
  154, 155-7
Katina (Theodossiou), 221
Keiser, Elfriede, *219*
Koch, Dr. Walter A., 219, 247
Koestler, Arthur, 110
Korsch, Dr. Hugo, 211-2
Krafft, Karl Ernst, 14, 26, 193, 209-10, *210*,
  212-15, 260, 262-7

Lane, Edward William, 176-7
Laplace, Pierre de, 183
Lavater, Johann, *162*
legal position of astrologers, England, 178,
  182 ; U.S.A., 196
Leo, 44, 66, *66*, 68, 75, 88-91, 292
Leo, Alan, 15, 35, 191-2, *192*, 195 ; trial, 198
Leo, Bessie, 191
Leverrier, Urbain, 183, *184*
Lévi, Eliphas (Alphonse Louis Constant),
  178, *179*
Lewi, Grant (Scorpio), 186
Libra, 21, 53, 93, 293
Lichtenberger, Johannes, 150, *150*
Lilly, William, 28, 35, 49, 63, 76, 164-5, *164*,
  172, 175, 214, 276, 281
Lincoln, Abraham, 96, 101
Lind, Ingrid, 20, 38, 44, 62, 66, 68, 77, 81,
  85, 88, 91, 95, 98, 100, 101, 146, 168,
  183, 186, 224, *231*, 258
local sidereal time, 245
London, 17, *69*, *175* ; table of houses for, 324
Long, Huey, 88
Louis XI, king of France, 277
Louis XIV, king of France, 88, 91, 167, 169,
  175, 278
Louis XVI, king of France, *15*
Lowell, Percival, *184*
Luther, Martin, 150, 170
Lyndoe, Edward, 199, 204, *204*, 207

magic, 49, 62, 126-8, *181*
Mallarmé, Stéphane, 99
mandala, *222*
Manilius, Marcus, 32, 38, 117
Mansfield, Katherine, 93
Mao Tse-tung, 30
Marco Polo, 30, 176
Margaret, Princess, *29*
Margesson, Maud, 195-6

Marie Thérèse, queen to Louis XIV of
  France, 278
Marlowe, Christopher, 158, *159*
Mars, 40, 55, 56-8, 80, 95, 195, *253*, 290
Marx, Karl, 85
Mason, Zoltan, 47
Mass Observation, 204-5
Mästlin, Michael, 156
Mather, Increase, 172, 280
medieval astrology, 137-8
medical astrology, 14, 21, 47, 49-50, 52, 58,
  126-8, *136*, 151-2
Medici, Giovanni de, 151 ; Lorenzo de, 88, 146
Médicis, Catherine de, *139*
medium coeli (M.C.), 23, *23*, 41, 244, 247, *248*
Melanchthon, Philip, 15
Melton, John, 279-80, *279*
Mercury, 50-3, 85, 91, 137, *252*, 290
Mesopotamian astrology, see Babylonia
meteorological astrology, *19*, 30
Mézières, Philippe de, 148
Middle Ages, see medieval
mid-heaven, see medium coeli
Miller, Henry, *11*, 288
Milton, John, 96, 120
Modern Astrology, magazine, 191, *192*
Montaigne, Michel de, 158
Montefeltro, Guido de, 143
Montgomery, Field Marshal Viscount, *56*, 218
Moody, T. H., 180-2
Moon, 46-50, 68, 83, 86, 103, *179*, 190, 193,
  224, *252*, 290
Moore, Marcia, 228
Morgan, J. P., 10, 198
Morier, James, 176
Morrish, Furze, 38, 47, 60, 64, 65, 66, 68,
  77, 82-3, 85, 88, 89, 92, 93, 96, 98, 100,
  101-2, 105, 223-4, 267
mundane astrology, *19*, 20, 110, 200
Mussolini, Benito, 58, *89*, 95, 201, *216*,
  218, 298
Mysore University, 228

nadi granthams, 10
Napoleon, Emperor, *43*, 49, 88, 98
natal astrology, see genethliacal
Naylor, R. H., 200, 205, *205*, 207
Nazis, 8, 16, 210-7, *210*, 220
Nebelmeier, Felix, 210, 218
Nechepso, 35, 126
Nechepso and Petosiris, Revelations of, 115,
  120
Nectanebus, king of Egypt, 278
Nehru, Pandit Jawaharlal, 287
Nelson, Horatio, Viscount, 57, 96
Neptune, 66-8, 95, 182, *184*, *253*, 291
Nero, Roman emperor, 122
New Statesman and Nation, 34, 205
New York, 17 ; table of houses for, 325
newspaper astrology, 32, 199, 204, *204*,
  207, 208, 232

347

Acknowledgments

Key to picture positions : (T) top (C) center (B) bottom ; and combinations, e.g. (TL) top left

Aero Photo, Paris : 123 (B)
Alexandra Palace Race Track : 197(BR)
American Federation of Astrologers : 227, 233(BR)
Associated Press : 239(B)
Banque Nationale pour le Commerce et l'Industrie : 50
André Barbault *Défense et l'Illustration de l'Astrologie*, Éditions du Seuil : 47
Bayerische Staatsbibliothek, Munich : 127
Bettmann Archive : 43(T), 48(T)
Biblioteca Estense, Moderna : 149
Biblioteca Vaticana : 138
Bibliotèque Nationale : 15, 71, 82
A. and C. Black Ltd., photo : Gordon Anthony : 229
Bodleian Library photo : Oxford University Press : 136
British Museum (photographs reproduced by courtesy of the Trustees) : 159(B) ;
   photo John Freeman : 53, 72, 81, 174, 175, 180, 181(BL), 272, 275, 276, 279, 283(L) ;
   photo David Swann : 12(T and B), 20(L), 27, 33(L and R), 51, 61, 74, 75, 108, 109(T), 114, 118(TL), 119(TL), 120, 121, 122, 129(L), 141(T and B), 142(T), 147(T), 150, 152(T), 155(T), 157, 162, 163, 164(BL), 171, 177, 243
Photo : Mike Busselle : 203, 230, 233(BL), 268(B)
J. Calder Ltd., photo : Alan Daiches : 11(B)
Culver Pictures Inc. : 199
Debeurme et Louvegnies, Paris : 237(B)
Doris Chase Doane *Astrology, 30 Years Research*, The Church of Light Inc. : 265
Ebertin Verlag : 221(B), 290
Éditions Rencontre : 173(CR)
Elle, Paris : 206(C)
Elliott and Fry Ltd. : 11(CL)
Eva, Milan : 206(T)
Hugh Evelyn Ltd. : 137
© W. Foulsham and Co. Ltd. : 248-9
Ernst L. Freud : 195
horoscopes cast by Arthur Gauntlett : 29(B), 78
Dr. Geuber : 45(T)
Giancolombo News, Milan : 18
René Groebli : 45(B)
Ara Guler : 111
© Philippe Halsman : 87(R)
Margaret Hone : 250
by courtesy of the Imperial War Museum : 56
Institut Belge d'Astrologie Scientifique : 233(T)
by permission of the International Publishing Co., Edinburgh, from one of the Leo textbooks : 324-5

Franz Jung : 222
Behram Kapadia : 109(B), 124, 189, 207
Elfriede Keiser : 219, 221(T)
Keystone Press : 29(T), 59, 63, 69, 99, 185(C and B)
Keystone Press, Tokyo : 238, 239(T)
K. E. Krafft, *Astro-biology* : 24-5
Frau K. E. Krafft : 266
Sam Levin, Camera Press : 54(R)
Leykham A. G., Graz : 19(BL), 152(B)
Herbert List : 19(BR)
Joseph Norman Lockyer *Dawn of Civilization* Thames and Hudson Ltd. : 113
London Express News : 43(B), 65(BL), 241
Lowell Observatory : 184(BR)
Mansell Collection, photo Alinari : 115, 129(R)
horoscopes cast by Jeff Mayo : 249, 251, 263, 298-301
Middle East Archive, photo Alistair Duncan : 17
Mount Wilson and Palomar Observatories, California, U.S.A. : 9
Müller et Cie, Neuhausen am Rheinfall, Switzerland : 268-9
Musée du Louvre : 26(R), 118(B) ; photo Chuzeville, 54(L)
Museo Archaeologico, Florence : 119(TR)
Nationale Forschungs und Gedenkstätten der klassischen deutschen Literatur in Weimar : 225(B)
National Film Archives : 84(B), 101
National Gallery, London : 92
by courtesy of the Trustees of the National Maritime Museum, Greenwich : 184(TL)
Musée de la Tapisserie de la Reine Mathilde, Bayeux : 171(TR)
The Nautical Almanac, by permission of Controller of H.M.S.O. : 302-23, 327-43
The New York Sun Inc. : 173(BR)
Nixa Records Ltd. reproduced by permission of Pye Records Ltd. : 11(CR)
Odhams Press : 204
R. Oldenbourg, Munich : 153
by permission of Her Majesty's Postmaster General : 234(B)
Pictorial Press Ltd. : 19(T), 216
Planet News : 31, 200, 286
Paul Popper Ltd. : 67, 89
Radio Times Hulton Picture Library : 26(L), 79, 87(L), 94, 184(CL), 191, 205(L), 208, 283(L), 285, 343(B)
Rascher Verlag, Zurich : 224, 225
Real Cartuja Valldemosa, Mallorca : 102
Rolls Prestcold, photo David Swann : 236
Royal Astronomical Society, photo David Swann : 166(T)
Royal Shakespeare Company, photo Angus McBean : 161
Rudaux et Vaucouleurs *L'Astronomie*, Larousse Éditeurs : 65(T), 72-3 (drawn by John Messenger)

Sanforized Service, Manchester: 237(T)
by courtesy of the Director, Science Museum,
     London: 65(BR), 117, 154, 184(TR), 185;
     photo David Swann: 37
Staatliche Museen, Berlin: 119(B)
Stevens Press: 206(B)
David Swann: 33(B), 145, 246, 259
Swiss National Tourist Office: 90
Theosophical Society: 188
© 1939 James Thurber: 97
Topix Picture Service: 240(T)
Twentieth Century Fox: 13, 14
Uffizi Gallery, Florence, photo G. B. Pineider:
     107, 135(T); photo Scala: 135(B)
Ullstein Verlag, Berlin: 213
Uni-Dia-Verlag, Stuttgart: 110
Universitätsbibliothek, Heidelberg, photo
     Lossen: 254-5
Joseph Wilpert *Die Römischen Mosaiken
     und Malereien der Kirchlichen Bauten*,
     Herder and Co. (1917): 131
John Wood: 57, 210
Mrs. W. B. Yeats, photo: Reading University:
     11 (TL and TR)
Yerkes Observatory: 184(BL)
Dr. Adrian M. Ziegler: 240(B)
Acknowledgment is made for permission to
     reprint excerpts from the following works:
     The English Physician and Complete Herbal
     by Nicholas Culpeper, published by Arco
     Publications.
Old Moore's Monthly Messenger (1908),
     now incorporated in *Foulsham's Original
     Old Moore's Almanack*
Crome Yellow by Aldous Huxley, published by
     Chatto and Windus Ltd.; reprinted in U.S.A.
     by permission of Harper and Row Inc.
Nehru's Letters to his Sister, ed. Krishna
     Nehru Hutheesing, published by Faber and
     Faber Ltd.
Henry Miller: His World of Urania by Sydney
     Omarr, published by Villiers Publications Ltd.